Classroom Companion: Business

More information about this series at https://link.springer.com/bookseries/16374

Benedicto Kulwizira Lukanima

Corporate Valuation

A Practical Approach with Case Studies

Springer

Benedicto Kulwizira Lukanima
Department of Finance and Accounting
Universidad del Norte
Barranquilla, Colombia

ISSN 2662-2866 ISSN 2662-2874 (electronic)
Classroom Companion: Business
ISBN 978-3-031-28266-9 ISBN 978-3-031-28267-6 (eBook)
https://doi.org/10.1007/978-3-031-28267-6

This Springer imprint is published by the registered company Springer Nature Switzerland AG
The registered company address is: Gewerbestrasse 11, 6330 Cham, Switzerland

To my family

Preface

Corporate valuation is an important subject in the corporate finance field. It plays a significant decision-making role among users such as finance professionals, managers, analysts, and investors. Valuation of companies, however, requires competent people: with knowledge, skills, and attitude to achieve acceptable valuation results. The subject is, therefore, among vital courses in many universities worldwide.

From my experience in teaching corporate valuation, many students tend to perceive it as a complex subject, which requires advanced level knowledge in quantitative analysis like statistics, mathematics, and econometrics. Several useful textbooks are available to support the learning process: they differ according to topic coverage, scope, depth, width, approach, and so on. Depending on target learners, some textbooks are better than others in terms of specific aspects such as conceptualization, simplicity, technicality, practicality, and illustrations. To ensure complete syllabus coverage, several textbooks are normally required or recommended: it is difficult to find an "all in one" textbook.

This book tries to address this limitation by bringing together most of the necessary learning materials required in any valuation syllabus. It intends to simplify valuation in order to suit better the needs of beginners, but without diluting the materials for advanced readers. Its design and approach allow readers to choose materials based on their general and specific needs at different levels of learning. The language used in this book is simple and straightforward. The aim is to make valuation an interesting and enjoyable course from the outset.

As a teaching and learning material, the usefulness of book cuts across the following key features: key valuation concepts, guidance for practical application, reflection on reality, guide for decision-making, combination of simplicity and complexity to suit beginners and experts, and wide topic coverage to suit most syllabi. It is designed to be a primary textbook in corporate valuation courses or as supplemental material for related courses like corporate finance, financial analysis, and financial management. For undergraduate beginners, the book provides basic materials in a simplified approach, taking them step by step to intermediate level. To suit the needs of graduate students, the book expands the materials on each topic, which address the art of valuation and taking into account technical challenges facing analysts in the valuation field. Moreover, valuation practitioners, company managers, analysts, and other decision-makers will find this book suitable as a supplement material and a guide to valuation.

In terms of approach, to help readers follow the concepts, this book starts with simple examples to address a particular aspect, then proceeds with real-world illustrations using real data. Readers can, therefore, easily link concepts with reality for a better understanding. Moreover, this book stands out from other books by making extensive use of news to inform readers about the reality of value and valuation. It, therefore, enhances readers' ability to critical analysis. The philosophical point of view here is that even "basic" materials should not fall short of "sufficient details." In other words, this book presents basic materials comprehensively. More importantly, this book is designed and presented in a manner that engages readers directly on each concept through specific learning features such as key points and examples.

In each valuation aspect, the book gives more emphasis on understanding the related practical challenges and different possible ways of addressing them. The aim is to give readers a sense of understanding the reality of valuation, not simply as a numerical subject, as most people tend to think, but as a combination of objective and subjective aspects. Overall, the book makes readers understand "the art of valuation" in relation to existing linkages between firm's objective, management role in value creation, investors' decisions, and the valuation role of financial information. Through using this book, students are expected to master valuation using the most commonly applied models.

Topic Coverage

Regarding coverage, this book is designed to cover the most common valuation topics available in many valuation syllabi of higher learning education, which mainly treat corporate valuation as a combination of accounting and finance. With few exceptions, the common coverage in company valuation syllabi of many universities tends to include topics like discounted cash flow, relative valuation, financial statement analysis, financial forecasting, and the cost of capital. In order to meet the needs of these topics, a combination of several textbooks is usually recommended: the most popular combination is to include textbooks related to corporate finance, financial statement analysis, and business valuation. The selection of topics in this book has considered this diversity of reading requirements, thereby making it a possible single-stop bookshelf for corporate valuation.

While financial accounting is usually a prerequisite for valuation courses, some students tend to have weak accounting and finance backgrounds, thereby limiting their ability to master valuation. This book addresses this problem by incorporating basic and advanced valuation-related aspects of accounting and finance. First, the book presents financial information as a vital ingredient for performing corporate valuation. Second, the book presents key concepts of value and valuation and basic techniques of cash flow discounting. Therefore, the book gives confidence to anyone who is interested in performing valuation, regardless of the level of accounting and finance background.

Selected topics are organized in four parts, each linking to one another as follows:

Part 1: The Concept of Value, Existence of a Firm, and The Objective Value Maximization

This part of the book is about conceptualization of value. It prepares readers to understand the meaning of value and how it can be created or destroyed. The idea is that, when performing valuation, it is very important to be aware of key questions like: Why value? What value? Value for who? Where does value come from? How is value measured? and so on. There are four chapters in this part, covering the following topics:

Chapter 1. An Overview of Corporate Valuation: The chapter introduces the reader to the concept of value and valuation approaches, clarifies different definitions of value, explains the importance of valuation, and discusses different valuation processes and their suitability for specific circumstance.

Chapter 2. Corporate Value Creation: The chapter covers corporate finance concepts relating to value by giving an overview of the firm as a unit of value creation and management. It informs readers about the reasons for the existence of a firm, its main objective, its stakeholders, and its financial management. Specific focus is put on clarifying value by comparing and contrasting it with related value concepts like profit versus cash flow, book value versus market value, and value versus price. The conflict of interest between business owners and managers is also discussed, taking into account its implication on value.

Chapter 3. Time Value of Money: The chapter prepares readers to understand the concept of cash flow discounting. It introduces the concept of time value of money, from which valuation is built. The aim is to educate readers about the time factor in valuation, while addressing issues relating to present value and future value. Readers without or with limited background in finance valuation concepts will use this part of the book as a foundation for progressing to valuation techniques.

Chapter 4. Security Markets and Valuation: The chapter makes an introduction to security markets (stocks and bonds) and their implications to value and valuation. The focus here is to acquaint readers with these security markets and their relationship with valuation. It prepares readers to apply stock markets and bond markets information in estimations of key valuation variables such as cost of equity and cost of debt, which are detailed in subsequent chapters.

Part 2: Financial Information as a Source of Valuation Inputs

This part covers financial information because value is created through business operations, in which results of operations are reported in financial statements. It introduces readers to the sources and nature of financial information, from which valuation data originates. The aim is to help learners understand the sources of value (value drivers) and valuation data. While there are many types of financial performance measurements, this book puts more emphasis on performance indicators that are mostly applicable in valuation, namely profitability, financial leverage, market perception, and free cash flows. In presenting these variables, a clear explanation is given of their implication on value, their relevance in valuation, and their applicability in particular valuation models. It covers the following six chapters:

Chapter 5. Overview of Financial Information: The chapter acquainting readers with the type and nature of financial information. Such information covers the financial position (balance sheet), the state of operations (income statement), and the flow of cash (cash flow statement).

Chapter 6. The Basics of Financial Statement Analysis: The chapter introduces the two major approaches of financial statement analysis, namely comparative analysis and financial ratio analysis.

Chapter 7. Profitability Analysis: The chapter focuses on selected key profitability ratios, aiming at demonstrating their implications in corporate valuation.

Chapter 8. Financial Leverage Analysis: The chapter focuses on practical relevance and application of leverage analysis. It considers its different versions by breaking them down according to potential effect on shareholders' wealth and business survival.

Chapter 9. Market Perception Analysis: The chapter presents the concept of investors' market perception and how it can be reflected and analyzed using ratios.

Chapter 10. Free Cash Flows: This chapter introduces cash flow as a key valuation variable. It builds on financial statements to introduce the concept of free cash flow and illustrate how it is calculated.

Part 3: The Cost of Capital

This part covers the cost of capital, a vital input for intrinsic valuation. Topics focus on understanding capital structure, the meaning, and estimation of cost of capital. While the concept of cost of capital can be easily understood, estimating the cost of capital is usually not a straightforward practice: challenges and limitations are clarified. Each chapter takes readers step by step from basics to advanced knowledge about the cost of capital. An overview of the cost of capital is aimed at understanding capital structure decisions and its implications on the cost of capital and value,that is, the relationship between cost of capital and value and its relevance in valuation. Then it develops into estimation of different components of the cost of capital, that is, the cost of equity and the cost of debt. In each of these components, different approaches are presented, discussed, and illustrated with simple examples as well as applied with practical data. Special emphasis is put on the suitability of different estimation approaches, considering both theoretical and practical limitations. It covers the following three chapters:

Chapter 11. Overview of Capital Structure and Cost of Capital: The chapter presents the general concept of capital structure and cost of capital.

Chapter 12. The Cost of Equity: The chapter takes a critical approach, considering theoretical views and practical aspects in addressing estimation challenges. It provides conceptual overviews of the estimation methods and uses practical examples to illustrate estimations of CAPM variables.

Chapter 13. The Cost of Debt: The chapter uses three concepts to explain cost of debt and estimation approach, hereafter referred to as effective interest rate approach (EIR), corporate default spread approach (CDS), and yield to maturity approach (YTM). Special emphasis is given on practical application and limitations of each approach.

Part 4: Intrinsic Valuation

This part covers intrinsic valuation, which is the application of discounted cash flow valuation models. Having been acquainted with required knowledge about cash flows and discount rates, readers are now progressing a further step to valuation of firm and equity. A clear distinction is made on the use of free cash flow to the firm (FCFF) and free cash flow to equity (FCFE) for direct estimation of firm value and equity value, respectively, and possible indirect estimations (from firm value to equity value and vice versa). Moreover, dividend discount models are presented for equity valuation.

The selection of topics in this part has considered the most commonly applied intrinsic valuation approaches and models. In applying free cash flows, two approaches are presented, namely the Cost of Capital approach (CC) and the Adjusted Present Value approach (APV). These two approaches are presented distinctively in order to provide a profound understanding of each. Moreover, for the same reason, we dedicate one chapter covering dividend discount models. Materials in each of the topics are presented with the aim of giving learners knowledge about the sources of valuation data, the ability to collect and extract data, making choices about the appropriate valuation models, addressing the limitations associated with valuation, analyzing valuation information, and making recommendations about value. To support these aims, a chapter is introduced for comparing and contrasting different valuation models and analyzing special issues like the value of growth and the present value of growth opportunities. The chapters are organized as follows:

Chapter 14. Estimating Growth Rates: The part starts with probably the most challenging aspect in valuation: estimation of growth rates, which is a vital input in cash flow forecasting. We believe that, upon reading this book, readers will acknowledge the complexity of growth rate estimation. This phenomenon, therefore, is presented to give readers an easy way of understanding the nature of complexity in estimating growth rates and how to address the limiting factors.

Chapter 15. Free Cash Flow Discount Models—Cost of Capital Approach: The chapter covers valuation with the cost of capital approach to estimate firm and equity value. The key variables are FCFF, FCFE, and discount rates (WACC and cost of equity).

Chapter 16. Free Cash Flow Discount Models—Adjusted Present Value Approach: The chapter introduces the APV approach and focuses on its distinction from CC approach. The key variables are FCFF and discount rates (unlevered cost of equity).

Chapter 17. Dividend Discount Models: The chapter focuses on explaining dividend discount models and practical limitations to guide analyst judgments on model suitability for specific valuation needs. More attention is given on estimating valuation variables from original data and decision about an appropriate valuation model.

Chapter 18. Further Issues with Cash Flow Discount Models: To expand learners' knowledge, this chapter gives additional explanation on valuation application, decision, and limitations.

Part 5: Relative Valuation

This part covers relative valuation, which is the application of valuation multiples. Topics are carefully selected and organized into four chapters. The layout of topics takes readers from the overview of relative valuation, whereby basic issues are introduced. The aim is to provide an initial understanding of the meaning of relative valuation, types of valuation multiples, and fundamental principles. Special emphasis is given on one of the challenging issues in relative valuation, that is, determination of comparable companies or peers. A comprehensive discussion is presented on the criteria for selecting peers and value drivers. This is followed by a general overview on application issues such as data collection, inspections, computation of value, interpretation, and practical limitations. While acknowledging the existence of numerous multiples, this book chooses to concentrate on the most practically applied multiples. Selected cases are used to illustrate practical application and limitations. The chapters are organized as follows:

Chapter 19. Overview of Relative Valuation: The focus of this chapter is to prepare learners to apply relative valuation effectively. It introduces the overall concept of relative valuation, its fundamental principles, and its significance in corporate valuation.

Chapter 20. Relative Equity Valuation: This chapter focuses on acquainting readers with an understanding of the most relevant equity value multiples. Readers will learn about five equity multiples, namely price to earnings (P/E), price to earnings growth (PEG), price to sales (P/S), price to book (P/B), and price to cash flows (P/CF).

Chapter 21. Relative Enterprise Valuation: This chapter focuses on acquainting readers with an understanding of the most relevant enterprise value (EV) multiples. The focus is on four multiples, namely EV to EBITDA, EV to EBIT, EV to sales, and EV to free cash flow.

Chapter 22. Application of Relative Valuation: This chapter is dedicated to explaining its real-world application of relative valuation. The aim here is to give readers a feeling of the reality and significance of relative valuation.

Special Learning Features

In this book, each valuation aspect or concept is presented in a way that addresses conceptual and practical questions such as: What is it? Who uses it? Where is it found and used? How is it done and applied? When to apply it? Why is it so? And which one is more suitable? These are the things that take readers from common theoretical concepts to real-world application. The approach, therefore, does not only intend to provide knowledge and skills, but also to build learners' ability to make appropriate choices and decisions to suit practical valuation challenges. Specifically, to make this book unique, it features the following aspects:

Learning Approach

It takes readers from knowledge-based approach of learning to application-based approach. While basic concepts are presented comprehensively, the book tries as much as possible to show readers *how to do it* in reality. This distinctive feature is reflected on the following practical elements:

Information: This book shows readers how information is a powerful aspect in performing valuation: it makes valuation either possible or impossible, accurate or inaccurate, and so on. Therefore, in each valuation variable, the book takes the reader step by step from understanding to applying information by addressing questions like: What information? Why is it relevant? Where to find it? How to extract data from it? When to use it? And how to apply it?

Methods: Indeed, valuation is a technical field that requires the use of quantitative methods such as mathematics and statistics. While this is important, this book is designed to show readers that valuation can be performed fully even with a minimum level of prior quantitative skills. To achieve this learning approach without diluting the reality of valuation, a careful balance is made between the selection of quantitative materials and conceptual materials. With the use of this book, therefore, a basic knowledge level in Excel application is, indeed, reasonably sufficient to perform valuation.

Reality

This book leads readers from conceptualization to understanding the reality about a particular concept. This is where readers broaden their knowledge about basic valuation concepts by taking it towards practical application. To achieve this goal, the book tries as much as possible to use real-world information and related data through the following features:

- *Cases*: The book tries as much as possible to use illustrative cases based on real-world data. Each case is conceived and designed to address a specific valuation

issue using a careful selection of case companies. While these cases are described with text, they are also presented in the form of exhibits, thereby making them usable as stand-alone materials where necessary.
- *News insights*: This book utilizes a wide range of news materials from different sources (e.g., Financial Times, The Economist, Bloomberg, CNN Finance, Reuters, Yahoo Finance). The idea is to make readers understand that valuation is not mainly about numbers and formula, but also the story surrounding a company (e.g., shareholders, analysts, regulators, lenders). This is because a company exists for a purpose and value is created from internal and external factors. News headlines and contents are carefully selected to fulfil the learning objective of a particular concept.
- *Quotes*: This book covers a number of quotes aiming at expanding knowledge about a particular concept. They show readers the reality about different perceptions and understanding of people's views on theoretical and practical valuation aspects. These quotes, thus, come from a diverse selection of people such as CEOs, investors, analysts, academics, news contributors, and other authors.

Presentation

This book is presented in a way that makes its easy-to-use, engaging, flexible, time saving, and interesting. Moreover, it gives readers a probably complete package of learning materials in different formats but for the same purpose.
- *Chapter introduction*: Each chapter commences with a brief introduction about what it covers. It makes the reader clear why materials in that chapter are important and how they are related to materials in other chapters. Overall, introductory statements show linkages among selected topics in different chapters and within the book. Moreover, each chapter introduction is supported by a list of expected learnings outcomes.
- *Self-contained chapters*: The organization of topics and presentation of this book makes each chapter as self-contained as possible. Thus, each chapter fulfils the complete need of a particular theme or topic. For example, a reader interested in estimating growth rates simply needs to focus on ▶ Chap. 14. This approach gives the book a wider room to be applied at different levels of learning, depending on course structures of different learning institutions.
- *Key points*: Most textbooks prefer to place key points or closing summary materials at the end of chapters or the book. In this book, however, key points (hereafter referred to as *banners*) are placed on the same page in which a particular concept is presented. These banners, therefore, serve as flags aiming at two purposes. First, they allow readers to have a quick eyeball of a particular concept before even embarking into deep details. Second, they serve as recapitulating materials for immediate conceptualization after reading the detailed

materials. Students preparing for final exams may use these banners as tools for quick concept review, while simultaneously referring to detailed materials on the same page.

- *Thinking*: While materials in this book are comprehensive, readers are expected to build and enhance their ability to think beyond what they have read or learnt in classrooms. This book, therefore, includes a large number of thinking-capacity questions (hereafter, they are referred to as *Think*), reflecting on a particular basic concept or practical problem relating to valuation. The aim is to give readers a pause for a critical view of the presented issues before proceeding to the next stage.
- *Practical assignments*: Materials in this book are designed to give readers active engagement at different stages of learning. To fulfil this goal, the book gives readers a room to apply a particular concept by working on a practical question (hereafter referred to as *Apply*), which is placed immediately after a concept or practical issue. The aim here is to give readers time to pause and grasp both concepts and application before proceeding.
- *Revisions:* Each chapter contains review questions to cover almost all concepts within that particular chapter. Where applicable, revisions include computations and analytical questions. These are placed at the end of chapters.
- *Exhibits*: Many textbooks use exhibits simply as references to support text materials. In this book, however, exhibits are designed and presented to serve two purposes: a reference to concepts within text and as stand-alone learning materials. That is, each exhibit is fully independent with all the information the reader needs to have in relation to a particular learning aspect. Depending on the objective of an exhibit, coverage includes, but not limited to, background information, data, worked examples, illustrative cases, news insights, instructions, explanations, analysis, and summary tables. As stand-alone materials, readers with limited time will find these exhibits very useful tools for quick conceptualization and revision.
- *Bibliography:* Each chapter includes a bibliography in order to direct readers to alternative readings relating to the topic covered within it.

Ancillary Materials

This book comes with the following ancillary materials:

- *Slides*: Each chapter is accompanied by slides to serve as teaching and reading materials for teachers and students, respectively.
- *Excel illustrations*: Each chapter with illustrative examples is supported with Excel illustrations to help readers with revisions.
- *Working data*: All practical cases are supported by working data to enable readers replicate the illustrations for revision purposes. Data supplements are also available for learnings, practices, and assignments.

Proposed Syllabi

While this book focuses on company valuation, its wide topic coverage makes it suitable for related corporate finance courses. The following course outlines are proposed:

Subject: Corporate Finance/Managerial Finance

- Corporate Decision and Value Creation (▶ Chap. 2)
- Interest Rates and Time Value of Money (▶ Chap. 3)
- Security Markets (▶ Chap. 4)
- Overview of Financial Information (▶ Chap. 5)
- Financial Statement Analysis (▶ Chap. 6)
- Profitability Analysis (▶ Chap. 7)
- Financial Leverage Analysis (▶ Chap. 8)
- Estimating Free Cash Flow (▶ Chap. 10)
- Overview of Capital Structure and Cost of Capital (▶ Chap. 11)
- Capital Asset pricing (▶ Chap. 12)
- The Cost of Equity (▶ Chap. 12)
- The Cost of Debt (▶ Chap. 13)
- Stock Valuation: Discounted Cash Flow (▶ Chaps. 15, 16, and 17).

Subject: Financial Statement Analysis

- Financial Information (▶ Chap. 5)
- Tools of Financial Statement Analysis (▶ Chap. 6)
- Comparative Analysis (▶ Chap. 6)
- Financial Ratios (▶ Chap. 6)
- Profitability Analysis (▶ Chap. 7)
- Financial Leverage Analysis (▶ Chap. 8)
- Market value analysis (▶ Chap. 9)
- Free Cash Flow (▶ Chap. 10)
- Valuation Ratios (▶ Chap. 19)
- Equity Value Ratios (▶ Chap. 20)
- Enterprise Value Ratios (▶ Chap. 21)

Subject: Investment Analysis and Security Valuation

- Corporate Decision and Value Creation (▶ Chap. 2)
- Interest Rates and Time Value of Money (▶ Chap. 3)
- Security Markets (▶ Chap. 4)

- Overview of Financial Information (▶ Chap. 5)
- Financial Statement Analysis (▶ Chap. 6)
- Overview of Capital Structure and Cost of Capital (▶ Chap. 11)
- The Cost of Equity (▶ Chap. 12)
- The Cost of Debt (▶ Chap. 13)
- Equity and Firm Valuation: Discounted Cash Flow Analysis (▶ Chaps. 15, 16, and 17).
- Equity and Firm Valuation: Relative Valuation (▶ Chaps. 19, 20, and 21).

Benedicto Kulwizira Lukanima
Barranquilla, CO, USA

Acknowledgments

Writing this book was a long and tough journey which took almost 3 years to be completed. It could, therefore, not be a success without the contribution of several individuals and institutions. I am grateful to all of them.

My foremost gratitude goes to my father and mother for their role in my education and career development, and my family for sacrificing my absence during the writing process.

Professor Glen Arnold inspired me to write this book. I had read and liked his book *Corporate Financial Management* during my postgraduate studies at Salford University, where he was teaching. Knowing him personally as an author of such a useful finance book was key to my conception of this book.

Starting the writing process required advice and guidance from experienced authors and colleagues. I would like to thank Prof. Mike Jackson (Hull University Business School, United Kingdom), Prof. Peijie Wang (University of Plymouth University, United Kingdom), Dr. Gabriel Komba (Mzumbe University, Tanzania), and Dr. Jahir Lombana (Universidad del Norte, Colombia).

Support from Universidad del Norte (Colombia) was vital. Through subscription to data sources (Bloomberg) and academic materials, I was able to access and obtain all the information required to make this book a success. Special thanks to the administration of Business School: Dr. Octavio Ibarra Consuegra (former dean), Dr. Maria Clemencia Sierra Peñas (current dean), Luis Sánchez Barrios (academic director), and Yuli Paola Gómez Bravo (head of finance and accounting department).

Apart from subscribed data sources, this book utilizes information from a wide range of sources. I am indebted to many publicly available information and data sources, including the following: Damodaran: Stern Business School (US), Nasdaq (US), CNBC (US), CNN Money (US), Reuters (UK), Bloomberg (US), Forbes (US), Financial Times (UK), Seeking Alpha (US), Yahoo Finance (US), Investing.com (Spain, Cyprus, Israel, China), New York Times (US), The Wall Street Journal (US), Simply Wall Street (Australia), The Economic Times (India), RTT News (US), The National News (UAE), Fitch (US), Moody's (US), S&P Global (US), The World Bank, The Balance (US), Statista (German), Investment Week Magazine: invetmentweek.co.uk (UK), MarketWatch: marketwatch.com (US), NerdWallet (nerdwallet.com) (US), Zacks Investment Research (US), GlobeNewsWire Inc. (US), The Motley Fool (US), Hollywood Reporter (US), Financial Poise (US), CFA Institute (US), KPMG (Netherlands), Financial Management Magazine-FM (UK), The Business Roundtable—BR (US), Business Wire Inc. (US), Accounting Today (US), Dynamic Business (Australia), PR Newswire (US), Times Colonist (Canada), International Capital Markets Association-ICMA (Switzerland), International Monetary Fund-IMF (US), Stockhouse (Canada), McKinsey & Company (US), and The Channel Company-CRN (US), PwC (UK).

Special thanks to Springer: Nitza Jones for considering my book proposal and for her valuable guidance; Maria David and Krishnakumar Pandurangan for their valuable support from the proposal stage to final submission.

Contents

IV Intrinsic Valuation

The Concept of Value, Existence of a Firm, and the Objective Value Maximization

Contents

An Overview of Corporate Valuation

Contents

Supplementary Information The online version contains supplementary material available at https://doi.org/10.1007/978-3-031-28267-6_1.

B. Kulwizira Lukanima, *Corporate Valuation*, Classroom Companion: Business, https://doi.org/10.1007/978-3-031-28267-6_1

1.1 Introduction

Valuation is one of the important topics in the business field, and it plays a key role in many areas of finance such as corporate finance, mergers and acquisitions (M&A), and portfolio management. Although the term "valuation" seems to be common, many people may be unaware of its core components. There are different ways in which valuation can be performed—hence, it is not an absolute process. Therefore, different analysts recommend different values for the same company or equity, simply because of different valuation approaches depending on valuation purposes and the suitability of valuation approaches. From this point of view, the definition of value (or valuation) depends on the valuation approach—for example, we have intrinsic value, relative value, market value, and book value.

This chapter provides an overview of corporate valuation. Specifically, this chapter clarifies different definitions of value, explains the importance of valuation, and discusses different valuation processes and their suitability for specific circumstances.

Learning Outcomes

- Define different concepts of value
- Describe different valuation approaches
- Explain the importance of valuation
- Understand the valuation process

1.2 Meanings of Value

In a nutshell, value simply means how much something is worth. Nevertheless, corporate valuation categorizes value in different ways depending on valuation approaches. It is, therefore, important to be more specific when talking about value to reflect on what it represents. Let us consider the following key valuation terms: "market value," "book value," "intrinsic value," "relative value," and "fair market value." To understand these value concepts, let us look at different valuation approaches in the next section.

Banner 1.1 Meaning of Value
Value is a measure of wealth—how much something is worth.

Exhibit 1.1 Value and Valuation Approaches

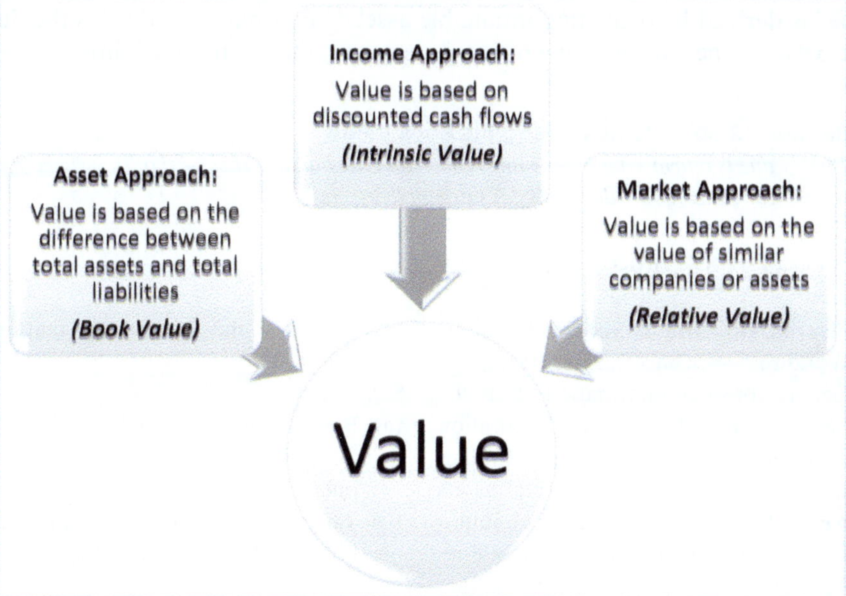

Source: Author's construct

1.3 Value and Valuation Approaches

Valuation approaches are commonly categorized as asset-based, income-based, and market-based. The key distinctive features of these three valuation approaches are summarized in Exhibit ▸ 1.1 and explained below.

Think 1.1

Should we have the same meaning of value for different valuation approaches? Why?

1.3.1 Asset-Based Approach

1.3.1.1 The Value Concept of the Asset Approach

The asset approach is based on the notion that shareholders' equity is the difference between total assets and total liabilities. In its basic form, therefore, the estimated value is a "book value." It is calculated on the basis of the historical cost of an asset, adjusted for loss of value (due to depreciation, amortization, or impairment costs of assets), and excludes the value of intangible assets (e.g., goodwill, trademark, etc.). Hence, book value is a backward-looking measure of value. From shareholders' perspective, this is the value that they should receive upon company

1

liquidation (i.e., net worth)—that is, the total asset value minus all financial obligations and minority interest. Depending on the valuation purpose, book value can also be adjusted to reflect tangible value or fair market value. "Tangible book value" is derived by deducting intangible assets. "Fair market value" is the difference between the current value of total assets and that of total liabilities.

Banner 1.2 Book Value vs. Tangible Book Value

Book value is a firm's net asset value reported in the balance sheet—that is, owners' net worth. Tangible book value excludes intangible assets.

Exhibit 1.2 Book Value vs. Market Value

Illustrative Example (See Excel Workings—▶ Chap. 1, Sheet E.1.2)

Let us consider information from the balance sheet of Chevron Corporation as of December 31, 2020, with all values in US$ (Zacks.com 2022). Total assets were US$239.79 billion of which intangible assets comprised US$4.4 billion. Total liabilities were US$107.06 billion, whereas minority interest was US$0. On 31 December 2020, Chevron stocks were trading at US$85.2 per share (Yahoo Finance, 2022). The company had 1.87 billion shares outstanding.

(a) What is the company's book value?
(b) What is the company's tangible book value?
(c) What is the company's market value?

Solution

(a) Book value = US$239.79 – US$107.06 – US$0 = US$132.73 billion
(b) Tangible book value = US$132.73 billion – US$4.4 = US$128.33 billion
(c) Market value = US$85.2 × 1.87B = US$159.82 billion

Sources of Data:

Zacks (2022) ▶ https://www.zacks.com/stock/quote/CVX/balance-sheet

Macrotrends (2022) ▶ https://www.macrotrends.net/stocks/charts/CVX/chevron/shares-outstanding

1.3.1.2 Practical Application

The usefulness of the asset-based approach is wide depending on the premises of value—either going-concern valuation or liquidation valuation. It has, however, limited use in operating businesses but more use in real estates and holding companies. For example, in a going-concern situation, lenders tend to analyze a company's ability to borrow and pay debt or use the asset value as collateral. In a liquidation situation, the asset approach can be used to determine a buying or selling price (e.g., mergers and acquisitions). Moreover, this approach can be used when other valuation approaches are not suitable. It is important, however, to note that the application of this approach depends on the availability of data, necessary to make vital adjustments like intangible assets and other obligations.

Banner 1.3 Market Value
Market value is the value based on market perception—that is, how much it is worth in the market.

Book values tend to be applied in conjunction with market value. "Market value" is the value based on market perception. It is based on the maximum price at which investors are willing to either buy or sell an asset in the market. It is the total value of a company's outstanding shares (market capitalization). Market value is forward-looking as it depends on expectations about the future of a business. Exhibit ► 1.2 provides an example to distinguish between book value and market value, whereas Exhibit ► 1.3 summarizes some of the key differences.

Investors usually compare book value and market value to gauge the market confidence of a company. To explain this, let us use the example of Chevron Corporation. The company had a book value of US$128.33 billion and a market value of US$159.82 billion in December 2020. From this example, a greater market value than book value signifies investors' positive perception about the company—they believe that the company has a better future, and, hence, its worth is US$31.48 billion more than the balance sheet value. In contrast, a lower market value than a book value would suggest a negative market perception of the company—its future prospect is believed to be weak. Quotes ► 1.1 presents some selected quotes showing how book value and market value are applied in investment decision-making. Overall, value investors prefer investing in stocks whose market value is lower than its book value—popular investors like Ben Graham and Warren Buffet have derived success from this investment strategy.

Moreover, book value tends to be more applicable to capital-intensive companies because they have a significant amount of physical assets. However, it has limited application in companies with a significant amount of intangible assets.

Think 1.2
Why should the premises of value (going-concern or liquidation) be considered in valuation?

Exhibit 1.3 Book Value vs. Market Value

	Book value	Market value
Source of information	Internal source of information prepared by the company (the balance sheet)	External source of information from the market (perception of the market)
Frequency of information	Low frequency—usually available annually and(or) quarterly	High frequency—usually available hourly, daily, weekly, and monthly
Base	Historical cost of assets	Current stock value (market capitalization)

1

	Book value	Market value
Calculation	(Total assets—total liabilities—minority interest) or (total assets—total liabilities—minority interest)—intangible assets	Common shares outstanding x current stock price
Reliability	Subjected to accounting issues—value can be influenced by accounting manipulation and policies relating to depreciation and asset impairment	Value is a consensus among investors—willing buyers and willing sellers. It is what assets (in books) will sell currently. However, the market is not always right—the company can be unfairly valued (overvalued or undervalued)

Quotes 1.1 Application of Book Value and Market Value

Quote 1.1.1 Value Investors

» Value investing—buying stocks that are cheap on measures such as earnings or book value—is having a renaissance. Up to last Thursday, large value stocks beat more expensive "growth" stocks by the most of any 50-day period since the technology bubble burst in 2000–01, with the exception of the post-vaccine rebound early last year" ... Cliff Asness, founder of quantitative fund manager AQR, thinks it is plausible that the bond-yield rise was the shock that changed investor views on growth stocks. "It's a catalyst not because of solid economic reasons but because catalysts for when irrationality will blow up are behavioral magic, not economics. (James Mackintosh, Senior columnist, markets, The Wall Street Journal)

James Mackintosh, February 1, 2022, The Wall Street Journal

Quote 1.1.2 Ben Graham, Warren Buffet, and Charlie Munger

» Ben Graham is ascribed as being the father of value investing. The intellectual framework he brought to investors was using the available accounting to measure value of a business. His way of measuring was book value, the total assets minus all liabilities. By figuring out this number, he could then divide this metric by the total shares outstanding to understand how much book value per share (what some may call net worth) a company had versus what the price the shares were trading for in the stock market...

...Warren Buffett (Trades, Portfolio) was hugely influenced by his teachers concepts early in his career. In later years, after being introduced to Charlie Munger (Trades, Portfolio) and witnessing what they saw with their investment in Sees Candy, he began to think much more about the future of a business than the current balance sheet. (Smead Capital Management)

Smead Capital Management, February 1 2022, Yahoo Finance

1.3.2 Income-Based Approach

1.3.2.1 The Value Concept of the Income Approach

The income approach is based on cash flow discounting models. Depending on the premises of value, the two major categories of income-based valuation are "income capitalization" and "cash flow discounting." The income capitalization approach is applied to estimate the asset value based on "actual" cash flows generated by those assets. The major assumption is that the past is a good representative of the future. The applicable discount rate on this approach is known as the capitalization rate, which is usually a market rate of return. The cash flow discount approach uses "expected" cash flows, considering their past, current, and future positions.

Banner 1.4 Intrinsic Value
Intrinsic value is the value estimated from discounting future cash flows—also known as economic value.

"Intrinsic valuation," therefore, falls under the income-based approach, in which the estimated value is referred to as the "economic value" or "intrinsic value." The philosophical basis of intrinsic value is that the main determinants of value are cash flows, growth, and risk. While growth is used to forecast cash flows, risk is incorporated in the discount rate (cost of capital). Therefore, the intrinsic valuation process includes cash flow projections, estimated lifetime of investment, and the appropriate discount rate. Depending on valuation models, the term "cash" carries different meanings such as free cash flow to the firm (for firm value), free cash flow to equity (for equity value), dividends per share (for equity value), face value and coupon interest (for bond value), and so on. In its simplest form, a cash flow discount equation can be presented as follows:

$$Value = \Sigma \frac{CF_t}{(1+r)^t}$$

where CF is the expected cash flow, t is the period in which the cash flow is generated, and r is the discount rate (cost of capital). Refer to ▶ Chap. 3 for understanding the concept of "time value of money." A simple example of estimating an intrinsic value is presented in Exhibit ▶ 1.4.

There are different types of cash flow discount valuation models. This book discusses and illustrates intrinsic valuation in ▶ Chaps. 11–18.

Think 1.3
Why cash flow, growth, and risk should be regarded as the main determinants of value?

1

Exhibit 1.4 Intrinsic Value

Illustrative Example (See Excel Workings—► Chap. 1, Sheet E.1.4)

An asset is expecting to generate cash flows over the next 8 years as indicated in the table below. The estimated discount rate is 8% throughout the lifetime of cash flows. Calculate the asset value.

Period	1	2	3	4	5	6	7	8
Cash flows (US$ million)	10.00	12.50	8.00	8.90	11.00	12.40	9.00	10.20

Solution

Period	1	2	3	4	5	6	7	8
Cash flows (US$ million)	10.00	12.50	8.00	8.90	11.00	12.40	9.00	10.20
Present value @8%	9.26	10.72	6.35	6.54	7.49	7.81	5.25	5.51

Value = the sum of present values = US$58.93 million

1.3.2.2 Practical Application

Despite its complexity, this approach is widely applied among professional analysts because it fulfills the concept of time value of money. The point is that investments are made now, but cash flows will be generated in the future—value is the present value of expected cash flows. We will discuss its application in comparison with the market-based approach in the next section.

1.3.3 Market-Based Approach

1.3.3.1 The Value Concept of the Market Approach

The market-based approach is used to value an asset by comparing values (or prices) of similar assets (peers)—that is, assets with identical characteristics. Value-based benchmarks are determined from selected value drivers like earnings, sales, cash flows, book value, etc. "Relative valuation" is a market approach—sometimes referred to as "extrinsic valuation" because it is not based on economic fundamentals. The estimated value is referred to as "fair market value" or "relative value."

Banner 1.5 Relative Value

Relative value is the value of any asset estimated by comparing the market prices of similar or comparable assets—also known as fair market value.

The root of relativity is that the value of an asset is whatever the market is willing to pay for it based upon its characteristics and performance compared to a single (e.g. P/E) or multiple (e.g. P/E, PEG, BP) peer benchmarks. In corporate valuation, a benchmark measures the average performance of other similar companies depending on one or more value drivers. Relative valuation, therefore, involves the selection of a group of comparable firms (peers), selection of value drivers, and analysis of performance indicators (valuation multiples or ratios).

For example, if we intend to value Chevron Corporation, we must first identify its appropriate peer group. There are many different types of value drivers and valuation multiples applied in relative valuation, but, here, they are categorized into two:

- *Equity value multiples*: These are used to estimate equity value. The most applied multiple is the price–earnings (P/E) ratio, but there are others too, such as price-to-book (P/B), price-to-sales (P/S), and so on.
- *Enterprise value multiples:* These are used to estimate an enterprise (firm value). Although there are different types of enterprise value multiples, the most applied are enterprise value/earnings before interest and taxes (EV/EBIT) and enterprise value/earnings before interest and taxes, depreciation, and amortization (EV/EBITDA).

A simple example about relative valuation is presented in Exhibit ▶ 1.5. In this book, relative valuation is covered in ▶ Chaps. 19–22.

Exhibit 1.5 Relative Value

Illustrative Example (See Excel Workings—▶ Chap. 1, Sheet E.1.5)

ABC company reported its earnings for the fourth quarter of 2021 as follows: earnings per share (EPS) is US$5, whereas EBITDA is US$120 million. Its peer group, which comprises five companies, has an average P/E ratio of 8 and an average EV/EBITDA of 5.

(a) What is ABC's equity value?

(b) What is ABC's enterprise value?

Solution

Value = value driver x peer benchmark

Equity value = US$5 × 8 = US$40 per share

Enterprise value = US$120 million × 5 = US$600 million

1.3.3.2 Practical Application

Intrinsic value and relative value are based on completely different valuation philosophies—the former is absolute, whereas the latter is relative. We should not, therefore, expect the same valuation results (if any). Quotes ▶ 1.2 provides a practical picture about their application. Generally, while intrinsic value seems to have great use among analysts and professionals, relative value appears to have more practical application among investors. Nevertheless, a better conclusion about value should be based upon a combination of both intrinsic and relative values.

1

Exhibit ▶ 1.6 presents a brief comparison between intrinsic and relative values. Both intrinsic and relative values tend to be applied in comparison with market values to determine whether a company or stock is undervalued or overvalued.

Exhibit 1.6 Intrinsic Valuation vs. Relative Valuation

	Intrinsic valuation	Relative valuation
Financial information	Used for determining cash flows (i.e., free cash flow to the firm, cash flow to equity and dividend) and estimating growth rates	Used for determining value drivers (e.g., earnings, sales, book value, free cash flows, etc.) and estimating growth rates
Market information	Used for estimating the cost of capital, risk analysis, credit ratings, etc.	Used for determining valuation multiple variables (i.e., stock price and enterprise value), peer companies, etc.
Valuation approach	Discounting of expected cash flows Generally a complex process, usually performed by valuation experts	Valuation multiples of peer companies Generally an easy process and can be performed by nonexperts
Reliability	Value is acceptable if it makes sense because a true intrinsic value is almost impossible to estimate Immune from market irrationality and mispricing	Value is acceptable if it makes sense because a true relative value is almost impossible to estimate Exposed to market irrationality and mispricing
Worthiness	Value considers only the company to be valued. It reflects the real value of an asset	Value considers other companies (peers). It may not represent the real worthiness of an asset but a comparative value to the market
Limitations	Involves many assumptions An analyst's subjective judgments can influence value Exposed to cash flow forecasting errors	Involves fewer assumptions The definition of a peer group is not universal—the selection of peers can influence value Getting "similar" companies is almost impossible Valuation can be misleading if comparable companies are mispriced

Quotes 1.2 Application of Intrinsic Value and Relative Value

▪ Quote 1.2.1 Conclusion Can Be Wrong

» The discounted cash flow (DCF) model is universal. So, what do I mean by this? And what are first principles? Let's take P/E ratios. Though every valuation multiple can be expanded into a DCF model, P/E ratios aren't necessarily shortcuts to the DCF model. When misapplied, they can lead to the wrong conclusions about a company's value. (Brian Nelson, CFA)

Brian Nelson, Valuentum Analysts, January 19, 2022, CFA Institute

- **Quote 1.2.2 Use Suitable Cash Flows**

» As Sempra operates in the integrated utilities sector, we need to calculate the intrinsic value slightly differently. Instead of using free cash flows, which are hard to estimate and often not reported by analysts in this industry, dividends per share (DPS) payments are used. Unless a company pays out the majority of its FCF as a dividend, this method will typically underestimate the value of the stock (Analyst, Simply Wall St.)
Analyst, January 25, 2022, NASDAQ

- **Quote 1.2.3 Contradicting Values from Different Approaches**

» Deciding if you should use a relative valuation model over an intrinsic valuation model can be a difficult choice for many investors. For instance, while my relative valuation model tells me ICON Public Limited Company's (NASDAQ:ICLR) is overvalued by 86.29%, my discounted cash flow (DCF) model signals a 19.91% undervaluation instead. Which model do I listen to and more importantly why? (Analyst, Simply Wall St, 2018)
Analysts, November 9, 2018, Yahoo Finance

- **Quote 1.2.4 Do Not Rely on a Single Approach**

» As part of our stock-selection process, we build a discounted cash-flow ('DCF') valuation model where we estimate the intrinsic value per share of companies... there's a lot of problems with just looking at the valuation multiple of a company. (Valuentum Analysts, Seeking Alpha)
Valuentum Analysts, February 1, 2022, Seeking Alpha

1.4 Why Corporate Valuation?

To understand the importance of corporate valuation, let us look at the following two key aspects—What do we value? What is the valuation motive?

Think 1.4
Is it possible to perform valuation without a motive? Explain.

1.4.1 What Do We Value?

Corporate valuation is built around the capital structure. Therefore, it focuses on two main aspects—firm value and equity value—although debt valuation is also practiced. In this book, we focus on both firm value and equity value.

Banner 1.5 Equity Value
Equity value is the value attributed to equity holders—it is the true value of owners' investments.

1.4.1.1 Equity Value

Equity is an important component of the capital structure because it represents business ownership. Due to their ownership status, common shareholders can be regarded as "internal investors." Therefore, we value equity to determine the true value of owners' investment in a company. From this point of view, a proper equity valuation should use variables with direct effect or interest to equity holders. For example, in intrinsic valuation, we use free cash flow to equity (or dividend), discounted at the cost of equity. In relative valuation, although there are several value drivers, the use of earnings per share (EPS) is dominant. Depending on a company's capital structure, we can also value preference equity—these investors do not have an ownership status, and, hence, they can be regarded as "external investors."

Banner 1.6 Firm Value

Firm value is the value attributed to a company—it is the true value of all investments.

1.4.1.2 Firm Value

When a company is fully financed by equity (an unlevered firm), firm value is the equity value. However, many companies tend to fund investments through both equity and debt. Therefore, firm value is the value of all investments (assets), regardless of how they were financed. From this point of view, firm valuation models use variables of interest to both equity holders and debtholders. For example, intrinsic valuation applies free cash flow to the firm (unlevered cash flows), discounted at the weighted average cost of capital (WACC)—the cost of all sources of finance. In relative valuation, value drivers that do not account for leverage (e.g., EBIT, EBITDA, sales, etc.) tend to be applied.

1.4.2 Valuation Motives

Like any kind of financial analysis, valuation should be performed with a motive. Primarily, valuation is a tool to help in decision-making because it includes identifying sources of value creation as well as value destruction. In the real world of corporate finance, we face several decisions—at corporate and individual levels—which require an upfront understanding of value and valuation. Among others, those decisions include takeovers, stock trading, public offering, managerial compensation schemes, and so on. Let us outline the key motives for valuation.

1.4.2.1 Investment and Financing Decisions

Any rational investor would like to know the value of a firm or stock before making a reasonable investment decision. In stock markets, for example, prices are determined by market perceptions about the firm. Several analysts follow those stocks and value them continuously. The purpose of valuing them is to help investors make informed decisions—whether to sell, buy, or hold stocks. For portfolio investment decision and management, valuation is vital for ascertaining overpricing or underpricing of financial securities. For example, when investors believe that the stocks of a firm have been undervalued, they will line up into buying now, expecting appreciation of their value in the future. On the contrary, if stocks have been overvalued, then investors will prefer to sell them now, expecting their value to fall in future. In public offering, a financing strategy, valuation is useful for justifying the stock price to be offered to the public. During initial public offering (IPO), both undervaluing and overvaluing of stocks may be detrimental to the firm's future value.

1.4.2.2 Mergers and Acquisitions (M&A)

Mergers and acquisitions involve negotiations about the values of the merging firms (mergers) or the target firm (acquisitions). Valuation, therefore, provides vital information to strengthen the negotiating power of the decision-makers in a deal. It should be noted that both sides (the merging firm and the bidding or target firm) need to know the right price for the deal—this price is determined by value, among other factors. In mergers, valuation tends to focus on synergy—added value from merging. In acquisitions, the bidder requires valuation to determine the maximum price to pay for the acquisition. For the target firm, valuation helps in ascertaining the minimum price to offer.

1.4.2.3 Management Motivation

One of the main issues in corporate governance is the principal-agency problem (refer to ► Chap. 2 for a detailed discussion). Among strategies to minimize this problem is executive compensation schemes, which are mostly determined by the ability of managers to create value. Hence, valuation is important for quantifying value creation attributable to executives to be compensated.

1.4.2.4 Identifying Value Drivers

Although it is important to know value, it is even more important to be aware of what drives such value. Valuation plays a vital role in identifying and stratifying value drivers. The analysis of key value drivers can be a powerful way to bring managers' attention on activities that will have more impact on value. In turn, managers will use this vital information to ensure that strategies and decision-making are aligned with the true drivers of value for their firm.

1.4.2.5 Strategic Decisions

Firms make many strategic decisions that may not be done appropriately without valuation. Among others, strategic decisions include whether to keep on the business, sell the business, merge, expand the business, or acquire another business. In strategic planning, valuation is fundamental for determining policies and means of enhancing value creation. This would also include measures like determining product lines, customer segments, country locations, and so on.

1

Exhibit 1.7 The Corporate Valuation Process

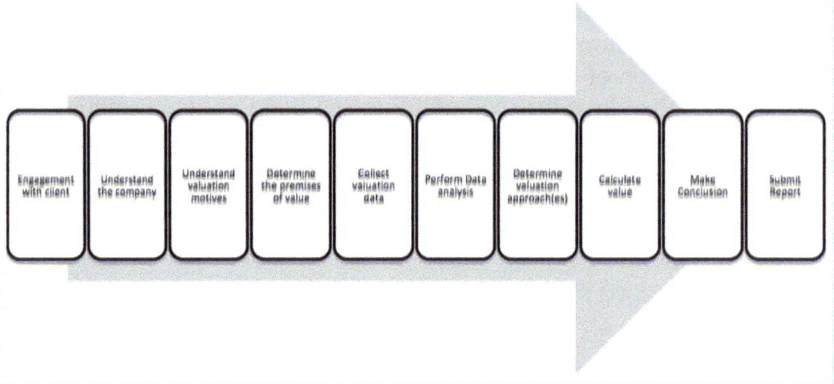

Source: Author's construct.

1.5 The Valuation Process

Corporate valuation can be described as the process of estimating an economic or fair value of a firm or equity. There is no standard series of steps to be followed in this process. However, valuation should comply with certain universal rules and principles, regardless of the order of valuation steps. Here, we describe the following key steps:

- **Engagement**

Usually, valuation starts with an engagement with the client—a person or entity on whom valuation will be performed (e.g., a willing seller or buyer, an investor, a court of law, etc.). This stage is important because it sets the foundation for the rest of the valuation process by defining key aspects like the scope of valuation, obligations of parties involved, valuation time frame, renumerations, and other requirements.

- **Understanding the Company**

Understanding the company is extremely crucial because every business is unique. It is, therefore, necessary to gather fundamental information about the company, such as its sector or industry, nature of business operations, strategies, investments, long-term plans, and so on. Such sets of information are helpful in identifying key valuation aspects such as access to valuation data, choice of valuation approach, possible valuation challenges (and solutions), and expertise requirements.

- **Understanding the Motive for Valuation**

As described earlier, there are several motives for valuation. Analysts, therefore, tend to value companies according to their specific purpose, which, in turn, influences valuation decisions like an approach to use and assumptions to make.

Consequently, any such decision will influence the conclusion about value. For example, if valuation is motivated by a takeover (buy) decision, then it is likely to aim at ensuring a cheaper takeover price (a low value). In contrast, a motive to sell a company should prefer a valuation conclusion with a higher price.

Alongside the motive, valuation considers the "basis of value"—the perspective of different parties in valuation—to reach a consensus about value. There is always tension between the involved parties like a willing seller and a willing buyer. The basis of value normally involves legal obligations (i.e., regulation, law, contract, etc.). Consider the case of DFC Global Corp. in ▸ Quotes 1.3.2, where a value decision had to be determined through the court of law.

- **Determining the Premises of Value**

Businesses can be valued under two different premises—either a going-concern premise or a liquidation premise.

Going-concern: A going-concern valuation assumes that a company or assets will continue to operate in its current form. Therefore, this premise focuses on the value of a business (not individual assets), considering not only its existing investments but also the potential future of its investments and operations and not as a collection of business assets.

Liquidation: It is vital to note that a going-concern valuation is distinct from an asset-based valuation, in which assets are valued separately. Cases of asset-based valuation include liquidation valuation and M&A (mergers and acquisitions). Liquidation valuation assumes that a company or assets (separately or jointly) will not continue operating in its current form. An M&A valuation assumes that the buyer may acquire synergy (i.e., more value than the fair value).

- **Collecting Valuation Data**

Information is one of the key aspects of valuation. This step involves gathering relevant company data (both financial and nonfinancial) and market data. Financial data are mainly extracted from financial statements (balance sheet, income statement, and cash flow statement). Nonfinancial data include aspects that will affect the future of the company's investments, finances, and operations—for example, ownership structure, strategic plans, contracts, agreements, obligations, etc. Market data may include competitors (peers), market price, economic data, and other performance benchmarks. Data collection should consider the notion of "garbage in garbage out"—that is, incorrect data lead to incorrect value and vice versa.

- **Performing Data Analysis**

The valuation process requires a profound quantitative and qualitative analysis of the company's past, current, and future positions. The analysis of historical performance, combined with the current situation and expectations, is vital for projecting future performance. It should be noted that valuation is a forward-looking process, in which consideration is made on the basis of aspects like growth, future cash flows, and risk.

1

Determining the Valuation Approach(es)

The selection of a suitable approach and its application depends on specific valuation considerations such as valuation motive, basis, premises, and availability of data, to mention a few. Nevertheless, a desirable value should be estimated from a combination of more than one approach.

Performing Valuation

This step entails the application of selected models to estimate value. It involves aspects like calculations of variables and adjustments. Estimation of value can be challenging depending on several factors—the selection of valuation methods, nature of valuation variables, reliability of data, correctness of projections, computational errors, etc.

Making a Conclusion About Value

The result of the valuation process is a conclusion of value—what is the firm value? What is the equity value? This conclusion is basically an opinion, arrived at after a thorough analysis of the entire valuation process, which should be presented in a report. The report is expected to be critical by justifying key decisions like assumptions, selection of models and variables, reconciliation of calculated value(s), and sense-making of values.

Submitting the Valuation Report

A valuation report should be submitted to the client. Sometimes the report submission process may start with a preliminary report (draft) to allow the client to review it—there may be suggestions about assumptions, corrections of facts, etc. Alternatively, a final signed report can be issued without a draft. However, room is given for follow-up discussions with the client in case of any issues that require attention. Exhibit ▶ 1.8 shows the key features of an ideal valuation report.

Think 1.5

From the valuation process, would you consider valuation as a science or art? Give examples to support your answer.

Exhibit 1.8 Key Features of a Valuation Report

REPORT SECTION	DETAILS
Executive Summary	A brief statement about the valuation report: purpose, approaches and methods, conclusion of value and recommendations
Introduction	General and specific aspects of valuation including, but not limited to the following: the assignment, scope, definitions of value, premises of value, sources of information, intended use, limitations, and organisation of the report
About the Company	A brief history and business operations
Economy and Industry	Overview of the economy and industry/sector: issues with impact on company performance and value such as inflation, interest rates, growth, financial markets, industry performance, government policies and regulations, etc.
Financials	Key historical financial data and forecasts
Valuation Approaches	Description of valuation approaches and methods, decisions about selected methods and valuation variables, application of approaches and calculation of value
Analysis and Conclusion	Analysis of valuation results, limitations, opinions, conclusion of value, recommendations
Appendices	Supporting materials like detailed financial statements, data, calculations, certification, etc.

Source: Author's construct

1.6 Art or Science?

There is a debate among valuation experts and professionals about whether valuation is a science or art or something else. Clearly, the debate is not conclusive. The valuation approaches (asset-based, income-based, and market-based) are universal—they can be considered as the "science of valuation." However, the application of these approaches involves things like forecasting of cash flows and estimation of valuation variables (like cost of capital and growth rates)—they can be considered as the "art of valuation." A practical example is evident in ▶ Quotes 1.3.2 and 1.3.4—valuation is more art than science. A detailed account of this phenomenon can be read in the study by Fabozzi et al. (2017). Brown (1998) considers valuation as an art—not science (see ▶ Quote 1.3.5), but in the words of Damodaran (a renowned valuation professor), valuation is neither a science nor art but "a craft" (see ▶ Quote 1.3.6).

Quotes 1.3 Art or Science?

▪ Quote 1.3.1 Sense-Making and Adjustments?

» I couldn't sleep. I knew something was wrong. The numbers just didn't make sense. For years, pipeline energy analysts seemed to be adjusting their valuation models for pipeline master limited partnership (MLP) stocks in order to explain what was happening to the price…But why? Why adjust the models for one set of companies and not for another? Cash is cash and value is the measure of cash going into and out of a business. There aren't different rules for different companies. Valuation is universal. (Brian Nelson, CFA)

Brian Nelson, Valuentum Analysts, January 19, 2022, CFA Institute

▪ Quote 1.3.2 Valuation Cannot Be 100% Precise

» A good valuation is 75% art and 25% science because it takes into account the story behind the numbers of a business. Appraisals fall down when there isn't enough support for the story behind it. It's based not on just what happened, but on why things happened. (Schubring, Analyst)

Darren Dahil, Contributor, October 30, 2016, Forbes

▪ Quote 1.3.3 The Case of DFC Global Corp.

» On August 1, 2017, the Delaware Supreme Court reversed the Delaware Court of Chancery's3 appraisal decision involving the acquisition of DFC Global Corp. (DFC), a publicly traded pay-day lending firm by private equity firm Lone Star. As a result, the case was returned to the Chancery court for further consideration. The Chancery court had determined that the sales process was competitive but concluded that because of the potential overhaul of pay-day industry regulations, DFC's publicly traded share price was an unreliable estimate of fair value. The Chancery court therefore decided to use a weighted average of the merger price, DCF estimates, and comparable sales analyses to determine fair value. Each of the three factors was given a one-third weight. The resulting estimate of fair value was 8.4% above the $1.3 billion merger price. (Donald M. DePamphilis, Researcher)

Donald M. DePamphilis, 2019, *Elsevier*

Quote 1.3.4 Valuation Is More Art Than Science

» The application of the income and market approaches have many areas of subjective judgment that practitioners make based on their experience and knowledge. Consideration and reconciliation of multiple approaches allows practitioners to gain confidence in estimating how much your business is worth. However, the subjective nature of a business valuation makes it more of an art than a science. (Steven Fischoff, Senior Director at Alvarez & Marsa)

Steven Fischoff, Senior Director at Alvarez & Marsa, July 1, 2021, Financial Poise

Quote 1.3.5 Valuation Is an Art Not Science

» As an art form, valuation had adopted the status of a mystical skill. Closely guarded secrets were passed down from one generation of valuers to another, with the reason for adopting certain practices being explained by years of accumulated wisdom. This approach was probably explainable in a world that had little real information, was inactive and relied on the belief that property had some special value that set it apart from other forms of investment. The need to justify a valuation or an investment decision was not something that could be realistically applied to property. (Gerald R. Brown, Salford University)

Gerald R. Brown, Professor of Property Development & Asset Management, University of Salford, March 1, 1998, Emerald Insight

Quote 1.3.6 Valuation Is a Craft

» In a science, if you get the inputs right, you should get the output right. The laws of physics and mathematics are universal and there are no exceptions. Valuation is not a science. In an art, there are elements that can be taught but there is also a magic that you either have or you do not. The essence of an art is that you are either a great artist or you are not. Valuation is not an art. A craft is a skill that you learn by doing. The more you do it, the better you get at it. Valuation is a craft. (Damodaran, Stern)

Aswath Damodaran, Finance Professor of Finance at Stern, New York University.

From the valuation process described in the previous section, it is reasonable to say that valuation is not a straightforward process—it combines many things such as approaches, assumptions, individual decisions, quantitative and qualitative aspects, and so on. Hence, the conclusion of value depends on how an analyst makes decisions about each aspect in the valuation process. Clearly, valuation is not more about numbers and calculations as many people tend to think. It is not a purely "objective" exercise; any preconceptions and biases that an analyst brings to the process tends to influence value. "Subjectivity" is, therefore, a key aspect of valuation. That is, the numbers should be supported and justified by a story behind them.

Let us look at two valuation aspects—objectivity and subjectivity:

Objectivity: This valuation aspect is mainly about what happens in a company and the economy in measurable terms like financial performance and price performance; it is therefore a quantitative aspect. For example, if the balance sheet reports an asset value of US$12 billion, that is, an objective variable—then it is what it is. If a stock is trading at US$4 per share, then that is what it is. An analyst cannot say the asset value is US$20 billion or the stock is trading at US$5 per share.

Subjectivity: This valuation aspect is about factors related to analyst judgments or decisions, which tend to influence valuation results. They may include things like choice of valuation methods, assumptions, opinions about value, and so on. For example, there may be different opinions about the growth rate of a company's cash flows—some analysts would suggest higher growth rates, whereas others lower growth rates. An analyst whose client's valuation motive is to sell a company is likely to aim at applying a higher growth rate for a higher selling price to gain bargaining power. In contrast, a motive to buy would aim at a lower growth rate of the target company. A practical example of subjectivity is evident from Quotes ▶ 1.3—when values do not make sense, analysts adjust their valuation models (see ▶ Quote 1.3.1). In the case of DFC Global Corporation, valuation variables were disputed in the court of law (see ▶ Quote 1.3.3).

Banner 1.7 Science or Art?
The valuation process is both objective and subjective. It is reasonable to consider valuation as a science and art.

1.7 Value vs. Price

Now, let us clarify another important aspect of valuation—price—to distinguish it from value. This distinction is vital for understanding more about why we need valuation. As we already know, value is a measure of how much something is worth. Price, on the other hand, is what you pay for an asset (see Quotes ▶ 1.4). Usually, the price of an asset tends to be different from its value. If more is paid on an asset than its actual value, then that asset is considered expensive (overpriced). If less is paid than its value, then it is cheap (underpriced). If the price is equal to its value, then the asset is said to be fairly priced.

Banner 1.8 Value vs. Price
Price is what you pay, whereas value is what you receive.

To explain the distinction between value and price, let us use a simple example of an auction. Assume that this is an auction of an extremely rare antique (an asset). In addition, assume that the action comprises three persons: the auctioneer (seller), buyer A, and buyer B. The seller presents an asset at the auction while knowing his preferred value (say US$20)—he will accept any bid equal to or more than US$20. The seller is neither obliged to disclose his desired value tag nor explain to the two buyers the criteria for the estimated value. On the other hand, each of the two potential buyers knows the assets and the reasons why they need it. Buyer A wants to buy this antique as an important gift to his wife, who admires it a lot. For him, this is a must-buy item—he gives it a value of $120. Buyer B is a pawn shop owner—she wants to resell the item for profit. She knows that the item can be sold in the market for at least US$95. Since her goal is to make a profit or break even, she sets a maximum bid of US$95—this is how much she values it. The auction starts and bids change hands between buyers A and B, until the price reaches US$100. At this price level, buyer B withdraws her interest—buyer A wins the bid and pays US$100.

What does this mean? The values set by the two buyers are fundamental—they are driven by purpose or utility: For buyer A, the value of the asset is driven by the desire to make his wife happy at US$120—he pays US$100 (undervalued). For buyer B, the asset is not worth more than US$95—at US$100, it is overvalued. The seller, who needs only US$20, receives US$100 (overvalued). Therefore, the value of the same item is different among the three aspirants. The market price of US$95 is what all willing buyers and willing sellers agree upon. By paying US$100, bidder A has paid more than the market value but less than his desired value.

Quotes 1.4 Value vs. Price

▪ Quote 1.4.1 What You Pay vs. What You Get!

» …the market value of the bonds and stocks that we continue to hold suffered a significant decline along with the general market. This does not bother Charlie and me. Indeed, we enjoy such price declines if we have funds available to increase our positions. Long ago, Ben Graham taught me that 'Price is what you pay; value is what you get.' Whether we're talking about socks or stocks, I like buying quality merchandise when it is marked down. (Warren Buffett, Board Chairman, Berkshire Hathaway Inc.)

Letter to Shareholders of Berkshire Hathaway, February 27, 2009.

▪ Quote 1.4.2 Arbitrary vs. Fundamental

» The most important distinction between price and value is the fact that price is arbitrary, and value is fundamental (Phil Town, Forbes Councils Member)

Phil Town, Forbes, January 4, 2018.

Think 1.6

Why should an asset price differ from its value? What are the possible factors affecting value? What are the possible factors affecting price?

In security markets (e.g., stock markets), analysts use valuation to estimate value—depending on valuation methods, they tend to have different value options. Usually, the estimated asset value tends to influence its price—often, an asset sells at or near the estimated value. However, it is highly common to see assets being traded (priced) far away from their estimated values—overvalued or undervalued. This is because investors and analysts tend to have different perceptions about asset values. Eventually, there should be a consensus between willing sellers and willing buyers—this is the market price or value.

Review Questions

1. What is the general meaning of value?
2. Use examples to define value according to the following valuation approaches:
   (a) Asset-based approach
   (b) Income-based approach
   (c) Market-based approach
3. With examples, explain why is it important to value firms.
4. Define the following valuation terms:
   (a) Intrinsic value
   (b) Relative value
   (c) Book value
   (d) Market value
   (e) Fair value
   (f) Economic value
5. Explain the difference between firm value and equity value.
6. With an example, explain why investors tend to use book value in conjunction with market value.
7. What is the meaning of the following premises of value and why should they be considered in valuation?
   (a) Going-concern valuation
   (b) Liquidation valuation
8. Explain the practical use of the asset-based valuation approach.
9. Explain the practical use of the income-based valuation approach.
10. Explain the practical use of the market-based valuation approach.
11. What are the main determinants of value according to intrinsic valuation?
12. Explain the difference between intrinsic value and relative value.
13. Use examples to explain the practical use of intrinsic value and relative value.
14. Why is it important to understand the motive for valuing a firm or equity?
15. Describe different valuation motives.
16. If you consider valuation as a scientific and artistic process, indicate which of the following aspects explain the science or art of valuation:
    (a) Intrinsic valuation applies cash flow discount models.
    (b) An analyst uses different methods to estimate the cash flow growth rate. He finally makes a decision about what is the growth rate to apply.
    (c) Financial statements, from which we extract valuation data, are prepared and presented according to financial reporting standards.
    (d) We use financial statements and economic information to make forecasts of valuation variables.
    (e) Beta, a valuation variable, is calculated by dividing the covariance of stock returns and market returns by the variance of market returns.

1

(f) An analyst decides to use a 10-year government bond yield to determine the risk-free rate for estimating the cost of equity.
(g) An analyst uses the P/E ratio to calculate price multiples for equity relative valuation.
(h) Valuation applies cash flows instead of profit to estimate firm or equity value.

17. Explain the difference between value and price.

Bibliography

Brown, G.R. (1998), The idea that valuation is an art, not a science, is hardly mentioned these days, *Journal of Property Valuation, and Investment*, 16 (1). doi: https://doi.org/10.1108/jpvi.1998.11216aaa.001

DePamphilis, D. M (2019), Mergers and Acquisitions Cash Flow Valuation Basics, In: *Mergers, Acquisitions, and Other Restructuring Activities: An Integrated Approach to Process, Tools, Cases, and Solutions* 10th ed., Elsevier Inc., *177 – 205,* doi: https://doi.org/10.1016/C2017-0-02823-9

Fabozzi, F. J., Focardi, F. M., & Jonas, C. (2017), *Equity Valuation: Science, Art, or Craft*? Issue 4, CFA Institute.

Fischoff, S. (2021), Business Valuation Is More Art Than Science, Available vis Financial Poise, https://www.financialpoise.com/art-of-business-valuation/ .Accessed on July 1, 2021.

Mackintosh, J. (2022). Value Investing Is Back. But for How Long? A bounce in bond yields is good news for dividend payers. Available via The Wall Street Journal. https://www.wsj.com/articles/value-investing-is-back-but-for-how-long-11643726540. Accessed February 01, 2022.

Nelson, B. (2022). Investing's First Principles: The Discounted Cash Flow Model. Available via CFA. https://blogs.cfainstitute.org/investor/2022/01/19/investings-first-principles-the-discounted-cash-flow-model/. Accessed January 19, 2022.

Corporate Value Creation

Contents

Supplementary Information The online version contains supplementary material available at https://doi.org/10.1007/978-3-031-28267-6_2.

B. Kulwizira Lukanima, *Corporate Valuation*, Classroom Companion: Business, https://doi.org/10.1007/978-3-031-28267-6_2

2.1 Introduction

To understand corporate valuation, it is important to have general knowledge about a firm and financial management because valuation takes place only in the existence of a financial object, such as a firm. This is where movements of financial resources take place: starting from injection of capital (financing) and buying assets (investing) to generating revenues (operating). Corporate valuation, therefore, plays a significant role in determining whether managers create or destroy value from financial resources. Indeed, valuation entails provision of vital information about the performance of a company in all aspects of value creation such as financial management, which includes functions like planning, capital structuring, and effective utilization of resources. Whether value is created or destroyed depends on whether finances are well or poorly managed. A firm with sufficient financial resources can perform poorly if those resources are not effectively managed, thereby destroying value. Likewise, a business with scarce resources can advance into successful performance if those scarce resources are effectively managed, thereby creating value.

This chapter, therefore, introduces the key concepts of value creation by firms through the financial management process. It starts with defining finance and describing the financial management process, the key financial decisions, and the role of the finance manager in value creation. Moreover, this chapter explains the perceived objective of a firm from a financial perspective and describes the value creation process as an important aspect of achieving such an objective. Finally, it explains the agency cost problem in order to enlighten the tension between business ownership and control.

Learning Outcomes

- Understand the existence of a firm and its implication in value creation
- Describe the role of corporate finance and financial management in value creation
- Explain the main goal of a firm
- Describe the different types of managerial decisions and their implications in corporate value
- Explain the concept of shareholder wealth maximization
- Understand the agency cost problem and its implication in value creation

2.2 Corporate Finance and Value Creation

Corporate finance can be defined as the process of resource allocation and value creation through investments. It deals with how investors allocate their funds over time and how those funds are managed to increase value. Value creation is a complex process, which involves interactions among different players like investors, firms, managers, financial markets, government, suppliers, and customers. Together, these players facilitate the availability of funds, investments, and operations in dynamic economic conditions with uncertainty. Exhibit ▶ 2.1 describes the process of value creation according to The International Federation of Accountants (IFAC 2020)—it involves defining, creating, delivering, and sustaining value.

Banner 2.1 Value Creation
Value creation is an integral function of finance, embodied in an interactive process that includes both internal (firm) and external (economic) factors, in which value should be created through the use of financial resources.

Exhibit 2.1 Value Creation

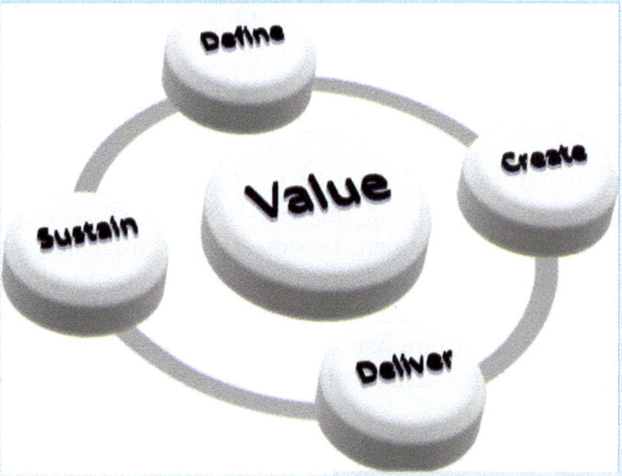

The International Federation of Accountants (IFAC) describes value creation as a process comprising four elements: value definition, value creation, value delivery, and value sustainability.

- *Who defines value?* Value is defined by different players such as investors, customers, and other stakeholders.
- *How is value created?* Value is created through an integrated system comprised of an organization's purpose, strategy, and business model. This integrated system involves raising capital, allocating resources, and managing relationships.
- *To whom and how is value delivered?* Value is delivered "to ever-more demanding and sophisticated stakeholders through responsible products and services, and through new channels, at an appropriate price."
- *How is value sustained?* Sustainability of value is achieved through internal retention and protection. These require appropriate reinvestment of resources, rewarding shareholders (through returns on investments (ROIs)), and meeting the needs of the overall society.

Exhibit ▶ 2.2 summarizes the complex nature of value creation, which includes a firm's internal and external factors. Some of these factors can be clearly identified in Quotes ▶ 2.1. For instance, management roles in financial performance can be considered an internal factor, whereas a pandemic like the coronavirus disease of 2019 (COVID-19) and customer satisfaction can be regarded as external factors. Let us describe each of the components that influence value in a firm.

Banner 2.2 A Firm

A firm is the center of value creation as an existing body that facilitates resource allocation and value creation.

2.2.1 A Firm

A firm is an entity that enables the collection of assets, investments, and the process of revenue generation. It comprises people (such as investors and employees) and assets. Overall, a firm can be viewed as a system with complementary contractual arrangements to mitigate conflicting interests between investors and managers (employers). Moreover, a firm is a unity that facilitates interactions between investors, financial markets, government, and other stakeholders. It, therefore, allows the inflow and outflow of financial resources in the process of value creation. A firm can take different forms such as a corporation, a partnership, or sole proprietorship.

Exhibit 2.2 The Complex Nature of Value Creation

Figure 2.1 depicts the interaction between a firm, the unit in which value is created through allocation and management of financial resources. Investors inject their funds into the firm, expecting to receive rewards (returns) from their

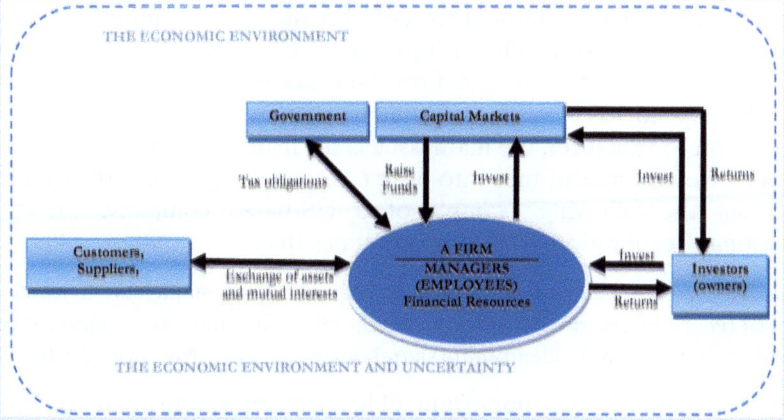

Fig. 2.1 Interaction Between a Firm and External Environment
Source: Author's construct

investments. From the firm's perspective, these funds are regarded as capital. This is where the cost of capital comes into play because capital is not free. To be regarded as a value creator, the firm should generate higher returns than the cost of capital.

The firm then uses capital to run business operations, which involve acquisition of assets, production of goods or services, and sales. Therefore, other players are involved in facilitating the firm's business operations. For example, the firm needs suppliers of goods or raw materials as well as customers to buy its products. It also has obligations to pay taxes to the government.

Capital markets provide a vital ground for the firm to raise funds (by selling stocks or bonds). They also provide investment opportunities to both the firm (as an entity) and investors (as individuals) through buying financial securities. This where investors can create their own investment portfolios apart from the firm.

Overall, the firm and other players exist within a particular economic environment, which includes other firms (competitors). It is, therefore, a complex environment in which the firm faces decision challenges during the course of its operations. Although funds are invested now, rewards are expected only in the uncertain future. Therefore, in creating value, the firm strives to generate returns (for its investors) while simultaneously facing risks (uncertainties).

For value to be realized, the firm should generate cash flows (not just profits). Hence, value can be estimated by calculating the present value of future cash flows (forecasts), discounted at the cost of capital.

2.2.2 Investors

Like a firm, investors form the core of corporate valuation due to their positions as business owners and capital fund providers. Investors invest capital into businesses either directly or indirectly. Direct injection of capital can occur through initial public offering or lending to the firm, whereas indirect investment can occur through buying stocks or bonds in secondary markets.

In relation to valuation, the main issue is the firm's obligation to its shareholders. When investors inject funds into businesses, they expect rewards (returns). Let us consider the following example of a US-based company, Crown Castle International Corporation. The company states that

> ...under the leadership of its Board of Directors and management team, has a proven record of creating significant shareholder value and has...generated returns and distributed cash dividend to its shareholders—(Globe Newswire 2020).

This statement shows two important obligations of the firm to its investors—"value" and "returns."

External investors (preference shareholders or debtholders) have fixed claims on the firm—the firm is obliged to pay them regardless of its performance. In contrast, internal investors (owners) do not have fixed claims: their rewards primarily depend on the performance of the firm. From a financial perspective, returns can be derived from several aspects of business performance. For example, a shareholder's returns can come from either dividends or capital gains from increased stock value. Although shareholders may have several motives to invest in a business, their main goal is to maximize their wealth. A firm plays a role in ensuring that this goal is achieved. If shareholders are not satisfied with the performance of a company, they can withdraw their investments. By doing so, the ultimate outcome would be the firm's collapse.

Banner 2.3 Investors
Investors comprise both business owners (internal investors) and lenders (external investors), to whom the firm has a primary obligation of generating returns (rewards).

2.2.3 Managers

Usually, investors tend to entrust other people (managers) to run a business on their behalf. Managers are, therefore, employees of the investors (owners) whose goal should be shareholders' value maximization. Consider again the following statement from Crown Castle International Corporation:

> ...under the leadership of its Board of Directors and management team..." the company "...has a proven record of creating significant shareholder value (Globe Newswire 2020).

Managers, therefore, are the building blocks of a company as they perform core functions, such as planning, organizing, staffing, directing, and controlling. Their main role is to achieve effective utilization of resources provided by investors and generate more resources through value creation. Usually, firms tend to have several managers to play different roles depending on their organizational structures—a finance manager is among them, whose main responsibility is to manage financial resources.

Banner 2.4 Managers
Managers are employees who are entrusted to run a firm on the behalf of investors (owners). They have an obligation to serve the interest of owners while creating value.

2.2.4 Other Players

A firm cannot exist without interactions with external players such as customers, suppliers, government, and capital markets. Similarly, the objective of value maximization cannot be achieved without other players. Hence, the value performance of a firm partly depends on its ability to associate with other players on all managerial aspects, including financial management. For instance, a business can sell more of its products if it maintains a good relationship with both its existing and potential customers. An increase in sales would imply an increase in profitability, with the other factors being equal. Financial management can play a significant role in this through a proper debtors' management system. When products are sold on credit, the role of financial management is to ensure a positive response while collecting accounts receivable and, at the same time, maintaining a good relationship with customers.

Likewise, a firm depends on supplies to provide for inventories: either as finished goods ready for sale or as raw materials for production. One of the performance indicators in financial management is how a firm can meet its financial obligations to suppliers. Thus, a firm must have enough funds to pay for its supplies; otherwise, it will not have anything to sell or produce if suppliers lose confidence. If a firm acquires it supplies on credit, then financial management should ensure a timely payment of accounts payable.

Governments determine the atmosphere in which firms exist depending on several factors such as country laws, taxation policies, investment incentives, political stability, key infrastructure, and so on. In value creation, one of a firm's responsibilities is to analyze the implication of government in its performance and take appropriate decisions. In doing so, a firm should abide by the laws and regulations set by the government, including the obligation to pay taxes.

There is a long list of other players in a firm's value creation process. They include, among others, professional bodies relating to the firm's business, environmental activists, analysts, lenders, academicians, politicians, and so on. In one way or another, directly or indirectly, they influence financial decisions and the overall performance of a firm.

2.2.5 Capital Markets

Capital markets are vital for value creation because they are major sources of finance and investment opportunities. In valuation, we consider the linkage between investors and capital markets, on one hand, and between a firm and capital markets, on the other. This linkage is also highly crucial in a firm's strategic decisions that affect its value. For example, a firm may decide to raise capital by either issuing stocks or borrowing from capital markets. This is a question of financing decision. In addition, a firm may decide to invest by buying stocks of other companies or issuing corporate bonds. This is a question of investment decision. Any such decisions will eventually have implications in aspects like the ability of a firm to create value, investors' perception, and investment decisions.

2.2.6 The Economy

All businesses exist in a particular economic environment. Irrespective of its type –small or large, domestic or international, private or public, and so on—a firm exists in an economy that influences its performance. Such an economic environment comprises all agents necessary for the existence of a firm. Such agents include people (such as customers, supplies, policymakers, investors, etc.), economic variables (such as interest rates, exchange rates, inflation, population, individual income, living standard, etc.), institutions (such as government, financial markets, regulators, etc.), competitors, and other factors that can have either a direct or indirect impact on the firm.

Together, all these agents constitute a dynamic business environment in which the future is always uncertain. One of the essential considerations in value creation is the uncertainty surrounding business operations. For example, plans that are made now should consider what is likely to happen in the future, even though not everything that is expected tends to be realized. Decisions that are made now are expected to have a long-term impact on the firm. However, due to uncertainty, no one knows for sure what that future impact will be. Hence, creation and management of value require continuous dynamic adjustments from time to time, which align business operations with the changing conditions of the economy. Poor economic performance is likely to have a negative impact on the firm. For instance, unemployment may be associated with decreased sales because peoples' affordability to buy diminishes; inflation may lead to higher production costs due to an increase in raw material prices; and poor economic policies may disincentivize investments. Due to this, value creation is a rather complex process.

Quotes 2.1 The Complex Nature of Value Creation

▪ Quote 2.1.1 Value Creation Can Face Threats

» COVID-19 is the greatest threat to value creation we've seen in generations. As a result, many companies are juggling a handful of pressing priorities, including protecting cash flows, ensuring long-term value creation, and delivering positive societal impacts. The CFO and finance function can partner with management to overcome the challenges associated with understanding and driving long-term value creation. (IFAC CEO Kevin Dancey)

Michael Cohn, July 2, 2020, Accounting Today

▪▪ Quote 2.1.2 Composition of Value, Creation, Delivery, and Sustenance

» With an estimated 80 percent of enterprise value now made up of non-financial assets such as brand recognition, human capital and customer satisfaction, organizations that understand how to create and deliver value will be better positioned to achieve sustainable success. (Barry Melancon, CEO of the Association of International Certified Professional Accountants)

Michael Cohn, July 2, 2020, Accounting Today

▪▪ Quote 2.1.3 Manager's Role in Value Creation Is Complex

» Financial performance is just one component of an organization's true value - in fact, what's on the balance sheet is now estimated to be just one-fifth of a business's value. That's one of several reasons the CFO's role in value creation is growing more complex. (Neil Amato, Senior Editor at Financial Management magazine)

Neil Amato, June 25, 2020, Financial Management (FM)

2.3 Managerial Decisions and Value Creation

Managers, who run firms, make decisions affecting both the firm's and shareholders' values. These decisions are aligned with the management of all processes associated with efficient acquisition and deployment of both short- and long-term financial resources. Usually, the management function involves other overlapping and interlinking roles such as strategic management, risk management, and operations management. However, achieving these roles requires the support of corporate financial management through its primary strategic decisions, namely, financing decisions, investment decisions, and dividend decisions.

The process of value creation starts when investors inject capital into a company. Managers are responsible for decisions that will have consequences on the firm's value (for the company) and equity value (for company owners). They make decisions on what assets to acquire (investment decision), where to raise funds and how to pay for them (financing decision), and what to do with the profits generated (dividend decision). With other factors being equal, good decisions would create value, whereas bad decisions would destroy value.

Although the decision-making process is complex, Dobbs et al. (2010) outline four principles to assist managers in making sound decisions: the core-of-value principle, the conservation-of-value principle, the expectations treadmill principle, and the best-owner principle. Let us briefly reflect on these principles by referring to Crown Castle's Highlights—Comments on Letter from Elliott (Globe Newswire 2020).

The core-of-value principle: Value is driven by two variables, growth and returns on capital. Crown Castle managers, in their response to a letter from investors (Elliott), defend their position about value creation by mentioning two value variables—returns and cash flow—while emphasizing growth. They state:

> …we have delivered: site rental revenue growth of 67%; 61% growth in Adjusted EBITDA and 73% AFFO growth, resulting in 39% growth in AFFO per share and a corresponding increase in dividends per share of 37%.

The conservation-of-value principle: Value is simply created through improving cash flows, irrespective of the amount of financial resources used. Crown Castle clearly acknowledges undertaking heavy investments (approximately $30 billion over 10 years) and related outcomes such as "…unique portfolio of assets…, unparalleled capabilities and strong customer relationships…," etc. Nevertheless, what matters most is its goal to its shareholders: cash flow in the form of an annual dividend growth from 7% to 8% per share.

The expectations treadmill principle: Value creation intends to meet investors' expectations about performance, whereby managers will always strive to meet those expectations; the higher the expectations, the better the performance should be. Crown Castle's highlights respond to what investors expect from the company's performance. In a letter to the company, investor views indicated their expectations for higher returns as they recommended the ROI-focused fiber investment approach and increase in dividends per share to $7.00 in 2021 and $8.00 in 2023.

T*he best-owner principle*: An owner's capabilities tend to influence value because "no business has an inherent value in and of itself; it has a different value to different owners or potential owners" (Dobbs et al. 2010). For example, Elliott (an investor) is pushing the company (Crown Castle International Corp) to improve its strategic focus and value, through a letter to the company. The company responded by defending its strategy, stating:

> …we remain confident in our ability to generate compelling value for our shareholders, including through our goal of growing our dividend per share 7% to 8% per year…

Despite their response, managers were obviously under pressure to create more value. A similar example can be drawn from ► Quote 2.2.4, in which CoreLogic's board of directors rejects an acquisition proposal from two of its investors to protect the interests of other investors. In this rejection, the board's decision clearly puts value creation at the center for all shareholders, regardless of their differences: it considers the two investors as "opportunists." In one of its comments, Paul Folino, Chairman of the Board, said:

> …Our Board is open to all viable paths to increasing shareholder value, and we are willing to meet with Senator and Cannae, but given CoreLogic's strong momentum, increasing margins, accelerating growth, and multi-faceted value-creation model, we are unanimous in our belief that CoreLogic will be able to deliver significantly more value to shareholders than this opportunistic proposal (Business Wire 2020).

Quotes 2.2 Managerial Decisions and Value Creation

▪ Quote 2.2.1 Decisions for Value Creation Can Be Challenging

> With significant subscriber growth achieved during this period we have spent a lot of time reflecting on how our investments have enabled growth. The key learning for us as a business is the need to take a disciplined approach to technology investments to ensure that there is not only alignment with strategy but ownership from our team. With all industries subject to volatility and disruption, there can be a tendency for technology decisions (or any investment decisions) to be fueled by competitive reaction or even fear—this will result in expensive projects and diluted enterprise value. To ensure we remained disciplined and focused on value accretive technology, we asked four primary questions: (1) Does the investment align with our strategic objectives? (2) What technology do we need to realize our strategy? (3) Who will own the technology and how do we engage the entire organization? And (4) How do we learn before committing? (David Jackson, CEO of 28 by Sam Wood, Australia)
>
> *David Jackson, July 8, 2020, Dynamic Business*

▪ Quote 2.2.2 Managers Should Be Aware of Value Creation Principles

> It's one thing for a CFO to understand the technical methods of valuation - and for members of the finance organization to apply them to help line managers monitor

and improve company performance. But it's still more powerful when CEOs, board members, and other nonfinancial executives internalize the principles of value creation. Doing so allows them to make independent, courageous, and even unpopular business decisions in the face of myths and misconceptions about what creates value (Richard Dobbs, Bill Huyett, and Tim Koller, McKinsey & Company)

Richard Dobbs, Bill Huyett, and Tim Koller, November 1, 2010, McKinsey Quarterly

Quote 2.2.3 Shareholders' Influence on Value Creation

» While we admire Crown Castle's investments in the wireless tower industry, we believe that the company's expansion away from its core and into fiber infrastructure has detracted from shareholder returns and will continue to detract from shareholder returns unless significant changes are made....Fiber infrastructure businesses can be attractive investments, but it is our considered view that Crown Castle's fiber strategy has not been successful and that the return on these investments has significantly underperformed... Elliott believes this consistent underperformance is directly attributed to the company's fiber strategy, which has yielded disappointing returns despite $16 billion of investment. (Jesse Cohn & Jason Genrich, Crown Castle International Corp, US)

Elliott Management Corp, July 6, 2020, Cision PR Newswire

Quote 2.2.4 Different Value for Different Owners

» Dear Fellow Shareholder,

As you may know, CoreLogic recently received an unsolicited acquisition proposal for $65.00 per share in cash from two of its shareholders, Senator Investment Group LP and Cannae Holdings Inc. After a careful and thorough review, conducted in consultation with our independent financial and legal advisors, the Board unanimously rejected the proposal based on its belief that the proposal significantly undervalues CoreLogic, is opportunistically timed, fails to address serious regulatory concerns, and is not in the best interests of shareholders other than Senator and Cannae (The CoreLogic Board of Directors)

Calif Irvine, July 7, 2020, Business Wire

Think 2.1

Why should value creation be regarded as a complex process? State your views while reflecting on information from Quotes ▶ 2.1 *and Quotes* ▶ 2.2.

Banner 2.5 Managerial Decisions and Value Creation

In making sound value-creating decisions, managers should focus on enhancing returns and growth while improving cash flows, balancing expectations of different investors, and managing external pressure.

2.4 Major Types of Managerial Decisions

In this section, we outline the three main managerial decisions—investment decisions, financing decisions, and dividend decisions. Our focus here is on understanding what each of these decisions mean as well as the key factors influencing them. As indicated in Exhibit ▶ 2.3, together, these decisions should target shareholders' value creation.

Exhibit 2.3 Managerial Decisions

The following are the key questions regarding the major types of managerial decisions:

Financing decisions: How do we raise funds and how to repay the cost of such funds?

Investment decisions: What do we do with the available funds regarding long-term investments or assets?

Dividend decisions: How do we use our earnings?

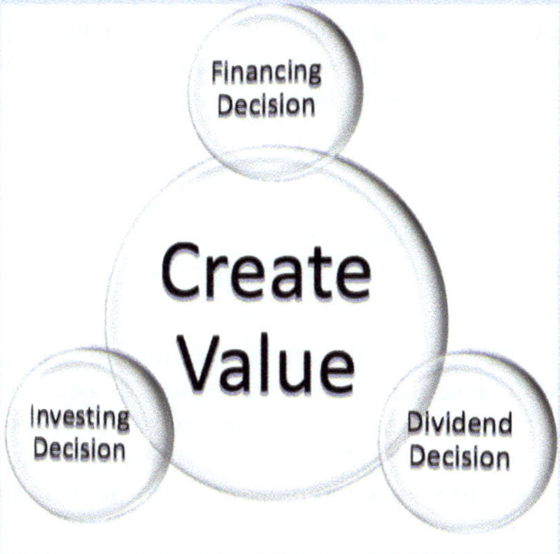

Source: Author's construct

2.4.1 Investment Decisions

Investment decisions are about what to do with the available funds. For example, should we invest in buying bonds or stocks? Should we construct a building or buy machinery? Should we acquire another company? The list goes on. It is important to note that investment decisions tend to be aligned with financing decisions. Ferrara (1966) suggests that investment decisions should be based on usual cash flow analysis, whereas financing decisions should consider the cost of alternative sources of finance. This suggestion is consistent with the "core-of-value principle" presented by Dobbs et al. (2010).

It should be noted that investment decisions, like any other decisions, are made in a world of uncertainly; hence, we should not expect the outcomes to always be right. There is a possibility of making decision mistakes. Making mistakes is not a problem, but the problem is whether those mistakes result from a reasonable level of judgment or from unacceptable motives for managers' self-interests. Sometimes poor decisions are made by lack of important information, lack of knowledge, and failure of decision-makers to exercise due diligence. A good case example is Motorola, a US-based technology company. In 2008, David Phillips presented the following news headline on CBS News: "Poor Investment Decisions Add to Motorola's Woes." (CBS News, November 4, 2008). Overall, the news article showed that investment decisions at Motorola failed to consider the changing nature and speed of mobile technology, leading to poor financial performance. The article said:

» Motorola reported an operating loss of 397 million dollars, or $0.18 a share, for the third quarter ended September 30, as revenues fell 15 percent to 7.48 billion dollars. The mobile phone maker, still stumbling from its failure to design smartphones to compete against the likes of Apple's iPhone and Blackberry models from Research in Motion, now has a new misstep to deal with poor returns on its in-house fund, called the SigmaFund (CBS News, November 4, 2008).

Banner 2.6 Investment Decision
Investment decisions are about how to use available funds to create value.

Whereas investment decisions should aim at creating value, sometimes those decisions are motivated by managers' behavioral factors associated with agency problems. Thus, managers make decisions that maximize their personal interest at the expense of shareholders' value (Denis 1992). Investment decisions can also be influenced by close ties between a company and informed creditors such as banks (Kang et al. 2000).

2.4.2 Financing Decisions

Financing decisions are about how to raise funds and how to repay the cost of such funds. The focus of a financing decision is to make investment decisions possible, and it represents the firm's options for meeting its financing need through internal and external sources. Internal financing (usually from retained profits) is ideal for meeting short-term investment needs. External financing sources are usually preferred for long-term investment decisions. The main common sources of long-term finance are issuing shares or borrowing. Each of these financing alternatives have implications in the status of the firm in several aspects, such as capital structure, control, value of the firm, risk, investors' perception, cost of capital, tax expenses, and so on.

Issuing shares involves inviting investors to inject money into a firm with the expectation of receiving returns either in the form of profits (dividends) or appreciation of the share value. In doing so, an investor becomes a shareholder (or owner) of the firm. Borrowing is about acquiring funds from lenders (such as banks or bond markets) and promising a series of fixed payments (to repay the debt and interest). It is, therefore, essential for decision-makers to analyze how a certain source of finance would affect value.

Banner 2.7 Financing Decisions
Financing decisions are about raising capital to fund value-creating investments.

Basically, the decision to raise capital and the choice of the source of finance depends on several factors such as leverage, production flexibility, sales stability, profitability, and so on. These factors are outlined here:

Operating leverage: Usually, firms tend to avoid overall higher risks (i.e., a combination of business and financial risks), to minimize the overall risk. A high operating leverage and a high financial leverage imply a high overall risk to a firm. There is also a link between operating leverage and risk of stocks. With other factors being equal, the higher the operating leverage, the higher the overall risk of the firm's stocks and its systematic risk (Lev 1974). This, in turn, affects investors' perception of the firm. For rational decision-making, therefore, a firm having a higher operating leverage (high business risk) is expected to opt for a low financial leverage (less debt than equity), and vice versa (Dotan and Ravid 1985).

Flexibility of productivity: Production flexibility is linked to dynamic adjustments in the operating leverage, hence influencing financing decisions. However, production flexibility depends on the operating adjustment costs. Hence, the relationship between production and a financing decision is supported by tax effects (Ravid 1988). This is because tax deductibility is not unique to debt but affects all inputs purchased by a firm. According to Mauer and Triantis (1994), smaller operating adjustment costs tend to increase the present value of the net interest tax shields of capitalization costs, thereby becoming an incentive for debt financing.

Sales stability: According to Taggart (1977), there is a link between sales stability and financing decision, as explained by liquid assets. This concept contends that since liquid assets facilitate a firm's transactions, their levels should vary in positive proportion to sales levels. However, the firm incurs costs to maintain the required level of liquid assets. Therefore, a firm with stable sales is likely to opt for debt finance as it is sure of incurring fixed charges on the cost of debt (i.e., interest).

Profitability: Firms that generate high profits, and hence higher returns on investment, have preference for internal financing (Vanacke and Manigart 2007). Therefore, they might prefer less external financing, especially for short-term financing needs. According to Fama and French (1998), profitability conveys information about dividends and debts, thereby influencing investors' perceptions of the firm and their willingness to provide capital funds. On one hand, profitability partly assures shareholders' motive for dividend returns, whereas interest paid to lenders affects the profitability of the firm on the other hand, depending on the significance of the interest tax shield.

Growth: Some evidence suggests that firms with high growth prefer internal financing alternatives. They can, however, be forced toward external sources (especially equity) when there are no alternatives from retained earnings (Vanacke and Manigart 2007). Moreover, debt finance increases risk exposure, thereby reducing the willingness of managers to use debt. As shown in the study by Dang (2010), firms with high growth potential tend to use less debt finance, and, as pointed out in the study by Alonso et al. (2005), debt has a negative influence on the market value of a firm when there is a growth opportunity. Byoun (2008) explains the growth aspect in relation to the evolution of the capital structure of a firm in different growth stages (life cycle). He shows that firms at the mature stage tend to prefer internal financing, whereas those at the developing stage use equity to maintain financial flexibility. Overall, growth opportunities tend to be externally financed by equity instead of debt to avoid debt overhang and mitigate the potential risk problem. Hence, firms with poor investment opportunities tend to grow slowly while relying on debt financing (Myers 1977; Lewis et al. 2003).

Target capital structure and control: Firms usually establish the target capital structure, which keeps a certain level of debt/equity ratio. Therefore, financing decisions try to achieve and maintain the target capital structure through a dynamic comparison with the actual capital structure. On the control side, more equity finance would imply more shareholder control. A study by Croci et al. (2011) suggests that family firms tend to be more reluctant than nonfamily firms to using equity finance; instead, they prefer debt finance because it does not dilute owners' control of a business. Moreover there exists management–shareholder control tension, usually relating to managerial control of voting rights. In this aspect, capital structure decision can be used to change management control rights (Stulz 1988).

Management attitude: Depending on risk perceptions, management may be either conservative or aggressive. Conservative managers tend to prefer avoiding risks, hence avoiding debt finance. Aggressive managers tend to take higher risks, an incentive for opting for debt finance. Overall, capital structure decisions are based on managerial analyses and influences. Obviously, the overall goal of managerial decisions should be to maximize shareholders' wealth. However, there is concern about managerial conflicts of interest that may induce managers to not act in the best interest of shareholders. This concern is usually explained in relation to the agency problem. Agrawal and Mandelker (1987) show that some big corporations have been trying to reduce this problem through managerial incentives that provide managers proportional ownership in corporations.

Financial strength: Firms whose present financial conditions are mediocre would prefer to avoid issuing long-term debt as this could be associated with higher issuing costs and increased financial risk. Firms with good financial positions are likely to be more flexible in financing decisions because they can easily access capital markets to raise funds in either equity or bonds. Consequently, higher financial flexibility (resulting from lower capitalization costs) tends to increase the tax shield value of debt financing (Mauer and Triantis 1994).

Tax effect: Taxes have implication in the benefit from interest expenses. If the tax rates are relatively high, leading to substantial relief from interest expenses, then a firm may be attracted to more debt finance. MacKie-Mason (1990a) provides strong evidence of the effect of tax on the financing structure, suggesting that tax shields affect financing decisions when they have a significant effect on marginal tax rates.

Lenders and credit ratings: Lenders and rating agencies play a significant part in analyzing the performance of companies. Therefore, they may play some advisory roles in the implication of certain financing decisions. Additionally, lenders determine the availability of capital and allow for the possibility of firms to access and afford the cost of capital. Some studies show the extent of decision criteria of whether financing is made publicly or privately regardless of either debt or equity (Mackie-Mason 1990b; Saá-Requejo 1996).

Capital market conditions: A firm's optimal capital structure depends on both long- and short-term changes. Considering the state of capital market, a firm will make financing decisions depending on its ability to combine long- and short-term finance. The condition of capital markets refers to efficiency and is important due to several reasons, such as: it affects the price of new stocks or bonds that a firm will issue and hence the value of funds that the firm can raise; it affects the cost of capital, which, in turn, affects capital budgeting decisions; and so on. Ooi et al. (2008) show some evidence of firms' market-timing behavior in which financing decisions vary alongside variations in securities' costs in the capital market. For instance, firms may issue new equity in periods coinciding with periods of high stock valuation, while preferring debt when the long-term rate is low and the credit spread is narrow.

Investors' influence: Investors are the owners of a firm. Therefore, their perception of a certain source of finance is important for influencing managers' decisions. Perceptions differ depending on several factors such as risk preferences, control motives, and so on. Shareholders who prefer strengthening their control status in the firm would not advocate the issue of new equity to finance investments. Instead, they are likely to influence the use of debt finance. There has been a debate on whether shareholders should possess decision-making powers in a firm. This debate has been mainly focused on the role of shareholders' decision control in value creation. Harris and Raviv (2010) argue that shareholders should not control all the major decisions, even if they have a value-creating agenda.

Size of the investment: Major investments are usually financed by external finance, whereas small investments can be easily financed by internal funds.

Think 2.2

If financing decisions are influenced by several factors, what should be the main criteria for managers to reach financing decisions?

2.4.3 Dividend Decisions

A dividend refers to a proportion of profits that is paid to shareholders as a reward for their investment. A dividend decision, therefore, is about what proportion of earnings should be paid to owners and what should be retained within the firm. These decisions are usually made by the firm's board of directors. We can categorize the decision structure into two: high payout and low payout. A "high-payout" decision means that, in distributing earnings, dividend payments take a higher proportion than retained earnings. A "low-payout" decision is when a company uses most (or all) of its earnings to reinvest rather than pay dividends.

Essentially, dividend decisions can be referred to as residual decisions mainly because they are made when firms start generating profits and determine investment opportunities. That is, firms with the potential for wealth-creating investments are likely to opt for a low payout (retain a large proportion of its earnings to finance growth through further investments), whereas those without the same are likely to opt for a high payout (pay more dividends and retain less earnings). A low payout implies that more shareholder wealth will be created by the firm. Shareholders with dividend motives can create their own dividends, referred to as "homemade dividend" by Miller and Modigliani (1961). With a high payout, shareholders will have an alternative for "self-value creation" by investing somewhere. Let us consider the following two situations:

2.4.3.1 Implications of a High Payout

A company uses most of its earnings to pay dividends, thereby reducing the use of internal funds for investments. This may imply slow growth if the company does not have alternative means to fund its worth-creating investments. However, the firm can use external sources of capital, thereby incurring a higher marginal cost of capital. With other factors being equal, the higher the cost of capital, the lower the firm value.

This decision, on the other hand, can be favorable to shareholders who are able to create their own value—"self-created value"—from individual investment portfolios.

Exhibit 2.4 Dividend Decisions

Dividend decisions split profit earnings between the amount to be distributed to shareholders and the amount to be retained by the firm. ◘ Figure 2.2 depicts a dividend decision and its implications in value creation. Like other managerial decisions, managers ought to consider several factors because dividend decisions can affect shareholder's value in different ways like the amount of taxes shareholders pay, shareholders' capital gain, long-term financing decisions, and growth.

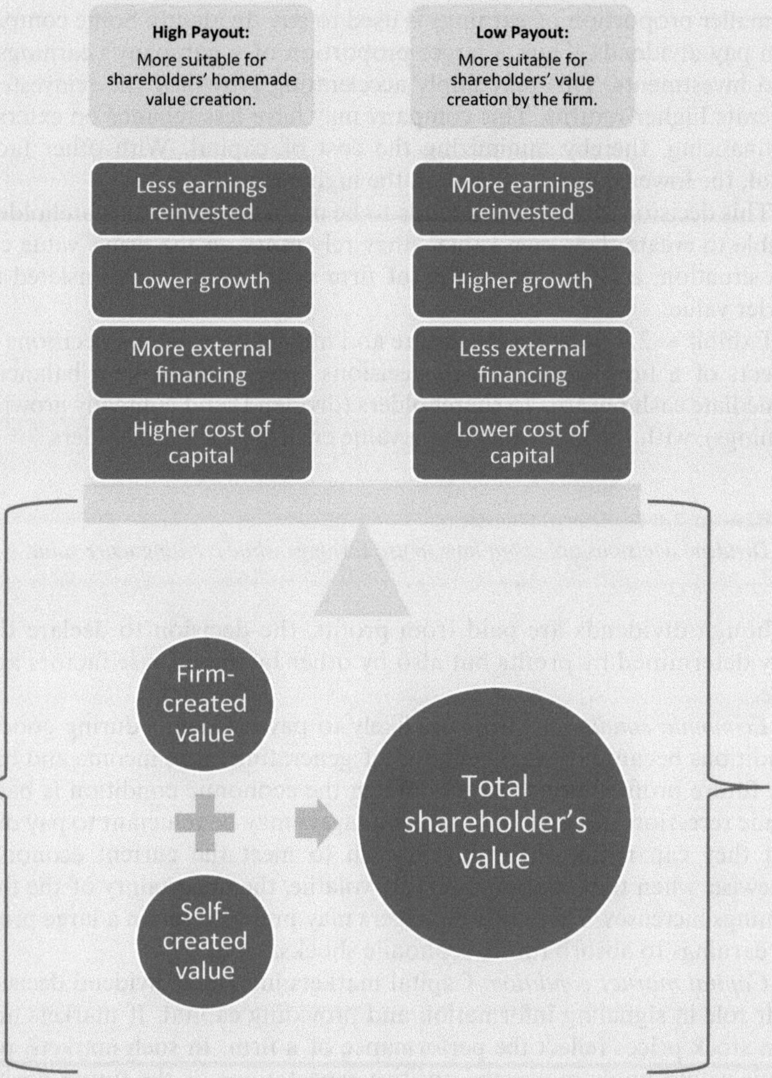

Fig. 2.2 Dividend decisions and shareholder value

Irrespective of the dividend decision that a firm makes, shareholder value creation is the main goal. For shareholders, this depends not only on value created by the firm but also on value created by each individual investor through other investment opportunities. Thus, a high or low dividend payout may be irrelevant. This, however, depends on the market response to dividend decisions. For a higher payout, although investors receive higher immediate cash, they are likely to lose capital gain due to possible falling of stock prices: lower growth expectations tend to lower stock prices. A lower payout has an opposite impact on stock prices. *Source:* Author's construct

2.4.3.2 Implications of a Low Payout

A smaller proportion of earnings is used to pay dividends. Some companies never even pay dividends. Thus, a larger proportion of a company's earnings is used to fund investments. This may imply accelerating growth if the reinvested earnings generate higher returns. This company may have less reliance on external sources of financing, thereby minimizing the cost of capital. With other factors being equal, the lower the cost of capital, the higher the firm value.

This decision, nevertheless, tends to be more favorable to shareholders who are unable to create their own value—they rely more on the firm's value creation. In this situation, a larger proportion of firm value should be translated into shareholder value.

Exhibit ▸ 2.4 portrays the nature and impact of dividend decisions on various aspects of a firm. Overall, such decisions "intend to strike a balance" between immediate cash rewards to shareholders (dividend) and company growth (retained earnings), with the main goal being value creation for shareholders.

Banner 2.8 Dividend Decisions

Dividend decisions are about how to use earnings while creating more value.

Although dividends are paid from profits, the decision to declare them is not only determined by profits but also by other factors. These factors are outlined here.

Economic condition: Firms are likely to pay dividends during good economic conditions because of the likelihood of generating more income and having positive future profitability prospects. When the economic condition is bad, like economic recession and high inflation, managers may be reluctant to pay dividends so that they can retain the available cash to meet the current economic shocks. Likewise, when the economy is highly volatile, the uncertainty of the firm's future earnings increases. Therefore, managers may prefer to retain a large proportion of the earnings to absorb future economic shocks.

Capital market condition: Capital markets influence dividend decisions due to their role in signaling information and providing capital. If markets are efficient, then stock prices reflect the performance of a firm. In such markets, paying dividends would imply managers' positive expectations of the future position of the firm. Therefore, firms in favorable markets are expected to implement liberal dividend decisions (a high payout ratio), whereas those in unfavorable markets would follow conservative dividend policies (a low payout ratio). Aivazian et al. (2003) provide evidence that firms in emerging capital markets tend to have more unstable dividend payments than do those in advanced markets like the United States.

Contractual provisions: Sometimes, contractual provisions for dividend decisions are made between lenders and a firm. The aim of such provisions is to restrict dividend payments to protect the interests of the lenders and allow the firm to meet its financial obligations to finance providers. For example, lenders may agree with the firm that dividends shall not be paid unless the firm has paid at least 40% of a loan or when the firm's liquidity ratio is less than 1:1.

Legal aspects: Legal provisions on dividends are usually stipulated in the Companies Act, in which restrictions are made on the extent of dividend payments and the conditions in which such payments can or cannot be made. For example, dividends cannot be paid out of capital, and a firm cannot declare dividends unless it has met other creditors' obligations.

Shareholders' influence: Although the decision to declare dividends lies with the firm's board of directors, shareholders play a certain influencing role in such decisions. The central point is that dividend decisions affect the market value of a firm's stocks and the value of the firm. Some investors are more interested in capital gain (increased market value of the firm) than regular returns from dividends. In that case, shareholders are likely to influence decisions that lead to more retained earnings than dividend payouts; they consider a dividend as "irrelevant" (see Miller and Modigliani (1961) and some empirical evidence in the studies by Black and Scholes (1974), Miller (1986), and Bernstein (1996)). Other shareholders simply prefer receiving dividends, and they believe that a firm ought to pay dividends (Graham and Dodd 1934). Moreover, in conditions in which capital gains are highly uncertain due to other economic factors, risk-averse shareholders may prefer receiving dividends as far as the firm is able to pay them; they follow a "bird-in-the-hand" attitude, which is supported by some studies (see, for example, Gordon and Shapiro (1956), Lintner (1962), and Walter (1963), among others). Therefore, firms may have different dividend decisions for different groups of shareholders according to their preferences. Overall, dividend payments send a signal about the performance of a firm.

Financial strength: The financial condition of a firm determines its ability to finance wealth-generating investments as well as meet its debt obligations. When a firm is in a good financial condition and has a good income-generating pattern, it may decide to use its internal earnings to finance investments rather than using external financing sources that are associated with a high cost of capital. Alternatively, a good financial condition indicates the ability of a firm to borrow. Hence, a firm that can access external sources of financing through debts can exhaust that borrowing opportunity and let some of its profits be distributed to owners in the form of dividends. However, a firm with financial difficulties, like big debt obligations, will not have a motive for dividend payout.

Earning stability and liquidity: Earning stability reflects less uncertainty in the firm's future cash flows. Therefore, firms with stable earnings are likely to have a higher dividend payout than are those with unstable earnings. However, stable earnings do not necessarily imply a strong liquidity position. Since dividend payments imply cash outflows, a firm will require a strong liquidity position to afford dividend payments.

Ownership and control: Control relates to the voting powers of shareholders and managers and the agency problem. Hence, shareholders and managers exert tension over the decision control of a firm. Eckbo and Verma (1994) conducted a study based on Canadian firms where managers tend to own large amounts of voting stocks. Their results suggest a close relationship between the voting powers of owner-managers and cash dividends, in which cash dividends decrease with increase in voting powers and are almost none when owner-managers have absolute voting control of the firm.

2

Management attitude: In firms, decisions are made by managers whose personal attitudes tend to have significant influence on their decision-making ability. Managers with conservative attitudes are likely to declare lower dividends in favor of strengthening the financial position of the firm by retaining larger proportions of profits. A study on NASDAQ (National Association of Securities Dealers Automated Quotations) firms, by Baker et al. (2002), suggests that some managers believe that a high dividend payout is not in the interest of shareholders. On the other hand, managers with liberal minds would pay more dividends and retain fewer earnings. Partington (1985) provides evidence of how managers consider dividends as a way of satisfying shareholders and supporting share prices, whereas Baker et al. (1985) show that other managers believe that dividend payments enhance value.

Think 2.3

If dividend decisions are influenced by several factors, what criteria should managers use to make their dividend decisions?

Exhibit 2.5 The Interactive Role of Financial Management

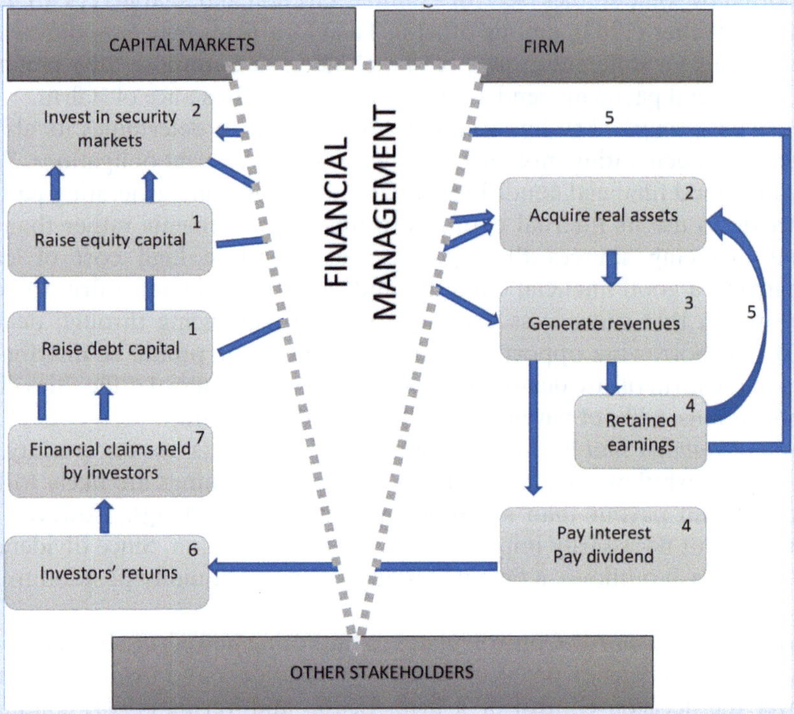

This figure considers the overall role of a finance manager and the overlapping role of financial management. The finance manager is expected to ensure linkage not only between the firm and capital markets but also other stakeholders. From number (1) to number (7), it can be summarized as follows:

(1) Raise capital from security markets in the form of equity or debt or both.
(2) Use the available funds raised from capital markets to acquire real assets and/or invest in security markets by buying equity or bonds.
(3) Generate revenues from business operations (use of real assets) and/or from other investments in security markets.
(4) Meet financial obligations by paying interest on debt. Depending on the dividend policy, use profits to pay dividends while retaining some earnings to increase shareholders' equity.
(5) Make decisions on the use of retained earnings—it can be used to acquire additional real assets and/or invest in security markets (stocks and bonds).
(6) The fulfillment of investors' financial obligations (paying interest and dividend) generates returns on their investments.
(7) Good returns enable investors to meet their financial claims held in capital markets. The fulfillment of financial obligations to investors creates a good relationship with the capital market and increases investors' confidence of the company. This, in turn, creates more investment opportunities and access to more funds for more value creation (1).

Source: Author's construct

2.5 The Role of Financial Management in Value Creation

Corporate financial management is an extremely important function of value creation due to its role in achieving fundamental managerial decisions and creating a link between financial functions and other functions of a firm such as operations, human resources, production, marketing, and so on. Specific functions of financial managing differ across firms, depending on factors like the size of the firm, nature of business or industry, and so on. For example, in large firms, financial management is more concerned with financial strategic aspects. In small firms, financial management may be deal with preparing accounting information and producing financial reports. Overall, the general role of financial management is overlapping and integrated into all other functions of a firm through planning, organizing, directing, and controlling the financial activities of the firm.

Exhibit ▶ 2.5 summarizes the interactive role of financial management and the general functions of a finance manager. Overall, financial management is responsible not only for managing a firm's financial functions but also for creating and managing linkage between the firm and external players like capital markets and other stakeholders. Both internal and external stakeholders play a role in the creation of value. Moreover, although all employees of the firm are expected to achieve value maximization, the finance manager acts as the key person in the process of value creation.

Think 2.4

Why is financial management considered to play a significant role in value creation?

Banner 2.9 Value-Creating Role of Finance Management

Financial management is an extremely important function of value creation. It plays a significant role in linking major managerial decisions to capital markets and other stakeholders.

2.6 Understanding the Main Goal of a Firm

2.6.1 What Should Be the Main Goal of a Firm?

As stated earlier, managers make many decisions on the behalf of investors (owners). However, "what do managers' decisions intend to achieve?" Is it to maximize profit, maximize growth, command market shares, eliminate competitors, or satisfy customers? Perhaps, it may be more important to know the short- and long-term implications of any decisions made. For example, if managers decide to improve profitability, is that improvement going to be short- or long-term? In whose interest will it be? Is it to generate enough cash to pay creditors or to improve employees' remunerations? Or is it aiming to strengthen the firm's ability to pay dividends to shareholders or to retain as much cash for future reinvestments? Obviously, each of these questions are important to the firm. Why are they important? Different firms have different goals—financial and nonfinancial—depending on several reasons. However, over many years, the perceived main goal of a firm has been to "maximize shareholders' wealth." Other objectives –generating cash flows, improving growth, generating returns, and paying dividends—and all decisions made on the basis of those objectives should target the same goal: shareholder wealth maximization, as depicted in Exhibit ▶ 2.6.

Exhibit 2.6 The Main Goal of a Firm

A firm can have many financial and nonfinancial objectives to achieve in the short and long terms. Financial objectives include, but are not limited to, profit maximization, improving returns, improving growth, paying dividends, and improving cash flows. Nonfinancial goals may include customer satisfaction, corporate social responsibility, leading market shares, etc. However, irrespective of the objectives set by a firm, its long-term target should be to maximize shareholders' value.

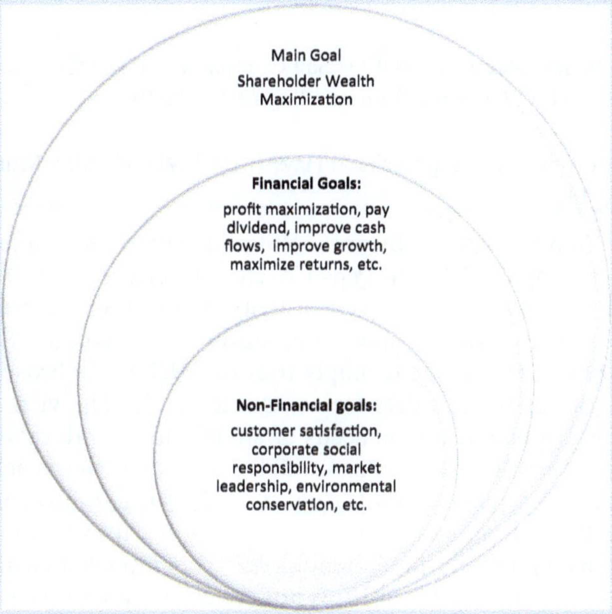

Source: Author's construct

Banner 2.10 The Main Goal of a Firm
Irrespective of how many objectives a firm intends to achieve, shareholder wealth maximization is the main perceived goal.

2.6.2 Debate About the Main Goal of a Firm

There is, however, debate regarding the shifting view of the main goal of a firm. In ▶ Quote 2.3.1, for example, an analyst (Steve Denning) is concerned about the deterioration of shareholders' value at the expense of other goals. The analyst was commenting on several news headlines regarding the doctrine of shareholder wealth. His views were based on the following news headlines, following a chief executive officer (CEO)'s statement from the Business Roundtable, August 2020:

- Shareholder Value Is No Longer Everything, Top C.E.O.s Say (David Gelles & David Yaffe-Bellany, The New York Times, August 19, 2019)

- CEO group says maximizing shareholder profits can't be main goal (Jena, McGregor, The Washington Post, August 19, 2019)

» Group of US corporate leaders ditches shareholder-first mantra (The Financial Times, August 19, 2019)

» Move Over, Shareholders: Top CEOs Say Companies Have Obligations to Society (David Benoit, The Wall Street Journal, August 19, 2019)

» Profits and Purpose: Can Big Business Have It Both Ways? (Alan Murray, Fortune, August 19, 2019)

It is important to note that the Business Roundtable represents the CEOs of 192 large companies (Apple, Walmart, PepsiCo, etc.). Over the last two decades, since 1997, the same Roundtable has been consistently advocating the interests of shareholders as the principal role of any corporation (see ▶ Quote 2.3.2 and 2.3.3). Overall, the new CEO's statement simply tries to redefine the broad roles of business—to focus on all stakeholders (see ▶ Quote 2.3.4). The view seems to shift commitment toward balancing the needs of shareholders with other stakeholders such as customers, employees, suppliers, and communities. Nevertheless, according to Jane McGregor (Washington Post, August 19, 2019), a group of investors' associations "respectfully disagree[s]" with the statement because it "undercuts notions of managerial accountability to shareholders." This implies that the new CEO's statement (Business Roundtable 2019) is not conclusive about what should be the main goal of a firm—it simply reignites the debate that has existed over many years, even before Friedman's doctrine of 1970.

Think 2.5
Why should shareholder wealth maximization be regarded as the main goal of a firm?

Quotes 2.3 Shareholder Wealth Maximization vs. Other Goals

▪ Quote 2.3.1 Eroding Shareholders' Value?

» ...By 2019, maximizing shareholder value has come to be seen as leading to a toxic mix of soaring short-term corporate profits, astronomic executive pay, along with stagnant median incomes, growing inequality, periodic massive financial crashes, declining corporate life expectancy, slowing productivity, declining rates of return on assets and overall, a widening distrust in business. (Steve Denning, Forbes)
Steve Denning, August 19, 2019, Forbes

▪ Quote 2.3.2 Focusing on Shareholders' Value

» The paramount duty of management and of boards of directors is to the corporation's stockholders. (CEO's Statement on Corporate Governance)
BRT Statement, September 1997, Business Roundtable

Quote 2.3.3 Why Focus on Shareholders' Value?

> The interests of other stakeholders are relevant as a derivative of the duty to stockholders.
>
> *BRT Statement, September 1997, Business Roundtable*

Quote 2.3.4 Focusing on Stakeholders' Value

> While each of our individual companies serves its own corporate purpose, we share a fundamental commitment to all of our stakeholders…We commit to deliver value to all of them, for the future success of our companies, our communities and our country. (CEO's Statement on The Purpose of a Corporation)
>
> *BRT Statement, August 19, 2019, Business Roundtable*

Quote 2.3.5 Debate on the Firm' Goal

> In its more corrosive application—the one that is inculcated in business schools, enforced by corporate lawyers and demanded by activist investors and Wall Street analysts—maximizing shareholder value has meant doing whatever is necessary to boost the share price this quarter and the next. Over the years, it has been used to justify bamboozling customers, squeezing workers and suppliers, avoiding taxes and lavishing stock options on executives. Most of what people find so distasteful about American capitalism—the ruthlessness, the greed, the inequality—has its roots in this misguided notion about what business is all about (Steven Pearlstein, investment analyst)
>
> *Steve Denning, August 19, 2019, Forbes*

2.6.3 Shareholder Wealth Maximization Vs. Profit Maximization

2.6.3.1 Misconception

There has always been a misconception among people about profit and wealth some people think that profit maximization is the same as wealth maximization. This notion is incorrect. Profit maximization means making the maximum profits possible during a financial period: it is a short-term measure of value. In reality, some firms never achieve profit maximization despite aiming for it. Even profit-making firms do not always maximize shareholders' wealth. In the CEO's statement (Business Roundtable 2019), the difference between maximizing profit and maximizing value is not clearly articulated. The terms "profit" and "value" seem to be used interchangeably, building on Milton Friedman's doctrine of 1970, which is regarded as the pioneer of firms' primary role - to generate returns to shareholders. While the matter of profit maximization vs. shareholder wealth maximation is debatable, our focus is on shareholders' wealth maximization. In this section, we show the difference between profit maximization and wealth maximization in favor of shareholders.

Banner 2.11 Shareholders' Wealth vs. Profit

Profit is a short-term measure of value, whereas wealth is a long-term measure of value.

Exhibit ▶ 2.7 provides a simple illustrative example to clarify the problem of profit as a measure of value. Some people use profitability indicators to measure how much wealth a firm is creating for shareholders. Such indicators include profit margins and returns on capital employed. In this example, we compare two firms, A and B. We see that firm B generated more profits than did firm A during the same financial period. However, firm A generated higher returns to shareholders than did firm B. As a quick indicator of performance, investors were better off in firm A but only during that financial period. That is, even if firm A generated more returns, this does not necessarily mean that it is maximizing shareholders' value—these are simply book figures: they show nothing about the source of such profits.

Therefore, the problem with accounting profit is the fact that it does not reflect all the information about value creation –cash flows, growth, and risk. Indeed, profits tend to be affected by several value-destroying factors such as accounting manipulation, managers' personal objectives, and noncash items. Consequently, profits do not consider the market value of a firm: they only reflect historical book values. Value should be driven by cash flows as discussed in the next section.

Think 2.6

Can you identify value from a profit figure reported in the income statement? Explain.

Exhibit 2.7 Illustrative Example

Shareholder Wealth Maximization vs. Profit Maximization

Suppose there are two firms, A and B, of relatively the same size and operating in the same industry. However, managers of these firms have different attitudes regarding profitability and value creation. Managers of firm A are risk-averse, and, hence, they have made decisions to take costly insurance policies and other risk management measures that cut a significant slice of the profits generated by the firm. On the other hand, managers of firm B have decided to cancel most of the firm's insurance policies and other risk management contracts as a cost-cutting strategy aiming at increasing reported profits. Consequently, firm B reports higher profits than does firm A, as indicated in Exhibit 2.7.1.

■ **Exhibit 2.7.1** Financial results of firm A vs. firm B

	Firm A ($ millions)	Firm B ($ millions)
Sales	120	200
Net profit	30	40
Total equity	350	600
Total assets	600	900

Question: If you invest in both firms A and B, will you better off with firm A or firm B?

A simple answer is that the lower profits reported by firm A are likely to be more value-creating than the higher profits reported by firm B. This is because of the higher risk in firm B—its future is more uncertain, thereby threatening its long-term profitability and survival. Although firm A reports lower profits, it is likely to have a better long-term position and is hence more valuable.

To use the financial results, let us analyze the performance indicators relating to profitability, as indicated in ■ Exhibit 2.7.2. As we have seen, firm B has generated more profits than firm A during the same period. However, firm A has generated higher returns to shareholders than firm B. For the investor, therefore, firm A, despite reporting lower profits, is more attractive than firm B, at least during that financial period.

■ **Exhibit 2.7.2** Performance of firm A vs. firm B

	Firm A	Firm B
Net profit margin	30%	20%
Return on equity	9%	7%
Return on assets	5%	4%

2.6.3.2 The Real World

There are real examples of corporations that have collapsed despite reporting high accounting profits. The Enron scandal is one of the most cited examples. The collapse of Enron was sudden and unexpected because, a few months before filing for bankruptcy, the company was regarded as one of the best in the United States in terms of innovation, growth, and management. This excellent image was only visible because of the hidden reality of its true picture. Later, the truth was revealed that Enron was in a difficult financial condition as early as 2000, but managers were able to manipulate accounting statements to hide the financial trouble. Indeed,

2

the company was performing poorly in its business operations and burdened with massive debt obligations. The nature and origin of its collapse was then regarded as a "financial scandal" because the accounting system was able to hide the clear picture of the company's true condition. Even corporate governance practices failed. On one hand, the independent auditors did not disclose the problem. On the other hand, the board members, who were expected to protect the interests of the investors, were unwilling to challenge the company's managers. Moreover, analysts in stock markets failed to flash a warning signal to investors about the expected financial trouble.

In short, Enron's managers were destroying value at the expense of misleading accounting profits. Probably, a major question arising from the Enron case would be: How do businesses make profits? Is it always a good performance indicator when companies report high profits? Nevertheless, the financial reports relating to such profits never provide sufficient information on how profits are made. Hiding useful information has been a policy and practical aspect of many companies under the umbrella of "confidentiality for competitive reasons."

Brennan (2003) gives the following comments on the consequences of such practices:

> As a result of the Enron bankruptcy, the once well-respected accounting profession came under indictment for injudicious, if not iniquitous, practices, which have undermined investor confidence in all firms and threaten to drastically depress the entire equity market in the United States.

Exhibit ▶ 2.8 summarizes the key distinctions between profit maximization and shareholder wealth maximization.

Exhibit 2.8 Shareholder Wealth Maximization vs. Profit Maximization

	Profit maximization	Wealth maximization
Goals	Short-term profit goals may be at the expense of long-term profitability and value	Long-term goals for wealth creation regardless of the level of profits
Risks and uncertainties	Profits may not consider the risks associated with how the profits are made	Considers the uncertainties and risks associated with business operations
Time value of money	Profitability returns are only a single period measure. They only reflect the state of a firm during a specific period	Wealth maximization focuses on the entire life of a firm, considering the future returns to shareholders and time value of money
Value measures	Profits are based on book values from operations during a specific period.	Wealth creation is measured by the market value of the firm's stocks, which reflects investors' perception of the firm

	Profit maximization	Wealth maximization
Managerial motives	Profits may be realized from managers' personal objectives that may destroy shareholder value as in the case of Enron and others	Wealth maximization avoids personal objectives and focuses on shareholders' value
Accounting problems	Profit figures arise from accounting reports, which may be subjected to manipulations	Wealth maximization goals avoid most of the accounting problems. The focus is on cash flows rather than profits

2.6.4 Cash Flow vs. Profit

2.6.4.1 Accrual Basis of Accounting and Noncash Items

In accrual basis of accounting, we recognize credit sales as revenue even though no cash has been received. Likewise, expenses are recognized even if no payment has been made. Therefore, some of the items from which profits are calculated are non-cash items, such as depreciation, credit sales, and credit purchases. To overcome the effect of accounting problems, wealth maximization should consider cash flows instead of profits.

Cash flows represent the entire financial health of a company. They are derived by considering all cash items of a firm during a certain period. These cash items not only come from operations but also financing and investment activities such as purchase and disposal of assets and liabilities.

Think 2.7

Why should cash flow be considered a more superior measure of value than accounting profit?

Here are some examples to justify the valuation relevance of cash flows against accounting profits:

1. *Credit sales:* A firm reports sales revenues on credit sales by creating debtors—no cash has been received. Sometimes the firm will be required to spend extra financial resources to collect money from debtors. In some cases, the firm may offer discounts as a means of encouraging debtors to pay, which, in turn, reduces the amount of cash revenues received. Moreover, some debtors tend to default, thereby forcing the firm to write them off as bad debts. This concept is illustrated in Exhibit ► 2.9.

Exhibit 2.9 Illustrative Example

Cash Flow vs. Profit

Scenario 1: Credit Sales

Exhibit 2.9.1 shows a firm's extent of its operating performance during a financial period. Suppose a firm buys merchandise worth $150 million on cash payment and sells its merchandise on credit worth $200 million. Thus, we can

2

distinguish accounting profit from cash flow based on the impact of credit sales. In this example, although a profit of $50 million has been made, no cash has been received therein despite paying $150 million on inventories. Unless the firm can collect cash from its customers (debtors), the net cash flow is negative $150 million.

Scenario 2: Credit Purchases

Exhibit 2.9.2 shows a firm's extent of its operating performance during a financial period. Now, suppose the firm purchases its merchandise on credit at $150 million and all are sold at $200 million on cash. In this case, the firm seems to be profitable with $50 million and highly liquid with cash of $200 million. This cash is sufficient to clear its accounts payable of $150 million and maintain a cash balance of $50 million.

Exhibit 2.9.1 The effect of credit sales

Profit ($millions)		**Cash flow ($millions)**	
Sales revenue	200	Cash inflow	0
Less cost of goods sold	150	*Less* cash outflow	150
Profit	50	Net cash flow	(150)

Exhibit 2.9.2 The effect of credit purchases

Profit ($millions)		**Cash flow ($millions)**	
Sales revenue	200	Cash inflow	200
Less cost of goods sold	150	*Less* cash outflow	0
Profit	50	Net cash flow	200

2. *Cost of goods sold*: Accounting profit recognizes the cost of goods sold from credit purchases, yet cash has not been paid for them. As a result, the firm is obligated to its creditors (current liabilities). Such a payment obligation can sometimes be difficult when the firm faces liquidity problems. In Exhibit 2.9.2, however, the firm does not have liquidity problems. The accounting profit is reported as $50 million, whereas cash is $200 million because of cash sales. However, the firm still has an obligation of $150 million to its suppliers. If all creditors are paid now, then a profit of $50 will be equal to cash balance.
3. *Inventory*: When a firm purchases goods for sale, either on cash or credit terms, the value of such purchases is not recorded as expenses in the income statement. Instead, it is recognized as current assets (inventories) in the balance

sheet. This happens only after selling them, when inventories change status from being assets to being cost of goods sold (expenses).

4. Accounting profit does not consider cash outflows and inflows relating to investment and financing activities. Here are a few examples:
   (a) The acquisition of assets such as land, buildings, and so on moves cash out of the firm. However, this movement of cash is not accounted for in determining profits. Instead, only depreciation on those assets, a noncash charge, is recognized.
   (b) The issue of shares brings in cash to the firm (cash inflow), but it is not recognized in calculating accounting income.
   (c) In connection to shares, when a firm pays dividends, cash flow is affected as it moves out of the firm. However, in calculating accounting profit, dividend expenses are not recognized.
   (d) Borrowing brings cash into the firm and creates a debt: this cash in not income and is hence not recognized in calculating profits. Even when the loan is paid, it does not constitute expenses in the income statement, which does not affect the profit.
   (e) In relation to debt, accounting profit recognizes the cost of that debt, which is charged as interest expenses.

From these few examples, accounting income may not be a good measure of value. In contrast, cash received or paid is extremely important for analyzing the value created for shareholders or firms. Indeed, in the short and medium terms, some firms can survive even without cash: for example, by delaying paying debts. However, in the long run, a business may not survive without having enough cash to meet its financial obligations.

Banner 2.12 Cash vs. Profit
Valuation considers cash flows as a better proxy for wealth maximization than accounting profit.

2.6.4.2 The Real World

Let us use some selected news insights relating to three case companies, GE (General Electric Co.), Telia, and ASIX Electronics. The news reports are based on the financial results for the fourth quarter of 2019.

In the case of GE, reporters Alwyn Scott and Rachit Vats used the headline: "GE Shares Jump 10% on Profit Beat, Higher 2020 Cash Target" (Reuters, January 29, 2020). The reporters imply that investors' reaction, which drove GE's stock prices up by 10%, was influenced by both profit and cash flows. However, it is the cash flow forecast target that seems to carry more weight. They describe it as "bullish cash target," meaning an expected rise in cash, which they also describe as "the new target marked a confident step up from GE's 2019 target of $0 to $2 billion in cash."

Link: ▶ https://uk.reuters.com/article/us-general-electric-results/ge-shares-jump-10-on-profit-beat-higher-2020-cash-target-idUKKBN1ZS1EW

2

In the case of Telia, the headline by Reuters was "Telia profit tops forecast, sees lower operational cash flow" (Reuters, January 29, 2020). In summary, the company reported higher profits than expectations but lower operating cash flows. According to the reporter, cash flows seem to be more important for investors and are described as "a measure closely eyed by investors to gauge future dividend capacity." Impliedly, higher profits are only meaningful if they turn into cash.

Link: ▶ https://www.nasdaq.com/articles/telia-profit-tops-forecast-sees-lower-operational-cash-flow-2020-01-29

In the case of ASIX, the Simply Walls St. had the headline "Is There More To The Story Than ASIX Electronics's Earnings Growth?" (Simply Wall St., January 30, 2020). The reporters acknowledge the importance of profits, but clearly caution that "statutory profits are not always the best tool for understanding a company's true earnings power." Instead, profits should be considered relative to how they can be converted into cash. They, therefore, recommend the use of a financial measure known as the "accrual ratio," which measures "how well a company converts its profit to free cash flow." A consensus is that investors tend to be concerned with both profit and cash flows but exercise caution when it comes to the power of profitability. An important point regarding the ASIX case is reflected in the following quote: "Happily for shareholders, ASIX Electronics produced plenty of free cash flow to back up its statutory profit numbers."

Link: ▶ https://simplywall.st/stocks/tw/semiconductors/gtsm-3169/asix-electronics-shares/news/is-there-more-to-the-story-than-asix-electronicss-gtsm3169-earnings-growth/

2.7 Agency Cost: Ownership and Control

Agency cost is one of the vital aspects of corporate value creation. This is mainly because, for achieving the goal of shareholder (principal) wealth maximization, managers (agents) should avoid aiming for personal gains. Therefore, there are two key issues relating to the agency cost: conflicts of interest and measures to overcome those conflicts.

Think 2.8

Who should be given top priority if conflicts of interest exist among business owners, managers, and other stakeholders?

2.7.1 Conflicts of Interest

The agency theory suggests that there are three types of conflicts of interest that exist within a firm: conflict between owners and managers; conflict among owners; and conflict between owners and the firm's stakeholders. Each of these types of conflicts tend to influence how firms create or destroy value.

2.7.1.1 Conflict Between Owners and Managers

This is the most common type of conflict due to its overall sensitivity to shareholder wealth maximization. The agency problem starts with the existence of a firm, which involves "separation of ownership and control" (see Jensen and Meckling 1976; Fama and Jensen 1983) in relation to the main goal of the firm—"maximization of owners' wealth." For small firms, management and ownership can be vested in the same person, the capital provider. However, for large firms, separation between management and ownership is inevitable. Since owners cannot run businesses on their own, they appoint managers to operate on their behalf. On the other hand, since it is assumed that all rational people aim at maximizing their wealth, managers may not necessarily act toward maximizing owners' wealth but rather their own wealth.

Thus, the agency problem arises due to the "conflict of interest" between the owners of a firm (principle) and the managers (agent). The problem can also be referred to as the "principle-agent problem" or the "agency dilemma." The idea behind this problem is that managers are empowered to make decisions that impact shareholders' wealth. Nevertheless, those decisions may be motivated by managers' interests, different or contradictory to those of the owners. Indeed, managers tend to be more informed than owners (the question of asymmetric information); hence, owners may not be in a better position to know whether managers are acting in their (owners) best interest.

From this conflict of interest arises the "agency cost," in which the owners bear the cost known as the "agency cost of equity." This cost entails measures usually taken by owners to limit divergences from their interest through establishing appropriate incentives for managers. These are known as "monitoring costs," designed to limit the aberrant activities of their managers—they include auditing, structuring, insurance costs, and so on. Jensen and Meckling (1976) viewed independent auditing as a crucial monitoring aspect that aims at increasing the value of the firm. A detailed account of the role of auditing in reducing the agency problem is found in the study by Watts and Zimmerman (1983).

On the other hand, managers incur "bonding costs." According to Cohen and Uliana (1990) there are several examples of bonding costs, which include excessive levels of management remuneration; shirking (neglect of duty); appropriation of corporate resources in the form of excessive levels of perks; avoiding investing corporate resources in potentially profitable ventures to the detriment of the shareholders; pursuit of sales growth at the expense of profits or shareholder wealth; empire building by managers; employee welfare objectives; and manipulation of dividend policy at the expense of shareholder wealth creation.

Despite several efforts that aim at minimizing the agency problem, sometimes there is a divergence between the manager's decisions and those decisions that would maximize owners' wealth. In monetary terms, any reduction of owners' welfare, which is caused by decision divergence, is also an agency cost. This cost is known as "residual loss."

Moreover, there may be other indirect costs, which arise from loss of opportunities. For example, there may be an investment opportunity that is expected to create more wealth for shareholders. However, upon undertaking such an investment, managers should sacrifice some benefits or even lose jobs. Even though this type of cost is unquantifiable, it has effects on both the owners and managers.

2.7.1.2 Conflict Among Investors

There are two major categories of investors in a firm. The first category can be referred to as internal investors (owners). These are investors with a controlling or majority stake in the firm. The second category can be referred to as external investors, who have a minority or noncontrolling stake in the firm. They mainly include debtholders and preferred equity holders. A conflict of interest arises when the controlling owners (agents) fail to provide assurance to the noncontrolling investors (principals) that their decisions and actions are not exploitative. From this type of conflict arises another agency cost known as the "agency cost of debt." This cost is associated with an increase in the cost of debt imposed by external investors, as a protective measure against owners.

2.7.1.3 Conflict Between Owners and Other Stakeholders

Stakeholders (such as suppliers, clients, regulators, government, employees, creditors, etc.) are as important to a firm as any other parties. The agency relationship between owners and stakeholders considers owners as agents and stakeholders as principals. Hence, a conflict arises when stakeholders feel that the owners benefit at their (stakeholders) expense.

2.7.2 Solutions for the Agency Problem

Several possible solutions are usually proposed to minimize the agency problem. The proposed measures include a combination of owners' wealth-based incentive schemes (low agency cost) and some degree of monitoring (high agency cost).

2.7.2.1 Performance-based Incentive Schemes

The justification for performance-based incentives stems from the reasoning that managers will act in the best interest of owners when performance is linked to their remunerations. These include share option schemes and other special rewards.

2.7.2.2 Share Option Schemes

This involves giving managers or employees the right to purchase shares in an enterprise at a fixed price as part of their remuneration. The objective is to motivate managers to make value-creating decisions. This measure, however, is subject to challenges because some of the factors that tend to influence shareholders' value are beyond the control of managers—they are external factors, which include interest rates, exchange rate volatility, government policies, natural disasters, and economic conditions. Hence, share option schemes cannot be regarded as effective measures to the agency problem. This, consequently, has shifted interest toward the so-called "performance-based share options," in which remunerations to managers are not only based on shares but also a certain performance measurement such as earnings per share (EPS), return on assets (ROA), return on equity (ROE), and so on. However, performance-based share options are subject to criticism because of the shortcomings of accounting performance indicators. There have been concerns about the possible manipulation of accounting performance measures by managers. Empirical evidence of accounting manipulations are available—examples include the cases of Enron and Baring Bank, among others. Stern (1974) provides a detailed discussion on the shortcomings of relying on accounting performance measures.

2.7.2.3 Value Creation Rewards

These are mechanisms that reward managers based on their ability to create value for the capital employed. One of the most popular measurement criteria is economic value added (EVA), which evaluates the extent to which managers have created or destroyed value for capital employed. According to Milunovich and Tsuei (1996), EVA encourages managers to act as owners through enforcing capital discipline. Therefore, linking managers' remunerations to change in EVA entails linking remunerations to owners' wealth creation.

2.7.2.4 Controls and Monitoring

From owners' perspective, the term "control" means their capability to elect the board of directors. It does not mean active managerial decision-making in a firm. However, at least it covers the fundamental decision of appointing the top managers of a firm. The two main ways in which owners can control a firm's management include: (1) their ability to influence how a firm should be managed and (2) their voting rights at annual general meetings.

The ability to change top managers is a control mechanism that gives owners power to influence some decisions. A study by Weisbach (1995) shows that changing management helps reverse the previous poor investment decisions made by exhausted managers. However, whereas business owners can have an indirect influence on changing top managers, the most fundamental change that they can make directly is the board of directors. Nevertheless, the board of directors tends to be regarded as a weak link between owners and managers because, in most cases, it tends to be influenced or controlled by the top management. This aspect can be exemplified by the case of Korean Air from the following quote of news headline "Korean Air parent shareholders join forces to oust management"

> Three key shareholders of Korean Air's parent company joined forces to oust the airline's current management, saying on Friday the airline and its parent needed professional executives and they would work together in an upcoming shareholders' meeting. The statement comes amid a family feud between the South Korean flag carrier's CEO and group chairman Cho Won-tae and his sister ahead of a shareholders meeting in March. Cho's sister, Heather Cho, a former Korean Air executive whose 'nut rage' incident in 2014 made global headlines, has accused her brother of disobeying their late father's will for the family to work together for the management of the group. Heather Cho, local activist fund KCGI and Bando Engineering & Construction, shareholders in Korean Air parent company Hanjin KAL, said in a joint statement the airline and parent Hanjin Group's 'current management situa-

tion is a serious crisis and it cannot be improved by the current management,' and professional managers must be introduced. 'To this end, we agreed to actively cooperate in activities for the growth and development of Hanjin Group, including exercising voting rights and putting forth proposals at the upcoming Hanjin KAL shareholders' meeting.' (Joyce Lee, Reuters, January 31, 2020)

2.7.2.5 Threats

To induce managers to work in the best interest of owners, some threats like dismissal and takeovers tend to be used. A dismissal threat means that shareholders can make the decision to dismiss the top managers. A takeover threat serves as an external control mechanism for ensuring managers maximize owners' wealth. Usually, a firm will be a target for takeovers when its share value decreases persistently. This means that managers will strive to work for increasing value to avoid losing their positions should takeovers occur.

Review Questions

1. Explain how the existence of a firm and its finance providers necessitates the need for valuation.
2. Mention the different types of a firm's investors and how they can influence value creation.
3. Why should shareholder wealth maximization be regarded as the main goal of a firm?
4. What is the main role of managers in creation of firm's and shareholders' value?
5. Outline the key stakeholders of a firm and explain their role in a firm's value creation and valuation.
6. Explain the differences between the following aspects relating to valuation:
   (a) Wealth maximization vs. profit maximization
   (b) Cash flow vs. profit
   (c) Value vs. price
   (d) Firm value and shareholder value
   (e) Book value vs. market value
7. With examples, explain how a firm can generate profits yet still face cash problems.
8. List the main three types of financial decisions and explain how those decisions are linked to value creation.
9. With examples, explain how each of the following financial decisions can either create or destroy value:
   (a) Operating decision
   (b) Financing decision
   (c) Investment decision
10. Explain why financial management should be regarded as a key aspect in shareholder value maximization.
11. Demonstrate how financial management can create an important linkage between a firm, capital markets, and stakeholders. Explain the role of that linkage in value creation.

12. With examples, explain how each of the following financial transactions can affect profits but not cash flows, or cash flows but not profits, or both profits and cash flows.
    (a) Merchandises worth US$25 million are sold, but US$10 million is on credit.
    (b) Merchandises worth US$14 million are purchased, but only US$5 million are paid for.
    (c) Equipment worth US$50 million are acquired and paid for. The payment is financed by a portion of a long-term loan worth US$86 million. The depreciation charge on equipment is 5% straightforward annually. The interest rate on loan is 10% annually.
    (d) A company issues new 1 million shares at US$2 per share. The issuance cost is 2%, which is paid to a syndicate of brokers.
    (e) A debt worth US$26 million is paid, including interest of US$7 million.
    (f) A company pays dividends on 1 million common shares at $0.5 per share.
13. Why is the agency cost problem important in explaining shareholder wealth maximization?
14. In relation to the agency cost phenomenon, outline different types of conflicts of interest and explain how they can affect value.
15. What is the difference between agency cost of equity and agency cost of debt?
16. Use an example to explain the different measures that are commonly used to manage the agency cost problem.

Bibliography

Agrawal, A. & Mandelker, G. M. (1987), Managerial Incentives and Corporate investment and Financing Decisions, *The Journal of Finance*, 42 (4), 823-837. https://doi.org/10.2307/2328293

Aivazian, V., Booth, L. & Cleary, S. (2003) Dividend policy and the organization of capital markets, *Journal of Multinational Financial Management*, 13 (2), 101-121. https://doi.org/10.1016/S1042-444X(02)00038-5

Alonso, P. A., Iturriaga, F. J. L & Sanz, Juan A. R (2005), Financial decisions and growth opportunities: a Spanish firm's panel data analysis, *Applied Financial Economics*, 15(6), 391-407. https://doi.org/10.1080/09603100500039201

Amato, N. (2020). The CFO's role in value creation, Available at Financial Management, https://www.fm-magazine.com/news/2020/jun/cfo-role-in-value-creation.html Accessed June 25, 2020.

Baker, H. K., Gail E. F. & Richard B. E., (1985), A Survey of Management Views on Dividend Policy, *Financial Management* 14 (3), 78-84. https://www.jstor.org/stable/3665062

Baker, H. K., Gary E. P. & Theodore, E. V., (2002), Revisiting Managerial Perspectives on Dividend Policy, *Journal of Economics and Finance* 26, 267-283. https://doi.org/10.1007/BF02759711

Bernstein, P.L., (1996), Dividends: The Puzzle, *Journal of Applied Corporate Finance.* 9 (1), 16-22. https://doi.org/10.1111/j.1745-6622.1996.tb00097.x

Black, F., & Scholes, M. S. (1974), The Effects of Dividend Yield and Dividend Policy on Common Stock Prices and Returns, *Journal of Financial Economics* 1 (1), 1-22. https://doi.org/10.1016/0304-405X(74)90006-3

Brennan, D. M. (2003), Enron and Failed Futures: Policy and Corporate Governance in the Wake of Enron's Collapse, Social Text. Duke University Press No.77, 21(4), 35-50. https://doi.org/10.1215/01642472-21-4_77-35

BRT (1997), Statement on Corporate Governance, Available vis The Business Roundtable (BR), https://cdn.theconversation.com/static_files/files/693/Statement_on_Corporate_Governance_Business-Roundtable-1997%281%29.pdf?1566830902 Accessed January 3 2021.

BRT (2019), Statement on the Purpose of a Corporation, Available via The Business Roundtable (BR), https://s3.amazonaws.com/brt.org/BRT-StatementonthePurposeofaCorporationwithSignaturesOctober2022.pdf Accessed January 3 2021.

Byoun, S. (2008), How and When Do Firms Adjust Their Capital Structures toward Targets? *The Journal of Finance*, 63(6), 3069-3096. https://doi.org/10.1111/j.1540-6261.2008.01421.x

Calif, I. (2020). CoreLogic Board Unanimously Rejects Opportunistic Acquisition Proposal from Senator and Cannae. Available at Business Wire, https://www.businesswire.com/news/home/20200707005439/en/CoreLogic-Board-Unanimously-Rejects-Opportunistic-Acquisition-Proposal Accessed July 7th 2020.

CBS News (2008), available at CBC News. http://www.cbsnews.com/8301-505123_162-35040134/poor-investment-decisions-add-to-motorolas-woes/ . Accessed November 4, 2008.

Cohen, T. & Uliana, E. (1990). An evaluation of corporate ownership structures on employee, management and shareholder compensation for JSE companies, *De Ratione*, 4(1), 7-14. https://doi.org/10.1080/10108270.1990.11435010

Croci, E. D., John A. & Gonenc, H. (2011), Family Control and Financing Decisions, *European Financial Management*, 17(5), 860-897. https://doi.org/10.1111/j.1468-036X.2011.00631.x

Cohn, M, (2020). Global accounting groups urge long-term value creation amid coronavirus. Available at Accounting Today, https://www.accountingtoday.com/news/global-accounting-groups-urge-long-term-value-creation-amid-coronavirus. Accessed July 02, 2020.

Dang, V. (2010). Leverage, Debt Maturity and Firm Investment: An Empirical Analysis, Journal of Business Finance and Accounting, 38 (1-2), 225-258. https://doi.org/10.1111/j.1468-5957.2010.02215.x

Denis, D. J. (1992), Corporate Investment Decisions and Corporate Control: Evidence from Going-Private Transactions, *Financial Management*, 21(3), 80-94. https://www.jstor.org/stable/3666021

Dobbs, R., Huyett, B., and Koller, T. (2010), The CEO's guide to corporate finance, Available at McKinsey Quarterly, November 2010. https://www.mckinsey.com/capabilities/strategy-and-corporate-finance/our-insights/the-ceos-guide-to-corporate-finance Accessed July 28 2020.

Dotan, A. & Ravid, A. S. (1985), On the Interaction of Real and Financial Decisions of the Firm under Uncertainty, *The Journal of Finance*, 40 (2) 501-517. https://doi.org/10.2307/2327897

Dynamic Business (2020). "Speed to market is critical:" A CEO's steps for using tech to grow fast, Available at Dynamic Business, https://dynamicbusiness.com.au/topics/technology/speed-to-market-is-critical-a-ceos-steps-for-using-tech-to-grow-fast.html Accessed July 8 2020.

Eckbo, E. B., & Verma, S. (1994), Managerial share ownership, voting power, and cash dividend policy, *Journal of Corporate Finance*, 1(1), 33-62. https://doi.org/10.1016/0929-1199(94)90009-4

Elliott (2020). Elliott Management Recommends Changes at Crown Castle. Available at Cision PR Newswire, https://www.prnewswire.com/news-releases/elliott-management-recommends-changes-at-crown-castle-301088355.html Accessed July 6th 2020.

Fama, E. F., & French, K. R. (1998), Taxes, Financing Decisions, and Firm Value, *The Journal of Finance*, 53 (3) 819-843. https://www.jstor.org/stable/117379

Fama, E. F., & Jensen M. C. (1983), Separation of ownership and control, *Journal of law and Economics*, 26(2), 301-315. https://www.jstor.org/stable/725104

Ferrara, W. L. (1966). Should Investment and Financing Decisions Be Separated? *The Accounting Review*, 41(1), 106-114. https://www.jstor.org/stable/242528

Financial Times (2020). Available at Financial Times, https://www.ft.com/content/674fe822-43be-11ea-a43a-c4b328d9061c Accessed January 31, 2020.

Friedman, M. (1970), The Social Responsibility of Business is to Increase its Profits, Available at The New York Times Magazine, September 13, 1970, https://www.nytimes.com/1970/09/13/archives/a-friedman-doctrine-the-social-responsibility-of-business-is-to.html Accessed March 21, 2022.

Globe Newswire (2020), Crown Castle Highlights Compelling Opportunity for Value Creation and Growth Comments on Letter from Elliott, Available at https://www.globenewswire.com/news-release/2020/07/06/2058010/0/en/Crown-Castle-Highlights-Compelling-Opportunity-for-Value-Creation-and-Growth.html, Accessed on July 6 2020.

Gordon, M. J., & Shapiro, E. (1956), Capital Equipment Analysis: The Required Rate of Profit, *Management Science* 3, 102-110. https://www.jstor.org/stable/2627177

Graham, B. and Dodd, D. (1934) *Security Analysis*, McGraw-Hill: New York. Pp. xi, 725.

Harris, M., and Raviv, A. (2010). Control of corporate decisions: shareholders vs. management. *The Review of Financial Studies* 23(11), 4115–4147. https://doi.org/10.1093/rfs/hhq081

IFAC (2020). The CFO and Finance Function Role in Value Creation, Available at IFAC, IIRC, CIMA, AICPA, Joint Report, June 25, 2020. https://www.integratedreporting.org/wp-content/uploads/2020/06/The-CFO-and-Finance-Function-Role-in-Value-Creationv3.pdf Accessed May 2, 2021.

Jensen, M. C. & Meckling, W. H. (1976). Theory of the Firm: Managerial Behavior, Agency Costs, and Ownership Structure. *Journal of Financial Economics*, 3(4), 305-360. https://doi.org/10.1016/0304-405X(76)90026-X

Kang, J., Shivdasan, A., & Yamada, T. (2000), The Effect of Bank Relations on Investment Decisions: An Investigation of Japanese Takeover Bids, *The Journal of Finance*, 55 (2) 2197-2218. https://doi.org/10.1111/0022-1082.00284

Lee J. (2020). Korean Air parent shareholders join forces to oust management, Available at Nasdaq https://www.nasdaq.com/articles/korean-air-parent-shareholders-join-forces-to-oust-management-2020-01-31 Accessed January 31 2020.

Lev, B. (1974), On the Association Between Operating Leverage and Risk, *The Journal of Financial and Quantitative Analysis*, 9(4), 627-641. https://doi.org/10.2307/2329764

Lewis, C. M. R., Richard J. & Seward, J. K. (2003). Industry conditions, growth opportunities and market reactions to convertible debt financing decisions, *Journal of Banking and Finance*, 27, 153-181. https://doi.org/10.1016/S0378-4266(01)00212-6

Lintner, J. (1962), Dividends, Earnings, Leverage, Stock Prices and Supply of Capital to Corporations, *The Review of Economics and Statistics* 64, 243-269. https://doi.org/10.2307/1927792

MacKie-Mason, J. K (1990a), Do Taxes Affect Corporate Financing Decisions? *The Journal of Finance,* 45(5), 1471-1493. https://doi.org/10.1111/j.1540-6261.1990.tb03724.x

Mackie-Mason, J. K., (1990b), Do Firms Care Who Provides Their Financing, in R.G. Hubbard, (Ed)., Asymmetric Information, Corporate Finance and Investment: NBER Report.

Mauer, D. C. & Triantis, A. J. (1994), Interactions of Corporate Financing and Investment Decisions: A Dynamic Framework, *The Journal of Finance*, 49 (4) 1253-1277. https://doi.org/10.1111/j.1540-6261.1994.tb02453.x

Miller, M. H., (1986), Behavioral Rationality in Finance: The Case of Dividends, *Journal of Business* 59(4), 451-468. https://doi.org/10.1086/296380

Miller, M. H., & Modigliani, F. (1961), Dividend Policy, Growth, and the Valuation of Shares, *Journal of Business* 34 (4), 411-433. https://doi.org/10.1086/294442

Milunovich, S. & Tsuei, A. (1996). EVA in the computer industry, *Journal of Applied Corporate Finance*, 9(1), 104-115. https://doi.org/10.1111/j.1745-6622.1996.tb00108.x

Myers, S., (1977). Determinants of corporate borrowing. *Journal of Financial Economics* 5 (2), 147–175. https://doi.org/10.1016/0304-405X(77)90015-0

Ooi, J. T., Ong, S, & Li, L. (2008), An Analysis of the Financing Decisions of REITS: From a Capital Market Perspective, IRES Working Papers Series 2008-004, National University of Singapore.

Partington, G. H., (1985), Dividend policy and its Relationship to Investment and Financing Policies: Empirical Evidence, *Journal of Business Finance and Accounting* 12 (4), 531-542. https://doi.org/10.1111/j.1468-5957.1985.tb00792.x

Ravid, A. S (1988), On Interactions of Production and Financial Decisions, *Financial Management,* 17(3), 87-99. https://doi.org/10.2307/3666075

Saá-Requejo, J. (1996), Financing Decisions: Lessons from the Spanish Experience, *Financial Management*, 25(3), 44-56. https://doi.org/10.2307/3665807

Simply Wall St. (2020). Is There More To The Story Than ASIX Electronics's (GTSM:3169) Earnings Growth? Vailable at Simply Wall St. https://simplywall.st/stocks/tw/semiconductors/gtsm-3169/asix-electronics-shares/news/is-there-more-to-the-story-than-asix-electronicss-gtsm3169-earnings-growth/ Accessed January 30 2020.

Stern, J. M. (1974), Earnings per share don't count, *Financial Analysts Journal*, 30 (4), 39-45. https://www.jstor.org/stable/4529716

Stulz, R., (1988), Managerial control of voting rights: Financing policies and the market for corporate control, *Journal of Financial Economics*, 20, 25–54. https://doi.org/10.1016/0304-405X(88)90039-6

Taggart, R. A. (1977). A Model of Corporate Financing Decisions, *The Journal of Finance*, 32(5), 1467-1484. https://doi.org/10.1111/j.1540-6261.1977.tb03348.x

Town, P. (2018). The Important Differences Between Price And Value, Available at Forbes, https://www.forbes.com/sites/forbesfinancecouncil/2018/01/04/the-important-differences-between-price-and-value/#7b1189324237. Accesses January 4th 2018.

Vanacke, T & Manigart, S (2007), Incremental Financing Decisions in High Growth Companies: Pecking Order and Debt Capacity Considerations. Working Papers 07/475 of Faculty of Economics and Business Administration, Ghent University, Belgium. https://econpapers.repec.org/scripts/redir.pf?u=http%3A%2F%2Fwps-feb.ugent.be%2FPapers%2Fwp_07_475.pdf;h=repec:rug:rugwps:07/475

Walter, J. E., (1963), Dividend Policy: Its Influence on the Value of the Enterprise, *Journal of Finance* 18 (2), 280-291. https://doi.org/10.1111/j.1540-6261.1963.tb00724.x

Watts, L. R. & Zimmerman, J. L. (1983), Agency Problems, Auditing, and the Theory of the Firm: Some Evidence, *Journal of Law and Economics*, 26(3), 613-633. http://www.jstor.org/stable/725039.

Weisbach, M. H. (1995), CEO turnover and the firm's investment decisions, *Journal of Financial Economics*, 37 (2), 159-188. https://doi.org/10.1016/0304-405X(94)00793-Z

Time Value of Money

Contents

Supplementary Information The online version contains supplementary material available at https://doi.org/10.1007/978-3-031-28267-6_3.

B. Kulwizira Lukanima, *Corporate Valuation*, Classroom Companion: Business, https://doi.org/10.1007/978-3-031-28267-6_3

3.1 Introduction

Time value of money (TVM) is a crucial concept in corporate valuation. Think about the popular English proverb that "time is money." That is, wasting time means losing money. In the real world, every aspect of human activity takes time—that is, time is valuable because, in the end, it is translated into returns. Now, suppose that you have won a lottery worth $10,000 and you are asked: "We would like to pay your money; do you prefer to receive it now or next week?" In addition, suppose that you borrowed $5000 from a friend and you were on the way to pay him. However, you friend gives you a choice: "You can pay me now or next month if you like." How would you respond to these questions? This chapter presents the concept of time value in relation to corporate valuation.

Learning Outcomes

- Understand the concept of time value of money (TVM)
- Explain the relationship between the present value (PV) and future value (FV)
- Understand the role of interest rate in adjusting the value of money in a time horizon
- Explain the main factors affecting time value of money
- Calculate the present and future values of cash flow streams
- Relate time value of money to shareholder wealth maximization
- Understand the timing of money for value maximization

3.2 Time Value of Money

Time value of money (TVM) is extremely important for explaining wealth creation in a firm. Hence, managers need to consider TVM in all aspects of strategic decisions. As described by Hilshleifer (1985), investment is "the present sacrifice for future benefit." That is, there is a time lap between now and the future, in which the value of investment cash flows will change with time. From this point of view, when investors inject money into a business, they sacrifice their money's current consumption. In doing so, they carry forward the present value of their money. However, the value of money today is not the same as that in the future; money tends to be more valuable now than in the future. Therefore, by injecting money into a company, investors require compensation for sacrificing their money—"opportunity cost." An ideal compensating factor is interest (cost of money), which is regarded as the price of money, measured as a percentage rate paid on money invested or saved. This compensation intends to cover for other factors that affect the value of money, such as time, inflation, and risk.

Time: This is an important factor for determining the value of money. Essentially, rational people would prefer to hold money now than in the future. However, time allows for a postponement of current consumption for earning interest in the future.

Inflation: This is a steady rise in the general price levels of goods in a market. It is a measure of the purchasing power of money. A rational compensation requires interest rates to be higher than inflation rates. For example, if the inflation rate is 6% and the interest rate is 6%, then no compensation is made on inflation, and, hence, no wealth will be created; instead, a loss of money can be realized after accounting for taxes. However, with the same 6% rate of inflation, if the interest rate is 9%, then there is a compensation of 3% on inflation, with other factors being constant (see ▸ Quote 3.1.1)

Risk: This arises due to uncertainty about the future. It indicates the danger that the expected yields from an investment may not be realized. Again, interest rates carry a compensation margin for risks. Under normal circumstances, high-risk investments are associated with high interest rates, and vice versa.

Therefore, other factors being equal, the future value of cash flow streams will decrease as a function of three factors: an increase in the preference for current consumption, an increase in expected inflation, and an increase in uncertainty about future cash flows.

Think 3.1

You may have heard on different occasions about the popular phrase "time is money." How do you interpret this phrase?

Exhibit 3.1 Time Value factors

Overlapping value factors	Time value factors		
	Time	**Interest**	**Money**
Time	The period in which money is held or sacrificed	The opportunity cost of money, in which the gain from interest varies with time	Cash flows relating to use of money. It can comprise cash outflows (invested money) and cash inflows (income from investment, borrowed money, etc.). The amount of money to be earned depends on the time horizon of cash flows
Inflation	Inflation changes with time	Interest carries a compensating value for inflation	Fall of the purchasing power of money over time due to inflation
Risk	Risk tends to increase with time: the longer the time horizon in future, the higher the expected risk	Interest carries a compensating margin for risk	The variability of expected future cash flows (risk) can affect the value of money

Banner 2.1 Time Value of Money
The value of money today is not the same as that in the future; money tends to change value over time.

3.3 Future Value Vs. Present Value

The time value of money has two forms: future value and present value. "Future value" can be defined as the value at some future time, of the present amount of money or a series of cash flows, determined by a given rate of interest (opportunity cost). "Present value" is the current value of the future amount of money or a series of cash flows, determined by a given interest rate. ▶ Exhibit 3.1 summarizes the three elements determining the time value of money: holding period of money (time), opportunity cost of money (interest), and money (cash flows).

The earlier an investment is made, the more the time to earn interest and the more the increase in the value of money, with other factors being equal. Moreover, the more the money is invested, the greater the returns are expected to be earned, and vice versa. Indeed, investing even a small amount of money is worthier than not investing at all. The goal should be to earn a compensation (which is reflected in the opportunity cost) that exceeds (or is at least equal to) the cost of the three overlapping value factors. Alternatively, we can say that interest rates (opportunity cost) carry information about time, inflation, and risk: the higher the interest, the more the value to be earned in future or the lower the present value of future cash flows, and vice versa.

Quotes 3.1 The Time Value of Money

▪ Quote 3.1.1 The Pace of Inflation vs. Interest Rate

» Inflation Eats Away At Your Savings

The money you have safely tucked away in savings loses value if the interest earnings are not keeping pace with inflation. With inflation running around 7% and your savings earning less than a half percent, your account is losing six and a half percent due to inflation. (Jonathan Dash, Forbes Council Member)

Jonathan Dash, January 26, 2022, Forbes

▪ Quote 3.1.2 The Effect of Inflation and Interest Rate

» The government doesn't sell Canada Premium or Savings bonds any longer as the rates were so low. Government bonds are currently all under 1.5%, even for a thirty-year bond. The risk with these rates of return is that your capital will be eroded by inflation and income taxes. Low interest rates and inflation deteriorates the purchasing power of your cash over the years, especially after you factor in income taxes. Within non-registered accounts, interest income is fully taxed and has zero deferral,

which makes the 'what ends up in your pocket' even worse. (Kevin Greebard, Portfolio Manager and Director of Wealth Management with The Greenard Group)
Kevin Greebard, January 31, 2020, Times Colonist

In ► Quotes 3.1.2, Kevin Greebard, a portfolio manager, presents a real example (based on Canadian cases) to demonstrate how inflation and interest rates affect the time value of money. In the next section, we use some simple illustrations to explain the three factors (time, interest, and money) more clearly.

Think 3.2
Why is interest rate regarded as the opportunity cost of holding money? Why investing and holding money are known as mutually exclusive choices?

3.4 The Time Factor

Time tends to affect the value of money, depending on the interest rate—simple interest or compound interest. "Simple interest" is the interest earned or paid only on the principal amount of money. This means that there is no interest earned on interest, and, hence, the interest payment is constant over time. "Compound interest" is the interest earned from both the principal and interest—that is, the money earned on interest is reinvested to earn more money. To earn or pay interest, there must be the principal, which is the original amount of money invested or borrowed. To illustrate this concept, we look at both the future and present values.

Banner 3.1 The Time Effect
The value of money changes over time: the longer the time from now. the lower the value and the lower the purchasing power.

3.4.1 The Future Value

► Exhibit 3.2 compares the effect of simple interest and compound interest on future values. ◘ Exhibit 3.2.1 shows how time affects the value of money when simple interest is earned. That is, given a simple interest of 8%, the interest to be earned annually is constant at $400. Likewise, the amount to amount to be reinvested is $5000 each year. Overall, the purchasing power of $5000 now diminishes with time—that is, the value of $5000 today is the same as $7000 in year 5. ◘ Exhibits 3.2.2 and 3.2.3 show how time affects the value of money when compound interest is earned. We can note that the interest is not constant because it earns interest too. Hence, the deposit is also compounded, increasing from $5000 to $8602.44 in year 5.

◘ Exhibit 3.2.4 shows that compound interest generates more money than simple interest. ◘ Exhibit 3.2.5 indicates that as time increases, the gap between the amount earned on simple interest and compound interest increases in favor of compound interest.

3

Banner 3.2 Future Value

How much cash will I earn (or pay) in the future if I invest (or borrow) a certain amount of cash at a certain rate of interest today?

Exhibit 3.2 The Time Factor: Future Value

Illustrative Example (See Excel Workings—▶ Chap. 3, Sheet E.3.2)

Miss Costancia wants to invest $5000 in a fixed deposit account for 5 years. The deposit is made at the end of the current year, with interest to be earned at the end of each year. How much interest on cash flow will she earn during the deposit time under the following conditions: (1) if the bank pays a simple interest rate of 8% per year and (2) if the bank pays a compound interest rate of 8% per year?

Solution

1. Simple Interest Rate

The calculation of simple interest is relatively simple. The general formula to calculate the total interest to be earned can be written as follows:

$$S_i = P(i)t$$

where S_i = simple interest earned; P = present value (principal); i = interest rate, and t = time to maturity. Therefore, the total interest to be earned in 5 years is $2000: that is, $5000(0.08)5 = $2000. This means that a constant amount of $400 is earned from interest every year over a period of 5 years. We can also calculate the annual interest earned by multiplying $5000 by 8%. The total future value (FV) of the deposit after 5 years is obtained by simply adding together the principal and interest earned as follows:

$$\text{FV} = P + S_i = \$5000 + \$2000 = \$7000$$

Exhibit 3.2.1 presents the results for the 5 years of investment.

2. Compounded Interest Rate

The general formula for calculating the future value (FV) of a single deposit like this is as follows:

$$FV = P(1+i)^t$$

From our example, using this formula, the future values in each period are calculated in Exhibit 3.2.2. It should be noted that the amount of interest earned in year 1 is the same as the amount earned on simple interest. The interpretation from this table is that the value of $5000 today is the same as $5400 in year 1, $5832 in year 2, $6298.56 in year 3, $6802.44 in year 4, and $7346.64 in year 5. Again, this means that the value of money diminishes over time.

In Exhibit 3.2.3, we can see that the interest earned in each year is reinvested to earn more interest next year. For example, an interest of $400 is earned in year 1 and reinvested in year 2 to earn $32 (i.e., $400(0.08) = $32). The total amount of interest earned in year 2 is $432. This includes the interest on principal (i.e., $5000(0.08) =$400) and the interest on interest (i.e., $400(0.08) = $32). Another way to calculate the total interest is to multiply the total

Exhibit 3.2.1 Time value of money with simple interest rate

Amount ($)	Year 0	Year 1	Year 2	Year 3	Year 4	Year 5
Deposit	5000.00	5000.00	5000.00	5000.00	5000.00	5000.00
Total interest earned		400.00	400.00	400.00	400.00	400.00
Total amount to be reinvested		5000.00	5000.00	5000.00	5000.00	**5000.00**
Cumulative total interest		400.00	800.00	1200.00	1600.00	**2000.00**
Total amount	**5000.00**	**5400.00**	**5800.00**	**6200.00**	**6600.00**	**7000.00**

Exhibit 3.2.2 Compound interest calculation using formula

Year	Calculation	Total cash ($)
0		**5000.00**
1	$FV = 5000(1+0.08)^1$	5400.00
2	$FV = 5000(1+0.08)^2$	5832.00
3	$FV = 5000(1+0.08)^3$	6298.56
4	$FV = 5000(1+0.08)^4$	6802.44
5	$FV = 5000(1+0.08)^5$	**7346.64**

Exhibit 3.2.3 Time value of money with compound interest rate

Amount ($)	Year 0	Year 1	Year 2	Year 3	Year 4	Year 5
Principal	5000.00	5000.00	5400.00	5832.00	6298.56	6802.44
Interest on interest			32.00	34.56	37.32	40.31
Total interest earned		400.00	432.00	466.56	503.88	544.20
Total amount to be reinvested		5400.00	5832.00	6298.56	6802.44	**7346.64**
Cumulative total interest		400.00	832.00	1298.56	1802.44	**2346.64**
Total amount		**5400.00**	**5832.00**	**6298.56**	**6802.44**	**7346.64**

3

Exhibit 3.2.4 Compound interest vs. simple interest

	Simple interest	Compound interest
Total interest ($)	2000.00	2346.64
Total amount ($)	7000.00	7346.64

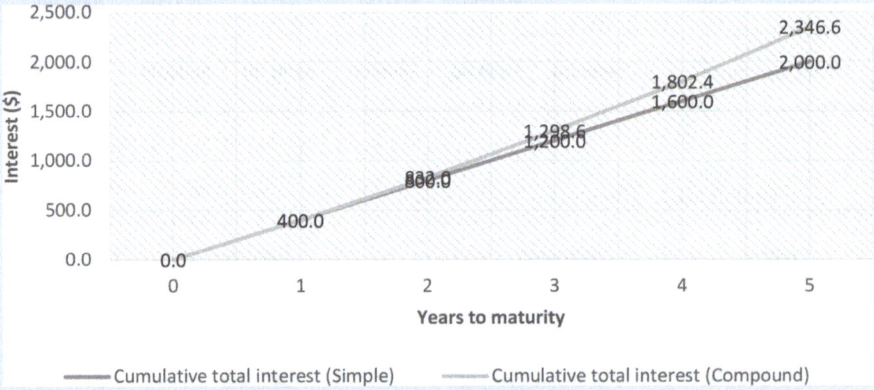

Exhibit 3.2.5 Cumulative total interest earned

amount reinvested by the interest rate. In year 2, for example, this is $5400(0.08) = $432.

The total amount of interest earned on principal and interest after 5 years is $2346.64, making the total cash flow of $7346.64. This is the same as summing the original principal and interest earned (i.e., $5000 + $2346.64 = $7346.64).

3.4.2 The Present Value

Let us use the same information in ▶ Exhibit 3.2, but in a different context, to explain and illustrate the meaning of present value. In calculating the future value, the investor's question is "how much money will I earn in the next five years if I deposit $5000 at a compounded interest of 8%?" Now, suppose that the investor is expecting to earn $7346.64 at the end of year 5 from today. His question would be "What is today's value of $7346.64 to be earned in the next five years if the interest rate is 8%?"

▶ Exhibit 3.3 illustrates how to calculate the present value of the expected future cash flow. In ◘ Exhibits 3.3.1 and 3.3.2, we see the purchasing power of \$7346.64 in the next 5 years declining over time to just \$5000 today. This loss of purchasing power is due to the time value, which ranges from \$2356.64 in 5 years to 0 today—that is, the longer the period to maturity, the lesser the purchasing power of money and the lesser the time value.

Banner 3.3 Present Value

What is today's value of a certain amount of money to be earned (or paid) in the future on an investment (or borrowing) at a certain interest rate?

Exhibit 3.3 The Time Factor: Present Value

Illustrative Example (See Excel Workings—▶ Chap. 3, Sheet E.3.3)

Miss Asela is expecting to receive \$7346.64 at the end of the next 5 years. If the interest rate is 8% compounded annually: (1) What is the present value of her expected earnings? (2) Show how the value of her money will change at the end of each year toward year 5.

Solution

(1) The general present value (PV) formula is as follows:

$$PV = \frac{FV}{(1-i)^t}$$

Therefore, the present value of \$7346.64, in 5 years, is \$5000, which is calculated as follows:

$$PV = \frac{\$7346.64}{(1+0.08)^5} = \$5000$$

(2) ◘ Exhibit 3.3.1 shows how values change each year from today (year 0) to the final year (year 5). We should note that the amount of money to be earned is the same (\$7346.64), but the time value decreases with the increase in the time to maturity. For example, we can say that the value of \$7346.64 in year 5 is equal to \$6802.44 in year 4 (the time value is \$544.20), the value of \$7347.64 in year 5 is equal to \$5400.00 in year 1 (time value is \$1946.64), and so on.

Observation

Present value = future value – time value

Future value = present value + time value

Time value = future value – present value

3

Exhibit 3.3.1 Time value of investment with compound interest

Year	Time to maturity	Calculation	Present value ($)	Time value ($)
0	5 years	PV = 7346.64/(1+0.08)^5	5000.00	2346.64
1	4 years	PV = 7346.64/(1+0.08)^4	5400.00	1946.64
2	3 years	PV = 7346.64/(1+0.08)^3	5862.00	1484.64
3	2 years	PV = 7346.64/(1+0.08)^2	6298.56	1048.08
4	1 year	PV = 7346.64/(1+0.08)^1	6802.44	544.20
5	0 year	PV = 7346.64/(1+0.08)^0	7346.64	0.00

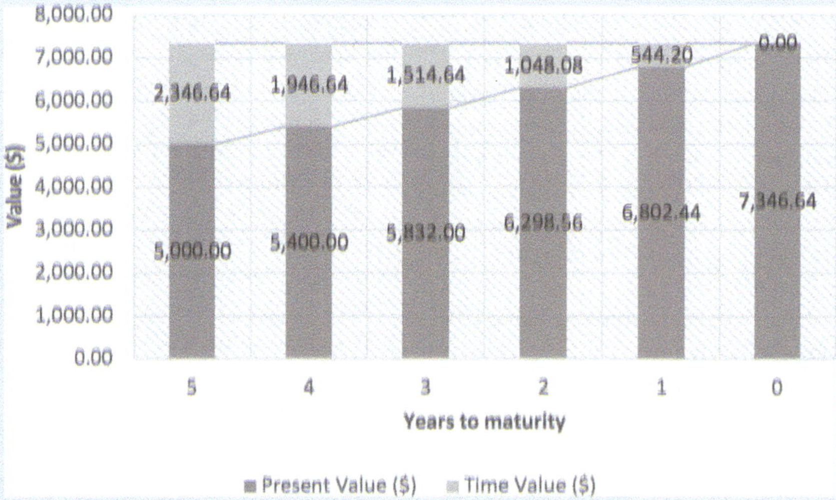

Exhibit 3.3.2 The time value effect

3.5 The Interest Factor

Interest affects time value of money—the higher (lower) the interest, the more (less) the money to be earned or paid at a given time in the future. Regardless of the size of interest, the value of money changes with time—more value now than in future. Moreover, as pointed out earlier, interest rates carry information about the risks related to the use of money (e.g., investment or financing) and inflation—a higher interest rate generally suggests higher risk and inflation, and vice versa.

Now, let us see how interest rates affect the time value of money under both aspects, namely, future value and present value. ▶ Exhibits 3.4 and 3.5 illustrate how interest rates affect the time value of money and how the size of interest rates influences the magnitude of change in the time value of money. Overall, we see two aspects relating to the interest factor in relation to time (see ◘ Exhibits 3.4.2 and 3.5.3).

1. The effect of the interest rate's size: Higher interest rates have more impact than do lower interest rates on the magnitude at which the value of money changes (increases or decreases) with time.
2. The effect of time: For any size of interest rate, the magnitude of change in the value of money is higher on longer maturities than on lower maturities.

Banner 3.4 The Interest Factor

(1) Given the time to maturity, the value of money varies depending on the size of the interest rate, and (2) the higher the interest rate, the greater the effect on the time value of money, and vice versa

Exhibit 3.4 The Interest Factor: Future Value

Illustrative Example (See Excel Workings—▸ Chap. 3, Sheet E.3.4)

Now, let us assume that Miss Asela has $5000 available for investment for 5 years. However, there is a possibility of earning different interest rates compounded annually—5%, 8%, 10%, and 12%. How will these interest rates affect the future value of her investments over the next 5 years?

Solution

The formula for calculation is the same as in the previous example (see ▸ Exhibit 3.2). The effect of the interest rate is shown in ◘ Exhibit 3.4.1 and plotted in ◘ Exhibit 3.4.2.

◘ **Exhibit 3.4.1** Interest and future value of money

Year	5% Interest ($)	8% Interest ($)	10% Interest ($)	12% Interest ($)
0	5000.00	5000.00	5000.00	5000.00
1	5250.00	5400.00	5500.00	5600.00
2	5512.50	5832.00	6050.00	6272.00
3	5788.13	6298.56	6655.00	7024.64
4	6077.53	6802.44	7320.50	7867.60
5	6381.41	7346.64	8052.55	8811.71

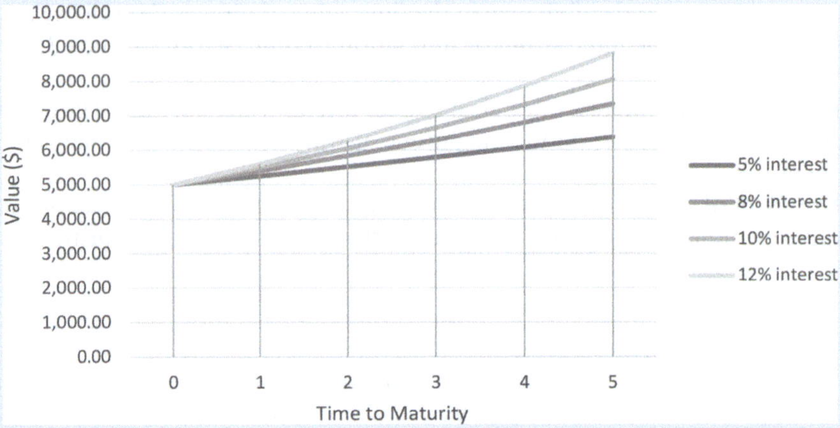

Exhibit 3.4.2 Interest and future value of money

Observation

The effect of the interest rate's size: Higher interest rates have more impact than do lower interest rates on the magnitude at which the value of money changes (increases or decreases) with time. For example, the future values of $5000 in year 4 are $6607.53 (at 5%), $6802.44 (at 8%), $7320.50 (at 10%), and $7867.60 (at 12%).

The effect of time: For any size of interest rate, the magnitude of change in the value of money is higher on longer maturities than on lower maturities. For example, at 5% interest, the value of $5000 today is equal to $5250.00 (year 1), $5788.13 (year 3), and $6381.41 (year 5).

Exhibit 3.5 The Interest Factor: Present Value

Illustrative Example (See Excel Workings—► Chap. 3, Sheet E.3.5)

- **Example 1: A Desired Today's Value**

An investor wants to know how much he should earn in the future to earn an equivalent of $5000 today. The possible interest rates are 5%, 8%, 10%, and 12%. How much should he earn if earnings are expected in year 1, year 2, year 3, year 4, or year 5?

Solution

To find the answer to the investor's question, we calculate future values, each year toward maturity, of the desired value of $5000 at each interest rate. The results are presented in Exhibits 3.6.1 and 3.5.3.

Example 2: An Expected Future Value

An investor is expecting to earn $10,000 at the end of year 5 from now. He poses two questions: (1) what is the present value of his expected earnings at different rates of interest and (2) what will be the value of those earnings each year before maturity?

Solution

To find the answer to the investor's questions, we calculate the present values of $10,000 at each interest rate, each year toward maturity. Exhibits 3.5.2 and 3.5.4 present the values calculated at different interest rates and time to maturity from 5 years to zero.

Observation

The effect of the interest rate's size: Higher interest rates have more impact than do lower interest rates on the magnitude at which the value of money changes (increases or decreases) with time. For example, to have a value of $5000 today, the investor will have to earn more money in the future with higher interest rates than with lower interest rates. As indicated in Exhibit 3.5.1, if earnings are expected in year 5, at each interest rate, the investor should earn $6381.41 (at 5%), $7346.64 (at 8%), $8052.55 (at 10%), and $8811.71 (at 12%).

The effect of time: For any size of interest rate, the magnitude of change in the value of money is higher on longer maturities than on lower maturities. For example, at 12% interest, the value of $10,000 in year 5 is equal to $8928.57 (year 4), $7117.80 (year 3), and $5674.27 (now).

Exhibit 3.5.1 Desired present value of money

Year	Time to maturity	5% Interest ($)	8% Interest ($)	10% Interest ($)	12% Interest ($)
0	5 years	5000.00	5000.00	5000.00	5000.00
1	4 years	5250.00	5400.00	5500.00	5600.00
2	3 years	5512.50	5832.00	6050.00	6272.00
3	2 years	5788.13	6298.56	6655.00	7024.64
4	1 year	6077.53	6802.44	7320.50	7867.60
5	0 year	6381.41	7346.64	8052.55	8811.71

3

Exhibit 3.5.2 Expected future value of money

Year	Time to maturity	5% Interest ($)	8% Interest ($)	10% Interest ($)	12% Interest ($)
0	5 years	7835.26	6805.83	6209.21	5674.27
1	4 years	8227.02	7350.30	6830.13	6355.18
2	3 years	8638.38	7938.32	7513.15	7117.80
3	2 years	9070.29	8573.39	8264.46	7971.94
4	1 year	9523.81	9259.26	9090.91	8928.57
5	0 year	10,000.00	10,000.00	10,000.00	10,000.00

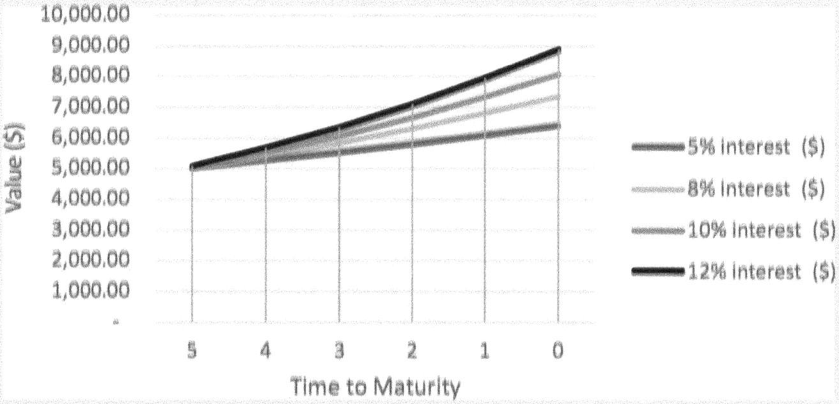

Exhibit 3.5.3 Desired present value of money

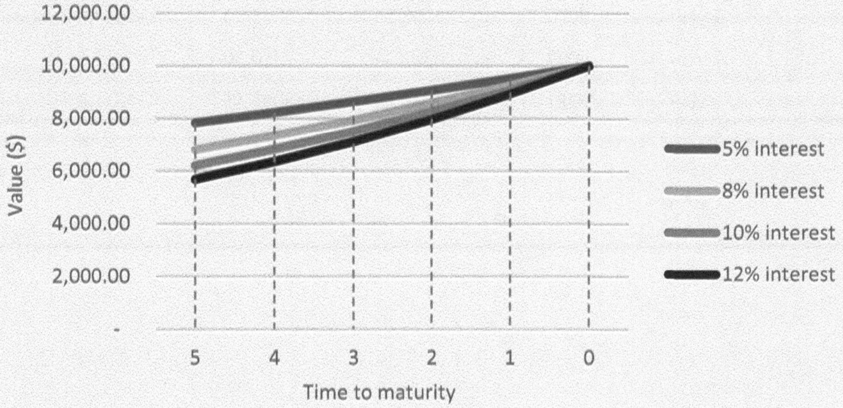

Exhibit 3.5.4 Expected future value of money

Think 3.3
Why should a higher interest rate have a greater impact on the change of value than a lower interest rate?

3.6 The Size of Money

So far, we have seen how both time and interest affect the time value of money. However, the size of money is also extremely important for determining the value of money and the magnitude at which time and interest affect that value. This aspect is illustrated in ▶ Exhibits 3.6 and 3.7 on two situations, the future value and the present value, respectively. Overall, we note that at a given interest rate and time, the larger the size of money, the higher the future value or present value. For example, if a bank offers an interest rate of 10% on a fixed deposit account for a fixed period (say 2 years), a person who invests $15,000 will earn more money than a person who invests $10,000. Equally, someone who invests nothing will earn nothing.

Banner 3.6 The Size of Money
The size of money determines the magnitude at which time and interest rate affect the value of money: the bigger the amount of money, the higher the rate at which time and interest affect value, and vice versa.

Exhibit 3.6 Size of Money: Future Value

Illustrative Example (See Excel Workings—▶ Chap. 3, Sheet E.3.6)

Suppose that you have $31,000 for investing into a bank's fixed deposit account. The bank offers an interest of 10% annually for 5 years.

(a) Show how the future value of money will change each year over the next 5 years if you deposit the following amounts in separate accounts: $1000, $5000, $10,000, and $15,000.
(b) What is the future value of all your investments in (a) above during maturity (year 5)?
(c) What would be the future value of your money if there were all deposited into a single account, earning the same interest rate for 5 years?

Solution

Exhibits 3.6.1 and 3.6.2 show the calculated future values for each investment in (a) and investment in (b). The horizontal axis shows future values at the end of each year. We can see that the graphs are not straight but upward curving toward maturity. This implies that the rate at which time and interest affect future values is different for each size of money—the more the amount of money invested, the higher the increase in the rate of future value. However, the total

3

Exhibit 3.6.1 Future value of money

Time 0	Invest $1000	Invest $5000	Invest $10,000	Invest $15,000	*Total $31,000*	Invest $31,000
1 year	1100.00	5500.00	11,000.00	16,500.00	*34,100.00*	34,100.00
2 years	1210.00	6050.00	12,100.00	18,150.00	*37,510.00*	37,510.00
3 years	1331.00	6655.00	13,310.00	19,965.00	*41,261.00*	41,261.00
4 years	1464.10	7320.50	14,641.00	21,961.50	*45,387.10*	45,387.10
5 years	1610.51	8052.55	16,105.10	24,157.65	*49,925.81*	49,925.81

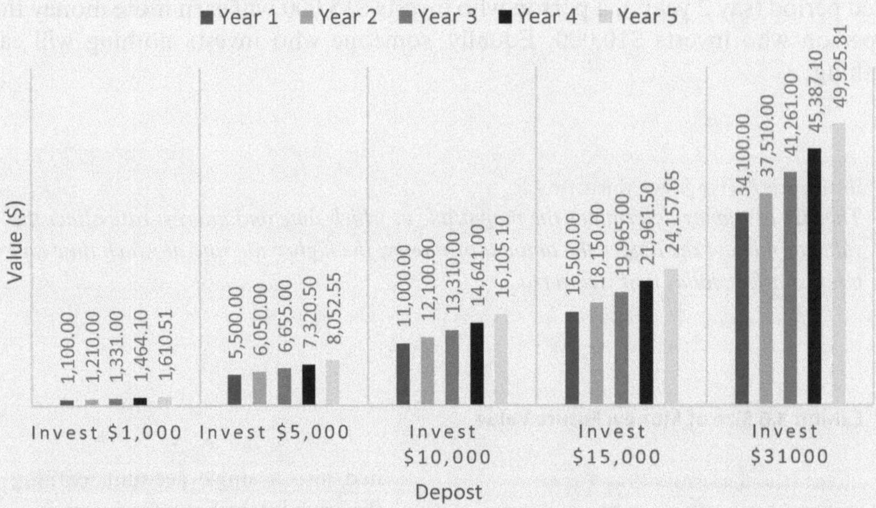

Exhibit 3.6.2 Future value of money

future value is the same for investments in (a) and a single investment in (c).

Observation

The general observation is that the magnitude at which time and interest affect future values increases over time. Exhibit 3.7.2 depicts the patterns of the expected future values over 15 years. Clearly, the earning gap between a smaller and a bigger investment widens with time. This also suggests that the rate at which money is earned increases with the amount of money invested: the more the money invested, the higher the rate at which money is earned, and vice versa. That is to say, at a specific interest rate and time, more money earns more money.

Exhibit 3.7 Size of Money: Future Value

Illustrative Example (See Excel Workings—► Chap. 3, Sheet E.3.7)

Suppose that you expect to pay $55,000 at the end of the next 20 years on separate bank loans, which charge an interest of 10% annually.

(a) Show how the present values of the payments will change every 2 years to maturity if your obligations are distributed as follows: $2000, $8000, $15,000, and $30,000.
(b) What is the present value of all your obligations in (a) above?
(c) What would be the present value of your obligation if you borrowed on a single account.

Solution

Exhibit 3.7.1 shows the calculated present values for each obligation every 2 years to maturity in year 20. The present values are plotted in Exhibit 3.7.2 for a clear view. Clearly, the graphs are not straight but curving toward maturity. The rate at which the present values change is greater for larger loans than for smaller loans. The total present value is the same for all obligations in (a) and a single obligation in (c).

Observation

From Exhibit 3.7.2, the gap between the obligation future values and present values declines at increasing rates toward the present period. The rate at which the present values change is higher for larger loans than for smaller loans. This means that at a given interest rate and time, large amounts of money are more penalized by time value than are small amounts of money.

Exhibit 3.7.1 The present value of money

Time	Time to maturity	Loan $2000	Loan $8000	Loan $15,000	Loan $30,000	*Total $55,000*	Loan $55,000
0	20 years	297	1189	2230	4459	*8175*	8175
2	18 years	360	1439	2698	5396	*9892*	9892
4	16 years	435	1741	3264	6529	*11,970*	11,970
6	14 years	527	2107	3950	7900	*14,483*	14,483
8	12 years	637	2549	4779	9559	*17,525*	17,525
10	10 years	771	3084	5783	11,566	*21,205*	21,205
12	8 years	933	3732	6998	13,995	*25,658*	25,658
14	6 years	1129	4516	8467	16,934	*31,046*	31,046
16	4 years	1366	5464	10,245	20,490	*37,566*	37,566
18	2 years	1653	6612	12,397	24,793	*45,455*	45,455
20	0 years	2000	8000	15,000	30,000	*55,000*	55,000

3

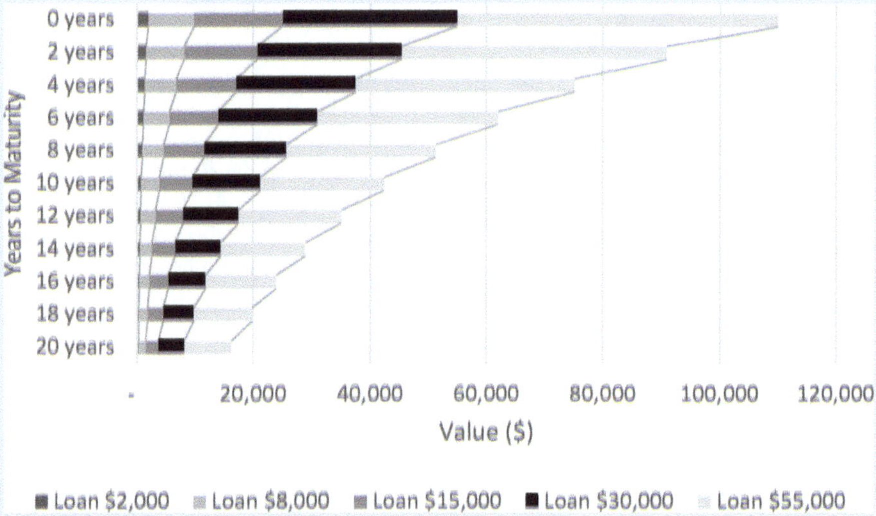

Exhibit 3.7.2 The present value of money

3.7 The Timing of Money

The timing of money simply means that when cash flows occur ("patterns of cash flows"),—it can be now or later (e.g., next month, next year, a few years to come, etc.). Moreover, the timing can affect annuities or mixed cash flows. Hence, the timing of money affects value. To explain this aspect, we use a simple example in ▶ Exhibits 3.8 and 3.9. We consider five companies with an equal total future cash flow (i.e., $82,000) in the next 5 years but different patterns of cash flow size and timing. Company E is expected to earn a large proportion of its total cash flow in earlier years, whereas company F delays most of its future cash flows. Company G has annuity cash flows. In company H, all future cash flows will be earned in the first year, whereas in company I, all cash flows will be generated in the terminal year (see Exhibits 3.8.1 and 3.9.1).

Banner 3.7 The Timing of Money (Present Value)
At a given interest rate, the more value that is realized, the sooner the timing in which more cash flows are generated, and vice versa. An increase in interest rates reduces the value of money, whereby the sooner the timing in which more cash flows are generated, the lower the proportion of value lost, and vice versa.

Exhibit 3.8 The Timing of Money

Illustrative Example (See Excel Workings—► Chap. 3, Sheet E.3.8)

Five companies have the following patterns of expected cash flows, summing $82,000. All cash flows will occur at the end of each year over the next 5 years.

(a) Calculate the present value of each company's cash flows if the interest is 6% annually.
(b) Repeat (a) if the interest rate rises to 15%.
(c) Rank the companies according to their present values from 1 to 5 (5 = the highest value, 1 = the lowest value).
(d) Indicate how the rise of the interest rate from 6% to 15% affects the present value of each company. Rank them according to their percentage change in value from 1 to 5 (5 = the highest change, 1 = the lowest change).

Solution.

Observation

From Exhibit 3.8.4, we can observe the following key points: (1) Regardless of the interest rate, the sooner the cash flows are generated, the more the value, and vice versa. (2) The more the cash flows are delayed, the more the sensitivity of value to change in the interest rate, and vice versa.

Exhibit 3.8.1 Cash flow profiles of different companies

Year	Company E ($)	Company F ($)	Company G ($)	Company H ($)	Company I ($)
1	35,000	1000	16,400	82,000	0
2	22,000	8000	16,400	0	0
3	16,000	16,000	16,400	0	0
4	8000	22,000	16,400	0	0
5	1000	35,000	16,400	0	82,000

Exhibit 3.8.2 Present values (interest rate = 6%)

Year	Company E ($)	Company F ($)	Company G ($)	Company H ($)	Company I ($)
1	33,019	943	15,472	77,358	0
2	19,580	7120	14,596	0	0
3	13,434	13,434	13,770	0	0
4	6337	17,426	12,990	0	0
5	747	26,154	12,255	0	61,275
Total	*73,117*	*65,077*	*69,083*	*77,358*	*61,275*

3

Exhibit 3.8.3 Present values (interest rate = 15%)

Year	Company E ($)	Company F ($)	Company G ($)	Company H ($)	Company I ($)
1	30,435	870	14,261	71,304	0
2	16,635	6049	12,401	0	0
3	10,520	10,520	10,783	0	0
4	4574	12,579	9377	0	0
5	497	17,401	8154	0	40,768
Total	*62,661*	*47,419*	*54,975*	*71,304*	*40,768*

Exhibit 3.8.4 Present value: sensitivity to change in interest rates

Interest	Company E	Company F	Company G	Company H	Company I
Value at 6% ($)	*73,117*	*65,077*	*69,083*	*77,358*	*61,275*
Value rank (6%)	*4*	*2*	*3*	*5*	*1*
Value at 15% ($)	62,661	47,419	54,975	71,304	40,768
Value rank (15%)	*4*	*2*	*3*	*5*	*1*
Change ($)	−10,455	−17,659	−14,107	−6054	−20,507
Change (%)	−14.3%	−27.1%	−20.4%	−7.8%	−33.5%
Rank	2	4	3	1	5

Exhibits 3.8.2 and 3.8.3 present the calculated present values at the interest rates of 6% and 15%, respectively. Exhibits 3.9.2 and 3.9.3 present the calculated future values at the interest rates of 6% and 15%, respectively. Exhibits 3.8.4 and 3.9.4 rank the five companies according to the present and future values, starting from the highest value (ranking 1) to the lowest value (ranking 5). Regardless of the interest rate, company H is the most valuable (ranking 1) because all its cash flows are generated in the most current period. In contrast, company I is the least valuable (ranking 5) because all its cash flows are delayed until the terminal period. Likewise, cash flows of company E are more valuable than those of company F because the former gains a larger proportion of its cash flows earlier than the latter. Company G, whose cash flows are evenly distributed, ranks mid (ranking 3).

Banner 3.8 The Timing of Money (Future Value)
At a given interest rate, more future value is realized the sooner the timing in which more cash flows are generated, and vice versa. An increase in interest rates increases the future value, whereby the sooner the timing in which more cash flows are generated, the higher the proportion of increases in value, and vice versa. Such an increase in value intends to maintain the same purchasing power of money in the present.

Exhibit 3.9 The Timing of Money

Illustrative Example (See Excel Workings—▶ Chap. 3, Sheet E.3.9)

Five companies have the following patterns of expected cash flows. The total amount of cash is $82,000. All cash flows will occur at the end of each year over the next 5 years.

(a) Calculate the future value of each company's cash flows if the interest is 6% annually.
(b) Repeat (a) if the interest rate rises to 15%.
(c) Rank the companies according to their future values of money.
(d) Indicate how the rise of the interest rate from 6% to 15% affects the future value of money for each company. Rank them according to their percentage change in value.

Solution.

Observation

From ◘ Exhibit 3.9.4, we can observe the following key points: (1) Regardless of the interest rate, the sooner the cash flows are generated, the more the value, and vice versa. (2) The more the cash flows are delayed, the less the sensitivity of value to change in the interest rate, and vice versa.

◘ **Exhibit 3.9.1** Cash flow profiles of different companies

Year	Company E ($)	Company F ($)	Company G ($)	Company H ($)	Company I ($)
1	35,000	1000	16,400	82,000	0
2	22,000	8000	16,400	0	0
3	16,000	16,000	16,400	0	0
4	8000	22,000	16,400	0	0
5	1000	35,000	16,400	0	82,000

3

Exhibit 3.9.2 Future values (interest rate = 6%)

Year	Company E ($)	Company F ($)	Company G ($)	Company H ($)	Company I ($)
1	44,187	1262	20,705	103,523	0
2	26,202	9528	19,533	0	0
3	17,978	17,978	18,427	0	0
4	8480	23,320	17,384	0	0
5	1000	35,000	16,400	0	82,000
Total	*97,847*	*87,088*	*92,448*	*103,523*	*82,000*

Exhibit 3.9.3 Future values (interest rate = 15%)

Year	Company E ($)	Company F ($)	Company G ($)	Company H ($)	Company I ($)
1	61,215	1749	28,684	143,419	0
2	33,459	12,167	24,942	0	0
3	21,160	21,160	21,689	0	0
4	9200	25,300	18,860	0	0
5	1000	35,000	16,400	0	82,000
Total	*126,034*	*95,376*	*110,575*	*143,419*	*82,000*

Exhibit 3.9.4 Future value: sensitivity to change in interest rates

Interest	Company E	Company F	Company G	Company H	Company I
Value at 6% ($)	*97,847*	*87,088*	*92,448*	*103,523*	*82,000*
Value rank (6%)	*4*	*2*	*3*	*5*	*1*
Value at 15% ($)	*126,034*	*95,376*	*110,575*	*143,419*	*82,000*
Value rank (15%)	*4*	*2*	*3*	*5*	*1*
Change ($)	28,188	8288	18,127	39,895	0
Change (%)	28.8%	9.5%	19.6%	38.5%	0.0%
Rank	4	2	3	5	1

▫ Exhibits 3.8.4 and 3.9.4 also show the sensitivity of both present and future values to changes in the interest rates from 6% to 15%. Regarding the present values (▫ Exhibit 3.8.4), company I, which is the least valuable (ranking 1 in value terms), is the most affected (ranking 5 in terms of sensitivity to change in the interest rate). Its present value of money drops by 33.5%. This is contrary to company H with only a 7.8% loss of value. Similarly, the present value in company F is more affected than that of company E with 27.1% and 14.3% change, respectively. Company G is mid (ranking 3 in terms of sensitivity). The ranking of future values is different (▫ Exhibit 3.9.4). Company H's future value is the most affected by the increase in the interest rate (38.5% change), whereas company I's future value is the least affected (0% change). ▸ Exhibit 3.10 compares both the present and future values in terms of sensitivity rankings.

Banner 3.9 Present vs. Future Value

The timing in which money is generated affects the value sensitivity of interest rates: the sooner the money is generated, the lower the sensitivity of the present value and the higher the sensitivity of the future value.

Exhibit 3.10 The Timing of Money: Present Value vs. Future Value

Illustrative Example (See Excel Workings—▸ Chap. 3, Sheets E.3.8 and E.3.9)

▸ Exhibits 3.10.1 and 3.10.2 compare the present and future values of the five companies regarding the following aspects:

1. Sensitivity to change in the interest rate from 6% to 15%
2. Ranking of sensitivity: 5 = the most sensitive company, 1 = the least sensitive company

Observation

The timing in which money is generated affects the value sensitivity of interest rates: the sooner the money is generated, the lower the sensitivity of the present value and the higher the sensitivity of the future value.

▫ **Exhibit 3.10.1** Sensitivity to change in interest rates (from 6% to 15%)

Interest	Company E	Company F	Company G	Company H	Company I
Present value	−14%	−27%	−20%	−8%	−33%
Future value	29%	10%	20%	39%	0%
Rank (present value)	2	4	3	1	5
Rank (future value)	4	2	3	5	1

3

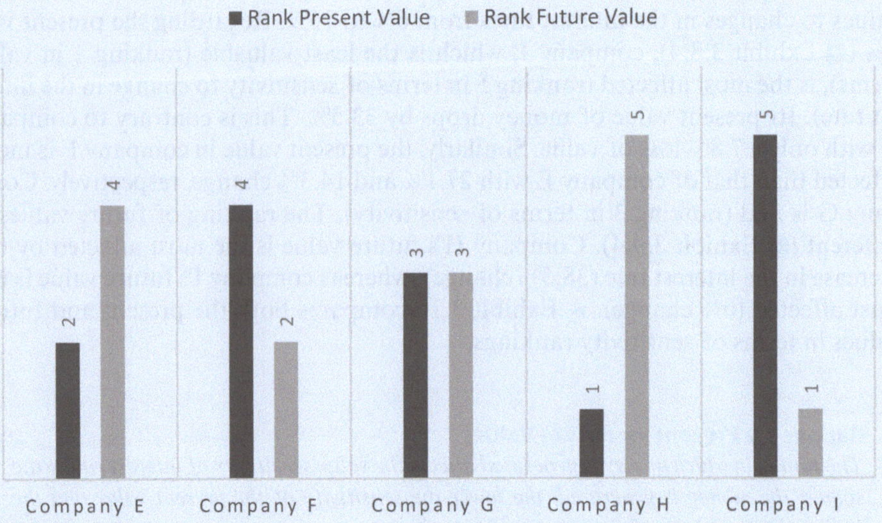

Exhibit 3.10.2 Ranking: sensitivity to change in interest rates (from 6 % to 15%)

Think 3.4

If your goal is to maximize value, and you are asked to choose between early cash flows or delayed cash flows on the following transactions, what would be your response?

(a) *Payment of your bank loan*
(b) *Payment of your warehouse rent*
(c) *Receipt of your house rent*
(d) *Receipt of salary*

3.8 Annuity Cash Flows

This section uses annuity cash flows to explain another important aspect of the timing of money—are the cash flows realized in the beginning or end of the payment or receipt period? Each of this aspect is defined briefly and illustrated with simple examples. The same concept is applied to mixed patterns of cash flows.

An annuity refers to a series of cash payments or receipts of an equal amount occurring at a specified time of equal installments. Such kinds of cash streams are common in financial transactions like hire purchases, insurance premium, mortgage payments, loan payments, and so on. An annuity payment or receipts can be made at the end or beginning of a specified period—this is referred to as an "ordinary annuity." There are several common examples of ordinary annuities. For instance, in bond markets, coupon interest tends to be paid at the end of the payment period. This also applies to payments relating to mortgages, salaries, and some utility bills. In contrast, an annuity occurring at the beginning of a period is called an "annuity due." Some examples include house rents and insurance premium.

3.8.1 The Future Value of Annuity

The calculation of the future value of annuity cash flows depends on the patterns of the cash streams: that is, whether it is an ordinary annuity or an annuity due. Exhibits 3.11 and 3.12 show how to calculate the future values of the two types of annuities. Exhibit 3.13 shows how the differences in the patterns of cash flows influence future values. It can be noted that, for both ordinary annuities and annuity dues, the longer the period between now and the future, the wider the difference between the present and future values. That is, the value difference narrows as we approach maturity. This also means that the sooner the money is earned or invested, the higher its future value.

Exhibit 3.11 Ordinary Annuity: Future Value

Illustrative Example (see Excel Workings—▶ Chap. 3, Sheet E.3.11)

▶ Exhibit 3.11.1 shows the patterns of an ordinary annuity. Since the cash flows occur at the end of the respective periods (1, 2 …*n*), the general formula for calculating the future value of an ordinary annuity (FVOA) can be expressed as follows:

$$FVOA_n = \Sigma CF_t (1+i)^{n-t}$$

where CF = cash flow; i = discount rate; n= number of periods to maturity; and t = cash flow time, which counts from period 1. Therefore, for the respective final future period, $t = n$.

Example

Suppose that Mr. Galembana has acquired a loan from a bank, which requires him to repay the loan and interest at constant installments of $1000 annually for a period of 5 years. Galembana and the bank have agreed that all payments must be made at the end of the year. What will be the future value of these cash flows for the loan period if the interest rate is 10%?

Solution

▶ Exhibit 3.11.2 depicts the pattern of the cash flows over years of loan repayments as they occur at the end of each year:

To calculate the future value of an ordinary annuity (FVOA) like this, the following general formula is applied:

Thus,

$$FVOA_n = \Sigma CF_t (1+i)^{n-t}$$

$$FVOA_5 = \$1000(1.10)^{5-1} + \$1000(1.10)^{5-2} + \$1000(1.10)^{5-3} + \$1000(1.10)^{5-4} + \$1000(1.10)^{5-5}$$

$$FVOA_5 = \$1000(1.10)^{4} + \$1000(1.10)^{3} + \$1000(1.10)^{2} + \$1000(1.10)^{1} + \$1000(1.10)^{0}$$

$$FVOA_5 = \$1464 + \$1331 + \$1210 + \$1100 + \$1000 = \$6105$$

These future values at the end of each period and the total in year 5 are depicted below in ▶ Exhibit 3.11.3.

Observation

The future values for payments made in early years are higher than those made in later years. That is, the longer the time to maturity, the more the interest rates penalize the future values.

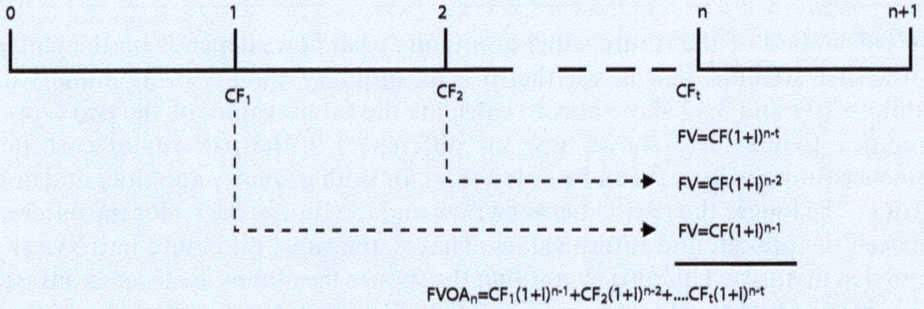

Exhibit 3.11.1 Patterns of an ordinary annuity

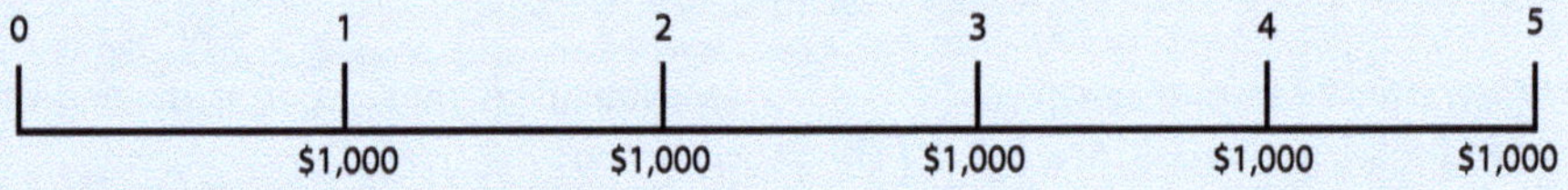

Exhibit 3.11.2 Patterns of an ordinary annuity

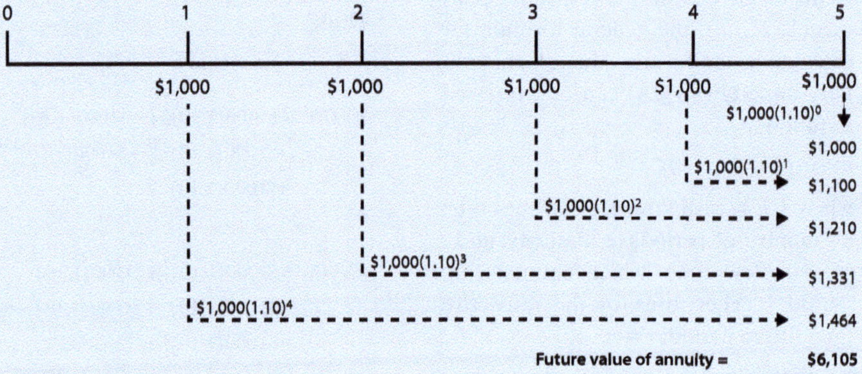

Exhibit 3.11.3 Future value of an ordinary annuity

Exhibit 3.12 Annuity Due: Future Value

Illustrative Example (See Excel Workings—► Chap. 3, Sheet E.3.12)

Exhibit 3.12.1 shows the patterns of an annuity due. Since the cash flows occur at the beginning of the respective periods, the general formula for calculating the future value of an annuity due (FVAD) can be expressed as follows:

$$FVAD_n = \Sigma CF_t (1+i)^{(n-t)}$$

where CF = cash flow; i = discount rate; n= number of periods to maturity; and t = cash flow time, which counts from period 0.

Example

Phina has rented a building for her business and will be paying $1000 each year for 5 years. According to an agreement with the landlord, all payments must be made at the beginning of the year. What will be the future value of the cash flows for the renting period if the interest rate is 10%?

Solution

Exhibit 3.12.2 depicts the pattern of the cash flows over years of loan repayments as they occur at the beginning of each year:

To calculate the future value of this annuity due (FVAD), we apply the same general formula. However, this time, the cash flow period (t) starts counting now (i.e., period 0).

Thus,

$$FVAD_n = \Sigma CF_t (1+i)^{(n-t)}$$

$$FVAD_5 = \$1000(1.10)^{5-0} + \$1000(1.10)^{5-1} + \$1000(1.10)^{5-2} + \$1000(1.10)^{5-3} + \$1000(1.10)^{5-4}$$

$$FVAD_5 = \$1000(1.10)^5 + \$1000(1.10)^4 + \$1000(1.10)^3 + \$1000(1.10)^2 + \$1000(1.10)^1$$

$$FVAD_5 = \$1611 + \$1464 + \$1331 + \$1210 + \$1100 = \$6716$$

These future values at the end of each period and the total in year 5 are depicted below in ► Exhibit 3.12.3.

Observation

The future values for payments made in early years are higher than those made in later years. That is, the longer the time to maturity, the more the interest rates penalize future values.

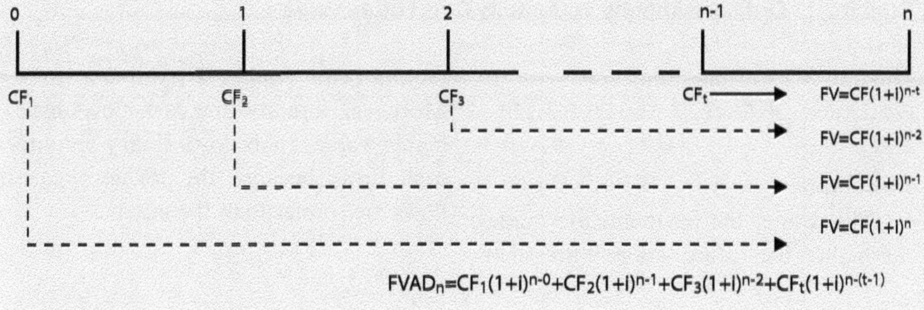

Exhibit 3.12.1 Patterns of an annuity due

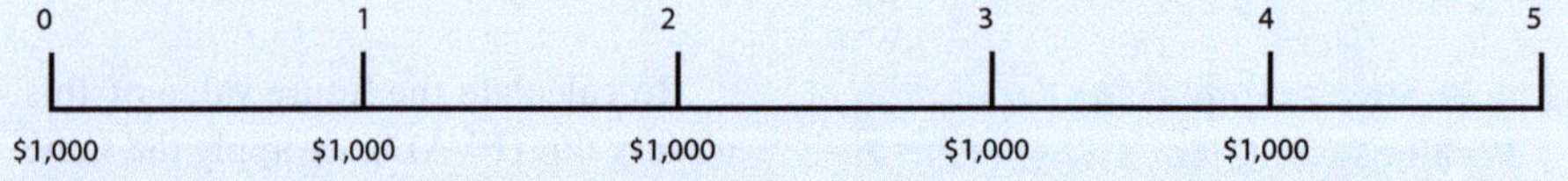

Exhibit 3.12.2 Patterns of an annuity due

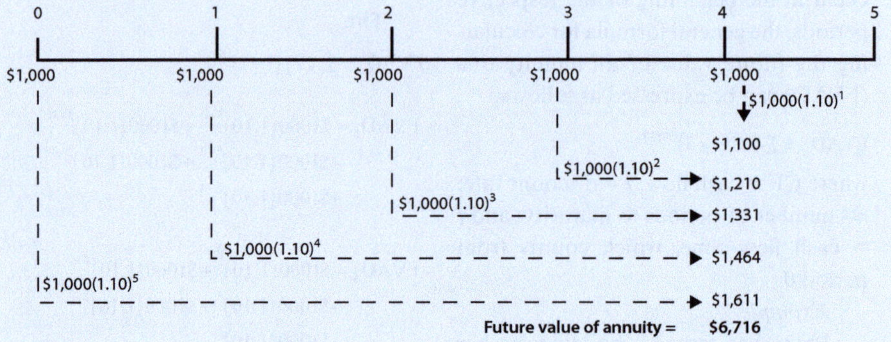

Exhibit 3.12.3 Future value of an annuity due

From ▶ Exhibit 3.13, it can also be observed that with equal cash flows, interest, and payment period, the future values of an annuity due are higher than those of an ordinary annuity. For example, in year 5, the value is $1100 for an annuity due and $1000 for an ordinary annuity. Thus, the total future value in year 5 is $6105 on an ordinary annuity and $6716 on an annuity due. This difference is because the time to earn or pay money is sooner in an annuity due than in an ordinary annuity. Thus, the difference is $611 = $6716 − $6105 or the sum of all differences in Exhibit 3.13.1. This implies that the sooner the money is earned or invested, the higher the future value it creates, with other factors being equal.

Exhibit 3.13 Ordinary Annuity vs. Annuity Due: Future Value

Illustrative Example (See Excel Workings—▶ Chap. 3, Sheets E.3.11 and E3.12)

Observation

The sooner the payments are made, the higher the future value, with other factors being equal (Exhibit 3.13.2). Moreover, annuity due cash flows have higher values than do ordinary annuity cash flows because the former's cash flows are sooner than the latter's.

Exhibit 3.13.1 Future values of annuities

Period	Payment 1	Payment 2	Payment 3	Payment 4	Payment 5	Total payment
Annuity due ($)	1611	1464	1331	1210	1100	6716
Ordinary annuity ($)	1464	1331	1210	1100	1000	6105
Difference ($)	146	133	121	110	100	611

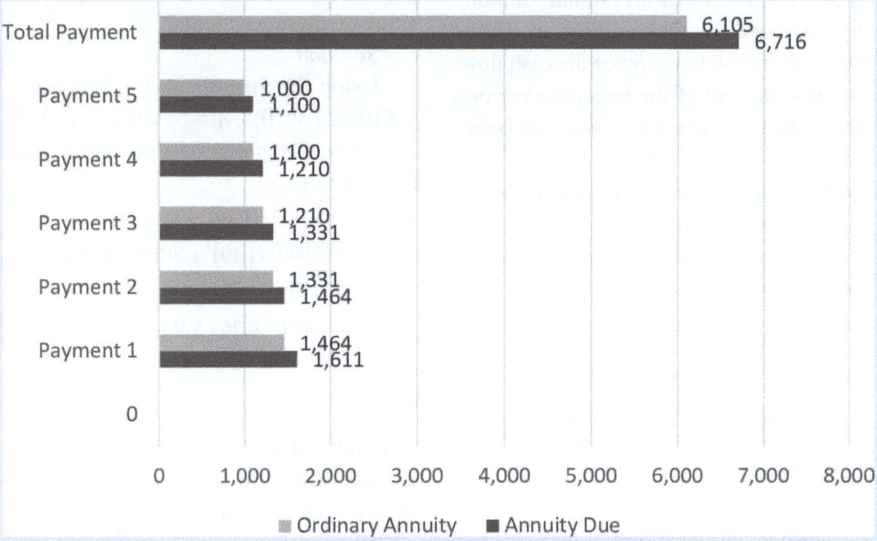

Exhibit 3.13.2 Future values of annuities

Banner 3.10 Ordinary Annuity vs. Annuity Due—Future Value

Given the same amount of money, interest, and payment period, the future values of an annuity due will be higher than those of an ordinary annuity. This is because money is realized sooner in an annuity due than in an ordinary annuity.

3.8.2 The Present Value of Annuity

▶ Exhibit 3.14 depicts the pattern of the present values of an ordinary annuity, whereas an illustrative example of an annuity due is provided in ▶ Exhibit 3.15. Like in future values, at the same interest rate and time to maturity, the present values of an annuity due are higher than those of an ordinary annuity. For example, in ▶ Exhibit 3.14,

Jordan expects to pay $1000 each year on an ordinary annuity basis. In Exhibit ▶ 3.15, Joseline is also expecting to pay $1000 but on annuity dues. Although the interest rate (10%) and time to maturity (5 years) are the same for both, the present values of their payments differ significantly. The present values of their total payments are $3791 and $4170, respectively. The difference is, therefore, $379. A comparison between the two types of annuities is presented in ▶ Exhibit 3.16.

Exhibit 3.14 Ordinary Annuity: Present Value

Illustrative Example (See Excel Workings—▶ Chap. 3, Sheet E.3.14)

The present value of an ordinary annuity is calculated by discounting its future streams of cash flows. Since the cash flows occur at the end of the respective periods, the present value counts from the beginning of the first period of cash flow streams (◼ Exhibit 3.14.1). Therefore, the general formula for calculating the present value of an ordinary annuity (PVOA) can be expressed as follows:

$$PVOA_n = \Sigma CF_t / (1+i)^t$$

where CF = cash flow; i = discount rate; n= number of periods to maturity; and t = cash flow time, which counts from period 1.

Example

Jordan has acquired a loan from a bank, which requires him to repay the loan and interest at constant installments of $1000 annually for a period of 5 years at an interest of 10%. All payments should be made at the end of the payment period. What is the present value of these payments?

Solution

Using the formula above, where CF = $1000, i = 10%, n = 5, and t = 1, 2, 3, 4, and 5, the present values are calculated as follows:

$$PVOA_5 = \$1000/(1.10)^1 + \$1000/(1.10)^2 + \$1000/(1.10)^3 + \$1000/(1.10)^4 + \$1000/(1.10)^5$$

$$PVOA_5 = \$909 + \$826 + \$751 + \$683 + \$621 = \$3791$$

$$PVOA_5 = \$3791$$

◼ Exhibit 3.14.2 displays the patterns of cash flows and the respective present values as calculated above.

Observation

The sooner the payments are made, the higher the value, with other factors being equal.

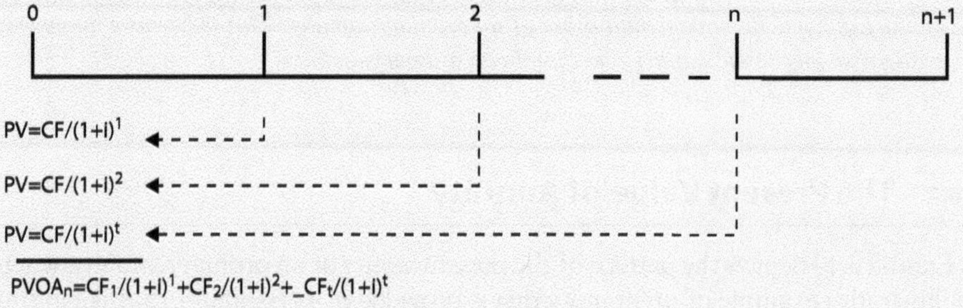

◼ **Exhibit 3.14.1** Patterns of an ordinary annuity

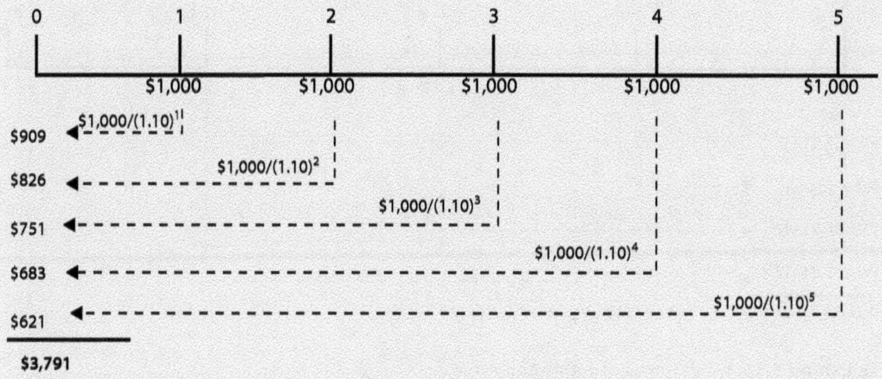

Exhibit 3.14.2 The present value of an ordinary annuity

Exhibit 3.15 Annuity Due: Present Value

Illustrative Example (See Excel Workings—▶ Chap. 3, Sheet E.3.15)

Since the cash flows occur at the beginning of the respective periods, the general formula for calculating the present value of an annuity due (PVAD) can be expressed as follows (Exhibit 3.15.1).

$$PVOA_n = \Sigma CF_t / (1+i)^t$$

where CF = cash flow; i = discount rate; n = number of periods to maturity; and t = cash flow time, which counts from period 0.

Example

Joseline has an insurance policy of $1000, which requires her to make payments at the beginning of each year. The average annual interest rate is 10%. She expects to hold the insurance for 5 years from now. What is the present value of her payments?

Solution

Using the formula above, where CF = $1000, i = 10%, n = 5, and t = 0, 1, 2, 3, 4, and 5, the present values are calculated as follows:

$$PVAD_5 = \$1000/(1.10)^0 + \$1000/(1.10)^1 + \$1000/(1.10)^2 + \$1000/(1.10)^3 + \$1000/(1.10)^4$$

$$PVAD_5 = \$1000 + \$909 + \$826 + \$751 + \$683$$

$$PVAD_5 = \$4170$$

Exhibit 3.15.2 displays the patterns of cash flows and the respective present values as calculated above.

Observation

The sooner the payments are made, the higher the value, with other factors being equal.

3

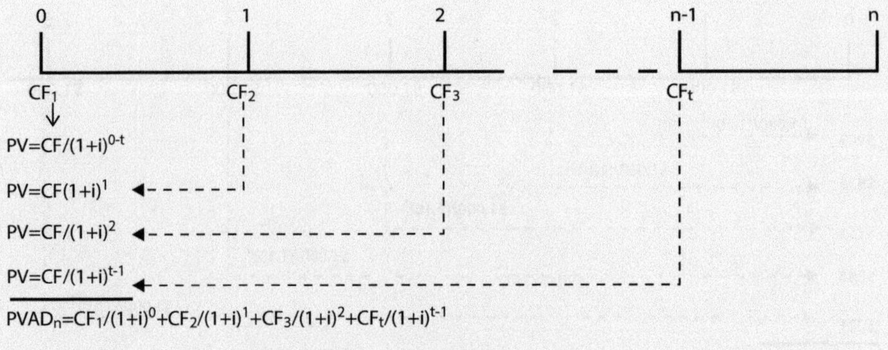

Exhibit 3.15.1 Patterns of an annuity due

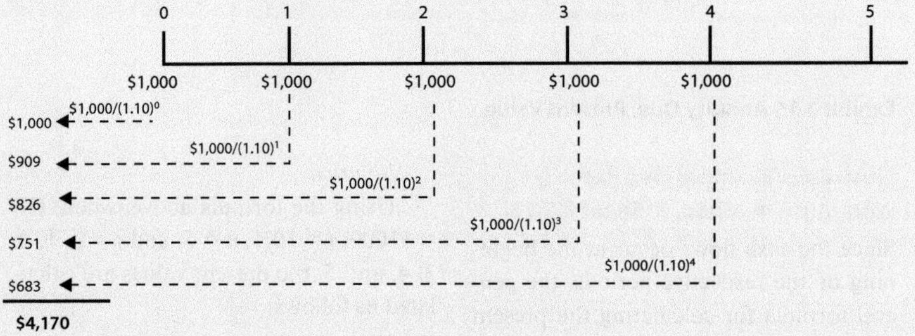

Exhibit 3.15.2 The present value of annuity due

Exhibit 3.16 Ordinary Annuity vs. Annuity Due: Present Value

Illustrative Example (See Excel Workings—► Chap. 3, Sheets E3.14 and E.3.15)

Observation

The sooner the payments are made, the higher the future value, with other factors being equal (Exhibits 3.16.1 and 3.16.2). Moreover, annuity due cash flows have higher values than do ordinary annuity cash flows because the former's cash flows are sooner than the latter's.

Exhibit 3.16.1 The present values of annuities

Period	Payment 1	Payment 2	Payment 3	Payment 4	Payment 5	Total payment
Annuity due ($)	1000	909	826	751	683	4170
Ordinary annuity ($)	909	826	751	683	621	3791
Difference ($)	91	83	75	68	62	379

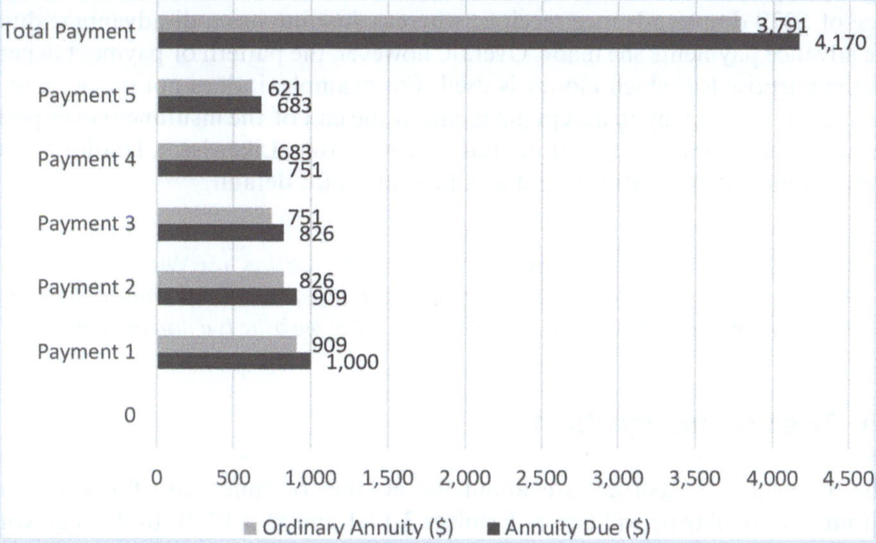

Exhibit 3.16.2 The present values of annuities

Banner 3.11 Ordinary Annuity vs. Annuity Due—Present Value

Given the same amount of money, interest, and payment period, the present values of an annuity due will be higher than those of an ordinary annuity. This is because money is realized sooner in an annuity due than in an ordinary annuity.

3.8.3 Losers and Winners

3

Who wins and who loses? The benefit or advantage of each type of annuity depends on whether the future cash flows are related to either payments or receipts. Ordinary annuities usually offer more advantage if cash flows are related to future payment obligations. In our examples (see Exhibit ▶ 3.13), the future values relating to Galembana's and Phina's obligations are $6105 on ordinary annuities and $6716 on annuity dues, respectively. Therefore, Galembana is a winner because his payments are delayed by a year—he gains $611. On the other hand, Phina is a loser of the same value ($611) because she makes payments 1 year in advance.

Likewise, while Galembana (the payer) is the winner, the bank (the receiver) is the loser. That is, annuity dues tend to be more advantageous on cash flows relating to receipts, whereas ordinary annuities are more advantageous on cash flows relating to obligations. For instance, in Exhibit ▶ 3.16, Joseline's insurer has an advantage of $379 due to advance receipts, whereas Joseline has a disadvantage due to the advance payments she made. Overall, however, the pattern of payment depends on the purpose for which money is used. For example, it does not make sense for an insurance company to accept payments at the end of the insurance cover period because the money to be paid intends to cover risks. Likewise, a landlord would prefer immediate payment of rent as a protection for default.

Banner 3.12 Ordinary Annuity vs. Annuity Due—Losers and Winners
Annuity due cash flows are more advantageous on receipts, whereas ordinary annuity cash flows are more advantageous on obligations. The opposite is a disadvantage.

3.9 The Frequency Effect

The frequency of cash flows is about the number of times cash flows in or out within a particular period (see ▶ Exhibits 3.17.1 and ◘ 3.17.2). In the real world, streams of cash flows occur at different frequencies like annually, semiannually, quarterly, monthly, and even daily. Frequency, therefore, affects the time value of money. One could ask you a question: "If you have money to invest, in which frequency will you prefer earning money?" Is it annually, or semiannually, or quarterly? And so on. Obviously, your decision will be based on an option that gives you more value. With other factors being equal, the main influencing factor determining value is the number of payment periods per year (m) and interest rate (i) over a certain number of years to maturity (n). This aspect is illustrated with examples in Exhibit ▶ 3.17.

Think 3.5
Suppose that you have invested in the stocks of a company, which pays dividends regularly. The following options are available for dividend payment per share: $5 annually, $2.5 semiannually, and $1.25 quarterly. Which frequency option do you think will add more value?

Exhibit 3.17 The Frequency Effect on Time Value of Money

Illustrative Example (See Excel Workings—▶ Chap. 3, Sheet E.3.17)

Example: Future Value

Joseline has $20,000 to invest in a fixed bank deposit, which pays 12% interest compounded annually. The bank also offers other frequency options in which the compounded periodical interest rates will be as follows: 6% semiannually and 3% quarterly. Joseline wants to decide on the frequency in which she should earn the interest over 2 years if she makes a single deposit on 1 January 2012 and receives payment at the end of each payment period until 31 December 2013. What is the future value of her earnings in 2 years for each category of payment frequency?

Solution

The future values for Joseline's cash flow streams are calculated as follows:

$$FV = Deposit(1+interest)^n$$

where n = number of payment periods

$$FV(Annually) = \$20{,}000(1+12\%)^2 = \$25.088$$

$$FV(Semiannually) = \$20{,}000(1+6\%)^4 = \$25{,}250$$

$$FV(Quarterly) = \$20{,}000(1+3\%)^8 = \$25{,}335$$

▶ Exhibit 3.17.3 shows the flow of cash for each payment period and the total

Exhibit 3.17.1 Number of payments and interest rates: 1 year

Frequency	Number of payments	Interest rate
Annually	1	12%
Semiannually	2	6%
Quarterly	4	3%
Monthly	12	1%

Exhibit 3.17.2 Number of payments and interest rates: 2 years

Frequency	Number of payments	Interest rate
Annually	2	12%
Semiannually	4	6%
Quarterly	8	3%
Monthly	24	1%

value in maturity as on 31 December 2013.

Observation 1

Given the same amount of money invested today, the same compounded interest rate, and the same maturity period, the higher the frequency of payments, the higher the future value of the investment money.

Example: Present Value

Now, let us suppose that Joseline desires to earn $50,000 in 2 years. The bank provides the following fixed deposit rates: an interest of 12% annually or 6% semiannually or 3% quarterly. How much should Joseline deposit today to achieve her desired earnings?

Solution

To answer this question, we can determine the present value factor using the information from ◘ Exhibit 3.17.3 by dividing the initial deposit ($20,000) by the total future value at the end of the investment maturity period. Thus, the present value factors for annual, semiannual, and quarterly frequencies are as follows: on 2 payments annually $20,000/$25,088 = 0.79719; on 4 payments semiannually $20,000/$25,250 = 0.79209; and on 8 payments quarterly $20,000/$25,335 = 0.78941. That is, if Joseline wants to earn $1.00 in 2 years, she should deposit $0.79719 for annual payment frequencies, $0.79209 for semiannual frequencies, or $0.78841 for quarterly frequencies. This means the higher the compounding frequency, the less the money we need to invest now to generate $1.00 in the future.

Thus, the amount to be invested today is obtained by multiplying the desired earnings ($50,000) by each of the present value factor. The results are displayed in ◘ Exhibit 3.17.4.

Observation 2

For a given desired future value and time to maturity, the amount to be invested or saved today is lower for higher payment frequencies and higher for lower frequency payments.

◘ **Exhibit 3.17.3** The frequency effect on the future value: 2 years

Frequency	Date	Deposited ($)	Interest ($)	Value ($)
Annually	Jan 1, 2012	20,000	-	20,000
Interest = 12%	Dec 31, 2012		2400	22,400
Number of payments = 2	Dec 1, 2013	22,400		
	Dec 31, 2013		2688	**25,088**
Semiannually	Jan 1, 2012	20,000	-	20,000
Interest = 6%	Jun 30, 2012		1200	21,200
Number of payments = 4	Jul 1, 2012	21,200		
	Dec 31, 2012		1272	22,472
	Jan 1, 2013	22,472		

Exhibit 3.17.3 (continued)

Frequency	Date	Deposited ($)	Interest ($)	Value ($)
	Jun 30, 2013		1348	23,820
	Jul 1, 2013	23,820		
	Dec 31, 2013		1429	**25,250**
Quarterly	Jan 1, 2012	20,000	-	20,000
Interest = 3%	Mar 31, 2012		600	20,600
Number of payments = 8	Apr 1, 2012	20,600		
	Jun 30, 2012		618	21,218
	July 1, 2012	21,218		
	Sept 30, 2012		637	21,855
	Oct 1, 2012	21,855		
	Dec 31, 2012		656	22,510
	Jan 1, 2013	22,510		
	Mar 31, 2013		675	23,185
	Apr 1, 2013	23,185		
	Jun 30, 2013		696	23,881
	Jul 1, 2013	23,881		
	Sept 30, 2013		716	24,597
	Oct 1, 2013	24,597		
	Dec 31, 2013		738	**25,335**

Exhibit 3.17.4 The frequency effect on the present value: 2 years

	Annually	Semiannually	Quarterly
Compounded frequency	2 payments	4 payments	8 payments
Target amount	$50,000	$50,000	$50,000
Compounded interest	12%	6%	3%
PV factor	0.79719	0.79209	0.78941
Amount to be invested	**$39,860**	**$39,605**	**$39,470**

In ▶ Exhibit 3.17.3, we show Joseline's status of her future value if she deposits \$20,000 in a bank, which offers three options of payment frequencies at compounded interest rates as follows: 12% annually, 6% semiannually, and 3% quarterly. We see that the quarterly payment frequency provides the highest future value (i.e., \$25,335), whereas the annual payment frequency provides the lowest future value (i.e., \$25,088). The semiannual frequency is mid at \$25,250. In ▶ Exhibit 3.17.4, we show how much Joseline should invest today if she desires to earn \$50,000 in 2 years at an interest of 12% annually, 6% semiannually, or 3% quarterly. We see that the amount to be invested is the smallest for the highest frequency (quarterly) and the biggest for the lowest frequency (annually)—\$39,470 (quarterly), \$39,605 (semiannually), and \$39,860 (annually). This implies that more compounded interest is earned when the payment frequency increases.

Banner 3.13 The Frequency Effect
Given the same amount of money, the same compounded interest rate, and the same maturity period, the higher the frequency of payments, the more the value, and vice versa.

3.10 Effective Interest Rate (EIR) Vs. Annual Percentage Rate (APR)

So far, we have seen that compounding frequency affects the time value of money, in which the higher the frequency, the higher the value. This is because the higher the frequency, the more often the interest earns interest. Effective interest rate (EIR) can adjust the nominal interest rates for such compounding frequency effects. For example, if a fixed-income deposit pays 1% interest each month, then the effective interest rate should be more than 1% because compounding the interest causes a marginal increase in the principal each month. Therefore, with the number of compounded periods per year (m) and the number of years to maturity (n), we can calculate the EIR using the following general formula:

$$\text{EIR} = \left(1 + \frac{i}{m}\right)^{mn} - 1$$

In technical terms, the interest rate (i) is referred to as the "stated annual interest rate" or the "quoted annual interest rate." Its common name in practice is the "annual percentage rate" (APR)—it is the rate that financial institutions (lenders) are required to publish in accordance with the law. This rate is simply calculated by multiplying the "periodic interest rate" (r) by the "number of compounded periods per year" (m) in which money is earned or paid (i.e., APR = rm). For example, for a weekly payment frequency, the number of compounded periods is 52 (i.e., there are 52 weeks in a year), for a monthly payment frequency, the number of periods is 12 (i.e., there are 12 months is a year), and so on. Therefore, if the APR is 4% annually, and the payment frequency is monthly (i.e., 12 payments per year), the EIR will be slightly greater, calculated as follows:

$$\text{EIR} = \left(1 + \frac{0.04}{12}\right)^{12} - 1 = 4.07\%$$

This aspect is illustrated in ▶ Exhibit 3.18, which shows the EIRs calculated for different compounding frequencies. The future values are also calculated to correspond to each frequency. Under each period to maturity, the highest future value arises from the highest frequency (weekly), whereas the lowest value arises from the lowest frequency (annual). Overall, we can say that the higher the compounding frequency, the greater the EIR, the more the value, and vice versa.

Banner 3.14 Effective Interest Rate (EIR)
Effective interest rate (EIR) is the actual interest rate earned or paid after adjusting the nominal interest rate for compounding payment frequencies.

The distinction between the EIR and the APR can be clearly seen in ◘ Exhibits 3.18.1 and 3.18.2. In this example, the APR is 12%, regardless of changes in compounded frequencies and years to maturity. In contrast, the EIR varies with frequencies and maturity periods. These aspects, consequently, affect values as demonstrated by calculating future values with maturities in 1 and 2 years. Whereas the future value with the APR does not vary, those with the EIR vary with frequency: the higher the frequency, the higher the value. For example, when maturity is 1 year, the future values with the EIR range from $22,400 (annually) to $22,547 (weekly). It is also important to note that when the frequency is annual, both the APR and EIR yield the same value (in this case, it is $22,400 in 1 year and $25,088 in 2 years). In addition, we observe that values calculated from periodical interest rates (r) are identical to those from the EIR. Using periodical interest rates, with the present amount of money (P), the future values (FV) are calculated using the following formula:

$$FV = P(1-r)^{mn}$$

Exhibit 3.18 Effective Interest Rate (EIR) vs. Annual Percentage Rate (APR)

Illustrative Example (See Excel Workings—▶ Chap. 3, Sheet E.3.18)

Suppose that the annual percentage rate (APR) published by a bank is 12%. Mr. Jordan has $20,000, and there is an investment opportunity to deposit this money into a bank account. The bank also offers other frequency options in which the compounded frequencies are annual, semiannual, quarterly, monthly, fortnightly, and weekly.

(a) Demonstrate how the frequency factor affects the APR and the EIR.
(b) Considering the frequency factor, show how Jordan's future values will differ between the APR and the EIR.

3

Solution

(a) Frequency does not have an effect on the APR because it is an annual rate. The effect of frequency on the APR, nevertheless, is reflected in the periodical interest rates (r), such that APR = rm. In contrast, frequency affects the EIR as depicted in the following formula:

$$\text{EIR} = \left(1 + \frac{i}{m}\right)^{mn} - 1$$

Exhibit 3.18.1. compares the APR with the EIR. For any number of frequencies and maturities, the APR is constant, whereas the EIR increases with an increase in frequencies.

(b) Exhibit 3.18.1 also displays futures values based on periodical interest rates, the APR, and the EIR. For each type of interest rate, future values are calculated as follows:

Based on the periodical interest rates (r):

$$FV = P(1+r)^{mn}$$

Exhibit 3.18.1 Comparison between EIR and APR

Frequency	Number of periods (m)	Maturity (years)	Periodic rate (r)	APR	EIR	(r) future value ($)	APR future value ($)	EIR future value ($)
Annual	1	1	12.00%	12.00%	12.00%	22,400	22,400	22,400
Semiannual	2	1	6.00%	12.00%	12.36%	22,472	22,400	22,472
Quarterly	4	1	3.00%	12.00%	12.55%	22,510	22,400	22,510
Monthly	12	1	1.00%	12.00%	12.68%	22,537	22,400	22,537
Fortnightly	26	1	0.46%	12.00%	12.72%	22,544	22,400	22,544
Weekly	52	1	0.23%	12.00%	12.73%	22,547	22,400	22,547
Annual	1	2	12.00%	12.00%	25.44%	25,088	25,088	25,088
Semiannual	2	2	6.00%	12.00%	26.25%	25,250	25,088	25,250
Quarterly	4	2	3.00%	12.00%	26.68%	25,335	25,088	25,335
Monthly	12	2	1.00%	12.00%	26.97%	25,395	25,088	25,395
Fortnightly	26	2	0.46%	12.00%	27.05%	25,411	25,088	25,411
Weekly	52	2	0.23%	12.00%	27.09%	25,418	25,088	25,418

Based on the annual percentage rate (APR):

$$FV = P(1 + APR)^n$$

Based on the effective interest rate (EIR):

$$FV = P(1 + EIR)$$

Observations

When using the APR, future values for 1-year and 2-year maturities are $22,400 and $25,088, respectively. These values are not affected by frequency but the time to maturity.

In contrast, the use of periodical interest rates and the EIR provides similar future values, which increase proportionally to the increase in both frequency and maturity: that is from $22,400 (annually, 1 year) to $22,544 (weekly, 1 year) and from $25,088 (annually, 2 years) to $25,418 (weekly, 2 years).

When the frequency is annual, all three interest rates yield the same values: that is $22,400 (1-year maturity) and $25,088 (2-year maturity).

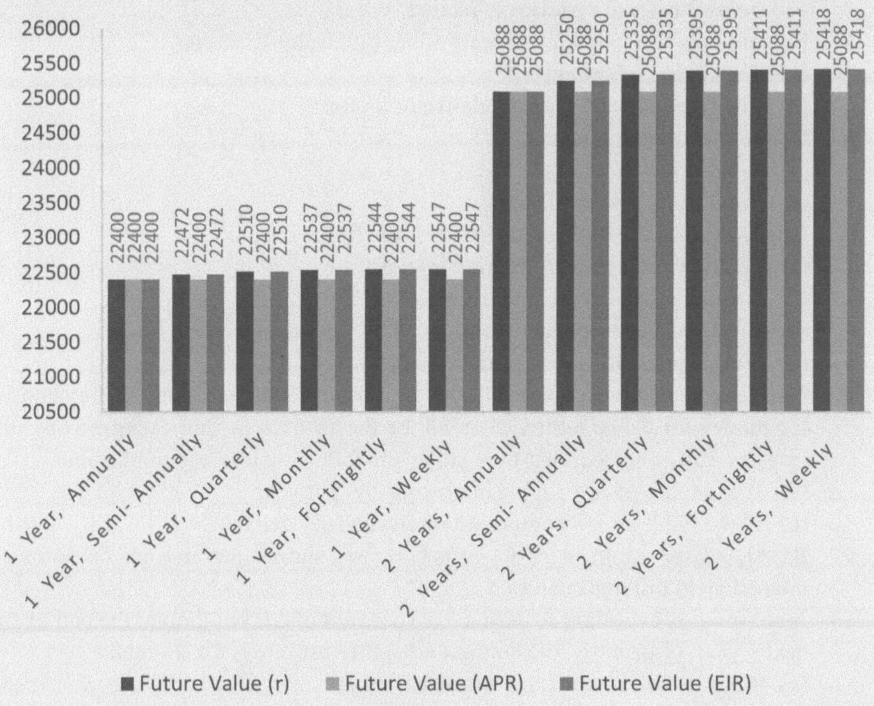

Exhibit 3.18.2 Comparison between EIR and APR

Banner 3.15 The Frequency Effect—Types of Interest Rates

When the compounded frequency is annual, the three types of interest rates (periodical interest rate, annual percentage rate, and effective interest rate) will yield the same values.

Otherwise, values will increase (decrease) with the increase (decrease) in frequencies when periodical interest rates and effective interest rates are applied.

3

Review Questions

1. Explain the meaning of time value of money.
2. In relation to valuation, why is it important to understand time value of money?
3. Outline the main factors effecting time value of money by explaining the effect of each of those factors.
4. Present values and interest rates are negatively related, whereas future values and interest rates are positively related. Why?
5. Explain how the following aspects affect time value of money:
   (a) The timing of money
   (b) The frequency of money relative to interest
6. Define the following terms:
   (a) Inflation
   (b) Purchasing power of money
7. Briefly explain the differences between the following:
   (a) Fixed interest rate vs. floating interest rate
   (b) Ordinary annuity vs. annuity due
   (c) Future value vs. present value
   (d) Simple interest vs. compounded interest
8. Mr. Tengule wants to invest $12,000 in a fixed deposit account. If he deposits the money for 6 years, then what will be the amount of interest earned by this investor during the deposit time under the following interest conditions?
   (a) If the bank pays a simple interest of 6% per year
   (b) If the bank pays a compound interest of 6% per year
9. Based on your results in (6) above, explain why simple interest and compounded interest yield different values.
10. A company is expecting to earn a fixed amount of $1.5 million at the end of the next 5 years. Currently, the compounded interest rate is 6% annually.
    (a) What is the present value of the earnings?
    (b) Show how the value of such earnings will change at the end of each year prior to the earning year.
    (c) Interpret your results in (b) above.
11. If you invest $50,000 today at a compounded interest rate of 8% annually, then what will be the future value of your money at the end of the next 4 years?
12. A company is expecting to earn money in the future from its current investments. The management's desire is to obtain the present value of $12 million from those earnings, which are expected at the end of next 3 years.

(a) How much should the company earn in order to fulfill its desired present value if the annual interest rates are 6%, 10%, and 15%?
(b) From your answers in (a) above, under which interest rate should the company earn more money in the future to obtain the value of $12 million today? Explain your answer.
(c) Explain the relationship between the size of interest rate and present value.

13. Phina is expecting to earn $5000 from her business in the next 5 years. Assume that the different possibilities of annual interest rates are 5%, 8%, and 12%.
    (a) Calculate the present value of her expected earnings for each of the interest rate possibilities.
    (b) What will be the value of her earnings at the end of each year until 5 years?
    (c) Under what interest rate does she obtain more value today? Explain why.
14. A bank offers an opportunity to invest in a fixed deposit account at an interest of 12% annually.
    (a) Show how the future value of your money will change each year if you invest the following amount of money today: $6000, $15,000, $24,000, and $35,000.
    (b) Based on your answers in (a) above, explain how the size of money affects the rate at which the interest rates affect future values.
15. Joseline expects to pay the following amounts of money on her debt portfolio with four different lenders: $1000, $5000, $12,000 and $22,000. All lenders charge an interest of 10% annually.
    (a) What is the present value of each of Joseline's obligations if payables are due in the next 10 years from today?
    (b) Show how the value of each of her obligations will change each year from now until the end of year 10.
    (c) Based on your analysis, explain the relationship between the size of money and the magnitude at which interest rates penalize the present values.
16. Consider the following flow of cash for three companies, A, B, and C. The total cash for each company is $22,500. Cash flows will occur at the end of each year over the next 5 years. The interest rate is 10% annually.

Year	Company A ($)	Company B ($)	Company C ($)
1	10,000	500	4500
2	7000	1000	4500
3	4000	4000	4500
4	1000	7000	4500
5	500	10,000	4500

    (a) Calculate the present value of each company's cash flows.
    (b) Calculate the future value of each company's cash flows as in the end of year 5.

(c) Which company's cash flows are more valuable today, and why?
(d) Which company's cash flows are more valuable at the end of year 5, and why?
(e) Based on your answers above, explain the relationship between the size of money, timing of money, and interest rate.
(f) Replicate (a) and (b) above if the interest rate rises to 15%. Show which company's present value and future value will be more affected by changes in the interest rates, and why?
(g) Replicate (a)–(f) if cash flows occur in the beginning of each year.

17. Consider the following flow of cash for three companies, X, Y, and Z. Cash flows will occur at the end of each year over the next 5 years. The interest rate is 10% annually.

Year	Company X ($)	Company Y ($)	Company Z ($)
1	45,500	0	0
2	0	0	0
3	0	45,500	0
4	0	0	0
5	0	0	45,500

(a) Calculate the present value of each company's cash flows.
(b) Calculate the future value of each company's cash flows as in the end of year 5.
(c) Which company's cash flows are more valuable today, and why?
(d) Which company's cash flows are more valuable at the end of year 5, and why?
(e) Based on your answers above, explain the relationship between the size of money, timing of money, and interest rate.
(f) Replicate (a) and (b) above if the interest rate rises to 15%. Show which company's present value and future value will be more affected by changes in interest rates, and why?
(g) Replicate (a)–(f) if cash flows occur in the beginning of each year.

18. The table below shows five different profiles of expected flow of money in the next 6 years. Cash flows occur at the end of each year. The interest rate is 8% compounded annually.

Year	Profile 1 ($)	Profile 2 ($)	Profile 3 ($)	Profile 4 ($)	Profile 5 ($)
1	12,500	600	5433	32,600	0
2	9500	1000	5433	0	0
3	6000	3000	5433	0	0
4	3000	6000	5433	0	0

Year	Profile 1 ($)	Profile 2 ($)	Profile 3 ($)	Profile 4 ($)	Profile 5 ($)
5	1000	9500	5433	0	0
6	600	12,500	5433	0	32,600

Now consider the following transactions and determine a cash flow profile or combination of profiles (where applicable) that will have the most value benefit for a particular earning or payment obligation. Use calculations and brief explanations to support your decisions.

(a) Grace has a payment obligation relating to her loan portfolio with a bank, in which she should pay $32,600 in the next 6 years.
(b) Valentine is expecting to receive $32,600 over the next 6 years as revenues from supplying farm equipment to a cooperative union.
(c) A construction company has ordered equipment worth $32,600. Payments should be completed within the next 6 years. The supplier offers a 2% discount of the total cost if at least 50% of it is paid within the next 3 years. The discount is not mandatory. Provide your answers in the perspective of both the construction company and the supplier.
(d) ABC company is expecting to earn $32,600 over the next 6 years following its sales. The company is also expected to spend $32,600 on its financial obligations within the same period.
(e) XYZ company is expecting to earn $32,600 over the next 6 years following its sales. The company is also expected to spend $32,600 on its financial obligations within the same period. The interest rate is expected to rise from 8% to 10%, which will be applicable from year 4 to the end.

19. A company has $150,000, and there is an investment opportunity to deposit this money into a bank account that pays 12% interest compounded annually. The bank also offers other frequency options in which the compounded periodical interest rates will be as follows: 6% semiannually and 3% quarterly. The investment will last for 3 full years, and money will be earned at the end of the payment period.
    (a) What is the future value and present value of the earnings for each category of payment frequency?
    (b) What is the most favorable frequency if the objective is to maximize value?
20. The annual percentage rate (APR) published by banks is 10.5%. Victor is anticipating investing $100,000 into a fixed deposit account at RT Bank for 1 year. The returns from this deposit can be earned upon a choice of the optional payment frequencies: annual, semiannual, quarterly, monthly, fortnightly, and weekly.
    (a) Show how the effective interest rate (EIR) differs from the annual percentage rate (APR) for each frequency.
    (b) Based on EIRs, show how the frequency of payment will affect the value of Victor's investment.

Bibliography

Greebard, K. (2020), Decline in the value of your cash savings, Available at Times Colonist, https://www.timescolonist.com/business/kevin-greenard-decline-in-the-value-of-your-cash-savings-1.240659451 Accessed January 31 2020.

Hilshleifer, J. (1985), Investment Decision Criteria, UCLA Department of Economics Working Paper 365, University of California, March 1985. http://www.econ.ucla.edu/workingpapers/wp365.pdf Accessed March 12, 2021.

Security Markets and Valuation

Contents

Supplementary Information The online version contains supplementary material available at https://doi.org/10.1007/978-3-031-28267-6_4.

B. Kulwizira Lukanima, *Corporate Valuation*, Classroom Companion: Business, https://doi.org/10.1007/978-3-031-28267-6_4

4.1 Introduction

Financial security markets form part of financial markets, which include equity markets, debt markets, and others (hybrid security markets and derivative markets). In ▶ Chap. 2, the linkage between a firm and financial markets was discussed. Overall, these markets facilitate business transactions, asset fair pricing, and risk sharing. This chapter focuses on stocks and bonds by explaining their implications in valuation. Jointly, they play a significant role in valuation because they provide opportunities for raising capital and making investments. Moreover, here, these markets are used to reflect on a firm's capital structure, which represents ownership (stocks) and leverage (debts). Moreover, the key determinants of security prices and their implications in valuation are discussed.

Learning Outcomes

- Explain the role of stock and bond markets
- Outline the key players in stock and bond markets
- Understand the role of stock market analysts
- Explain the key determinants of stock and bond prices
- Understand bond credit ratings and their implications in corporate valuation
- Explain the valuation implications of stock and bond markets
- Understand the sources of security market information

4.2 An Overview of Security Markets

Security markets are financial markets in which securities are issued by companies, purchased by investors, and subsequently transferred among investors. Their primary function is to facilitate the flow of capital from one party (those with excess) to another (those in deficit). These markets include equity security markets, debt security markets, hybrid security markets, and derivative markets.

Generally, these markets are categorized into two—primary markets and secondary markets. In "primary markets," new securities are issued for the first time and made available for the public to purchase—the issuer receives the proceeds. For example, a company can raise capital through issuing new stocks in terms of initial public offers (IPOs) or issuing corporate bonds. Consequently, the newly issued securities can be listed under trade in "secondary markets" (security exchange markets), where they are regarded as old (previously issued) securities. Secondary markets allow securities to change hands among investors through trading (buying and selling), thereby facilitating a dynamic and competitive pricing mechanism.

Banner 4.1 Role of Security Markets

Security markets create funding and investment opportunities for companies and investors.

Exhibit ▶ 4.1 shows the difference between primary and secondary markets. The linkage between two parties (the issuer and the purchaser) facilitates the flow of funds depending on the need of each party. The objective of an issuer is to raise capital to fund short- or long-term needs. The objective of a purchaser is to invest, expecting returns that reflect the risk of the investments.

Exhibit 4.1 Primary vs. Secondary Markets

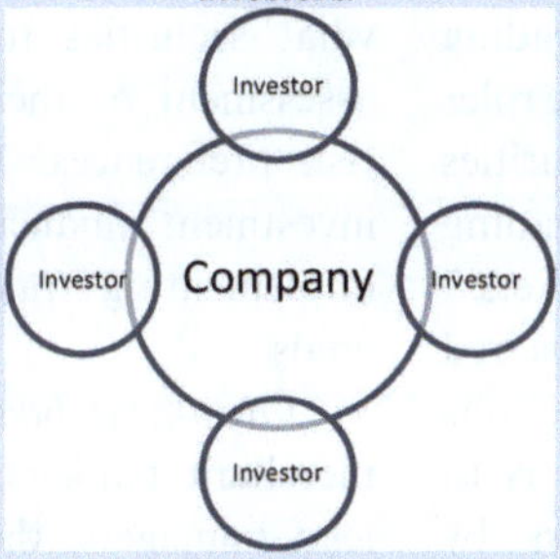

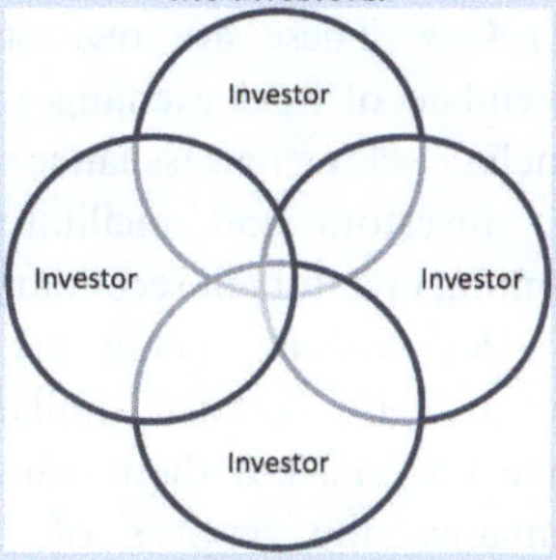

	Primary market *Investment linkage is between the issuer (company) and investors. There is no linkage among the investors.*	Secondary market *Investment linkage is among investors. There is no direct linkage between the issuer and the investors.*
Meaning	Securities are issued for the first time	Securities are traded after initial issue
Intermediation	Underwriters, the issuing registerer, merchant banks, collection banks, portfolio managers, etc.	Security brokers
Relationship	Direct purchase from the company	Trading among investors
Trading	Only once	Unlimited
Objective	To raise large capital	Investment with liquidity
Price	The price is fixed by company analysts	The price fluctuates due to market forces
Proceeds	A company gets the proceeds (capital)	Investors gain profit/loss or returns
Valuation	Book value	Market value

4.3 The Key Players in Security Markets

Several individuals and organizations play different roles in security markets, as outlined in Exhibit ▶ 4.2. Here, we categorize them into five groups: (1) "corporations," which need capital funding; (2) "capital providers," who transfer funds to corporations through investments (e.g., investment specialists and individual investors); (3)

"intermediaries," such as brokers and investment bankers, who play an intermediary role between corporations and capital providers; (4) "advisers" (e.g., investment advisors, underwriters, and credit rating agencies), whose role is to analyze securities and offer advisory services to corporations and investors; and (5) "regulators" (e.g., governments, central banks, and security market authorities), whose role is to ensure smooth running of security markets, compliance, and safeguard the interests of all players. It is important to understand that all these players do not work in isolation—they have interactive and overlapping roles in a security market system.

Exhibit 4.2 The Key Players in Security Markets

Brokers: These are registered trading members of stock exchanges whose roles include selling new issuance of securities to investors and facilitating trading among investors in secondary markets.

Sub-brokers: These are registered agents who perform similar functions like brokers, but their main role is to enhance the services of brokers by reaching a larger number of investors.

Investment Specialists: There are several investment specialists in stock markets such as asset management companies, portfolio managers, and investment advisors.

Asset Management Companies: These are investment specialists who help investors in selecting and managing a portfolio of securities. They are allowed to offer securities, thereby participating in a pool of money for creation of investment portfolios.

Portfolio Managers: These are also investment specialists, but, unlike asset management companies, they do not offer any security (and hence are not allowed to pool money from investors). Instead, they act on behalf of the investor by creating and managing a portfolio.

Investment Advisers: These are specialists who help investors' decisions on what securities to buy based on an assessment of their specific needs and risk preferences. They also engage in investment financial planning and in implementing strategies to suit investors' goals.

Investment Bankers: Also known as merchant bankers, issue managers, or lead managers, they play a significant role in facilitating the initial issuance of securities by helping an issuer access the security market. Their specific duties include, but are not limited to, evaluating the capital needs, structuring an appropriate instrument, participating in pricing the security, and managing the entire issue process until the securities are issued and listed on a stock exchange.

Underwriters: An "underwriter" is a term used to describe primary market specialists who are engaged in evaluating security risk and price for a fee. They buy (underwrite) securities of issuing companies to sell in the public market. For example, investment bankers perform the underwriting function.

Credit Rating Agencies: These are expert companies that provide a professional opinion about the ability of an issuer to meet obligations. They evaluate the issuer's financial conditions, considering economic conditions, and give credit ratings, which help investors assess the default risk of a security.

Regulators: Security markets are regulated according to a specific country's requirements as well as international requirements. Generally, regulatory organs include regulatory authorities of countries (to protect the interest of investors), central banks (to manage government securities), and security exchanges (to manage security trading).

4.4 Stock Markets

Stock markets allow companies to raise capital through issuing stocks, thereby creating investment opportunities in the market. In this section, we focus on the implication of valuation in stock markets, the role of stock analysts, and price determinants.

Think 4.1

If you are one of the owners of a company, would you prefer you company's stocks to be listed for public trading? Give reasons.

4.4.1 The Role of Stock Markets

4.4.1.1 Primary Market: Initial Issuance of Stocks

Companies use IPOs (initial public offers) and FPOs (follow-on public offers) to issue stocks for the first time—usually, the main goal is to raise a large amount of capital to finance new investments or expand the existing ones. Therefore, in the company's balance sheet, the value of initial offering is presented as "paid-in capital" (the original source of shareholders' equity) or "additional paid-in capital" (a new issue of equity). Thus, paid-in capital represents the amount of capital directly contributed by investors or owners, hence increasing total shareholders' equity (the book value). To explain this aspect, we use Exhibit 4.3.1. From the balance sheet of the Coca-Cola Company, 7,040 million shares were issued to raise US$1,760 million (paid-in capital at $0.25 par value) and were still outstanding in 2020 and 2021. "Capital surplus" (also known as a share premium) is additional paid-in capital in which stocks are sold at more than the par value—it was US$18,116 million and US$17,601 million in 2021 and 2020, respectively. It should be noted that the par value is a fixed price.

Banner 4.2 The Value of Initial Stock Offering

The value of an initial stock offering is reflected in the company's balance sheet as paid-in capital, thereby increasing shareholders' equity (the book value).

4.4.1.2 Secondary Market: Stock Trading

After the initial offer, some companies issue stocks for trading in secondary markets (stock exchanges) like the New York Stock Exchange (NYSE), NASDAQ (National Association of Securities Dealers Automated Quotations), and Dow Jones (the United States), London Stock Exchange (the United Kingdom), Tokyo Stock Exchange (Japan), Dar es Salaam Stock Exchange (Tanzania), Bogota Stock Exchange (Colombia), and so on. Companies whose stocks are listed in exchange markets are, therefore, referred to as "public companies," and, hence, it is mandatory that they publish their financial reports quarterly and/or annually. Like IPOs, the goal of stock listing is to raise capital. Moreover, listed stocks provide investment opportunities to the public (investors) through buying and selling at competitive pricing. Unlike IPOs, stock prices in secondary markets are not fixed—they are determined by investors' perceptions about company performance, considering the market forces of supply and demand. ▶ Exhibit 4.3.2 displays market information regarding the Coca-Cola Company. This information from Yahoo Finance indicates the company's stocks trading on the NYSE on 18 March 2022—the stock price closed at US$60.20, leading to a total market value (market capitalization) of US$260.56 billion.

Banner 4.3 The Value of Stock in Secondary Markets

The value of stocks in secondary markets is reflected in quoted prices, which are determined through competitive pricing. The total value is known as market capitalization (market value).

Apart from raising capital and creating investment opportunities, public stock trading has other advantages like promoting the company's image and brand, enhancing the visibility of the company and its products, and enhancing transparency, accountability, and liquidity, among others. These advantages, however, come with side effects like strict compliance with market rules, undervaluation risk, floating and listing costs, and being subject to public scrutiny.

Quotes 4.1 The Information Role of Stock Markets

- **Quote 4.1.1 Creating the Possibility to Analyze Company Fundamentals and Market Information for Investment Decisions**

» ...Diving in, Coca-Cola's revenue and earnings both topped Wall Street estimates. Accordingly, quarterly revenues grew by 10% to $9.46 billion from last year's $8.61 million. Net income for the quarter came in at $2.41 billion, up by an impressive 65% year-over-year from $1.46 billion. Accordingly, earnings per share were $0.56 in comparison with last year's $0.34. Financials aside, Wells Fargo (NYSE: WFC) analyst Chris Carey reiterated his Overweight rating on KO stock. The analyst believes that momentum could continue due to strong top line performance driven by higher pricing and mix delivery. Given the strong quarter from Coca-Cola, will you be buying KO stock? (Jonathan Phillip, Contributor at NASDAQ).

Jonathan Phillip, Contributor at NASDAQ, February 22, 2022, NASDAQ

■ Quote 4.1.2 Enhancing Information Flow and Improving Efficiency

» ...developed and liquid stock markets are expected to play a key role by aggregating information about economic activity and firms' fundamentals; information that in turn might be useful for firms' managers, capital providers and regulatory authorities. In this sense, stock prices are expected to improve efficiency by directing capital towards more productive uses. (Alvaro Pedraza 2015).

Alvaro Pedraza, Research Economist, February 24, 2015, The World Bank

Banner 4.4 Information Role of Stock Markets
Stock markets allow for the availability of vital information for performing company analysis and valuation, thereby helping decision-making and improving performance.

4.4.1.3 Information Role of Stock Markets

Let us use two concepts, market value and book value, to explain the role of stock markets in information dissemination. According to Firth (1977), stock markets facilitate security valuation in which properly valued stocks signal the allocation of scarce capital. For example, let us compare the Coca-Cola Company's book value and market value in ▶ Exhibit 4.3.3. The fact that the book value (US$5.73 per share) is less that the market value (US$60.10 per share) implies a positive market perception about the company. That is, the market believes that the company's fundamentals are strong—hence, they are willing to invest as they expect more value in the future. This perception becomes a motivation for the company for efficient resource allocation toward improving performance and creating more value. Similarly, reflecting on ▶ Quotes 4.1.1, a stock analyst uses the company's fundamentals relative to stock market information to guide investor decisions with the question, "Will you buy the stock?" Moreover, the following news headlines are among many others, which highlight the information role of stock markets—that is, stock prices reflect the available information:

1. Tesla stock up as it plans for a stock split vote to pay stock dividend: *By Niloofer Shaikh, SA News Editor (Seeking Alpha, March 28, 2022)*
2. Top Wall Street analysts see long-term upside in these stocks even amid investor uncertainty: *By Brock Ladenheim, Tiranks.com (CNBC, March 27, 2022)*
3. Ahead of Market: 12 things that will decide stock action on Monday: *By Pawan Nahar, ETMarkets.com (The Economic Times, March 27, 2022)*

Overall, the information role of stock markets can be summarized as follows: Stock markets are viewed as stimulators of performance through efficient allocation of resources (see ▶ Quotes 4.1.2); in the absence of stock markets, investors would not have an easy access to information; market information influence stock pricing (see news headlines 1 and 2 above); and analysts rely on stock market information to guide investors (see news headline 3). Overall, stock market information plays vital roles in valuation and investment decisions.

4

Exhibit 4.3 Reflection of Securities in the Company Balance Sheet

Illustrative Example (See Excel Workings—▶ Chap. 4, Sheet E.4.3)

Exhibit 4.3.1 presents the balance sheet of the Coca-Cola Company. The focus is to reflect on the initial issuance of security by identifying the two major securities (debt and equity). Exhibit 4.3.2 reflects on secondary market activities, showing the varying nature of stock prices (market valuation). The book value of equity (balance sheet) is compared with the market value in Exhibit 4.3.3.

Exhibit 4.3.1 Balance sheet reflection of security markets
The Coca-Cola Company: Balance Sheet as of 31 December (US$ Millions)

	31 Dec 2021	31 Dec 2020
Current assets		
Cash and cash equivalents	9684	6795
Short-term investments	1242	1771
Total cash, cash equivalents, and short-term investments	10,926	8566
Marketable securities	1699	2348
Trade accounts receivable, less allowances of $516 and $526, respectively	3512	3144
Inventories	3414	3266
Prepaid expenses and other current assets	2994	1916
Total current assets	22,545	19,240
Equity method investments	17,598	19,273
Other investments	818	812
Other noncurrent assets	6731	6184
Deferred income tax assets	2129	2460
Property, plant, and equipment—net	9920	10,777
Trademarks with indefinite lives	14,465	10,395
Goodwill	19,363	17,506
Other intangible assets	785	649
Total assets	94,354	87,296
Current liabilities		
Accounts payable and accrued expenses	14,619	11,145
Loans and notes payable	3307	2183
Current maturities of long-term debt	1338	485

Exhibit 4.3.1 (continued)

	31 Dec 2021	31 Dec 2020
Accrued income taxes	686	788
Total current liabilities	19,950	14,601
Long-term debt	38,116	40,125
Other noncurrent liabilities	8607	9453
Deferred income tax liabilities	2821	1833
The Coca-Cola Company shareholders' equity		
Common stock—$0.25 par value; authorized—11,200 shares; issued—7040 shares	1760	1760
Capital surplus	18,116	17,601
Reinvested earnings	69,094	66,555
Accumulated other comprehensive income (loss)	−14,330	−14,601
Treasury stock, at cost—2715 and 2738 shares, respectively	−51,641	−52,016
Equity attributable to shareowners of the Coca-Cola Company	*22,999*	*19,299*
Equity attributable to noncontrolling interests	*1861*	*1985*
Total equity	24,860	21,284
Total liabilities and equity	94,354	87,296

Source: Coca-Cola reports (2022)

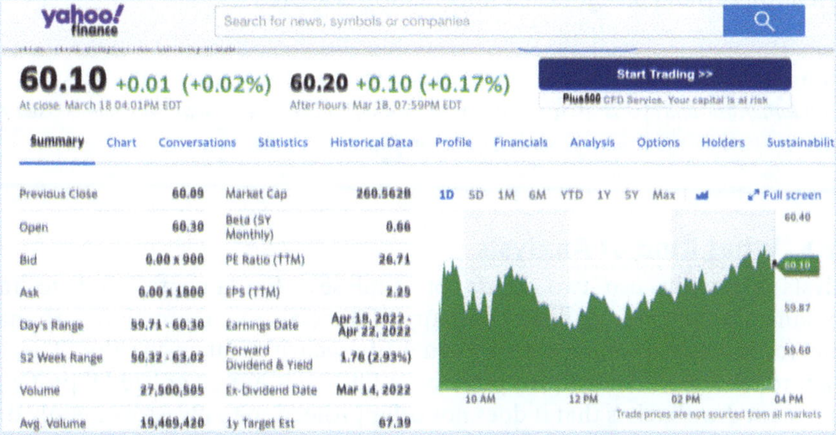

Exhibit 4.3.2 The Coca-Cola Company: stock trading information
Source: Yahoo Finance (2022)

Exhibit 4.3.3 The Coca-Cola Company: book value vs. market value

Information	Value
Market value as on 18 March 2022 (US$ millions)	60,562.00
Total equity in the balance sheet as on 31 Dec 2021 (US$ million)	24,860
Stock value per share as on 18 March 2022 (US$)	60.10
Book value per share as on 31 Dec 2021 (US$)	5.73

Notes: The number of common shares outstanding is 4335.47 million. The book value per share is determined by dividing the total equity by the number of common shares outstanding, that is, US$24,860 million/4335.47 million = US$5.72 per share

4

4.4.2 The Role of Stock Analysts

Stock analysts are market experts who follow companies, analyze their performance, estimate stock value, and publish their opinions for public use. They, therefore, play a vital role in investment decisions and risk management. According to Chugh and Meador (1984), stock analysts follow an extremely comprehensive evaluation process, which encompasses firm-specific factors and economic factors (qualitative and quantitative). Nevertheless, it is the information role of security markets that enables analysts' work—the markets provide vital information and data in various forms such as news, financial reports, company releases and briefings, investors opinions, etc. Probably, the most important feature of stock market information is the speed in which information is shared.

Banner 4.5 The Goal of Fundamental Analysis vs. Technical Analysis

Fundamental analysis is used to determine value, whereas technical analysis is used to identify patterns (trends) in security performance.

4.4.2.1 What Kind of Analysis

Analysts normally use two kinds of analyses—fundamental and technical. "Fundamental analysis" utilizes company's financials in conjunction with market factors (economy, sector, industry) to quantify security's intrinsic value. This analysis approach follows a complex process and hence is more applied by professionals. Its main drawback is that it does not offer protection to investors mainly due to its inability to anticipate future events, which are unrelated to company financials, leading to market volatility (risk). "Technical analysis," on the other hand, utilizes market information such as stock prices and trading volume. Its goal is not to determine value but to identify patterns that can be used to forecast the future. It, therefore, applies tools like moving average charts (long-term and short-term), which are easy to use. This approach is, therefore, more favored by nonprofessionals like individual investors and traders.

Think 4.2

If you were to choose between fundamental analysis and technical analysis, what would be your pick? Give reasons.

4.4.2.2 Why Are Analysts Important?

The primary goal of stock analysts is to provide "estimates." These estimates are forward-looking measures of performance on key indicators like earnings, growth, return on equity, and so on. They, therefore, set benchmarks against which companies' performance is interpreted—"beating estimates or failing estimates." A company that beats the estimates is viewed as a good performer, whereas a company failing estimates is viewed as a poor performer. Hence, analysts are like stock market "watchdogs" who give rating opinions on stocks such as "buy," "sell," or "hold" to signify that the stock is undervalued (buy), overvalued (sell), or undefined (hold). Specifically, analysts do the following:

1. "Give estimates" before companies announce their financial reports. Here, they rely on the company's guidance, economic conditions, and their own analysis.
2. "Participate or attend company press conferences" during the announcement of financial reports. These conferences, which discuss the reports, tend to reflect on the performance indicators in relation to the factors affecting them.
3. "Give opinions" after the announcement of financial results. Analysts communicate the results in conjunction with their expert opinions (interpretations): what are the reasons for beating or failing to beat the estimates?

Banner 4.6 The Role of Stock Analysts

The primary goal of stock analysts is to provide estimates, which form the basis of giving opinions about stock performance relative to the overall financial performance of a company.

4.4.2.3 Are Analysts Right?

There is no straightforward answer to this question—it depends on the analyst's objective of following a particular stock. Some analysts follow stocks on behalf of investors (buyers), whereas others do so on behalf of liquidators (sellers). A "buy-side" analyst tends to align with undervaluation, whereas a "sell-side" analyst tends to align with overvaluation, thereby influencing bullish and bearish expectations, respectively. Exhibit ► 4.4 shows an example of vital information normally presented by stock analysts. The Wall Street Journal (WSJ) depicts how different analysts rated and recommended Block Inc. (US: NYSE). From these facts, we can summarize the following key valuation implications:

1. Analysts' estimates, both individual and consensus, can deviate from actual results—for example, Q1 2021.
2. Analysts' estimates, both individual and consensus, can be somehow correct—for example, Q2 2021.
3. Analysts' estimates, both individual and consensus, can be correct—for example, Q3 and Q4 2021.
4. The fact that many analysts recommend a "buy," signifies that they are driven by bullish expectations—for example, 3 months (23 analysts), 1 month (29 analysts), and current (30 analysts), whereas only 2 analysts recommend a "sell" on the 3 coverages.
5. Valuation results are never precise—just estimates. Therefore, a range is always given (highest, mean, and lowest). For example, the price range is between $120 (lowest) and $240 (highest), whereas the median is $178.

Think 4.3

Why should analysts' estimates be either right or wrong? What does it imply when the estimates deviate from actuals?

To be right or wrong depends on the perspective of the analyst and sometimes conflict of interest. For example, some buy-side analysts (e.g., those working for investment banks or mutual funds) can have investment motives for companies they follow—they are likely to give a buy rating (before buying) and a sell rating (after buying). It is, therefore, better not to rely on one analyst. Instead, a comparison of several analysts, considering their performance records and understanding the companies they work for, should help determine a desirable rating. Some market institutions provide consensus information about stock ratings from several analysts. For example, let us consider the following description from NASDAQ Analyst Research.

> Nasdaq Analyst Research provides analyst research for ratings consensus and a summary of stock price targets. Analysts evaluate the stock's expected performance in a given time period based on their research and their own opinions. Analyst ratings can be used in addition to other personal research work prior to making investment decisions (NASDAQ, 23 March 2022).

Banner 4.7 Caution When Using Analyst Estimates

We can deduce three key aspects of how analysts' estimates should be used effectively: (1) ratings are based on two things—objectivity (research) and subjectivity (opinions), and (2) there can be a consensus, but (3) investment decisions should not rely only on analysts' ratings but also on one's own analysis.

Exhibit 4.4 Stock Analysts

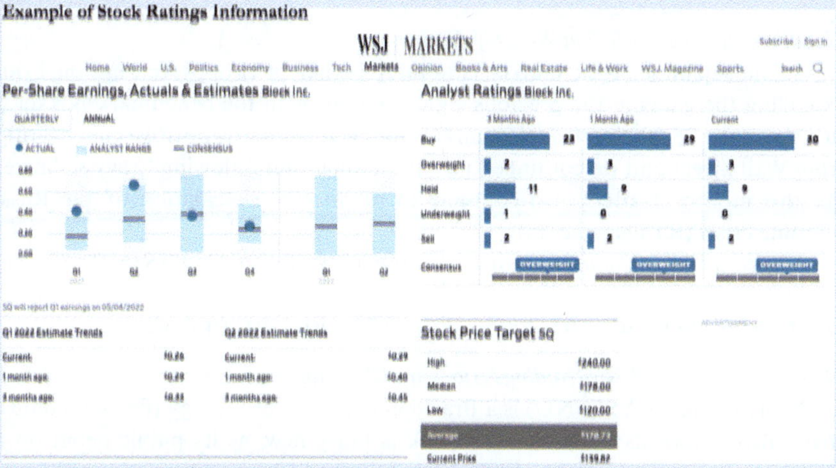

Example of stock rating information
Source: The Wall Street Journal (23 March 2022)

4.4.3 Determinants of Stock Prices

In primary markets, IPO prices are fixed following expert analysis of the company's financial condition and performance, considering other factors like comparable companies and economic condition. In secondary markets, however, the main determining factor of stock prices is market forces of supply and demand for the stocks, which influence trading (buying and selling). Trading transactions begin with the availability of stocks (supply) and the interest to buy those stocks (demand). Hence, stock prices move up and down from time to time. With other factors being constant, a low supply (demand) drives the price up (down), and vice versa.

Several factors influence the supply and demand of shares. An IPO increases supply, whereas share repurchase reduces supply. Investors, on the other hand, are the key drivers of demand. Depending on their investment motives and perceptions, investors' positive (negative) perceptions on companies will increase (decrease) the demand for the stocks. Notwithstanding, investors' influence on demand is associated with other factors. First, there are the company's internal factors, which are related to financial performance (fundamentals) and stock price performance (technical). Second, there are market factors, which cannot be controlled by the company such as economic growth, inflation, interest rates, etc.

Quotes 4.2 Determinants of Stock Market Prices

■ Quote 4.2.1 Market Linkages and Economic Factors

» *Headline: Japanese Market Notably Higher*

...The Japanese stock market is notably higher in choppy trading on Friday, extending the gains in the previous eight sessions, with the benchmark Nikkei 225 just above the 28,200 level, as the markets follow the broadly positive cues overnight from Wall Street and on continued upward momentum following heavy selling earlier this month. Traders also continue to monitor the escalation of the Russia-Ukraine crisis (RTTNews.com)

RTTNews.com, Contributor at NASDAQ, March 24, 2022, NASDAQ

■ Quote 4.2.2 Demand and Supply—Post-IPO Price Performance

» *Headline: Don't Call Nu Holdings Stock an IPO Flop Just Yet*

Nu Holdings (NYSE: NU) is a Brazilian financial technology (fintech) company that's also known as Nubank. NU stock is fairly new, as its public debut on the New York Stock Exchange took place late last year. IPO investing can be risky, and so can international investing. There's certainly no guarantee that the Nu Holdings share price will recover from its post-IPO slump. Yet, it's entirely possible that NU stock will just be a late bloomer. Sometimes, there's a delayed reaction as Wall Street can take a while to warm up to a newly listed company... Going back to the beginning, Nu Holdings established a price range of $10 to $11 per share, but then reduced the IPO range to $8 to $9 per share. Finally, NU stock commenced trading on the New York Stock Exchange on Dec. 9, 2021, at around $9. Likely due to the buildup of investor enthusiasm, the stock shot up right out of the gate, hitting $12.24 on Dec. 10. As that enthusiasm declined, so did the share price. By March of 2022, NU stock had collapsed to $6 before pushing back toward $8. (David Moadel 2022)

David Moadel, Contributor at NASDAQ, March 23, 2022, NASDAQ

■ Quote 4.2.3 Dividend and Stock Repurchase Policy

» *Headline: Two Reasons Why Devon Energy Stock Is Likely to Keep Rising This Year*

...Devon Energy (NYSE: DVN) was the best performing stock in the S&P 500 last year. This was because of its super generous dividend and buyback policy. DVN stock is on its way again this year. Year-to-date (YTD) it's up 37.63% as of March 22, at $66.63 per share. And now, with Devon's significantly higher buyback policy, there are two good reasons to believe it could move much higher: its dividends will likely rise, and its buybacks will push DVN stock higher. (Mark R. Hake, Investor Place)

Mark R. Hake, Contributor at NASDAQ, March 23, 2022, NASDAQ

The reality of these factors can be reflected from the selected news headlines in Quotes ▶ 4.2 –for example, the following factors can be noted: the influence of US markets on Japanese markets; the effect of the Russia–Ukraine war (▶ Quote 4.2.1); risk factors (IPO risks and international risks), investor perceptions, expectations, and demand (▶ Quote 4.2.2); and company internal factors—dividend and stock repurchase policy (▶ Quotes 4.2.3). These are just few among many other factors.

Apply 4.1 Determinants of Stock Market Prices
Search for any four news articles, which report on the stock performance of any company or companies. Generally, the news articles will highlight the factors influencing the current performance of stocks, i.e., company factors or market factors or both. The four articles should focus on four different companies either separately or collectively. From the articles, answer the following questions:
(a) Identify and list a company's specific factors affecting its stock price performance.
(b) Identify and list the market factors effecting the stock price performance of the company or entire market.
(c) Based on your views, explain how the factors listed in (a) and (b) affect stock prices.
(d) Give your views about the possible valuation implications of those factors and your explanations in (c).

4.5 Bond Markets

Bond markets (also known as debt markets, fixed income markets, or credit markets) allow participants to raise capital and invest through primary markets (new issue of bonds) and secondary markets (bond trading). Although there are many types of bond instruments, this chapter focuses on the role of corporate bonds and government bonds due to their application in corporate valuation. Specific emphasis is placed on bond pricing, yields, and credit ratings.

▪ Primary Markets: Initial Issuance of Bonds

Like stocks, the new issue of bonds intends to raise large amount of funds. Let us see the following typical example of issue statement from Ecopetrol's bond issuance prospectus:

> We expect the net proceeds from the sale of the notes will be approximately US$1,978,040,000 (after giving effect to underwriting discounts but before expenses). We intend to use the net proceeds for general corporate purposes, including but not limited to financing our investment plan in the 2020–2021 period (Ecopetrol's Bond Prospectus Supplement for 6.875% due 2030).

Thus, the bond issuer is a borrower, whereas the buyer is an investor—the process that creates interest obligations (for the issuer) and interest income (for the investor). In the issuer's balance sheet, bonds are incorporated within other debts like bank loans. For example, the Coca-Cola Company is an issuer of several corporate bonds (see ◘ Exhibit 4.5.1). Hence, the long-term debt appearing in its balance sheet (◘ Exhibit 4.3.1) comprises bonds, among other debts.

Banner 4.8 The Value of Initial Bond Issuance
The value of initial bond issuance is determined by a fixed issue price and the number bonds to be issued, and it is reflected in the company's balance sheet among other debts.

Exhibit ▶ 4.5 shows some information relating to bond issuance and trading. Typically, the most relevant information for new bond issuance include face value, coupon rate, issue date, maturity date, and issue price.

4

Exhibit 4.5 The Key Features of a Bond

Illustrative Example (See Excel Workings—▶ Chap. 4, Sheet E.4.5)
▫ Exhibit 4.5.1 presents key information from selected corporate bonds, followed by the definitions of each term. ▫ Exhibit 4.5.2 depicts the varying nature of bond prices in secondary markets.

▫ **Exhibit 4.5.1** Example of corporate bond variables

Key variables	Coca-Cola	Coca-Cola	Apple Inc.	Exxon	Ecopetrol
Coupon rate	3.2%	2.900%	3.0%	0.789%	6.875%
Installments per year	2	2	2	4	2
Face value	$1,000	$1,000	$1,000	$1,000	$1,000
Issue date	01 Nov 2013	25 May 2017	20 Jun 2017	20 Jun 2017	29 Apr 2020
Maturity date	01 Nov 2023	25 May 2027	20 Jun 207	20 Jun 207	29 Apr 2030
Issue price (%)	100	99.60	99.77	100	99.11
Issue price	$1,000	$996	$997.7	$1,000	$991.1
Issue price status	Par	Discount	Discount	Par	Discount
Market price (%)	107.16	99.3	100.55	99.54	106.25
Market price	$1,071.6	$993	$1,005.5	$995.4	$1,062.5
Market Price status	Premium	Discount	Premium	Discount	Premium

Source: Business Market Insider (1 April 2022)

Definition of Bond Variables
Face Value

This value, which is also known as par value, indicates what the bond is worth on maturity date. It is the value the bondholder (investors) will receive from the issuer (borrower). Face value is also used to determine the interest payments (coupons), and they are always in monetary denominations such as \$100, \$1000, \$5000, and \$10,000. It should be noted that face value is not the price of a bond—i.e., it is not what an investor pays for the bond.

Issue Price and Market Price

"Issue price" is the quoted fixed price of a bond—the amount to be paid for the bond on new issuance. For example, in ◘ Exhibit 4.5.1, issue prices were quoted on respective issue dates.

"Market price" is the trading price quoted in secondary markets, which fluctuates throughout its life in response to several variables, including interest rates and time to maturity. In ◘ Exhibit 4.5.1, for example, market prices were quoted on the trading day of 1 April 2022. ◘ Exhibit 4.5.2 shows an example of bond price fluctuations for the Coca-Cola Company.

It should be noted that bond prices tend to be quoted as a percentage of face value to enable comparability among different bonds with different denominations. They can be less than the face value (at discount), greater than the face value (at premium), or equal to the face value (at par).

Coupon Rate

Coupon interest rate is the percentage rate, which determines installment payments on a bond depending on the face value. For example, in ◘ Exhibit 4.5.1, if the coupon rate for Coca-Cola is 3.2% and the face value is \$1000, then the annual interest payment is \$32 (i.e., \$16 for each of the two installments annually).

In most cases, the coupon interest rate is fixed throughout the life of the bond. However, some coupons can be floating with a benchmark index such as the money market index (e.g., LIBOR (London Interbank Offered Rate) or Euribor) or inflation (price index).

Some bonds do not have coupons and are known as "zero-coupon bonds."

Issue Date and Maturity Date

"Issue date" is the date at which the new issue of the bond is made, whereas "maturity date" is the final payment date of the bond. The number of years from the issue date to the maturity date is referred to as "term," "tenor," or "maturity." For example, in ▸ Exhibit 4.5.1, the maturity of the 6.875% Ecopetrol's bond is 10 years.

Yield

The term "yield" refers to the rate of return received from investing in the bond—it is an opportunity cost of investment. The yield can be described as "current yield" or "yield to maturity."

"Current yield" is simply the annual return on a bond, which is determined by dividing the annual coupon payment by the current market price.

"Yield to maturity" is the internal rate of a return on a bond held to maturity—it equates the price of the bond to the present value of future payments (face value and interest). It is, therefore, the annual return on the bond if held to maturity, considering when it is bought and the price paid for it.

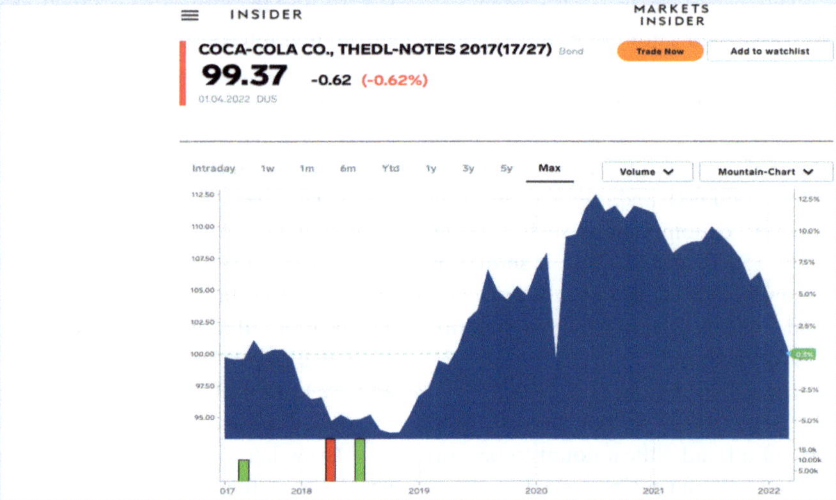

Exhibit 4.5.2 Example of the bond price chart—The Coca-Cola Company
Source: Business Market Insider (1 April 2022)

Secondary Markets: Bond Trading

Some bonds are listed for trading in secondary markets, e.g., stocks, thus creating investment opportunities through trading. While some bonds trade publicly in exchanges, others trade over-the-counter (OTC) through brokerage and dealership networks. Here, the price of a bond becomes the "market price," thereby fluctuating over time. For example, in ▶ Exhibit 4.5.2, we see the bond price (Coca-Cola 2.90% coupon for 2027) fluctuating between discount and premium from the issue date to 1 April 2022. The role of secondary markets is explained further in the next section.

Banner 4.9 The Value of Bonds in Secondary Markets

The value of a bond in secondary markets varies from time to time depending on market forces of supply and demand.

4.5.1 The Role of Bond Markets

4.5.1.1 Government Bonds

Governments issue bonds to finance their spending, making them the world's largest bond market. According to the International Capital Market Association (ICMA), as of August 2020, the overall size of the global bond markets, in terms of US$ equivalent notional outstanding, was approximately $128.3 trillion. This volume comprised of $87.5 trillion SSA (Supranational, Sovereigns, and Agencies) bonds (68%) and $40.9 trillion corporate bonds (32%). In the SSA category, the sovereign bond market alone constituted $63.7 trillion (73%) (see ICMA 2020).

To understand the role of government bonds, the International Monetary Fund (IMF) (2001:2) highlights the following points:

» …Bond markets link issuers having long-term financing needs with investors willing to place funds in long-term, interest-bearing securities…

…A mature domestic bond market offers a wide range of opportunities for funding the government and the private sector, with the government bond market typically creating opportunities for other issuers...

…Government bonds are the backbone of most fixed-income securities markets in both developed and developing countries...

…They provide a benchmark yield curve and help establish the overall credit curve.

To emphasize the role of government bonds, Quotes ▶ 4.3. presents some selected news contents, reflecting on the effect of the Russia–Ukraine War of 2022. Clearly, government bonds signal to almost all economic sectors in terms of current performance and the future. That is, economic variables and activities tend to adjust to news about government bonds.

Quotes 4.3 The Role of Government Bonds

▪ Quote 4.3.1 US Market—Signal Economic Conditions

» *Headline: Treasury yields invert, traders weigh U.S. recession risk*

The bond market on Monday continued to flash warning signs that the U.S. economy could be headed for a recession after U.S. Treasury yields inverted again (Samantha Subin & Vicky McKeever, Contributors at CNBC)

Samantha Subin and Vicky McKeever, April 4, 2022, CNBC

▪ Quote 4.3.2 Indian Market—Domestic Reaction to International Markets

» *Headline: Bond market has already priced in lot of inflation, rate hikes, says RBL Bank's Anand Bagri*

Yields on 10-year US bonds—a global benchmark for debt—have surged a massive 69 basis points over a month. Bond prices and yields move inversely. By contrast, India's 10-year benchmark yield has climbed only seven basis points, primarily because the market was spared any central government bond supply. While inflation risks at home are seen driving up Indian sovereign borrowing costs, the market has already priced in a lot of the risk… (Anand Bagri, RBL Bank's Head of Domestic Markets)

Bhaskar Dutta, April 4, 2022, The Economic Times

Quote 4.3.3 Global Markets—Effect on Investment Decisions

» *Headline: Bond markets in historic downturn as central banks battle inflation*

Global bond markets have suffered their deepest downturn since at least 1990 as investors brace themselves for rapid rises in interest rates from central banks that are battling the highest inflation in decades. (Tommy Stubbington & George Steer, Financial Times)

Tommy Stubbington and George Steer, March 23, 2022, Financial Times

Quote 4.3.4 Emerging Markets—Reflection on Monetary Policy and Investment Decisions

» *Headline: Here's how traders are betting on emerging market debt*

Traders of emerging-market debt have a new challenge: predicting which central banks will be first to stop rate rises, and then buying bonds from those countries. While that might sound premature to investors digesting the Federal Reserve's first interest-rate increase since 2018, Latin America has emerged as the front-runner in this high-stakes game after nations in the region began aggressive tightening about a year ago. Brazil indicated a rise in May would probably be its last after boosting rates almost 10 percentage points in 13 months. And central banks in Chile and Colombia raised borrowing costs last month by less than economists forecast.

Bloomberg, March April 11, 2022, The National News

Quote 4.3.5 Flight to Safety

» *Headline: How to Endure the Big Decline in Bonds*

It's been a horrible start of the year for the bond market, the worst in decades. If you hold bonds in a mutual fund or exchange-traded fund, it's highly likely that your quarterly statement next month will show that you have lost money. ...Does it make sense to hold bonds if they are losing money? It may be painful to hold bonds now, but there are good reasons to do so, especially Treasuries. Mr. Page, who is the author of the book 'Beyond Diversification: What Every Investor Needs to Know About Asset Allocation,' said Treasuries are safe and provide insurance when stocks and other investments fall. 'The expected return on bonds is low and they aren't providing all of the benefits of diversification that they have in the past, but they will, I think, continue to deliver in a crisis, when you get an extreme flight to safety.' (Jeff Sommer, Analyst at The New York Times)

Jeff Sommer, Analyst, April 1, 2022, The New York Times

Think 4.4

From Quotes ▶ 4.3, *discuss the following questions: (a) what was (were) the main factor(s) influencing the international bond market in March–April 2022? (b) Why should investors and policymakers be concerned about the situation in bond markets during that period?*

4.5.1.2 Corporate Bonds

Corporate bonds are issued and traded domestically and internationally. Statistics from the ICMA (2020) show that, in terms of the country of incorporation, as of 2020, the US corporate bond market was dominant ($10.9 trillion), followed by China ($7.4 trillion). These two countries had a 45% share of the total global corporate bond market. Financial institutions alone had 53% ($21.5 trillion) of outstanding global corporate bonds. These facts can be used to justify the following roles of corporate bonds:

1. Corporate bonds allow companies to raise money. A corporate bond is issued by a company to raise money without necessarily borrowing from banks or issuing additional stocks. According to Mizen and Tsoukas (2014), the Asian Crisis of 1997–8 has taught us a lesson on the danger of relying solely on bank credits.
2. Investors in bond markets gain fixed returns (income). Unlike stocks (where dividends are not compulsory), returns from bonds are always fixed. Although corporate bonds carry a higher risk than government bonds, they tend to offer more attractive yields. For example, in April 2022, one of the Coca-Cola Company's bonds (for 2024) had a yield of 2.76% compared to the highest yield on US treasuries (2.55% on the 5-year note).
3. Companies with corporate bonds are susceptible to credit ratings. This enables companies to be ranked for quality and risk by credit rating agencies.

In addition, Quotes ▶ 4.4 show the reality of the role of corporate bonds.

Quotes 4.4 The Role of Corporate Bonds

- **Quote 4.4.1 Source of Business Funding, Investment, and Job Creation**

» *Headline: Why corporate bonds are important*

Corporate bonds can be an important source of funding for European companies, which can use the proceeds from bond sales to invest in growth and job creation. They offer businesses access to alternative, more diverse sources of funding. They also offer new investment opportunities for European savers.

European Commission (2022)

- **Quote 4.4.2 Alternative to Bank Loans—Reflection on the Asian Crisis of 1997–8**

» *Headline: Why corporate bonds are important*

The presence of an active and efficient domestic capital market, in particular, the bond market, would give corporations an alternative means of raising debt capital in the event that banks were unable to do so, thus ameliorating any potential adverse effect that a bank-credit crunch may have on the economy.

The Emerging Markets Committee of the International Organization of Securities Commissions (2002)

4.5.2 Bond Pricing

As mentioned earlier, bond market prices vary from time to time due to market forces of supply and demand. However, factors such as interest rates (yield to maturity), coupons, and maturity can be used to determine the fair price. Mathematically, it can be presented as follows:

$$P_B = \sum_{t=1}^{n} \left[\frac{c}{(1+i)^t} \right] + \frac{M}{(1+i)^n}$$

where P_B is the market price of the bond, i denotes the rate of return (yield or interest rate), t is the payment period from now to maturity, c is the coupon payment in the nth installment, and M is the face value (principal). Alternatively, the general pricing formula for a coupon bond is as follows:

$$P_B = c \times \frac{(1-(1+i)^{-n}}{i} + \frac{M}{(1+i)^n}$$

where n denotes the number of installment payments to maturity. The price of a zero-coupon bond can, therefore, be calculated as follows:

$$P_B = \frac{M}{(1+i)^t}$$

The price, therefore, reflects the value of expected cash flows on the bond (coupon and principal), considering the opportunity cost of investment (interest rate). The proxy for general interest rates is usually determined by governments (official interest rates or government bond yields). An example is illustrated in Exhibit ▶ 4.6.

Exhibit 4.6 Determinants of Bond Price

Illustrative Example (See Excel Workings—▶ Chap. 4, Sheet E.4.6)

A corporate bond was issued last year with a face value of $1,000 and offered a 3.2% coupon to be paid semi-annually. The interest rate was 3.2%. The bond's maturity is 5 years. Show how the bond price will be affected by changes in the interest rates under the following conditions:

(a) If today, the interest rates fall to 2.2%

(b) If today, the interest rates rise to 4.2%

Solution

The number of payments to maturity equals years to maturity multiplied by the payment frequency per year. Interest rate per payment installment equals annual interest rate divided by number of installments per year. The price of a bond is calculated by discounting the expected future cash flows (coupon and face value) using the following formula:

$$P_B = \sum_{t=1}^{n}\left[\frac{c}{(1+i)^t}\right] + \frac{M}{(1+i)^n} = c \times \frac{(1-(1+i)^{-n}}{i} + \frac{P}{(1+i)^n}$$

$$P_B\,(Last\ Year) = \$16 \times \frac{(1-(1+1.6\%)^{-10}}{1.6\%} + \frac{\$1,000}{(1+1.6\%)^{10}} = \$1,000$$

The following table summarizes the data and calculation results.

	Falling interest rates from 3.2% to 2.2%		Increasing interest rates from 3.2% to 4.2%	
Key facts	**Last year**	**Today**	**Last year**	**Today**
Coupon rate	3.20%	3.20%	3.20%	3.20%
Annual installments	2	2	2	2
Interest rates	3.20%	2.20%	3.20%	4.20%
Face value ($)	1000.00	1000.00	1000.00	1000.00
Time to maturity (years)	5	4	5	4
Price ($)	1000.00	1,038.09	1000.00	963.53
Yield to maturity	3.20%	2.20%	3.20%	4.20%
Price status	Par	Premium	Par	Discount

Observations:

1. The bond that was issued a year ago still pays the same coupon today (it is an old bond).
2. The fall in interest rates today (from 3.2% to 2.2%) makes the bond more valuable than new bonds (at par) paying just a 2% coupon rate. Today, an investor who sells the 3.2% bond before maturity is likely to gain a higher price than it was a year ago. Higher prices imply lower yield to maturity of the bond for investors who buy the old bond at the new higher price. Hence, "lower interest rates lead to higher bond prices and lower bond yields."
3. The rise in interest rates today (from 3.2% to 4.2%) makes the bond less valuable than new bonds (at par) paying a higher coupon of 4.2%. Today, an investor who sells the 3.2% bond before maturity is competing with new bonds (at par) offering a higher coupon rate 4.2%. The old bond is likely to be less attractive, causing a fall in price. Hence, higher "interest rates lead to lower bond prices and higher bond yields."

4.5.3 Bond Pricing and Risk Factors

Bonds, like any other financial securities, are susceptible to different types of risks. Here, we explain the three major risks—interest rate risk, inflation risk, and credit risk.

4.5.3.1 Interest Rate Risk

Considering fixed interest bonds, changes in the prevailing interest rates are reflected in bond pricing as follows (refer to Exhibit ▶ 4.6):

1. A fall in interest rates will make the existing bonds more valuable. This is because they have higher coupons as they were previously sold in a higher interest rate environment. The price of older bonds should, therefore, increase because investors can respond to falling interest rates by charging a "premium."
2. A rise in interest rates will make the existing bonds less valuable. This is because they have lower coupons as they were previously sold in a lower interest rate environment. The price of older bonds should, therefore, fall because they should be trading at a "discount."

Banner 4.10 Bond Sensitivity to Interest Rates

Bond prices and interest rates are inversely proportional. With other factors being constant, an increase (decrease) in interest rates is associated with a decrease (increase) in bond prices. The magnitude of sensitivity, however, depends on the coupon size and time to maturity.

As defined in Exhibit ▶ 4.5, the actual return on a bond held to maturity is the yield to maturity. Bond yields tend to move in the same direction as interest rates. The higher the yield, the lower the price, and vice versa. Therefore, on a short-term basis, bond values should increase with falling interest rates and decrease with rising interest rates. Nevertheless, in the long term, rising interest rates can boost returns on a bond portfolio because the money from the maturing bonds is reinvested in bonds with higher yields. In contrast, the long-term returns can potentially hurt by the falling interest rates because the money from the maturing bonds may be reinvested in new bonds that pay lower rates. Bond price sensitivity to changes in interest rates is the phenomenon known as interest rate risk.

Quotes 4.5 Determinants of Bond Price

- **Quote 4.5.1 European Markets: Bond Yields and Interest Rates**

» *Headline: Euro zone bond yields soar as rate hikes bets jump on hawkish ECB*

Euro zone government bonds yields soared on Thursday as money markets rushed to price in more than four rate hikes from the ECB this year as President Christine Lagarde chose not to repeat her past comment that a 2022 rate hike was very unlikely.

Yoruk Bahceli and Dhara Ranasinghe, February 3, 2022, Reuters

▪ Quote 4.5.2 Global Markets: The Long-Term Bullish Bond Market Reverses

» *Headline: Why the Bond Market Turned Bearish After a Decades-Long Bull Run*

For decades, the bond market was mostly a one-way street: Prices kept going up as borrowing rates went lower, even sending yields negative in some places. But now the opposite is happening. Bond returns are falling the most on record as yields surge. Investors are scrambling to sort through the impact of the inflation that's come in the pandemic's wake, questions about how fast central banks will do to growth

Greg Ritchie and Olivia Cherry, April 3, 2022, Bloomberg

▪ Quote 4.5.3 US Market: Inflation, Yield, and Price

» *Headline: Treasury yields rise slightly following lighter than expected inflation data*

U.S. Treasury yields were slightly higher on Tuesday after wholesale inflation data came in lighter than expected. The yield on the benchmark 10-year Treasury note moved 1 basis point higher to 2.149%. The yield on the 30-year Treasury bond added less than a basis point to reach 2.489%. Yields move inversely to prices and 1 basis point is equal to 0.01%

Tanaya Macheel and Vicky McKeever, March 15, 2022, CNBC

Although several factors influence the interest rate risk, its effect on a bond depends on two factors relating to the bond itself—maturity and coupon rate.

The coupon effect: With other factors being equal (e.g., maturity and bond quality), a rise in the interest rate will generally cause a greater price decline in bonds with lower coupon rates. That is, bonds with lower coupon rates tend to have a higher interest rate risk than do similar bonds offering higher coupon rates. For example, consider two different bonds, one with a 2.2% coupon and the other with a 4.2% coupon. Other factors being constant, the rise in the interest rate will cause more decline in the price of the 2.2% coupon bond than the 4.2% coupon bond.

The maturity effect: Maturity affects bond sensitivity to interest rates. With other factors being equal (e.g., coupon and bond quality), the price of a bond with longer maturity will be more sensitive to changes in interest rates than a similar bond with shorter maturity. Therefore, coupon rate considers a risk premium for maturity—that is, the longer the maturity, the higher the coupon, and vice versa.

Exhibit ▶ 4.7 summarizes the relationship between interest rates and bond prices, considering both old and new bonds. The theoretical factors affecting bond pricing are available in the literature (e.g., Malkiel 1962; Bremmer and Kesselring 1992; Barber 2022) as well as some empirical evidence from several studies (e.g., Barber 2010; Luo et al. 2016, among others). The reality of this phenomenon can also be reflected from the news headlines in Quotes ▶ 4.5.

4

Exhibit 4.7 Interest Rate Risk

Change in interest rates	Response in bond markets	
	Old bonds	**New bonds**
Rising rates	Lower interest rate than new bonds	Higher interest rate than old bonds
	The coupon becomes lower	The coupon become higher
	The bond becomes less attractive	The bond becomes more attractive
	Falling price	High price
	Trade at discount	Trade at premium
Falling rates	Higher interest rate than new bonds	Lower interest rate than old bonds
	The coupon becomes higher	The coupon becomes lower
	The bond becomes more attractive	The bond becomes less attractive
	Increasing price	Low price
	Trading at premium	Trading at discount

4.5.3.2 Inflation Risk

Inflation, which is simply the general rise in the prices of goods and services, causes a decline in purchasing power. Its effect on bond value is, therefore, on the cash flows (coupon and principal)—inflation reduces the purchasing power of investment income from bonds. For investors holding bonds, therefore, the increase in inflation risk is a big concern because it forces yields up and values down. A good example is evident from ▶ Quote 4.5.3. Moreover, Jeff Sommer (New York Times) uses the following phrase to describe the effect of inflation on bond markets:

> Hammered by high inflation and the start of interest rate increases by the Federal Reserve and other central banks, the bond market is having a horrendous year—producing painful losses on a scale last seen in the 1980s (New York Times, 25 March 2022).

Banner 4.11 Inflation Risk
Inflation reduces the purchasing power of investment income from bonds.

4.5.3.3 Credit Risk

Credit (or default) risk is the risk that the debt issuer will fail to fulfill (i.e., paying interest and principal), leading to default. The yield, therefore, is expected to incorporate a credit risk compensation for investors. Moreover, although credit risk is directly related to bonds, it basically affects stock investments too. This is because a company's default will also affect stock returns – that is, declining g stock value (capital gain) and/or inability to pay dividends (dividend yield). The next section explains credit risk ratings.

Banner 4.12 Credit Risk
Credit risk is the risk that the debt issuer will default.

4.5.4 Credit Risk and Credit Rating

Credit ratings use quantitative measures to estimate the ability of a government or a company to fulfill its financial obligations. In other words, credit ratings show the creditworthiness of an issuer or their possibility to default on a debt. Whereas there are several credit rating agencies globally, the market share is commanded by three independent agencies—Standard & Poor's (S&P), Moody's Investor Services (Moody's), and Fitch IBCA (Fitch).

The ideal rating scales (long-term) of the three rating agencies are presented in Exhibit 4.8.1. It is possible to make a comparison across different ratings regardless of lettering differences. For example, an Aa1 rating from Moody's is equivalent to an AA+ rating from S&P and Fitch. The qualities of the ratings are ranked between two extreme spectrums: the highest quality (top) and the lowest quality (bottom). Thus, the quality of a bond declines as you move from top to bottom of the scale. For example, the top ratings (Aaa and AAA) represent the highest credit quality (almost no default), whereas the bottom ratings (C and D) are regarded as junk (default). Information about the rating methodologies is available on the rating agencies' websites. It should be noted that credit ratings are subject to review from time to time to reflect the changing circumstances of the issuers and external factors affecting their creditworthiness. For example, Exhibit 4.8.2 shows the downgrading of Ensco and the reasons for the rating action.

Exhibit 4.8 Credit Ratings

Exhibit 4.8.1 Credit rating scales

Moody's	S&P	Fitch	Credit worthiness
Aaa	AAA	AAA	*Prime:* An obligor has EXTREMELY STRONG capacity to meet all financial commitments.
Aa1	AA+	AA+	*High Grade*: An obligor has VERY STRONG capacity to meet all financial commitments, differing from the highest-rated obligors only by a small degree.
Aa2	AA	AA	
Aa3	AA−	AA−	
A1	A+	A+	*Upper Medium Grade*: An obligor has STRONG capacity to meet all financial commitments but is somewhat more susceptible to the adverse effects of changes in circumstances and economic conditions than obligors in higher-rated categories.
A2	A	A	
A3	A−	A−	
Baa1	BBB+	BBB+	*Lower Medium Grade:* An obligor has ADEQUATE capacity to meet all financial commitments. However, adverse economic conditions or changing circumstances are more likely to lead to a weakened capacity of the obligor to meet all financial commitments.
Baa2	BBB	BBB	
Baa3	BBB−	BBB−	
Ba1	BB+	BB+	*Non-investment Grade (Speculative)*: An obligor is LESS VULNERABLE in the near term than other lower-rated obligors. However, this obligor faces major ongoing uncertainties and exposure to adverse business, financial, or economic conditions, which could lead to the obligor's inadequate capacity to meet all financial commitments.
Ba2	BB	BB	
Ba3	BB−	BB−	
B1	B+	B+	*Highly Speculative*: An obligor is MORE VULNERABLE than the obligors rated "BB," but this obligor currently has the capacity to meet all financial commitments. Adverse business, financial, or economic conditions will likely impair the obligor's capacity or willingness to meet all financial commitments.
B2	B	B	
B3	B−	B−	
Caa1	CCC+	CCC+	*Substantial Risks*: An obligor is CURRENTLY VULNERABLE and is dependent upon favorable business, financial, and economic conditions to meet all financial commitments.
Caa2	CCC	CCC	
Caa3	CCC−	CCC−	
Ca	CC	CC	*Extremely Speculative*: An obligor is CURRENTLY HIGHLY VULNERABLE.
	C	C	*Default Imminent*: An obligor is CURRENTLY HIGHLY VULNERABLE to nonpayment. This may be used where a bankruptcy petition has been filed.

Exhibit 4.8.1 Continued

Moody's	S&P	Fitch	Credit worthiness
C	RD	RD	*In Default*: An obligor has failed to meet one or more of the financial obligations (rated or unrated) when it became due.
	SD	D	
	D		

MOODY'S
INVESTORS SERVICE
Rating Action: Moody's downgrades Ensco to B2

Global Credit Research - 06 Oct 2017

Approximately $4.7 billion of rated debt affected

New York, October 06, 2017 -- Moody's Investors Service, ("Moody's") downgraded Ensco plc's (Ensco) Corporate Family Rating (CFR) to B2 from B1, Probability of Default Rating (PDR) to B2-PD from B1-PD and senior unsecured notes to B2 from B1. The Speculative Grade Liquidity Rating was affirmed at SGL-1. The rating outlook is negative. This concludes the rating review that was initiated on May 31, 2017.

"The downgrade reflects increased financial leverage and diminished liquidity cushion following the Atwood acquisition, the anticipated decline in earnings and cash flow from ongoing contract expirations, and the weak fundamentals of the offshore drilling industry," said Sajjad Alam, Moody's Senior Analyst. "Ensco's credit metrics will be pressured at least through 2018 despite maintaining good liquidity, a high-quality rig fleet and a diversified global exposure."

Exhibit 4.8.2 Rating review: example
Source: *Moody's (2017)*

It is important to understand that credit ratings are "opinions," as indicated in each of the following definitions by the three agencies:

» Fitch Ratings publishes credit ratings that are forward-looking opinions on the relative ability of an entity or obligation to meet financial commitments (Fitch 2022)

» Moody's long-term ratings are opinions of the relative credit risk of fixed-income obligations with an original maturity of one year or more (Moody's 2022)

» Credit ratings are forward looking opinions about an issuer's relative creditworthiness (S&P 2022)

Credit ratings, therefore, are vital for investment decisions and corporate valuation because they are forward-looking and standardized for consistency. In the words of S&P:

» …They provide a common and transparent global language for investors to form a view on and compare the relative likelihood of whether an issuer may repay its debts on time and in full (S&P 2022).

Apply 4.2 Determinants of Bond Prices
Search for corporate bond trading in secondary markets. The bonds should be categorized as follows: (1) two bonds must differ in terms of coupon and maturity and (2) two bonds must differ in terms of coupon but must have equal time to maturity. For each of the bonds, determine the following variables: par value, issue price, market price, coupon interest, coupon frequency, time to maturity, and credit rating. Also search for information about the prevailing market interest rate applicable for the bonds. Then, answer the following questions:

(a) Calculate the price of each of the selected bonds.
(b) Compare bonds in category (1), and explain how the bonds will be affected by any change in the interest rates.
(c) Compare bonds in category (2), and explain how the bonds will be affected by any change in the interest rates.
(d) Compare all the bonds and comment on the default probability of each bond.

4.6 Implications of Valuation in Stock and Bond Markets

Generally, security markets play vital roles in valuation in different ways. Generally, in their role as sources of capital and investment opportunities, they facilitate the estimation of key valuation variables like the cost of capital, valuation multiples, investment returns, risks, and so on. More importantly, security markets simplify the access to company information and valuation data.

Specifically, we can mention the following valuation variables to reflect on the role of security markets. The applications of these variables are found in the subsequent chapters of this book.

1. *Market Valuation*: Secondary markets, unlike primary markets, create valuation. Stocks and bonds trading in secondary markets facilitate a competitive pricing mechanism, which determines the security values depending on market forces.
2. *Cost of Capital*: The weighted average cost of capital is estimated using the market values of the respective sources of capital. Stock markets provide information about market capitalization (i.e., the market value of the equity portion in the capital structure). Bond markets help in estimating the market value of a debt. Moreover, the estimation of the cost of equity and the cost of debt relies on other market variables like risk-free rate, market return, beta, and so on. Refer to ▶ Chaps. 11–▶ 13.
3. *Cost of Equity*: The cost of equity can be estimated using the capital asset pricing model (CAPM) and/or dividend growth model (DGM). Stock markets provide vital information for estimating CAPM variables (market returns and beta) and DGM variables (dividend per share and stock market prices). Refer to ▶ Chaps. 12 and ▶ 13.
4. *Cost of Debt*: Both corporate and government bonds have implications in debt valuation in different ways. Corporate bond yields can be used to estimate the cost of debt using the yield to maturity approach. The default spread approach

uses government bond yields, adjusted for corporate default risk. Vulnerability in credit markets tends to affect credit ratings, which, in turn, effect valuation. Refer to ► Chap. 13.

5. *Risk-free Rate:* Bond markets enable the estimation of the risk-free rate, which is based on government bond yields. Moreover, credit ratings allow for adjustments for a specific country's risk, which should be accounted for in the risk-free rate. Refer to ► Chaps. 12 and ► 13.
6. *Investment Returns*: Investors in security markets expect returns on their investment portfolios. In stock investments, returns come from the appreciation of stock value (capital gain) and/or dividend yield. Stock markets provide information for determining the return variables (capital gain and dividend yield). Similarly, bond markets are vital for providing information about bond yields. Refer to ► Chaps. 12 and ► 13.
7. *Present Value of Growth Opportunities (PVGOs)*: Valuation uses the PVGOs to evaluate the growth potentials of the stock relative to a company's performance on earnings. Stock markets provide vital information for determining the PVGO variables (i.e., stock market price, earnings per share (EPS), and the cost of capital). See ► Chap. 18.
8. *Valuation Multiples*: Relative valuation relies on market information to determine valuation variables for multiples (e.g., price–earnings (P/E) ratio, enterprise value/earnings before interest, taxes, depreciation, and amortization (EV/EBITDA), etc.). Refer to ► Chaps. 19–► 22.
9. *Economic Value Added (EVA)*: Security markets enable the estimation of economic valued added (EVA), which basically compares investment-required returns with the actual returns generated by a company. Refer to ► Chap. 7.
10. *Credit Risk:* Corporate valuation considers credit risk in different ways. Government credit risk is applicable in CAPM to determine the risk-free rate (see ► Chap. 12). Corporate credit risk is vital for estimating some valuation variables like the cost of capital (see ► Chap. 13) and the probability of default (see ► Chap. 16). Moreover, relative valuation considers credit risk, among others, to define a company's peer group (see ► Chap. 19).
11. *Decision-making:* Valuation results (intrinsic value or relative value) are normally compared to market values to determine the market price of an asset – overvalued, undervalued, or fairly priced. This comparison is useful for decision-making among investors. Refer to ► Chaps. 15–► 22.

4.7 Types and Sources of Security Market Information

Information about security markets is vital not only for investment decisions but also for corporate valuation. For publicly trading securities, information and valuation data can be easily accessible from several sources (free and paid), thanks to the Internet and online technological tools. Nevertheless, it may be difficult to find information on most private companies. This section outlines the types of information generally required for valuation and their sources.

- **General Information**

The availability of security information has been simplified by different sources, which provide quality data in different forms such as historical, current, and forecasts. These sources include Yahoo Finance, investing.com, Reuters, CNN Money, Bloomberg, PCQuote.com, Fin Box, and SmartMoney.com, to mention a few. Overall, most of these sources provide valuable information such as security prices, yields, dividends, company profiles, security analysis, earnings, brokerage services, updated financial reports, etc.

- **Company Information**

Company information is the starting point for understanding the characteristics of the security to be valued. Such information include company profile, ownership, management and organizational structure, nature of products, industry segment, competitors, capital structure, security issuance, and so on.

Sources of Information: Respective companies' websites can be a starting point. Other sources include security exchange websites (e.g., Nikkei, NASDAQ, the Financial Times Stock Exchange (FTSE), etc.), general market websites (e.g., investing.com, Yahoo Finance, Wall Street Journal, Bloomberg, Morning Star, etc.), credit rating agencies (e.g., Moody's, Fitch, S&P, etc.), and market analysts following the company, among others.

- **Domestic Market Conditions**

This type of information relates to what is happening in a company's domicile country. It includes key economic variables like interest rates, economic growth, inflation, national income (gross domestic product (GDP)), monetary policies, taxation, and regulations, among others.

Sources of Information: This information is usually available from local newspapers (both hard and online) and economic reports from different agents such as central banks, news bulletins, journals, and domestic security exchanges. Moreover, some international organizations publish country-level data—for example, the World Bank, the International Monetary Fund (IMF), World Trade Organization (WTO), and so on.

- **International Market Conditions**

International market conditions (e.g., wars, international market performance, oil prices, economic crises, etc.) tend to affect domestic markets. For example, a surge in international oil prices is likely to influence domestic market inflation.

Sources of Information: Information about international markets tends to be presented in the form of news and market analysis. News provides qualitative reflections on the reality of security markets and stories behind quantitative information. There are many sources of market and company news at the international level. These include the most popular ones like Bloomberg, Financial Times (UK), Yahoo Finance, CNN Money, etc.

- **Industry Information**

Industry information is vital for valuation because it provides benchmarks for company performance. Key industry (sector) information include demand, supply, market share, earnings, growth, investment returns, risks, and so on.

Sources of Information: Information about the domestic industry can be found in domestic market reports, news, and security exchange websites. Internationally, this information can be available from international market indices (e.g., S&P 500 etc.)

- **Security Prices and Returns**

Security price information is one of the pillars of valuation. This type of information includes price quotes, historical data (stock prices, bond prices, market indices, dividend yields, and bond yields), and security returns.

Sources of Information: Almost all exchanges worldwide provide stock and bond price data (where applicable). A comprehensive list of international exchanges and their websites can be retrieved from Yahoo Finance. Some websites, are dedicated to bonds, for example investing.com, Investing in Bonds, World Government Bonds, among others.

- **Financial Reports**

Valuation relies much on financial information, which provide data about the historical performance of finances, investments, and operations. This type of information is presented in the balance sheet (financing and investing), income statement (operating), and cash flow statement (cash position).

Sources of Information: All public companies are required by law to publish their financial statements (annually and/or quarterly). This information is, therefore, public and should be available at most sources such as company websites, security exchanges, market websites, etc.

Review Questions

1. What is the primary role of security markets and why are they important?
2. What is the main difference between primary security markets and secondary markets?
3. Mention and define the key players in security markets. Explain their roles.
4. Explain how the initial offering of a stock is reflected in a company's financial statements.
5. Define the following terms as applicable in the balance sheet of a company:
   (a) Par value
   (b) Authorized shares
   (c) Issued shares
   (d) Share premium
   (e) Paid-in capital
6. What are the main advantages and disadvantages of listing stocks in secondary markets?
7. Explain the role of information in stock markets and its implication in valuation.

8. ABC company has just published its financial reports. The balance sheet shows the following information: paid-in capital $25 million, share premium $8 million, and total equity $40 million. The company has 4 million shares outstanding, currently trading at $1.5 per share. (a) What is the market perception about ABC company? (b) What performance does the market expect from the company?
9. XYZ company has just published its financial reports. The balance sheet shows the following information: paid-in capital $30 million, share premium $12 million, and total equity $50 million. The company has 2 million shares outstanding, currently trading at $2.2 per share. (a) What is the market perception about XYZ company? (b) What performance does the market expect from the company?
10. Based on information in questions 9 and 10, briefly explain the role of security markets.
11. Explain the difference between fundamental analysis and technical analysis.
12. Describe the main role of stock market analysis.
13. Explain how investors should make effective use of stock analysts' estimates.
14. Explain the main determinants of stock market prices under the following categories:
    (a) Company's internal factors
    (b) Market factors
15. Mention and explain the main factors influencing the supply and demand for stocks.
16. Explain how bond prices are determined in primary markets and secondary markets.
17. Define the following terms related to bonds:
    (a) Face value
    (b) Coupon interest
    (c) Yield to maturity
    (d) Current yield
    (e) Maturity
    (f) Issue price
    (g) Market price
    (h) Zero-coupon bond
18. Explain why bond prices tend to be quoted in percentage?
19. In bond pricing, what is the meaning of the terms "par," "premium," and "discount?"
20. A 5-year corporate bond has a face value of $1,000 and a coupon interest rate of 5.2% to be paid semiannually. This bond was issued a year ago at the price of 102%, and it is currently trading at 99% (refer to Excel workings—▶ Chap. 4, Sheet R20).
    (a) How many payments will the bond make to its maturity? How much to be paid in each installment?
    (b) In dollar terms, what is the issue price and market price?
    (c) Considering its current trading price, state whether the market interest rate should be greater or less than the coupon interest. Explain why.

(d) Calculate the bond price on issue date if the market interest rate is 6.0%. Show whether the bond price is at par, premium, or discount.
(e) Calculate the bond price today if the market interest rate has fallen to 5.2%. Show whether the bond price is at par, premium, or discount. How does the fall in interest rate affect investors?
(f) Calculate the bond price today if the market interest has risen to 7.0%. Show whether the bond price is at par, premium, or discount. How does the rise in interest rate affect investors?

2. Mention and explain the factors determining the fair price of a bond.
3. Explain the effect of interest rates on bond prices under the following situations:
   (a) Bond A whose coupon rate is less than the interest rate versus bond B whose coupon rate is greater than the interest rate
   (b) Bond A with a maturity of 5 years versus bond B with a maturity of 20 years.
4. What is credit risk and why is it important in investment decisions and valuation?
5. Explain the relationship between interest rates and inflation and how they affect bond yield and value.

Bibliography

Bahceli, Y. & Ranasinghe, D. (2022). Euro zone bond yields soar as rate hikes bets jump on hawkish ECB, Available at Reuters, https://www.reuters.com/world/europe/euro-zone-bond-yields-soar-rate-hikes-bets-jump-hawkish-ecb-2022-02-03/ Accessed February 3, 2022.

Barber, J.R. (2010). A General Relationship between Prices of Bonds and their Yields, *Quarterly Journal of Finance and Accounting,* 49(3/4), 75–85. http://www.jstor.org/stable/23074631

Barber, J.R. (2022). Power law bond price and yield approximation, *The journal of risk finance,* 23 (1), 14-31. doi: https://doi.org/10.1108/JRF-10-2020-0217

Bloomberg (2022). Here's how traders are betting on emerging market debt, Available at National News, https://www.thenationalnews.com/business/markets/2022/04/12/heres-how-traders-are-betting-on-emerging-market-debt/ Accessed April 11, 2022.

Bremmer, D. & Kesselring, R. (1992). The Relationship Between Interest Rates and Bond Prices: A complete proof, *American Economist*, 36 (1), 85, pg. 85-86. https://www.proquest.com/scholarly-journals/relationship-between-interest-rates-bond-prices/docview/200684196/se-2?accountid=41515

Lal C. Chugh, & Meador, J. W. (1984). The Stock Valuation Process: The Analysts' View. *Financial Analysts Journal,* 40(6), 41–48. http://www.jstor.org/stable/4478786

Dutta, B. (2022). Bond market has already priced in lot of inflation, rate hikes, says RBL Bank's Anand Bagri. Available at Economic Times, https://economictimes.indiatimes.com/markets/expert-view/bond-market-has-already-priced-in-lot-of-inflation-rate-hikes-says-rbl-banks-anand-bagri/articleshow/90633564.cms Accessed April 4, 2022.

EMCIOSC (2002) The Development of Corporate Bond Markets In Emerging Market Countries, (EMCIOSC) The Emerging Markets Committee of the International Organization of Securities Commissions, May 2002. https://www.iosco.org/library/pubdocs/pdf/IOSCOPD127.pdf

Firth M. (1977) The Role of the Stock Market. In: The Valuation of Shares and the Efficient-Markets Theory. Studies in Finance and Accounting. Palgrave, London. doi: https://doi.org/10.1007/978-1-349-15819-5_1

Fitch (2022), Rating Definitions, Available at https://www.fitchratings.com/products/rating-definitions, Accessed on May 16th 2022.

Hake, M. (2022). Two Reasons Why Devon Energy Stock Is Likely to Keep Rising This Year, Available at Nasdaq, https://www.nasdaq.com/articles/two-reasons-why-devon-energy-stock-is-likely-to-keep-rising-this-year Accessed March 23, 2022.

ICMA (2020). Bond Market Size, International Capital Market Association, August 2020, https://www.icmagroup.org/market-practice-and-regulatory-policy/secondary-markets/bond-market-size/

IMF (2001), Developing Government Bond Markets, The World Bank, https://doi.org/10.5089/9780821349557.069

Ladenheim, B. (2022). Top Wall Street analysts see long-term upside in these stocks even amid investor uncertainty. Available at CNBC, https://www.cnbc.com/2022/03/27/top-analysts-say-buy-stocks-like-nike-nividia.html. Accessed March 27, 2022.

Luo, J., Ye, X., & Hu, M. (2016). Counter-Credit-Risk Yield Spreads: A Puzzle in China's Corporate Bond Market. *International Review of Finance*, 16(2), 203-241. https://doi.org/10.1111/irfi.12079

Macheel, T. & McKeever, V. (2022). Treasury yields rise slightly following lighter than expected inflation data. Available at CNBC, https://www.cnbc.com/2022/03/15/us-bonds-treasury-yields-fall-with-focus-on-russia-ukraine.html. Accessed March 15, 2022.

Malkiel, B. G. (1962). Expectations, Bond Prices and the Term Structure of Interest Rates, *Quarterly Journal Economics*, 76(2), 197-218. https://doi.org/10.2307/1880816

Market Insider (2022), Bonds, https://markets.businessinsider.com/bonds Accessed April 1, 2022.

Mizen, P., & Tsoukas, S., (2014), What promotes greater use of the corporate bond market? A study of the issuance behaviour of firms in Asia *Oxford Economic Papers,* 66 (1), 227–253, https://doi.org/10.1093/oep/gpt005

Moadel, D. (2022). Don't Call Nu Holdings Stock an IPO Flop Just Yet, Available at Nasdaq, https://www.nasdaq.com/articles/dont-call-nu-holdings-stock-an-ipo-flop-just-yet Accessed March 23, 2022.

Moody's (2017), Moodys Downgrades Ensco to B2, Moody's Global Credit Research, 6th October, 2017. https://www.moodys.com/research/Moodys-doMoody's%20Global%20Credit%20Research,%206th%20October,%202017wngrades-Enscos-senior-unsecured-notes-to-B3-affirms-B2--PR_377875?cy=arg&lang=es-ar Accessed May 14th 2022.

Moody's (2022), Rating Scale and Definitions, Available at https://www.moodys.com/sites/products/productattachments/ap075378_1_1408_ki.pdf Accessed May 14th 2022.

Nahar, P. (2022). Ahead of Market: 12 things that will decide stock action on Monday. Available at Economic Times, https://economictimes.indiatimes.com/markets/stocks/news/ahead-of-market-12-things-that-will-decide-stock-action-on-monday/articleshow/90475929.cms Accessed March 27, 2022.

Nasdaq (2022). Analyst Research. Available at https://www.nasdaq.com/market-activity/quotes/analyst-research Accessed March 23, 2022.

New York Times (2022), Bad Tidings From the Bond Market, Available at nytimes.com https://www.nytimes.com/2022/03/25/business/bond-market-inflation-recession.html Accessed March 25, 2022.

Pedraza, A. (2015). The informational role of stock prices, Available at The World Bank Blogs, https://blogs.worldbank.org/allaboutfinance/informational-role-stock-prices Accessed February 24, 2015.

Phillip, J. (2022). Best Stocks To Invest In 2022? 4 Consumer Staples Stocks to Watch. Available at Nasdaq, https://www.nasdaq.com/articles/best-stocks-to-invest-in-2022-4-consumer-staples-stocks-to-watch Accessed February 12, 2022.

Ritchie, G. & Cherry, O. (2022). Why the Bond Market Turned Bearish After a Decades-Long Bull Run, Available at Bloomberg, https://www.bloombergquint.com/quicktakes/why-a-decades-long-bond-bull-market-turned-so-bearish-quicktake Accessed April 3, 2022.

RTT News (2022). Japanese Market Notably Higher. Available at Nasdaq, https://www.nasdaq.com/articles/japanese-market-notably-higher-1 Accessed March 24, 2022.

S&P (2022), Intro to credit ratings, Available at https://www.spglobal.com/ratings/en/about/intro-to-credit-ratings Accessed May 14th 2022.

Shaikh, N. (2022). Tesla stock up as it plans for a stock split vote to pay stock dividend, Available at Seeking Alpha, https://seekingalpha.com/news/3817875-tesla-stock-up-as-it-plans-for-a-stock-split-vote-in-the-form-of-a-stock-dividend Accessed March 28, 2022.
Sommer, J. (2022). How to Endure the Big Decline in Bonds, Available at The New York Times, https://www.nytimes.com/2022/04/01/business/bond-market-decline.html Accessed April 1, 2022.
Stubbington, T. & Steer, G. (2022). Bond markets in historic downturn as central banks battle inflation. Available at Financial Times, https://www.ft.com/content/40237918-8153-4ade-af3d-f4f1de724de8 Accessed March 23, 2022.
Subin, S. & McKeever, V. (2022). Treasury yields invert, traders weigh U.S. recession risk. Available at CNBC, https://www.cnbc.com/2022/04/04/us-bonds-treasury-yields-invert-ahead-of-fed-minutes.html Accessed April 4, 2022.
WSJ (2022). WSJ Markets, Available at Wall Street Journal, https://www.wsj.com/market-data/quotes/SQ/research-ratings Accessed March 23, 2022.

Financial Information as a Source of Valuation Inputs

Contents

An Overview of Financial Information

Contents

Supplementary Information The online version contains supplementary material available at https://doi.org/10.1007/978-3-031-28267-6_5.

B. Kulwizira Lukanima, *Corporate Valuation*, Classroom Companion: Business, https://doi.org/10.1007/978-3-031-28267-6_5

5.1 Introduction

Financial information is essential for several corporate aspects like performance analysis and decision-making. In addition, it is a source of vital inputs required in all valuation models. For instance, some valuation models utilize free cash flows to estimate the intrinsic value. Likewise, relative valuation models utilize financial metrics like earnings, book value of equity, dividends, and so on. Therefore, knowledge about financial information and its application in valuation is essential for any valuation expert. Indeed, each component of financial information conveys a message about the condition of a firm such as its financial strength, risks taken, growth prospects, and so on.

This chapter, therefore, aims at acquainting readers with the type and nature of financial information. Such information covers a firm's financial position (the balance sheet), the state of its operations (the income statement), and the flow of cash (the cash flow statement).

Learning Outcomes

- Explain the existence of a business and its reflection in financial statements
- Understand the flow of a company's financial resources and how it is reported in financial statements
- Explain the nature of information in the different types of financial statements
- Explain information linkages between the income statement, the balance sheet, and the cash flow statement
- Understand the use of financial information and its implication in valuation

Banner 5.1 Financial Statements and the Flow of Resources
Financial statements summarize information about the flow of financial resources in a company, considering the linkages to the economy (i.e., capital markets, customers, suppliers, government, etc.)

5.2 The Existence of a Firm and the Flow of Financial Resources

Financial information signifies the existence of a firm, beginning with injection of funds in the form of capital (refer to ▶ Chap. 4 for the role of security markets) for a return (refer to ▶ Chap. 11 for cost of capital). Therefore, the flow of financial resources and the reporting of financial information are inseparable—they commence immediately with the establishment of a firm. Exhibit ▶ 5.1 depicts the interactive nature of information flow in financial statements.

The subsequent sections illustrate and explain the items of a financial statement and their implication in valuation, considering the following three aspects:

1. The state of financial position

2. The state of operations
3. The state of cash flows

Exhibit 5.1 The Interactive Nature of Financial Information

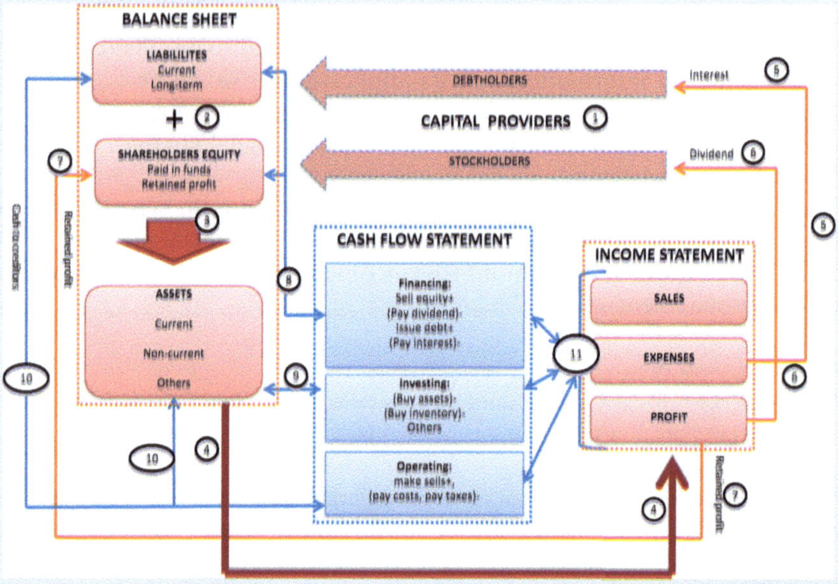

Notes:

1. *Balance Sheet*: Financial resources (capital) are injected into businesses by investors, i.e., stockholders (owners), debtholders (lenders), or both.

   Financial resources from different sources are presented in the balance sheet as liabilities (funds owed to external providers) and shareholders' equity (funds belonging to owners). Long-term liabilities represent resources obtained for long-term obligations (e.g., long-term loans, bonds, etc.), whereas current liabilities represent resources obtained for short-term use (e.g., credit purchases, accruals, etc.).

   Shareholders' equity includes profits obtained from business operations (the income statement). The connection between a balance sheet (equity) and an income statement (profit) reflects the role of operational performance in growth—earnings can improve growth if reinvested to generate more returns.

   Capital resources from both external providers and internal sources are invested, including acquiring assets (long- and short-term investments).

2. *Balance Sheet/Income Statement*: The efficient use of assets is reflected in business operations through generating income (profits).

3. *Income Statement*: In capital markets, investors expect returns. A firm has the obligation to pay interest to the debtholders. This is a financing expense.

   In capital markets, investors expect returns. Depending on the company's dividend policy, part of the profits can be plowed back to investors in the form of dividends. It should be noted that a dividend is not regarded as an expense—it is the use of profit.

   Another part of the profit is retained as an internal source of capital, which increases owners' equity.

4. Cash Flow Statemen: The flow of cash for business financing (the balance sheet) is reported in the cash flow statement.

   The flow of cash for investments (the balance sheet) is reported in the cash flow statement.

   The flow of cash for operating activities (the income statement) is reported in the cash flow statement.

   Cash expenses are categorized according to their nature: operating expenses, financing expenses, and investment expenses.

Think 5.1

1. What makes a balance sheet different from an income statement?
2. Why do the balance sheet and income statement recognize both noncash items and cash items?
3. Why is a cash flow statement important?

Banner 5.2 Capital Funds and Valuation Implications
The flow of resources in a firm starts with the injection of funds (capital). This aspect is reflected while estimating the cost of capital, which is a vital input in intrinsic valuation.

5.3 The State of Financial Position

This type of information is provided by a statement of financial position, commonly known as the "balance sheet"—it shows the financial health of a firm "as at" a certain financial reporting period. ▶ Exhibit 5.2 shows an illustrative example: "FAIDA Ltd statement of financial position as at 31 December 2011." The phrase "as at" is important because it shows the cumulative nature of balance sheet information—that is, the financial position of a company from the time of its establishment.

Basically, a balance sheet presents the flow of financial resources relating to financing ("where does the capital come from?") and investing ("how do we use the capital to acquire business resources?"). Therefore, the "sources of finance" (liabilities and equity) must equal the "financial resources" (assets) and can be presented as follows:

$$\text{Assets} = \text{Liabilities} + \text{Equity}$$

Banner 5.3 The Nature of Information in a Balance Sheet
A balance sheet reports the cumulative state of financial position "as at" a reporting period.

Items in a balance sheet tend to be listed in a particular order. In ▶ Exhibit 5.2, the listing order is based on generally accepted accounting principles (GAAP), which are used here to explain the balance sheet. It should be noted, however, that other different reporting orders also exist.

5

Exhibit 5.2 Information About the Financial Position

Example

FAIDA Ltd statement of financial position as at 31 December

	2012 ($ millions)	2011 ($ millions)	Change ($ millions)
Assets			
Cash and cash equivalents	119	113	+6
Accounts receivable	420	435	−15
Inventory	700	636	+64
Prepaid expenses	10	10	0
Accumulated tax prepaid	15	12	+3
Total current assets	*1264*	*1206*	*+58*
Investments (long-term)	60	50	+10
Property, plant, and equipment	1200	1020	+180
Less accumulated depreciation	369	310	+59
Net property, plant, and equipment	*831*	*710*	*+121*
Other assets (long-term)	213	223	−10
Total noncurrent assets	*1104*	*983*	*+121*
Total assets	**2368**	**2189**	**+179**
Liabilities and equity			
Accounts payable	100	114	−14
Notes payable	304	299	+5

	2012 ($ millions)	2011 ($ millions)	Change ($ millions)
Accrued tax	36	24	+12
Other accruals	100	100	0
Total current liabilities	540	537	+3
Long-term debt	630	523	+107
Shareholders' equity			
Preferred stock	749	749	0
Common stock ($100/par)	210	210	0
Retained earnings	239	170	+69
Total equity	1198	1129	+69
Total liabilities and equity	**2368**	**2189**	**+179**

Notes: The "Change" column shows how each of the balance sheet line item changed in one financial year. This column is solely presented for illustration purposes: firms are not obliged to present this in their reporting of financial statements. In this example, the net change on both sides of the balance sheet equation is $179 million: that is, the difference between $2368 (2012) and $2189 (2011). The increase in assets is equal to the increase in liabilities and equity

5.3.1 Items Relating to Business Financing

As illustrated in ► Exhibit 5.1, a business starts with capital injection. The major sources of long-term financing are usually equity (owners) and debt (nonowners) (refer to ► Chap. 4 for the role of capital markets), borrowing (debt finance), or both. Now, let us use ► Exhibit 5.2 to understand the type of information in the financing section and the order of presentation.

5.3.1.1 Long-term Debt

A long-term debt includes loans and capital lease obligations, with maturities of more than a year. Therefore, the use of a long-term debt creates a "long-term liability" to the firm. For example, FAIDA Ltd had a long-term debt of $523 million in 2011 and $630 million in 2012, showing an increase of $107 million. Essentially, a debt creates a financial obligation to repay it along with the interest therein. Interest expenses are reported in the statement of income (see ► Exhibits 5.1 and 5.5).

5.3.1.2 Equity

Depending on the company, the two categories of equity are preferred equity and common equity. "Preferred stockholders" do not have ownership status. Hence, they have fixed claims on dividends—the firm is obliged to pay them dividends. In contrast, "common shareholders" hold the ownership status. Hence, they do not obligation have fixed claims on dividends—they can be paid based only upon the discretion of the firm. For example, FAIDA Ltd's equity comprised of common equity worth $210 million and preferred stock worth $749 million, which were unchanged between 2011 and 2012. The total equity also included retained earnings. This is an additional book value created from business operations and reported in the income statement. The cumulative earnings created as at 31 December 2012 was US$239 million—an increase of $69 million from $170 million in 2011. Therefore, the common stockholders' equity (or net worth) was $380 million in 2011 and $449 million as of 2012.

Short-term financing arises from current liabilities. For FAIDA Ltd, the current liabilities ($537 in 2011 and $540 in 2012) indicate that the company acquired some of its short-term resources through notes payable (short-term debt), accounts payable (such as credit purchases of merchandises), accrued tax (from unpaid or deferred taxes), and other accruals (which may include interest, salaries, and bills). Usually, the company has an obligation to fulfill its short-term financial obligations within one financial year.

Banner 5.4 Liabilities and Equity

Liabilities and equity represent information about how a firm finances its businesses. The order of reporting liabilities and equity follows the payment priority from top to bottom.

5.3.1.3 The Order of Listing

The order of reporting liabilities and equity follows the priority of payment—that is, starting with items that should be paid first. For example, FAIDA Ltd may have obligations to its suppliers (accounts payable) due within 30 days; short-term loans (notes payable) due within 3 months; the government (accrued tax) within 3 months; and bondholders (long-term debt) due between 1 year and 15 years. Equity holders are the final claimants. This aspect is depicted in ▶ Exhibit 5.3.

Exhibit 5.3 Balance Sheet Components: The Order of Listing Liabilities and Equity

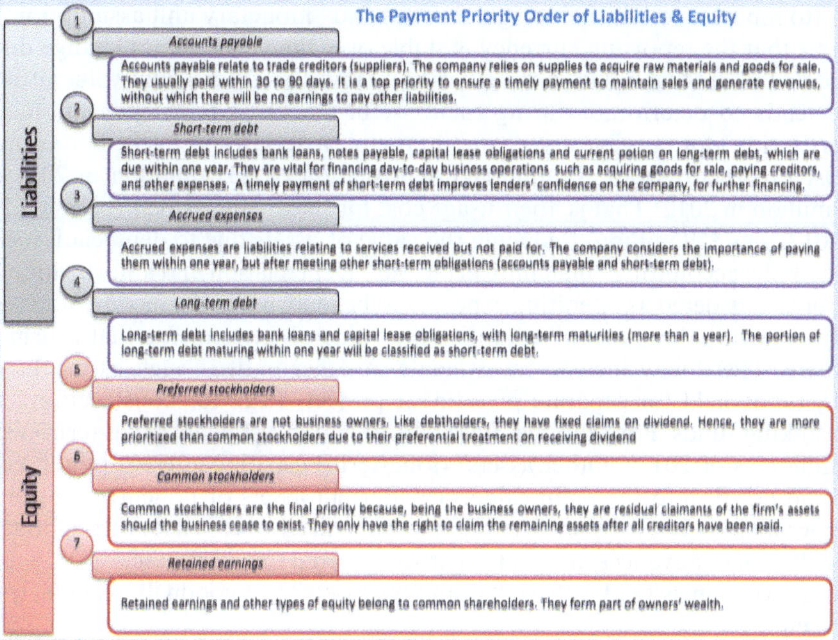

Think 5.2

Why is it important to list equity and liabilities in the order of payment priority?

5.3.2 Items Relating to Acquisition of Business Resources

As illustrated in ▶ Exhibit 5.1, equity and liabilities are financial resources required for financing investments (tangible assets and other investments). Investments, therefore, have future economic values measured in monetary terms. ▶ Exhibit 5.2 shows the business resources in the asset section, which are explained below.

5.3.2.1 Noncurrent Assets

Noncurrent assets are intended for long-term use (more than one financial year). Depending on the company and nature of business, assets include investments in other companies, "tangible" assets acquired by the firm (e.g., property, plant, and equipment), "intangible" assets (e.g., goodwill, patents, and trademarks), and other assets (those not included in the investments, fixed, or intangible asset categories).

"Property, plant, and equipment" are reported by the historical cost of acquiring them. For example, in FAIDA Ltd, the book value of property, plant, and equipment was $1020 million in 2011 and $1200 million in 2012. This means, additional assets were acquired between 2011 and 2012 at $180 million. The reporting of original cost is to comply with two accounting aspects, namely, “the cost principle” (to report assets at their original costs) and “monetary unit assumption” (to presume that the reporting currency is stable over time and cannot change due to economic factors like inflation or deflation). However, the original value of some assets tends to deteriorate during their useful life—that is, “depreciation” and “amortization” for tangible assets and intangible assets, respectively. For example, FAIDA Ltd reported an accumulated depreciation of $310 million in 2011 and $369 million in 2012. That is, their usage cost for one financial year (between 2011 and 2012) was $59 million. Reducing the value of assets due to depreciation complies with the accounting “matching principle.” Depreciation and amortization are, therefore, considered as operating expenses to be reported in the income statement.

“Investments (long-term)” comprise the value of investments that a firm has elsewhere. These may include investments in other entities such as stocks and bonds, funds held for separate investment projects (e.g., for construction), and bond sinking funds. For example, FAIDA Ltd had investments (long-term) worth $60 million as of 2012. “Other assets” (long-term) usually represent minor assets, which do not fit into the main categories (current assets or noncurrent assets)—examples include bond issue costs that are amortized to expenses throughout the life of the bond, advances, prepaid expenses, differed tax assets, etc.

Some companies tend to have “intangible assets” like goodwill, patents, trademarks, etc.

5.3.2.2 Current Assets

Current assets are intended for short-term use. They represent financial resources that can be converted into cash within one financial year. Sometimes, certain current assets can be reported at values less than their historical cost. For instance, to comply with the “matching principle,” accounts receivable can be reported at a lower value if the firm has doubts about some debtors. For example, in 2012, FAIDA Ltd had $420 million in accounts receivable. If the company had anticipated collecting only $400 million, then doubtful debtors worth $20 would have been reported as a “provision for doubtful receivables.” Any receivables deemed uncollectable can be written off and treated as “bad debtors’ expense” in the income statement. Similarly, the “conservatism principle” may force inventories to be reported at a lower cost. Usually, this happens after the process of inventory valuation. For example, FAIDA Ltd reported inventories at $700 million in 2012. If, however, the cost of these inventories had dropped (say by $50 million), then the company would have reported only $650 million to reflect the current cost of the inventories after valuation.

Banner 5.5 Assets

Assets represent information about the financial resources owned by a firm. The order of listing asset items depends on their ability to be easily converted into cash.

5.3.2.3 The Order of Listing

Assets are usually reported in the order of their liquidity—starting with the most liquid assets (those that can be easily converted into cash at a fair market value). ► Exhibit 5.4 explains the liquid nature of assets.

Exhibit 5.4 Balance Sheet Components: The Order of Listing Assets

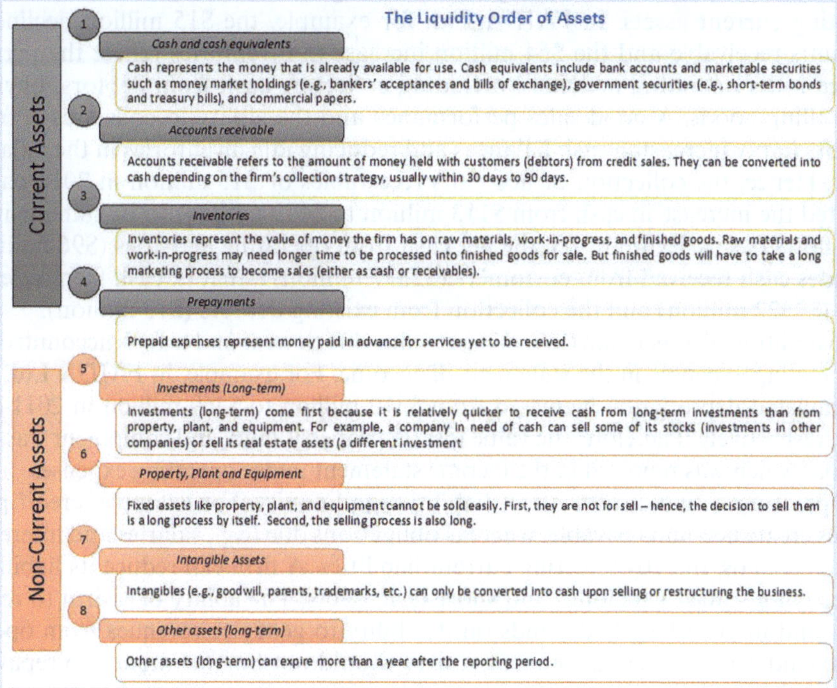

Think 5.3

Why is it important to list assets in the order of liquidity?

5.3.3 Changes in the Financial Position

From the original historical cost, each of the balance sheet items (assets, liabilities, and equity) can change (increase or decrease) over time. A change, therefore, is a quick historical performance indicator. Overall, a positive change in total assets (or total liabilities and equity) signifies growth, whereas a negative change signifies deterioration. For example, FAIDA Ltd grew from \$2189 million in 2011 to \$2368 million in 2012. The financial performance is a result of several factors, which explain the overall performance of the firm: that is, performance in its operating activities, financing activities, and investment activities.

5.3.3.1 How Does Operating Performance Affect the Financial Position?

There are several ways in which core business operations affect a firm's financial position. As depicted in ▶ Exhibit 5.1, operating activities affect balance sheet items. For instance, operating activities include sales, purchase of inventories, and paying bills. Therefore, business operations create accounts receivable (from credit sales) and inventories (from the purchases of goods or raw materials), thereby affecting current assets. In FAIDA Ltd, for example, the $15 million decline in accounts receivable and the $64 million increase in inventories reflect the performance in its operating activities, including collecting cash from debtors, buying, and selling goods. A good sales performance and the ability to collect cash from debtors imply increasing cash balances and reducing idle inventories in the balance sheet. Hence, the collection of accounts receivables of $15 million in 2012 partly affected the increase in cash from $113 million to $119 million. In its statement of cash flows (see ▶ Exhibit 5.7), the net cash from operating activities ($96 million) includes cash received from customers ($2337 million)—that is, cash from sales in 2012 ($2322 million) and the collection from existing debtors ($15 million).

In addition, depreciation (loss of asset value due to wear and tear) is accounted for as operating expenses in the statement of income. For example, in FAIDA Ltd, the accumulated depreciation increased from $310 million to $369 million in 2011 and 2012, respectively. Therefore, the value lost on property, land, and equipment was $59 million, which was reported in the income statement under operating expenses.

Operating activities also affect liabilities and equity. For example, credit purchases create accounts payable, whereas obligations due (e.g., salaries and interests) create accruals, thereby affecting current liabilities. A firm can reduce its liabilities by repaying some of its long- and short-term debts. The ability of a firm to repay debts and interest largely depends on its ability to generate revenues from operations. Under normal circumstances, a firm should not borrow money to repay its current debts. Regarding equity, operating performance affects the amount of retained earnings (i.e., from profits), which, in turn, can increase or decrease owner's equity. In FAIDA Ltd, profits from business operations increased total equity by $69 million between 2011 and 2012.

5.3.3.2 How Does Financing Performance Affect the Financial Position?

Financing activities relate to capital structure decisions and short-term financing. An increase (decrease) in liabilities can result from an increase in borrowing (repaying debts). For example, the long-term debt of FAIDA Ltd increased from $523 million in 2011 to $630 million in 2012. The borrowed amount of $107 million might have been used to fund additional long-term capital investments. Similarly, a change in equity arises from issuing new shares or repurchasing of shares. In our FAIDA Ltd example, there was no change in common stocks and preferred stocks. However, obtaining debts or attracting new investors partly depend on investors' perception about the financial health of a firm. An attractive history of the ability to fulfill financial obligations and generating investment returns will create a positive perception about the company.

5.3.3.3 How Does Investing Performance Affect the Financial Position?

Investment activities can either increase or reduce an asset's value. Either way, they will affect the overall financial position in different ways. For example, FAIDA Ltd increased its capital investment by $179 million in 2012, which included $180 million in property, plant, and equipment and $10 million in other investments.

Banner 5.6 Change in the Financial Position
The overall performance of a firm is extremely important for strengthening its financial position. Hence, changes in the financial position reflect performance in all business activities—operating, financing, and investing.

5.4 The State of Business Operations

The state of business operations is about how a firm generates revenues from its core business activities, which is summarized in the income statement. Unlike the balance sheet, the income statement reports the operating performance "for" the reporting period—that is, a change in wealth only during that specific period. For example, "FAIDA Ltd statement of income for the year ended 31 December 2012."

Exhibit 5.5 Information About the State of Business Operations

Example

FAIDA Ltd statement of income for the year ended 31 December

	2012 ($ millions)
Sales/revenues	2322
Cost of goods sold	1680
Gross income	642
Operating expenses	425
Operating income	217
Interest expenses	65
Income before tax	152
Income tax	61
Net income	**91**
Cash dividends	*22*
Retained earnings	*69*

Exhibit 5.6 Income Statement Components: The Order of Listing

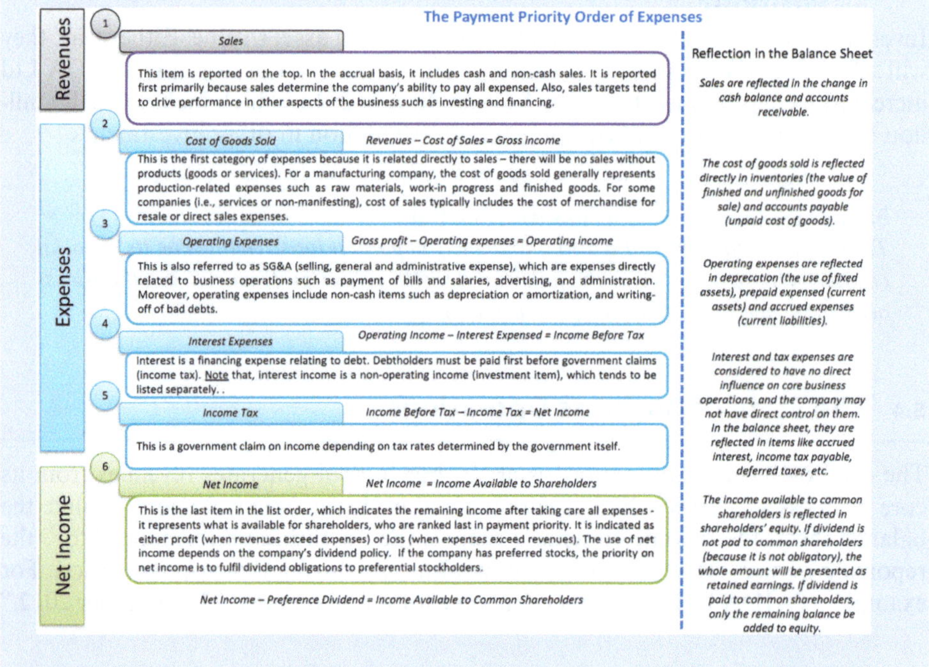

5.4.1 Income Statement Components

The main components of an income statement are "revenues" and "expenses," and the product is profit (also referred to as "income" or "earnings"). Therefore, the following general equation is applicable.

$$\text{Revenues} - \text{Expenses} = \text{Net income}$$

▶ Exhibit 5.5 shows an example of income statement items. A comprehensive income statement can show more details than this. ▶ Exhibit 5.6 clarifies the order of listing of income statement items, in which expenses are listed in the order of payment priority.

Banner 5.7 Nature of Information in an Income Statement

In an income statement, the word "for" indicates a change in a firm's wealth within a single operating period and not cumulatively. Expenses are listed in the order of payment priority.

Think 5.4
Why is it important to list expenses in the order of payment priority?

5.5 The State of Cash Flow

In accrual basis of accounting, several items are recognized and reported in the statement of income and in the balance sheet even if no cash has been received or paid. The statement of cash flows, therefore, addresses the movement of cash. It addresses several issues that the balance sheet and the statement of income fail to address such as the source and use of cash as well as adjustments for noncash items. Let us reflect on the following items from the income statement and the balance sheet.

5.5.1 Noncash Items in an Income Statement

In an income statement, the calculation of profit includes noncash items. Therefore, profit is generally not a measure of cash generated from operating activities. The following are examples of noncash items in an income statement.

(a) Usually, "sales" is accounted for when goods are delivered to customers as cash is rarely received immediately. Instead, credit sales creates debtors—it is reported in the balance sheet to show an increase in "accounts receivable."
(b) "Operating expenses" are not necessarily accounted for when cash is actually paid. When a firm buys merchandises, the cost of goods is always accounted for when the goods are received because immediate payments are not always made. Moreover, services (like bills, advertisements, wages, etc.) are recognized before they are paid for. Instead, a liability is created and reported in the balance sheet as "accounts payable" and "accrued expenses."
(c) "Depreciation" or amortization is accounted for in expenses, but they are noncash items. In the balance sheet, it reflects the loss of asset value over their useful life—"accumulate depreciation."
(d) "Bad debts" are accounted for as expenses, but they do not constitute any cash outflow. They simply reflect the writing-off of doubtful debtors, thereby reducing "accounts receivables" without cash being received.

5.5.2 Noncash Items in a Balance Sheet

Similarly, values in a balance sheet do not necessarily mean cash value. Let us look at the following examples:

(a) A balance sheet shows cumulative values of "capital expenditure" (such as property, plant, and equipment) and "current assets" (e.g., inventories) but no indication of the amount and source of "cash" (not money) spent on those assets in the reported period. Some of these assets might have been obtained on loan arrangements (e.g., hire purchase, capital lease, credit purchase, etc.). Indeed, a balance sheet does not indicate how much of its asset funding comes from internal sources (retained earnings) or external sources (debt or equity).

(b) The cumulative "debt" value neither tells the amount of cash received (additional debt) nor the amount of cash paid (reduced debt) for the reported period.
(c) "Dividend" payments move cash out of business, but they are neither considered in the income statement nor in the balance sheet.

The above points explain the importance of a cash flow statement. It is noteworthy that intrinsic valuation uses cash as a measure of value and not profit. Cash position is a key factor in determining a company's ability to finance some investments to support growth; otherwise, it should borrow or issue stocks. Moreover, cash position is a good indicator of a firm's liquidity and its ability to meet its financial obligations such as paying debts, paying bills and salaries, developing new products, and so on. A cash flow statement, therefore, shows cash inflows and outflows and indicates a change in the firm's cash position "for" the reported financial period. For example, "FAIDA Ltd statement of cash flows for the year ended 31 December 2011" (see ▶ Exhibit 5.7).

A statement of cash flows is divided into three major categories according to the major business activities, namely, operating activities, investment activities, and financing activities. In ▶ Exhibit 5.7 is an example of a cash flow statement, in which we use FAIDA Ltd to explain its components.

Banner 5.8 The Cash Flow Statement
A statement of cash flows summarizes cash inflows and outflows and indicates a change in a firm's cash position "for" the reported financial period.

5.5.3 Cash from Operating Activities

In ◘ Exhibits 5.7.1 and 5.7.2, cash from operating activities is presented using both a "direct approach" and an "indirect approach," respectively. Let us use FAIDA Ltd to explain items included in a cash flow statement.

5.5.3.1 Direct Reporting

(a) "Cash received from customers" includes net sales of $2322 million (from the income statement) and an additional $15 million received from debtors (a decrease of accounts receivable in the balance sheet).
(b) "Cash paid to suppliers" includes the following: $1680 million of the cost of goods sold (from the income statement), plus $64 million increase in inventory (from the balance sheet), plus the $14 million decrease in accounts payable (from the balance sheet). This means that FAIDA Ltd spent $1744 million to buy inventories in 2012 and $14 million to settle liabilities relating to suppliers from the previous period.

"Cash paid for operating expenses" includes $425 million spent on operating expenses (from the income statement), minus adjustment for noncash charges ($59 million on depreciation).

(c) "Tax paid" includes $61 million relating to the 2012 tax obligation (from the income statement) and $3 million tax paid in advance (increase in accumulated tax prepaid in the balance sheet).
(d) "Interest paid" in 2012 is $65 million (from the income statement), and this implies that cash moved out of the business.
(e) "Accrued tax" ($12 million) is a result of an increase in accrued tax from $24 million in 2011 to $36 million in 2012. This implies that cash remained in the company.

5.5.3.2 Indirect Reporting

(i) A "net income" of $91 million (from the income statement) includes both cash and noncash items from revenues and all expenses for 2012.
(ii) "Depreciation" ($59 million) is added to the net income to adjust for noncash charges—it was deducted as an expense in the calculation of net income.
(iii) On "accounts receivable," the $15 million decrease shows the amount of cash received from debtors in 2012.
(iv) On "inventories," the increase of $64 shows the cash amount that the company paid to its suppliers in 2012.
(v) Accumulated "tax prepaid" increased by $3 million (from the balance sheet). This is the amount of cash paid on tax advances in 2012.
(vi) "Accrued tax" ($12 million) is a result of an increase in accrued tax from $24 million in 2011 to $36 million in 2012. This implies that cash remained in the company.
(vii) On "accounts payable," $14 million is the amount of cash paid to suppliers in 2012. It is a decrease in accounts payable in the balance sheet from $114 million as of 2011 to $100 million as of 2012.

5.5.3.3 Notes on Interest and Dividends

1. When using the indirect approach, interest is not directly listed because it was included in the calculation of net income.
2. Basically, interest and dividends are either financing (expenses) or investment (income) items. In a cash flow statement, dividends are usually classified under financing activities. However, it is a debatable matter to classify interest under operating activities. Neither the International Financial Reporting Standards (IFRSs) nor GAAP provides conclusive answers. While GAAP "requires" interest to be presented under operating activities, IFRSs simply "suggest" the following:

> Interest and dividends received and paid *may* be classified as operating, investing, or financing cash flows, provided that they are classified consistently from period to period. (IAS 7.31).

5

Exhibit 5.7 The State of Cash Flow

Exhibit 5.7.1 FAIDA Ltd statement of cash flow for the year ended 31 December

	2012$ millions	Remarks
Cash from operating activities		
Cash received from customers (+)	2337	a
Cash paid to suppliers and operations (−)	(2124)	b
Tax paid (−)	(64)	c
Interest paid (−)	(65)	d
Accrued tax (+)	12	e
Net cash provided (used) by operating activities	96	
Cash from investment activities		
Increase in property, plant, and equipment (−)	(180)	f
Increase in long-term investments (−)	(10)	g
Decrease in other long-term assets (+)	10	h
Net cash provided (used) by investment activities	(180)	
Cash from financing activities		
Increase in notes payable (+)	5	i
Increase in long-term debt (+)	107	j
Cash dividends paid (−)	(22)	k
Net cash provided (used) by financing activities	90	
Increase (decrease) in cash and cash equivalents	6	l
Cash and cash equivalents at the beginning of the year	113	m
Cash and cash equivalents at the end of the year	119	n

Exhibit 5.7.2 FAIDA Ltd statement of cash flow for the year ended 31 December

	2012 ($ millions)	Remarks
Cash from operating activities		
Net income (+)	91	i
Depreciation (+)	59	ii

Exhibit 5.7.2 (continued)

	2012 ($ millions)	Remarks
Decrease in accounts receivable (+)	15	iii
Increase in inventories (−)	(64)	iv
Increase in accumulated tax prepaid (−)	(3)	v
Increase in accrued tax (+)	12	vi
Decrease in accounts payable (−)	(14)	vii
Net cash provided (used) by operating activities	96	

Note: The "Remarks" column is not part of the cash statement reporting requirements, but it only shows the letters and numbers corresponding to illustrative explanations on how each of the cash item figure was obtained

5.5.4 Cash from Investment Activities

(f) On "property, plant, and equipment," the cash outflow was $180 million, indicating an increase of gross value from $1020 million in 2011 to $1200 million in 2012 (from the balance sheet).
(g) On "investments (long-term)," a change from $50 million in 2011 to $60 million in 2012 is the amount of cash spent—i.e., $10 million (from the balance sheet).
(h) A decrease in long-term assets may be due to disposal of some assets or withdrawal of investments (long-term). The company received $10 million of cash.

5.5.5 Cash from Financing Activities

(i) On "short-term debt," the cash received was $5 million—notes payable increased from $299 million in 2011 to $304 million in 2012 (from the balance sheet).
(j) On "long-term debt," the cash received was $107 million—long-term debt increased from $523 million in 2011 to $630 million in 2012 (from the balance sheet).
(k) On "dividends," the cash paid to shareholders was $22 million.

5.5.6 Net Change in Cash Position

(l) In all, $6 million is the sum of all cash inflows and cash outflows, that is, cash generated from operating activities ($96 million) minus cash used in investment activities ($180 million) plus cash used in financing activities ($90 million).

In the balance sheet, this is also the difference between cash balance as of 2011 (US$113 million) and that as of 2012 (US$119 million).

(m) $113 million is the cash balance as of December 31, 2011 (from the balance sheet).

(n) $119 million is the cash balance as of December 31, 2012 (from the balance sheet).

Think 5.5

Why is it important to classify interest under operating activities in a cash flow statement?

5.6 Valuation Implications of Financial Information

Financial statements have a vital role in corporate valuation. Hence, any analyst ought to be profoundly acquainted not only with the details in financial statements but also their relation to value and valuation. Moreover, as explained in ▸ Chap. 4, security market prices reflect information about the financial performance of companies. Let us consider the followings aspects:

As pointed out in ▸ Chap. 1, cash is a key valuation input. The income statement can be used in conjunction with the balance sheet to forecast future cash flows. Moreover, as depicted in ▸ Exhibit 5.1, the statement of cash flows merges the movement of cash from both the statement of income (operating activities) and the balance sheet (financing and investment activities).

Intrinsic valuation, which discounts cash flows to estimate value, utilizes information from financial statements to determine free cash flows (see ▸ Chap. 10), estimates the cost of capital (see ▸ Chap. 11), and estimates growth rates (see ▸ Chap. 14). Relative valuation uses financial statements to analyze companies and determine peers and value drivers such as earnings per share (EPS), earnings before interest and taxes (EBIT), earnings before interest, taxes, depreciation, and amortization (EBITDA), etc. (see ▸ Chap. 19).

Financial statements are vital for fundamental analysis and for choosing valuations models, which suit specific characteristics of a company. For instance, financial statements can be used to analyze the source and use of funds. Long-term source of funds can provide information about the stability of capital structure and the cost of capital. By examining the historical financing trend, it is possible to determine the stability of capital structure, which, in turn, helps determine the cost of capital assumptions. Regarding the use of funds, more value is expected if a large proportion of funds are used for long-term rather than short-term investments. The relationship between long-term investments and long-term sources is also vital for predicting the potential growth of future cash flows. The use of long-term sources to finance short-term operations may imply liquidity problems and potential slow growth. A company with a potential for cash flow growth should be able to use internally generated funds (earnings) to fund short- and long-term financial obligations. Selling assets to fund debt payment is also a sign of solvency problem that can lead to financial distress.

Security markets tend to respond when companies release financial reports (refer to ▶ Chap. 4). The responses are always reflected in prices (i.e., market valuation). Nevertheless, despite their importance, the relevance of financial statements in market valuation varies due to several factors. According to Hail (2013), income statements can be less relevant in countries with strong institutions, whereas a balance sheet becomes more relevant in the presence of common laws and investor protection, strict disclosure requirements, and integrated markets. Moreover, the relevance of financial statements varies among industries and sectors (Govindarajan et al. 2018)—financial statements may be less relevant in digital companies (e.g., Uber, Amazon, and the like) than capital-intensive companies (e.g., General Electric, Toyota, Chevron Corporation, etc.). The authors first pose the following question:

Why do investors react negatively to financial statement losses for an industrial firm but disregard such losses for a digital firm?

Then, they present the following arguments:

One reason is that our current financial accounting model cannot capture the principle value creator for digital companies: increasing return to scale on intangible investments. This becomes clear when you look at a company's two most important financial statements: the balance sheet and the income statement. For an industrial company dealing with physical assets and goods, the balance sheet presents a reasonable picture of productive assets and the income statement provides a reasonable approximation of expenses required to create shareholder value. But these statements have little salience for a digital company, which often has assets that are intangible in nature and appreciate in value with use, and ecosystems that extend beyond the company's boundaries. So as digital companies become more prominent in the economy, and physical companies become more digital in their operations, they will also have to dramatically alter the manner and ways by which they convey their value to outside investors (Govindarajan et al. 2018: *Harvard Business Review*).

Think 5.6

Will it be possible to value a company without using any information from financial statements? Give reasons.

Review Questions

1. In terms of the nature of information, explain the main differences between a balance sheet, an income statement, and a cash flow statement.
2. With examples, explain why financial statements are important in corporate valuation.

3. Demonstrate how financial statements are linked to each other and their overlapping relationships.
4. The relevance and use of financial statements for corporate valuation differ across sectors and industries. Do you agree? Explain with examples.
5. Which of the following companies' financial statements are likely to be more relevant or less relevant in valuation? Give reasons to support your answers.
   (a) Meta (Facebook)
   (b) Shell
   (c) Citi Bank
   (d) Ernest and Young
   (e) Apple
   (f) Amazon
   (g) Google (Alphabet)
   (h) General Motors
6. Mention the items contained in the following balance sheet components and explain their implication in corporate valuation:
   (a) Financing
   (b) Investing
7. Explain the order in which the following items are listed in a balance sheet:
   (a) Assets
   (b) Liabilities
   (c) Equity
8. How do the following aspects affect changes in the financial position of a company?
   (a) Operating activities
   (b) Investment activities
   (c) Financing activities
9. Explain the meaning of the following phrases as applied in financial statements:
   (a) Balance sheet "as at" or "as of"
   (b) Income statement "for"
   (c) Cash flow statement "for"
10. With examples, explain why a company can have high profits but no cash.
11. Explain how financial statements can be used for fundamental analysis and their implication in corporate valuation.

Bibliography

Govindarajan, V., Rajgopal, S., & Anup Srivastava, A. (2018), Why Financial Statements Don't Work for Digital Companies, Harvard Business Review, February 26, 2018, https://hbr.org/2018/02/why-financial-statements-dont-work-for-digital-companies

Hail, L. (2013). Financial Reporting and Firm Valuation: Relevance Lost or Relevance Regained? *Accounting and Business Research*, 43 (4), 329-358. https://doi.org/10.1080/00014788.2013.799402

The Basics of Financial Statement Analysis

Contents

Supplementary Information The online version contains supplementary material available at https://doi.org/10.1007/978-3-031-28267-6_6.

B. Kulwizira Lukanima, *Corporate Valuation*, Classroom Companion: Business, https://doi.org/10.1007/978-3-031-28267-6_6

6.1 Introduction

Financial statements provide quantitative information for different purposes and are extremely useful when properly analyzed and interpreted. This chapter, therefore, introduces the two major approaches to financial statement analysis, namely, comparative analysis and financial ratio analysis. Overall, financial statement analysis is vital for measuring performance over time across companies and industries. It is, therefore, one of the key analytical tools of corporate valuation, as presented in the subsequent chapters of this book.

Learning Outcomes

- Explain financial statement analysis and its role in corporate valuation
- Understand comparative analysis of financial statements
- Explain the difference between horizontal and vertical analyses of financial statements
- Apply comparative analysis to measure company performance
- Understand financial ratio analysis
- Describe different categories of financial ratios
- Calculate and interpret key financial ratios
- Explain the relevance of financial statement analysis to different aspects of performance measurement and decision-making
- Explain the factors of effective financial statement analysis

6.2 The Role of Financial Statement Analysis

There are several ways of measuring business performance, which target the different functional levels of a company, namely, strategic, managerial, and operational. Performance measurement requires performance indicators, which may include both financial and nonfinancial measures. Although there are many tools for measuring performance (e.g., balanced scorecards, result-based management, and so on), this chapter focuses on financial measures based on financial statements. The two major categories of financial statement analyses are comparative analysis and financial ratio analysis.

Banner 6.1 The Primary Role of Financial Analysis
The primary role of financial analysis is to help in decision-making amongst different users of financial information, including value analysts.

The need for financial statement analysis primarily arises because financial information is vital for sound decision-making amongst different users of such information, including value analysts. Among many, financial analysis is used to measure how a company's financial resources are utilized to generate earnings and cash and create value; to assess whether a company has achieved its objectives by comparing performance measures (such as profitability, liquidity, asset management) with the targets; and to motivate and control performance through benchmarking, action-taking, and improvement. Lenders like banks, apart from requiring collateral, use financial performance to ascertain the financial health of a company and its ability to fulfill financial obligations—hence, this has implications in the cost of debt.

6.3 Comparative Analysis

Comparative analysis involves horizontal and vertical analyses of financial statements. This section explains the two types of comparative analyses with illustrative examples, considering their usefulness and practical application.

Banner 6.2 Horizontal Analysis

Horizontal analysis compares periodical changes in the individual line items of financial statements.

6.3.1 Horizontal Analysis

Horizontal analysis is about comparing periodical changes in financial line items (e.g., revenues, expenses, cash, accounts payable, long-term debts, etc.)—it is a "time series analysis," which expresses changes in both "monetary" and "percentage" terms While monetary values provide a broader picture of the factors affecting the performance of specific financial items, percentage changes provide more useful information for interpretation as they show both the direction and magnitude of change. To illustrate horizontal analysis, the financial statements of FAIDA Ltd are used in ▶ Exhibits 6.1 and 6.2.

Trend percentages are useful when analyzing changes over many years, aiming to track the possible causes of those changes. This aspect is illustrated in ▶ Exhibit 6.2 using the income statement information of FAIDA Ltd over 12 years. A better way to interpret trend percentages is to use graphs (see ◘ Exhibit 6.2.3).

Exhibit 6.1 Horizontal Analysis: Balance Sheet

Illustrative Example (See Excel Workings—▶ Chap. 6, Sheet E.6.1)

This example shows how to calculate and present horizontal analysis in a balance sheet. It covers two financial periods, i.e., 2011 and 2012. Three columns are included to show monetary changes, percentage changes, and trend percentages. Explanations are given below.

FAIDA Ltd: statement of financial position as of 31 December

	2012 ($ millions)	2011 ($ millions)	Change ($ millions)	Percentage change	Trend percentage
Assets					
Cash and cash equivalents	119	113	+6	5%	105%
Accounts receivable	420	435	−15	−3%	97%
Inventory	700	636	+64	10%	110%
Prepaid expenses	10	10	0	0%	100%
Accumulated tax prepaid	15	12	+3	25%	125%
Total current assets	*1264*	*1206*	*+58*	*5%*	*105%*
Investments (long-term)	60	50	+10	20%	120%
Property, plant, and equipment	1200	1020	+180	18%	118%
Less accumulated depreciation	369	310	+59	19%	119%
Net property, plant, and equipment	*831*	*710*	*+121*	17%	117%
Other assets (long-term)	213	223	−10	−4%	96%
Total noncurrent assets	*1104*	*983*	*+121*	*12%*	*112%*
Total assets	2368	2189	+179	*8%*	*108%*
Liabilities and equity					
Accounts payable	100	114	-14	−12%	88%
Notes payable	304	299	+5	2%	102%
Accrued tax	36	24	+12	50%	150%
Other accruals	100	100	0	0%	100%
Total current liabilities	540	537	+3	1%	101%
Long-term debts	630	523	+107	20%	120%
Shareholders' equity					

	2012 ($ millions)	2011 ($ millions)	Change ($ millions)	Percentage change	Trend percentage
Preferred stock	749	749	0	0%	100%
Common stock ($100/par)	210	210	0	0%	100%
Retained earnings	239	170	+69	41%	141%
Total equity	1198	1129	+69	6%	106%
Total liabilities and equity	2368	2189	+179	8%	108%

6

Monetary Change

A monetary change is calculated by subtracting the line item value of the current year (2012) from that of the previous year (2011). For example, for cash and cash equivalents ($119 million – $113 million = $6 million), the change is an increase in cash and cash equivalents and hence a "+" sign is used. For accounts receivable ($420 million – $435 million = –$15 million), the change is a decrease in accounts receivable and hence a "–" sign is used. The same applies to all the line items.

Percentage Change

A percentage change is calculated by dividing the monetary change by the previous period's value, multiplied by 100. For example, for cash and cash equivalents ($6 million/$113 million) × 100 = 5%. The interpretation is that cash and cash equivalents increased by 5% between 2011 and 2012. Likewise, for accounts receivable (–$15 million/$435 million) × 100 = –3%, meaning that the accounts receivable declined by 3% between the two periods.

Trend Percentages

Trend percentages show changes in line items in terms of the base year, which is set to 100%. In this balance sheet, the base year is 2011. For example, the trend percentage for cash and cash equivalents is 100% + 5% = 105%. This means that cash and cash equivalents increased by 5% (from 100% to 105%) from the base year to the current year. For accounts receivable, the trend percentage is 97% (i.e., 100% + –3% = 97%), meaning that the accounts receivable declined by 3% (from 100% to 97%) from the base year to the current year.

Observations

With horizontal analysis, it is possible to make general and specific interpretations. There are several ways to make a comparative interpretation depending on the purpose of the analysis. However, normally, the main goal is to examine the possible effects of changes.

Let us look at the following examples. A 3% decrease in accounts receivable suggests improvement in the collection of cash from debtors. A 5% increase in cash and cash equivalents may imply either an improvement in cash collection or an inability to use the cash. A 10% increase in inventories may suggest either slow sales or purchases of more inventories than the ability to deliver or sell. Likewise, a 12% decrease in accounts payable is an indication of improved performance in managing trade creditors.

Exhibit 6.2 Percentage Trend: Income Statement

Illustrative Example (See Excel Workings—► Chap. 6, Sheet E.6.2)

This example shows how to calculate and present percentage trends. It covers the historical period from 2001 to 2012. Exhibit 6.2.1 presents the historical operating performance (income statement), whereas Exhibits 6.2.2 and 6.2.3 present the percentage trends in tabular and graphical forms, respectively. Exhibit 6.2.4 shows the historical use of profits.

Exhibit 6.2.1 FAIDA Ltd statement of income for the year ended 31 December ($ millions)

Income statement	2012	2011	2010	2009	2008	2007	2006	2005	2004	2003	2002	2001
Net sales	2322	2229	2140	2054	1972	1834	1706	1586	1475	1180	944	755
Cost of sales	1680	1596	1516	1440	1368	1286	1209	1137	1068	801	601	451
Gross income	642	633	624	614	604	548	497	450	407	379	343	305
Operating expenses	425	400	376	353	332	305	281	258	238	178	134	100
Operating income	217	234	248	261	272	243	216	191	169	201	210	204
Interest expenses	65	59	53	47	40	35	32	28	24	22	17	14
Income before tax	152	175	196	214	232	207	184	163	145	179	192	190
Income tax	61	70	78	85	93	83	74	65	58	72	77	76
Net income	91	105	117	128	139	124	111	98	87	107	115	114
Cash dividends	*22*	*55*	*97*	*120*	*137*	*119*	*100*	*93*	*68*	*88*	*94*	*104*
Retained earnings	*69*	*50*	*20*	*8*	*2*	*5*	*11*	*5*	*19*	*19*	*21*	*10*

Exhibit 6.2.2 FAIDA Ltd horizontal trend percentages for income statement

Trend percentages	2012	2011	2010	2009	2008	2007	2006	2005	2004	2003	2002	2001
Net sales	307%	295%	283%	272%	261%	243%	226%	210%	195%	156%	125%	100%
Cost of sales	373%	354%	336%	320%	304%	285%	268%	252%	237%	178%	133%	100%
Gross income	211%	208%	205%	202%	198%	180%	163%	148%	134%	124%	113%	100%
Operating expenses	424%	398%	374%	352%	331%	304%	280%	258%	237%	178%	133%	100%
Operating income	106%	114%	121%	128%	133%	119%	106%	94%	83%	98%	103%	100%
Interest expenses	468%	421%	379%	341%	290%	255%	227%	204%	174%	156%	125%	100%
Pretax income	80%	92%	103%	112%	122%	109%	97%	86%	76%	94%	101%	100%
Income tax	80%	92%	103%	112%	122%	109%	97%	86%	76%	94%	101%	100%
Net income	80%	92%	103%	112%	122%	109%	97%	86%	76%	94%	101%	100%
Cash dividends	21%	53%	93%	115%	131%	114%	95%	89%	65%	85%	90%	100%
Retained earnings	690%	500%	200%	80%	20%	50%	110%	50%	190%	190%	210%	100%

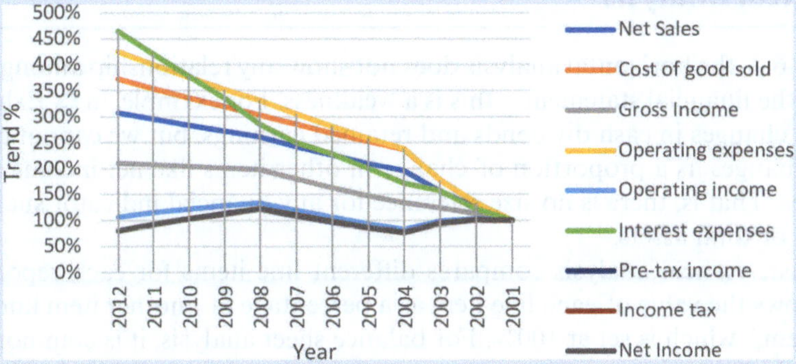

Exhibit 6.2.3 FAIDA Ltd horizontal trend percentages for statements of income from 2001 to 2012

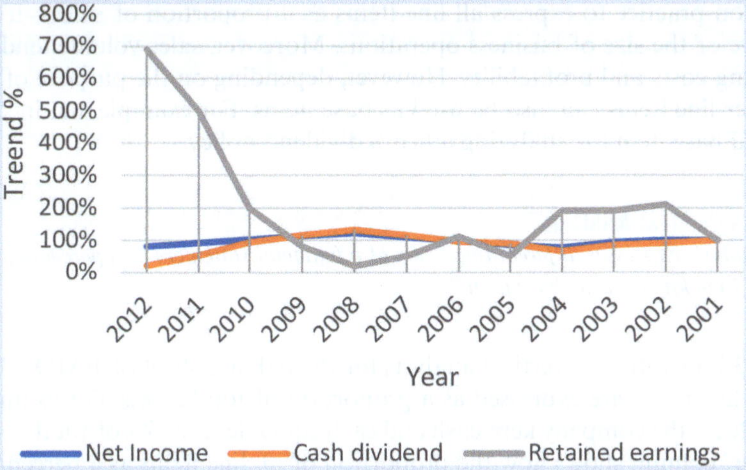

Exhibit 6.2.4 FAIDA Ltd use of net income

Observations

Overall, the company shows growth in its business operations. From the base year 2001 onward (100%), sales increased by 307%, directly proportional to the increase in the cost of goods sold and expenses. However, the magnitude of increase in operating expenses and interest expenses exceeded that of the increase in the operating income. The outcome was a downward trend in net income, except during 2004–2008. This suggests that the company performed better in generating revenues than in managing expenses. The company's dividend policy seemed to be shifting from a high payout to a high plowback—despite the declining net income, retained earnings have grown at a high rate in recent years. The change in cash dividends was directly proportional to the change in net income, implying that no external sources of funds were used to pay the dividends. Generally, the company's profitability performance was stable.

6.3.2 Vertical Analysis

In ▶ Exhibit 6.2, the horizontal analysis does not show any relationship among the line items in the financial statement—this is a weakness. For example, in ◘ Exhibit 6.2.4, we see changes in cash dividends and retained earnings, but we cannot consider those changes as a proportion of change in other items like net income and sales revenues. That is, there is no size reference for any financial indicator such as sales volume or total assets.

In contrast, vertical analysis compares different line items for each reported period. It shows the value of each line item as a percentage of another item known as a "base item," which is set at 100%. For balance sheet analysis, it is common to express each individual item as a percentage of the "total assets"—it should be noted that total assets equal total liabilities and equity. Total asset is used as a base item because it is a proxy for either company size or wealth. For income statements, it is a common practice to express all line items as a proportion of sales—it is a good measure of the size of business operations. Moreover, sales volume tends to drive operating costs and profitability. However, depending on the purpose of the analysis, other line items can also be used as base items. For example, net income can be a good base item for analyzing a firm's dividend policy.

Banner 6.3 Vertical Analysis

Vertical analysis expresses different line items of a financial statement as a percentage of another item known as a "base item."

▶ Exhibit 6.3 illustrates the vertical analysis for the balance sheet of FAIDA Ltd, in which the line items are expressed as a proportion of total assets. For example, in 2012 and 2011, the company kept cash and cash equivalents at 5% of total assets. The "Change" column shows how the proportion of all line items as a percentage of total assets changes between the two periods. For example, as a percentage of total assets, the total current assets declined by 2%, whereas noncurrent assets increased by 2% in 2012.

Exhibit 6.3 Vertical Analysis: Balance Sheet

Illustrative Example (See Excel Workings—▶ Chap. 6, Sheet E.6.3)

This example uses the balance sheet to show vertical analysis, whereby total asset is the base item for two periods (2011 and 2012).

FAIDA Ltd common size balance sheet as at 31 December

	2012 ($ millions)	2011 ($ millions)	Percentage of total assets		
			2012	2011	Change
Assets					
Cash and cash equivalents	119	113	5%	5%	0%
Accounts receivable	420	435	18%	20%	−2%
Inventory	700	636	30%	29%	1%
Prepaid expenses	10	10	0%	0%	0%
Accumulated tax prepaid	15	12	1%	1%	0%
Total current assets	*1264*	*1206*	53%	55%	−2%
Investments (long-term)	60	50	3%	2%	0%
Property, plant, and equipment	1200	1020	51%	47%	4%
Less accumulated depreciation	369	310	16%	14%	1%
Net property, plant, and equipment	*831*	*710*	35%	32%	3%
Other assets (long-term)	213	223	9%	10%	−1%
Total noncurrent assets	*1104*	*983*	47%	45%	2%
Total assets	**2368**	**2189**	**100%**	**100%**	**0%**
Liabilities and equity					
Accounts payable	100	114	4%	5%	−1%
Notes payable	304	299	13%	14%	−1%
Accrued tax	36	24	2%	1%	0%
Other accruals	100	100	4%	5%	0%
Total current liabilities	540	537	23%	25%	−2%
Long-term debts	630	523	27%	24%	3%
Shareholders' equity					
Preferred stock	749	749	32%	34%	−3%
Common stock ($100/par)	210	210	9%	10%	−1%

	2012 ($ millions)	2011 ($ millions)	Percentage of total assets		
			2012	2011	Change
Retained earnings	239	170	10%	8%	2%
Total equity	1198	129	51%	52%	−1%
Total liabilities and equity	**2368**	**2189**	**100%**	**100%**	**0%**

Observations

On investment activities, as a percentage of total assets, the company had more current assets than noncurrent assets—the proportion of the current assets declined by 2%, i.e., from 55% to 53%, whereas the proportion of noncurrent assets increased by the same percentage from 45% to 47%. Most of the current assets were tied up in inventories and accounts receivable, whereas property, plant, and equipment took a larger share of the noncurrent assets.

On financing activities, as a percentage of total assets, the company relied more on debts (notes payable, preference stock, and long-term debts), which jointly made 72% and 71% compared to just 10% and 9% common equity in 2011 and 2012, respectively. This implies high leverage.

6

▶ Exhibit 6.4 illustrates the vertical analysis for the income statement of FAIDA Ltd for 12 years from 2001 to 2012, using net sales as the base item. ◘ Exhibit 6.4.1 presents a common size income statement. For example, in 2012, the cost of goods sold were $1680 million and net sales was $2322 million—thus, the cost of goods sold is presented as 72% of net sales (i.e., $1680 divided by $2322). Similarly, the net income, which was $91 million in 2012, is presented as 4% of net sales (i.e., $91 divided by $2322). ◘ Exhibit 6.4.2 depicts the relationship between each line item and base item for an easy interpretation. ◘ Exhibit 6.4.3 shows the use of net income—it expresses dividends and retained earnings as a percentage of the net income (base item).

Exhibit 6.4 Vertical Analysis: Income Statement

Illustrative Example (See Excel Workings—▶ Chap. 6, Sheet E.6.4)

This example uses the income statement in ◘ Exhibit 6.2.1 to show the vertical analysis, whereby the base item is sales. The analysis covers a long period from 2001 to 2012. ◘ Exhibits 6.4.1 and 6.4.2 present the analysis table and graph, respectively—it should be noted that net sales is set at 100%. ◘ Exhibit 6.4.3 analyzes dividend policy using net income as the base item.

Exhibit 6.4.1 FAIDA Ltd common size income statement for the year ended 31 December (2001–2012)

	2012	2011	2010	2009	2008	2007	2006	2005	2004	2003	2002	2001
Net sales	100%	100%	100%	100%	100%	100%	100%	100%	100%	100%	100%	100%
Cost of goods sold	72%	72%	71%	70%	69%	70%	71%	72%	72%	68%	64%	60%
Gross income	28%	28%	29%	30%	31%	30%	29%	28%	28%	32%	36%	40%
Operating expenses	18%	18%	18%	17%	17%	17%	16%	16%	16%	15%	14%	13%
Operating income	9%	10%	12%	13%	14%	13%	13%	12%	11%	17%	22%	27%
Interest expenses	3%	3%	2%	2%	2%	2%	2%	2%	2%	2%	2%	2%
Pretax income	7%	8%	9%	10%	12%	11%	11%	10%	10%	15%	20%	25%
Income tax	3%	3%	4%	4%	5%	5%	4%	4%	4%	6%	8%	10%
Net income	4%	5%	5%	6%	7%	7%	7%	6%	6%	9%	12%	15%
Cash dividends	1%	2%	5%	6%	7%	6%	6%	6%	5%	7%	10%	14%
Retained earnings	3%	2%	1%	0%	0%	0%	1%	0%	1%	2%	2%	1%

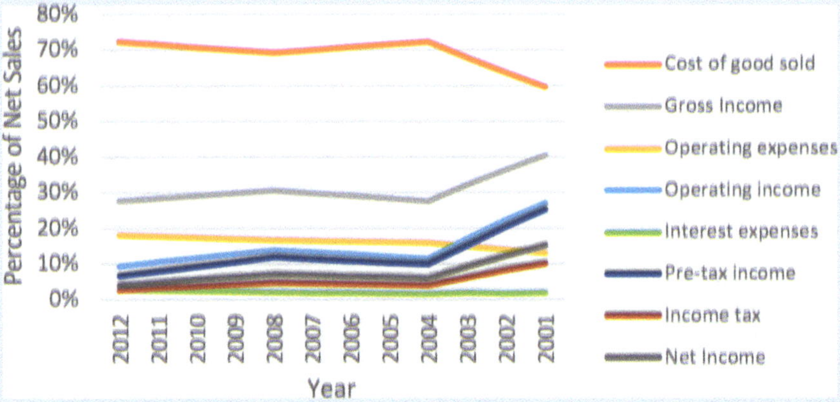

Exhibit 6.4.2 FAIDA Ltd percentage of net sales for the period ended 31 December (2001–2012)

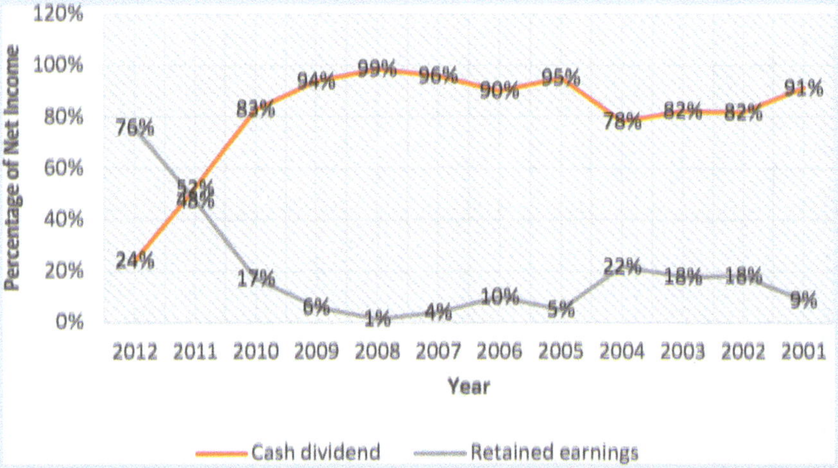

Exhibit 6.4.3 FAIDA Ltd dividend decisions

Observations

Overall, as it is normally the case, the cost of goods sold tends to make up the largest proportion of sales revenues. The proportions of other expenses tend to decline from top to bottom of the income statement following the order of payment priority. Similarly, proportions of income tend to decline from top (gross income) to bottom (net income) depending on the proportion of expenses.

Each specific line item can be interpreted separately. For example, as a percentage of sales, the cost of goods sold increased each year from 60% in 2001 to 72% in 2012, leading to a decline in the percentage of gross income from 40% to 28% during the same period. Moreover, the percentage of operating expenses increased each year from 13% to 18% between 2001 and 2012, whereas the percentage of operating income declined significantly from 27% to 9%. For the company's managers, this trend is alarming—they may be required to examine the performance of managing and controlling operating expenses. The effect of operating expenses is clearly reflected in the percentage of net income. It should be noted that that interest expenses are fixed claims, whereas income tax expenses depend on the operating income.

Regarding dividend policy, the company maintained a high payout ratio for many years. However, there seemed to be a strategy to gradually replace the high payout ratio by a high plowback ratio, starting from 2008 to 2012—the payout ratio declined from 99% in 2008 to 24% in 2012.

6.3.3 Practical Relevance

"Horizontal analysis" is a vital performance analysis tool, aiming to track changes and examine the possible cause of such changes. Let us use our example in ▸ Exhibit 6.2 (horizontal analysis) to elaborate this point.

The net income of FAIDA Ltd declined from 2001 to 2004, despite an increase in sales revenues. What was the cause? There may be several factors, but, during the same period, the company experienced an increase in both cost of goods sold and operating expenses. The increase in expenses could be due to either internal factors (the ability of the company to manage and control expenses) or external factors (economic condition affecting all companies).

Later, from 2005 to 2008, the net income showed a steady increase that was proportional to the increase in sales and a slight decline in the cost of goods sold and operating expenses. What was the cause of this change? Perhaps, the company implemented some cost-cutting strategies after learning from its past performance.

A decline in net income was then observed from 2008 to 2012 alongside declining sales, but there was an increase in the cost of goods sold and operating expenses. The rate of increase in interest expenses was also higher than before. What was the cause of this change? It is probable that the company's cost-cutting strategies had little impact on the net income. Why? It may be that performance was mostly driven by external influences, which were beyond the company's control. For example, the global financial crisis of 2008 might have contributed to higher costs relating to raw materials and production or, perhaps, the company had not recovered from the effects of the 2008 financial crisis.

"Vertical analysis" measures the extent of performance of an individual financial item in relation to another item. It is, therefore, suitable for analyzing performance across companies regardless of their size. The interpretation focuses on how a particular financial item relates to a selected base item—this can then be compared across industries, competitors, or peers. Using FAIDA Ltd as an example, several comments can be made on its performance (see ▶ Exhibits 6.3 and 6.4).

From the "balance sheet," between 2011 and 2012, more than 50% of the company's wealth was tied up in current assets: that is, 55% in 2011 and 53% in 2012, with inventories taking the lion's share (about 30%). However, current liabilities constituted 25% and 23%, in 2011 and 2012, respectively, of total financial resources, equal to the most liquid assets (cash and cash equivalents and accounts receivable). This is an indication of high liquidity—even if inventories were not sold out, the most liquid assets could clear out all current liabilities. Equity seems to be a major source of long-term finance with almost half of its contribution going to total wealth (i.e., 52% and 51% in 2011 and 2012, respectively). However, preferred stocks took the largest share with 34% and 32%, in 2011 and 2012, respectively. With long-term debts contributing to 24% and 27%, respectively, the company depended on external financing for more than half of its long-term financing sources. Hence, the company had more fixed than discretional obligations to its investors (preference dividends and interest expenses), thereby coming under pressure to generate more profits.

Regarding the "income statement," the cost of goods sold had been taking a significant slice of the company's sales revenues, which is normal. However, the main concern would be an increase of 12% from 60% in 2001 to 72% in 2012. This may imply the need for managers to scrutinize the operating performance of raw materials and production costs. Operating expenses ranged between 13% and 18% of revenues, which could be considered stable despite a steady increase of 5% over the past 12 years. The proportion of net income to revenues declined over time (from 15% in 2001 to just 4% in 2012) due to a proportional increase in expenses. Although the company never incurred losses, profitability as a percentage of revenues is alarming.

6.3.4 Valuation Implications

Comparative analysis is highly useful in valuation as a quick indication of the future direction of the company. It is noteworthy that valuation uses historical information to forecast the future and examine the strength of a company's fundamentals. Let us look at one of the key variables, net income, which has implication in growth and stock market price. While horizontal analysis can show trends in the utilization of net income, vertical analysis can help explain the causes of such trends. For example, FAIDA Ltd, between 2001 and 2012, seemed to have implemented two different dividend policies. A remarkable change in the payout ratio was evident from 2009 onward, whereby the payout ratio started to decline from 99% in 2009 to 24% in 2012. From the valuation perspective, this change implies more growth and a possible increase in value, with other factors being equal (refer to ▶ Chap. 14 for estimation of growth rates and ▶ Chap. 18 for the present value of growth opportunities). A trendy increase in retained earnings may be interpreted as a strategy to reduce reliance on external financing (debts).

Apply 6.1 Comparative Analysis

Chevron (United States), Shell (United Kingdom), and Sasol (South Africa)

Data: See Excel Workings—▶ Chap. 6, Sheet A.6.1

The data sheet presents income statements from 2009 to 2021. Use Excel to perform a comparative analysis of the three companies as follows:

(a) *Horizontal Analysis:* Use 2009 as the base year. Calculate trend percentages for each of the income statement items and present a result table. Present graphs, examine trends, and explain the possible causes. Search and explain any real-world events likely to have influenced the performance of each company.

(b) *Vertical Analysis*: Use revenues as the base item. Perform vertical analysis for the historical period (2009–2021). Compare performance across the three companies, and give comments for each financial statement item. Search and explain any real-world events likely to have influenced performance in the industry and each company.

(c) Explain the usefulness of your analysis to different users of financial statements.

6.4 Financial Ratios

As we have seen, comparative analysis focuses on financial items from each financial statement separately—there is no comparison between balance sheet items and income statement items. Ratios, in contrast, express the relationships between items of a single or more financial statements or between financial statements and market values. This section provides an overview of the different categories of ratios to help understand their meanings, calculations, interpretations, and applications. A comprehensive analysis of selected ratios is presented in ▶ Chaps. 7–9.

Banner 6.4 Financial Ratios

Financial ratios express the relationships between two of more financial variables, from either a single financial statement or multiple financial statements or market values.

6.4.1 The Main Categories of Ratios

Financial ratios can be categorized according to their purposes as follows: profitability ratios, liquidity ratios, efficiency ratios, leverage ratios, and market value ratios. ▶ Exhibit 6.5 summarizes the structures of selected ratios (numerator and denominator) for each category and indicates the sources of information. It should be noted that the list of ratios presented here is not exhaustive, as they are many other ways of categorizing them.

Exhibit 6.5 Categories of Financial Ratios and Selected Measurements

Exhibit 6.5.1 Profitability ratios

	Numerator	Denominator
Gross margin	Gross profit (*income statement*)	Sales (*Income statement*)
Net profit margin	Net profit (*income statement*)	Sales (*income statement*)
Return on assets	Operating profit (*income statement*)	Total assets (*balance sheet*)
Return on equity	Net profit (*income statement*)	Common equity (*balance sheet*)

Exhibit 6.5.2 Liquidity ratios

	Numerator	Denominator
Current ratio	Current assets (*balance sheet*)	Current liabilities (*balance sheet*)
Quick ratio	Quick assets (*balance sheet*)	Current liabilities (*balance sheet*)
Defensive interval	Quick assets (*balance sheet*)	Average daily cash outflow from operations (*income statement*)

Exhibit 6.5.3 Efficiency ratios

	Numerator	Denominator
Asset turnover	Sales (*income statement*)	Total assets (*balance sheet*)
Inventory turnover	Cost of goods sold (*income statement*)	Inventories (*balance sheet*)
Accounts receivable turnover	Sales (*income statement*)	Accounts receivable (*balance sheet*)
Accounts payable turnover	Purchases (*income statement*)	Accounts payable (*balance sheet*)

■ **Exhibit 6.5.4** Leverage ratios

	Numerator	**Denominator**
Debt-to-equity ratio	Total liabilities (*balance sheet*)	Total common equity (*balance sheet*)
Debt ratio	Total liabilities (*balance sheet*)	Total assets (*balance sheet*)
Equity ratio	Total common equity (*balance sheet*)	Total assets (*balance sheet*)

■ **Exhibit 6.5.5** Market perception ratios

	Numerator	**Denominator**
Price to earnings	Stock price (*stock markets*)	EPS (*income statement*)
Dividend yield	Cash dividends (*income statement*)	Stock price (*stock markets*)

6.4.1.1 Profitability Ratios

What Do They Measure?

Profitability ratios measure the ability of a company to generate profits from its operations and efficiently use financial resources to generate returns. ■ Exhibit 6.5.1 summarizes these ratios in terms of their structure and sources of information.

Banner 6.5 Profitability Ratios

Profitability ratios measure the ability of a company to generate profits from its operations and efficiently use assets and capital to generate returns.

Relevance of Profitability Ratios

Users of financial information may want to know: (a) "to what extent do business operations generate profit?" and (b) "is a company generating enough profit relative to its financial resources?" Profitability ratios can answer these questions. While interpreting a company's profitability performance, investors and other users of financial information can compare performance over time and across industries and sectors. Examples to calculate these ratios are presented in Exhibit ▶ 6.6, whereas practical applications are elaborated in ▶ Chap. 7.

Exhibit 6.6 Profitability Ratios

Illustrative Example (See Excel Workings—► Chap. 6, Sheet E.6.6)

The following information was extracted from the financial statement of FAIDA Ltd In 2012, the company reported gross income and net sales revenues of $642 million and $2322, respectively. Operating income, pretax income, and net income were $217, $152, and $91, respectively. Total assets were $2189 and $2368 in 2011 and 2012, respectively, whereas common equity was $380 and $449, respectively. Capital employed was $1651 in 2011 and $1828 in 2012.

Calculate the following profitability ratios for 2012:

(a) Gross margin
(b) Net profit margin
(c) Return on assets (ROA)
(d) Return on equity (ROE)

Solution

(a) Gross Margin

$$\textit{Gross margin} = \frac{\textit{Gross profit}}{\textit{Sales}} = \frac{\$642}{\$2322} \times 100 = 27.6\%$$

Interpretation: After paying off inventory costs, FAIDA Ltd still had 28% of sales revenue to cover its operating costs.

(b) Net Profit Margin

$$\textit{Net profit margin} = \frac{\textit{Net profit}}{\textit{Sales}} = \frac{\$91}{\$2322} \times 100 = 3.9\%$$

Interpretation: After considering all expenses, the company generated 4% profits from sales.

(c) Return on Assets (ROA)

$$ROA = \frac{\textit{Operating profit}}{\textit{Average total assets}} = \frac{\$217}{\$2279} \times 100 = 9.5\%$$

Interpretation: Every dollar that FAIDA had invested in assets during the year 2012 produced $0.95 of the operating income.

(d) Return on Equity (ROE)

$$ROE = \frac{\textit{Net profit}}{\textit{Average common equity}} = \frac{\$91}{\$415} \times 100 = 22\%$$

Interpretation: Every dollar of common shareholder's equity earned about $0.22 in 2012. That is, common shareholders earned a 22% return on their investment.

6

Think 6.1

Why should we use net income as a numerator in calculating ROE and operating income as a numerator in calculating ROA?

6.4.1.2 Liquidity Ratios

What Do They Measure?

Although profitability is the most popular measure of operating performance, it does not indicate a company's ability to fulfill its short-term financial obligations like paying creditors, bills, and wages. Recall that profit does not mean cash.

Liquidity ratios address this issue by asking: "is a company able to generate sufficient funds to fulfill its day-to-day business operations?" The ratios, therefore, focus on working capital management—the relationship between current assets and current liabilities.

The most common types of liquidity ratios are current ratios, quick ratios, and defensive interval (see ◘ Exhibit 6.5.2). Although they measure the same thing, the ratios differ in defining liquidity. "Current ratio" considers all current assets, assuming that they can all be easily converted into cash within a short period of time. "Quick ratio" considers only the most liquid assets. "Defensive interval" focuses on a firm's ability to survive under difficult financial conditions.

Banner 6.6 Liquidity Ratios

Liquidity ratios measure the ability of a firm to meet its day-to-day (short-term) financial obligations.

Current Ratio

Measurement: Current ratio considers all current assets, thereby measuring the overall liquidity position of a firm as follows:

$$\text{Current ratio} = \frac{\text{Current assets}}{\text{Current liabilities}}$$

Generally, a current ratio is considered low when it is less than 1 (e.g., 0.8:1), which implies a liquidity problem. Similarly, it is considered high when it is greater than 1 (e.g., 3:1), implying a no-liquidity problem. ▶ Exhibit 6.7 presents an example for calculating current ratio.

"What is a desirable ratio?" There is no straightforward answer—it depends on several factors. Current ratios vary across industries and the nature of working capital (types of current assets and current liabilities). For example, industries that require holding up large inventories for long time (e.g., metal and car manufacturing) tend to have higher current ratios than do those with quick inventory movements (e.g., retail supermarkets and food processing). As a common rule of thumb, a current ratio of 2:1 is considered generally favorable. However, a good current ratio should be proportional to the operating cycle (OC): the period between when cash is invested in current assets and when such an investment generates cash.

Banner 6.7 Current Ratios

Current ratios measure the overall liquidity of a company by relating all current assets to current liabilities. It is particularly more relevant for managers and creditors.

Think 6.2

What should be the main challenge likely to face managers in making decisions about a desired current ratio or quick ratio?

Quick Ratio

Measurement: One of the drawbacks of current ratio is the inclusion of all current assets regardless of how quickly they can be converted into cash. "Quick ratio (acid test)" addresses this limitation by excluding inventories from the current assets—the focus is on assets, which can be easily converted into cash at market price close to their book value. Therefore, quick ratio can be expressed as follows:

$$Quick\ ratio = \frac{Quick\ assets}{Current\ liabilities}$$

▶ Exhibit 6.7 presents an example for calculating quick ratio.

Assets Excluded: Inventories tend to be excluded from current assets because they must be sold first before they become cash. If a company is unable to sell its inventories due to adverse conditions, then the current ratio can overstate its liquidity position. It is also reasonable to exclude prepaid expenses because they will never be converted into cash—they simply reduce the financial obligations to services paid for but not received.

6

Caution on Quick Assets: It is important to examine the proportion of quick (defensive) assets that a firm maintains. Cash is the most defensive asset because it is readily available for use. Cash equivalents (marketable securities) can be converted into cash relatively quicker than accounts receivable. The amount of accounts receivable at a particular time depends on sales and credit policy. The speed of collecting cash from debtors depends on several factors such as credit policy and economic conditions.

Banner 6.8 Quick Ratios

Quick ratios measure the overall liquidity status of a firm by considering only current assets that can be quickly converted into cash. Like current ratios, they are particularly more relevant for managers and lenders, especially those who hold a more conservative view of liquidity.

Defensive Interval

Measurement: Both current ratio and quick ratio compare current assets and current liabilities while ignoring operating expenses. However, liquidity is necessary to enable a company to pay operating expenses and finance current liabilities. A concern is that a company is expected to use revenues to cover operating costs. However, the question is: "how would a firm pay for operating expenses if there is no sales due to adverse business conditions?" Defensive interval addresses this question by measuring the number of days a business can survive at its current level of operations if there are no cash inflows from operating activities. The ratio is expressed in number of days as follows:

$$\textit{Defensive interval} = \frac{\textit{Quick assets}}{\textit{Average daily cash outflow from operations}}$$

▶ Exhibit 6.7 presents an example for calculating the ratio.

Banner 6.9 Defensive Interval

Defensive interval measures the ability of a firm to survive during difficulties when no cash is received from operating activities. It is relevant for managers with a view of knowing the future liquidity position of a firm.

Think 6.3

Under what circumstances can defensive interval be used for decision-making? What types of decisions should be related to it?

Exhibit 6.7 Liquidity Ratios

Illustrative Example (See Excel Workings—▶ Chap. 6, Sheet E.6.7)

The following information was extracted from the financial statement of FAIDA Ltd (all figures in millions). In 2011 and 2012, total current assets were $1206 and 1264, whereas total current liabilities were $537 and $540, respectively. In 2012, cost of goods sold was $1680, operating expenses were $425, and depreciation was $59. The breakdown of current assets and liabilities is presented below.

	2012 ($ millions)	2011 ($ millions)
Cash and cash equivalents	119	113
Accounts receivable	420	435
Inventory	700	636
Prepaid expenses	10	10
Accumulated tax prepaid	15	12
Total current assets	*1264*	*1206*
Accounts payable	100	114
Notes payable	304	299
Accrued tax	36	24
Other accruals	100	100
Total current liabilities	540	537

Required
Calculate the following liquidity ratios (assuming a year with 365 days):
(a) Current ratio
(b) Quick ratio
(c) Defensive interval

Solution
(a) Current Ratio

$$Current\ ratio = \frac{Current\ assets}{Current\ liabilities}$$

$$\text{Current ratio for 2011}: \$1206 / \$537 = 2.2$$

$$\text{Current ratio for 2012}: \$1264 / \$540 = 2.3$$

Interpretation: In 2011 and 2012, the company had enough current assets to pay off 2.2 and 2.3 times its current liabilities, respectively. That is, for each $1 of current liabilities, the company had $2.2 and $2.3 of current assets, respectively.

(b) Quick Ratio

$$Quick\ ratio = \frac{Quick\ assets}{Current\ liabilities}$$

Note: Quick assets are calculated as current assets excluding inventories, prepaid expenses, and accumulated tax prepaid. In other words, quick assets include only cash and cash equivalents and accounts receivable. Thus, quick assets in 2011 and 2012 were $548 and $539, respectively (all figures in millions).

$$\text{Quick ratio for 2011}: \$548 / \$537 = 1.00$$

$$\text{Quick ratio for 2012}: \$539 / \$540 = 1.02$$

Interpretation: In 2011, the company was able to pay almost all (100%) of its current liabilities from its quick assets. However, in 2012, the company could pay all its current liabilities from quick assets and keep 2% excess quick assets (102%–100%).

(c) Defensive Interval

$$Defensive\ interval = \frac{Quick\ assets}{Average\ daily\ cash\ outflow\ from\ operations}$$

Note: Assuming 365 days in a year, the average daily cash outflow (expenses) from operations can be estimated by dividing the total cash outflow from operations by 365. For FAIDA Ltd, the total cash outflow from operations in 2012 is calculated as follows (all figures in millions): to the cost of goods sold ($1680), add operating expenses ($425) and subtract depreciation ($59) = $2046.

Thus, in 2012,

$$Defensive\ interval = \frac{\$539}{\$2046 / 365} = 96\ days$$

Interpretation: Given its level of operations, FAIDA Ltd had approximately 96 days of the most liquid assets to cover its operating cash outflows.

Relevance of Liquidity Ratios

Overall, liquidity ratios are vital tools for managers, investors, and creditors because they show the strength of a company to settle its short-term financial obligations without necessarily depleting its long-term financial resources. Regardless of the ratio type, the higher the ratio, the higher the liquidity. Interpreting liquidity ratios is basically relative and ambiguous. While an extremely high ratio may imply idle resources (poor management), a low ratio would mean poor liquidity.

Regarding current ratio and quick ratio, prospective lenders desire higher current ratios. However, for managers, the size of ratio matters only if it implies efficient management of working capital. Generally, a low ratio (<1) alerts managers to improve liquidity. Defensive interval is not a substitute but rather a supplement of both current ratio and quick ratio when there are uncertainties in business operations. Usually, there are periods of good sales and bad sales, but business operations should continue. These operations will incur costs despite dropping sales or without sales. Visionary managers use defensive interval to estimate operating survival days without necessarily being forced to borrow.

Moreover, liquidity ratios can be used to compare performance across companies in the same industry but with caution—there can be variations in the types of current assets (their ability to be easily converted into cash) as well as working capital policies. For example, a low quick ratio may not be a problem if a company takes strategic measures to negotiate quick receipts from its debtors alongside agreeing to a longer period to pay creditors. This aspect is elaborated in ▶ Exhibit 6.8.

Exhibit 6.8 Liquidity Ratios of Two Different Companies

Illustrative Example (See Excel Workings—▶ Chap. 6, Sheet E.6.8)

This example compares the liquidity positions of two companies from the same industry. The aim is to explain the relevance of the ratios.

	Company A ($ 000)	Company B ($ 000)
Cash and cash equivalents	60,000	1000
Accounts receivable	30,000	24,000
Inventories	5000	70,000
Total current assets	*95,000*	*95,000*
Accounts payable	25,000	15,000
Notes payable	12,000	10,000
Accrued expenses	3000	15,000
Total current liabilities	*40,000*	*40,000*

	Company A ($ 000)	Company B ($ 000)
Total cash operating expenses	102,000	98,000
Current ratio	2.4:1	2.4:1
Quick ratio	2.3:1	0.6:1
Defensive interval	322 days	93 days

Observations

Both companies A and B have an equal current ratio, but A has a higher quick ratio than B. Despite equality in the current ratio, A's liquidity is stronger due to a large proportion of cash and cash equivalents compared to other current assets. If, however, cash takes a larger share in cash and cash equivalents, it is possible to doubt A's efficiency in using financial resources—that is, keeping idle cash is to sacrifice profitability for low risk. However, if A is highly levered (debt obligations), a high cash balance can be justified by the need to repay debt. Company B can be considered to have higher liquidity risk and financial distress if it is highly levered.

Firm A can survive for more days (322) than B (93), even though A has higher operating expenses than B. This explains the importance of a good proportion of defensive assets to operating expenses. Company A's proportion of quick assets to operating expenses is 88% compared to B with only 26%.

6.4.1.3 Efficiency Ratios

What Do They Measure?

Business resources are acquired to run business operations, aiming to generate revenues and profits and maximize shareholders' wealth. Efficiency ratios (also known as "operation efficiency ratios," "activity ratios," "asset usage ratios," or "turnover ratios") measure how well business resources are utilized to generate revenues or profits. There are several types of management efficiency ratios, but, here, we focus on a few of them, namely, asset turnover (AT), receivables turnover, inventory turnover (IT), and payables turnover (see ◘ Exhibit 6.5.3). We also show how they relate to a firm's operating cycle and cash conversion cycle (CCC). ▶ Exhibit 6.9 presents examples to calculate and interpret the ratios.

Banner 6.10 Efficiency Ratios

Efficiency ratios measure the ability of a firm to generate revenues (sales) from its financial resources.

Asset Turnover

Measurement: Asset turnover (AT) measures the ability of a firm to maximize the number of times its assets are turned over by its sales revenues. The ratio is presented as follows:

$$Asset\ turnover = \frac{Sales}{Average\ total\ assets}$$

The higher the turnover, the better the performance, and vice versa—the more sales are generated per each dollar of asset value, the better (see example in ▶ Exhibit 6.9).

Banner 6.11 Asset Turnover
Asset turnover measures how much sales is generated per each unit of asset value. A higher turnover is generally desirable.

Inventory Turnover

Measurement: Inventory turnover (IT) measures the number of times inventories are turned over during a reported financial period—that is, a firm's ability to convert inventories into sales. The ratio is expressed as follows:

$$Inventory\ turnover = \frac{Cost\ of\ goods\ sold}{Average\ inventories}$$

A higher ratio indicates a quick movement of products—no holding of too many inventories and/or products that are highly marketable. A low ratio indicates slow-moving products—it takes a longer time from obtaining products to selling them. Thus, IT can be used to estimate the days in inventory (DI) ratio, which measures the number of days taken to sell inventories. Assuming a 365-day year, this can be calculated as follows:

$$Days\ in\ inventory = \frac{365}{IT}$$

An example is given in ▶ Exhibit 6.9.

Generally, a higher IT (a lower DI) ratio is desirable, but, this depends on other strategies and policy issues relating to profitability performance. For instance, a higher IT (a lower DI) ratio that deprives cost reduction opportunities may be more unfavorable than a lower IT (a higher DI) ratio that creates profit-maximizing opportunities. For example, when suppliers offer discounts for ordering large quantities of inventories, it is an opportunity to reduce the cost of goods sold, thereby increasing profitability. Whereas ordering large quantities will increase average inventories and reduce the IT (increase DI) ratio, it aims at value maximization in the long term.

Banner 6.12 Inventory Turnover

Inventory turnover measures the ability of a firm to convert its inventories into sales revenues. A higher turnover is generally desirable.

Accounts Receivable Turnover (ART)

Measurement: Accounts receivable turnover (ART) is a quick indicator of the number of times a firm can turn its accounts receivables into cash, and it is expressed as follows:

$$\textit{Accounts receivable turnover} = \frac{\textit{Sales}}{\textit{Average accounts receivable}}$$

6

The term "sales" in this analysis refer to "net sales"—that is, sales after deducting allowances for returns and discounts. Accounts receivable refers to "net accounts receivable"—that is, receivables after deducting allowances for doubtful debtors.

A higher ART ratio indicates a shorter period from credit sales to collecting cash from customers, and vice versa. Hence, the average number of days taken to collect cash from debtors can be estimated using a days in accounts receivable (DAR) ratio. Assuming a 365-day year, this can be expressed as follows:

$$\textit{Days in accounts receivable} = \frac{365}{\textit{ART}}$$

Generally, a high ART (a low DAR) is desirable because it indicates better performance in collecting cash from debtors. An example is given in Exhibit ▶ 6.9.

Banner 6.12 Accounts Receivable Turnover

Accounts receivable turnover measures the number of times a firm can turn its accounts receivables into cash. A higher ratio is generally desirable.

Accounts Payable Turnover (APT)

Measurement: Accounts payable turnover (APT) measures the number of times accounts payables are turned during a finance period. It is a quick indicator of the frequency in which a company pays its trade creditors (suppliers). It is expressed as follows:

$$\textit{Accounts payable turnover} = \frac{\textit{Total purchases}}{\textit{Average accounts payable}}$$

whereby

$$\textit{Total purchases} = \textit{cost of goods sold} + \textit{change in inventories}$$

If a firm has made a significant amount of cash purchases, then adjustments should be made to exclude cash purchases from total purchases.

Using APT, the number of days it takes to pay the suppliers can be determined as follows:

$$Days\ in\ accounts\ payables\left(DAP\right)=\frac{365}{APT}$$

An example is given in ► Exhibit 6.9. A higher APT (a lower DAP) ratio indicates the higher frequency (shorter time) it takes for a firm to pay its suppliers—a lower APT (a higher DAP) suggests the opposite. However, a desirable ratio depends on several factors such as payment agreements with suppliers and the financial capabilities of the firm. Through credit purchases, a company creates a liability (carrying forward payments) while preserving some cash that can be directed to other revenue-generating activities. Therefore, a higher APT (a lower DAP) is favorable from the suppliers' perspective but not necessarily from the firm's perspective. To some companies, delaying payments can be a way to solve liquidity problems. It can, however, hamper suppliers' trust.

Banner 6.13 Accounts Payable Turnover

Accounts payable turnover measures the frequency at which a firm pays off its trade creditors. A desirable ratio depends on several factors, but a higher turnover is generally favorable to creditors.

Operating Cycle

Measurement: An operating cycle (OC) is the time length (days) taken to covert debtors and inventories into cash. It is, therefore, calculated as the sum of DAR and DI as follows:

$$Operating\ cycle = Days\ in\ accounts\ receivable + Days\ in\ inventories$$

A lower OC is generally desirable. Moreover, an OC is normally applied to measure a company's liquidity relative to its current ratio. The first step is to calculate operating cycle turnover (OCT), which is expressed as follows:

$$Operating\ cycle\ turnover\left(OCT\right)=\frac{365}{OC}$$

Then, the OCT is compared to the current ratio. A greater OCT than the current ratio indicates insufficient operating current assets to cover operating current liabilities during a specified operating cycle. Short-term debts might be used to finance some of the operating liabilities. An OCT less than the current ratio suggests that sufficient assets were available to cover the current asset turnover. An example is given in ► Exhibit 6.9.

Banner 6.14 Operating Cycle

An operating cycle measures the number of days a firm takes to convert its receivables and inventories into cash.

Cash Conversion Cycle

Measurement: Credit purchases (accounts payable) affect the time length taken to convert operating resources into cash. However, the OC does not account for the number of days it takes to pay suppliers (DAP). To consider this aspect, we use the cash conversion cycle (CCC), which is calculated as follows:

$$Cash\ conversion\ cycle(CCC) = OC - DAP$$

The CCC (sometimes called "cash cycle" or "trading cycle") measures the average time length taken to generate cash from trading activities –acquiring inventories, selling them, collecting cash from customers, and paying trade creditors. A shorter period is generally desirable as it indicates more operating efficiency and better cash management. An example is given in ▶ Exhibit 6.9.

Banner 6.15 Cash Conversion Cycle

A cash conversion cycle measures the number of days that a firm takes to generate cash from operating activities: acquisition of inventories, selling them, and paying suppliers.

The cash conversion cycle is extremely important for measuring the ability of managers to manage working capital. Poor working capital management may have significant detrimental effects on the value of a firm through affecting profits, liquidity, and operating risks. A firm with inefficient use of its current assets is likely to face cash flow problems, which, in turn, may affect it borrowing position.

Exhibit 6.9 Efficiency Ratios

Illustrative Example (See Excel Workings—▶ Chap. 6, Sheet E.6.9)

The following information was extracted from the financial statement of FAIDA Ltd for 2011 and 2012 (all figures in millions). Respectively, total equity in 2012 and 2011 was $1198 and $1129, whereas long-term debts were $630 and $523. Total assets were $2189 and $2368, respectively. Sales revenue was $2322 and $2229, respectively. Cost of goods sold in 2012 was $1680. Moreover, in 2012 and 2011, inventories were $700 and $636, whereas accounts receivable was $420 and $435, respectively.

Required

Calculate and interpret the following efficiency ratios for 2012:

(a) Asset turnover
(b) Inventory turnover and days in inventory
(c) Accounts receivables turnover and days in accounts receivable
(d) Accounts payables turnover and days in accounts payable
(e) Operating cycle and its turnover
(f) Cash conversion cycle

Solution

(a) Asset Turnover

$$AT = \frac{Sales}{Average\ total\ assets}$$

$$AT = \frac{\$2,322}{(\$2,189 + \$2,368)/2} = 1.02\ times$$

Interpretation: For each $1 of total assets, the company was able to generate $1.02 of sales in 2012.

(b) Inventory Turnover

$$IT = \frac{Cost\ of\ goods\ sold}{Average\ inventories} = \frac{\$1,680}{(\$700 + \$636)/2} = 2.5\ times$$

$$Days\ in\ inventory\,(DI) = \frac{365}{IT} = \frac{365}{2.5} = 145\ days$$

Interpretation: In 2012, the company was able to turn over its inventories approximately 2.5 times, taking approximately 145 days to sell them.

(c) Accounts Receivable Turnover

$$ART = \frac{Sales}{Average\ accounts\ receivable} = \frac{\$2322}{(\$420 + \$435)/2} = 5.4\ times$$

$$DAR = \frac{365}{ART} = \frac{365}{5.4} = 67\ days$$

Interpretation: In 2012, the company was able to turn over its accounts receivable approximately 5.4 times, taking 67 days on average to collect cash from debtors.

(d) Accounts Payable Turnover

$$APT = \frac{Total\ purchases}{Average\ accounts\ payable}$$

$$APT = \frac{\$1680 + (\$700 - 636)}{(\$100 + \$114)/2} = 16\ times$$

$$DAP = \frac{365}{APT} = \frac{365}{16} = 22\ days$$

Interpretation: In 2012, accounts payable was turned approximately 16 times, taking 23 days on average to pay suppliers.

(e) Operating Cycle

$$OC = DI + DAR = 145 + 67 = 212\ \text{days}$$

$$OCT = \frac{365}{OC} = \frac{365}{212} = 1.7\ times$$

Interpretation: In 2012, it took 212 days to convert inventories and debtors into cash. The current ratio in 2012 was 2.3—compared to OCT (1.7), and this suggests that the company's current assets were sufficient to cover operating current liabilities during the operating cycle of 212 days.

(f) Cash Conversion Cycle

$$CCC = \frac{\frac{\$700 + \$636}{2}}{\frac{\$1680}{365}} + \frac{\frac{\$420 + \$435}{2}}{\frac{\$2322}{365}} - \frac{\frac{\$100 + \$114}{2}}{\frac{\$1744}{365}} = 190\ days$$

Interpretation: In 2012, it took 189 days on average to generate cash from acquiring inventories, selling them, collecting from customers, and paying suppliers.

Relevance of Efficiency Ratios

Generally, efficiency ratios are applied as managerial performance indicators of the usage of financial resources like capital and assets as well as for the overall management of debtors and trade creditors. These ratios are, therefore, relevant for managers, lenders, customers, investors, and analysts. They can be used to motivate performance improvement in several operational aspects like cost management, procurement, and public relationship.

To determine the level of performance, benchmarks can be selected for competitors and the industry, and they can be analyzed over years to evaluate progress and track the factors affecting performance.

Think 6.4

If you are a finance manager in a company with cash problems, would you rather delay paying suppliers or borrow to speed up payments. Give reasons considering the impact of both delay payment and the cost of debt.

6.4.1.4 Leverage Ratios

What Do They Measure?

Leverage ratios measure a company's ability to fulfill its financial obligations—it is a measure of financial risk. Overall, the ratios compare financial obligations (debt) to business resources such as debt to equity total, debt to assets, and so on (refer to Exhibit 6.5.4). That is, "what is the overall debt load of a company compared to its equity or assets?" Or "how much of the company assets belong to the shareholders rather than creditors?" A company is less levered when most of its assets belong to shareholders, and vice versa. Examples to calculate leverage ratios are presented in ▶ Exhibit 6.10. Practical applications are discussed in ▶ Chap. 8.

Banner 6.16 Leverage Ratios

Leverage ratios measure a company's financial risk—that is, its ability to fulfill its financial obligations.

Relevance of Leverage Ratios

Leverage ratios are used to assess the risk of financial distress arising from managers' capital structure decisions. For instance, the "debt-to-equity ratio" (i.e., total liabilities to common equity) shows the proportion of company financing coming from creditors compared to common equity holders: a ratio of 50% means that shareholders can cover liabilities twice and a ratio of 100% implies that shareholders and creditors have equal stake in the company's assets. "Total liabilities to total assets" shows the ability of a company to pay off its total liabilities with its assets—it indicates the overall liability burden and ability to pay it off: a ratio of 50% suggests low risk because assets are twice liabilities; a ratio of 100% means a company will have to deplete all its assets to pay off liabilities. "Total common equity to total assets" measures the percentage of assets that is financed by owners' equity. It indicates how much assets the investors should retain if a company is liquidated to pay all its liabilities. A higher equity ratio is a sign of investors' confidence of the company.

Exhibit 6.10 Leverage Ratios

Illustrative Example (See Excel Workings—► Chap. 6, Sheet E.6.10)

The following information was extracted from the financial statement of FAIDA Ltd (all figures in millions). In 2012 and 2011, the company reported total equity of $1198 and $1129 (including common shareholders' equity of $449 and $380), respectively. Total liabilities were $1170 and $1060, whereas total assets were $2368 and $2189 in 2012 and 2011, respectively.

Calculate the following leverage ratios for 2012, whereby debt is defined as total liabilities.

(a) Debt-to-equity
(b) Debt-to-total assets
(c) Equity-to-total assets

Solution

(a) Debt-to-Equity

$$\textit{Debt-to-equity ratio} = \frac{\textit{Total liabilities}}{\textit{Shareholders' equity}} = \frac{\$1170}{\$449} = 2.61 = 261\%$$

Interpretation: Shareholders' (owners') equity is 261% short to cover all liabilities. The leverage is generally high.

(b) Debt-to-Total Assets (Debt Ratio)

$$\textit{Debt ratio} = \frac{\textit{Total liabilities}}{\textit{Total assets}} = \frac{\$1170}{\$2368} = 0.49 = 49\%$$

Interpretation: If liquidated, only 49% of the assets will be used to settle all liabilities, retaining 51% of the current asset value. The leverage is generally low.

(c) Equity-to-Total Assets (Equity Ratio)

$$\textit{Equity ratio} = \frac{\textit{Shareholders' equity}}{\textit{Total assets}} = \frac{\$449}{\$2368} = 0.19 = 19\%$$

Interpretation: In all, 19% of assets are financed by owners' equity. If liquidated, the assets will cover 81% of all liabilities.

Think 6.5

What types of leverage ratios are likely to be more relevant to the following: (a) common shareholders, (b) debtholders, and (c) all investors? Explain your opinions.

6.4.1.5 Market Value Ratios

What Do They Measure?

Market value ratios measure (Exhibit 6.5.5) market perception about company performance. They compare stock market prices to performance measures like earnings and dividends. See the example in ▶ Exhibit 6.11, and refer to ▶ Chap. 9 for further details and practical application.

Banner 6.17 Market Value Ratios

Market value ratios are relevant to investors for analyzing stock price trends, which can help predict the future market value of stocks.

Relevance of Market Value Ratios

Overall, market value ratios are used to analyze stock price trends to help predict the future market value. They indicate investors' expectations on their investment returns in terms of key measures like earnings per share (EPS), dividend per share (DPS), and capital gains (CG). Thus, analysts and investors can use these ratios to determine whether stocks are overvalued, undervalued, or fairly priced.

The "price–earnings (P/E)" ratio, which compares stock price (numerator) to earnings per share (denominator), shows how much the market is willing to pay for a stock relative to earnings per share. It is, therefore, relevant to investors for determining a fair market price based on expectations about EPS. For dividend companies, higher expected earnings are usually associated with expected higher dividends and/or expected appreciation of the stock value. Generally, a higher P/E ratio implies investors' positive perception and higher demand of company's stocks, and vice versa. "Dividend yield (DY)," which compares DPS (numerator) to stock price (denominator), shows investors how their investments generate returns in the form of cash dividends, considering growth opportunities. Market value ratios are more useful when comparing peer companies or the industry.

Exhibit 6.11 Market Value Ratios

Illustrative Example (See Excel Workings—▶ Chap. 6, Sheet E.6.11)

On 31 December 2018, FAIDA Ltd reported a net income of $122 million. The company paid a total of $35 million in cash dividends, which was distributed to preference stockholders ($25 million) and common stockholders ($10 million). The number of common shares outstanding at the end of the period was 5 million. Its stocks were trading at $32.5 per share.

Calculate and interpret the following market value ratios as on 31 December 2018:

1. P/E ratio
2. DY ratio

Solution

(a) P/E Ratio

$$PE\ ratio = \frac{Market\ price\ per\ share}{EPS}$$
$$= \frac{\$32.5}{\$19.4} = 1.68$$

$$EPS = \frac{Earnings\ available\ to\ common\ shareholders}{Number\ of\ common\ shares\ outstanding}$$

Earnings available to common shareholders are calculated by subtracting the preference dividends from the net income (i.e., $122 – $25 = $97 million). EPS is $19.4 (i.e., $97/5).

Interpretation: Investors are willing to pay $0.68 more for every dollar of earnings.

(b) DY Ratio

$$DY = \frac{Dividend\ per\ share}{Market\ price\ per\ share}$$
$$= \frac{\$2}{\$32.5} = 0.06 = 6.0\%$$

Interpretation: Investors received 6.0% investment returns in the form of dividends—that is, $0.06 cash dividends for every dollar of investment market value.

6.4.2 Valuation Implications

Ratio analysis plays an important role in examining company performance to achieve the main goal of shareholders' wealth maximization. Although ratios are generally based on historical performance, they help predict the future, considering other factors like economic condition, competition, and so on. To analyze value, ratios tend to be applied in different ways like comparative company analysis (relative valuation), growth estimation, and risk analysis. Some of these aspects are discussed in ▸ Chaps. 7–9.

Apply 6.2 Financial Ratios: WALMART

Data: See Excel workings—▸ Chap. 6, Sheet A.6.1)

Use the financial statements of Walmart to analyze its performance from 2016 to 2021 on the following aspects:

(a) Profitability
(b) Liquidity
(c) Efficiency
(d) Leverage
(e) Market perception

Think 4.6

Reflecting on market perception ratios, are investors better off in companies with high dividend payouts or low dividend payouts? Explain with examples.

6.5 Effective Financial Statement Analysis

Financial statements carry information about a company's financial performance without directly showing the performance drivers. It is not enough to say, for example, that the ROE increased by 5% from 2010 to 2011. This percentage increase means nothing without answering key questions such as: Why 5%? What are the factors that affected it? What is the performance of the peers of the industry? Is the performance good or bad?

Financial ratios, therefore, should not be interpreted rigidly by solely relying on accounting information because the numbers reflect what happened outside the book of accounts. For example, sales depends on demand and the overall economic condition in which a firm operates. Therefore, the use of financial ratios requires multidimensional analysis of factors to distinguish the way companies set their policies and strategic decisions that affect financial performance.

Banner 6.18 Effective Financial Statement Analysis

An effective financial statement analysis should consider both a firm's internal factors and external factors as well as quantitative and qualitative measurements.

"Internal factors" are a firm's specific factors and are within its control, for example, corporate strategies, managerial decisions, management and staff quality, organizational policies, culture, financial capability, credibility, organizational structure, board of directors, and so on. "External factors" are industry-specific or economic, beyond a firm's control but they influence performance, such as demand, purchasing power of people, inflation, government policies, regulations, political stability, exchange rate volatility, and so on. For instance, the Covid-19 pandemic, and a surge in oil prices due to low supply (amid Russia-Ukraine war) affected performance in almost all companies.

Consider the following quote relating to Orvana Minerals, a multi-mine gold and copper producer:

> *A variety of inherent risks, uncertainties, and factors, many of which are beyond the Company's control, affect the operations, performance and results of the Company and its business, and could cause actual events or results to differ materially from estimated or anticipated events or results expressed or implied by forward looking statements (Marketwire Canada, August 17, 2012).*

The quote was extracted from a news article titled "Orvana Announces Changes to Board of Directors" following the company's release of financial projections—forward-looking statements. Orvana's management identified several internal and external factors expected to affect its projections. Some of those factors are summarized in ▶ Exhibit 6.12 together with their implications.

Overall, financial statement analysis should help companies improve performance and other users (e.g., investors, lenders, suppliers, customers, and so on) make good decisions. Hence, performance should be analyzed on the basis of three dimensions—the past, the present and the future. Moreover, the overall performance of a firm cannot be judged by single or double ratios—a group of ratios should be used.

Exhibit 6.12 Internal and External Factors Affecting Performance

Case Example: Orvana Minerals

The following table provides a real case example of factors to consider for effective financial statement analysis. It should be noted that a performance driver can be both an internal factor (if the company can implement some control measures) and an external factor (if the company cannot control it).

Performance driver	As an internal factor	As an external factor
Fluctuations in the price of gold, silver, and copper	The company can implement hedging strategies against price volatility	The company cannot control global market prices
The need to recalculate estimates of resources based on actual production experience	Estimates are based on managerial decisions	
Failure to achieve production estimates	Production performance depends on the firm's internal capabilities	Production can be influenced by external factors such as natural disasters and government policies
Variations in the grade of ores mined		The company cannot control the grade of minerals
Variations in the cost of operations	Company's costing and cost management	External forces can affect operational costs
Availability of qualified personnel	Recruitment policy and capability	Availability of qualified personnel
The company's ability to obtain and maintain all necessary regulatory approvals and licenses	Internal policies and strategies	Regulatory environments
The company's ability to use cyanide in its mining operations	Financial resources	Regulatory environment and environmental policies
Risks generally associated with mineral exploration and development	Financial resources	Mining regulations, government policies, and availability of minerals

Performance driver	As an internal factor	As an external factor
The company's ability to acquire and develop mineral properties and to successfully integrate such acquisitions	Financial resources	Industry competitors, regulations, and policies
The company's ability to obtain financing when required on acceptable terms	Financial resources and financial management	Presence of strong capital markets
Challenges to the company's interests in its property and mineral rights		Regulatory environments
Current, pending, and proposed legislative or regulatory developments or changes in political, social, or economic conditions in countries in which the company operates		Regulations and policies, economic conditions, political risks, etc.
General economic conditions worldwide	Risk management, financial management, etc.	Domestic and global economic conditions
Risks and uncertainties	Risk management	Unforeseen events

Source: Summarized from *Marketwire Canada (August 17, 2012)*

6.6 Limitations of Financial Statement Analysis

Users of financial statements should be cautious when interpreting and drawing performance conclusions. Several factors can limit financial statement analysis, including the following:

Reliability: Financial statements are subjected to reliability issues—the quality of accounting information can be affected by factors like diversity in accounting practices, accounting manipulation, and subjective motives.

The Timing and Duration of Financial Reporting: Regulators require companies to publish financial reports (annually, quarterly, or trailing quarters or 12 months). However, there are neither universal standards nor rules to be followed by companies to determine financial reporting dates or duration. This limits comparative performance analysis among firms.

Basis of Preparing Financial Statements: The basis on which financial statements are prepared differ across firms. Among others, these differences include treatment of inventories, depreciations, amortization of intangibles and preliminary expenses, treatment of extraordinary items, and asset valuations. These differences limit comparability among firms.

Inflation Effects: Financial statements are prepared and presented on historical cost without adjustments for inflation. If two companies purchased assets at different periods, then inflation will have different effects on those assets—that is, historical cost-based financial statements will mislead their current values.

Stop and Think 4.7

Reflecting on the limitations of financial statement analysis, suggest and explain some possible solutions in addressing each of the limiting factors.

Review Questions

1. What is the main role of financial statement analysis?
2. With examples, explain how financial statement analysis can be useful to each of the following users of financial information:
   (a) Company's management
   (b) Investors
   (c) Lenders
   (d) Suppliers
   (e) Debtors
   (f) Analysts
3. Explain the difference between horizontal and vertical analyses of financial statements.
4. With examples, describe the usefulness of horizontal and vertical analyses of financial statements.
5. In horizontal financial statement analysis, what is the difference between percentage changes and trend percentages? What is the practical use of each?
6. Explain why the effect of company size can limit the application of horizontal analysis in comparing the performances of different companies.
7. Define the following aspects as applied to comparative analysis of financial statements:
   (a) Horizontal trend percentages
   (b) Vertical trend percentages
8. Explain why the effect of company size cannot limit the application of vertical analysis in comparing the performances of different companies.
9. Define the following aspects as applied to comparative analysis of financial statements:
   (a) Base year
   (b) Base item
10. What is the commonly applied base item in vertical analysis of a company's financial position? Give reasons to support your answer.
11. What is the commonly applied base item in vertical analysis of a company's business operations? Give reasons to support your answer.
12. Use examples to explain the valuation relevance of the following financial statement analysis aspects:
    (a) Horizontal analysis
    (b) Vertical analysis
    (c) Financial ratios

13. What is the difference between comparative financial statement analysis and financial ratio analysis?
14. Describe the main categories of financial ratios and explain their practical use.
15. Based on their purpose, suggest the types of ratios that are likely to be the most relevant to each of the following users of financial information:
    (a) Company's management
    (b) Investors
    (c) Lenders
    (d) Suppliers
    (e) Debtors
16. In profitability ratios, what is the difference between profit margins and returns?
17. How can you interpret the following profitability ratios?
    (a) Gross margin = 45%
    (b) Net profit margin = 8%
    (c) Return on assets = 25%
    (d) Return on equity = 12%
    (e) Return on capital employed = 10%
18. How can you interpret the following liquidity ratios?
    (a) Current ratio = 3: 1
    (b) Current ratio = 1: 1
    (c) Current ratio = 0.7: 1
    (d) Quick ratio = 4: 1
19. In terms of relevance, what is the difference between current ratio and quick ratio? Use examples to support your explanations.
20. Explain the practical relevance of defensive interval.
21. Under what circumstances can defensive interval be used for decision-making?
22. How can you interpret the following efficiency ratios?
    (a) Capital turnover = 4.3 times
    (b) Inventories turnover = 7.9 times
    (c) Receivables turnover = 22.5 times
    (d) Payables turnover = 12 times
23. What does it imply when a company's capital turnover is less than 1?
24. What are the key decision criteria for determining the ideal level of the following ratios?
    (a) Inventories turnover
    (b) Accounts payable turnover
25. Define the following terms and explain their role in measuring the efficiency of working capital management.
    (a) Operating cycle
    (b) Cash conversion cycle
26. Do efficiency ratios supplement profitability ratios? Explain.
27. Explain the main uses of financial leverage ratios.
28. How can you interpret the following leverage ratios?
    (a) Total liabilities to shareholders' equity = 0.45
    (b) Total liabilities to shareholders' equity = 1.24
    (c) Total liabilities to total assets = 0.50

(d) Total liabilities to total assets = 1.0
(e) Shareholders' equity to total assets = 2.4
(f) Shareholders' equity to total assets = 0.83

29. What type of leverage ratio is likely to be more relevant to the following users of financial information?
    (a) Lenders
    (b) Investors
    (c) Managers
    (d) Suppliers
30. Explain the importance of the following ratios:
    (a) Price to earnings
    (b) Dividend yield
31. Reflecting on market perception ratios, are investors better off in companies with high dividend payouts or low dividend payouts? Explain with examples.
32. How can you interpret the following market perception ratios?
    (a) P/E = 0.65
    (b) P/E = 1.00
    (c) P/E = 5.9
    (d) DY = 6.2%
    (e) DY = 100%
    (f) DY = 103%
33. The following information was extracted from the financial statement of ABC Plc for 2017 and 2018 (all figures in millions). In 2018, the company reported net sales revenues and gross profit of \$4600 and \$1450, respectively. Cost of goods sold was \$3245, operating expenses were \$910, and depreciation was \$123. EBIT, pretax income, and net income were \$430, \$306, and \$190, respectively. The company paid a total of \$90 cash dividends, which was distributed to preference stockholders (\$60) and common stockholders (\$30). The company's financial reporting period is 30 June annually. The number of common shares outstanding on 30 June 2018 was \$2, in which its stocks were trading at \$22.8 per share. Additional information is provided in the following table:

	2018 (\$ millions)	2017 (\$ millions)
Cash and cash equivalents	240	224
Accounts receivable	850	890
Inventory	1420	1300
Prepaid expenses	25	30
Accumulated tax prepaid	34	25
Accounts payable	220	231
Notes payable	613	600
Accrued taxes	84	53
Other accruals	215	286

	2018 ($ millions)	2017 ($ millions)
Long-term debt	1268	1050
Common equity	950	800
Total equity	2450	2300
Total liabilities	2380	2.200

6

Calculate the following ratios for 2018 and interpret your results:
- (i) Gross margin
- (ii) Net profit margin
- (iii) Return on assets
- (iv) Return on equity
- (v) Return on capital employed
- (vi) Current ratio
- (vii) Quick ratio
- (viii) Defensive interval
- (ix) Capital turnover
- (x) Inventory turnover
- (xi) Accounts receivables turnover
- (xii) Accounts payables turnover
- (xiii) Operating cycle
- (xiv) Cash conversion cycle
- (xv) Total liabilities to shareholders equity
- (xvi) Total liabilities to total assets
- (xvii) Total equity to total assets
- (xviii) P/E ratio
- (xix) Dividend yield

34. In financial statement analysis, why is it important to consider information beyond financial statements?
35. With examples, explain how a firm's specific factors and external factors can affect financial performance.
36. Outline the key factors limiting effective financial statement analysis. Give examples to support your answers.

Bibliography

Market wire Canada (2012), Orvana Announces Changes to Board of Directors, Available at Market Wire Canada http://www.stockhouse.com/News/CanadianReleasesDetail.aspx?n=8592757 Accessed August 17, 2012.

Wall Street (2022). 2021 financial statement confirms growth course - Martin Esser appointed to the Management Board as CFO, https://www.wallstreet-online.de/nachricht/15386594-dgap-news-2021-financial-statement-confirms-growth-course-martin-esser-appointed-to-the-management-board-as-cfo Accessed April 29th, 2022.

Profitability Analysis

Contents

Supplementary Information The online version contains supplementary material available at https://doi.org/10.1007/978-3-031-28267-6_7.

B. Kulwizira Lukanima, *Corporate Valuation*, Classroom Companion: Business, https://doi.org/10.1007/978-3-031-28267-6_7

7.1 Introduction

Profitability is the most important performance measure used in business operations. Although it does not imply value, profit maximization signifies investment returns (interest and dividends paid to debtholders and shareholders) and growth potential (retained earnings). Therefore, investors and other users of financial statements tend to be more attentive to news about profitability than other financial metrics, thus making it the most important ratio in financial analysis. This chapter, therefore, takes a special interest and focuses on the key profitability ratios, aiming to demonstrate their implications in corporate valuation.

Learning Outcomes

- Analyze a company's performance in sales and cost of goods sold
- Analyze a company's performance in managing and controlling expenses
- Analyze a company's performance in financial resource efficiency
- Choose relevant profitability ratios for specific purposes
- Understand the industry factor in profitability analysis
- Apply profitability ratios to analyze economic value added
- Understand the valuation implications of profitability ratios

7.2 Profitability Performance

Making profits is a process that depends on several factors, both company-specific (internal) and economic (external). Overall, profitability arises from sales after taking care of expenses at different stages of business operations, with the goal being profit maximization. Profitability analysis, therefore, focuses on measuring the performance of the following key aspects: sales and cost of goods sold, management and control of expenses, and financial resource efficiency. It should be noted, however, that the profit maximization goal does not mean value maximization (refer to ▶ Chap. 2).

Banner 7.1 Profit Maximization

Profit maximization signifies investment returns (interest and dividends) to debtholders and shareholders and growth potential (retained earnings).

7.3 Performance in Sales and Cost of Goods Sold

Sales performance is a key driver of corporate profitability performance after taking care of expenses, starting with those directly related to sales (cost of goods sold or cost of sales). The difference between sales revenues and cost of sales is gross profit (earnings before both operating and nonoperating expenses). Therefore, gross profit should be sufficient enough to cover all other expenses—otherwise, a company will incur a loss. Normally, cost of sales and operating expenses tend to be driven by sales targets.

Think 7.1

What are the possible measures to maximize sales and minimize cost of sales?

How Is It Measured?

To measure the ability of a firm to manage and control the cost of goods sold, we use the "gross margin" or the "gross profit" ratio (refer to ▶ Chap. 6). While judging performance, one must keep in mind that a lower (higher) margin means a lower (higher) gross income as a percentage of sales—it reflects the firm's ability to maximize sales and minimize cost of sales.

Banner 7.2 Gross Margin

The gross margin measures the ability of a firm to manage and control its cost of sales.

What Is the Relevance of the Gross Margin?

The gross margin is particularly relevant for operational managers in different sections relating to sales, production, logistics and supplies, costing and pricing, and the like. When margins show a declining trend and are lower than those of competitors (or the industry), it is required that the firm focuses its attention on improvement.

In value creation, the gross margin can have several implications. First, it can affect cash flows because cash flows arise from income. Second, the ability to increase sales depends on a company's marketing strategies, which imply marketing expenses—the gross margin should be sufficient to support those expenses. Investors, therefore, are interested in the gross margin as an indicator of possible earnings and cash flow risks. An extremely narrow gross margin is dangerous because even a small fluctuation in sales or cost of sales may cause a significant impact on earnings or cash flows.

Kovar (2020) explains how the gross margin is related to company value. In mergers and acquisitions (M&A), target companies' gross margins are more relevant than both earnings before interest and taxes (EBIT) and net income because "the buyer will be looking to reduce redundancies like dual marketing departments after an acquisition" (Linda Rose, principal at RoseBiz, Encinitas, a California-based M&A adviser to technology services companies). Hence, "maximizing company value depends primarily on increasing recurring revenue, customer satisfaction, and financial fitness."

7.4 Performance in Operating Expenses

After cost of sales, another item that takes a share of sales revenues is "operating expenses." The difference between cost of sales and operating expenses is operating income or earnings before interest and taxes (EBIT)—interest and taxes are excluded to focus on expenses that companies control directly.

▪ **How Is It Measured?**

An appropriate ratio to measure a firm's ability to manage its operating expenses is the "operating profit margin," which is expressed as follows:

$$Operating\ profit\ margin = \frac{EBIT}{Sales} \times 100$$

Performance analysis should consider both historical performance across companies and industry benchmarks. A lower (higher) margin means that a company generates a lower (higher) percentage of EBIT relative to its sales—an increased ratio (historical analysis) or a higher ratio (based on benchmarks) is desirable as it indicates better performance.

Banner 7.3 Operating Profit Margin

The operating profit margin measures a firm's ability to manage and control its operating expenses.

▪ **What Is the Relevance of the Operating Profit Margin?**

The operating profit margin reflects a firm's performance in operating expenses, which are usually addressed by strategic decision-makers, operational managers, and other related personnel. It is relevant to investors (debtholders and shareholders) as an indicator of a company's ability to fulfill its investment obligations—pay interest and/or dividends. Moreover, the operating margin is a useful input for determining the relative value of growth (RVG), considering that growth is a driver of value (refer to ▸ Chap. 18).

7.5 Performance in Overall Expenses

A company's overall performance in managing expenses should consider not only operating expenses but also nonoperating expenses—interest and taxes. Whether interest and tax expenses should be jointly analyzed (when using EBIT) depends on the purpose of the analysis. Companies influence neither interest rates nor income tax rates—these are determined by lenders and governments. When including only interest expenses, we use earnings before tax (EBT); assuming that companies have some control over their interest expenses, they have the power to make decisions on the amount of debt (financing decisions). Moreover, the exclusion of taxes enables comparability among companies (within the industry) due to possible differences in tax rates and tax liabilities.

▪ How Is It Measured?

From the earlier point of view, the profit margin is based on earnings before tax (EBT) to arrive at the "pretax profit margin" as follows:

$$Pretax\ profit\ margin = \frac{EBT}{Sales} \times 100$$

If, however, the focus is on all expenses regardless of their controllability, then the appropriate margin is based on earnings after tax (EAT). This is known as the "net profit margin (NPM)" and is calculated as follows:

$$Net\ profit\ margin = \frac{EAT}{Sales} \times 100$$

Banner 7.4 Pretax Profit Margin

The pretax profit margin measures the ability of a firm to manage and control its operating and financing expenses.

▪ What Is the Relevance of the Pretax Profit Margin?

The pretax profit margin conveys important information about the two key aspects relating to value creation: the ability to generate revenues and the ability to be cost-effective in operating and financing decisions. As firms strive to boost their profits, a higher (lower) pretax profit margin is a sign of efficiency (inefficiency) in business operations, which indicates sales maximization and cost minimization. For company analysts and investors, the pretax margin is suitable to compare companies in the same peer group or industry, regardless of differences in their sizes. It is, therefore, relevant to market analysts and investors, reflecting organic growth, which influences value.

Banner 7.5 Net Profit Margin

The net profit margin measures the ability of a firm to manage and control all its expenses.

▪ What Is the Relevance of the Net Profit Margin?

The net profit margin indicates a firm's strategic position on pricing and costing. It is probably the most popular profitability measure due to its relevance to almost all users of financial statements. A lower (higher) ratio is an indication of a lower (higher) safety margin—the risk of profits depleting if sales drop. Shareholders, therefore, use the net profit margin to analyze a company's ability to maximize value in the long term (LT) through dividends (cash flows) and growth (reinvestment of retained earnings).

Banner 7.6 Performance in Managing Expenses

When comparing the profitability performance of two or more companies, the smaller the difference between the gross margin and operating margin (or net profit margin), the better the company's performance in managing its operating (or nonoperating) expenses.

Think 7.2

When it comes to profit margins, why do some companies perform better than others in the same industry?

The Industry Factor

It is essential to consider the industry factor because profit margins differ significantly across industries and sectors—some industries tend to have naturally higher margins than do others. Hence, comparative analysis should be applied to similar companies or to those within the same industry—a company is doing well if it outperforms its peers or the industry.

7

► Exhibits 7.1–7.3 elaborate this aspect using selected case companies, covering five fiscal years. These are case analyses of six US companies selected from three different sectors (two companies from each sector): Walmart and PriceSmart (consumer staples), Exxon Mobil and Chevron Corporation (energy), and Amazon and Wayfair (consumer discretionary). The three cases show different methods of performance analysis, considering three aspects—the time trend, sector benchmark, and the influence of external factors. Clearly, each sector has unique business characteristics that are reflected in their profit margins. For example, the energy sector shows the highest gross margin (45.3%) but the lowest net profit margin (1.0%). The other two sectors, consumer staples and consumer discretionary, differ slightly. Consumer staples show a higher gross margin (37.0%) but a lower net profit margin (3.9%). The difference between gross margins and operating margins is almost 32.1% (energy), 29.8% (consumer discretionary), and 25.6% (consumer staples). This implies that the energy sector has the highest operating expenses, whereas the consumer staples sector has the lowest.

Exhibit 7.1 Analysis of Profit Margins

Case Example: Walmart vs. PriceSmart (See Excel Workings—► Chap. 7, Sheet E.7.1)

This is a case of two companies: Walmart and PriceSmart (consumer staples). Company performance is analyzed based on sector benchmarks and historical trends (see ■ Exhibit 7.1.1). It should be noted that the two companies have different fiscal years: Walmart (31 January) and PriceSmart (31 August).

Average Sector (Consumer Staples) Performance of US Companies by January 2020: the gross profit margin

(GPM) was 36.3%, the operating income margin (OPM) was 10.7%, and the net profit margin (NPM) was 5.5%.

Analysis

General: Overall, they show identical performance trends, moving together up and down, suggesting an identical influence of external factors. Performance in margins was generally stable.

Specific: Walmart had a higher GPM (25% average) than did PriceSmart (16% average)—the difference was approximately 9% on a 5-year average. This implies that Walmart performed better than did PriceSmart in sales maximization relative to minimization of cost of goods sold but was below the sector average (36.3%). The two companies were almost equal in OPM and NPM but below the sector average (10.7% on OPM and 5.5% on NPM). However, PriceSmart was better than Walmart in managing operating expenses.

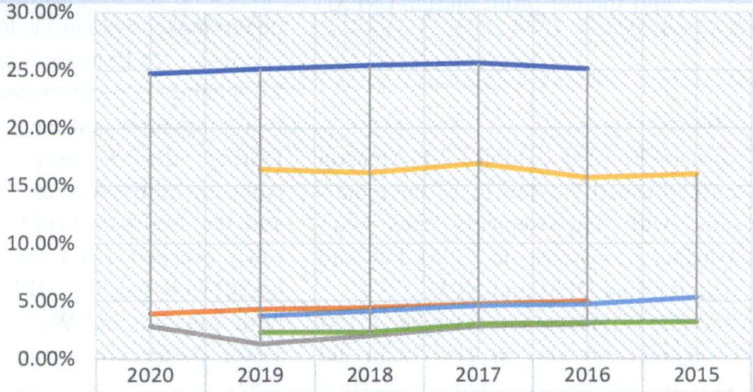

	2020	2019	2018	2017	2016	2015
Walmart GPM	24.70%	25.10%	25.40%	25.60%	25.10%	
Walmart OPM	3.90%	4.30%	4.40%	4.70%	5.00%	
Walmart NPM	2.80%	1.30%	2.00%	2.80%	3.00%	
Price Smart GPM		16.40%	16.10%	16.90%	15.70%	16.00%
Price Smart OPM		3.70%	4.10%	4.60%	4.70%	5.30%
Price Smart NPM		2.30%	2.30%	3.00%	3.10%	3.20%

Exhibit 7.1.1 Walmart vs. PriceSmart

Exhibit 7.2 Analysis of Profit Margins

Case Example: Amazon vs. Wayfair (See Excel Workings— ▶ Chap. 7, Sheet E.7.2)

This is a case analysis of two companies in the same sector (consumer discretionary). Company performance is analyzed based on sector benchmarks and historical trends.

Average Sector (Consumer Discretionary) Performance of US Companies by December 2019: the gross profit margin (GPM) was 37.0%, the operating income margin (OPM) was 7.2%, and the net profit margin (NPM) was 3.9%.

Analysis

General: From ▣ Exhibit 7.2.1, Amazon outperformed Wayfair in all three margins, with improvements each year. Wayfair was stable on GPM but had deteriorating OPM and NPM.

Specific: Amazon had a higher GPM (ranging from 33% to 41%) than did Wayfair (24% average). This implies that Amazon performed better than Wayfair in sales maximization relative to minimization of cost of goods sold. Amazon's OPM showed yearly improvement (from 2.1% to 5.1%), whereas Wayfair's OPM deteriorated (from -3.6% to -10.2%). A similar trend was evidenced on NPM, whereby Amazon had a significant rise from just 0.6% to 4.10% compared to a significant decline in Wayfair from -3.4% to -10.8%. Overall, Wayfair was inefficient in managing expenses. Its investors should have been worried about possible value destruction if the company continued to make losses in the long term.

Sector: ▣ Exhibits 7.2.2, 7.2.3, and 7.2.4 compare performance between the two companies and against the sector. During the 5 years (2015–2019), Amazon outperformed both Wayfair and the sector on GPM. Wayfair narrowly overperformed the sector, except in 2017. Regarding OPM and NPM, both Amazon and Wayfair were below sector performance throughout the 5 years.

	2019	2018	2017	2016	2015
Amazon.com GPM	41.00%	40.20%	37.10%	35.10%	33.00%
Amazon.com OPM	5.10%	5.30%	2.30%	3.10%	2.10%
Amazon.com NPM	4.10%	4.30%	1.70%	0.70%	0.60%
Wayfair Inc. GPM	23.50%	23.40%	23.70%	23.90%	24.00%
Wayfair Inc. OPM	-10.20%	-7.00%	-4.80%	-5.80%	-3.60%
Wayfair Inc. NPM	-10.80%	-7.40%	-5.20%	-5.80%	-3.40%

▣ **Exhibit 7.2.1** Amazon vs. Wayfair

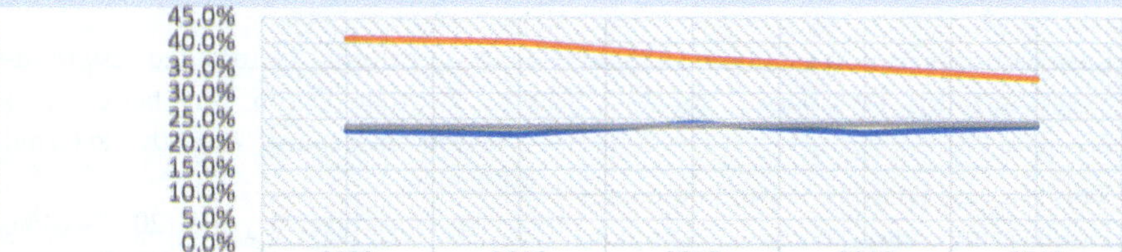

	2019	2018	2017	2016	2015
GPM (sector)	22.7%	21.9%	24.1%	22.2%	23.5%
GPM (Amazon)	41.0%	40.2%	37.1%	35.1%	33.0%
GPM (Wayfair)	23.5%	23.4%	23.7%	23.9%	24.0%

Exhibit 7.2.2 Company vs. sector—gross profit margin

	2019	2018	2017	2016	2015
OPM (sector)	5.9%	6.0%	9.2%	10.5%	12.6%
OPM (Amazon)	5.1%	5.3%	2.3%	3.1%	2.1%
OPM (Wayfair)	-10.2%	-7.0%	-4.8%	-5.8%	-3.6%

Exhibit 7.2.3 Company vs. sector—operating profit margin

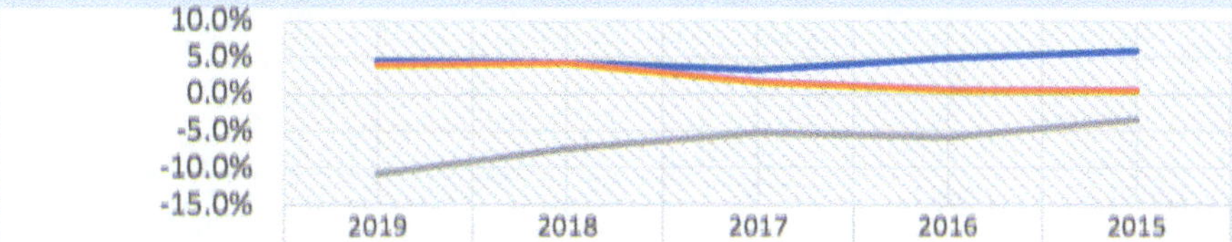

	2019	2018	2017	2016	2015
NPM (sector)	4.6%	4.3%	3.3%	4.9%	5.9%
NPM (Amazon)	4.1%	4.3%	1.7%	0.7%	0.6%
NPM (Wayfair)	-10.8%	-7.4%	-5.2%	-5.8%	-3.4%

Exhibit 7.2.4 Company vs. sector—net profit margin
Source of Data: Finbox.com (2020)

Exhibit 7.3 Analysis of Profit Margins

Case Example: Exxon vs. Chevron (See Excel Workings—▶ Chap. 7, Sheet E.7.3)

This is a case analysis of two companies in the same sector (energy). Company performance is analyzed based on sector benchmarks, historical trends, and sector-specific factor (oil prices).

Average Sector (Energy) Performance of US Companies by December 2019: the gross profit margin (GPM) was 45.3%, the operating income margin (OPM) was 13.2%, the net profit margin (NPM) was 1.0%.

Analysis

General: Overall, as depicted in ▪ Exhibit 7.3.1, the two companies show identical performance trends on OPM and NPM, suggesting an identical influence of external factors on the two variables. However, Exxon's GPM was more stable than Chevron's, suggesting that the external factors had less influence or that Exxon was better than Chevron in dealing with the external influences.

Specific: Over 5 years (2015–2019), Chevron was within the GPM sector average (45.3%) and outperformed Exxon—the average difference between the two companies was 13.4%. However, Exxon performed better than did Chevron on both OPM and NPM. This means that Exxon was more efficient than Chevron in managing operating expenses. Moreover, the two companies outperformed the NPM sector average (1%) but were below the OPM sector average (13.2%).

Sector-Specific Factor: ▪ Exhibits 7.3.2 and ▪ 7.3.3 use crude oil prices to examine the possible external factors affecting sector performance. Clearly, revenue and cost of goods sold of the two companies tend to move together with oil prices.

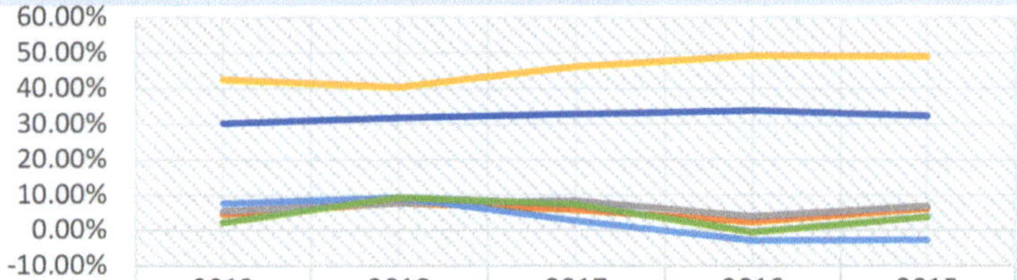

	2019	2018	2017	2016	2015
Exxon Mobil GPM	30.20%	31.70%	32.90%	33.80%	32.20%
Exxon Mobil OPM	4.60%	7.70%	5.90%	2.30%	6.00%
Exxon Mobil NPM	5.60%	7.50%	8.30%	3.90%	6.70%
Chevron Corp. GPM	42.70%	40.50%	46.20%	49.30%	49.10%
Chevron Corp. OPM	7.50%	9.20%	2.70%	-2.90%	-2.60%
Chevron Corp. NPM	2.10%	9.30%	7.20%	-0.50%	3.70%

▪ **Exhibit 7.3.1** Exxon Mobil vs. Chevron Corporation

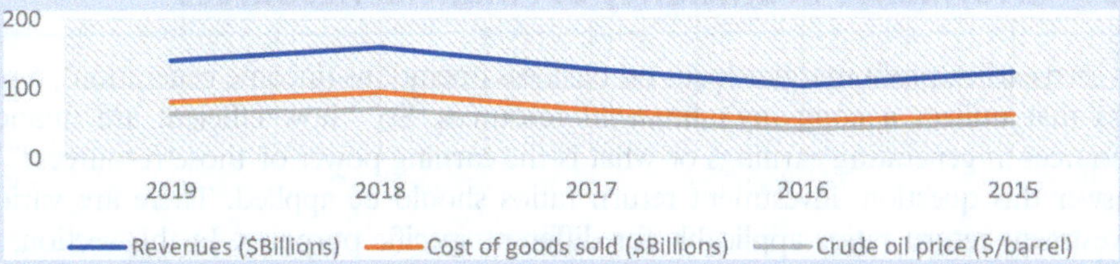

Exhibit 7.3.2 The influence of oil prices—Chevron

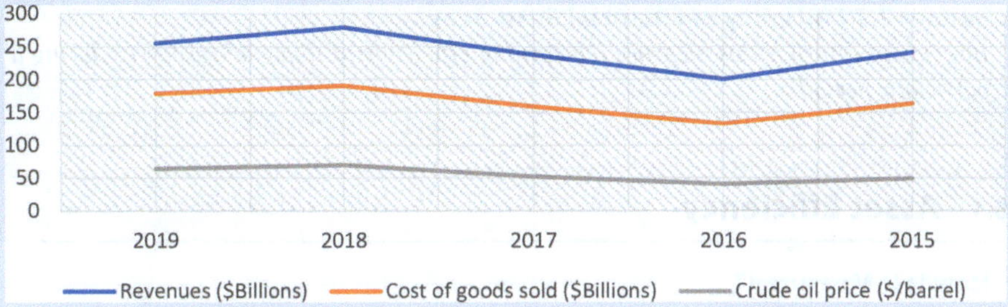

Exhibit 7.3.3 The influence of oil prices—Exxon
Source: Finbox.com (2020)

Apply 7.1 Profitability Margins

Ford Motor Co., General Motors Co., and Toyota Motor Corp.

Data See Excel workings—► Chap. 7, Sheet A.7.1–3

The data sheet presents financial statements for 5 years. Use Excel to perform the following analysis:

(a) Calculate the profit margins (the 5-year trend): the gross margin, operating margin, pretax profit margin, and net profit margin.
(b) Use graphs to interpret and analyze performance. Make specific comments on the following aspects: cost of goods sold, operating expenses, and all expenses.
(c) Explain valuation implications of the company's profitability performance.

Think 7.3

What is the possible valuation effect of a company like Wayfair, whose net profit margin deteriorates from time to time?

7.6 Performance in Efficiency of Financial Resources

As seen earlier, profit margins focus on business operations (income generation), a process that utilizes a company's financial resources. So, "how efficient are financial resources in generating earnings or what is the earning power of those resources?" To answer this question, investment return ratios should be applied. There are various investment return ratios applicable for different specific purposes. In this section, we focus on the following: return on assets (ROA), return on capital employed (ROCE), return on invested capital (ROIC), and return on equity (ROE).

Banner 7.7 Efficiency of Financial Resources
Investment return ratios measure the earning efficiency of financial resources during a particular period.

7.6.1 Asset Efficiency

- **How Is It Measured?**

To measure the performance of total assets to generate earnings, "return on assets (ROA)" is used. Total assets mean all company resources—equal to total liabilities and equity. However, the numerator in ROA can vary according to the purpose of the analysis. If the focus is on returns for all investors (debtholders and equity holders), then the appropriate measure is operating income (EBIT). This also applies when excluding the leverage (financing) and tax effects, which differ across companies. The ROA ratio is expressed in percentage as follows:

$$ROA = \frac{EBIT}{Average\ total\ assets} \times 100$$

If the focus is on shareholders' earnings, then the appropriate measure is net income or earnings after tax (EAT)—"earnings available to shareholders." The ROA ratio is now expressed as follows:

$$ROA = \frac{Net\ income}{Average\ total\ assets} \times 100$$

Refer to the example in ▶ Chap. 6 on how to calculate ROA. ▶ Exhibit 7.4 breaks down ROA according to return drivers.

Banner 7.8 Return on Assets (ROA)
Return on assets (ROA) measures the performance of total assets in generating earnings during a specified period.

Think 7.4
When analyzing investment returns, why do we use average in the denominator?

What Is the Relevance of ROA?

ROA is a relevant performance measure when considering investment returns extensively and excessively. That is, ROA accounts for all resources at a company's disposal (shareholders' funds, borrowed funds, current assets, and current liabilities). It is, therefore, appropriate for analyzing asset intensity across companies and industries. On the other hand, ROA is used as a guide to track managers' performance in resource utilization over time.

When applied with EBIT, ROA measures the earning power of resources regardless of managers' financing decisions (leverage effect), thus making it relevant when comparing companies—it avoids distortions due to differences in leverage and tax rates. When applied with net income, ROA is more relevant for investors, intending to know the earning power of their total financial resources and considering leverage effects. Hence, the ratio can be misleading when comparing companies, but it is more appropriate when analyzing performance over time.

Regarding valuation, ROA can be compared to a company's overall required rate of return (cost of capital). Since the main goal is maximizing value, a better (worse) performance is when ROA exceeds (trails) the cost of capital—a company generates excess (shortage) returns.

Exhibit 7.4 Return on Assets: Performance Drivers

This exhibit breaks down ROA into its drivers: that is, profitability and asset turnover.

Applying EBIT

When using EBIT, the profitability component is the operating margin, whereas the turnover component is asset turnover, such that:

$$ROA = Operating\ margin \times Asset\ turover$$

$$ROA = \frac{EBIT}{Sales} \times \frac{Sales}{Average\ total\ assets}$$

Asset turnover expresses the number of times assets are turned over by sales revenues in a reported period—that is, how much sales is generated per each dollar of the total resources. The higher the turnover, the better the performance, and vice versa. This breakdown provides more details on the extent to which operating activities and assets contribute to asset efficiency.

Let us consider the following case example (Walmart):

The operating margin was 3.9% in 2019. Revenues during the same period was \$514.4 billion. Total assets in 2019 and 2018 were \$291.3 billion and 204.5 billion, respectively. The asset turnover in 2019 was, therefore, 2.4 times (or 240%): that is, \$514.4/[(\$291.3+\$204.5)/2]. This means that for each \$1 of its assets, the company was able to generate \$2.4 of sales revenues in 2019. ROA was 9.3% (i.e., 3.9% times 240%). That is, when generating ROA, the asset turnover had more contribution (5.4%) than the operating margin (3.9%).

Applying Net Income

When using earnings after tax (EAT), ROA can be broken down into net profit margin and asset turnover, such that:

$$ROA = Net\ profit\ margin \times Asset\ turover$$

$$ROA = \frac{EAT}{Sales} \times \frac{Sales}{Average\ total\ assets}$$

When analyzing performance over time, the decline of ROA signifies trouble. It is, therefore, important to examine the factors leading to such troubles. For example, ROA can decline due to a mismatch between capital spending (investment) and sales growth, which can be caused by both internal and external factors.

Banner 7.9 Relevance of ROA

Return on assets (ROA) is relevant for managers, investors, and analysts, as it intends to gauge the earning power of all business resources. Managers create (destroy) value if ROA exceeds (trails) the cost of capital.

7.6.2 Capital Efficiency

■ How Is It Measured?

When focus is on the performance of capital to generate income, several ratios can be used depending on the specific purpose. This section explains the following three ratios: "return on capital employed (ROCE)," "return on invested capital (ROIC)," and "return on equity (ROE)." Usually, ROCE and ROIC are applicable when focusing on the income available to all investors (debtholders and shareholders) but solely generated from core business operations. Therefore, the most appropriate income measure is net operating profit after tax (NOPAT), although EBIT can also be used on ROCE. NOPAT is important because it measures earning performance without financial leverage: that is, its allows comparability among companies with different capital structures. ROE is applicable when focusing on shareholders' returns.

Banner 7.10 Return on Capital Employed (ROCE)

ROCE measures the earning performance of long-term capital (long-term debts and equity), which a company has.

Banner 7.11 Return on Invested Capital (ROIC)

The difference between ROCE and ROIC is that ROIC focuses on the capital invested and is used to generate earnings within the reported financial period.

Return on Capital Employed (ROCE)

Generally, ROCE focuses on the performance of long-term capital (i.e., long-term debts and equity) to generate returns to both debtholders and equity holders. Although there are various versions of ROCE, here, we present the NOPAT version, which can be expressed as follows:

$$ROCE = \frac{NOPAT}{Capital\ employed} \times 100$$

Return on Invested Capital (ROIC)

"Return on invested capital (ROIC)" is like ROCE in the use of NOPAT. However, ROIC focuses on capital invested and is used to generate earnings within a financial period. It, therefore, measures investment returns regardless of financing sources. The general formula can be expressed as follows:

$$ROIC = \frac{NOPAT}{Invested\ capital} \times 100$$

Usually, when calculating ROIC, the invested capital (IC) is taken from the beginning of the year, although it is not uncommon to apply the invested capital either at the end of the year or as a 2-year average. The rationale is that capital expenditure during a year should have been fully utilized to generate income during the same year. Overall, there are variations in the way that analysts define and calculate invested capital. ▶ Exhibit 7.5 explains how to calculate NOPAT and invested capital, whereas vital adjustments are explained in ▶ Exhibit 7.8. A comprehensive example is illustrated in ▶ Exhibit 7.9 using the case of Walmart.

Exhibit 7.5 How to Calculate NOPAT and Invested Capital

Net Operating Profit After Tax (NOPAT)

The following methods can be used to determine NOPAT: the EBIT approach and the EAT (earnings after taxes) approach. Each of these approaches requires some adjustments to arrive at the target NOPAT depending on the available information.

With the "EBIT approach," NOPAT is simply EBIT adjusted for tax, such that:

$$NOPAT = EBIT\,(1 - Tax\ rate)$$

The "EAT approach" starts with after-tax profits to arrive at EBIT. However, some income statements tend to include bottom-line items related to nonbusiness operations (e.g., gains or losses from currency fluctuations, gains from one-time transactions, etc.). Therefore, NOPAT can be calculated as follows:

$$EBIT = \left(\begin{array}{l} EAT + Interest\ expenses + Taxes + \\ Nonoperating\ loss - Nonoperating\ gain \end{array} \right)$$

$$NOPAT = EBIT\,(1 - Tax\ rate)$$

It should be noted that NOPAT considers tax benefits (savings) earned on interest expenses. In valuation, interest tax benefits are expected to add value to shareholders whose earnings depend on the after-tax profits.

Invested Capital (IC)

There are two major approaches to calculating invested capital: the financial (or capital) approach and the operating (or asset) approach.

The financial approach (or the capital approach)

This approach focuses on financing needs to fund the net assets. It is, therefore, the sum of total debt and total equity, "minus" nonoperating assets, such that:

$$IC = Total\ debt + Total\ equity - Nonoperating\ assets$$

"Total debt" includes loans and capital lease obligations (both short- and long-term). "Total equity" means common stocks, preferred stocks, additional paid-in capital, retained earnings, bad debt reserve, and capitalized expenses (e.g., research and development (R&D) and marketing expenses). "Nonoperating assets" include cash and cash equivalents (e.g., cash from interest income and dividends received as well as marketable securities). They may be subtracted depending on analysts' views on active assets—some analysts tend to exclude them because ROIC should focus on the earning efficiency of an active investment.

The *operating approach (or the asset approach)*

This approach focuses on asset requirements to run business operations. It is, therefore, a measure of company's efficiency to use capital. Invested capital is therefore the sum of net working capital, noncurrent assets, intangible assets, and other operating assets.

$$IC = Net\ working\ capital + Tangible\ noncurrent\ assets + Intangible\ assets + Other\ operating\ assets$$

"Net working capital" includes current assets "minus" noninterest-bearing current liabilities. It can be negative for companies with a negative cash conversion cycle—they sell inventory and collect cash from debtors but delay paying suppliers. Tangible "noncurrent assets" include net plant, property, and equipment and other long-term investments. "Intangible assets" should always include goodwill and other intangible assets deemed to have a sale value. "Other operating assets" may include miscellaneous items such as deferred tax assets, derivative and hedging assets, and so on. To include or exclude an item in invested capital depends on one key question: can the same level of NOPAT be achieved without that item? Include the item if the answer is no. Exclude it if the answer is yes.

7

Think 7.5

When determining ROIC, nonoperating assets are excluded from invested capital. How can this be justified?

Think 7.6

Between the financial approach and the operating approach, which do you think is better for determining invested capital?

Return on Equity (ROE)

"Return on equity (ROE)" focuses on the returns generated for shareholders. Depending on the purpose of analysis, ROE can have two main versions, namely, "return on owners' equity" and "return on shareholders' equity." The general formula for ROE, which basically focuses on all shareholders (both common and preference), can be expressed as follows:

$$ROE = \frac{Net\ income}{Average\ total\ equity} \times 100$$

If the focus is on the owners (common shareholders), then the appropriate income measure is "earnings attributed to common shareholders" (which can be net income if no preference shareholders). Moreover, equity should consider "owners' equity" (which excludes preferred equity from total equity). This ROE version can be expressed as follows:

$$ROE = \frac{\text{EAC}}{Average\ owners' equity} \times 100$$

A comprehensive example is illustrated in ▶ Exhibit 7.9 using the case of Walmart.

Banner 7.12 Return on Equity (ROE)

ROE measures the profitability performance, focusing on returns generated for shareholders.

Banner 7.13 Return Analysis and Investment Decisions

*Leaving the question of price aside, the best business to own is one that over an extended period can employ large amounts of incremental capital at very high rates of return. (*Warren *Buffet, 1992).*

What is the Relevance of Return on Capital?

Returns (referring to ROCE, ROIC, ROA, and ROE) have extensive applications. Examining the return on capital over a period helps investors, managers, and analysts gauge whether a company's ability to generate returns to investors is improving, deteriorating, or stagnant. Let us consider the following quote:

> Leaving the question of price aside, the best business to own is one that over an extended period can employ large amounts of incremental capital at very high rates of return. The worst business to own is one that must, or *will*, do the opposite - that is, consistently employ ever-greater amounts of capital at very low rates of return. Unfortunately, the first type of business is very hard to find: Most high-return businesses need relatively little capital. Shareholders of such a business usually will benefit if it pays out most of its earnings in dividends or makes significant stock repurchases (Warren Buffet, 1992).

As pointed out by Buffet (1992), return on capital influences investment decisions—favorable returns motivate investors to inject more funds, and vice versa. Hence, companies that generate high returns on capital are likely to grow faster than are companies with low returns. That is, return on capital is a good indicator of a company's competitive advantage over both accessing capital and protecting its long-term profitability from core business operations.

To determine the value creation ability, investment returns tend to be compared to the cost of capital (weighted average cost of capital (WACC) and cost of equity), as illustrated in ▶ Exhibit 7.9. It should be noted, however, that ROIC is regarded as a superior measure of value creation because it focuses on long-term value and core business operations. Generally, for a company to be considered a value creator, its ROIC should be at least 2% more than its cost of capital—Walmart was, therefore, a value creator. Regarding the valuation implication of ROIC, let us consider the following quote:

> » Return on Capital or Return on Invested Capital (ROIC) is something I think about a lot. The list of metrics I look at when I analyze businesses is long: revenue growth, operating margins, free cash flow, payout ratios, etc. But if I could look at only one metric about a business to judge the quality of that business- ROIC would be the metric. Good businesses generate high returns on capital, and they do so with consistency. Return on capital is important because it is a fundamental driver of valuation. Businesses that can generate higher returns on capital can invest less in capital expenditures and thus generate more free cash flow to distribute to shareholders. Since value is the present value of future cash flows, this makes these businesses more valuable all else being equal (Scuttlebutt Investor, December 17, 2016).

ROE is an indicator of the rate of growth of shareholders' net worth (equity) through business operations. 7 Chapter 14 shows how ROE is used in estimating growth rates of earnings and free cash flows to equity. However, caution should be exercised when applying ROE due to its insensitivity to leverage variations. A change in the capital structure by increasing debts (high leverage) increases financial risk, but lower earnings may still indicate a higher ROE. That is, owners will earn higher returns at the expense of a higher risk of financial distress. Hence, ROE is more meaningful when retained earnings are reinvested.

Think 7.7

Assume two companies A and B from different industries: A is a technology company, whereas B is a manufacturing company. If their ROICs are 25% and 12%, respectively, should we consider company A to be a better value creator than company B? Discuss.

The Industry Factor

Investment returns vary across industries or sectors due to differences in business models. For instance, capital-intensive industries (e.g., telecommunication, car manufacturing, road construction, etc.) require huge asset investments to generate small returns. In contrast, asset-light industries (e.g., entertainment, online services, etc.) can generate high returns with low capital or investments.

An analysis by Jiang and Koller (2006) provides evidence about ROIC variations by industry for nonfinancial US companies from 1963 to 2004. While the average ROIC for US companies stood between approximately 9.5% and 10%, variations across industries ranged between 27% (pharmaceuticals, biotechnology) to approximately 6% (utilities). Trainer (2019) presents an analysis of ROIC by sectors between 2000 and 2019, corroborating Jiang and Koller—the lowest and highest ROICs were evident for the utilities and technology sectors, respectively.

To explain this aspect, a case analysis of three companies from different industries is presented in ► Exhibit 7.6: Alphabet Inc. (Internet content and information industry), Target Corporation (retail consumer staples industry), and Exxon Mobil Corporation (oil and gas integrated industry). The analysis compares the size of investment, business operation, and investment returns.

Exhibit 7.6 The Industry Factor

Case Examples: Alphabet, Exxon, and Target (See Excel Workings—► Chap. 7, Sheet E.7.6)

This illustrative case explains the causes of return variations across companies in different industries. The selected three companies are incomparable due to industry differences and business models. Therefore, this analysis is not meant to compare performance. ◘ Exhibit 7.6.1 compares invested capital, revenues, and operating income. Exxon is the largest company in terms of investments and revenues, whereas Target is the smallest.

The Industry Factor

Exxon (a capital-intensive company) generates higher revenues than does Alphabet (an asset-light company)—but Alphabet generates higher operating income than does Exxon. ◘ Exhibit 7.6.2 reflects on businesses models based on percentage proportions of investments relative to operations (revenues

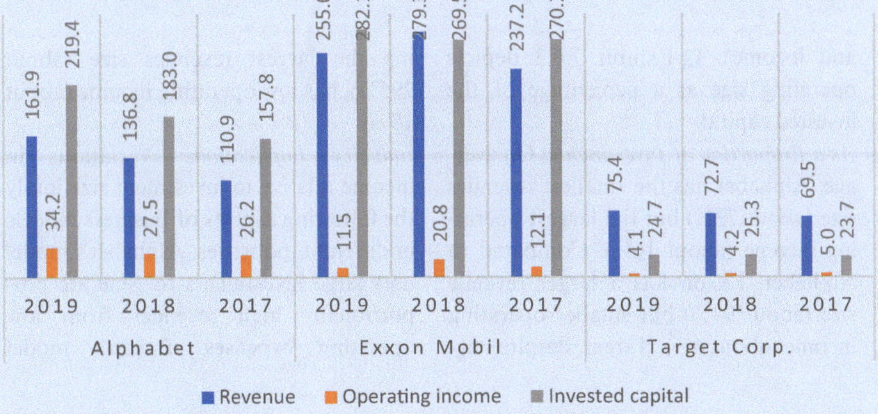

◘ **Exhibit 7.6.1** Investment size and business operations (US$ billions)

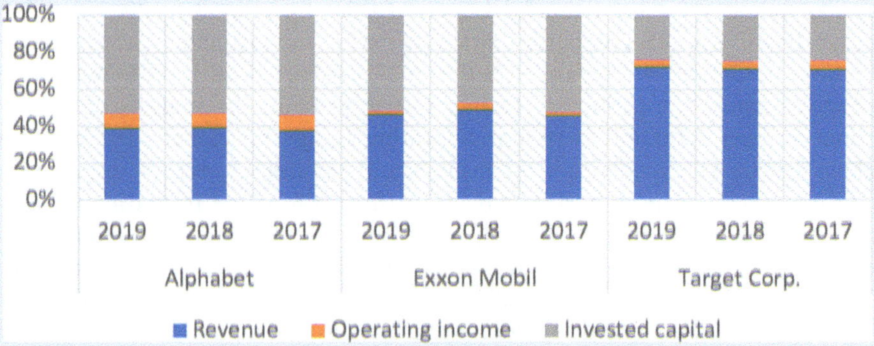

Exhibit 7.6.2 Business model reflected in investments and operations

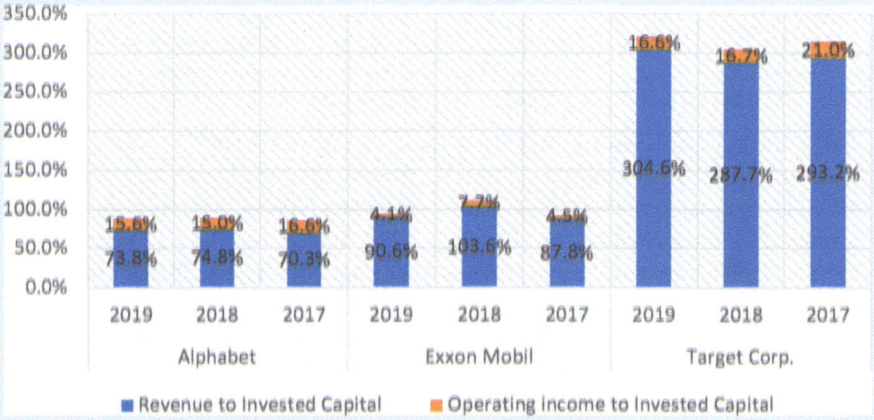

Exhibit 7.6.3 Proportion of income to invested capital

and income). Exhibit 7.6.3 depicts operating size as a percentage of the invested capital.

As a Proportion of Investments: On average, Alphabet has the smallest revenues size (about 73%) but the largest operating income (about 16%). Compared to Alphabet, Exxon has a larger revenue size (about 94%) but smaller operating income (about 5%). Target, despite having the largest revenues size (about 295%), has low operating income (about 18%).

Industry Implications: Variations in income relative to investment size imply the following aspects of business models in different industries: Alphabet's model uses large investments to generate proportionally high revenues from low operating expenses. Exxon's model requires massive capital investments to generate proportionally high revenues from high operating expenses. Target's model requires small capital investments to generate proportionally high revenues from high operating expenses.

Profitability: ▫ Exhibit 7.6.4 presents the profitability ratios of the three companies. Alphabet's operating margin is the highest—it has low operating expenses. Exxon and Target are generally equal in operating margins—they both have high operating expenses. Due to huge capital requirements and small operating margins, Exxon, like other companies in the same industry, has the lowest ROIC and ROE. Target and Alphabet almost match on ROIC—it should also be noted that the two companies match on the percentage of operating income to invested capital (see ▫ Exhibit 7.6.3).

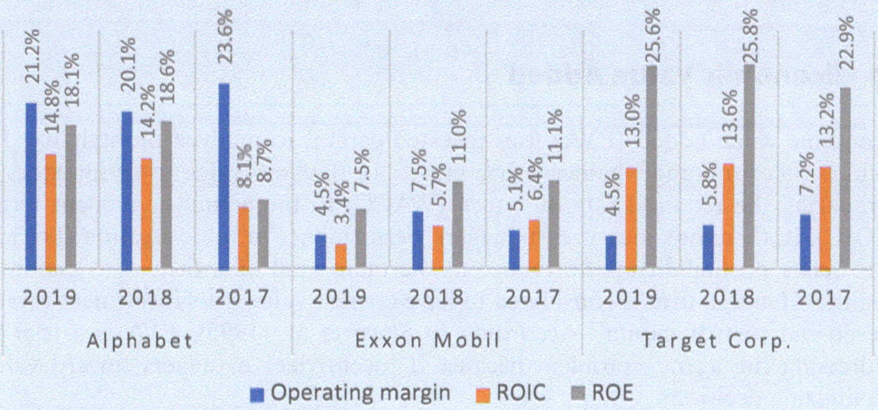

▫ **Exhibit 7.6.4** Profitability analysis
Source of Data: Bloomberg (2020)

Think 7.8

When analyzing the earning power of financial resources, we use book values instead of market values. Is this appropriate? Discuss.

Banner 7.14 Profitability and the Industry Factor

Efficiency in capital usage to generate earnings varies across industries due to differences in business models, which determine capital requirements, revenue size, and proportion of operating expenses.

Apply 7.2 Efficiency on Usage of Financial Resources

Ford Motor Co., General Motors Co., and Toyota Motor Corp.

Data: See Excel Workings—► Chap. 7, Sheet A.7.1–3

The data sheet presents financial statements and WACC for 5 years. Use Excel to perform the following analysis:

(a) Calculate capital and asset usage ratios (the 5-year trend): ROA, ROE, and ROCE.
(b) Calculate ROIC. Explain your decisions on each adjustment item to arrive at NOPAT and invested capital.
(c) Use graphs to interpret and analyze performance. Make specific comments on the following aspects: excess returns, owner returns, and all investors' returns.
(d) Explain valuation implications of the company's efficiency in capital and asset usage.

7.7 Economic Value Added

Economic value added (EVA) uses invested capital to analyze profitability. The focus is on examining whether a firm creates or destroys value to its investors by comparing the required rate of return (WACC) to the actual investment return (ROIC). It, therefore, measures managers' performance in value creation. The idea is to relate profitability performance to the main goal of a firm—"to maximize wealth." Hence, a firm is considered to have created value if its investment returns exceed the cost of capital. According to Stern et al. (1995), EVA is a tool for addressing the agency problem because it incentivizes managers toward value-maximizing decisions.

Banner 7.15 Economic Value Added

EVA is a profitability measure, which focuses on whether a firm creates or destroys value by comparing the required rate of return (WACC) and the actual investment return (ROIC).

7.7.1 How to Calculate EVA

There are two approaches to calculating EVA, namely, the "excess return approach" and the "residual income approach." The key EVA inputs are NOPAT, invested capital (IC), and WACC.

The Excess Return Approach: This approach defines EVA as a product of excess returns (ROIC – WACC) and invested capital as follows:

$$EVA = \left(ROIC - WACC\right)IC$$

This implies that investors expect managers to generate excess returns (ROIC – WACC) from the use of financial resources (IC).

The Residual Income Approach: This approach defines EVA as the difference between after-tax operating income (NOPAT) and capital charges ((WACC)IC)) as follows:

$$EVA = NOPAT - (WACC)IC$$

This implies that investors expect managers to generate after-tax earnings (NOPAT) more than the cash flows required to compensate for risking their invested funds (IC).

7.7.2 The Relevance of EVA

The application of EVA in valuation is noteworthy. Overall, it is a tool that can be used to motivate managers to create value. A positive EVA signifies value creation from the invested capital, whereas a negative EVA shows value destruction. ► Exhibit 7.7 presents an example to calculate and interpret EVA. It should be noted that managers can destroy value (negative EVA), despite generating profits (NOPAT). This explains the importance of EVA—to measure managers' performance by considering the market value of the invested capital (the cost of capital). Otherwise, true value can be overstated by simply looking at book values.

Banner 7.16 Complexity of EVA

EVA adjustments can differ across companies to suit their specific circumstances, depending on specific business models, financing, and investment structures.

Exhibit 7.7 Economic Value Added

Illustrative Example (See Excel Workings—► Chap. 7, Sheet E.7.7)

The following information was extracted from the financial statement of FAIDA Ltd. In 2012, EBIT was $271 million, whereas the corporate tax rate was 40% percent. Invested capital in 2012 and 2011 was $2132 million and $1951 million, respectively.

Calculate EVA using both the excess return approach and the residual income approach under the following conditions: (a) if WACC is 6.8%, (b) if WACC equals ROIC, and (c) if WACC = 8.5%.

Solution:

$$NOPAT = EBIT(1 - Tax\ rate) = \$271(1 - 0.40) = \$162.6\ million$$

To calculate ROIC, we use the invested capital at the beginning of 2012 (i.e., the invested capital at the end of 2011). Some analysts use the average invested capital.

$$ROIC = \frac{NOPAT}{Invested\ capital} = \frac{\$162.6}{\$1951} = 8.33\%$$

(a) If WACC = 6.8%

The Excess Return Approach:

$$EVA = (ROIC - WACC)IC = (8.33\% - 6.8\%) \$1951 = \$29.9\,million$$

The Residual Income Approach:

$$EVA = NOPAT - (WACC)IC = \$162.6 - (6.8\%)\$1951 = \$29.9\,million$$

Interpretation: Managers created 1.53% more returns than required by investors (8.33% - 6.8% = 1.535). That is, earnings exceeded capital charges (\$162 - \$132.67) to create residual income (economic value) of \$29.9 million in 2012.

(b) If WACC = 8.33%

The Excess Return Approach:

$$EVA = (ROIC - WACC)IC = (8.33\% - 8.33\%)\$1951 = \$0\,million$$

The Residual Income Approach:

$$EVA = NOPAT - (WACC)IC = \$162.6 - (8.33\%)\$1951 = \$0\,million$$

Interpretation: Managers created returns required by investors. Earnings were just sufficient to recover capital charges (breakeven) in 2012. No economic value was created.

(c) If WACC = 8.5%

The Excess Return Approach:

$$EVA = (ROIC - WACC)IC = (8.33\% - 8.5\%) \$1951 = -\$3.24\,million$$

The Residual Income Approach:

$$EVA = NOPAT - (WACC)IC = \$162.6 - (8.5\%) \$1951 = -\$3.24\,million$$

Interpretation: Managers did not fulfill investors' required return by 0.17% (i.e., 8.33–8.5%). That is, capital charges exceeded earnings (\$162.6– \$165.89), thereby destroying economic value by \$3.24 million in 2012.

7

7.7.3 EVA Adjustment and Justifications

The example in ▶ Exhibit 7.7 is simple. The reality is that calculating EVA is a complex process due to the numerous adjustments required to determine NOPAT and the invested capital. The goal of adjustments is to transform financial statements from their conventional forms to determine economic profit and the market value of assets during a financial period. Consideration is on fulfilling the following three requirements:

Cash Flow for Valuation: Cash is the main valuation input—not profit. Hence, noncash items should be adjusted.

Capitalization of Operating Items: Some operating items (such as research and development, staff training, marketing, operating lease, etc.) may have long-term economic benefits. They should be capitalized. The aim is to encourage managers pursue investments with long-term benefits (value).

Unusual Items: Items deemed unusual (income or expenditures) should be adjusted.

▶ Exhibit 7.8 outlines the key adjustments and provides explanations to justify them. ▶ Exhibit 7.9 presents the case of Walmart to illustrate the adjustments. According to Stern et al. (1995), some companies may require more adjustments to suit their specific circumstances, depending on specific business models, financing, and investment structures.

Think 7.9

Based on the information in ▶ Exhibit 7.8, what do you think is the main limitation of ROIC to measure performance across companies?

Exhibit 7.8 EVA Adjustments

ROIC calculation is straightforward, but it can be complicated due to several required adjustments. What adjustments should be considered as not straightforward—good judgment is required and may differ among analysts, thus causing ROIC variations even for the same company. The most important practical consideration is to be consistent in making judgments to enable ROIC comparability across companies. Here are the potential adjustments to consider when determining NOPAT and invested capital.

Noncash Items

Noncash items (such as depreciation/amortization, allowances for bad and doubtful debts, deferred tax provisions, and allowances for inventory) represent over-prudence on the part of financial accountants, thereby understating the true value of invested capital. They should be treated with suspicion due to possible accounting manipulations on profits rather than any real costs. To determine NOPAT, noncash loses (expenses) should be added back to the net income, whereas noncash gains (benefits) should be deducted. To determine invested capital, the value of provisions and allowances should be added back.

Excess Cash

The concept of excess cash is ambiguous and debatable. It is generally the amount of cash that is more than what a company needs to run its business: hence, it is a nonoperating asset. Ambiguity arises from determining it—what is the maximum cash needed to run business operations, and why should there be a limit? There is no straightforward answer because cash requirements differ according to various factors like the nature of business, cash conversion cycle, and funding needs. Generally, there is no excess cash unless a company has reached all its cash needs for capital funding and day-to-day business operations. For instance, cash and cash equivalents can be regarded as excess cash if they exceed the total current liabilities: otherwise, there is no excess cash.

This brings in the treatment of cash and cash equivalents. Some analysts suggest that cash and cash equivalents should be included in invested capital because all assets should contribute to generate return on capital. Others argue that cash and cash equivalents should be excluded because they are not active assets. That is, capital and resource allocation should be separated by considering only the operating assets.

7

Intangible Assets

An important question is how significant are intangible assets and whether they impact operating earnings. Some intangibles result from mergers and acquisitions (M&A). Therefore, the inclusion of intangibles will constitute two types of returns: operating and acquisitive. If a significant portion of intangibles is acquisitive, then including them in the invested capital can be misleading if ROIC is not properly interpreted—the difference between ROIC (with intangibles) and ROIC (without intangibles) can be significant.

A practical application is to consider that acquired intangibles have a clear resale value—hence, if a company expects to engage in M&A activities, then an acquisitive invested capital is probably more reasonable than an operating invested capital. Another practical consideration is that intangibles like goodwill can lose value—the lost value should be written-off by adding it to the invested capital to lower ROIC. It is, however, debatable whether this treatment is appropriate for acquisitive assets. Since the goal of ROIC is to measure managers' asset efficiency, why should they be held responsible for acquisition deals in perpetuity?

Restructuring

Financial reporting considers restructuring charges (such as cost reduction strategies, branch closures, plant closures, relocations, etc.), which imply two items: writing-off assets as a noncash item and restructuring costs as a cash item. The treatment of asset write-offs follows the same principle as goodwill. However, restructuring charges do not require adjustments—they may reduce invested capital in the short term (by creating accrued expenses, a noninterest-bearing liability that reduces the net working capital) but increase it in the long term when a company spends cash to clear its accruals.

Operating Lease

Operating lease is an obligation (financing item) but is not capitalized in the balance sheet. In some companies, the lease can take a substantial portion of assets, and, hence, adjustments are required for both NOPAT and invested capital. For NOPAT, the treatment is to reclassify lease-related expenses from operating expenses (operating lease) to interest expenses (capitalized lease)—adjustments will be reflected in increased EBIT and reduced tax expenses (interest tax shield)—that is, depreciation on assets acquired under the lease and interest on lease liability. For invested capital, a capitalized lease implies adding debts and assets—that is, operating leases should be capitalized and added to the invested capital.

Noncontrolling Interest

Adjustment for minority interest is important for determining shareholder value and can be viewed from two angles: when other companies have minority interest in the analyzed company and when the analyzed company has minority interest in other companies. In the first and second angles, minority interest should be subtracted and added (from) to the invested capital, respectively—in both cases, taxes should be considered.

Development Items

A conventional account treats them as expenses because there is no reliable and common measure to determine their economic benefits. For some companies, R&D expenditure tends to be significant—if not capitalized, then invested capital is understated. A practical treatment, therefore, is twofold: the capitalized value should be added to the invested capital, whereas amortization should be expensed into the income statement—amortization rates vary across industries.

Share Repurchases

Although share repurchases can have a positive impact on earnings and ROE, their effect on ROIC is unlikely no matter how they are funded, either available cash or issue of new debt. If funded with "excess cash," then they cannot affect ROIC because neither NOPAT nor invested capital will change. Moreover, if funded with new debt, then NOPAT is not affected because it is unlevered (no leverage effect). Invested capital is also not affected because the increase in debt is offset by equity reduction (share repurchase). Therefore, there are no adjustments.

Economic vs. Accounting Depreciation/Amortization

Except for simplicity purposes, accounting depreciation does not necessarily reflect the true change in the value of assets during the period: the appropriate charge is the economic depreciation (decrease in the market value of an asset over time from influential economic factors). To reflect economic depreciation, adjustments should be made in NOPAT by adding (deducting) to (from) the net income accounting depreciation (economic depreciation). For invested capital, adjustment should be made to noncurrent assets to replace accounting depreciation for economic depreciation.

Deferred Taxes

The income statement reports tax expenses regardless of whether they may or may not have been paid (the prudence principle). Deferred taxes, therefore, refer to tax expenses that have not been paid during a financial year—the difference between tax expenses reported in the income statement and paid taxes. The principle of EVA is to consider "cash taxes" rather than the "accrual taxes." Cash taxes are calculated as: tax charges (per income statement) minus increase (add deduction) in the deferred tax provision and plus tax benefits on interest. NOPAT adjustment requires adding (deducting) to (from) the net income increase (decrease) in the provision for deferred taxes. For invested capital, provision for deferred taxes should be added.

7.7.4 Limitations of EVA

Although EVA is a superior profitability performance measure, it suffers from several limitations, as outlined below.

Complexity of Adjustments: To implement EVA, firms and analysts need to overcome several adjustment challenges. These include converting the conventional accounting information to suit EVA requirements, thereby contradicting accounting reporting standards and principles. Some companies are reluctant to apply EVA due to these challenges.

Limited Intercompany Comparisons: EVA applies criteria that are highly specific to a particular company—there is no consensus about the level of adjustments. If different analysts apply adjustments inconsistently, then EVA comparability across companies will be impaired.

Possible Accounting Manipulation: EVA determines performance on a year-to-year basis, thereby creating loopholes for possible accounting manipulations. For instance, finance managers may decide to choose short-term, early yield projects over longer-term, delayed-income streams and higher-yield projects. They might also abstain from value-creating investments like R&D or advertising costs, thereby limiting long-term prosperity.

Backward-Looking: The failure of EVA to use discounted cash flows in performance analysis implies that it is a backward-looking approach like other financial ratios. Although EVA uses measures like economic profit and market value of assets, the estimates of these values lack precision and objectivity.

Think 7.10

When calculating ROIC, how can you justify the use of the following variations in invested capital? (a) Average, (b) beginning of the current year, and (c) end of the current year.

Exhibit 7.9 Performance in Usage of Financial Resources

Case Example: Walmart (See Excel Workings—▸ Chap. 7, Sheet E.7.9)

This case illustrates how to calculate ROCE, ROIC, and ROE considering their various versions. It also explains the relevance of these ratios in real-world applications. Exhibit 7.9.1 presents the required financial data (Walmart) extracted from the income statement and the balance sheet. Calculations and analysis are presented in Exhibit 7.9.2–7.9.14.

Calculation of NOPAT

$$NOPAT = EBIT\left(1 - Tax\ rate\right)$$

The applicable tax rate is adjusted: dividing income tax by the adjusted pre-tax income. All adjustments and results are presented in Exhibit 7.9.2.

Exhibit 7.9.1 Walmart financials (in US$ billions)

	2020	2019	2018	2017	2016	2015
Operating activities						
EBIT	20.6	22.0	20.4	22.8	24.1	27.1
Nonoperating income (expenses)	−0.5	−10.5	−5.3	−2.3	−2.5	−2.3
Pretax income	20.1	11.5	15.1	20.5	21.6	24.8
Deferred income tax expense (benefits)	0.3	−0.5	−0.2	0.7	−0.7	−0.5
Interest expenses (excluding operating lease liability)	2.6	2.3	2.3	2.4	2.5	2.3
Income tax	4.9	4.2	4.6	4.2	4.6	8.0
Effective tax rate	24.4%	36.5%	30.4%	20.5%	21.3%	32.3%
Net income, excluding noncontrolling interest	14.9	6.7	8.9	13.6	14.7	16.5
Financing and investment activities						
Total current liabilities	77.8	77.5	78.5	66.9	64.6	65.3
Non-debt current liabilities	71.3	69.7	68.8	63.0	58.6	59.4
Short-term debts + lease obligations	6.5	7.8	9.7	3.9	6.0	5.9
Short-term borrowings	0.6	5.2	5.3	1.1	2.7	1.6
Short-term lease obligations	0.5	0.7	0.7	0.6	0.6	0.3
Current portion of LT debts	5.4	1.9	3.7	2.3	2.8	4.0
Long-term debts + lease obligations	65.7	58.8	47.1	53.6	53.2	50.3
Long-term borrowings	43.7	43.5	30.1	36.0	38.2	37.0
Long-term lease obligations	4.3	6.7	6.8	6.0	5.8	2.6
Operating lease liability	17.7	8.5	10.3	11.6	9.2	10.7
Owners' equity (excluding minority interest)	74.7	72.5	77.9	77.8	80.5	81.4
Minority interest	6.9	7.1	3.0	2.7	3.1	4.5
Total equity	81.6	79.6	80.9	80.5	83.6	85.9
Equity equivalents	4.3	4.5	1.9	2.7	1.9	3.6
Deferred tax liabilities	6.2	6.3	3.8	4.3	3.4	4.7
Deferred tax assets	*1.9*	*1.8*	*1.9*	*1.6*	*1.5*	*1.1*

(continued)

Exhibit 7.9.1 (continued)

	2020	2019	2018	2017	2016	2015
Accumulated other comprehensive net income (loss)	−12.8	−11.5	−10.2	−14.2	−11.6	−7.2
Cash and cash equivalents	9.4	7.7	6.8	6.9	8.7	9.1
Total current assets	61.8	61.9	59.7	57.7	60.2	63.3
Net property, plant, and equipment	105.2	104.3	107.7	107.7	110.2	114.3
Other long-term assets	47.7	46.0	30.0	27.1	22.8	23.6
Total intangible assets	*31.1*	*31.2*	*18.2*	*17.1*	*16.7*	*18.1*
Deferred tax assets	*1.9*	*1.8*	*1.9*	*1.6*	*1.5*	*1.1*
Derivative and hedging assets	*0.0*	*0.4*	*0.5*	*0.5*	*0.6*	*0.5*
Miscellaneous LT assets	*14.7*	*12.6*	*9.4*	*7.9*	*4.0*	*3.9*
Construction in progress (from Notes)	3.8	3.5	3.6	4.3	4.5	5.8
Total assets	236.5	219.3	204.5	198.8	199.6	203.5

7

Exhibit 7.9.2 NOPAT (all figures in US$ billions, except percentages)

	2020	2019	2018	2017	2016	2015
EBIT	20.6	22.0	20.4	22.8	24.1	27.1
Pretax income	20.1	11.5	15.1	20.5	21.6	24.8
Deferred income tax expense (benefits)[1]	0.3	−0.5	−0.2	0.7	−0.7	−0.5
Interest expenses (operating lease liability, 4.25%)[2]	0.8	0.4	0.4	0.5	0.4	0.5
Nonoperating income (expenses)[3]	−0.5	−10.5	−5.3	−2.3	−2.5	−2.3
Pretax income (adjusted)[1,2,3]	20.1	21.1	19.8	23.0	23.0	26.2
Income tax	4.9	4.2	4.6	4.2	4.6	8.0
Effective tax rate (adjusted)[4]	24.3%	19.9%	23.2%	18.3%	20.0%	30.5%
NOPAT = EBIT(1 − Tax, adjusted)	15.6	17.6	15.7	18.6	19.3	18.9

Notes: To adjust effective tax, we work from the pretax income to arrive at the adjusted pretax income: [1]added to eliminate the deferred income tax. [2]Deducted to account for capitalization of operating lease obligation (interest is calculated as a product of capitalized lease and discount rate (4.25%) and the average cost of debt). [3]Income (expenses) is deducted (added) to eliminate it. [4]Income tax divided by pretax income (adjusted)

Calculation of Invested Capital

The financial approach is applied with some adjustments (see ◘ Exhibit 7.9.3 in conjunction with data from ◘ Exhibit 7.9.1).

$$Invested\ capital = (Total\ debt) + (Total\ equity) - (Nonoperating\ assets)$$

Calculation of ROIC

To calculate ROIC for the current year, current-year NOPAT is used. However, invested capital can be treated in three different ways: (1) a 2-year average (using end-of-year invested capital), or (2) beginning of the current year (i.e., end of the previous year), or end of the current year. In this case, we calculate and show all three alternatives as indicated in ◘ Exhibit 7.9.4 (panel A). It is, therefore, practically common to have ROIC variations among analysts due to differences in adjustments and calculations—panel B compares ROIC from three different analysts.

Calculation of EVA

◘ Exhibit 7.9.5 presents EVA calculations using both the excess return approach and the residual income approach. For illustration purposes, we apply the average invested capital (refer to ◘ Exhibits 7.9.3 and 7.9.4). Other EVA versions (with beginning- and end-of-year invested capital) can also be calculated.

◘ **Exhibit 7.9.3** Invested capital: financial approach (all figures in US$ billions)

	2020	2019	2018	2017	2016	2015
Total debt[5]	72.1	66.5	56.8	57.6	59.2	56.2
Total equity (adjusted)[6]	98.7	95.7	92.9	97.5	97.0	96.7
Nonoperating assets[7]	0	0	0	0	0	0
Invested capital	170.8	162.2	149.8	155.0	156.3	152.9
Invested capital[8]	165.2	158.0	146.6	152.4	152.1	149.6

Notes: [5]Total debt = Short-term debts and lease obligations + Long-term debts and lease obligations + operating lease liability. [6]Total equity (adjusted) = Shareholders' equity, including minority interest + equity equivalents—other accumulated comprehensive income (loss), whereby, equity equivalents = deferred tax liabilities—deferred tax assets. [7]Nonoperating assets are defined as excess cash. To determine excess cash, we relate total current assets and twice-current liabilities: if current assets exceed current liabilities, then excess cash is either the lower of (a) cash and cash equivalents or (b) current assets—twice-current liabilities; if twice-current liabilities exceed current assets, then there is no excess cash. In all 6 years, total current liabilities exceeded the total current assets—hence, there was no excess cash. We also note that from 2017 to 2020, noninterest-bearing current liabilities exceeded total current assets, suggesting that Walmart relies more on suppliers to finance its working capital—it can sell inventory and collect cash from debtors before paying trade creditors. [8]Other analysts could have a different view and treat cash and cash equivalents as nonoperating assets—invested capital is slightly different in this case but can have a significant impact on some companies

Exhibit 7.9.4 ROIC

		2020	2019	2018	2017	2016
Panel A Based on invested capital	Average[9]	9.3%	11.3%	10.3%	12.0%	12.5%
	Beginning of year[10]	9.6%	11.8%	10.1%	11.9%	12.6%
	End of year[11]	9.1%	10.9%	10.5%	12.0%	12.3%
Panel B Other analysts	FinBox	10.4%	12.3%	12.9%	12.9%	13.2%
	Bloomberg	10.5%	10.4%	11.3%	12.2%	12.5%
	Guru Focus	11.3%	11.0%	11.8%	13.0%	13.3%

Notes: For example, in 2020, NOPAT was US$15.6 billion. The invested capital was US$170.8 billion and US$162.2 billion in 2020 and 2019, respectively. [9]ROIC 2020 = US$15.6/((US$170.8+US$162.2)/2)) = 9.3%. [10]ROIC 2020 = US$15.6/US$162.2 = 9.6%. [11]ROIC 2020 = US$15.6/US$170.8 = 9.1%

7

Exhibit 7.9.5 EVA

	2020	2019	2018	2017	2016
NOPAT	15.6	17.6	15.7	18.6	19.3
Invested capital (average)[12]	166.5	156.0	152.4	155.6	154.6
ROIC (based on the average invested capital)	9.3%	11.3%	10.3%	12.0%	12.5%
WACC[13]	6.0%	7.5%	6.5%	6.3%	6.7%
EVA = (ROIC − WACC) invested capital	5.6	5.8	5.8	8.9	8.9
EVA = NOPAT − WACC (invested capital)	5.6	5.8	5.8	8.9	8.9

Notes: [12]For example, the invested capital was US$170.8 billion and US$162.2 billion in 2020 and 2019, respectively. Invested capital 2020 (average) = (US$170.8+US$162.2)/2 = US$166.5 billion. EVA = (9.3% − 6.0%) US$166.5 = US$5.6 billion or EVA = US$15.6 − 6.0%(US$166.5) = US$5.6 billion. [13]WACC data were obtained from Bloomberg Terminal

Calculation of ROCE

To calculate ROCE, we use NOPAT and the average total capital (long-term debts and total equity): adjustments for total equity and long-term debts include long-term borrowings and lease obligations. Calculations are presented in Exhibit 7.9.6.

Exhibit 7.9.6 ROCE (all figures in $ billions, except percentages)

	2020	2019	2018	2017	2016	2015
NOPAT	15.6	17.6	15.7	18.6	19.3	18.9
Long-term debts	65.7	58.8	47.1	53.6	53.2	50.3
Total equity	81.6	79.6	80.9	80.5	83.6	85.9
Capital employed	147.3	138.4	128.0	134.2	136.8	136.2
ROCE[14]	10.9%	13.2%	12.0%	13.7%	14.1%	

Notes: [14]For example, in 2020, NOPAT was US$15.6 billion. Total capital was US$147.3 billion and US$138.4 billion in 2020 and 2019, respectively. ROCE 2020 = US$15.6/((US$147.3+US$138.4)/2)) = 10.9%

Exhibit 7.9.7 ROA and ROE

	2020	2019	2018	2017	2016	2015
EBIT	20.6	22.0	20.4	22.8	24.1	27.1
Net income, excluding minority interest	14.9	6.7	8.9	13.6	14.7	16.5
Total assets	236.5	219.3	204.5	198.8	199.6	203.5
Owners' equity	74.7	72.5	77.9	77.8	80.5	81.4
ROA (for all investors)[15]	9.0%	10.4%	10.1%	11.4%	12.0%	
ROA (for owners)[16]	6.5%	3.2%	4.4%	6.8%	7.3%	
ROE (for owners)[17]	20.2%	8.9%	11.4%	17.2%	18.2%	

Notes: [15]For example, in 2020, EBIT was US$20.6 billion and net income was US$14.9 billion. Total assets were US$236.5 billion and US$219.3 billion in 2020 and 2019, respectively. ROA 2020 = US$20.6/((US$236.5+US$219.3)/2)) = 9.4%. [16]ROA 2020 = US$14.9/((US$236.5+US$219.3)/2)) = 6.5%. [17]For example, in 2020, net income was US$14.9 billion. Owners' equity was US$74.7 billion and US$72.5 billion in 2020 and 2019, respectively. ROE 2020 = US$14.9/((US$74.7+US$72.5)/2)) = 20.2%

Calculation of ROA

Refer to data in Exhibit 7.9.1. Using total assets, two versions of ROA are presented in Exhibit 7.9.7: EBIT is applied when focusing on all investors' returns, whereas net income (equal to earnings to common shareholders) is applied when focusing on owners' returns.

Calculation of ROE

Refer to data in Exhibit 7.6.1 and results in Exhibit 7.9.7. To calculate ROE, both total equity and net income exclude minority interest—that is, owners' equity and earnings available to Walmart's common shareholders.

Analysis and Interpretation

Graphs in Exhibits 7.9.8, 7.9.9, 7.9.10, 7.9.11, 7.9.12, 7.9.13, 7.9.14, 7.9.15, and 7.9.16 are used to analyze and interpret Walmart performance regarding two aspects: historical performance and industry comparison. The cost of capital was used as a performance criterion on "excess returns"—economic value should be created if profitability returns exceed the cost of capital (WACC or cost of equity).

Historical Performance (2015–2020)

Overall, based on the "excess returns" analysis, the company performed well in generating returns to all its investors. Over 5 years, investors earned higher returns (ROIC and ROCE) than the required returns (WACC). Moreover, asset usage generated more returns (ROA) than financing cost (WACC). If reinvested properly,

Exhibit 7.9.8 ROIC excess returns

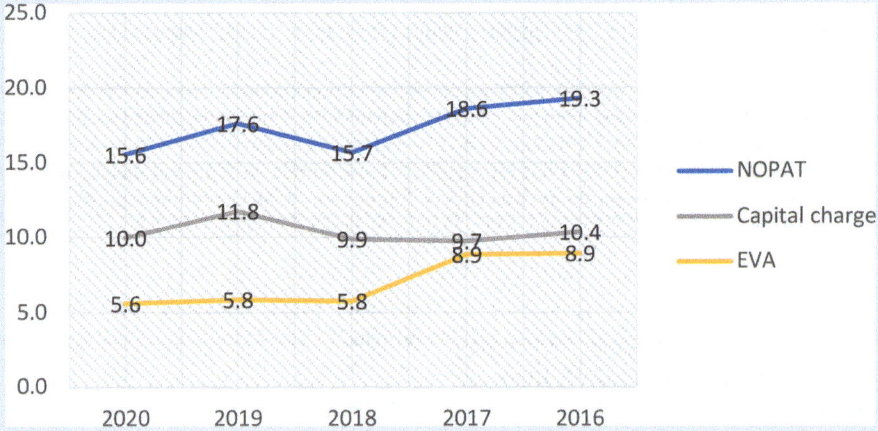

Exhibit 7.9.9 EVA

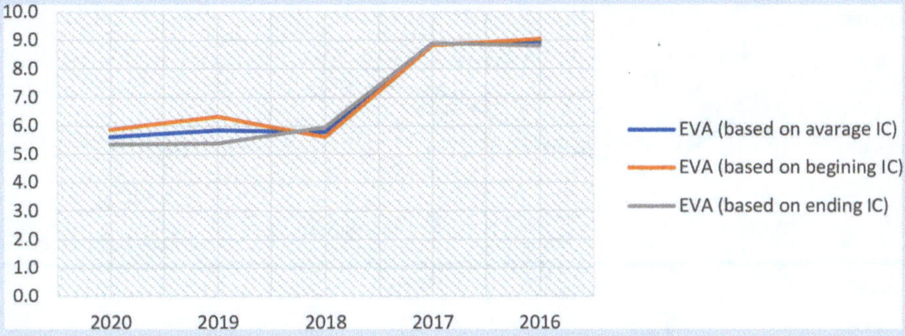

Exhibit 7.9.10 EVA

Exhibit 7.9.11 ROCE excess returns

Exhibit 7.9.12 ROA excess returns (for all investors)

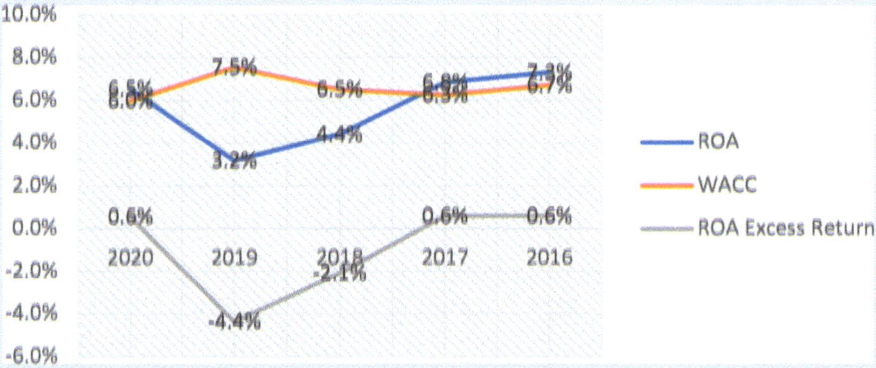

Exhibit 7.9.13 ROA excess returns (for owners)

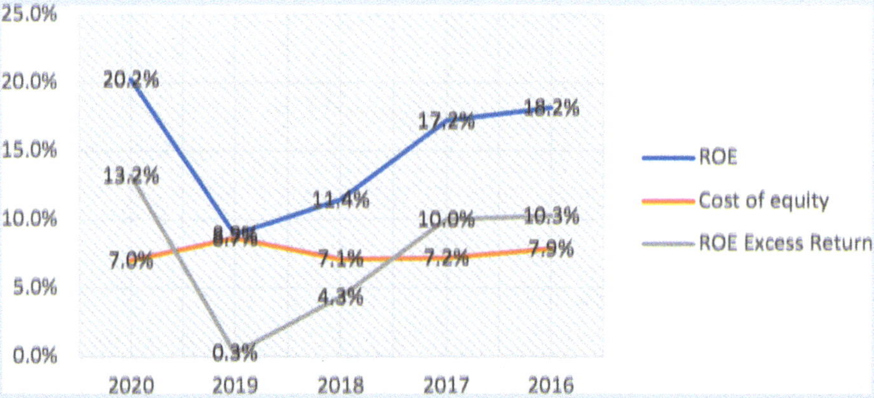

Exhibit 7.9.14 ROE excess returns

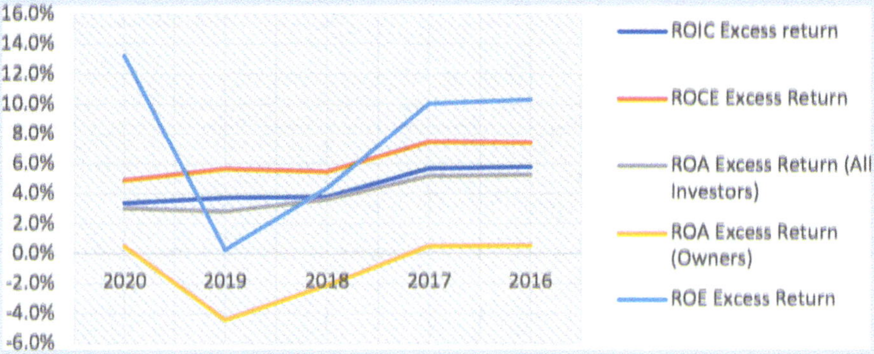

Exhibit 7.9.15 Comparison of excess returns

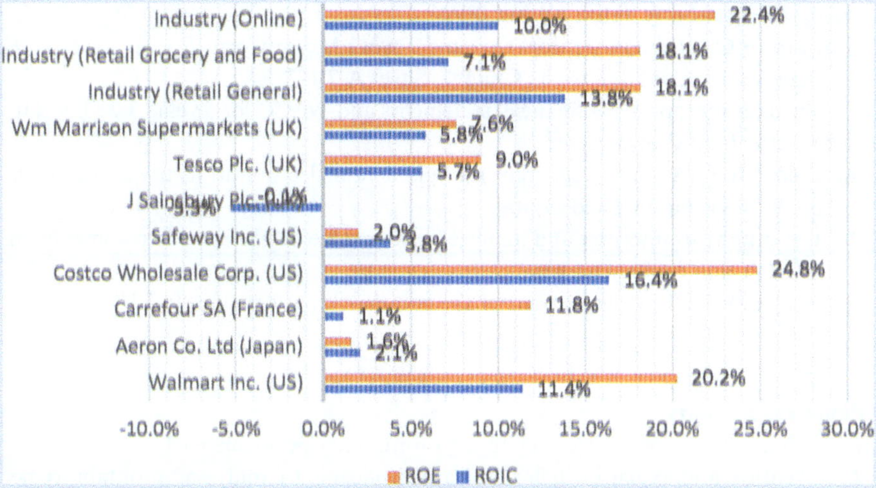

Exhibit 7.9.16 ROIC and ROE within the industry in 2020

then excess returns can accelerate growth to create more value. Nevertheless, excess returns show a downward trend parallel with deteriorating resource efficiency and rising capital charges (see Exhibits 7.9.8 and 7.9.11, 7.9.12, 7.9.13, and 7.9.14). This is reflected in the declining EVA from US$8.9 billion in 2016 to US$5.6 billion in 2020 (see Exhibits 7.9.9 and 7.9.11).

Focusing on owners, ROA is not the best for analyzing owners' returns because total assets are financed by all investors. However, it can be used as a quick indication of safety margin because owners are the ultimate claimants should the company be liquidated. As indicated in Exhibit 7.9.13, owners' ROA exceeded WACC in 2016, 2017, and 2020. Based on ROE (a superior measure of owners' returns), excess returns declined from 10.3% to 0.3% between 2016 and 2019, followed by a sharp increase in 2020.

Industry Comparison (2020)

Exhibit 7.9.16 compares Walmart's performance to that of selected global peers and the industry based on ROIC and ROE in 2020. Clearly, Walmart outperformed many competitors, only trailing behind its US rival, Costco Wholesale Corporation. It should be noted that Walmart is a multi-industry retailer in terms of classification due to its various business lines. In the category of general retail industry, the company was 3.1% below the industry ROIC performance but 2.1% above the industry ROE performance. In the retail grocery and food category, which is its main business line, Walmart outperformed the industry on both ROIC and ROE by 3.6% and 2.1%, respectively. In the retail online segment, Walmart's ROIC was above industry by 0.7%, whereas its ROE was below industry by 2.2%.

Apply 7.3 Economic Value Added (EVA)

Ford Motor Co., General Motors Co., and Toyota Motor Corp.

Data See Excel workings—► Chap. 7, Sheet A.7.1–3

The data sheet presents financial statements and WACC for 5 years. Use Excel to perform the following analysis:

(a) Calculate EVA (the 5-year trend). Explain your decision to justify adjustments on NOPAT and invested capital.

(b) Use graphs to interpret and analyze performance. Make specific comments on NOPAT and capital charges.

(c) Explain valuation implications of the company's performance in EVA.

Review Questions

1. What are the main factors effecting profitability performance?
2. Mention and explain which ratios are applicable to analyzing profitability performance relating to the following operating items?
   (a) Sales and cost of goods sold
   (b) Operating expenses
   (c) All expenses
3. Explain the relevance of the following profitability ratios:
   (a) Gross margin
   (b) Operating profit margin
   (c) Pretax profit margin
   (d) Net profit margin
4. Why is it important to consider industry factors when analyzing profitability performance?
5. With examples, explain how industry differences can influence the following profitability ratios?
   (a) Operating profit margin
   (b) Net profit margin
6. What is the main difference between profit margin ratios and asset efficiency ratios?
7. Explain the relevance of the following ratios:
   (a) Return on invested capital (ROIC)
   (b) Return on assets (ROA)
   (c) Return on equity (ROE)
8. Explain the difference between the following.
   (a) ROIC and ROCE
   (b) EBIT and NOPAT
9. Provide justification for using the following items to calculate ratios:
   (a) The use of EBIT to calculate ROA
   (b) The use of net income to calculate ROE
   (c) The use of NOPAT to calculate ROIC
   (d) The use of net income to calculate ROA

10 Why is ROIC considered the most superior of other efficiency ratios?
11. Define the following terms:
    (a) Excess returns
    (b) Capital charges
    (c) Economic value added (EVA)
12. What is the importance and practical application of EVA?
13. Explain the limitations of EVA.
14. When calculating EVA, what is the goal of adjusting NOPAT and invested capital?
15. Explain the possible valuation implications of the following:
    (a) ROE
    (b) ROIC
    (c) Net profit margin
    (d) EVA
16. The following information was extracted from the income statements of GEUZA Ltd for 2014 and 2015 (see the suggested solution in Excel workings—Sheet R.7).

Income statement data: GEUZA Ltd (figures in $ thousands)

	2015	2014
Operating income	8000	6000
Interest expenses	1500	1000
Income before taxes	6500	5000
Income tax expenses (30%)	1950	1500
Net income	4550	3500

Additional information is as follows:
   (a) The company implemented two projects relating to research and development: project A and project B.
   (b) The allowance for doubtful debts was $650,000 on 1 January 2014, $500,000 on 31 December 2014, and $700,000 on 31 December 2015.
   (c) For project A, $750,000 was incurred on R&D costs during each of the years 2014 and 2015. These costs were expensed in the income statement, as they did not meet the requirements of financial reporting standards for capitalization. Project A is not complete yet.
   (d) At the end of 2013, the company had completed another research and development project, project B. The total expenditure on this project had been $2,500,000, none of which had been capitalized in the financial statements. The product developed by project B went on sale on 1 January 2014, and the product was a great success. The product's life cycle was only 2 years, so no further sales of the product were expected after 31 December 2015.

(e) The company incurred noncash expenses of $80,000 in both years.
(f) The invested capital as per the statement of financial position was $31,000,000 on 1 January 2014 and $46,000,000 on 1 January 2015.
(g) The pretax cost of debt was 6% in each year. The estimated cost of equity was 11% in 2014 and 13% in 2015. The rate of corporate income tax was 30% during both years.
(h) The company's capital structure was 70% and 30% of equity and debt, respectively.
(i) There was nwo provision for deferred taxes.

Required:

Calculate NOPAT and invested capital for 2015 and 2014 considering the necessary adjustments. Provide justification for each adjustment. Calculate EVA for 2015 and 2014. Interpret the company' performance.

Bibliography

Buffet, W. (1993). To the Shareholders of Berkshire Hathaway Inc., https://www.berkshirehathaway.com/letters/1992.html Accessed March 03, 2021.

Jiang, B. & Koller, T. (2006), A long-term look at ROIC, Available at McKinsey https://www.mckinsey.com.br/business-functions/strategy-and-corporate-finance/our-insights/a-long-term-look-at-roic Accessed February 01, 2006.

Kovar, J.F. (2020). M&A Adviser To Solution Providers: To Boost Valuation, Get To 50 Percent Recurring Revenue, Available at CRN https://www.crn.com/m-a-adviser-to-solution-providers-to-boost-valuation-get-to-50-percent-recurring-revenue Accessed March 03, 2020.

Scuttlebutt Investor (2016). A good metric is hard to find—return on capital, http://www.scuttlebuttinvestor.com/blog/2016/12/10/return-on-capital-and-other-diversions Accessed December 17, 2016.

Stern J. M, Stewart, B.G, Chew, D. H (1995), The EVA Financial Management System, *Journal of Applied Corporate Finance*, 8(2), 32.46. https://doi.org/10.1111/j.1745-6622.1995.tb00285.x

Trainer, D. (2019), Long-Term Trends Revealed by Analyzing ROIC By Sector, Available at Forbes, https://www.forbes.com/sites/greatspeculations/2019/06/19/long-term-trends-revealed-by-analyzing-roic-by-sector/?sh=7bfbe4b92e87 Accessed June 19, 2019.

Financial Leverage Analysis

Contents

Supplementary Information The online version contains supplementary material available at https://doi.org/10.1007/978-3-031-28267-6_8.

B. Kulwizira Lukanima, *Corporate Valuation*, Classroom Companion: Business, https://doi.org/10.1007/978-3-031-28267-6_8

8.1 Introduction

Leverage arises from corporate financing decisions—to what extent borrowed money is used to fund investments. Borrowing is a vital strategic decision for three reasons. First, it can improve earnings and investment returns. Second, interest expenses create a tax shield, thereby reducing the net cost of debt. Third, leverage comes with financial risk regarding the ability to fulfill financial obligations. Therefore, balancing between the benefit and cost of leverage is essential for achieving the goal of value creation and shareholders' wealth maximization.

This chapter focuses on the practical relevance and application of leverage analysis. It considers its different versions by breaking it down according to its potential effect on shareholders' wealth and business survival.

Learning Outcomes

- Understand the meaning of financial leverage
- Understand the various categories and types of leverage ratios and their implications
- Analyze leverage implications in owners' funds
- Analyze leverage implications in all business resources
- Analyze leverage implications in business operations and interest expenses
- Explain the practical relevance of leverage ratios
- Understand the industry factor of financial leverage

8.2 The Concept of Financial Leverage

Capital structure decisions tend to combine two major sources of capital: funds from creditors (debts) and funds from shareholders (equity). Debt finance creates leverage, which has financial implications in a company and its shareholders. On one hand, a debt means incurring fixed interest obligations, thereby increasing financial risk. A firm with high leverage is likely to be more vulnerable to economic cycles as the debt-servicing obligation continues regardless of economic conditions and profitability performance. On the other hand, debt finance reduces tax bills because of the interest tax shield—corporate income taxes are paid from income after deducting interest expenses. Therefore, leverage is vital for analyzing the balance between financial risks and investment returns.

"Leverage ratios" (sometimes called capital structure ratios or capitalization ratios) are used to measure financial risks. There are various types of leverage ratios, but they generally show a proportional composition of debts relative to equity and assets. In their different forms, this chapter categorizes them as "debt to equity," "debt to asset," and "interest cover."

Banner 8.1 Leverage Focusing on Equity Holders

Debt-to-equity ratios measure leverage as a proportional composition of debt (or total liabilities) to common equity (or total equity). The higher the proportion of debt (or liabilities), the higher the financial risk attributable to shareholders, and vice versa.

8.3 Leverage Focusing on Shareholders

Common shareholders are the ultimate claimants of business resources should a company face bankruptcy. They are, therefore, the primary bearers of financial risks. To measure how much risks they bear, leverage ratios focus on the weight of financial obligations relative to shareholders' funds—that is the ability of common shareholders to meet their ultimate financial obligations at their different levels (i.e., long-term (LT) debts, total debts, and total liabilities).

When focusing on long-term debt (LT debt), the leverage ratio can be referred to as "long-term debt to equity" as follows:

$$LT\ debt\ to\ equity = \frac{Long-term\ debt}{Common\ equity}$$

This ratio is more meaningful when a firm has a large amount of long-term debt compared to short-term debt. Since only long-term debt is used as the numerator, the ratio can underestimate shareholders' financial risk. Hence, a broader measure of debt (i.e., total debt) can be more relevant for firms with a large amount of short-term debt. Therefore, "total debt" becomes the numerator as follows:

$$Total\ debt\ to\ equity = \frac{Total\ debt}{Common\ equity}$$

Additionally a more comprehensive measure of shareholders risk-bearing consider all shareholders' funds and all financial obligations. Hence, the numerator and denominator become total liabilities and total equity, respectively, as follows:

$$Total\ liabilities\ to\ equity = \frac{Total\ liabilities}{Total\ equity}$$

Exhibit ▶ 8.1 presents an example to illustrate the implication of leverage in shareholders' funds. Focusing on owners' equity (common equity), leverage ratios in 2012 and 2011 were greater than 100%. This implies that the company relied heavily on debt financing, exposing owners at high risk should the company face financial difficulties. Considering all shareholders (common and preference), leverage was just under 100%, leaving shareholders with a narrow safety cover.

Think 8.1

If leverage exposes shareholders to financial risks, then why should companies maintain high leverage in their capital structure?

The following news headline exemplifies the impact of leverage on shareholders:

» Carnival: Enormous Risk for LT Common Stockholders… Carnival has several improving metrics as COVID-19 wanes, which may make the stock tempting to investors. However, the company has taken on so much debt and issued so many shares that there will be nothing left on the bones for long-term common shareholders (Guichard 2022).

Exhibit 8.1 Leverage Analysis

Illustrative Example (See Excel Workings—► Chap. 8, Sheet E.8.1)

Exhibit 8.1.1 presents financial data of FAIDA Ltd in December 2012 and 2011.

Required:

Analyze the company's performance of the following leverage aspects:

(a) Ability to service long-term debt from owners' funds
(b) Ability to service total debt from owners' funds
(c) Ability to meet its total liability obligations from shareholder's funds
(d) Ability to service long-term debt from its total assets
(e) Ability to service total debts from total assets

Exhibit 8.1.1 FAIDA Ltd financials

	2012	2011
Total liabilities	1170	1060
Preferred stock	749	749
Common stock ($100/par)	210	210
Retained earnings	239	170
Total equity	1198	1129
Owners' funds*	449	380
Long-term debt	630	523
Total assets	2368	2189
Total debt	934	822
Gross income	642	633
Operating expenses	425	400
Operating income	217	234
Interest expenses	65	59

Note: *Owners' funds = total equity – preferred equity

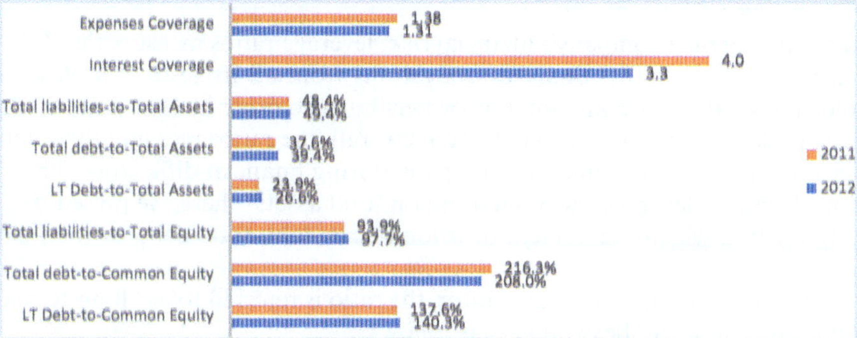

Exhibit 8.1.2 Leverage ratios: FAIDA Ltd

(f) Ability to meet its total liability obligations from its total assets
(g) Ability to service its interest obligations from its operating income

Solution:

Exhibit 8.1.2 presents the leverage ratios (refer to the formula on how to calculate). The implications are as follows:

Focusing on Owners' Funds

(a) Focusing on long-term debt and owners' equity, the shortage in 2012 and 2011 was 40.3% and 37.6%, respectively: that is, 140.3–100% and 137.6–100%, respectively. Risk increased in 2012.
(b) Focusing on total debt, common equity was less by 108% and 116.3%, respectively: that is, 208–100% and 216.3–100% respectively. Risk declined in 2012.
(c) Focusing on total liabilities, shareholders' funds in 2012 and 2011 exceeded financial obligations by 2.3% and 6.1%, respectively: that is, 97.7–100% and 93.9–100% respectively. Risk increased in 2012.

Focusing on Total Assets

(d) Looking at the long-term debt against total assets, leverage was 26.6% and 23.9% in 2012 and 2011, respectively. To clear the obligations, the company could liquidate its assets by 73.4% and 76.1%, respectively. Risk increased in 2012.
(e) Looking at total debt, the company could settle it and still operate under asset capacity by 60.6% and 62.4% in the respective periods. Risk increased in 2012.
(f) When total liabilities are considered, the leverage ratios were 49.4% in 2012 and 48.4% in 2011—that is, total assets exceeded total liabilities by 50.6% and 51.6% in the respective periods. The company could survive (below capacity) after liquidating a fraction of its assets to settle all financial claims. Risk increased in 2012.

Focusing on Interest Coverage

The company's ability to pay its interest expenses declined by 4 times in 2011 to 3.3 times in 2012. Risk increased in 2012.

8.4 Leverage Focusing on Company

When focusing on a company's financial risk, leverage ratios measure the ability of the company to fulfill its financial obligations from all its resources. Bearers of financial risks, therefore, are not only owners but also other investors and creditors (e.g., suppliers, clients, government, etc.). Overall, the ratios measure the extent to which total assets can protect the company during financial difficulties. There are various forms of leverage ratios focusing on total assets—here, we present the following three in which the numerator is long-term debt, total debt, or total liabilities.

When long-term debt is a numerator, the ratio is referred to as "long-term debt to total assets and can be expressed as follows:

$$LT\ debt\ to\ total\ assets = \frac{Long - term\ debt}{Total\ assets}$$

When a broader measure of debt (i.e., total debt) is applied, the ratio becomes "total debt to total assets," and can be expressed as:

$$Total\ debt\ to\ total\ assets = \frac{Total\ debt}{Total\ assets}$$

Moreover, when a comprehensive measure of leverage is used (i.e., total liabilities), the leverage ratio becomes "total liabilities-to-total assets," which can be expressed as:

$$Total\ liabilities\ to\ total\ assets = \frac{Total\ liabilities}{Total\ assets}$$

An illustrative example is presented in Exhibit ▶ 8.1. All three measures show that leverages in 2012 and 2011 were less than 50%, implying that the assets safely cover above 50% (see ◘ Exhibit 8.1.2). In case of financial difficulties, the company could settle all its financial obligations by liquidating less than 50% of its assets.

Banner 8.2 Leverage Focusing on a Company's Financial Risk
Debt-to-asset ratios measure leverage as a proportional composition of financial obligations to total assets. The higher the proportion of debt (or liabilities), the higher the financial risk, and vice versa.

8.5 The Power of Earning on Leverage

Leverage creates financial risks due to fixed interest obligations, which should be paid from operating earnings. Interest expenses, therefore, affect profitability despite tax bill savings. Normally, the essence of long-term debt is to finance long-term investments, whereas short-term debt should finance day-to-day business operations.

▪ Ability to Pay All Financial Obligations

Since business operations generate revenues, the prudent decision to acquire a debt can be measured by the ability of a company to improve its subsequent revenues. After taking care of the cost of goods sold, gross income should cover all operating obligations (including financing and taxes). The ability to cover current operating and financing obligations can, therefore, be measured by the ratio of gross profit to all expenses, excluding taxes (it should be noted that taxes depend on profit).

$$Expenses\ coverage(EC) = \frac{Gross\ income}{Operating\ expenses + Interest\ expenses}$$

The EC ratio, therefore, focuses on both operating and financial leverage. Unless gross income is sufficient to pay operating expenses, it will not be able to cover interest expenses. An example in Exhibit ▶ 8.1 shows that FAIDA Ltd could fulfill its interest obligations despite a slight decline in expenses cover from 1.38 times in 2011 to 1.31 times in 2012.

▪ The Safety Margin of Fixed Interest Obligations

After paying operating expenses, the operating income (earnings before interest and taxes (EBIT)) should cover interest expenses first before paying taxes. To analyze the ability of a firm to pay its interest from operating earnings, we use the "interest coverage" (IC) ratio (sometimes called times interest earned), which is expressed as follows:

$$Interest\ coverage(IC) = \frac{EBIT}{Interest\ expenses}$$

The ability to fulfill debt obligations increases with a high IC ratio. Although there is no standard measure of a good IC ratio, two times is considered a minimum safely margin. The example in Exhibit ▶ 8.1 shows the interest coverage of 3.3 times and 4 times in 2012 and 2011, respectively. Interest claimants were, therefore, safe in the two periods.

Overall, leverage should not be a problem if operating earnings can fulfill investors' returns—they should be sufficient to first pay debtholders (interest expenses) and second to keep earnings for shareholders. Consider the following quote referring to the leverage analysis of the company WideOpenWest Inc.

> » Neither WideOpenWest's ability to cover its interest expense with its EBIT nor its net debt to EBITDA gave us confidence in its ability to take on more debt. But the good news is it seems to be able to grow its EBIT with ease. Looking at all the angles mentioned above, it does seem to us that WideOpenWest is a somewhat risky investment as a result of its debt. That's not necessarily a bad thing, since leverage can boost returns on equity, but it is something to be aware of. Even though WideOpenWest lost money on the bottom line, its positive EBIT suggests the business itself has potential (Simply Wall St. 2022).

Think 8.2

Is it possible to have a negative interest cover? If yes, what does it imply?

Banner 8.3 Interest Coverage

Interest coverage is a measure of the ability to fulfill interest obligations from operating income. A higher ratio is preferable as it shows a higher safely margin in paying interest, and vice versa.

8.6 Practical Relevance of Financial Leverage Ratios

Leverage ratios are important for different purposes. As a measure of performance, lenders and management use leverage ratios to assess the potential capability of a firm to avoid bankruptcy and, at the same time, strengthen their ability to service debt obligations through improving profitability. Active investors use leverage ratios to analyze the creditworthiness of companies. A company is creditworthy if it can generate sufficient earnings to cover its debt obligations while avoiding excessive debts to minimize bankruptcy costs.

Exhibit ▶ 8.2 uses real-world cases to analyze and explain the relevance of leverage ratios. The cases compare leverage among four companies in two pairs, each representing companies from the same industry: Exxon Mobil and Chevron Corporation (oil and gas) and Apple Inc. and Microsoft (technology). The analysis covers five financial years, from 2015 to 2019. Generally, we can observe that the two companies in the oil and gas industry are less levered than those in the technology industry. However, regarding interest coverage, Apple and Microsoft are stronger than Exxon and Chevron. That is, despite their higher leverage, Apple and Microsoft show more potential for earnings-driven growth than do Exxon and Chevron.

Banner 8.4 Shareholders' Risk Cover

When financial obligations (debt and other liabilities) exceed equity, shareholders bear a high risk and a company would have to liquidate its assets to cover its financial obligations should there be financial difficulties.

Apply 8.1 Leverage Analysis

McDonald's, Starbucks, and Chipotle Mexican.

Data: See Excel Workings—▶ Chap. 8, Sheet A.8.1

The data sheet presents the companies' financials for 4 years. Use Excel to perform the following analysis:

(a) Calculate leverage ratios relevant for analyzing shareholders' financial risk.
(b) Calculate leverage ratios relevant for analyzing companies' financial risk.

(c) Calculate interest coverage.
(d) Use graphs to perform comparative analysis of the three companies over the 4 years.
(e) Explain valuation implications of each company's leverage.

Exhibit 8.2 Leverage Analysis

Illustrative Cases: Exxon Mobil vs. Chevron Corp. and Apple Inc. vs. Microsoft (See Excel Workings—▶ Chap. 8, Sheet E.8.2)

These cases show the relevance of leverage ratios by comparing the performance of companies in the same industry: case 1 —Exxon vs. Chevron and case —2 Apple vs. Microsoft. The aim is not to calculate the ratios but to analyze performance.

Exxon Mobil Vs. Chevron Corporation

Exhibits 8.2.1 and 8.2.2 present leverage ratios for Exxon Mobil and Chevron Corporation, respectively. Exhibits 8.2.3–8.2.5 compare the interest coverage and leverage between the companies and the industry. We can analyze historical performance as follows:

Focusing on Equity Holders: Both companies had equity capacity to fulfil all their financial obligations because leverage ratios were less than 100%. Regarding total debt and long-term debt, the two companies were almost within the same range, but Exxon's leverage in 2019 increased significantly to 27.5% and 16.1% from 19.7% and 10.7% in 2018, respectively. Considering total liabilities, Exxon's highest leverage was 93.6% in 2015, whereas Chevron's highest leverage was 77.9%. Shareholders' safety on total liabilities increased on

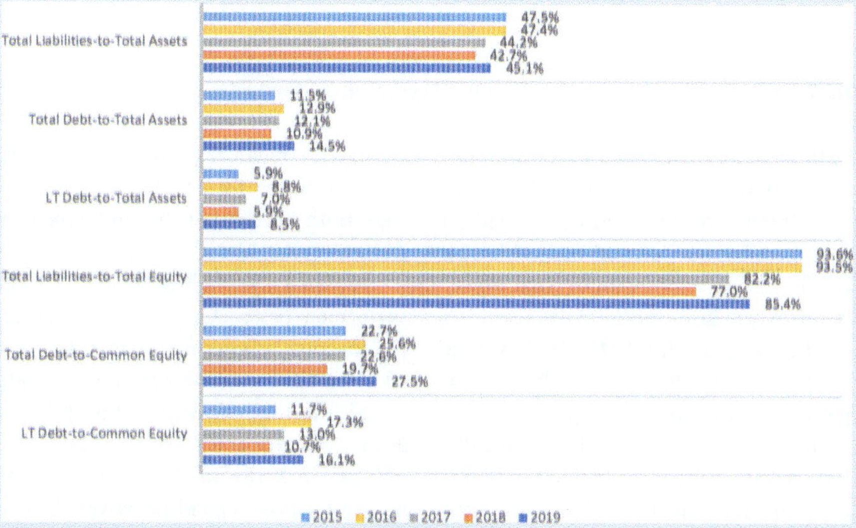

Exhibit 8.2.1 Financial leverage of Exxon Mobil

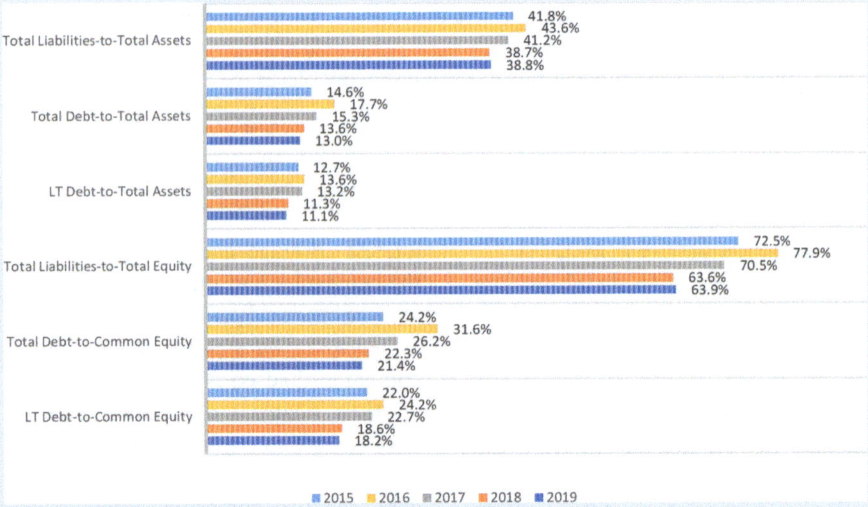

Exhibit 8.2.2 Financial leverage of Chevron Corporation

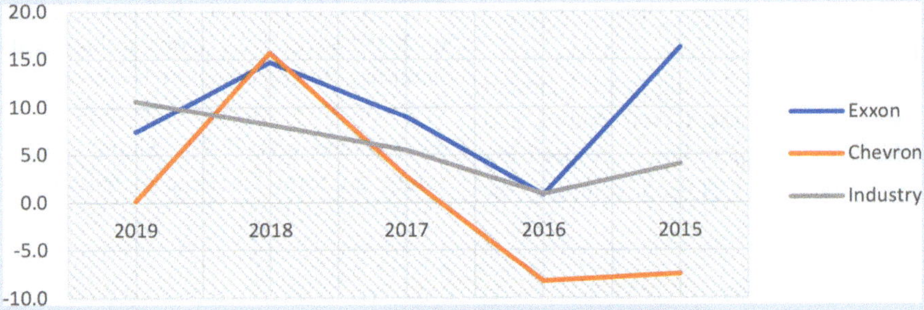

Exhibit 8.2.3 Interest coverage: Exxon, Chevron, and the industry

both companies, although Exxon maintained higher leverage than did Chevron. Compared to the industry median (petroleum refineries and related industries), the two companies had lower leverage (see Exhibit 8.2.4).

Focusing on Total Assets: Leverage ratios were less than 50% on both companies, but Chevron showed better overall historical improvement. Specifically, Exxon was stronger regarding long-term debt and total debt—its leverage ratios were lower than those of Chevron's. However, regarding total liabilities, Chevron outperformed Exxon, but they were both better than the industry (see Exhibit 8.2.5).

Focusing on Interest Cover: Exxon performed better. On a 5-year average, the coverage was approximately 10 times. Chevron's interest cover was lower despite significant improvement from 2016 to 2018 (outperformed Exxon and the industry in 2018). In 2015 and 2016, the negative ratios implied negative EBIT—earnings could not pay interest expenses.

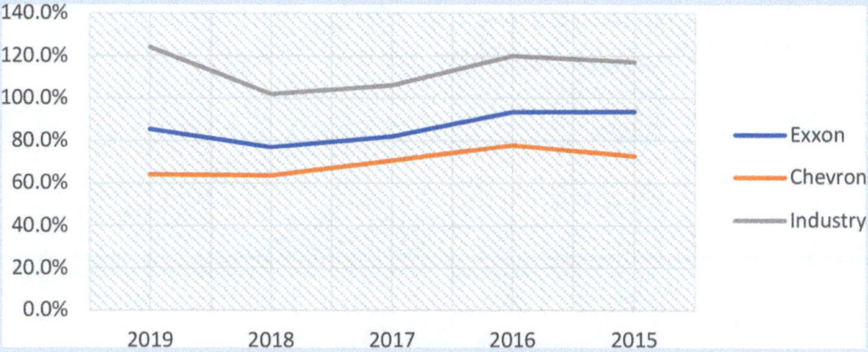

Exhibit 8.2.4 Total liabilities-to-total equity: Exxon, Chevron, and the industry

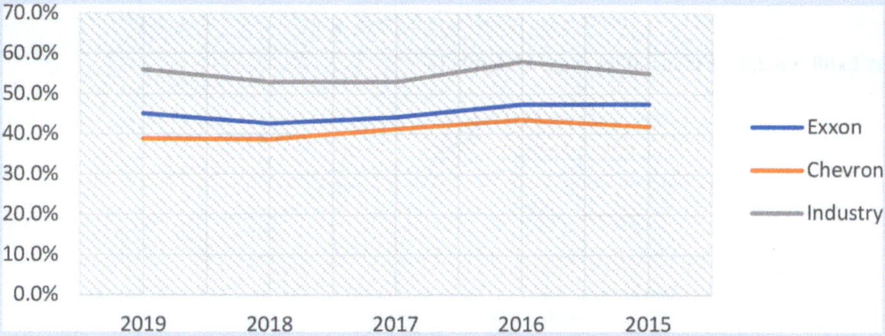

Exhibit 8.2.5 Total liabilities-to-total assets: Exxon, Chevron, and the industry

Overall, the company had a narrow and vulnerable safety margin on its interest obligations. Compared to the industry, Exxon's coverage ratio was above average, whereas Chevron's was below average, except in 2018. Moreover, the two companies (and the industry) moved together up and down, suggesting the influence of external factors (except in 2019).

Apple Inc. vs. Microsoft Corp.

Exhibits 8.2.6, 8.2.7, and 8.2.8 present leverage ratios for Apple Inc. and Chevron Corp. We can analyze historical performance as follows:

Focusing on Equity holders: Considering long-term debt, both companies maintained less than 100% leverage, except 101.5% for Apple in 2019—long-term debt did not threaten shareholders' equity. Regarding total debt, leverage for both companies increased over time to exceed 100% toward 2019. Overall, for both companies, the capacity of common equity to cover debt declined over time with a consistent increase in leverage between 2015 and 2019. Concerning total liabilities, leverage in both companies was above 100% with a systematic increase between 2015 and 2019: from 143.2% to 274% (for Apple) and from 118% to 180% (for Microsoft).

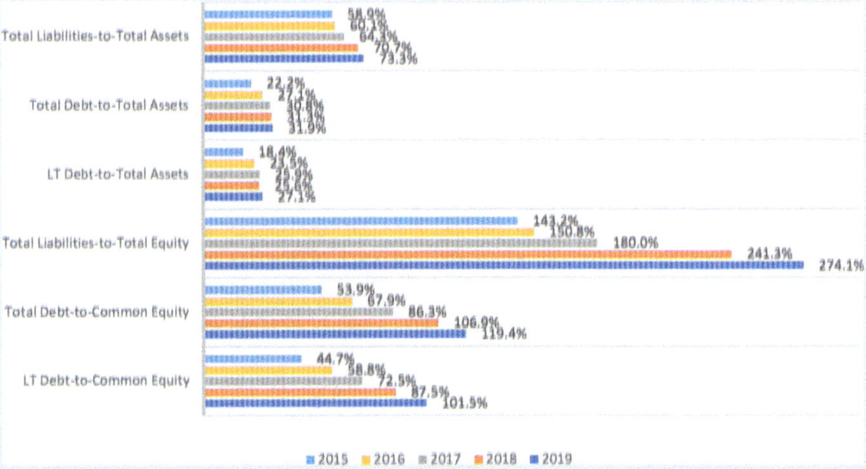

Exhibit 8.2.6 Financial leverage of Apple Inc.

8

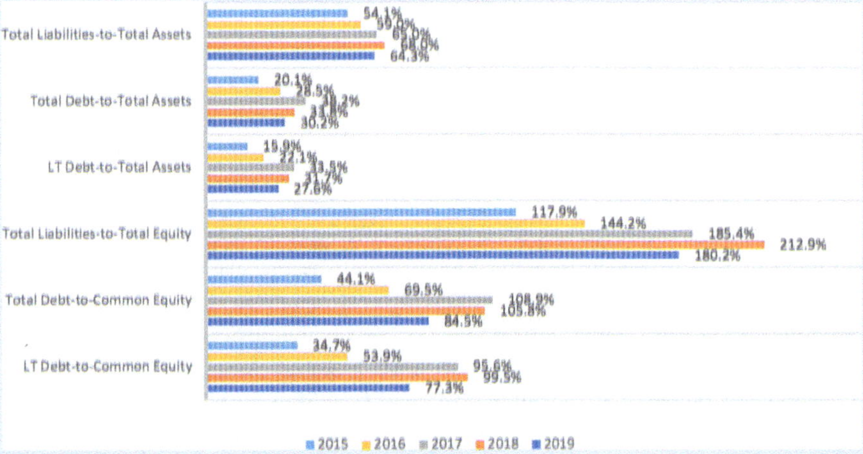

Exhibit 8.2.7 Financial leverage of Microsoft

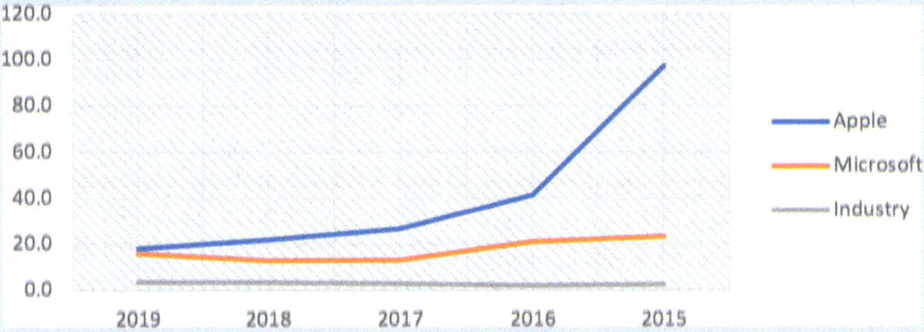

Exhibit 8.2.8 Interest coverage: Apple, Microsoft, and the industry
Source of Data: Bloomberg (2020)

Focusing on Total Assets: The two companies were generally identical regarding the ability of total assets to cover financial obligations—as a proportion of total assets, long-term debt and total debt were levered less than 50%, whereas total liabilities were less than 100%.

Focusing on Interest Cover: The two companies maintained high coverage ratios (more than two times) and significantly above the industry average. However, Apple outperformed Microsoft—their 5-year IC averages were approximately 51 times and 17 times, respectively. Despite maintaining a higher interest coverage ratio, Apple's performance declined dramatically from 97 times in 2015 to 18 times in 2019. In contrast, Microsoft's interest coverage was steady.

8.7 The Industry Factor

Leverage ratios differ across industries and even among companies within the same industry. Exhibit ▶ 8.3 shows variations in leverage ratios for selected sectors and industries in 2020. The commercial bank industry (financial) is among the highly levered, whereas Internet services and the social media industry (technology sector) is among the lowly levered (see ◘ Exhibits 8.3.1 and ◘ 8.3.4).

Among other reasons, capital intensity tends to attract high leverage. ◘ Exhibits 8.3.2 and ◘ 8.3.5 depict the proportion of interest coverage to leverage (debt to equity)—the proportion is higher in noncapital-intensive industries than in capital-intensive industries. This is because capital-intensive companies (e.g., oil and gas production, commercial banks, transport, logistics, etc.) use debt to fund their heavy asset investments but generate narrow earnings—it is the opposite for noncapital-intensive industries (e.g., consulting services, Internet services and social media, etc.). ◘ Exhibits 8.3.3 and ◘ 8.3.6 show the correlation between interest cover and leverage in 2020 under both sector and industry classifications. A negative correlation indicates low leverage is generally associated with higher interest coverage, and vice versa.

Generally, a company with a significantly lower leverage than industry benchmarks does not necessarily mean better performance—this may imply that the company did not optimize the leverage opportunity to generate earnings.

Banner 8.4 Industry Factor

Leverage and interest coverage differ significantly across sectors and industries as well as across companies within the same industry. This is mainly due to differences in capital intensity and business operation models.

Exhibit 8.3 Leverage Ratios by Sector and Industry (See Excel Workings—▶ Chap. 8, Sheet E.8.3)

8.8 Valuation Implications

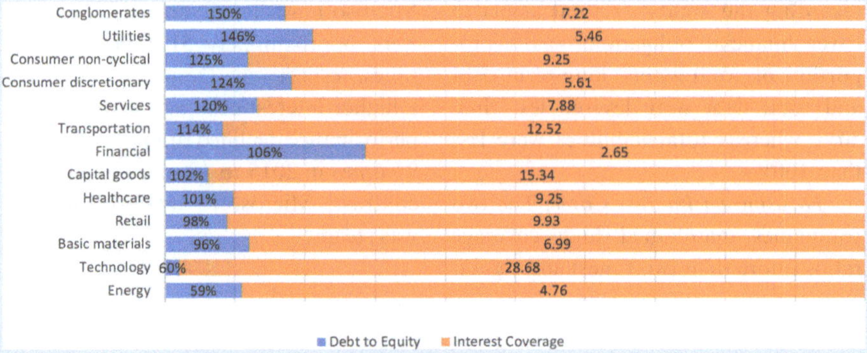

Exhibit 8.3.1 Leverage ratios by sector in 2020

Exhibit 8.3.2 Proportion of interest cover to debt to equity by sector in 2020

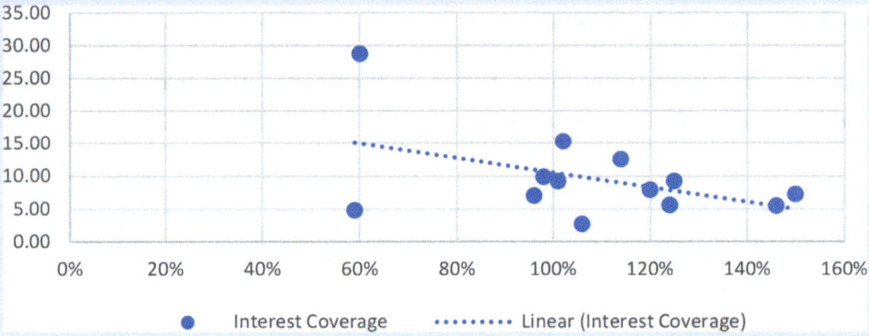

Exhibit 8.3.3 Correlation between interest cover and debt to equity (Sector Classification)

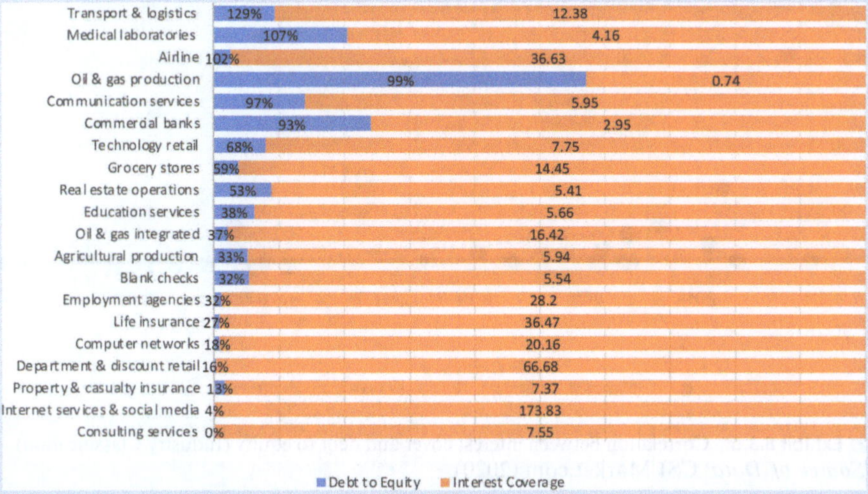

Exhibit 8.3.4 Leverage ratios by industry

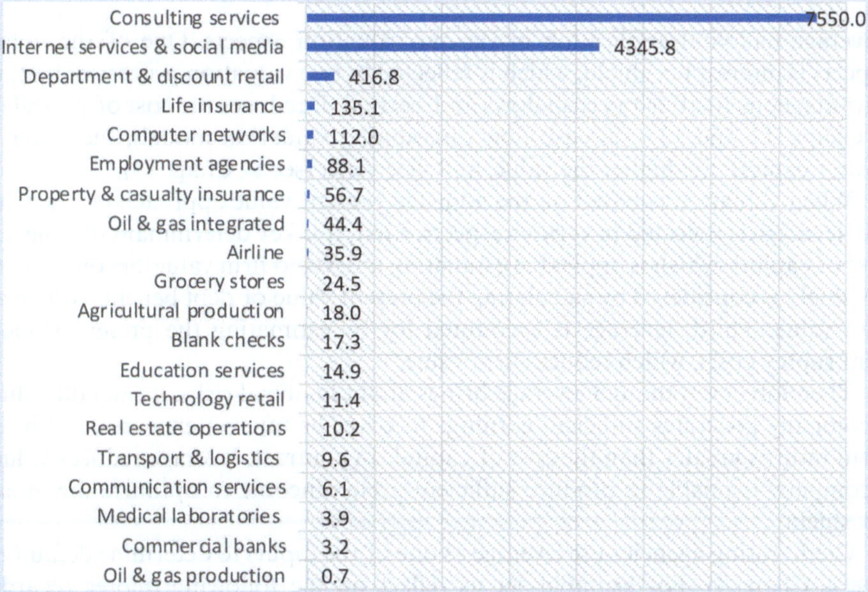

Exhibit 8.3.5 Proportion of interest cover to debt to equity by industry in 2020

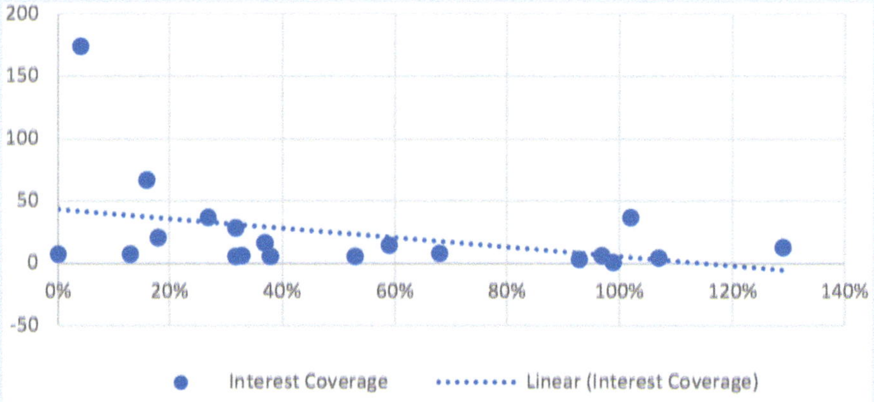

Exhibit 8.3.6 Correlation between interest cover and debt to equity (Industry Classification)
Source of Data: CSI Market.com (2020)

Leverage has vital application in various valuation aspects. One of the notable aspects is interest tax shield, which is reflected in two valuation processes: first, it is advantageous to after-tax cash flows and, second, it reduces the cost of capital (see ▶ Chaps. 11 and 13)—in cash flow discounting valuation models, the lower the cost of capital, the higher the value, and vice versa (see ▶ Chap. 15).

When valuation is based on the adjusted present value approach (see ▶ Chap. 16), leverage is reflected in various aspects. First, it is key determinant of unlevered cost of capital, which is applied in estimating unlevered firm value. Second, interest tax shield is considered by calculating the present value of debt benefits, which add firm value. Third, leverage is accounted for by estimating the present value of bankruptcy costs, which reduces firm value.

Therefore, even though leverage brings about financial risks, it can add value if a company generates sufficient earnings to cover its interest expenses and investment returns greater than the cost of capital. In contrast, leverage reduces value if a company is unable to produce sufficient pretax income to optimize the interest tax shield.

Credit rating agencies use leverage as one of the inputs to determine default risk (see ▶ Chap. 4). For example, let us reflect on the following quotes regarding Fitch's rating drivers for the company Solar Capital (Fitch, April 17, 2020):

> The affirmations reflect Fitch's view that Solar's asset coverage cushion will remain appropriate for its rating, despite expectations for negative portfolio valuation marks in the near term and an increase in credit issues in the medium term, given its ***relatively low leverage*** as of Dec. 31, 2019...

» ...Rating constraints for the business development companies (BDC) sector more broadly include the market ***impact on leverage***...

» Recently relaxed regulatory ***limits on leverage*** are an evolving sector headwind, which could contribute to increased risk profiles for individual BDCs...

» Solar's ***leverage ratio*** was 0.66X as of Dec. 31, 2019, which implied an asset coverage cushion of 40.6%. Solar's cushion is above the peer average and within Fitch's 'a' category ***leverage benchmark range*** of 33–60% for BDCs. Fitch believes Solar is relatively well-positioned as its portfolio can sustain a valuation decline of more than 33% before its asset coverage cushion falls to the low end of Fitch's 'BBB' category benchmark range of 11–33%...

Valuation Implication

Valuation application of leverage can be reflected in various aspects such as calculation of cost of capital, value of interest tax benefits, value of bankruptcy costs, and credit ratings.

Apply 8.2 Leverage Analysis

McDonald's, Starbucks, and Chipotle Mexican.

Data: See Excel workings—▸ Chap. 8, Sheet A.8.1

The data sheet presents the companies' financials for 4 years. Use Excel to perform the following analysis:

(a) Search for industry leverage ratios relevant for analyzing shareholders' and company's financial risk.

(b) Based on your calculations in ▸ Apply 8.1, analyze the three companies' leverage relative to the industry.

Review Questions

1. Why should companies use debt if leverage implies financial risk?
2. Explain the implication of financial leverage in the following aspects:
   (a) Tax expenses
   (b) Risk
   (c) Cost of capital
3. Explain risk implications of leverage in the following:
   (a) Shareholders
   (b) Company
4. When leverage ratios focus on owners' (or shareholders') financial risk, what is the implication of defining leverage using the following financial items:
   (a) Long-term debt
   (b) Total debt

   (c) Total liabilities
5. When leverage ratios focus on shareholders' financial risk, what is the implication of the following ratios?
   (a) Leverage ratio is 100%
   (b) Leverage ratio is 115%
   (c) Leverage ratio is 90%
   (d) Leverage ratio is 0%
6. When leverage ratios focus on a company's financial risk, what is the implication of the following ratios?
   (a) Leverage ratio is 100%
   (b) Leverage ratio is 115%
   (c) Leverage ratio is 90%
   (d) Leverage ratio is 0%
7. The following information was extracted from the financial statements of CPT Company.

	2021	2020
Total liabilities	4.36	3.96
Common equity	2.30	2.02
Long-term debt	3.30	2.95
Short-term debt	0.22	0.21
Total assets	6.65	5.98
Total equity	2.30	2.02
Total debt	3.52	3.16
EBIT	0.82	0.32
Interest expenses	0.03	0.04
Operating expenses	0.88	0.72
Gross income	1.71	1.04

   Required: Use the financials to analyze and explain implications of leverage aspects.
   (a) Shareholder's financial risk on total debt, long-term debt, and total liabilities.
   (b) Company's financial risk on total debt, long-term debt, and total liabilities.
   (c) Interest coverage from operating earnings.
8. Why is it important to consider the industry factor when analyzing financial leverage?
9. Explain valuation implications of financial leverage.

Bibliography

Fitch (2020), *Fitch Affirms Solar Capital Ratings at 'BBB-'; Outlook Stable,* https://www.fitchratings.com/research/corporate-finance/fitch-affirms-solar-capital-ratings-at-bbb-outlook-stable-17-04-2020

Guichard, B. (2022). Carnival: Enormous Risk For LT Common Stockholders. Available at Seeking Alpha, https://seekingalpha.com/article/4515978-carnival-enormous-risk-for-lt-common-stockholders Accessed June 02, 2022.

Simply Wall St. (2022). Wide Open West (NYSE:WOW) Takes On Some Risk With Its Use Of Debt, Available at Simply Wall St. https://simplywall.st/stocks/us/media/nyse-wow/wideopenwest/news/wideopenwest-nysewow-takes-on-some-risk-with-its-use-of-debt Accessed June 06, 2022.

Market Perception Analysis

Contents

Supplementary Information The online version contains supplementary material available at https://doi.org/10.1007/978-3-031-28267-6_9.

B. Kulwizira Lukanima, *Corporate Valuation*, Classroom Companion: Business, https://doi.org/10.1007/978-3-031-28267-6_9

9.1 Introduction

As discussed in the previous chapters, investors inject funds into companies, expecting rewards in the form of earnings and returns on their investments. Net earnings, reported in the income statement, belong to shareholders and can be distributed to them either directly in the form of "dividends" or indirectly through retained earnings to increase their net wealth. While earnings per share (EPS) is a book value, stock prices are driven by investors' market perception about the company. Hence, market price is a measure of the current shareholders' value created by the company.

This chapter, therefore, presents the concept of investors' market perception and how it can be reflected on and analyzed using ratios. That is, unlike other ratios, market perception ratios relate financial performance to market expectations.

Learning Outcomes

- Explain the meaning of market perception
- Relate market perception to capital market efficiency
- Analyze market perception using financial ratios
- Explain the relevance and valuation implications of market perception ratios
- Understand the industry factor of market perception ratios

9.2 The Concept of Market Perception

Market perception is about how investors perceive company performance based on their expectations. Perception is reflected in stock market prices—a positive perception implies investors' satisfaction, leading to an increase in price, whereas a negative perception implies dissatisfaction, leading to a fall in price. Market perception ratios (or market value ratios), therefore, relate financial performance (book value) to market performance (market value) to provide a more realistic measure of performance.

Banner 9.1 Market Perception
Market perception ratios analyze stock market perception of a company by comparing its stock price (market performance) and book value (financial performance).

9.2.1 Financial Performance

The most important financial performance items that attract investors' attention are earnings per share (EPS) and book value per share (BPS) of equity. Both EPS and BPS are determined by earnings available for common shareholders (EAC) and book value of equity (BVE), excluding preference equity, divided by the number of shares outstanding. While EPS focuses on profitability performance, BPS focuses on shareholders' wealth performance. Thus, EPS and BPS monitor growth in earnings and shareholder's net worth, respectively.

Banner 9.2 Earnings Per Share and Book Value Per Share

Both EPS and BPS are the most important financial measures because they entail shareholders' wealth. EPS is reflected in shareholders' wealth through retained earnings and/or dividends.

9.2.2 Market Performance, Information, and Efficiency

Market performance is measured through stock market price. There is, therefore, a link between market information, efficiency, and stock prices. Theoretically, if markets are efficient, then stock prices provide information that prices are fair (Fama 1970)—the stocks of the company are neither undervalued nor overvalued. However, stocks can be underpriced or overpriced, implying market imperfection, reflected in investors' perceptions.

Think 9.1

Why is it important to analyze market perception?

Exhibit 9.1 Market Perception Ratios

In ▫ Exhibit 9.1.1, market perception ratios (price–earnings (P/E), price-to-book (P/B), and dividend yield (DY)) use market price to assess investors' perception (expectations) of earnings (EPS), net worth (BPS), and dividends, respectively. Price, therefore, carries information about expectations. ▫ Exhibit 9.1.2 compares the ratios for three companies based on their financial performance and market response (price).

Exhibit 9.1.1 Structure of price–earnings, price-to-book, and dividend yield

9

Exhibit 9.1.2 Example of P/E, P/B, and DY

	Company A	Company B	Company C
Stock price ($)	200	375	600
Dividend per share ($)	25	25	0
Earnings per share ($)	186	155	155
Book per share ($)	297	196	710
ROE	19.20%	18.50%	9.24%
P/E	1.08	2.42	3.87
DY	12.50%	6.67%	0.00%
BP	0.67	1.91	0.85

9.3 Analyzing Investors' Perception of Earnings, Dividends, and Equity Value

There are several market perception ratios, but the most popular are "price–earnings" (P/E), "price-to-book" (P/B), and "dividend yield" (DY), which are covered in this chapter. As depicted in Exhibit ▶ 9.1, market price reflects investors' expectations about company performance on respective financial indicators.

Think 9.2
Is there any relationship between earnings and dividends? Explain.

9.3.1 Market Perception About Earnings

9.3.1.1 How Is It Measured?

The most important profitability measure attracting investors' attention is EAC (earnings available for common shareholders) due to its implications in their wealth—cash dividends (depending on dividend policy) and retained earnings (which affect the net worth in the balance sheet). Therefore, to measure market perception about earnings, the P/E ratio can be calculated as follows:

$$P/E = \frac{Market\ price}{EPS}$$

9.3.1.2 Relevance

First consider the following quote:

> A key metric that value investors always look at is the Price to Earnings Ratio, or P/E for short. This shows us how much investors are willing to pay for each dollar of earnings in a given stock and is easily one of the most popular financial ratios in the world. The best use of the P/E ratio is to compare the stock's current P/E ratio with (a) where this ratio has been in the past; (b) how it compares to the average for the industry/sector; and (c) how it compares to the market as a whole (Zack 2022).

A P/E greater than 1 signifies that EPS performance is above expectations and that investors are optimistic about increasing stock value in future. A P/E less than 1 signifies that EPS is below expectations and that investors are pessimistic about stock value in future. For example, in Exhibit 9.1.2, investors' earnings confidence is the highest on company C and the lowest on company A.

Nevertheless, it is vital to consider other factors when analyzing P/E. For example, new or infant companies can have high P/E ratios because investors bet on a potential future even if the current earnings are low or even negative. Mature companies can have low but stable P/E ratios. Overall, the market never relies solely on current earnings but also the stability of those earnings over time. Hence, a current higher P/E ratio is not necessarily an indication of good performance if long-term earnings are unstable—risk of volatile earnings. A high P/E may arise from a declining business rather than a positive market perception when the fall in earnings is not reflected in the current stock price.

Banner 9.3 P/E Ratio
A P/E ratio measures market perception about earnings performance. A higher P/E ratio is generally desirable as it shows more investors' confidence about earnings-driven value in future, and vice versa.

9.3.2 Market Perception About Dividends and Growth

9.3.2.1 How Is It Measured?

Dividend per share depends on dividend policy and has implication in growth—a higher (lower) payout ratio means less (more) earnings are reinvested. Investors' dividend preferences differ—dividend investors prefer immediate cash from the company, whereas non-dividend investors prefer growth of share value. Eventually, both dividends and growth of share prices have implication in shareholders' wealth maximization. "Dividend yield" (DY) can, therefore, be used to assess investors' perception of dividends relative to growth potentials.

$$DY = \frac{Dividend\ per\ share}{Market\ price}$$

9.3.2.2 Relevance

A higher (lower) DY ratio signifies that investors pay more (less) for cash dividends. Therefore, a high DY is generally favorable for dividend investors. However, when interpreting DY, other factors should also be considered, since it can be misleading when a company suffers from abnormally low stock prices (say due to factors like depression). Moreover, a low DY relative to the industry or peers can have two implications, either positive or negative. The positive side reflects market optimism about an impressive future; hence, the stock is attractive (high price) regardless of the current low dividend payout. The negative side is when a company simply fails to pay dividends due to financial difficulties.

9

To elaborate this point, let us compare companies A and B in ◘ Exhibit 9.1.2. DY is 12.5% for company A and 6.7% for company B. A dividend investor will prefer to invest in company A rather than in company B, and, if he is optimistic about stable dividends in the long run, then he can sell some of his stocks in company B to buy more stocks in company A. However, non-dividend investors can still prefer company B because they expect more value from its future earnings—its shares are more valuable than those of company A, despite a lower EPS today.

Reflect on the following quote:

> » The industrial giant's full-year guidance is under threat…Industrial giant 3M's (MMM -4.53%) stock is now yielding more than 4% and is very tempting for income-seeking investors. That's fair enough. If your primary focus is yield, go ahead, and buy the stock. However, it might be a different story for investors looking for capital appreciation. It seems highly likely that management will have to lower full-year guidance on its next earnings call, so if you buy the stock, be aware there's a high possibility of some negative near-term news flow (Samaha 2022).

Think 9.3

Why do dividend preferences differ among investors, and what is the implication on dividend yield?

Banner 9.4 Dividend Yield
Dividend yield measures investors' perception on dividends and growth potentials. A higher DY implies a lower price per each dividend, and vice versa.

9.3.3 Market Perception About Tangible Value

9.3.3.1 How Is It Measured?

Tangible value is measured by book value of equity, which shows how much is available for common shareholders should a company be liquidated and needs to pay all its liabilities. Hence, the appropriate ratio for tangible value is "price-to-book" (P/B). It compares the current market price to book value per share (BPS) of equity as follows:

$$P/B = \frac{Market\ price}{BPS}$$

9.3.3.2 Relevance

While P/E is the most applicable market perception ratio, conservative investors prefer a more tangible measure of value—book value of equity. The purpose of a P/B ratio is to help investors determine how much they are paying for their net worth (investment) in the company. It is, therefore, more suitable for capital-intensive companies (e.g., banks, airlines, etc.). A low P/B (less than 1) gives a quick indication of undervalued stocks (a negative market perception), whereas a high P/B (greater than 1) indicates that stocks are trading for more than the investment's book value and could be overvalued (a positive market perception).

Nevertheless, the P/B ratio alone may not provide a true picture about value—it should be interpreted with caution and conclusion should be drawn only after a thorough analysis of other factors. For example, an extremely low P/B ratio can signify a troubled company rather than an undervalued stock. The ratio, therefore, becomes more useful when analyzed in conjunction with asset efficiency indicators (e.g., return on equity (ROE)). For example, in ◘ Exhibit 9.1.2, company A has a lower P/B (0.67) than does company B (1.91), but it has a higher ROE (19.20%) than does company B (18.50%)—company A can be considered undervalued. However, this is not the case when comparing company B and company C whose P/B (0.85) and ROE (9.24%) are both lower than company C's.—this does not necessarily mean that company C's stocks are undervalued. A P/B ratio is, therefore, more appropriate when comparing companies with similar growth and profitability performance. Let us reflect on the following quote:

> ...a stock with a P/B ratio of 2 means that we pay $2 for every $1 of book value. Thus, the higher the P/B, the more expensive the stock...But there is a caveat. A P/B ratio less than one can also mean that the company is earning weak or even negative returns on its assets or that the assets are overstated, in which case the stock should

be shunned because it may be destroying shareholder value. Conversely, the stock's price may be significantly high—thereby pushing the P/B ratio to more than one—in the likely case that it has become a takeover target, a good enough reason to own the stock (Shah 2022).

Banner 9.5 Price-to-Book
P/B is a market perception ratio based on the balance sheet's tangible value. A higher (lower) ratio can be a typical indication of an overvalued (undervalued) stock.

Think 9.4
Why is it important to analyze P/B ratio in comparison to profitability performance ratios like ROE?

Exhibit ▸ 9.2 presents two case examples to illustrate market perception ratios. The cases explain market perception ratios using companies from different industries and dividend characteristics:

9

Think 9.5
Based on market perception, what is the impact on existing and potential investors of an undervalued and an overvalued stock? Which one reflects a positive market perception and which one reflects a negative one?

Exhibit 9.2 Market Perception Analysis

Illustrative Cases (See Excel Workings—▸ Chap. 9, Sheet E.9.2)

Case 1:

MFA Financial Investment and Garrison Capital Inc.

Exhibits 9.2.1, 9.2.2, and 9.2.3 present market perception ratios for MFA and Garrison, which are both US-based companies (financial services industry). Both companies' P/E ratios were above 1, implying a positive market perception of their earnings over 5 years (2015–2019). However, MFA showed better performance with a steady P/E increase, outperforming the industry from 2017 onward, whereas Garrison was below the industry throughout. In contrast, Garrison had a higher DY ratio with a faster historical increase, whereas both companies were above the industry. This signifies that MFA investors expected more value from earnings per share (hence a higher P/E) and were willing to pay more for lower dividends (hence, a lower DY)—it was the opposite for Garrison investors.

Regarding P/B ratio, it was less than 1 for both compan14.173ies and below the industry—MFA and Garrison stocks were likely to be undervalued, especially MFA's. The overall implication is that value investors in the companies had safety margins on their investments throughout the 5 years.

Case 2:

Apple Inc., Microsoft Corp., and Adobe Inc.

Exhibit 9.2.1 P/E ratio: MFA, Garrison, and the industry

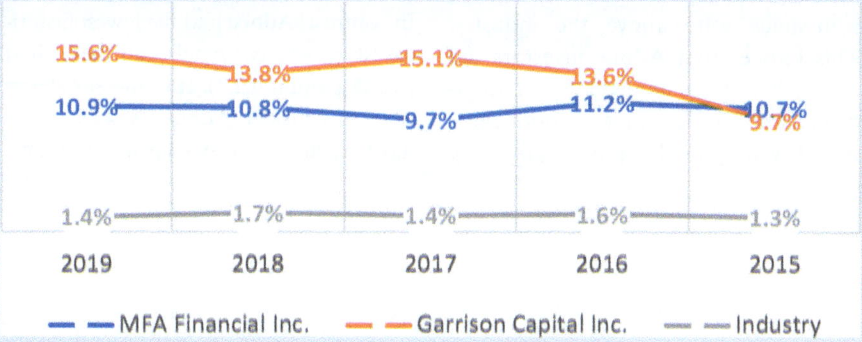

Exhibit 9.2.2 DY ratio: MFA, Garrison, and the industry

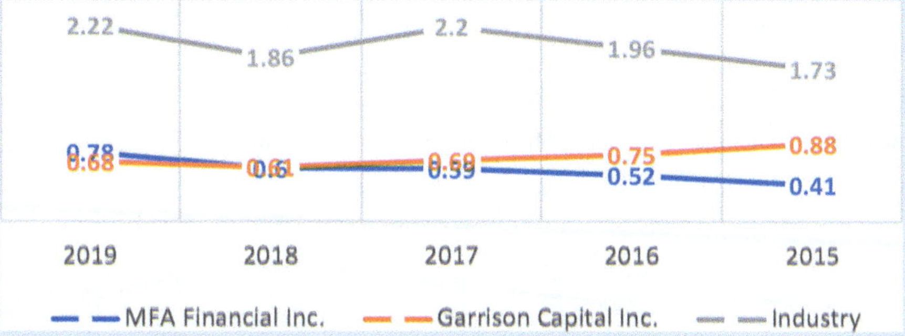

Exhibit 9.2.3 P/B ratio: MFA, Garrison, and the industry

Exhibits 9.2.4, 9.2.5 and 9.2.6 present market perception ratios for Apple, Microsoft, and Adobe (electronics general industry). All companies' P/E ratios were above 1, implying a positive market perception of their earnings over 5 years (2015–2019). However, Adobe, a non-dividend company, outperformed the other two (dividend companies) and the industry (except in 2018), with Apple being the lowest. For the dividend companies, DY declined over time, like the industry, but Microsoft maintained a higher DY. Both companies were above the industry. This implies that Adobe investors did not bother about immediate cash (dividends) and were optimistic about earnings-driven growth and value—they were willing to pay higher per share. Apple and Microsoft investors had moderate perceptions of earnings and growth—they matched earning expectations and dividend preferences.

Regarding P/B, the ratio was greater than 1 and above the industry for all three companies, signifying investors' high confidence about asset-driven value. Moreover, the three companies had an upward historical trend, following the industry, but Adobe investors were the most optimistic (highest P/B), whereas Apple investors were the least (lowest P/B, except in 2019). In contrast, Adobe had the lowest historical ROE, whereas Apple had the highest (see Exhibit 9.2.7). It is, therefore, possible to consider Adobe's stocks as the most expensive and Apple's the cheapest.

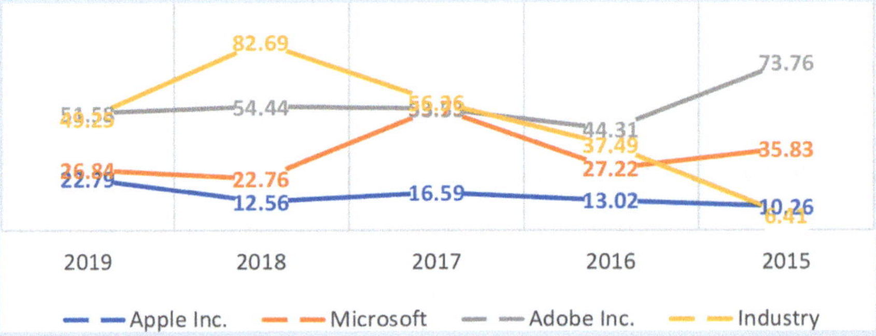

Exhibit 9.2.4 P/E ratio: Apple, Microsoft, Adobe, and the industry

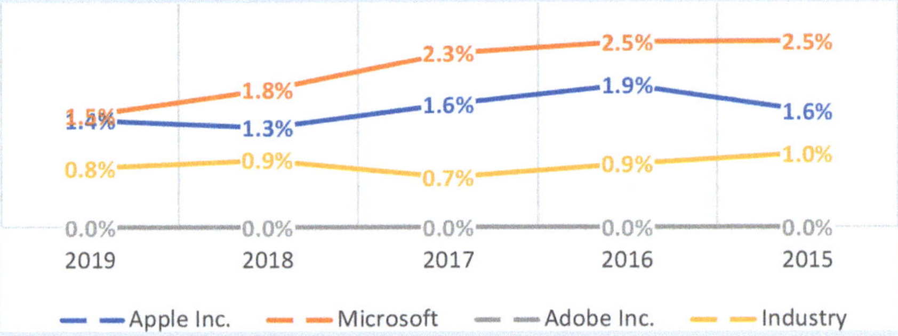

Exhibit 9.2.5 DY ratio: Apple, Microsoft, Adobe, and the industry

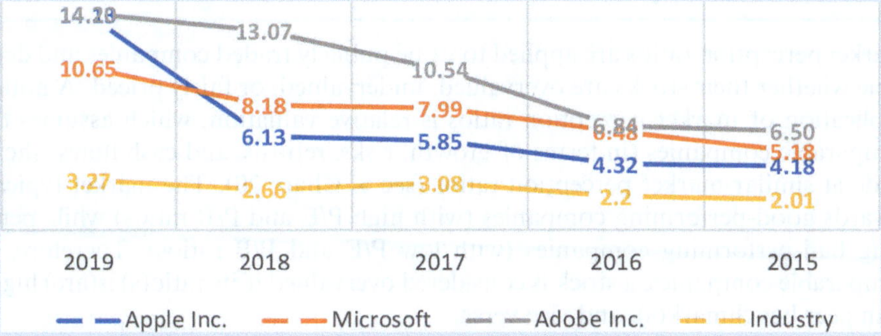

Exhibit 9.2.6 P/B ratio: Apple, Microsoft, Adobe, and the industry

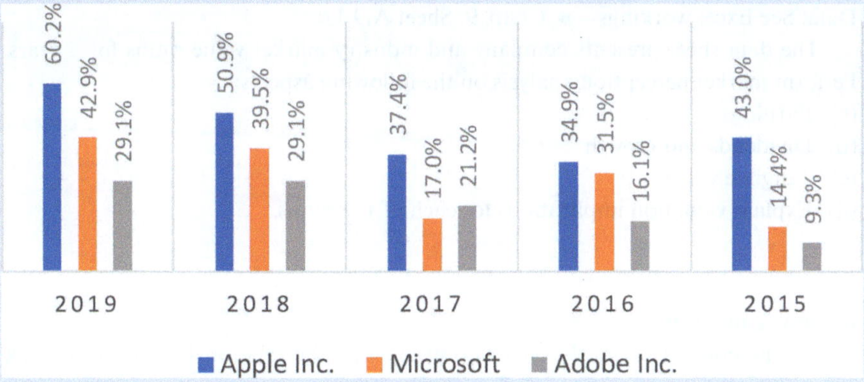

Exhibit 9.2.7 ROE: Apple, Microsoft, and Adobe

9.4 The Industry Factor

Like any other ratios, the industry effect is equally noticeable in market perception ratios. Capital-intensive companies (like manufacturing, banks, airlines, etc.) tend to have lower P/E and DY ratios than do noncapital-intensive companies (e.g., computer software, Internet and social media services, communication services, etc.). Therefore, as illustrated in Exhibit ▶ 9.2, these ratios should generally be analyzed by comparing companies within the same industry or sector and using industry benchmarks to determine whether a stock is overpriced or underpriced.

The P/B ratio is mainly useful for capital-intensive businesses whose assets are mostly tangible—it can be misleading when analyzing companies whose assets are mostly intangible. Moreover, the P/B ratio can be even more sensitive to specific company asset characteristics within the same industry.

9.5 Valuation Implication

Market perception ratios are applied to value publicly traded companies and determine whether their stocks are overvalued, undervalued, or fairly priced. A notable application of market perception ratios is relative valuation, which assumes that comparable companies (in terms of growth, risks, returns, and cash flows) should trade at similar market perception ratios (see ▶ Chap. 20). The market typically rewards good-performing companies (with high P/E and P/B ratios) while penalizing bad-performing companies (with low P/E and P/B ratios). Therefore, for comparable companies, a stock is considered overvalued if its ratio(s) is(are) higher than peer benchmark(s), and vice versa.

Apply 9.1 Market Perception Analysis: Chevron Corp. and Exxon Mobile

Data: See Excel workings—▶ Chap. 9, Sheet A.9.1

The data sheet presents company and industry market value ratios for 5 years. Perform market perception analysis on the following aspects:

(a) Earnings
(b) Dividends and growth
(c) Tangible value
(d) Explain valuation implications for each of the ratios.

Review Questions

1. In the context of market perception, explain the relationship between stock market price and company's financial performance.
2. Explain why the following financial variables are more relevant for analyzing market perception of companies:
   (a) Earnings available for common shareholders
   (b) Book value of equity
3. Why is it important to analyze market perception?
4. What is the relationship between earnings and dividends?
5. The following information relate to three companies in the same industry for the year 2021.

	Company X	Company Y	Company Z
Stock price ($)	12	64	35
Dividend per share ($)	0.86	0	1.4
Earnings per share ($)	14.3	45	45
Book per share ($)	33	28	15

Industry benchmarks were as follows: ROE (18.0%), P/E (1.2), DY (6.0%), and P/B (3.10).

Required:

(a) Calculate the following market perception ratios: P/E, DY, and P/B.
(b) For each of the three ratios in (a), analyze market perception of each company separately.
(c) For each of the three ratios in (a), analyze market perception by comparing the three companies and the industry.

6. Explain the practical relevance of the following ratios and the factors to consider when interpreting each of them.
   (a) P/E
   (b) DY
   (c) P/B
7. Why do dividend preferences differ among investors, and what is the implication on the DY ratio?
8. Why is the P/B ratio considered a tangible measure of value?
9. Which of the following aspects reflect positive or negative market perception? Explain the implication of each for existing and potential investors.
   (a) Undervalued stock
   (b) Overvalued stock
10. Why should the industry factor be considered in analyzing market perception ratios?

Bibliography

Fama, E. F. (1970). Efficient Capital Markets: A Review of Theory and Empirical Work. *The Journal of Finance*, 25(2), 383–417. https://doi.org/10.2307/2325486

Samaha, L. (2022). 3M's 4% Dividend Yield Isn't a Reason to Buy the Stock, Available at Fool https://www.fool.com/investing/2022/06/11/3ms-4-dividend-yield-isnt-a-reason-to-buy-the-stoc/ Accessed June 11, 2022.

Shah, K (2022). Buy These 5 Low Price-to-Book Value Stocks in June. Available at Nasdaq https://www.nasdaq.com/articles/buy-these-5-low-price-to-book-value-stocks-in-june Accessed June 1, 2022.

Zack (2022). Can Value Investors Choose Silver Standard Resources (SSRM) Stock?, Available at Nasdaq, https://www.nasdaq.com/articles/can-value-investors-choose-silver-standard-resources-ssrm-stock Accessed June 1, 2022.

Free Cash Flows

Contents

Supplementary Information The online version contains supplementary material available at https://doi.org/10.1007/978-3-031-28267-6_10.

B. Kulwizira Lukanima, *Corporate Valuation*, Classroom Companion: Business, https://doi.org/10.1007/978-3-031-28267-6_10

10.1 Introduction

Companies need cash to fund various business activities, such as purchasing inventories, paying bills, developing new products, acquiring assets, paying off debts, paying dividends, etc. A cash flow statement shows the movement of cash through the three main types of business activities (operating, investing, and financing) and cash balance for the financial period. However, cash balance is not free cash flow (FCF); it is a key variable in corporate valuation. None of the three financial statements (balance sheet, income statement, and cash flow statement) are designed to show free cash flows.

This chapter, therefore, reflects on financial statements and introduces the concept of free cash flow and how it is calculated.

Learning Outcomes

- Understand the concept of free cash flow
- Explain the appropriate financial statement adjustments for calculating free cash flows
- Calculate free cash flows using various approaches
- Understand the interpretation of free cash flows
- Explain the effect of corporate decisions on free cash flows
- Explain the limitations of free cash flows in relation to the agency cost problem
- Understand the practical complexities involved in calculating and using free cash flows
- Understand the valuation implications of free cash flows

10.2 The Concept of Cash and Free Cash Flow

Consider a cash flow statement (refer to ▶ Chap. 5), in which cash flows through three main business activities: operating activities (which include working capital), investment activities, and financing activities. Generally, cash should be free after fulfilling all the necessary requirements to continue business operations. Most items in investment activities (except capital expenditure that represents reinvestment into the business) and financing activities are typically discretional. Therefore, the general meaning of "free cash flow" (FCF) is a company's discretionary cash flow.

Exhibit 10.1 The Concept of Free Cash Flow

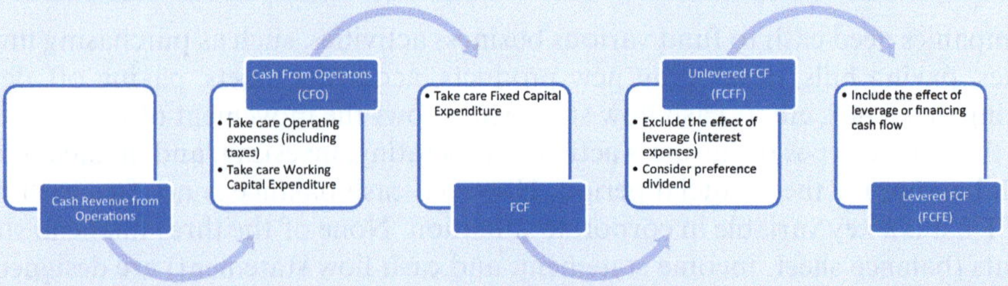

Cash from operations (CFO) is cash revenue remaining after taking care of the operating expenses (including income tax) and working capital expenditure. Free cash flow (FCF) is CFO after taking care of the fixed capital expenditure. Free cash flow to the firm (FCFF) is FCF after excluding the effect of leverage (interest expenses and interest tax shield)—it is available to all investors. Free cash flow to equity (FCFE) is FCFF after taking care of the financing activities (interest expenses, preference dividends, net debt, and net preference stock)—it is available to common equity holders (owners). In the absence of leverage (debt), FCF should be equal to FCFF. In the absence of leverage and preference stocks, FCF, FCFF, and FCFE should all be equal.

10

To be more specific, free cash flow is broken down to address the question of discretionary cash—"free cash to who?" The answer to this question involves two main categories of free cash flow relevant for valuation: (1) cash available to all investors (debtholders and equity holders)—"free cash flow to the firm (FCFF)," and (2) cash available to equity holders (owners)—"free cash flow to equity (FCFE)." These three FCF concepts, namely, CFO, FCFF, and FCFE, are depicted in ▶ Exhibit 10.1 and are elaborated in the following sections.

10.2.1 Free Cash Flow (FCF)

Refer to ▶ Exhibit 10.1. Starting from operating activities, cash flows into business in the form of revenues and flows out of business in the form of operating expenses (including taxes). The remaining cash goes into investments—short-term investments (working capital) and long-term investments (fixed capital). "Free cash flow (FCF)" is the cash available after taking care of the operating expenses and capital expenditure but includes interest expenses (a financing aspect), thereby ignoring the interest tax shield. It is, therefore, typically not suitable for firm intrinsic valuation.

Banner 10.1 Free Cash Flow (FCF)

FCF is cash available to the firm after taking care of the operating and investment activities and interest expenses.

Banner 10.2 Free Cash Flow to the Firm (FCFF)
FCFF is cash available to all investors after taking care of the operating and investment activities, excluding interest expenses, but considering the interest tax shield—it is unlevered FCF.

10.2.2 Free Cash Flow to the Firm (FCFF)

Refer to ▶ Exhibit 10.1. "Free cash flow to the firm (FCFF)" is cash remaining after taking care of the operating and investment activities but excluding interest expenses, thereby considering the interest tax shield. It is available to all finance providers (debtholders and equity holders). It should be noted that debtholders get priority because common equity holders are the ultimate claimants.

Since none of the financing activities have been considered, FCFF is referred to as "unlevered free cash flow"—it excludes the impact of debts (interest expenses and mandatory debt repayments). FCFF indicates the ability of a company to fulfill its financial obligations to debtholders and to pursue opportunities that enhance shareholders' (owners') value. For instance, if cash is always available to pay off debts, then there will be more financing opportunities for more investments, and vice versa. Hence, FCFF is typically applied in estimating a firm's intrinsic value (see ▶ Chaps. 15 and 16).

Banner 10.3 Free Cash Flow to Equity
FCFE is cash available after taking care of the operating, investment, and financing obligations—it is what belongs to business owners.

Banner 10.4 Financing Effect
In the absence of debts, FCF = FCFF
In the absence of debts and preference stocks, FCF = FCFF = FCFE

10.2.3 Free Cash Flow to Equity (FCFE)

Refer to ▶ Exhibit 10.1. Starting from FCFF, cash is prioritized to debtholders and preference stockholders (paying interest and preference dividends). The remaining cash (including net borrowing and net preference stock) belongs to the ultimate claimants (common equity holders). This is known as "free cash flow to equity (FCFE)" or "levered free cash flow" (because it considers the impact of debts). FCFE, therefore, indicates the ability of a company to create owners' value. Positive FCFE can be used either to enhance cash dividends or expand investments for growth. Prolonged negative FCFE may signify shareholders' value destruction. Hence, FCFE is typically applied in estimating equity intrinsic value (see ▶ Chap. 15).

Think 10.1
Is it a good decision to invest in a company with negative FCFE?

Banner 10.5 Lower vs. Higher Free Cash Flows
While higher cash flows generally signify a company's better financial health, lower (and negative) cash flows do not necessarily imply a failing business or poor performance.

10.3 Calculating Free Cash Flows

Calculating free cash flows is generally straightforward. However, to be correct, the process is not simply mathematical. It requires background work—to understand financial statement contents or items and the company. The goal is to determine what financial information to use depending on the company's nature of business.

10.3.1 Understanding Financial Statements

Typically, any of the following financial statement pairs is required to calculate either FCFF or FCFE: (1) income statement and balance sheet and (2) income statement and cash flow statement. However, it is essential to be conversant with financial items and the key adjustments to be made for a specific company.

10.3.1.1 Mismatches

In pair (1), the balance sheet is required to derive changes in capital expenditure and net financing, which are directly presented in the cash flow statement. Logically, for the same financial item (e.g., inventories), a change in the balance sheet should match that in the cash flow statement—but it is not uncommon to find mismatches (see ◘ Exhibit 10.2.1). There may be reasons like changes in accounting policies and reporting requirements. Does it matter? As long as financial statement pairs are consistently applied, mismatches will not affect the comparability across companies—pair (1) and (2) should not be used interchangeably to analyze different companies. Since the goal of free cash flows is to value companies (based on forecasts), what matters is the relationship between the overall change in working capital to the change in revenue. However, for simplicity, it is recommended to use pair (2), which is based on the company's interpretations of investing expenditure and financing.

Exhibit 10.2 Understanding Financial Statements and the Company

Illustrative Example (See Excel Workings—▶ Chap. 10, Sheet E.10.7B)

Exhibit 10.2.1 Amazon Inc.'s change in capital: balance sheet vs. cash flow statement

All in US$ millions	2021	2020	2019
Working capital (balance sheet)	−1313	31,549	11,959
Working capital (cash flow statement)	−19,611	13,481	−2438
Gross PPE (balance sheet)	−83,781	−66,280	−49,051
Gross PPE (cash flow statement)	−55,396	−35,044	−12,689

Note: The negative sign (−) means cash outflow (positive change of capital investment)

Exhibit 10.2.2 Netflix's noncurrent assets

All in US$ thousands	2021	2020	2019	2019
Total assets	44,584,663	39,280,359	33,975,712	25,974,400
Current assets	8,069,825	9,761,580	6,178,504	9,694,135
Total noncurrent assets	36,514,838	29,518,779	27,797,208	16,280,265
Gross PPE	1,939,759	1,454,973	981,226	786,800
Accumulated depreciation	−616,306	−494,790	−416,005	−368,519
Goodwill and other intangible assets	30,919,539	25,383,950	24,504,567	14,960,954
Other noncurrent assets	4,271,846	3,174,646	2,727,420	901,030

Exhibit 10.2.3 Ecopetrol's noncurrent assets

All in COP millions	2021	2020	2019	2019
Total assets	242,426,616	137,694,169	133,890,296	124,643,498
Current assets	51,695,747	22,834,374	23,364,461	27,030,612
Total noncurrent assets	190,730,869	114,859,795	110,525,835	97,612,886
Gross PPE	233,011,936	192,807,368	179,176,881	161,792,198
Accumulated depreciation	−106,528,888	−93,986,985	−85,433,036	−75,916,765
Goodwill and other intangible assets	20,194,840	2,149,322	1,643,020	1,570,669
Investments and advances	9,664,770	4,051,636	6,600,346	4,671,053

10.3.1.2 Financial Reporting Styles

Although financial statements are guided by reporting standards, they tend to be prepared and presented differently across companies and different sources (see PwC 2014). Hence, in calculating free cash flows, adjustments (such as noncash charges, interest, etc.) depend on how financial statements are presented.

10.3.1.3 Meaning of Signs

Another aspect to consider relates to signs (+ or −), which tend to cause confusion, calculation errors, and misinterpretation. For instance, a negative sign (−) may have different meanings in different financial statements: does it mean deduct (e.g., a positive number like expenses); does it represent a negative value (e.g., decline in receivables); or is it cash outflow? Likewise, what does a positive sign (+) represent? It may mean addition or a positive value or cash inflow. For example, in ◘ Exhibit 10.2.1, a negative sign (−) means cash outflow (increase in capital expenditure). In ◘ Exhibits 10.2.2 and 10.2.3, a negative sign (−) in accumulated depreciation does not mean decrease but deduct—this sign may not be indicated in some financial statements.

10.3.2 Understanding the Company

Examining the company helps determine the nature of its business, core business activities, recurring items, etc., which are vital for determining cash flow adjustments.

10.3.2.1 The Nature of Business

Companies differ in terms of industry and specific nature of business, which influence free cash flow calculations. Typically, financial items used to calculate free cash flow vary according to the nature of business. For example, PPE (property, plant, and equipment) is the largest item in a capital-intensive company like Ecopetrol but not in an online company like Netflix, dominated by goodwill and other intangibles (see ◘ Exhibits 10.2.2 and 10.2.3). Moreover, Ecopetrol's current assets are a small proportion of PPE, but Netflix is the opposite.

10.3.2.2 Core Business

In calculating free cash flow, the focus is on cash flow relating to core business activities—not on noncore activities. For example, Netflix's core business is its subscription-based streaming media service, which offers online streaming of a library of films and television programs, including those produced in-house. Its direct costs consist of licensing fees and the cost of producing its original content assets (through amortization). Licensing fees (intangibles) are typically a large, fixed capital expenditure (◘ Exhibit 10.2.2). In contrast, Ecopetrol engages in the exploration, development, and production of crude oil and natural gas—its large capital expenditure is PPE (◘ Exhibit 10.2.3).

10.3.2.3 Recurring Items

In calculating free cash flows, several adjustments should be made on financial statement items to determine cash flows from operating, investment, and financing activities—the goal is to adjust for noncash items. The rule of thumb is to adjust only the recurring items. For example, depreciation is a common noncash item, but there are several other items like deferred taxes, gains, losses on asset disposal, etc. By carefully examining a company's financial statements, the nonrecurring items should be identified and ignored during adjustments.

10.3.3 Approaches to Calculate Free Cash Flows

After scrutinizing the financial statements and the company's nature of business, free cash flows can be easily calculated using several approaches, which consider the general concept depicted in ▶ Exhibit 10.1.

▶ Exhibit 10.3 presents the financial statements of HIJ Company in 2020 and 2019 (balance sheet and income statement), which are used to explain and illustrate the different ways to calculate free cash flows. The overall approach (following ▶ Exhibit 10.1) is presented in ▶ Exhibit 10.4 with an example. Alternative approaches are presented in ▶ Exhibits 10.5 (FCFF) and 10.6 (FCFE).

Exhibit 10.3 Calculating Free Cash Flows from Income Statement and Balance Sheet

Illustrative Example (See Excel Workings—▶ Chap. 10, Sheet E.10.3)
(◘ Exhibits 10.3.1 and 10.3.2)

◘ Exhibit 10.3.1 HIJ Company's balance sheet for the year ended 31 December 2020

	2020 (US$ millions)	2019 (US$ millions)
Assets		
Cash	90	100
Accounts receivable	394	410
Inventory	696	616
Prepaid expenses	15	14
Total current assets	*1195*	*1140*
Noncurrent assets		
Property, plant, and equipment	1030	930
Less accumulated depreciation	329	299

(continued)

Exhibit 10.3.1 (continued)

	2020 (US$ millions)	2019 (US$ millions)
Net property, plant, and equipment	*701*	*631*
Investments (long-term)	50	50
Other assets (long-term)	223	223
Total assets	**2169**	**2044**
Liabilities and equity		
Accounts payable	110	110
Notes payable	290	295
Other accruals	100	100
Total current liabilities	500	505
Long-term debts	530	453
Shareholders' equity		
Common stock ($100/par)	200	200
Preferred stock	729	729
Retained earnings	210	157
Total equity	1139	1086
Total liabilities and equity	**2169**	**2044**

Exhibit 10.3.2 HIJ Company's income statement for the year ended 31 December 2020

	2020
Net sales	2211
Cost of goods sold	1599
Gross profit	612
Operating expenses	402
Earnings before interest and taxes (EBIT)	210
Interest expenses	59
Earnings before tax (EBT)	151
Income tax (39.74%)	60
Earnings after tax (EAT)	91
Preference dividends	38
Retained earnings	53

Exhibit 10.4 Calculating Free Cash Flows

Illustrative Example (See Excel Workings—▶ Chap. 10, Sheet E.10.4)

Notes: Examples are based on data from ▶ Exhibit 10.3. Explanations (superscripts 1–7) are given to clarify the key adjustments. Based on the concept in ▶ Exhibit 10.1, the overall step-by-step approach is as follows:

$$\text{CFO} = \text{Net income} + \text{Noncash charges} -{+}\text{Change in working capital}$$

$$\text{FCF} = \text{CFO} - \text{Fixed capital expenditure}$$

$$\text{FCFF} = \text{FCF} + (\text{Net interest expenses} + \text{Preference dividends})$$

$$\text{FCFE} = \text{FCFF} - \text{Net interest expenses} - \text{Preference dividends} + \text{Net borrowing} + \text{Net preference stock}$$

The general approach from net income to FCFE and data sources are presented in ◘ Exhibit 10.4.1. An example is provided in ◘ Exhibit 10.4.2.

◘ **Exhibit 10.4.1** Calculating CFO, FCF, FCFF, and FCFE: starting with net income

Action	Adjustment item	Source of information	Financial period
Start with	Net income	Income statement Cash flow statement	Current Current
Add	Noncash charges (Note 1)	Income statement Cash flow statement	Current Current
Deduct/ Add	Change in working capital (Note 2)	Balance sheet Cash flow statement	Previous and current Current
Result	CFO (Note 3)		
Deduct	Fixed capital expenditure (Note 4)	Cash flow statement Balance sheet	Current Previous and current
Result	FCF		
Add	Net interest expenses (Note 5)	Income statement	Current
Add	Preference dividends (Note 6)	Cash flow statement	Current
Result	FCFF		
Deduct	Net interest expenses (Note 5)	Income statement	Current
Deduct	Preference dividends (Note 6)	Cash flow statement	Current
Add	Net borrowing (Note 7)	Cash flow statement Balance sheet	Current Previous and current

(continued)

Exhibit 10.4.1 (continued)

Action	Adjustment item	Source of information	Financial period
Add	Net preference stock (Note 8)	Cash flow statement Balance sheet	Current Previous and current
Result	FCFE		

Exhibit 10.4.2 HIJ Company's free cash flows for the year ended 31 December 2020

	US$ millions
Net income (W1)	91
Add depreciation (W2)	30
Deduct/Add working capital investment (W3)	−65
CFO	***56***
Deduct fixed capital expenditure (W4)	−100
FCF	***−44***
Add net interest expenses (W5)	36
Add preference dividends (W6)	38
FCFF	***30***
Deduct net interest expenses (W5)	−36
Deduct preference dividends (W6)	−38
Add net borrowing (W7)	72
Add net preference stock (W8)	0
FCFE	***28***

Workings: Data from ► *Exhibit* 10.3

W1: Refer to the income statement. The net income was US$91 million in 2020.

W2: Based on the available data, depreciation is the only noncash charge (refer to the balance sheet). It is the difference between accumulated depreciation in 2020 and that in 2019: US$329 – US$299 = US$30 million.

W3: The working capital for 2020 is the difference between the working capital for 2020 and that for 2019—excluding cash and cash equivalents and notes payable (refer to the balance sheet). Thus, a change in working capital = (current assets – cash and cash equivalents) – (current liabilities – notes payables). Working capital in 2020 = [(US$1195 – US$90) – (US$500 – US$290)] – [(US$1140 – US$100) – (US$505 – US$295)] = US$65 million. A positive change implies cash outflow (−US$65).

W4: Fixed capital expenditure (land, property, and equipment) is the difference between the fixed capital expenditure in 2020 and that in 2019:

Exhibit 10.4.2 (continued)

US$1030 – US$930 = US$100 million (refer to the balance sheet). A positive change implies cash outflow (–US$100).

W5: The net interest expenses are tax-adjusted interest expenses (refer to the income statement): US$59(1 – 39.74%) = US$36 million.

W6: Refer to the income statement. Preference dividends were US$38 million in 2020.

W67: Net borrowing in 2020 is the difference between net borrowing in 2020 and that in 2019, which includes notes payable and long-term debts (refer to the balance sheet). Net borrowing = (US$290 + US$530) – (US$295 + US$453) = US$72 million. A positive change implies cash inflow.

W8: Net preference stock is the difference of net preference stock between 2020 and 2019. Net preference stock = US$729 – US$729 = US$0 million. A positive change implies cash inflow.

Notes for Exhibit 10.4.1

1. *Noncash Charges:* The focus is on noncash charges above the reported earnings (EBIT or net income) because they were deducted to determine the respective earnings—to add them is to remove them from the earnings. The most common noncash charge is "depreciation (amortization)" because they are obvious recurring items. However, there are several other noncash charges to consider such as restructuring charges and deferred taxes. "Restructuring charges" are noncash charges relating to losses or gains on disposal of long-term assets—losses (gains) are added (deducted) to be removed from the net income. "Deferred taxes" are included to reflect cash taxes. They should be carefully analyzed from time to time. The difference between book income (as per the income statement) and taxable income (as per tax assessment) should offset each other overtime, thereby reducing any effect on the overall cash flows. However, when continued increase in deferred tax liabilities is expected (not reversable), such increases should be added back to the net income. In contrast, any increase in deferred tax assets (not expected to reverse) should be deducted. Other noncash charges include stock-based compensation, impairment charges, asset write-off, and provisions and contingencies for future losses. Some analysis, however, argue against including stock-based compensations because they only affect equity holders and do not reflect real noncash. Overall, the rule of thumb is to include only the recurring items.

   Noncash charges = Depreciation + Amortization + Gains or losses on investments + Deferred taxes + Stock – based compensation + Impairment charges + Asset write – off + Provisions and contingencies for future losses.

2. *Working Capital*: Working capital is the difference between current operational assets (i.e., excluding cash assets) and current operational liabilities (i.e., excluding interest-bearing liabilities) in a financial period. Cash assets (cash and cash equivalents) are not considered because cash does not affect the operating

cash flow, since it appears at the bottom of the cash flow statement and including it will double the counting, and because cash equivalents are nonoperating assets. Likewise, any short-term interest-bearing debts (e.g., short-term loans, notes payable, etc.) are excluded from current liabilities because they constitute financing obligations to be included in net borrowing to calculate FCFE. The focus is to determine change in working capital. A negative (positive) change implies a decrease (increase) in working capital, reflecting cash inflow (outflow). Therefore, when calculating FCFF, a positive change is deducted (−), whereas a negative change is added (+) to reflect cash outflow and inflow, respectively.

3. *Cash from Operations*: CFO should be directly obtained from the cash flow statement (usually reported as net cash provided by operating activities). In the absence of direct data, CFO can be calculated using information from the income statement and the balance sheet.
4. *Fixed Capital Expenditure*: This is an investing item relating to operating capital, usually property, plant, and equipment or other forms of capital depending on the nature of business. Some companies (especially in the technology industry) tend to have recurring "capitalized software expenses," whereas others regularly undertake and report "business acquisitions": these items can be regarded as investments in operating capital only if they recur, relate to core business, and effect all investors—otherwise, they should be ignored. The focus is to determine cash outflow (inflow) from additions (reductions) to the fixed capital in a particular accounting period. Additions (cash outflows) can arise from purchase of new fixed capital and/or expenditure on capitalized improvements and repairs. Reductions in fixed capital investment (cash inflow) can arise from disposal or sale of some of the existing assets. The difference between outflows and inflows is referred to as "fixed capital expenditure." Between two periods, a positive (negative) change implies an increase (decrease) in capital expenditure and reflects cash outflow (inflow)—it is subtracted (added) when calculating FCFF.
5. *Net Interest Expenses = Interest Expenses (1 − Tax Rate)*. Interest expenses represent a financing obligation, which reduces tax bills. For example, if the tax rate is 35%, then the net effect on free cash flow is an increase in after-tax interest cost by only 65%. The cash flow statement treats interest expenses as an operating cash flow because it is deducted when calculating income—categorized under operating activities. In net income, it is added to be removed from expenses. When calculating FCFF, net interest expenses are added to reflect the cash available to all investors after considering the interest tax shield. When calculating FCFE, they are deducted to reflect the cash available to equity holders.
6. *Preferred Dividends:* Preference stocks are like debts in terms of a

firm's fixed financing obligations. Hence, preference dividends are a fixed claim just like interest expenses, except that the former is not tax-deductible. It is a bottom-line item, which is determined from net income. When calculating FCFF, preference dividends are added to reflect the cash available to all investors. It is deducted from FCFF when calculating FCFE to reflect the cash available to common equity holders.

7. *Net Borrowing*: Net borrowing reflects cash outflows (debt reduction) and cash inflows (debt issuance). Companies can borrow and repay debt at the same time to take advantage of the cheaper cost of debt. Alternatively, the debt can be simply rolled over to maintain the desired target leverage ratio. Net borrowing is, therefore, the difference between cash outflows and inflows. When calculating FCFE, net borrowing is added to reflect the cash available to common shareholders.
8. *Net Preference Stocks*: Preference stocks are hybrid stocks (characterizing partly equity and partly debt). When calculating FCFE, it should be treated like debt to determine the cash available to common shareholders. The focus is on net change in preferred equity because a company can issue new shares and repurchase the old ones simultaneously. Net preference stock is the difference between stock repayments and issuances.

10.3.4 Alternative Approaches to Calculate FCFF

There are several alternative approaches to calculate FCFF, which can be applied depending on the available data. Irrespective of the approach used, the results should be the same. ▶ Exhibit 10.5 presents examples to illustrate two approaches: EBIT and net income. Refer to notes in ▶ Exhibit 10.4 for detailed clarifications about adjustment items.

Exhibit 10.5 Calculating Free Cash Flows to the Firm (FCFF)

Illustrative Example (See Excel Workings—▶ Chap. 10, Sheet E.10.5)

Note: Examples are based on data from ▶ Exhibit 10.3.

Starting with EBIT

$$\text{FCFF} = \text{EBIT}\left(1-\text{Tax rate}\right)+\text{Noncash charges}+\text{Preference dividends}$$
$$-+\text{Change in working capital}-\text{Fixed capital expenditure}$$

The approach to calculating FCFF and data sources are presented in ◻ Exhibit 10.5.1. An example is provided in ◻ Exhibit 10.5.3.

Exhibit 10.5.1 Calculating FCFF: starting with EBIT

Action	Adjustment item	Source of information	Financial period
Start with	EBIT (1 - tax rate) (Note 9)	Income statement	Current
Add	Noncash charges	Income statement Cash flow statement	Current Current
Add	Preference dividends	Cash flow statement	Current
Deduct/ Add	Change in working capital	Balance sheet Cash flow statement	Previous and current Current
Deduct	Fixed capital expenditure	Cash flow statement Balance sheet	Current Previous and current
Result	FCFF		

9. *EBIT*: Consider the effect of interest and taxes on cash flow. Adjustments should be made to determine the net operating profit after tax (NOPAT, after-tax EBIT) because of the interest tax shield. Net interest expenses are included in EBIT.

10

Starting with Net Income

$$\text{FCFF} = \text{Net income} + \text{Net interest expenses} + \text{Preference dividends} + \text{Noncash charges} \\ -+\text{Change in working capital} - \text{Fixed capital expenditure}$$

The approach to calculating FCFF and data sources are presented in Exhibit 10.5.2. An example is provided in Exhibit 10.5.4.

Exhibit 10.5.2 Calculating FCFF: starting with net income

Action	Adjustment item	Source of information	Financial period
Start with	Net income	Income statement Cash flow statement	Current Current
Add	Net interest expenses	Income statement	Current
Add	Preference dividends	Cash flow statement	Current
Add	Noncash charges	Income statement Cash flow statement	Current Current
Deduct/ Add	Change in working capital	Balance sheet Cash flow statement	Previous and current Current
Deduct	Fixed capital expenditure	Balance sheet	Previous and current
Result	FCFF		

Exhibit 10.5.3 HIJ Company's FCFF: starting with EBIT

	(US$ millions)
EBIT (1 – tax rate) (W9)	127
Add noncash charges	30
Add preference dividends	38
Deduct/Add change in working capital	−65
Deduct fixed capital expenditure	−100
FCFF	30

Exhibit 10.5.4 HIJ Company's FCFF: starting with net income

	(US$ millions)
Net income	91
Add net interest expenses	36
Add preference dividends	38
Add Noncash charges	30
Deduct/Add change in working capital	−65
Deduct fixed capital expenditure	−100
FCFF	30

Workings:

W9: EBIT is adjusted for income tax to account for the interest tax shield (refer to the income statement): US$210(1 – 39.74%) = US$127 million.

10.3.5 Alternative Approaches to Calculate FCFE

Like FCFF, there are several alternative approaches to calculate FCFE, which can be applied depending on the available data. Irrespective of the approach selected, the results should be the same. ► Exhibit 10.6 presents and illustrates two approaches: CFO and net income. Refer to notes in ► Exhibit 10.4 for detailed clarifications about adjustment items.

Exhibit 10.6 Calculating Free Cash Flows to Equity (FCFE)

Illustrative Example (See Excel Workings—▶ Chap. 10, Sheet E.10.6)

Note: Examples are based on data from ▶ Exhibit 10.3.

Starting with CFO

FCFE = CFO – Fixed capital expenditure + Net borrowing + Net preference stock

The approach to calculating FCFE and data sources are presented in ■ Exhibit 10.6.1. An example is provided in ■ Exhibit 10.6.3.

■ **Exhibit 10.6.1** Calculating FCFE: starting with CFO

Action	Adjustment item	Source of information	Financial period
Start with	CFO	Cash flow statement	Current
Deduct	Fixed capital expenditure	Cash flow statement Balance sheet	Current Previous and current
Add	Net borrowing	Cash flow statement Balance sheet	Current Previous and current
Add	Net preference stock	Cash flow statement Balance sheet	Current Previous and current
Result	FCFE		

10

Starting with Net Income

FCFE = Net income + Noncash charges – +Change in working capital – Fixed capital expenditure + Net borrowing + Net preference stock

The approach to calculating FCFE and data sources are presented in ■ Exhibit 10.6.2. An example is provided in ■ Exhibit 10.6.4.

■ **Exhibit 10.6.2** Calculating FCFE: starting with net income

Action	Adjustment item	Source of information	Financial period
Start with	Net income	Income statement Cash flow statement	Current Current
Add	Noncash charges	Statement of income Cash flow statement	Current Current
Deduct/Add	Change in working capital	Balance sheet Cash flow statement	Previous and current Current
Deduct	Fixed capital expenditure	Cash flow statement Balance sheet	Current Previous and current

Exhibit 10.6.2 (continued)

Action	Adjustment item	Source of information	Financial period
Add	Net borrowing	Cash flow statement Balance sheet	Current Previous and current
Add	Net preference stock	Cash flow statement Balance sheet	Current Previous and current
Result	FCFE		

Exhibit 10.6.3 HIJ Company's FCFE: starting with CFO

	(US$ millions)
Cash from operations	56
Deduct fixed capital expenditure	−100
Add net borrowings	72
Add net issue preference stock	0
FCFE	28

Exhibit 10.6.4 HIJ Company's FCFE: starting with net income

	(US$ millions)
Net income	91
Add noncash charges	30
Deduct/Add change in working capital	−65
Deduct fixed capital expenditure	−100
Add net borrowing	72
Add net preference stock	0
FCFE	28

Think 10.2

Is free cash flow to equity (FCFE) available for preference shareholders too? Explain

The HIJ Company example is based on information from the balance sheet and the income statement (pair 1). To apply income statement and cash flow statement (pair 2), a practical case example of Amazon is illustrated in ▶ Exhibit 10.7. Amazon's diverse core businesses cover retail, subscriptions, and web services, among others, but retail remains the primary source of its revenue, with online and physical stores accounting for the biggest share.

Exhibit 10.7 Calculating Free Cash Flows From Income Statement and Cash Flow Statement

Case Examples: Amazon Inc. and Ecopetrol SA (See Excel Workings—▶ Chap. 10, Sheet E.10.7A and 10.7B)

Excel data present Amazon's financial statements for 4 years from 2018 to 2021 (in US$ millions) and Ecopetrol's financial statements for 16 years from 2006 to 2021. Cash flows are calculated for each company, but only Amazon's are presented here. The key step and adjustment items are as follows:

1. Determine noncash charges (see ◻ Exhibit 10.7.1). These items are listed in the cash flow statement (operations section).
2. Determine effective tax rates (see ◻ Exhibit 10.7.2). This item is calculated using information from the income statement by dividing income tax by pretax income.
3. Determine cash from operations (see ◻ Exhibit 10.7.3). This item is obtained from the cash flow statement.
4. Determine change in working capital. This is directly obtained from the cash flow statement. It includes accounts receivable, inventories, accounts payable, accrued expenses, and deferred liabilities.
5. Determine fixed capital expenditure. This is obtained from the cash flow statement. It includes two items: (1) net PPE and (2) net business purchase – this item is included because it is recurring and aligns with Amazon's core business operations.
6. Determine net borrowing. This is directly obtained from the cash flow statement. It includes net issuance and payment of debt (long-term and short-term).
7. Determine interest expenses. This is obtained from the income statement adjusted for income tax.
8. Determine net income. This is available in both the income statement and cash flow statement.
9. Determine EBIT. This is obtained from the income statement.
10. Determine net preference stock and preference dividends. Amazon did not have preference stocks and dividends.
11. Calculate free cash flows (see ◻ Exhibit 10.7.3). Alternative approaches can be applied to arrive at the same results.

Note: All figures are in US$ millions.

Exhibit 10.7.1 Amazon Inc.'s noncash charges

	2021	2020	2019
Depreciation amortization depletion	34,296	25,251	21,789
Deferred tax	−310	−554	796
Stock-based compensation (Note 1)	12,757	9,208	6,864
Other noncash items	−14,169	−2,653	−85
Noncash charges (total)	*32,574*	*31,252*	*29,364*

Exhibit 10.7.2 Amazon Inc.'s effective tax rate

	2021	2020	2019
Pretax income	38,151	24,178	13,976
Income tax	4791	2863	2374
Effective tax rate	12.56%	11.84%	16.99%

Exhibit 10.7.3 Amazon Inc.'s free cash flows: starting with net income

	2021	2020	2019
Net income	33,364	21,331	11,588
Add noncash charges	32,574	31,252	29,364
Deduct/Add working capital investment	−19,611	13,481	−2438
CFO	46,327	66,064	38,514
Deduct fixed capital expenditure	−57,381	−37,369	−15,150
FCF	−11,054	28,695	23,364
Add net interest expenses	1582	1452	1328
Add preference dividends	0	0	0
FCFF	−9472	30,147	24,692
Deduct net interest expenses	−1582	−1452	−1328
Deduct preference dividends	0	0	0

(continued)

Exhibit 10.6.2 (continued)

	2021	2020	2019
Add net borrowing	6291	−1104	−10,066
Add net preference stock	0	0	0
FCFE	−4763	27,591	13,298

Note 1: Stock-based compensation is sometimes excluded from noncash charges. However, for Amazon, it is reasonably included because it is a recurring item and is thus significant

Apply 10.1 *Free Cash Flows:* Amazon Inc.
Data: See Excel workings—▸ Chap. 10, Sheet E.10.7A

The data sheet presents the company's financial statements for 4 years from 2018 to 2021. Use Excel to calculate the free cash flows for 3 years (2019, 2020, and 2021) as follows:

(a) Free cash flow to the firm (FCFF)
  (i) Starting with EBIT
  (ii) Starting with net income
(b) Free cash flow to equity (FCFE)
  (i) Starting with CFO
  (ii) Starting with net income

Apply 10.2 Free Cash Flows: Ford Motor Co.
Data: See Excel workings—▸ Chap. 10, Sheet A.10.2

The data sheet presents the company's financial statements for 5 years from 2017 to 2021. Use Excel to calculate the free cash flows for 4 years (2018, 2019, 2020, and 2021) as follows:

(a) Free cash flow to the firm (FCFF) using different approaches
(b) Free cash flow to equity (FCFE) using different approaches
(c) Explain your judgment about the inclusion of adjustment items in (a) and (b) above.
(d) Comment on the company's free cash flow performance and its implications for the future.

10.4 Free Cash Flow and Agency Costs

Corporate and Investors' Decisions

The relevance of free cash flows is vivid in both corporate decisions and valuation. Overall, free cash flow informs companies and business owners about their spending ability free from any obligations. Corporate decisions regarding the use of free cash flows include dividend payments, share repurchases, change in leverage, and expansion. Investors, therefore, use free cash flows to establish managers' ability to create value, pay off debts, pay dividends, and repurchase shares.

Generally, positive, high, and consistently growing cash flows signify a company's financial health and desirability to investors. Low and consistently falling cash flows signify deteriorating financial health, calling the need for financial restructuring. Nevertheless, low cash flows do not necessarily imply a failing business. Some companies experience low (or negative free cash flows) because of growth-targeting decisions such as acquisitions and new investments. It is, therefore, necessary to not rely only on numbers but also examine what is hidden within the numbers. Among many reasons, high free cash flows may arise from disposal of assets, reduction in capital expenditure, delay in expenses and accounts payable payments, reduction in maintenance cost, and increase in accounts receivable. On the other hand, low free cash flows may result from increase in working capital, huge inventory order, larger capital investment, and other development projects.

The size of cash flows can also vary according to the industry—capital-intensive companies may experience low free cash flows due to extensive capital expenditure, whereas noncapital-intensive companies can be the opposite. Moreover, free cash flows are more relevant to nonfinancial companies, rather than banks and other investment companies.

Think 10.3
Why should a company have negative FCFF or FCFF and what are the implications?

Think 10.4
What does it imply when FCFE is greater than FCFF, and vice versa?

Banner 10.6 Free Cash Flows and Performance Measurement
Current performance should be judged not only by looking at free cash flow numbers but also by the use of cash and reasons for low or high free cash flows to determine long-term value implications.

Effect of Corporate Financing Decisions

While FCFE belongs to equity holders, companies make financial decisions about cash flows beyond FCFE—such as cash dividends, share repurchase, share issuance, and financial restructuring. Decisions relating to cash dividends, share repurchase, and share issuance do not affect both FCFF and FCFE. However, financial restructuring will have an effect on FCFE (not FCFF) because it alters the target debt ratio, which affects debt obligations and interest expenses—obligations to debtholders must be fulfilled before determining FCFE. For instance, a reduction in debt implies using more cash to pay off debts (reduce the net debt). This reduces the current FCFE but with a potential increase in the long term due to reduction in future interest expenses. The opposite occurs when more debt is raised. FCFE increases in the current year but potentially falls in the subsequent years. On the other hand, financing decisions do not affect FCFF because they constitute operating and investing cash flows, which are taken care of before financing activities.

Banner 10.7 Free Cash Flows and Financing Decisions

Financing decisions do not affect FCFF and FCFE, except leverage decisions, which affect only FCFE.

The Agency Cost Problem

Recall the agency cost concept in ▶ Chap. 2. Regarding free cash flow, agency cost can be reflected in managers' corporate decisions relative to performance and the use of free cash flow. Free cash flow is a vital performance measurement variable, which has implications in valuation. How do we judge managers' performance based on free cash flow? For instance, should low or negative cash flows be considered poor performance and high cash flows good performance? To answer these questions, we need to understand several issues amid manager's decisions, which affect free cash flows—why do some companies have low or negative free cash flows, whereas others have positive free cash flows? Moreover, we need to explain whether free cash flows are inevitable.

Low or negative FCFF does not imply poor performance if a company has spent a significant amount of cash for value-creating investments (good decision) instead of value-destroying investments (poor decision). In the long term, value-creating investments are expected to improve free cash flows to enhance both firm and shareholders' value, whereas value-destroying investments will damage free cash flows. The relationship between free cash flows and agency cost is explained in the literature (see, for example, Jenses 1986; Lang et al. 1991; DeAngelo et al. 2004; Richardson 2006). The overall argument is that there are agency costs associated with the availability of free cash flows, whereby cash could be wasted due to underutilization. Due to conflict of interest between managers and shareholders, generating free cash flows does not necessarily imply that managers will use it for shareholders' wealth enhancement. Free cash flow is value-creating if managers are capable of reinvesting it in growth-enhancing activities. Investments can be used to justify low or negative free cash flows, and agency costs can arise from managers' motives behind "overinvestment." While FCFF is cash flow left after the firm has invested in all available positive present value projects (see Jenses 1986), overinvestment is "investment expenditure beyond that required to maintain assets in place and to finance expected new investments in positive NPV projects" (Richardson 2006: 160). Hypothetically, managers endowed with free cash flow will invest it in negative net present value (NPV) projects rather than pay it shareholders.

Banner 10.8 Low Free Cash Flows and Agency Cost

When managers use cash in unproductive investments, lower free cash flows imply poor performance. However, when cash is used in productive investments, lower free cash flows do not imply poor performance.

Banner 10.9 High Free Cash Flows and Agency Cost
When managers use cash in productive investments, higher free cash flows imply good performance. However, when managers reject product investments to preserve cash, higher free cash flows do not imply poor performance.

Overall, free cash flows allow companies to pursue opportunities that enhance shareholder value—increasing dividends, developing new products, servicing debts, and repurchasing stocks. Hence, growing free cash flows may imply sustainable growth in operating income, whereas shrinking free cash flows may signify limited internal sources of cash to fund operations and growth. Nevertheless, a negative or declining free cash flow is not necessarily bad provided that it is temporary. Therefore, when using free cash flows to judge performance, it is always important to carefully examine the reasons for such performance. From the agency cost point of view, managers can squander positive free cash flows by investing unproductively, thereby contributing to inefficient usage of assets (Iskandar et al. 2012). In contrast, squandering negative free cash flows is only possible if a company can raise low-cost capital, which cannot be achieved without the scrutiny of capital markets (DeAngelo et al. 2006).

Consider the following two cases:

» *Motorola (a US-based company) during a 9-month period that ended in September 2008*: The company recorded investment impairment charges of US$288 million, most of it (US$145 million) related to temporary declines in certain Sigma Fund investments, a special investment vehicle managed by Gordian Knot Limited (a UK-based company), and US$83 million was attributed to an equity security held by the company as a strategic investment. Motorola reported an operating loss of US$397 million ($0.18 loss per share of which US$0.05 were from Sigma Fund), for the third quarter that ended on September 30 due to falling revenues by 15%. At the same time, the company was stumbling from its failure to design competitive smartphones to match Apple's iPhone and Blackberry models. Analysts commented that Sigma Fund was a poor investment—instead of investing in new, wireless smartphone technology, the company's decision led to investment wastage in significant impairments (Phillips 2008).

Think 10.5
In the case of Motorola, was the Sigma Fund investment a proper use of operating cash that could enhance long-term free cash flows? Explain.

» *Telia (a Swedish company) in 2019*: The company was undergoing major restructuring amid withdrawal from Central Asian markets to focus on its core Nordic and Baltic markets. Moreover, Telia had finalized two major acquisitions, buying Norway's Get in 2018 and Bonnier Broadcasting, the parent of Sweden's biggest commercial channel TV4, in 2019. These strategic investment decisions were reflected in the company's profitability and free cash flow performance at the end of 2019. Earnings before interest, taxes, depreciation, and amortization (EBITDA) increased from 6.68 billion crowns to 7.91 billion, beating analysts' estimates. The company was expecting an EBITDA growth of 2–5% in 2020, but free cash flow declined from 12.6 billion crowns in 2019 to 10.5–11.5 billion crowns in 2020 (Reuters 2020).

Think 10.6

In the case of Telia, should the expected decline in free cash flows be considered poor performance? Explain.

10.5 Valuation Implications

Free cash flows have significant implications in valuation. In intrinsic valuation, firm value is estimated by discounting expected FCFF using the cost of capital (weighted average cost of capital (WACC)), whereas equity value is estimated using FCFE discounted at the cost of equity (see ▸ Chaps. 15 and 16). In relative valuation, free cash flows can be applied as valuation multiples. For example, to determine enterprise value (EV), we can relate enterprise value (EV) to FCFF to form an EV/FCFF multiple. Moreover, to determine equity value, we can relate stock price (P) to FCFE to form a P/FCFE multiple (see ▸ Chap. 19).

10.6 Complexities of Free Cash Flow

There is doubt about the role of free cash flows in valuation. However, it is important to be aware of their complexities, which primarily arise from financial reporting, calculations, and interpretation. Therefore, free cash flows can have several limitations, as follows:

- There is no universal or standard definition for free cash flow—adjustments can differ significantly among analysts and so can the calculated FCFF and FCFE. Hence, the interpretation of free cash flows needs caution and requires an understanding of the calculation details. For instance, companies have some leeway when defining capital expenditure. Therefore, to compare performance and value across different companies, free cash flows should be determined from consistent definitions and adjustments.
- The current period's free cash flow is not necessarily an indication of future performance, which may be subjected to changes due to variation in vital drivers such as earnings, working capital, and fixed capital expenditure.
- The agency cost problem is debatable in terms of the essence of free cash flows. There is a consensus that free cash flows still provide financial flexibility through investments in value-creating projects. However, negative arguments point to the possibility of investing free cash flows in value-destroying projects. Moreover, since free cash flow is a measure of a firm's financial performance, managers can use several methods to influence free cash flow to attract investors. For example, to preserve cash, managers can delay payments of bills, putting off purchases of inventory, and rejecting valuable investments. To accelerate cash income, they can shorten debtors' collection period. In the current period, free cash flows may appear attractive but have negative long-term implications.

- Free cash flows are derived from core business operations. However, some companies generate a significant amount of cash from noncore business activities. Therefore, scrutiny is required to determine any significant income or expenses not directly related to the firm's normal core business.

Review Questions

1. What is the general meaning of free cash flow?
2. Explain the difference between free cash flow to the firm (FCFF) and free cash flow to equity (FCFE).
3. Why is FCFF also called unlevered free cash flow, and why is FCFE called levered FCF?
4. Under what circumstances should FCF and FCFF be equal?
5. Under what circumstances should FCF, FCFF, and FCFE be equal?
6. Why is free cash flow referred to as discretionary cash?
7. Explain why free cash flows are used to measure performance.
8. Why is FCF not suitable for intrinsic company valuation?
9. What is the valuation application of FCFF and FCFE?
10. Based on the agency cost problem, what are the limitations of free cash flows in business performance measurement?
11. Give examples of corporate decisions, which will affect the following cash flow components:
    (a) Cash from operations
    (b) Investing cash flows
    (c) Financing cash flows
12. Based on the free cash flow concept, give examples of financial items included in each of the following:
    (a) Operating cash revenue
    (b) Operating expenses
    (c) Working capital
    (d) Fixed capital investment
    (e) Net borrowing
    (f) Net preference stock
13. What is the impact of a negative FCFF or FCFE on the following aspects?
    (a) Managers' performance measurement
    (b) Valuation
14. Why is it important to examine financial statements before calculating free cash flows?
15. What factors should be considered when determining items to be included in each of the following cash flow variables?
    (a) Noncash charges
    (b) Capital expenditure
    (c) Working capital
16. Explain the treatment of the following items when calculating free cash flows.
    (a) Income tax

(b) Cash and cash equivalents reported in the statement of financial position
(c) Short-term debts
(d) Preference dividends
(e) New issues of preference shares

17. “Free cash flow is a contradictory measure of performance.” Discuss this statement reflecting on the agency cost problem.
18. How would you judge the performance of a company with negative FCFF or FCFE or both?
19. Explain how the following corporate decisions can affect FCFF and FCFE:
    (a) Dividends
    (b) Share repurchases
    (c) Share issues
    (d) Change in leverage
20. The following information pertains to financial statements of True Company. Calculate its FCFF and FCFE for 2021. Use any three approaches to calculate FCFF and FCFE.

True Company
Balance Sheet as at 31 December 2021

	2021 (US$ millions)	**2020 (US$ millions)**
Assets		
Cash	3853	3700
Marketable securities	698	1261
Receivables	20,988	18,866
Inventory	10,108	9463
Other current assets	3273	2585
Current assets	*38,920*	*35,875*
Property, plant, and equipment	63,631	56,527
Less accumulated depreciation	−32,291	−28,291
Net fixed assets	*31,340*	*28,236*
Investments (long-term)	17,308	13,623
Total assets	87,568	77,734
Liabilities and equity		
Notes payables	7602	5892
Accounts payable	3367	3167
Accrued expenses	11,801	11,276

	2021 (US$ millions)	2020 (US$ millions)
Other current liabilities	2506	1365
Current liabilities	*25,276*	*21,700*
Deferred charges	3861	3280
Long-term debts	11,943	10,825
Other long-term liabilities	3656	3420
Long-term liabilities	*19,460*	*17,525*
Total liabilities	44,736	39,225
Shareholders' equity:		
Common stock	6357	6341
Retained earnings	36,475	32,168
Total equity	*42,832*	*38,509*
Total liabilities and equity	87,568	77,734

True Company
Statement of Income for the period ended 31 December 2021

	2021 (US$ millions)	2020 (US$ millions)
Net sales	69,513	63,438
Cost of goods sold	30,723	27,701
Gross profit	38,790	35,737
R&D expenses	6554	6827
SGA expenses	20,709	21,289
EBITDA	11,527	7621
Depreciation and amortization	4000	4500
Earnings before interest and taxes (EBIT)	7527	3121
Interest expenses	1324	976
Earnings before tax (EBT)	6203	2145
Income tax	2543	879
Net income	3660	1266

Bibliography

DeAngelo, H., DeAngelo, L., and Skinner, D. J. (2004), Are dividends disappearing? Dividend concentration and the consolidation of earnings, *Journal of Financial Economics*, 72(3), 425-456, https://doi.org/10.1016/S0304-405X(03)00186-7

DeAngelo, H., DeAngelo, L., & Stulz, R. (2006). Dividend policy and the earned/contributed capital mix: a test of the life-cycle theory, *Journal of Financial Economics,* 81(2), 227-254. https://doi.org/10.1016/j.jfineco.2005.07.005

Iskandar, Takiah M., Bukit, Rina B., & Sanusi, Zuraidah M. (2012), The Moderating Effect of Ownership Structure on the Relationship between Free Cash Flow and Asset Utilization, *Asian Academy of Management Journal of Accounting and Finance*, 8(1), 69-89. https://www.researchgate.net/publication/286192000_The_moderating_effect_of_ownership_structure_on_the_relationship_between_free_cash_flow_and_asset_utilisation

Jenses, Michael (1986), Agency costs of free cash flow, Corporate Finance, and Takeovers, *American Economic Review*, 76(2), 323-329. https://www.jstor.org/stable/1818789

Lang, Larry H. P., Stulz, Renè M., & Walking, Ralph, A. (1991), A Test of Free Cash Flow Hypothesis: the case of bidder returns, *Journal of Financial Economics*, 29(2), 315-335. https://doi.org/10.1016/0304-405X(91)90005-5

Phillips, D. (2008). Poor Investment Decisions Add to Motorola's Woes, Available at CNBC, http://www.cbsnews.com/8301-505123_162-35040134/poor-investment-decisions-add-to-motorolas-woes/ Accessed November 4, 2008.

PwC (2014). *FRS and US GAAP: similarities and differences*, October, PwC, https://www.pwc.com/cz/en/ucetnictvi/ifrs-publikace/pwc-ifrs-and-us-gaap-similarities-and-differences.pdf

Reuters (2020). Telia profit tops forecast, sees lower operational cash flow, Available at Nasdaq, https://www.nasdaq.com/articles/telia-profit-tops-forecast-sees-lower-operational-cash-flow-2020-01-29 Accessed January 29.

Richardson, Scott (2006), Over-investment of free cash flow, *Review of Accounting Studies*, 11, 159-189. https://doi.org/10.1007/s11142-006-9012-1

The Cost of Capital

Contents

An Overview of Capital Structure and Cost of Capital

Contents

Supplementary Information The online version contains supplementary material available at https://doi.org/10.1007/978-3-031-28267-6_11.

B. Kulwizira Lukanima, *Corporate Valuation*, Classroom Companion: Business, https://doi.org/10.1007/978-3-031-28267-6_11

11.1 Introduction

As seen in ▶ Chap. 5, the existence of any business starts with capital. However, capital is not available free of charge. Typically, the main sources of capital are equity and debt—hence, capital providers (equity holders and debtholders) are investors who expect returns from a company. That is, a company ought to compensate its capital providers for sacrificing their funds—this compensation is the cost of capital. Therefore, "capital is not a cost, but it has a cost."

As mentioned in ▶ Chap. 1, the cost of capital is an essential input in intrinsic valuation. This chapter, therefore, presents the general concept of capital structure and cost of capital.

Learning Outcomes

- Explain the concept and meaning of capital structure and cost of capital
- Explain capital structure decisions and their implications in cost of capital
- Calculate the cost of capital from available information
- Understand the industry effect of cost of capital
- Understand the relevance of cost of capital
- Understand the key determinants of cost of capital

11.2 What is Cost of Capital?

In a world of various investment opportunities, capital providers (investors) have choices where to inject funds. These choices are driven by two major factors—risk and return. Hence, there is an opportunity cost of investment depending on the expected return relative to the expected risk. From an investor's perspective, the cost of capital is the required rate of return that could have been earned from alternative investments of equal risk. From a firm's perspective, the cost of capital is the rate of return required to persuade both existing and potential investors to invest into the firm.

Exhibit 11.1 Tension Between Investors and the Company

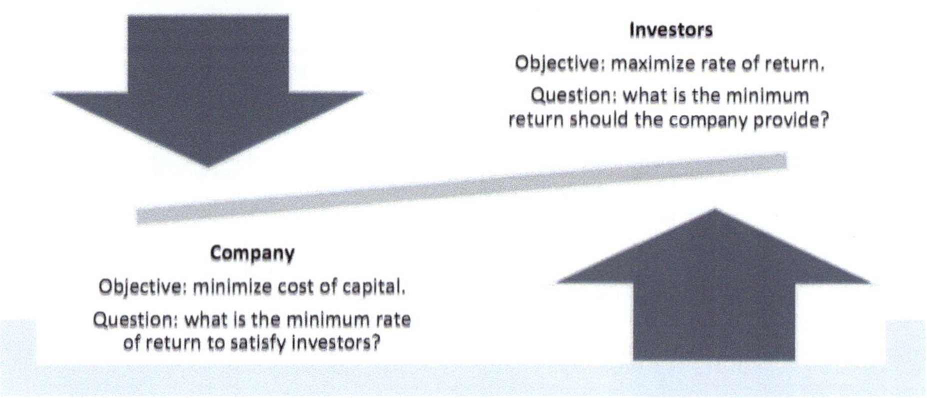

There are "two sides of the same coin." On one side of the coin, investors sacrifice their funds by providing capital to the company: they expect to receive a fair reward for foregoing other alternative investments or present needs. On the other side of the coin, company managers use capital to generate investment returns: they strive to fulfill investors' return expectations.

Basically, capital does not belong to the firm: it belongs to the investors. The firm is simply the user of investors' funds, who have discretion to withdraw should they be dissatisfied by the returns. Therefore, the cost of capital explains the existence of tension between investors (capital providers) and the company (capital recipient). While investors' goal is to maximize the rate of return, the company's goal is to minimize the cost of capital—"the return to investors is the cost to the company." This tension is depicted in ▶ Exhibit 11.1. For the company, to attract capital, the key questions are What is the minimum rate of return to satisfy investors? How can the company achieve the required rate of return through corporate strategic decisions and business operations?

Banner 11.1 Cost of Capital
The cost of capital (to the company) is the expected return (to investors) based on various components of the capital structure.

Think 11.1
Since there is tension between investors and the company, who determines the cost of capital?

11.3 Cost of Capital and Capital Structure

11.3.1 Weighted Average Cost of Capital

A capital structure typically comprises equity (common equity and preference equity) and debt, from which the cost of capital arises (see ▶ Exhibit 11.2). For an unlevered firm (with no debts), and without preference equity, the cost of capital is the cost of equity. However, when capital is raised from several sources (common equity, preference equity, and debt), the cost of capital is the weighted average of the financing mix and costs of each individual source of capital—weighted average cost of capital (WACC). An important point to consider is that the estimation of the cost of capital should be based on the same currency for all financing components.

Exhibit 11.2 Capital Structure and Cost of Capital

Depending on the company, an ideal capital structure comprises common equity, preference equity, and debt (see Exhibit 11.2.1). To calculate the cost of capital (WACC), market values (not book values) of each source of capital are used to reflect investors' perceptions (see Exhibit 11.2.2).

Weighted Average Cost of Capital (WACC)

Total Capital: This is the sum of market values of all capital structure components, typically common equity, debt, and preference equity.

Weight of Common Equity (W_e): This is the proportion of the common equity value to the total market value. The cost of common equity capital (k_e) is the required rate of return on common stocks and, as such, represents the minimum acceptable rate of return on the equity-financed portion of a company. Common shareholders have claims on residual earnings and retain control of investment decisions.

Weight of Debt (W_d): This is the proportion of debt to the total market value. The cost of debt capital (k_d) is the interest rate on the debt, considering the interest tax shield. Debtholders have fixed claims on interest but have no controlling powers over the company.

Weight of Preference Equity (W_p): This is the proportion of preference equity to the total market value. The cost of preference equity capital (k_p) is the fixed rate of dividend per share committed by the firm to preference equity holders, who represent a special type of ownership interest. While preference dividends are fixed, payments are subject to making profits. Unlike debts, there is no interest tax shield on preference dividends.

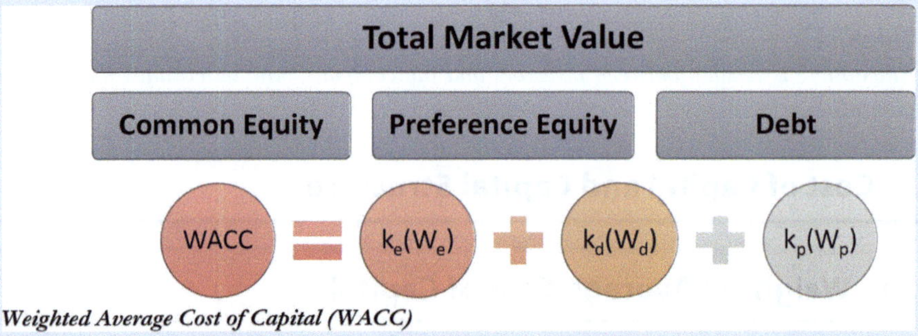

Exhibit 11.2.1 Capital structure

Illustrative Example (See Excel Workings—► Chap. 11, Sheet E.11.2)

Quadra J is a company with the following capital structure. Its corporate income tax rate is 33%. Calculate its cost of capital.

Solution:

$$WACC = W_e(k_e) + W_p(k_p) + W_d[(k_d(1-T_c)]$$

where

W_e, W_p, and W_d are the respective market value weights of common equity, preference equity, and debt. k_e, k_p, and k_d are the respective required rates of return on common equity, preference equity, and debt. T_c is the marginal tax rate.

$$\text{Total market value} = 55 + 20 + 25 = \text{US\$100 million}$$

$$W_e = 55/100 = 0.55 \text{ or } 55\%$$
$$W_p = 20/100 = 0.20 \text{ or } 20\%$$

$$W_d = 25/100 = 0.25 \text{ or } 25\%$$

$$\text{WACC} = 0.55(14\%) + 0.20(8\%) + 0.25[(8\%(1-33\%))] = 10.64\%$$

Exhibit 11.2.2 Quadra J company

Capital structure	Market value (US$ millions)	Required return
Common equity	55	4%
Preference equity	20	8%
Debt	25	8%

Think 11.2

Why are book values not used in determining capital weights for calculating WACC? Discuss.

11.3.2 Capital Structure Decisions

Corporate capital structure decisions are about choosing and arranging the financing mix from available sources such as common equity, preference equity, debt, and retained earnings. Each of these sources has different implications in the cost of capital, firm value, and equity value. Typically, capital structure decisions strive to minimize the cost of capital (from a firm's perspective) while maximizing the required rate of return (from investors' perspective).

11.3.2.1 Common Equity

Common equity is an inevitable financing mix because it represents ownership—there is no business without owners' equity. Capital structure decisions, therefore, dwell on the proportion of common equity relative to other sources (preference equity and debt). More equity than debt implies low leverage risk, but the cost of issuing equity tends to be higher than that of issuing debt. From investors' perspective, common equity holders take higher risk than debtholders due to two major reasons: first, they are the ultimate claimants of residual income after paying debtholders and, second, common dividends and capital gains are not guaranteed. Thus, the cost of equity tends to be higher than the pretax cost of debt. Moreover, for dividend companies, equity capital reduces retained earnings (an internal source of capital), leading the way to external sources (debts). Hence, dividend policy can influence financing decisions.

11.3.2.2 Debt vs. Preference Equity

According to Frank and Goyal (2009), a decision to use a debt aims at "reallocating some expected future cash flows away from equity claimants in exchange for cash up front." This is because debt obligations are fixed and reduce taxable income (interest tax shield)—the net income (with tax benefits) belongs to shareholders. Nevertheless, leverage increases the financial risk and cost of equity.

As mentioned in ▶ Chap. 10, preference equity is a hybrid security characterized partly by equity and partly by debt. Like debt, preference equity is associated with fixed obligations to the company (dividends), except that it is subject to after-tax income and hence has no interest tax shield. This explains why companies prefer debt to preference equity, considering the additional value from tax savings—although the tax benefits are also reflected in the decreased cost of debt, that benefit can be offset by an increase in the cost of equity due to leverage risk. ▶ Exhibit 11.3 demonstrates the difference between debt and preference equity and their impact on common shareholders, being the last claimants, they are affected by capital structure decisions (debt vs. preference equity).

Exhibit 11.3 Debt vs. Preference Equity: The Tax Effect

Illustrative Example (See Excel Workings—▶ Chap. 11, Sheet E.11.3)

Consider two firms D and P, which are the same in every aspect (industry, size, asset value, working capital, fixed capital expenditure, revenues, earnings before interest and taxes (EBIT), tax rate, etc.). Both D and P have common equity. But D includes debt (paying interest of US$120 million per year) while P includes preference equity (paying preference dividend of US$120 per year).

	Firm D (US$ millions)	Firm P (US$ millions)
EBIT	450	450
Interest expenses	120	0
Taxable income	330	450
Tax expenses (30%)	99	135

	Firm D (US$ millions)	Firm P (US$ millions)
Net income	231	315
Preference dividends	0	120
Earnings available to common equity holders	231	195
Change in working capital	45	45
Noncash charges	8	8
CFO	194	158
Fixed capital expenditure	102	102
FCFF (Note 1)	176	176
Net borrowing	10	0
Net preference equity	0	10
FCFE (Note 2)	102	66

Note 1: Free cash flow to the firm (FCFF) = Cash from operations (CFO) – Fixed capital expenditure + Interest expenses (1 – tax)
Note 2: FCFF = FCFF + Net borrowing + Net preference equity – Interest expenses (1 – tax) – Preference dividends

Leverage Effect

1. *Tax bills*: Debt reduces tax bills and creates an interest tax shield of US$36 million (i.e., 30% of US$120).
2. *Net income (available to common and preference equity holders)*: Debt reduces net income due to interest expenses but with tax savings (US$120 – US$36 = US$84 million and US$231 – US$315 = –US$84 million).
3. *Earnings available to common shareholders*: More earnings in firm D than in firm P due to the interest tax shield (US$231 – US$195 = US$36 million).
4. *Cash from operations (CFO):* More CFO in firm D than in firm P due to the interest tax shield (US$194 – US$158 = US$36 million).
5. *Free cash flow to the firm (FCFF)*: No effect.
6. *Free cash flow to equity (FCFE):* More FCFE in firm D than in firm P due to the interest tax shield (US$102 – US$66 = US$36 million).

11.1.1.1 Risk–Return Trade-off

Capital structure decisions affect shareholders' (owners') risk and return. Although an interest tax shield is a return advantage, it comes with leverage risks. Managers should make informed decisions about capital mix to minimize risks and maximize returns. Risk affects the cost of capital—from our definition, "it is the rate of return that could have been earned by investing into a different firm with 'equal risk'." However, from finance fundamentals, "the higher the risk, the higher the return." Hence, the cost of capital is expected to change in direct proportion to a change in risk. Unless managers take risk management measures, the cost of capital cannot be minimized.

11.1.1.2 Shareholders' Wealth Maximization

There is no doubt that a capital structure decision is a puzzling issue but affects corporate performance, including profitability. The most important performance consideration, however, is to achieve the main goal of the firm—to maximize shareholders' wealth. As illustrated in ► Exhibit 11.3, leverage can enhance FCFE, implying more owners' value. When making capital structure decisions, the main challenge is to achieve the optimal capital mix that maximizes value.

Think 11.3

Is an optimal capital structure achievable? Discuss.

11.1.1.3 An Optimal Capital Structure

11

Theoretically and empirically, the issue of optimal capital structure is complex and debatable (Titman 1984; Titman and Wessels 1988; Harris and Raviv 1991). The overall, argument, however, is that an optimal capital structure (if any) should maximize shareholders' wealth through minimization of the overall cost of capital. Since capital structure decisions focus on leverage, arguments for and against debts stem from three theories in particular, among others: "trade-off theory" focusing on optimizing the interest tax shield at the expense of bankruptcy costs; "pecking order theory" (Myers 1984), contending that managers' preference order of capital sources starts with internal funding (retained earnings), followed by external sources (debt), and, finally, issuance of new equity; and "agency theory" (see Jensen and Meckling 1976; Jensen 1986) in which leverage creates debt-related agency costs and bankruptcy costs; hence, an optimal capital structure should equate marginal costs of debt to its marginal benefits.

Banner 11.2 Capital Structure Decision
An ideal capital structure should aim at maximizing shareholders' value through minimizing the cost of capital, reducing the company's overall risk, and improving its cash flows while safeguarding owners' control.

11.4 The Industry Factor

Like any other financial ratio, capital structure decisions vary across industries (refer to ► Chap. 8 and Excel Sheet D.11.1). For instance, in industries with strong competition and volatile earnings, managers are likely to avoid fixed charge-bearing securities (debt and preference equity) in favor of low leverage. It is the opposite for industries with low business competition. Empirical studies about the industry effect on capital structure are many. Overall, industries with high profit margins and higher growth tend to have lower leverage ratios (Miao 2005; Talberg et al. 2008; Li and Islam 2019). Nevertheless, variations exist within companies in the same industry due to company-specific factors. Consequently, the industry effect on leverage is implied in the cost of capital.

11.5 Determinants of the Cost of Capital

There are various factors affecting the cost of capital, which can be split into three categories: fundamental factors, firm-specific factors, and economic factors (see ► Exhibit 11.4).

Banner 11.3 Determinants of the Cost of Capital
All factors determining the cost of capital point to one common concept: the higher the risk, the higher the returns and so the cost of capital.

Exhibit 11.4 Determinants of the Cost of Capital

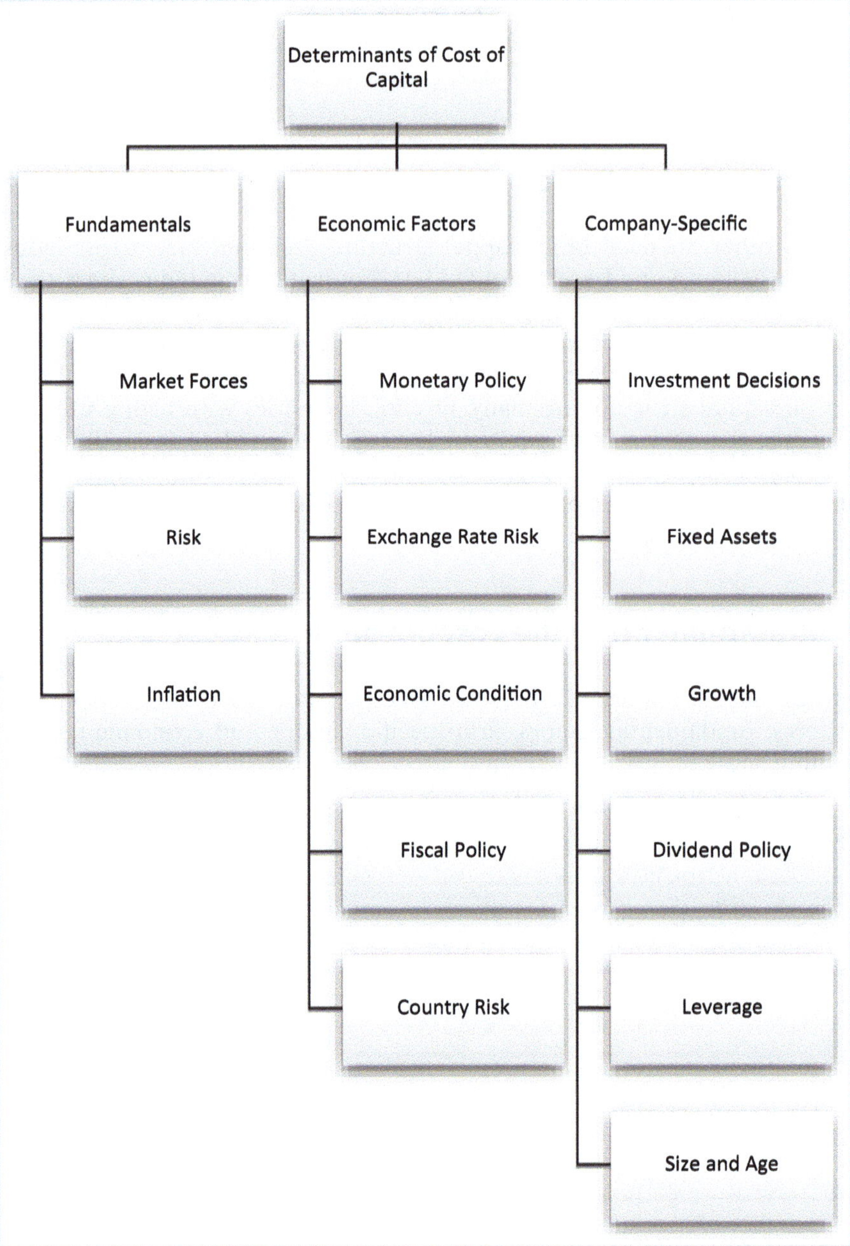

11.5.2.1 Fundamental Factors

Risk: Modigliani and Miller (1958) posed the following question when explaining the meaning of cost of capital:

> » What is the 'cost of capital' to a firm in a world in which funds are used to acquire assets whose yields are uncertain; and in which capital can be obtained by many different media, ranging from pure debt instruments, representing money-fixed claims, to pure equity issues, giving holders only the right to a pro-rata share in the uncertain venture?

In this question, the direct determinant of cost of capital is the risk associated with the use of capital (i.e., investments).

Market Forces: The pricing of securities in capital markets depends on market supply and demand forces, which also depend on general economic conditions. The supply of capital depends on the existence of those with excess funds, whereas demand depends on the presence of those with a shortage of funds. The basic principle of market forces posits that when demand for capital is higher than supply, the required rate of return tends to increase.

Inflation: Inflation reduces purchasing power. Hence, an increase in inflation is expected to be associated with an increase in the cost of capital, as investors require a higher rate of return to compensate for the loss in their purchasing power.

11.5.2.2 Firm-Specific Factors

Investment Decisions: Cost of capital depends on the risks associated with investments. Investors will require a higher risk compensation, the higher the risk of firms' projects. To attract investors, an attractive risk premium should be reflected in the required rate of return (cost of capital). Risk in firm's investments can be primarily influenced by the variability of the returns.

Leverage: Both operating leverage and financial leverage tend to affect risk. Operating leverage creates "business risk" from variability of asset returns due to volatility in operating earnings. On the other hand, financial leverage causes "financial risk," which is related to variability in returns to common stockholders due to capital structure decisions. Investors will require a higher rate of return when the total leverage increases.

Firm Size and Age: The size of a firm determines its financing needs, which affects its cost of capital. Large financing needs require managers to raise more capital, which tends to cause additional floatation costs associated with the issuance of securities, thereby increasing the marginal cost of capital. Moreover, as managers enter capital markets for large amounts of capital relative to the firm's size, capital suppliers may become skeptical of default risk, and hence higher risk compensation, thus leading to a higher cost of capital.

Growth: Growth affects the cost of capital in different ways. As a company grows bigger, it increases its ability to diversify, thereby reducing risk, and becomes less prone to bankruptcy—it will thus have a higher debt capacity. Moreover, growth tends to be associated with growth in earnings and dividends (for common shareholders), thereby affecting the cost of equity.

Fixed Assets: The proportion of fixed assets to total capital can have an impact on cost capital. Since fixed assets are for long-term use, they can either be underutilized or overutilized, thereby increasing the company's overall risk. Depending on asset efficiency, an increase in fixed assets or capital intensity can decrease the cost of capital, and vice versa. Consistent with the trade-off theory, the higher the tangibility of assets, the higher the use of cheaper capital (debt), as those assets become collateral.

Dividend Policy: Company's dividend policy affects payout ratio and retention ratio. A higher retention ratio increases the internal capital (retained earnings), which can reduce leverage, thus impacting the reduced cost of equity and the overall cost of capital.

11.5.2.3 Economic Factors

Monetary Policy: Through central banks, monetary policies influence the economy. The most important variable is interest rate. Lower interest rates are expected to boost economic activities through reduction in borrowing and lending rates and so is the cost of capital.

Fiscal Policy: Budget deficit and surplus can have an impact on the cost of capital. Budget surplus increases a government's ability to repurchase its securities from the market, thereby reducing interest rates. Deficit is the opposite because the government will have to fund its expenditure by selling its securities, thereby increasing money supply and inflation, leading to increasing the cost of capital. Likewise, selling government securities to financial institutions reduces banks' loanable funds, thereby increasing lending cost.

Economic Condition: Lower interest rates and inflation during good economic conditions and higher interest rates and inflation during bad economic conditions will be reflected in the cost of capital.

Country Risk: Country risk is associated with country-specific factors like political, social, policy, laws, and the economic environment. International investors consider country risk—the higher the risk, the higher the risk compensation, which should be reflected in the cost of capital.

Exchange Rate Risk: Foreign investments are associated with exchange rate risk, in which real returns on foreign investments depend on two factors: investment performance and foreign currency performance in comparison to the home currency. At investment maturity, depreciation of home reduces the net realized returns in home currency. Hence, foreign investors' required returns tend to consider compensation for exchange rate risk.

Think 11.4

Among the three categories of factors determining the cost of capital, which is the most influential? Discuss.

11.6 Relevance of Cost of Capital

Cost of capital is a vital decision-making tool for company managers and investors. This stems from the need to strike a balance between minimization of the cost of capital (from a firm's perspective) and maximizing the required returns (from investors' perspective). These decisions have implication on several aspects such as performance analysis, investment decisions, information signal, and valuation, among others (see ▶ Exhibit 11.5).

Exhibit 11.5 Relevance of Cost of Capital

Performance Analysis

Because companies incur cost to raise capital, its uses (investments) are expected to earn a return that is greater than the cost of capital to generate value. To measure performance on capital usage, WACC is compared to return on invested capital (ROIC)—a good performance is when ROIC is greater than WACC, implying managers' ability to create excess asset returns (for all investors). Cost of equity is compared to return on equity (ROE)—a good performance is when ROE is greater than the cost of equity, implying managers' ability to create excess equity returns (for owners). Overall, excess returns (on total capital or equity) imply that investment returns are sufficient to cover the cost of capital—hence, cost of capital can be regarded as a performance "target rate."

Investment Decisions

Companies raise capital to undertake various investments, which should generate value. The minimum returns from any worthwhile investment must be equal to the cost of capital associated with an investment. To create value, an investment should earn higher returns than the cost of capital. Hence, the cost of capital is applied in capital budgeting decisions, in which expected cash flows are discounted using the appropriate cost of capital ("discount rate"). An investment will be rejected on two criteria: if its net present value (NPV) is negative or if its internal rate of return (IRR) is less than the cost of capital.

Information Signals

From an investor's point of view, the cost of capital can indicate a firm's expected income against inherent risks. Usually, a high cost of capital may signify that the firm's present rate of earnings is less than expected while the inherent risk is high. It may also suggest an imbalance in the capital structure. In this regard, investors are expected to require a higher rate of return.

Valuation

Intrinsic valuation requires appropriate discount rates for cash flows. To estimate firm value, free cash flows to the firm (FCFF) are discounted using the cost of capital (WACC). Similarly, the cost of equity is used as a discount rate in equity valuation either using FCFE or dividends (refer to ▶ Chaps. 15–17).

Review Questions

1. Clearly explain the meaning of cost of capital.
2. What is the meaning of the following terms relating to the cost of capital?
   (a) Weighted average cost of capital (WACC)
   (b) Cost of debt
   (c) Cost of common equity
   (d) Cost of preference equity
3. Explain cost of capital under the following:
   (a) From an investor's perspective
   (b) From a firm's perspective
4. What decision challenges face corporate managers relating to the cost of capital?
5. "Capital is not a cost, but it has a cost." What is the meaning of this phrase?
6. Why is the cost of capital considered a crucial aspect of corporate finance?
7. Explain how a capital structure decision can affect a firm's cost of capital (WACC) and cost of equity.
8. When calculating WACC, will you use a capital structure's book value or market value? Provide reasons.
9. A firm is financed by common equity and debt whose market values are US$60 million and US$40 million, respectively. Shareholders require a rate of return of 12%, whereas the interest on debt is 9%. The firm's tax rate is 35%. What is the firm's cost of capital?
10. You are a finance manager in a company that is currently all-equity-financed (book value is US$290 million). The company intends to raise more capital (US$120 million) through either long-term debt (the interest rate is 7%) or preference shares (the dividend rate per share is 7%). The company's income tax rate is 30%. Would you choose debt or preference shares? Explain the implication of your decision in the firm's cost of capital and shareholder value.
11. A firm is financed entirely by equity with a market value of US$12 million. Shareholders' required rate of return is 8%. Corporate tax is 33%. Book value of equity is US$10 million. What is the firm's cost of capital?
12. Why are both risk and return vital for influencing the cost of capital?
13. What is the meaning of the following terms and how do they relate to the cost of capital?
    (a) Optimal capital structure
    (b) Risk–return trade-off
    (c) Leverage

Bibliography

Frank, M. Z., & Goyal, V. K. (2009). Capital Structure Decisions: Which Factors Are Reliably Important? *Financial Management,* 38(1), 1-37. https://doi.org/10.1111/j.1755-053X.2009.01026.x

Harris, M. & Raviv, A. (1991), The Theory of Capital Structure, *Journal of Finance* 46(1), 297–356. https://doi.org/10.1111/j.1540-6261.1991.tb03753.x

Jensen, M.C. (1986), Agency Costs of Free Cash Flow, Corporate Finance and Takeovers, *American Economic Review,* 76 (2), 323-329. https://www.jstor.org/stable/1818789

Jensen, M.C. & Meckling, W. H. (1976), Theory of the Firm: Managerial Behavior, Agency Costs and Ownership Structure, *Journal of Financial Economics* 3 (4), 305-360. https://doi.org/10.1016/0304-405X(76)90026-X

Li, L., & Islam, S. Z. (2019), Firm and industry specific determinants of capital structure: Evidence from the Australian market, *International Review of Economics & Finance*, 59, 425-437. https://doi.org/10.1016/j.iref.2018.10.007

Miao, J. (2005), Optimal Capital Structure and Industry Dynamics, *The Journal of Finance,* 60(6), 2621-2659, http://www.jstor.org/stable/3694799.

Modigliani, F., & Miller, M. H. (1958), The Cost of Capital, Corporation Finance and the Theory of Investment. *The American Economic Review*, 48(3), 261–297. http://www.jstor.org/stable/1809766.

Myers, S.C. (1984), The Capital Structure Puzzle, *Journal of Finance* 39(3), 575–592. https://doi.org/10.1111/j.1540-6261.1984.tb03646.x

Talberg, M., Winge, C., Frydenberg, S., & Westgaard, S. (2008) Capital Structure Across Industries, *International Journal of the Economics of Business*, 15(2), 181-200. https://doi.org/10.1080/13571510802134304

Titman, S. (1984), The Effect of Capital Structure on a Firm's Liquidation Decision, *Journal of Financial Economics* 13 (1), 137–151. https://doi.org/10.1016/0304-405X(84)90035-7

Titman, S., & Wessels, R. (1988). The Determinants of Capital Structure Choice. *The Journal of Finance*, 43(1), 1–19. https://doi.org/10.2307/2328319.

The Cost of Equity

Contents

Supplementary Information The online version contains supplementary material available at https://doi.org/10.1007/978-3-031-28267-6_12.

B. Kulwizira Lukanima, *Corporate Valuation*, Classroom Companion: Business, https://doi.org/10.1007/978-3-031-28267-6_12

12.1 Introduction

After defining the cost of equity in ▶ Chap. 11, this chapter covers the estimation of the cost of equity using the capital asset pricing model (CAPM). This model, despite its popularity, has practical limitations. Overall, estimating the cost of equity can be considered complex due to several reasons that are presented and discussed in this chapter.

This chapter takes a critical approach to addressing the estimation complexity and challenges by considering the theoretical views and practical aspects involved. It provides conceptual overviews of the estimation methods and uses practical examples to illustrate estimations of CAPM variables.

Learning Outcomes

- Understand the CAPM concept and its variables.
- Estimate CAPM variables from the original data.
- Apply the capital asset pricing model (CAPM) to estimate the cost of equity.
- Understand the practical limitations of CAPM.
- Use alternative betas to estimate the cost of equity for private firms.

12.2 Estimating the Cost of Equity: An Approach Overview

Estimating the cost of equity is generally not a straightforward process due to various assumptions and technical issues. While CAPM is the most applicable method, the cost of equity can also be estimated using the dividend growth model (DGM). Overall, both CAPM and DGM reflect investors' return expectations relative to a firm's performance and stock market predictions (see ▶ Exhibit 12.1). A major difference between CAPM and DGM is the assumption about the determinants of investors' required rate of return: CAPM focuses on market risks, whereas DGM is based on dividend yield and dividend growth (this is covered in ▶ Chap. 17).

12

Exhibit 12.1 Cost of Equity Estimation: CAPM vs. DGM

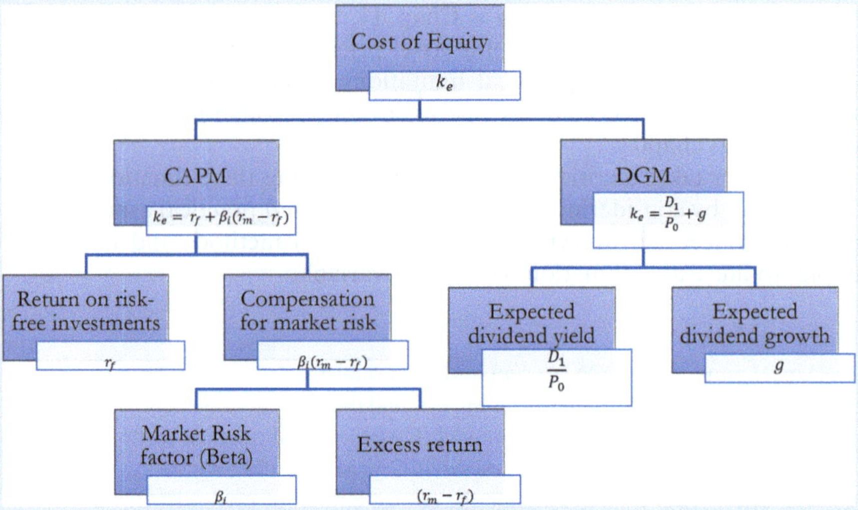

Estimation Variables

CAPM: *rf* is the risk-free rate, representing an expected rate of return from a risk-free investment, such as treasury bonds of a creditworthy government, *βi* (i.e., beta) is a measure of systematic risk (undiversifiable risk) related to a specific investment, and *rm* is the expected rate of return on the overall market portfolio.

DGM: D_1 is the expected dividend on an investment, *Po* is the current stock market price, and *g* is the expected dividend growth rate.

12.3 The Capital Asset Pricing Model (CAPM)

CAPM is an asset pricing model, which is built on the risk–return trade-off hypothesis (Markowitz 1959; Sharpe 1964; Lintner 1965; French et al. 1987). It portrays investors' expectations of earning higher-than-"normal" returns on their investments with higher risks—the higher the risk, the higher the return. This model is built on three behavioral aspects: (1) investors prefer more returns to less and risk must be compensated; (2) returns and variance of returns are investor's key considerations; and (3) investor's forecasts are homogeneous and markets are frictionless. Hence, CAPM assumptions are as follows:

- *Investors are Well-Diversified:* Investors do bother about diversifiable risk (unsystematic risk). They are concerned about systematic risk (undiversifiable) since it is inherent to all market participants and therefore drives their expected returns.
- *Single-Period Transaction Horizon:* All investors are myopic, having only one and the same holding period. To make a comparison between difference securi-

ties, a standardized holding period is required. For example, a return over 12 months should be compared with another return of the same time horizon.
- *Risk-Free Rate:* Investors can borrow and lend at a risk-free rate of return, which is therefore the minimum required rate of return. It is the benchmark rate at which additional returns depend on risk compensation.
- *Perfect Capital Market:* All securities are priced correctly: markets are frictionless (no taxes or transaction costs); all investors have the same expectations and equal access to perfect information; all investors are risk-averse, rational, and desire to maximize their own utility; and there are many buyers and sellers in the market.

According to CAPM, therefore, market risk is the sole systematic risk determining the cost of equity (see ▶ Exhibit 12.2). The general equation is presented as follows:

$$k_{ei} = r_f + \beta_i \left(r_m - r_f \right)$$

rf is the risk-free interest rate and the minimum required rate of return as it represents what an investor would have earned from a risk-free investment, usually proxied by securities of creditworthy governments (e.g., treasury bonds and bills).

βi(rm − rf) is the risk premium on a stock investment. *βi* is a measure of market risk (systematic risk) and cannot be eliminated through portfolio diversification; hence, the expected stock return (cost of equity) should be compensated for market risk premium (MRP) relative to excess market returns (*rm − rf*). The excess return is equal for all investors and depends on the expected rate of return on the overall market portfolio (*rm*) and the risk-free rate (*rf*). Therefore, beta, which is specific to each investment, is the only risk factor affecting the cost of equity—the higher the systematic risk, the higher the risk premium and so the higher the required rate of return.

▶ Exhibit 12.2 presents an illustrative example to calculate the cost of equity based on CAPM and how to interpret the results. Clearly, from ◘ Exhibit 12.2.1, investors in the same market have equal minimum required returns (risk-free rate) and excess market returns but different required rate of returns (costs of equity) on a specific investment—each investment has a unique beta.

Banner 12.1 Market Return

A market return represents the expected required rate of return on a market portfolio.

Banner 12.2 Risk-Free Rate

A risk-free rate is a theoretical rate of return on a riskless investment.

Banner 12.3 Beta

Beta is a measure of market risk, which is the only risk factor capturing systematic risk and determining the cost of equity according to CAPM.

12

Exhibit 12.2 CAPM and the Cost of Equity

Illustrative Example (See Excel Workings—▶ Chap. 12, Sheet E.12.2)

An investor is considering investing in stocks of different companies, which are trading in the same market. The expected market return is 6.8%. The risk-free rate is 2.2%. The investor has identified six stocks (X, Y, Z, U, V, and W), with different betas (see Exhibit 12.2.1).

Required:

(a) Calculate the cost of equity for each stock.

(b) Explain the relationship between beta and the cost of equity.

Solution:

- W1: The same risk-free rate is assumed for all the investors in the same market: 2.2%.
- W2: The same market risk premium (excess return) is assumed for the all investors due to the same expected market return and risk-free rate: 6.8% − 2.2% = 4.6%.
- W3: The stock risk premium is specific to each stock depending on its beta: β_i(6.8% − 2.2%).
- W4: kei = 2.2 % + βi(6.8 % − 2.2%)

As indicated in Exhibit 12.2.1 and depicted in Exhibit 12.2.2, the only variable affecting the cost of equity is beta—the higher the beta, the higher the risk premium and the cost of equity.

Exhibit 12.2.1 Investment portfolio: cost of equity for different stocks

	Stock X	Stock Y	Stock Z	Stock U	Stock V	Stock W
Beta	0.2	0.9	1.0	1.9	2.6	3.5
Risk-free rate (W1)	2.2%	2.2%	2.2%	2.2%	2.2%	2.2%
Market risk premium (W2)	4.6%	4.6%	4.6%	4.6%	4.6%	4.6%
Stock risk premium (W3)	1.1%	3.9%	4.6%	8.7%	12.0%	16.1%
Cost of equity (W4)	3.3%	6.1%	6.8%	10.9%	14.2%	18.3%

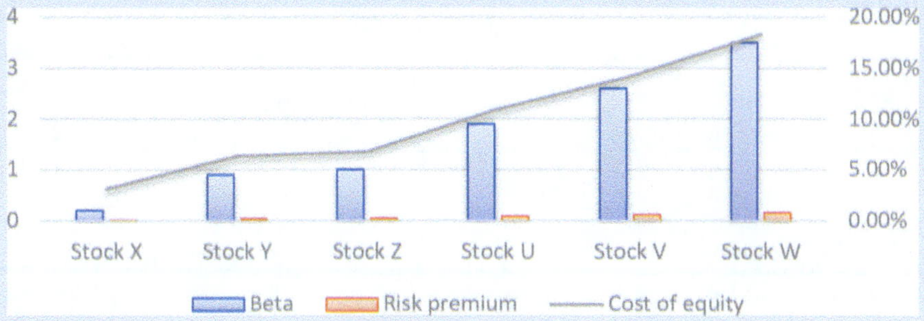

Exhibit 12.2.2 Relationship between beta and the cost of equity

12.3.1 CAPM and the Security Market Line (SML)

▶ Exhibit 12.3 explains the CAPM equation using the security market line (SML). Although various risk factors can influence systematic risk, CAPM recognizes only market risk, which is measured by beta. This risk originates from market variables, such as broad market returns, interest rates, total economy-wide resource holdings, aggregate income, recession, and so on—it cannot be eliminated through diversification because it affects all investments in a portfolio. Investors, therefore, are concerned with systematic risk because it is undiversifiable and not to the risk of individual investment returns ("unsystematic risk"), which is diversifiable and eliminable.

Think 12.1

Why should betas differ across stocks within the same market?

Banner 12.4 CAPM's Risk Factor

According to CAPM, only one risk factor drives the cost of equity—that is, market risk, which influences systematic risk.

Exhibit 12.3 CAPM and the Security Market Line

Illustrative Example (See Excel Workings—▶ Chap. 12, Sheet E.12.3)

To relate CAPM to the security market line (SML), consider a market comprising several stocks, which differ in several aspects, including risk and return profiles. Let us assume a market with eight stocks—A, B, C, D, E, F, O and U. The risk-free rate is assumed to be 4% and the expected market return is 7% so that the market risk premium is 3%.

The relationship between risk and expected return for each individual stock in the market is presented in

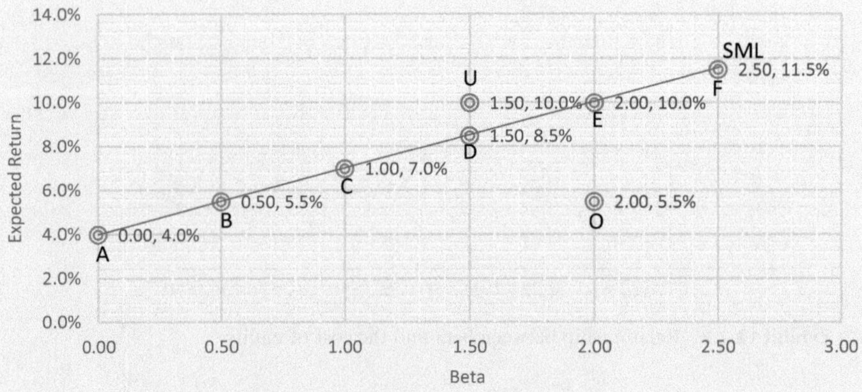

Exhibit 12.3.1 Systematic risk and the cost of equity

Exhibit 12.3.1. The security market line (SML) presents CAPM as a linear equation, whereby risk and return are directly proportional. Each point in the SML represents an individual asset—there are six assets from A to F. Each of these assets has its specific risk, measured by its own beta (*βi*)—there are different betas in the horizontal axis. The risk-free rate and market risk premium are the same for all stocks as indicated in the following CAPM equation:

$$k_{ei} = 4\% + \beta_i(7\% - 4\%)$$

The required rate of return (*ke*) for each stock (*i*) varies only with the level of its own sensitivity to the market risk factor (i.e., beta)—the higher the beta, the higher the cost of equity, with other factors being equal.

Let us examine the cost of equity for each stock at different levels of beta.

- *Case: Beta > 1*
  - An associated individual asset carries more risk than the market. This is an indication that stock returns are more volatile than market returns. For example, a beta of 1.05 suggests that stock returns are 5% more volatile than market portfolio returns. Therefore, the minimum required rate of return by investors should be greater than the market return—this applies to stocks D, E, and F. While the market return is 7%, the expected return for the three stocks is 8.5%, 10%, and 11.5%, respectively.

$$k_{ei} > r_m$$

- *Case: Beta < 1*
  - An associated individual asset carries less risk than the market. This is an indication that the stock returns are less volatile than the market portfolio returns. Here, investors of that asset are prepared to accept a rate of return that is less than the market return. For example, investors in stock B expect a return of 5.5% and a market return of 7%.

$$k_{ei} < r_m$$

- *Case: Beta = 1*
  - An associated individual asset and the market have equal market risk. This suggests a 100% correlation between stock returns and market returns. Therefore, when beta is 1.0, there will be no additional market risks and investors can expect a return that is equal to the market return—it is the same as a fully diversified portfolio. This is the case of stock C, for which the required rate of return is 7% (the same as the market return).

    $k_{ei} = r_m$

- *Is it possible to have beta = 0?*
  - Zero beta implies no systematic risk. In the CAPM intuition, if beta is zero, then the required rate of return should be equal to the risk-free rate. For example, if there exists an investment with the same characteristics as those of asset A, then its required rate of return would be 4%. However, such an asset is unlikely to exist. Instead, an investor can create a zero-beta investment through a portfolio of different assets.

    $k_{ei} = r_f$

- *Is it possible to have beta < 0 (negative)?*
  - A negative beta can occur when an individual stock return moves against market portfolio returns. This means, if that asset is added to the investment portfolio, then the risk of the portfolio will decrease. Hence, investors are prepared to accept a rate of return (on that asset) that is less than the risk-free rate. Intuitively, assets with negative betas create insurance against the market risk factor that may subsume several macroeconomic risk factors (that are not identified in the CAPM model). Hence, investing in assets with a negative beta is like paying for an insurance policy against risk.

    $k_{ei} < r_f$

- *Stocks outside the SML*
  - CAPM assumes that all assets along the SML are correctly priced—these are stocks A, B, C, D, E, and F. Assets outside the SML are unfairly priced—these are stocks O and U, which are overpriced and underpriced, respectively. A capital investment like O, which is below the SML, would not be efficiently priced to the buyer of that investment—it is expensive (overpriced). As a result, a higher return or a lower price would be required, leading to a higher cost of equity. A capital investment like U, which is above the SML, would not be efficiently priced for the seller of an asset—it is cheaper (underpriced). As a result, a lower return or a higher price would be required to justify the cost of equity.

Hence, the SML represents the relationship between the expected rate of return on an individual investment and its level of systematic risk as measured by beta. A unit increase in this risk is associated with a proportional increase in the required rate of return for an investment. In essence, according to CAPM, all assets along the SML are correctly priced (stocks A–F in ◘ Exhibit 12.3.1). However, in the real world, there is evidence of incorrect pricing of financial assets like stocks (underpriced or overpriced)—this is when assets fall outside the SML. Assets above the SML (like stock U) are underpriced because their expected returns are "too high," implying "too low" prices relative to a CAPM's "fair" price. On the other hand, assets below the SML (like stock O) are overpriced because their expected returns are "too low," implying "too high" prices relative to the "fair" price implied by CAPM. Moreover, whereas the SML is plotted as a straight line, this cannot be the case for real-world data because the true expected returns and true betas are unknown. If we use real-world data, only a "fitted" (estimated) SML can be plotted but not a "true" SML like that in ◘ Exhibit 12.3.1. In the real world, however, historical data are used assuming that they provide good and unbiased estimates of true beta and true expected rates of return.

12.3.2 Valuation Implications of CAPM Variables

We have seen that two factors determine the cost of equity—risk-free rate and market risk premium. We have also seen that only beta matters when stocks are trading in the same market. That is, the risk-free rate and market returns will have an equal impact on the cost of equity for all stocks in the market portfolio. However, it is important to understand that the cost of equity depends on the level of the risk-free rate and market returns. In valuation terms, the higher the cost of equity, the lower the equity value, and vice versa. Therefore, it is vital to understand the cost of equity sensitivity to both the risk-free rate and market returns.

► Exhibit 12.4 shows how the risk premium affects the cost of equity under two scenarios: first, when the risk premium is due to a change in the market return while the risk-free rate is constant and, second, when the risk premium is due to a change in the risk-free rate while the market return is constant.

Scenario 1: Sensitivity to Market Returns

1. With other factors being constant, an increase in market returns is associated with an increase in the market risk premium, whereas a decrease in market returns is associated with a decrease in the market risk premium—and changes in the cost of equity are directly proportional to changes in market returns.
2. With other factors being constant, a small change in market returns is associated with a greater change in the cost of equity for stocks with higher systematic risk—the higher the beta, the higher the sensitivity of the cost of equity to variations in the market return.

Banner 12.5 Systematic Risk and Market Return

At a constant risk-free rate, the cost of equity is more sensitive to changes in the market return for stocks with higher betas. Stocks with smaller betas have the opposite sensitivity effect.

In valuation terms, with other factors being equal, this implies the following: (1) A stock with higher systematic risk becomes less valuable when the risk premium increases due to an increase in the market return. (2) In contrast, a stock with higher systematic risk becomes more valuable when the risk premium decreases due to a decrease in the market return.

Think 12.2

Why is the market return important for investors' decision about the required rate of return on stocks?

Scenario 2: Sensitivity to the Risk-Free Rate

1. With other factors being constant, an increase (decrease) in the risk-free rate is associated with a decrease (increase) in the market risk premium.
2. The cost of equity becomes more sensitive to a change in the risk-free rate when the stock beta deviates away from the market beta of 1—a fully diversified portfolio.
   (a) When a stock "beta is less than 1," at a constant market return, any increase in the risk-free rate is associated with a positive change in the cost of equity (increase). The higher the risk-free rate, the higher the cost of equity, and vice versa. The lower the beta, the higher the rate of increase in the cost of equity, and vice versa.
   (b) When a stock "beta is greater than 1," at a constant market return, any increase in the risk-free rate is associated with a negative change in the cost of equity (decline). The higher the risk-free rate, the lower the cost of equity, and vice versa. The higher the beta, the higher the rate of decrease in the cost of equity, and vice versa.
   (c) When a stock "beta is 1," at a constant market return, any change in the risk-free rate does not affect the cost of equity—the change in the cost of equity is zero.

Banner 12.6 Systematic Risk and Risk-Free Rate

At a constant expected market return, any positive change in the risk-free rate is associated with the following impacts on the cost of equity:

- *Beta < 1: increase in the cost of equity*
- *Beta > 1: decline in the cost of equity*
- *Beta = 1: no change in the cost of equity*

In valuation terms, stocks whose "betas are less than 1" become less valuable when the market risk premium decreases due to an increase in the risk-free rate, with other factors being equal. In contrast, they become more valuable when the market risk premium increases due to a decrease in the risk-free rate, with other factors being equal. Stocks whose "betas are greater than 1" become more valuable when the market risk premium decreases due to an increase in the risk-free rate, with other factors being equal. In contrast, they become less valuable when the market risk premium increases due to a decrease in the risk-free rate, with other factors being equal. The value of a stock whose "beta equals 1" is not affected when the market risk premium changes due to a change in the risk-free rate.

Think 12.3

Why is the rate of return on riskless investments important for investors' decision?

Quotes 12.1 CAPM Variables

Quote 12.1 Why Does Only Systematic Risk Matter?

» Since investors can eliminate company-specific risk simply by properly diversifying portfolios, they are not compensated for bearing unsystematic risk. And because well-diversified investors are exposed only to systematic risk, with CAPM the relevant risk in the financial market's risk/expected return tradeoff is systematic risk rather than total risk. Thus, an investor is rewarded with higher expected returns for bearing only market-related risk. (David W. Mullins, Jr.)

David W. Mullins, Jr, January 1982, *Harvard Business Review.*

Exhibit 12.4 Valuation Implications of CAPM Variables

Illustrative Example (See Excel Workings—▶ Chap. 12, Sheets E.12.4A and B)

Let us consider the same stocks used in ▶ Exhibit 12.2 (X, Y, Z, U, V, and W), with the same betas as shown in ◘ Exhibit 12.4.1.

What happens to the cost of equity under the following two scenarios?

- *Scenario 1*: When the expected market return changes while the risk-free rate is the same (i.e., 2.2%). Different cases of variations in the market return and market risk premium are presented in ◘ Exhibit 12.4.2.
- *Scenario 2*: When the risk-free rate changes while the expected market return is the same (i.e., 6.8%). Different cases of variations in the risk-free rate and market risk premium are presented in ◘ Exhibit 12.4.3.

Cost of Equity Sensitivity to Change in the Risk-Free Rate

◘ Exhibit 12.4.4 shows how the cost of equity for each individual stock varies according to a change in the risk-free rate, with other factors being equal. In conjunction with ◘ Exhibit 12.4.5, we observe the following four aspects:

1. At a constant market return, the cost of equity becomes more sensitive to a change in the risk-free rate when the stock beta moves away from the market beta of 1.
2. At a constant market return, the sensitivity of the cost of equity to a change in the risk-free rate is positive when a stock beta is less than 1 (stocks X and Y)—the lower the beta, the higher the increase in the cost of equity (stock X), and vice versa (stock Y).

3. At a constant market return, the sensitivity of the cost of equity to a change in the risk-free rate is negative when a stock beta is greater than 1 (stocks U, V, and W)—the higher the beta, the higher the decrease in the cost of equity, and vice versa (of the three stocks, W has the highest beta, whereas U has the lowest).
4. At a constant market return, the sensitivity of the cost of equity to a change in the risk-free rate is zero when a stock beta is equal to 1 (stock Z)—the cost of equity does not change.

Cost of Equity Sensitivity to a Change in the Expected Market Return

▣ Exhibit 12.4.6 shows how the cost of equity for each individual stock varies according to a change in the expected market return, with other factors being equal. Variations in the market return affect the risk premium. In conjunction with ▣ Exhibit 12.4.7, we observe that as the systematic risk increases, a small change in the market return causes a greater change in the cost of equity, when the risk-free rate is constant. The cost of equity of stock X (the lowest beta) is the least sensitive to a change in the market return, whereas that of stock W (the highest beta) is the most sensitive.

▣ **Exhibit 12.4.1** Stock betas

	Stock X	Stock Y	Stock Z	Stock U	Stock V	Stock W
Beta	0.2	0.9	1.0	1.9	2.6	3.5

▣ **Exhibit 12.4.2** Stock market returns

	Case 1	Case 2	Case 3	Case 4	Case 5	Case 6
Expected market return	2.5%	5.0%	7.5%	10.0%	12.5%	15.0%
Market risk premium	0.3%	2.8%	5.3%	7.8%	10.3%	12.8%

▣ **Exhibit 12.4.3** Risk-free rates

	Case 1	Case 2	Case 3	Case 4	Case 5	Case 6
Risk-free rate	2.5%	3.0%	3.5%	4.0%	4.5%	5.0%
Market risk premium	4.3%	3.8%	3.3%	2.8%	2.3%	1.8%

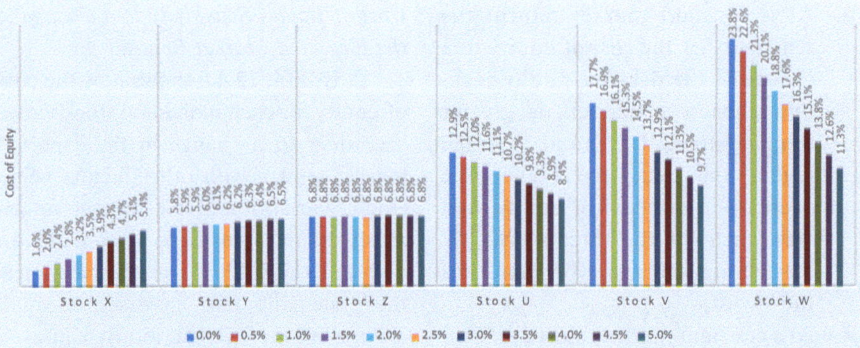

Exhibit 12.4.4 Cost of equity sensitivity to a change in the risk-free rate

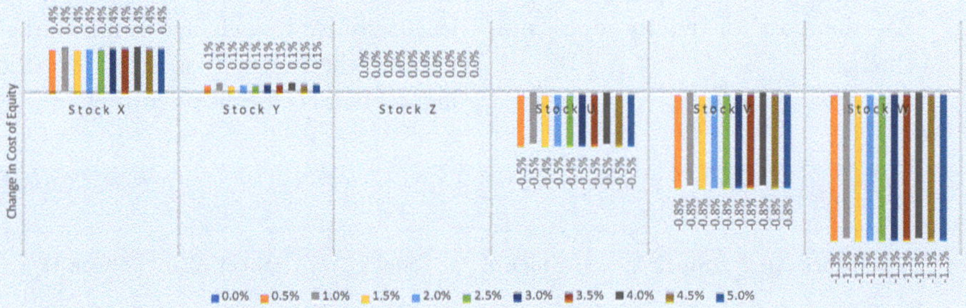

Exhibit 12.4.5 Change in the cost of equity to a 0.5% increase in the risk-free rate

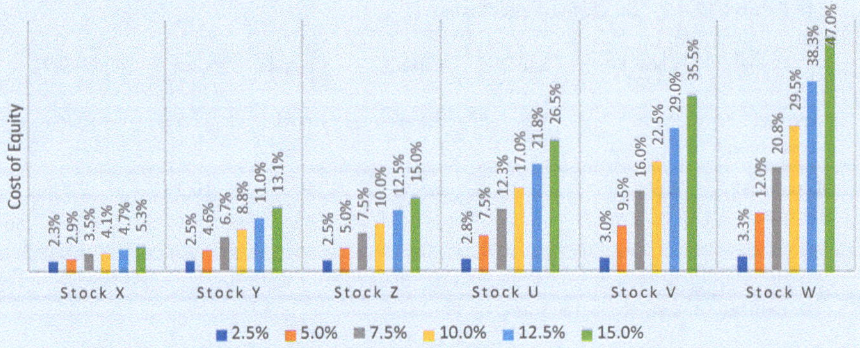

Exhibit 12.4.6 Cost of equity sensitivity to the expected market return

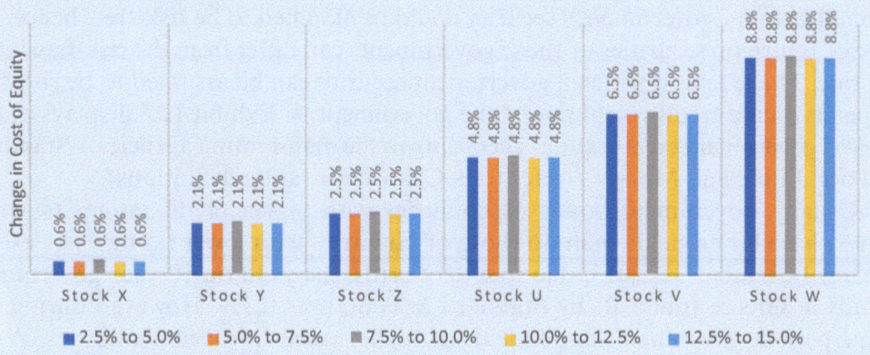

Exhibit 12.4.7 Change in the cost of equity to a 2.5% change in the expected market return

12.4 Estimating the Cost of Equity: CAPM Variables

After grasping the concept of CAPM and its variables, this section brings the concept to reality—how to estimate the cost of equity by determining each of the CAPM variables: risk-free interest rate, beta, and expected market return.

12.4.1 Risk-Free Interest Rate

It is almost unlikely to have an investment that is a 100% riskless. Some investments, however, are considered to be extremely low-risk, especially government securities—treasury bonds and bills. Returns or yields to maturity of these assets, therefore, are commonly used as proxies for risk-free interest rates.

12.4.1.1 Risk-Free Rate Variables

Governments issue various securities, and their yields vary according to maturity—the longer the maturity, the higher the yield. Moreover, even with the same maturity, yields differ across countries. For example, on 21 July 2020, 10-year bonds for the United States and Colombia had yields to maturity of 0.605% and 5.44%, respectively. However, there are several questions: Are these government securities risk-free assets? Which government's securities should be considered risk-free? Considering different maturities, which proxy must one use? These questions are answered in the following sections.

Not Every Government Security Is Risk-Free

Not all or every government's security could be assumed to be risk-free; hence, the rate of return on securities of those governments can differ from the risk-free interest rate. The extent to which a government security can be assumed to be risk-free depends on the creditworthiness of the government. ▶ Exhibit 12.5 displays examples of government credit ratings according to the major rating agencies—Standard & Poor, Fitch, and Moody's (refer to ▶ Chap. 4 for rating definitions).

Usually, government bonds of countries with higher credit ratings (such as AAA) have lower yields than do those of countries with lower ratings. For example, on December 31, 2013, due to a debt crisis, the yield on 10-year government bonds in Greece (rated B- by Standard & Poor) was 8.3%. However, during the same period, government bond yields of higher-rated European countries (AAA rating) were low: yields for Switzerland, Sweden, and Germany were 1.2%, 2.5%, and 1.9%, respectively. This implies that in countries with persistent economic difficulties, government bond yields should not be used as a reliable proxy for the risk-free interest rate, except after adjusting for risk factors.

A government bond with an AAA rating is prime-grade, and, hence, yields of its securities can be assumed to have a risk-free interest rate. A government bond with a CCC rating is highly risky, and, hence, yields of its securities cannot be assumed to have a risk-free interest rate. Each of these ratings is associated with a quantitative measure of risk, which can be referred to as sovereignty or government default spread (hereafter GDS). These spreads can be accessed from different sources, including Damodaran's valuation database, which is based on Moody's ratings.

Banner 12.7 Government Security Yields and Risk-Free Rate
Government security yields are generally acceptable as proxies for the risk-free rate. However, not all government securities are risk-free.

Determining a Risk-Free Rate

▶ Exhibit 12.5 illustrates how to determine the risk-free interest rate using US and Colombian cases. Two variables are typically required, government bond yield (GBY) and sovereignty default spread (GDS). The risk-free rate is the difference between the two variables, such that:

$$r_f = GBY - GDS$$

Exhibit 12.5 Determining the Risk-Free Interest Rate

Illustrative Case: United States and Colombia (See Excel Workings—▸ Chap. 12, Sheet E.12.5).

The following key steps apply in determining the risk-free interest rate:

1. Search for data on government bond yield of the appropriate maturity—in this example, we use 10-year bond maturity obtained from the website of World Government Bonds (see Exhibit 12.5.1).
2. Search for the government's credit rating from any credible source—in this example, we use Moody's ratings (see Exhibit 12.5.2).
3. Search for GDS data. In this case, we use Damodaran's database (see Exhibit 12.5.3).
4. Calculate the risk-free rate for each respective country as follows:

$$r_f = GBY - GDS$$

$$r_{f(US)} = 0.605\% - 0.00\% = 0.605\%$$

$$r_{f(Colombia)} = 5.440\% - 2.23\% = 3.21\%$$

Exhibit 12.5.1 Data for estimating a risk-free interest rate

Country	10-Year bond yield	Credit rating	GDS
United States	0.605%	Aaa	0.00%
Colombia	5.440%	Baa2	2.23%

Exhibit 12.5.2 Selected government bond ratings

Country	Moody's	S&P	Fitch
United States	Aaa	AA+	AAA
Germany	Aaa	AAA	AAA
Colombia	Baa2	BBB−	BBB−
Japan	A1	A+	A
Brazil	Ba2	BB−	BB−
Kenya		B−	B−

Exhibit 12.5.3 Risk-free interest rates

Country	GBY	GDS	*rf*
United States	0.605%	0.00%	0.605%
Colombia	5.440%	2.23%	3.210%

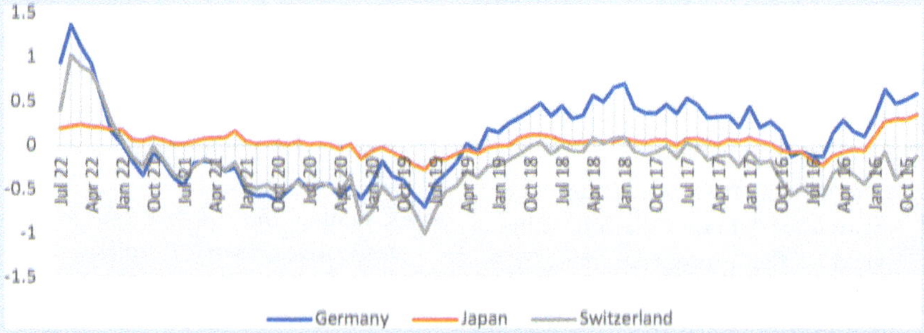

Exhibit 12.5.4 Negative bond yields: 10-year government bonds (Japan, Germany, and Switzerland). (*Sources of data:* ▶ Countryeconomy.com (21 July 2020), World Government Bonds (21 July 2020), Damodaran's database (July 2020), ▶ investing.com (July 2022))

12.4.1.2 Practical Considerations

With the availability of data, determining the risk-free interest rate can be straightforward, but there are several practical issues to consider as follows:

- **Negative Government Security Yields**

Some government securities tend to experience negative yields. For example, Exhibit 12.5.4 shows 10-year government yields for Japan, Germany, and Switzerland between September 2015 and July 2022. Negative yields occurred in some periods of 2016 and from 2019 to 2021. Japan had a zero yield in January 2019. Negative yields can be artificially temporal (e.g., Germany: June to September 2016) or persistent (e.g., Germany: May 2019 to December 2021). Typically, they arise from unorthodox monetary policies to curb temporal economic problems.

What does negative or zero yields imply? A negative yield is analogous to storage cost (pay for a safe cash deposit), whereby the net value of the stored cash declines in future by storage cost. Hence, investing in negative-yield government bonds implies paying a premium, expecting less money at maturity—an investor sacrifices some returns to the issuer (government). The main possible reason to buy bonds with negative yields is safety—to keep money in a safe deposit and pay for the storage cost.

Can negative yields be applied to estimate the cost of equity? A major valuation implication of negative or zero risk-free interest rates is the artificial (significantly low or negative) cost of equity and the overall cost of capital, which consequently lead to artificial or unrealistic valuation (highly overvalued equity or firm). Since CAPM does not rely on only one variable, a negative cost of equity can be overcome if the sum of the risk-free rate and risk premium is positive—even though the cost of equity is extremely low. With a negative risk-free rate, a negative cost of equity can be avoided depending on the beta and expected market return—that is, the cost of equity can be positive if the risk premium is large enough to offset the negative risk-free rate. For example, assume that the expected market return is 6.8% and the risk-free rate is −2.2%. Stock A's beta is 0.2, and stock B's beta is 0.9.

The market risk premium is 9%, whereas the stock risk premium (beta times the market risk premium) for A and B is 1.8% and 8.1%, respectively. Hence, A's cost of equity is negative (−0.4%), but B's cost of equity is positive (5.9%).

Alternatively, to avoid negative risk-free rates, a recent or average historical government bond yield can be used if the negative yield(s)) is (are) temporary. For example, if we were to use a 10-year German government bond yield to determine the risk-free rate in September 2016 (when the yield was −0.12%), a 1-year average yield (September 2015–2016) could be used, which was 0.22%.

Nevertheless, if negative yields are persistent, then an alternative proxy for the risk-free rate can be estimated using a benchmark country with similar credit ratings. One of the benchmarking approaches is based on the "International Fisher Parity (IFP)," which portrays that nominal interest rates in one country should be equal to those of another country, adjusted for inflation rate differentials as follows:

$$r_{f(\mathrm{A})} = r_{f(\mathrm{B})} + \left(f_{(\mathrm{A})} - f_{(\mathrm{B})}\right)$$

where $rf_{(\mathrm{A})}$ and $rf_{(\mathrm{B})}$ are the nominal rates in the target country A and benchmark country B, respectively, whereas $f_{(\mathrm{A})}$ and $f_{(\mathrm{B})}$ are their expected inflation rates, respectively. For example, in December 2021, the German and US 10-year government bond yields were −0.179% and 1.512%, respectively. Both countries were rated AAA by Fitch. The expected inflation in Germany and the United States was 3.1% and 4.6%, respectively. The US 10-year bond yield could be used as a benchmark to determine a proxy for the German risk-free rate as follows:

$$r_{f(Germany)} = r_{f(US)} + \left(f_{(Germany)} - f_{(US)}\right) = 1.512\% + (3.1\% - 4.6\%) = 0.012\%$$

A major limitation of the IFP approach, however, is that inflation differentials should not be negatively higher than the benchmark nominal bond yield—because the target nominal yield will be negative.

▪ Bond Volatility

One of the practical challenges in determining the risk-free rate arises when yields in government bonds experience high volatility during certain periods. For example, according to Ernest & Young Global Limited (2015), the debt crisis in some European countries (Portugal, Greece, Ireland, and Spain) seems to be associated with a significant increase in their government bonds during the period commencing from 2008 to 2014. Such high yields are regarded as "artificial" because they represent a particular turbulent period. In such circumstances, the use of government yields, as a proxy for risk-free rate, may be misleading.

▪ Maturity

Maturities of government securities vary. For example, from 1 month to 30 years for the United States and from 1 to 15 years for Colombia, and so on. So, what is the maturity that should we use? The answer is not straightforward—it depends on several factors. Government securities of short-term maturities (like 3 months,

6 months, up to 1 year) are almost risk-free. However, securities with long-term maturities bear some risk, depending on the creditworthiness of the government. Therefore, the choice of the risk-free rate should consider the objective of the analysis. Usually, we estimate the cost of capital for the purpose of valuing equity or for investment analysis. When determining a risk-free rate, the duration of the investments to be analyzed should be considered. The objective here is to try matching a particular risk-free rate to the investment duration, even if it cannot be a perfect match. For example, when valuing an investment with a short life (say 1 year), it may be more appropriate to use the 1-year treasury bill rate, especially if the investment generates most of its cash flows at the end of the year. If an investment has a regular pattern of cash flows throughout the year (like stock trading), then yields of government securities of shorter maturities (e.g., 3- and 6-month treasury rate) might be more appropriate. For investments with long lives, yields of government bonds with long maturities might be appropriate. It is important to note that the choice of bond maturity has implications in the risk-free rate and equity value—the higher the bond maturity, the higher the yield.

▪ Differences in Ratings

Credit ratings, which we use to determine government default spreads, can differ across rating agencies. For example, in ▶ Exhibit 12.5, whereas Fitch and Moody's rate the United States as prime-grade (Aaa or AAA), S&P downgrades it to just high-grade (AA+). When there are inconsistences in ratings, it is up to the analyst's discretion to decide what ranking to use. This can be guided by several criteria such as: What do the majority of the ratings show? How consistently has the government maintained a particular rating? What is the expected outlook associated with ratings? For example, it is reasonable to choose a prime (AAA) rating for the United States because, despite being rated so by two of the major agencies, it has maintained that rating over many years.

▪ Inflation Risk

Depending on the purpose of valuation, this risk-free rate can be adjusted for inflation to match the cash flows—using the nominal rate if valuation applies nominal cash flows and the real rate when cash flows are in real terms. The risk-free rate estimated from a government bond yield and a default spread is the nominal rate—it is not adjusted for inflation. Generally, inflation has two major implications in the risk-free rate. First, some analysts, for simplicity reasons, tend to assume that no government should default—a government can print more money to repay its domestic debts. However, more money supply tends to increase inflation, which affects the real returns on government securities that are assumed to be risk-free. With inflation, therefore, investors in government securities bear inflation risk. Second, inflation risk is more relevant when the risk-free interest rate is determined from a government bond yield of long maturity. Securities with short-term maturities (usually up to 1 year) have minimum inflation risk or probably none.

To adjust for inflations, the following equation can be used:

$$r_{f(real)} = \frac{1+r_f}{1-i} - 1$$

where $rf_{(real)}$ denotes the real risk-free rate and i is the inflation rate.

▶ Quotes 12.2 provides some analysts' insights into the effect of inflation on the risk-free interest rate.

▪ No Single Risk-Free Interest Rate

A risk-free interest rate is not absolute but is relative to an analyst's subjective judgments to choose the determinant variables—bond yield (and maturity) and default spread (the choice of credit rating). For example, two analysts will have completely different risk-free interest rates if one of them uses a 10-year bond yield while the other uses a 2-year bond yield. Consequently, for the same stock, different analysts may arrive at different estimates of the cost of equity.

Banner 12.8 Use Company's Domicile Country

A risk-free rate should be based on a company's domicile country (headquarters).

Think 12.4

Why is the proxy for a risk-free interest rate a challenging aspect in estimating the cost of equity?

Apply 12.1

Objective: Determine the risk-free interest rate for the purpose of estimating the cost of equity for the following companies:

1. Ecopetrol SA (Colombia):
   (a) Determine the risk-free rate for its stocks in the New York Stock Exchange (NYSE) (US market).
   (b) Determine the risk-free rate for its stocks in BVC (Colombian market).
2. Exxon Mobil (US-based):
   (a) Determine the risk-free rate for its stocks in the New York Stock Exchange (US market).
   (b) Determine the risk-free rate for its stocks in Sao Paulo (Brazil market).
3. For each of the cases (1) and (2) above, make assumptions about the purpose for which the risk-free interest rate is intended for, and provide reasons to justify your decisions about the selection of the proxy.
4. Replicate 1–3 for any company of your choice.

Quotes 12.2 Risk-Free Rate and Inflation

Quote 12.2.1 Ripple Effects of Low Interest Rates

» I still consider myself one of the younger folks at the energy trading firm where I work. The more tenured employees will sometimes talk about the early 1980s, when mortgage rates were north of 10%. 'Try paying that down quickly,' they'll quip, as we watch the 10-year Treasury note yield scroll by on the ticker—at around 0.7%...

The yield on Treasury bonds, especially the 10-year note, is often considered the risk-free rate, meaning it's the return you can earn while taking minimal risk. But that risk-free rate isn't looking terribly tempting. Annual inflation is running at just 1%. Inflation expectations for the next five years are under 2%. Nonetheless, those inflation rates are above both short- and intermediate-term Treasury yields. That means the after-inflation 'real' interest rate on Treasury is below 0%.

To earn inflation-beating gains, savers are relegated to taking more risk in higher-yielding corporate bonds or even the stock market. And, no, the bank isn't an alternative: During much of the 1980s and 1990s, savings accounts earned 1% to 4% after inflation. Today, the real yield at many banks is often more like negative 1%." (Mike Zaccardi, Financial Analyst)

Mike Zaccardi, CFA, CMT, August 28, 2020, ▶ *investing.com.*

Quote 12.2.2 Here's How Negative "Real Yields" Drive a Crowded Rally in Stocks, Gold, and Everything Else

» Deeply negative real yields—bond yields after accounting for inflation—are driving gains in all corners of financial markets. That's the growing view among market participants who say the decline of this key bond market indicator has driven increased risk-taking but also a surge in traditional safe havens like gold among investors who are looking for assets that offer higher returns and offset the losses arising from inflation. The 10-year real yield stood at around a negative 1.05%, derived from trading in Treasury inflation-protected securities. It hit its record low of negative 1.11% on Thursday (Sunny Oh, Analyst)

Sunny Oh, August 10, 2020, *Market Watch.*

Quote 12.2.3 Euro Zone Bond Yields Edge Down as Inflation Turns Negative

» Euro zone government bond yields nudged down on Tuesday as data showing that inflation in the b0loc plunged last month shifted the focus to next week's European Central Bank meeting. Inflation in the single currency bloc turned negative in August for the first time since May 2016 at minus 0.2%. Underlying inflation, closely watched by the ECB, also tumbled, suggesting the bloc's deepest recession is not temporary but could prove to be a longer-lasting drag. There was little immediate reaction in the markets, with some pointing to ECB board member Isabel Schnabel's Reuters interview on Monday, where she said the bank had no reason for now to add to its stimulus measures. But borrowing costs drifted lower as the session wore on, with Germany's 10-year bond yield last down 2 basis points at −0.41%, off recent highs that marked the highest levels since June (Yoruk Bahceli, Reporter)

Yoruk Bahcel, September 1, 2020, *Reuters.*

12.4.2 Expected Market Return

The objective of estimating the expected market return is to determine the excess return and the equity risk premium. This section explains and clarifies the meaning of expected market return, describes the information requirements, and shows different estimation methods.

12.4.2.1 Which Market?

It is first important to understand two issues regarding the expected market return: (1) stock market index in which the return is determined and (2) the concept of CAPM market return.

> **Banner 12.9 Expected Market Return**
> *According to CAPM, a market return is assumed to represent return on a portfolio made of all risky investment opportunities in a market.*

- **Stock Indices**

In application, a market rate of return is derived from a representative stock market index. These indices can be categorized into three geographical coverages: domestic market indices, regional market indices, and global market indices. In each of these categories, some stock markets have indices for specific segments relating to either company size or industry—such as large corporations, financial services, the energy sector, etc. For example, in North America, the major stock indices include Standard & Poor's 500 (S&P 500) (United States) NYSE Composite (United States), Dow 30 (United States), NASDAQ (National Association of Securities Dealers Automated Quotations) Composite (United S), and TSX 60 (Canada), to mention a few. In Europe, the major stock indices include Financial Times Stock Exchange (FTSE) 100 (England), *Cotation Assistée en Continu* (CAC) 40 (France), Deutscher Aktien Index (DAX) (Germany), Swiss Market Index (Switzerland), and Euronext 100 (Europe). Indices in Asia include Hang Seng (Hong Kong), Nikkel 225 (Japan), Shanghai SE Composite, etc. There are also indices in South America and Africa such as IPC (Mexico), Bovespa (Brazil), Nairobi Securities Exchange (NSE) 20 (Kenya), BSE (Botswana Stock Exchange) Domestic (Botswana), the Nigerian Stock Exchange (NSE) 30 (Nigeria), FTSE South Africa (South Africa), etc. Examples of global stock indices include Morgan Stanley Capital International (MSCI) and Global Dow.

- **The Concept of CAPM Market Return**

Conceptually, the CAPM market return is assumed to be a return on a portfolio made of all stocks in a market. For instance, if we intend to estimate the cost of equity for Amazon in the US market, then we need to use a stock index that best represents the all-stocks portfolio in the US market. However, it is worth noting that an index for an all-stocks portfolio does not exist—indices typically cover a particular segment of stocks. For example, S&P 500 includes only 500 stocks: a fraction of thousands of publicly traded stocks in the US market. FTSE 100 is a share index of 100 companies listed on the London Stock Exchange with the highest market capitalization, which represents about 81% of the entire market capitalization. The MSCI World Index (for 23 developed countries) measures the market performance of 4500 large and mid-cap companies that have a global presence. Therefore, in choosing an index for the purpose of estimating the expected market return, the aim is to simply have something that "somehow" or "closely" represents the respective stock investment portfolio. A normal practice is to use a broad stock index that includes many stocks in the market.

Banner 12.10 No Index for an All-Stocks Portfolio
An index that represents a portfolio of all stocks in the market does not exist, but an index that closely represents it does.

Think 12.5
Does the choice of stock index influence the estimation of the cost of equity? Explain.

12.4.2.2 Market Information

Typically, the expected market return tends to be estimated from historical market index data. The assumption is that the average of the past stock index returns constitutes an appropriate estimate of the future (market expectations). An acceptable and common practice is to use "close price" data, which can be presented under different names such as "price," "close," "last," etc. (see ▸ Exhibit 12.6). To clarify, close price can also be quoted as "adjusted close" to reflect the dividend information required to keep track of the performance of the stock. Because some stocks do not pay dividends, adjusted close limits comparability across stocks—hence, close price (unadjusted for dividends) is usually preferred.

It is not difficult to find stock market data for public companies. Numerous sources of such data exist such as Yahoo Finance, Google Finance in Google Sheets, ▸ investing.com, Wall Street Journal, Bloomberg, CNN Money, Reuters, etc. Thanks to the Internet and search engines like Google, it is easy to download data from several websites.

Banner 12.11 A Market Return Is Not Absolute
The estimation of a market return tends to be influenced by analysts' judgments about data frequency, sample period, and averaging methods.

Exhibit 12.6 Estimating a Market Return

Illustrative Case: For US Investors (See Excel Workings—▶ Chap. 12, Sheets E.12.6, D.12.1, and D.12.2)

This illustration shows how to estimate a stock market return. The following steps are used:

Step 1: Determine an appropriate stock index

Exhibit 12.6.1 displays a screenshot of the major US indices on 7 August 2020 (Yahoo Finance). It should be noted that there is a clear difference between S&P 500, Dow 30, and NASDAQ in terms of market price and day return (change). Assuming a US investment portfolio, S&P 500 is used as a case example. The same steps apply to other stock indices.

Step 2: Collect data

Collect historical stock index data from a reliable source. The frequency of data observations is usually available as daily, weekly, monthly, or annually. The appropriate frequency must be used depending on the purpose of estimation (this is clarified in the subsequent section). To estimate a market return, we use "close" quotes, (price quoted in the end of a trading day) as indicated in Exhibits 12.6.2 and 12.6.3.

Step 3: Calculate the percentage change

A change is simply the difference between the current close and the previous close. For example, in Exhibit 12.6.2, the change between February and January 1928 is −31 (i.e., 17.26 − 17.57) and the percentage change is −1.76%.

The following formula is used to calculated percentage changes (returns), depending on data frequency:

$$Price\ change\% = \frac{Current\ close - Previous\ close}{Previous\ close} \times 100$$

It can also be presented as:

$$Stock\ Return = \frac{Current\ close}{Previous\ close} - 1$$

For example, market data in Exhibit 12.6.2 are monthly. The percentage change for August 2020 is 2.54%, which is calculated as (3351.28 − 3271.12)/3271.12 or (3351.28/3271.12) − 1. The same calculation applies to the entire data sample.

Since data frequency is monthly, we have monthly percentage changes (i.e., monthly market returns). Depending on other data frequencies, market returns can be described as daily returns, weekly returns, or annual returns. For example, Exhibit 12.6.3 presents annual market returns like 9.54% in 2016 and −6.24% in 2018.

Step 4: Calculate the average market returns for the sample period

Determine the sample period and calculate the average stock market returns based on returns from step 3. Two averaging methods are available (arithmetic and geometric).

1. Arithmetic mean

   This is merely a simple average: the sum of all observations in the sample period divided by the number of observations.

2. Geometric mean

   Geometric mean is the *n*th root of the product of all *n* observations in a sample period, and it is presented as follows:

$$Average = \sqrt[n]{(Product\ of\ returns)} - 1$$

Avoiding negativity: Because a geometric mean uses products of observations, negativity should be removed by simply adding 1 or 100% to each observed change calculated in step 2 (see ◘ Exhibits 12.6.2 and 12.6.3 under the column "Change (%) + 100%."

◘ Exhibit 12.6.4 presents the average returns for selected sample periods. Regardless of the averaging method, the market returns should be interpreted according to data frequency and sample period. For example, the monthly average market return for 5 years to August 2020 is 0.86% or 0.78% and the annual average market return for 5 years to December 2019 is 10.38% or 9.43%.

Step 5: Calculate the annualized return

From Step 4, when the average returns are not based on annual data, they should be annualized to be applicable in the CAPM equation. For example, in ◘ Exhibit 12.6.4, annualization only applies to monthly average returns. The following formula is used:

$$Average\ market\ return(annualized) = (1 + average\ market\ return)^{12} - 1$$

where the average market return is obtained from step 4 above, and 12 represents the number of months in a year.

For example, 5 years' annualized arithmetic average return is calculated as follows:

$$Average\ market\ return(annualized) = (1 + 0.86\%)^{12} - 1 = 10.78\%$$

◘ Exhibit 12.6.5 presents all the calculated market returns in terms of the annual average. We can note that the calculated returns differ according to data frequency, sample period, and averaging method.

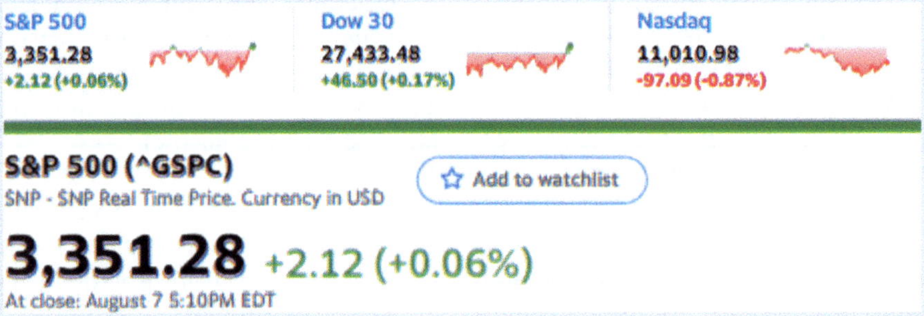

◘ **Exhibit 12.6.1** Stock market indices—quotation display. (*Source:* Yahoo Finance, August 8, 2020)

Exhibit 12.6.2 S&P 500 historical data: monthly

Date	Close	Change (%)	Change (%) + 100%
01/1928	17.57		
02/1928	17.26	−1.76%	98.24%
03/1928	19.28	11.70%	111.70%
04/1928	19.75	2.44%	102.44%
.	.	.	.
.	.	.	.
07/2020	3271.12	5.51%	105.51%
08/2020	3351.28	2.45%	102.45%

Source: Yahoo Finance (August 8, 2020)

Exhibit 12.6.3 S&P 500 historical data: annually

Date	Close	Change (%)	Change (%) + 100%
1928	24.35		
1929	21.45	−11.91%	88.09%
1930	15.34	−28.48%	71.52%
.	.	.	.
.	.	.	.
2018	2506.85	−6.24%	93.76%
2019	3230.78	28.88%	128.88%

Notes: These tables present only sections of historical data—the entire population for S&P 500 is dated from 1957, when the 500-stock index was adopted. Its origin, however, dates back to 1926 as a composite index
Source: Macro Trends (August 8, 2020)

Exhibit 12.6.4 S&P 500's historical average returns

Sample period	Average returns (annual frequency)		Average returns (monthly frequency)	
	Arithmetic	Geometric	Arithmetic	Geometric
5 Years	10.38%	9.43%	0.86%	0.78%
10 Years	12.86%	11.22%	0.99%	0.93%
15 Years	8.26%	6.76%	0.64%	0.56%
Since 1957	8.29%	6.96%	0.65%	0.56%
Since 1928	7.35%	5.52%	0.62%	0.47%

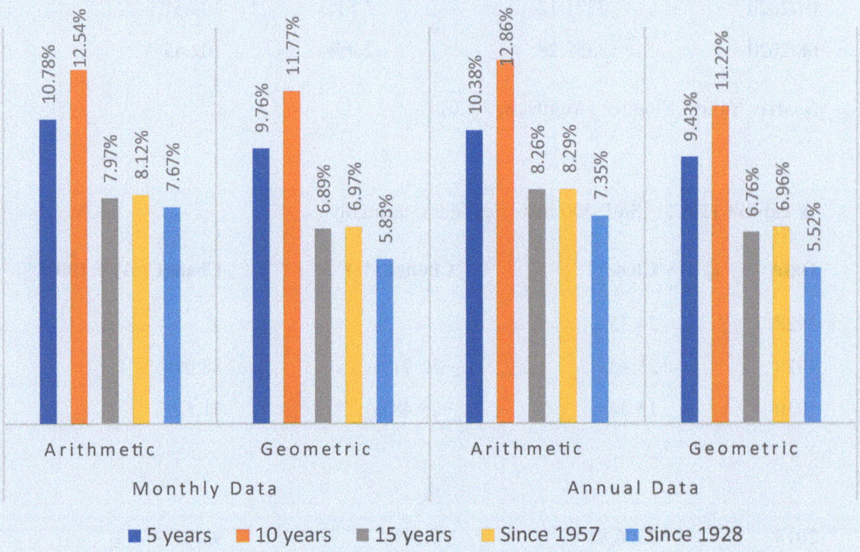

Exhibit 12.6.5 S&P 500's market returns for CAPM—arithmetic vs. geometric

12.4.2.3 Estimating Market Returns

Now that we are aware of the type of information, let us turn our attention to the practical estimation of market returns for the purpose of CAPM. Basically, a market return is estimated as an average return for a selected sample period—this averaging can be either arithmetic or geometric. This aspect is illustrated in ▸ Exhibit 12.6. The estimated market return is influenced by three main factors: data frequency, observation sample period, and averaging method (see ◘ Exhibit 12.6.5). An analyst has judgmental discretion of choice regarding these three factors, and, hence, like the risk-free interest rate, there is no absolute market return.

Think 12.6

Since estimated market returns differ according to analyst judgments and estimation methods, which one should be chosen in CAPM application? Explain.

12.4.2.4 Practical Considerations

The reality about stock market returns is far beyond the numbers—it is influenced by several factors, both objective and subjective. Let us discuss some of most important practical factors.

- **Arithmetic vs. Geometric Returns**

Arithmetic returns tend to be slightly higher than geometric returns (see ◘ Exhibit 12.6.5). A practical judgment is on "which of the two averaging methods is more appropriate." To answer this question, let us consider the following quote by Kolbe et al. (1984) debating the choice of market returns from the two methods for the purpose of capital budgeting analysis:

> Note that the arithmetic mean, *not* the geometric mean, is the relevant value for this purpose. The quantity desired is the rate of return that investors expected over the next year for the random annual rate of return on the market. The arithmetic mean, or simple average, is the unbiased measure of expected value of repeated observations of a random variable, not the geometric mean…the geometric mean underestimates the expected annual rate of return.

Butler and Schachter (1989) agree with Kolbe et al. (1984). However, they clarify that an arithmetic return is not an unbiased estimate of expected returns over periods greater than 1 year. The study by Cooper (1996) shows mixed views among analysts and academicians on the choice between arithmetic mean and geometric mean, depending on the purpose of the estimated cost of equity or cost of capital. Although the debate seems to be inconclusive, the following explanations may be a good guidance:

1. An arithmetic mean is more appropriate for observations that seem to be independent of each another: that is, stock prices in one period are not expected to affect prices in the next period. In technical terms, changes in stock prices (observed returns) are serially uncorrelated. For example, data with high-frequency observations (like daily or weekly) tend to be serially uncorrelated. That is, investors' gains in one day cannot easily influence the returns of the next day.

2. A geometric mean is more relevant when observed returns are dependent on each other. Usually, as we move to longer time horizons (like several months or years), returns tend to become more serially correlated. Annual data is an example: if an investor loses returns in 1 year, then there is still an opportunity to generate returns during the following years. Indeed, annual data are derived from calculating the average of returns during a particular year or picking returns at the end of the year. Hence, an accurate estimate of annual market returns for low-frequency data and a large sample period (for example, 5 years) can be achieved from a geometric mean rather than an arithmetic mean.
3. Overall, the purpose for which the cost of equity is estimated should be considered. An arithmetic mean represents an investor's expected returns at any given point in time (such as a day, a week, or a month). In contrast, a geometric mean usually represents returns that investors should expect over long horizons (such as 12 months, 5 years, 10 years, etc.). Therefore, if the purpose is to use the cost of equity (or the cost of capital) to discount cash flows over a long time horizon (e.g., 5 years, 10 years, etc.), then a geometric mean is more appropriate. In the context of CAPM, the time horizon (e.g., 10 years) is a single period. Otherwise, if the purpose is to analyze the value of a particular short period investment, and of course with the use of high-frequency data, then an arithmetic mean is more appropriate.

Banner 12.12 Arithmetic vs. Geometric Average
An arithmetic average is desirable when observed returns are independent of each other. A geometric average is desirable when observed returns are dependent on each other.

Sample Period

When estimating market returns, one of the key judgments is selecting an appropriate sample: "what should be the starting period and ending period?" In ▶ Exhibit 12.6, for example, data for S&P 500 were available from 1928—the 500-stock index was started in 1957. Generally, there is no standard sample for estimating market returns (see Zenner et al. 2008; Damodaran 2019b). However, it is important to understand the implication of sample size. Statistically, the larger the sample, the more its representativeness of the entire historical population. However, is such a long historical coverage a good predictor of the future? Such a statistical (and frequentist) conception is only relevant if we assume that, first, a series of historical data can provide realizations/observations of the same underlying random variable and, second, that the "population" concept is relevant in finance to describe something that we can observe through time. An intuitive thought is that the world has not been the same throughout that long historical period: things tend to change over time.

For S&P 500, the average annual historical return since 1957 is about 7–8%. Considering the most recent stock prices, a 5-year annual historical return is between 9% and 10%, whereas a 10-year return is between 11% and 13%. This means that stock market returns are not absolute—they vary from time to time. See further evidence in ▶ Quotes 12.3.

Therefore, the selection of the sample period should rather be based on a careful examination of the data to observe any significant shifts in stock market prices. Cutoff off points may consider structural break points caused by key events like economic depression, natural disasters, policy reforms, etc. Overall, the sample data to be selected should correspond to the period that suits the objective of valuation.

- **Inflation**

The historical data used in estimating market returns are nominal—hence, the annual market return is also a nominal return. Due to inflation, the real expected market return is likely to be lower. For example, if the annual historical return is 10% and the expected inflation rate is 3%, then the real rate of return should be approximately 7%. Inflation adjustment, however, is not a necessary condition in CAPM application.

Apply 12.2

Use any of the stock market index data to estimate the market return to be used in an CAPM equation.

(a) Collect the required data depending on the stock market of your interest. Show the sources of your data.
(b) Use both arithmetic and geometric methods of averaging. Interpret your results.
(c) Explain the criteria or reasons to justify your choices regarding data frequency and sample periods.

Quotes 12.3 Variations in Stock Market Returns

- **Quote 12.3.1 US Market—Market Returns Vary over Time**

» While 10% might be the average, the returns in any given year are far from average. In fact, between 1926 and 2014, returns were in that 'average' band of 8% to 12% only six times. The rest of the time they were much lower or, usually, much higher. Volatility is the state of play in the stock market. (Analysts James Royal & Arielle O'Shea)
James Royal and Arielle O'Shea, May 11, 2020, *Nerd Wallet*

- **Quote 12.3.2 US Market—Variations in Stock Market Returns**

» The average annualized total return for the US over the past 90 years is 9.8 percent… Yet equity returns come in waves, not in metered doses. The market gets on a roll, overshoots, retrenches, and sometimes—as in the 18 months that ended last November—just slides sideways. One of the market's more intriguing and mischievous traits is that it rarely produces the long-term 'average' return in a given calendar year. Looking now only at price returns (not counting dividends), a gain of 5 to 10 percent is one of the rarest results for stocks. According to data furnished by LPL

Financial senior market strategist Ryan Detrick, in the 89 years from 1928 to 2016, only six finished with a gain in that range that we think of as a 'typical' annual return (Analyst Michael Santoli)

Michael Santoli, June 18, 2017, *CNBC*

▪ **Quote 12.3.3 US Market—Positive Returns Outweigh Negative Returns**

» Negative stock market returns occur, on average, about one out of every four years. Historical data shows that the positive years far outweigh the negative years. The average annualized return of S&P 500 Index was about 11.69% from 1973 to 2016. In any given year, the actual return you earn may be quite different than the average return, which averages out several years' worth of performance (Analyst Dana Anspach & Roger Wohlner)

Dana Anspach and Roger Wohlner, June 29, 2020, *The Balance*

12.4.3 The Market Risk Premium

At this point, we know the information required for determining the market risk premium ($rm - rf$) and the decision challenges facing analysts when determining the two variables: the risk-free rate and market return. One of the key practical questions is: "how to determine the appropriate pair of market return and risk-free rate?"

Banner 12.13 Selection of Market Premium Variables

When estimating the market risk premium, consideration should be made in matching the two variables (market return and risk-free rate) in terms of the time horizon of the expected investment.

As discussed earlier, the purpose for which the cost of equity is estimated determines the method of estimating the market return. The choice of a risk-free rate can also be considered in the same way. When the objective is to analyze investments with a short lifetime, government securities with a short maturity (e.g., treasury bills) may be an appropriate match as a proxy for the risk-free rate, and the most likely method for estimating the market return would be the arithmetic mean with high-frequency data (i.e., monthly, weekly, and daily). In contrast, when the objective is to value assets for a long time horizon (say several years), it is more appropriate to use government securities with long maturity as a proxy for the risk-free rate, and the market return should be based on the geometric mean with low-frequency data (usually annual). According to Damodaran (2019b), the historical market return tends to vary according to estimation methods, and it has always ranged between 3% and 12%. Hence, the risk premium should also vary from time to time. For example, if the 10-year US treasury yield is 0.64%, then we can calculate the market risk premium using geometric returns in ▫ Exhibit 12.6.5—considering returns since 1957, the risk premium would be 6.32% (i.e., 6.96% − 0.64%), and considering 15-year market returns, the risk premium would be 6.12%.

Apply 12.3

Based on you results in ► Apply 12.1 and 12.2, determine the market risk premium to be used in the CAPM equation for Ecopetrol and Exxon.

(a) Make an assumption about the objective of the analysis.
(b) Make a decision about the market return and risk-free rate. Explain the criteria or reasons to justify your decision.
(c) Calculate the market risk premium and interpret the results.
(d) Replicate (a)–(c) for the company of your choice.

12.4.3.1 Different Concepts of Market Risk Premium

There are four vital concepts regarding market returns and risk premium—historical premium, expected premium, required premium, and implied premium (see ► Exhibit 12.7). Overall, the four concepts differ in the way they are determined or calculated. Historical equity risk premium, which is applicable in CAPM, is derived from observed stock market data, whereas the other three concepts (expected, required, and implied) are unobserved and tend to be lower than the historical premium (see ► Quotes 12.4).

Banner 12.14 Market Risk Premium Concepts

A historical premium is backward-looking and is equal for all investors—it is observable. Other forms of returns (expected, required, and implied) are forward-looking and are different for different investors—they are not observable.

Exhibit 12.7 Market Risk Premium

A "historical risk premium" is simply calculated from historical returns, as illustrated in ► Exhibit 12.6—it is, therefore, backward-looking.

An "expected risk premium" is derived from expected returns, which should not necessarily be equal to historical returns—several factors can determine the future performance in markets, and if the current historical period is regarded as good performance, then it is reasonable to expect a return lower than the most current historical return. For example, if the historical return is 10%, then the expected return can be lower (e.g., 5%, 6%, etc.). If the most current period performance is bad, then the expected return can be higher than the historical return.

A "required risk premium" is the premium required by an investor to hold the market portfolio. According to CAPM, both expected and required returns are assumed to be equal and so are expected and required risk premia.

An "implied risk premium" is more complex because it is derived not only by looking at market performance over time but also by considering several factors in the future. It can be calculated using expected future streams of cash flows from stock trading, in which the implied market return equates the present value of future cash flows to the current price paid in buying stocks. The key assumption is that stocks are correctly priced in the aggregate. The implied risk premium is, therefore, the difference between the implied market return and the risk-free rate. ◘ Exhibit 12.7.2 presents the implied risk premia for selected global stock markets.

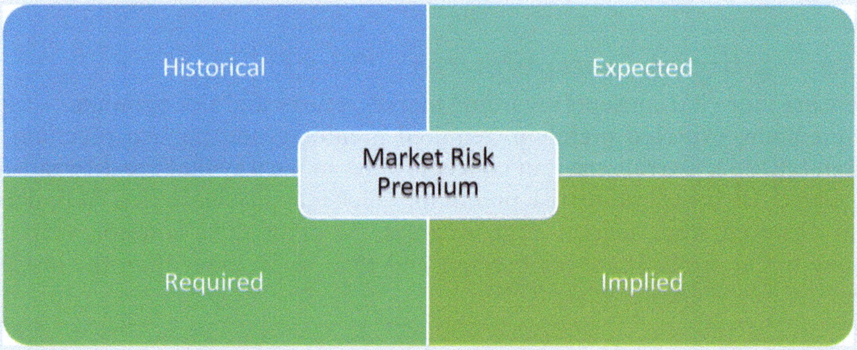

◘ **Exhibit 12.7.1** Different concepts of market risk premium

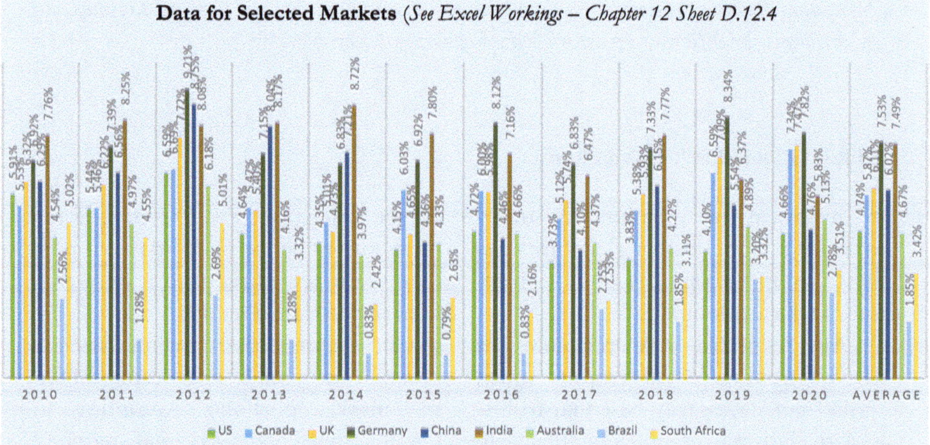

◘ **Exhibit 12.7.2** Implied market risk premia for selected markets (2010–2020). Data for selected markets (see Excel workings—▶ Chap. 12, Sheet D.12.4). (*Source:* Data were obtained from Market Risk Premia (2020) at ▶ http://www.market-risk-premia.com)

Quotes 12.4 Market Risk Premium

- **Quote 12.4.1 A Historical Premium Tends to Be Higher Than the Expected Risk Premium**

» The future equity risk premium for the UK market is set to be lower than the historical average, according to the London Business School. In its Global Investment Returns Yearbook 2002, the school finds that, factoring in current market volatility, the future equity risk premium for UK and world stock markets will be around 3.5% to 4%. This compares with a historical average premium for equity risk in the UK of around 5.8% over the past 100 years and 5.9% for the world market. The equity risk premium is defined as the difference between the return on stocks and bonds. Elroy Dimson, professor of finance at the London Business School and one of the authors of the report, said the average risk premium for UK equities relative to bonds increased in the second half of the twentieth century, rising from just 3.1% during the first 50 years to some 9.2% between 1950 and 2001. Dimson said this increase was down to factors such as increased productivity, accelerating technological change and improved management and corporate governance. (London Business School)
London Business School, 2002, *Investment Week.*

- **Quote 12.4.2 A Market Risk Premium Is Different Across Countries**

» …the United Kingdom (UK) has the lowest MRP alongside Germany and Norway. Greece, the Ukraine and Turkey all had average risk premiums of over 10% in 2020. Having a lower market risk premium may seem bad, but for countries such as the UK and Germany where rates have been consistent for several years, it is because the market is stable as an environment for investment. (Analyst James Cherowbrier)
James Cherowbrier, April 20, 2020, *Statista*

12.4.3.2 Which Risk Premium for Which Market?

From our definition, the market risk premium applies to all stocks in the same market. However, what is the boundary of stock markets? Is it for all stocks in the world or just for all stocks in one country or region? If the estimated market risk premium is based on data from one country, then is it possible to apply these data for analyzing investments in other countries or regions?

To answer these questions, we need to consider "country risk transfer." Some countries are riskier than others. For example, country credit ratings according to Moody's in 2020 are as follows: United States (AAA), Canada (AAA), Greece (B3), the United Kingdom (Aa2), and Colombia (Baa2). Investments in countries such as Greece or Colombia are exposed to higher risks than those in Canada, the United States, or the United Kingdom. Hence, stock market risk premium defers across countries according to country-specific risk (see ▶ Quote 12.4.2).

Should the differences in country risk matter when applying a stock market risk premium? There are two issues relating to market openness characteristics, which determine the degree of risk transmission across markets. (1) "Closed economies." If a country's risk is assumed to be idiosyncratic (i.e., that risk cannot be transferred to other countries), then it is possible to diversify risk through investing in several countries globally. However, this assumption is only valid if markets are not fully correlated, thereby ruling out the possibility of economic spillover effects from one market to another. In such circumstances, a stock market risk premium is the difference across countries. However, to assume that countries are uncorrelated may be hard to swallow in a world of openness and globalization. (2) "Open economies." If we assume that all investors hold portfolio investments globally, then a market risk premium should be the same globally. This assumption seems valid in today's world, where global investments are a commonplace practice as we see multinational corporations in different countries. However, some barriers and restrictions limit investment entries in some countries.

From these arguments, a more reasonable judgment is that stock risk premia should vary across countries. To use the same risk premium for different markets comes with exceptions. For example, if the market risk premium is based on US data, then it is possible to apply these data to other "developed" countries (e.g., Canada, Germany, the United Kingdom, etc.) with some adjustments—this aspect is discussed in the next section.

Banner 12.15 Market Risk Premium Differs Across Countries
While global stock markets can be considered borderless, each country tends to have a market risk premium that suits its specific risk factors.

12.4.3.3 Market Risk Premium Based on Mature Stock Markets

In the previous sections, we saw how a risk premium can be determined by subtracting the risk-free rate from the market return. In this section, we show alternative ways of estimating the risk premium based on mature stock markets like the United States, Canada, the United Kingdom, and so on, after adjusting for country-specific risk. According to Damodaran (2015, 2019a), mature markets are used as benchmarks to adjust for country-specific risk (refer to Damodaran's data and updates for credit ratings and default spreads https://pages.stern.nyu.edu/%7Eadamodar/New_Home_Page/datafile/ctryprem.html). To use the United States as a mature market, these approaches are presented here and illustrated in ▶ Exhibit 12.8.

- **Country Default Spread (DS)**

To determine the risk premium for a country, a default spread (DS) is added to the US market risk premium (MRP). Default spreads for different countries can be obtained from rating agencies (e.g., S&P, Moody's, and Fitch) or calculated using credit default swaps (CDSs). Thus, a market risk premium for a specific country (*MRPCountry*) is calculated as:

$$MRP_{Country} = MRP_{US} + DS$$

- **Relative Equity Market Volatility (REMV)**

This approach involves computing the ratio of equity volatility in an intended market to equity volatility in a mature market, which tends to be highly liquid. This ratio is then multiplied by the market risk premium in the mature market. Low-liquidity markets (like emerging markets and developing markets) tend to have a higher standard deviation than high-liquidity markets (like the United States and other developed markets), and even country risk is expected to be higher. Hence, equity market volatility is influenced by country risk, and, therefore, the market risk premium is calculated as:

$$MRP_{Country} = MRP_{US}\left(\frac{EMV_{Country}}{EMV_{US}}\right)$$

where, $EMV_{Country}$ and EMV_{US} denote equity market volatility (standard deviation) of the target country and the US market, respectively. Since REMV is sensitive to liquidity limitations, using this approach for low-liquidity markets may be misleading.

- **Scaled Default Spread (DS)**

This approach uses the country risk spread, scaled with the ratio of equity market volatility in a country to the volatility of its government bond. Unlike the relative market volatility, this approach overcomes some of the estimation drawbacks caused by liquidity variations in stock markets across different countries. The market risk premium is, therefore, calculated as follows:

$$MRP_{Country} = MRP_{US} + DS\left(\frac{EMV_{Country}}{BV_{Country}}\right)$$

where, $BV_{Country}$ represents the bond volatility (standard deviation) of the country.

- **Limitations**

Market correlation should be considered when using mature markets as a benchmark. Correlation tends to be high among markets of similar characteristics. A US-based market risk premium can be suitable for many advanced markets but not for several emerging and frontier markets. Even in some other developed stock markets, several risk factors can influence the risk premium—for example, political risk, inflation risk, market barriers, and economic stability, to mention a few.

Banner 12.16 Risk Premium and Market Correlation

To use a mature market as a benchmark to estimate the risk premium for another country, the two markets should be highly correlated.

12

Apply 12.4

Determine the US-based market risk premia for selected countries.

(a) Choose any five countries of your interest. Collect the required data depending on availability. Show the sources of your data.

(b) Calculate the market risk premium applying default spread approaches and relative equity market volatility.

(c) Explain the criteria or reasons to justify your choices of countries and discuss the possible limitations.

Think 12.7

Since there are several approaches to estimate the expected market return, which of them is the most favorable and why?

Exhibit 12.8 Market Risk Premium Based on Mature Stock Markets

Illustrative Case: Selected Markets (See Excel Workings—▸ Chap. 12, Sheet E.12.8)

This illustration shows how market risk premia can be determined using mature markets as a benchmark—the US market is used here. The following steps are used:

Step 1: Collect data

Exhibit 12.8.1 presents data sets relating to country risk spreads, equity volatility, and bond volatility.

Step 2: Determine the market risk premium for the benchmark market (in this case, the United States)

The market risk premium is 6.32%—the market return is based on geometric returns for annual data since 1957. The risk-free rate is proxied by a US 10-year treasury yield of 0.64% in August 2020.

Step 3: Calculate the country risk premia for each approach depending on data availability

Exhibit 12.8.2 presents the results.

Country Default Spread (DS): In this approach, three different measures of country default spreads are applied: ratings-based spreads, CDS-based spreads, and volatility-based (scaled) spreads. The general formula applicable for ratings-based and CDS-based spreads is as follows:

$$MRP_{Country} = MRP_{US} + DS$$

Example (Colombia):

$$\begin{aligned} \text{MRP} &= 6.32\% + 2.23\% \\ &= 8.55\%(\text{ratings} - \text{based spread}) \end{aligned}$$

$$\begin{aligned} \text{MRP} &= 6.32\% + 2.94\% \\ &= 9.26\%(\text{CDS} - \text{based spread}) \end{aligned}$$

For the volatility-based (scaled) spread, the following formula is applied:

$$MRP_{Country} = MRP_{US} + DS\left(\frac{EMV_{Country}}{BV_{Country}}\right)$$

Example (Colombia):

$$\begin{aligned} \text{MRP} &= 6.32\% + 2.23\%(12.58\% / 14.25\%) \\ &= 8.30\%(\text{ratings} - \text{based spread}) \end{aligned}$$

Relative Equity Market Volatility (REMV): This approach is based on equity market volatility (*EMV*) between a selected country and the United States, and it is applied as follows:

$$MRP_{Country} = MRP_{US}\left(\frac{EMV_{Country}}{EMV_{US}}\right)$$

Example (Brazil):

$$\text{MRP} = 6.32\%(19.82\% / 14.32\%) = 8.74\%$$

Exhibit 12.8.1 Country credit ratings, default spreads, and market volatility

Market	Rating	Country default spread		Volatility	
Country	Moody's	Rating-based	CDS-based	Equity	Bond
United States	Aaa	0.00%	0.40%	14.32%	NA
Canada	Aaa	0.00%	0.49%	NA	NA
Colombia	Baa2	2.23%	2.94%	12.58%	14.15%
Brazil	Ba2	3.53%	1.74%	19.82%	14.28%
Mexico	Baa1	1.87%	3.00%	15.24%	5.94%
Kenya	B2	6.46%	7.29%	11.08%	NA
South Africa	Ba1	2.93%	4.73%	15.64%	9.86%
Tanzania	B1	5.28%	NA	24.74%	15.48%
Greece	B1	5.28%	2.32%	23.72%	13.71%
Indonesia	Baa2	2.23%	3.10%	12.58%	10.77%
China	A1	0.83%	1.01%	22.31%	12.33%
India	Baa3	2.53%	3.01%	14.72%	8.01%

Notes: NA—information not available on these countries. Volatility is measured by standard deviations

Source: Data were obtained from Damodaran (2020) at ▶ http://pages.stern.nyu.edu/~adamodar/New_Home_Page/datafile/ctryprem.html

12

Exhibit 12.8.2 US-based market premia for selected countries

Market	Rating	Country default spread			Equity volatility
Country	**Moody's**	**Rating-based**	**CDS-based**	**Scaled**	**REMV**
United States	Aaa	6.32%	6.72%	NA	6.32%
Canada	Aaa	6.32%	6.81%	NA	NA
Colombia	Baa2	8.55%	9.26%	8.30%	5.55%
Brazil	Ba2	9.85%	8.06%	11.22%	8.74%
Mexico	Baa1	8.19%	9.32%	11.12%	6.72%
Kenya	B2	12.78%	13.61%	NA	4.89%
South Africa	Ba1	9.25%	11.05%	10.96%	6.90%
Tanzania	B1	11.60%	NA	14.76%	10.91%
Greece	B1	11.60%	8.64%	15.45%	10.46%
Indonesia	Baa2	8.55%	9.42%	8.92%	5.55%
China	A1	7.15%	7.33%	7.82%	9.84%
India	Baa3	8.85%	9.33%	10.97%	6.49%

NA not applicable

12.4.4 Beta (β)

Beta is a measure of systematic risk. Statistically, it measures the sensitivity of individual stock returns to market returns. Therefore, to estimate beta, a pair of historical data is required—stock returns (for individual stocks) and market returns (for the market portfolio).

Banner 12.17 Estimating Beta
Regardless of the method, beta is a measure of correlation between market returns and stock returns and their respective standard deviations.

12.4.4.1 Estimation Methods

Several methods exist for estimating beta, but the most applied are: (1) regression or correlation scatters, (2) covariance–variance ratio, and (3) slopes. All these methods define beta as the sensitivity of stock returns to market returns; they should produce the same results.

- **Linear Regression**

In this method, stock returns (a dependent variable) are regressed as a function of market returns (an independent variable) as follows:

$$S_t = c + \beta M_t + \varepsilon_t$$

where *St* and *Mt* represent stock returns and market returns for a given time (*t*), respectively; β is the stock beta to be estimated, c is a constant, and εt is the error term.

Thanks to Excel, a regression line can be easily obtained using "correlation scatters," which plot correlation points between stock returns and market returns and display the slope of the "straight line of best fit" for the points and the estimated beta coefficient.

- **Covariance–Variance Ratio**

In this method, beta is derived as a ratio of the covariance between stock returns and market returns to the variance of market returns as follows:

$$\beta = \frac{cov(S_t, M_t)}{Var(M_t)}$$

where *Cov*(*St*, *Mt*) represents the covariance between stock and market returns for a given period, whereas *Var*(*Mt*) is the variance of market returns for that period.

- **Slope**

This is the proportional change in stock returns to the change in market returns and can be presented as follows:

$$\beta = \frac{\Delta S_t}{\Delta M_t}$$

where ΔSt and ΔMt denote changes in stock returns and market returns over time, respectively.

▶ Exhibit 12.9 presents an example to estimate CAPM beta using Chevron Corporation. The following key points should be noted. Beta estimates differ across sample periods, data frequencies, and market indices. There are different views about choosing these estimation inputs, and, therefore, due to analysts' subjective judgments, beta is not absolute (see ◘ Exhibits 12.9.5 and 12.9.6).

Banner 12.18 Beta Is Not Absolute

Beta is influenced by analysts' judgments and choice of estimation variables: sample period, data frequency, and market index.

Think 12.8

Since analysts' judgments influence stock beta, are there any judgment criteria to determine which beta to use? Discuss.

Exhibit 12.9 Estimation of CAPM Beta

Illustrative Case: Chevron Corporation (See Excel Workings—▶ Chap. 12, Sheet E.12.9).

This illustration shows how to estimate CAPM beta. We use Chevron Corporation, a US-based company, as on 1 May 2019. The main steps are as follows:

Step 1: Make decision about inputs

Determine data inputs: sample period, data frequency, and stock market index. These issues are discussed in the next section (see the section "Practical Considerations"). To illustrate, we use various inputs as follows: two sample periods (2 years and 3 years); three frequencies (daily, weekly, and monthly), and three different indices; S&P 500, NYSE Composite, and DJIA (see Exhibit 12.9.1).

Step 2: Collect historical data

A pair of historical data on stock prices (Chevron) and stock market index was obtained from Yahoo Finance (see Exhibit 12.9.2). This is simply a section of data extract from monthly close price observation—refer to Excel workings for complete data. The same can be replicated for other frequencies.

Step 3: Calculate returns

A return is simply a price change between the current and previous period and is therefore calculated as follows for both individual stock and market index:

$$Return = \frac{P_t - P_{t-1}}{P_{t-1}}$$

where Pt and Pt_{-1} denote the current and previous close stock price (or index), respectively.

Exhibit 12.9.2 presents monthly returns for the market and the stock, denoted as Mt and St, respectively. For example, returns for June 2016 are calculated as:

$$M_t = (2098.860 - 296.950) / 296.950 = 0.001 : S_t = (104.830 - 101.000) / 101.000 = 0.038.$$

Step 4: Calculate beta (β)

Refer to the three formulas presented earlier. This illustration applies monthly data to a 3-year sample (1 May 2016–1 May 2019). Exhibit 12.9.3 shows the estimates from the three methods: regression, slope, and covariance–variance ratio. Exhibit 12.9.4 depicts the respective scatter graph, which includes a regression equation and the line of best fit. Exhibit 12.9.5 compares beta estimates from various choices on inputs (sample, frequency, and index).

Exhibit 12.9.1 Sample periods and frequencies

Frequency	3-Year sample period	2-Year sample period
Daily	9 May 2016–9 May 2019	9 May 2017–9 May 2019
Weekly	8 May 2016–6 May 2019	8 May 2017–6 May 2019
Monthly	1 May 2016–1 May 2019	1 May 2017–1 May 2019

Exhibit 12.9.2 Calculation of returns

Date	S&P 500	Chevron	*Mt*	*St*
May 2016	2096.950	101.000		
June 2016	2098.860	104.830	0.001	0.038
July 2016	2173.600	102.480	0.036	(0.022)
August 2016	2170.950	100.580	(0.001)	(0.019)
September 2016	2168.270	102.920	(0.001)	0.023
October 2016	2126.150	104.750	(0.019)	0.018

Exhibit 12.9.3 Calculation of beta

Method	Refer to Excel workings	Beta
$St = c + \beta Mt + \varepsilon t$	$St = -0.0015 + 0.7424Mt + \varepsilon t$	$\beta = 0.7424$
$\beta = \frac{cov(S_t, M_t)}{Var(M_t)}$	$Cov(St, Mt) = 0.0008$ $Var(Mt) = 0.0011$	$\beta = \frac{0.0008}{0.0011} = 0.7424$
$\beta = \frac{\Delta SR_t}{\Delta MR_t}$	$\frac{\Delta S_t}{\Delta M_t} = 0.7424$	$\beta = 0.7424$

12

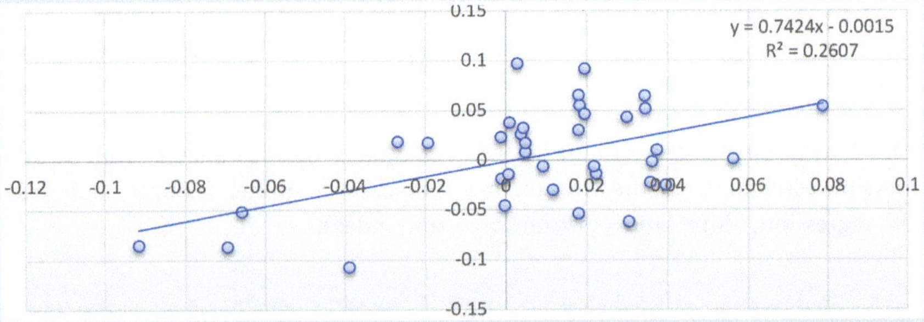

Exhibit 12.9.4 Scatter graph. *Notes:* In the regression equation, *y* represents stock returns (*St*), whereas *x* represents market returns (*Mt*). Beta is the coefficient 0.7424

Exhibit 12.9.5 Comparison of beta estimates for Chevron stocks

Sample	Index	Beta estimates of May 2019		
		Daily data	**Weekly data**	**Monthly data**
3-Year	S&P 500	0.88	0.79	0.74
	NYSE Composite	1.06	0.93	0.95
	DJIA (Global)	0.89	0.82	0.76
2-Year	S&P 500	0.87	0.88	0.78
	NYSE Composite	1.11	1.05	1.00
	DJIA (Global)	0.86	0.90	0.74

Exhibit 12.9.6 Different betas for different analysts: Chevron's stock

Other sources	Beta on 15 May 2019
NASDAQ	0.85
Financial Times (FT)	0.96
Yahoo Finance (3 years)	0.75
Reuters	1.23
Zack's	1.00
In Front Analytics (1 year)	0.93
In Front Analytics (2 years)	0.86
In Front Analytics (3 years)	0.79

Sources
Reuters (2019) ► https://www.reuters.com/finance/stocks/overview/CVX.NIn Front Analytics (2019) ► https://www.infrontanalytics.com/fe-en/30295NU/Chevron-Corp-/BetaYahoo Finance (2019) ► https://finance.yahoo.com/quote/CVX/Zack's (2019) ► https://www.zacks.com/stock/chart/CVX/fundamental/betaFinancial Times (2019) ► https://markets.ft.com/data/equities/tearsheet/summary?s=CVX:NYQNasdaq (2019) ► https://www.nasdaq.com/symbol/cvx

12.4.4.2 Practical Considerations

As seen in Exhibits 12.9.5 and 12.9.6, analysts' subjective judgments tend to influence beta estimates. This aspect is discussed here for practical considerations and decision-making about data frequency, sample period, and market index.

- **Data Frequency**

The choice of data frequency should depend on data properties and the trading pattern of the stocks to be estimated. In active stock markets, where stock prices are quoted almost continuously on a daily basis, beta can be estimated from high-frequency data like daily or weekly. The main advantage of high-frequency data is that these can easily capture most of the microstructural effects (see Williams 1977; Dimson 1979; Cohen et al. 1983). Nevertheless, not all stock markets have regular daily trading patterns—most infant markets experience "thin trading" characterized by infrequent activeness. The use of high-frequency data in these markets can cause serious estimation problems. Lower-frequency data (monthly) can be more suitable despite having their own concerns. Overall, the higher the frequency of data, the more the accuracy of beta estimates. Corporate analysts like Yahoo Finance and Bloomberg use monthly and weekly returns, respectively. Some analysts suggest the use of intraday data, but it is practically difficult to implement.

▪ Time Coverage (Sample Size)

As mentioned earlier, there is no standard sample size in estimating beta. However, for improving the accuracy of beta estimates, a reasonably large sample is required. The main problem, however, is that as you go further back in determining the initial date (an extremely large sample), there is a great chance of facing structural shifts in the observed returns or strategic changes in a firm's business—the true relationship between stock and market returns may have changed too. To consider data frequency, a larger sample may be more suitable for low-frequency data (e.g., monthly data) than for high-frequency data (e.g., daily data). For example, Yahoo Finance estimates beta using monthly returns covering 3 years, whereas Bloomberg uses weekly returns covering 2 years. However, for markets with thin trading, larger samples may be appropriate even with monthly data.

▪ The Market Index

Most stock markets have several indices, specific to segments of stocks or companies (e.g., large corporations, financial services, the energy sector, etc.). An important point to understand is that an index for all stocks in a market does not exist. The choice of an index should be based on its ability to represent stock returns relative to the market in which beta is being estimated. It is, therefore, more sensible to use a broad stock index that includes many stocks in the market, assuming active stock trading. In thin markets, where a broad index can include inactive stocks, the use of specific indices covering active stocks (or a geographical market or a class of companies) can be more appropriate.

For example, in ▶ Exhibit 12.9, a suitable index for estimating Chevron's stock beta is required. This is a US-based multinational company and can therefore be represented by several domestic and global indices such as Standard & Poor's 500 (S&P 500), New York Stock Exchange (NYSE) Composite, and Dow Jones Industrial Average (DJIA) Global. S&P 500's index is a market capitalization-weighted index of the 500 largest US publicly traded companies. The index is widely regarded as the best gauge of large-cap US equities. DJIA Global is for 30 large multinational companies (including Chevron). The NYSE Composite index is an index that measures the performance of all stocks listed on the New York Stock Exchange, which includes more than 1900 stocks, of which more than 1500 are US companies. Hence, beta should be interpreted relative to a selected index.

▪ Outliers

Outliers are abnormal returns in stock markets that do not reflect a true pattern of stock performance for the selected sample period because they are temporary. They can, therefore, cause over- or underestimation of beta. As a remedy, stock price data must be carefully examined to identify and avoid outliers—it may be necessary to omit abnormal observations or to choose a cutoff date that avoids them.

Apply 12.5

Refer to ▶ Apply 12.1–12.3 regarding Ecopetrol and Chevron.

(a) Determine the sample period and data frequency to suit beta estimation for each of the companies and respective stock markets.

(b) Calculate beta for Ecopetrol stocks in NYSE and BVC Colombia.

(c) Calculate beta for Chevron stocks in the United States.

(d) Calculate the cost of equity for each company considering investors in specific markets.

(e) Replicate (a)–(d) for any company of your choice.

12.4.4.3 Can Beta Be Negative?

Yes, it is possible to have a negative beta. However, what does it imply? We know that beta is a measure of systematic risk—the higher the beta, the higher the risk. Now, does a negative beta mean negative market risk? Does it make any sense? To answer these questions, we need to discuss how a negative beta occurs. From our definition of beta—a correlation between market returns and stock returns—a negative beta occurs when the two returns move in opposite directions due to several factors. For instance, when a company undergoes reforms or changes, the market tends to react to its stocks. If the market reaction causes a persistent change in the normal stock price direction, then a negative beta is likely to occur during that period.

Some examples of negative betas are available. Carrier Global Corporation had a beta of −0.84 relative to S&P 500; according to the analysis by Bob Ciura (2020) on July 27 2020, the company was experiencing an unexpected fall in its operating performance. In addition, according to Market Beat (▶ marketbear.com) on 27 August 2020, there were several stocks with negative betas relative to S&P 500, including Torm (−413.51), Eneva SA (−28.90), Zoom Video Communications (−1.15), Grasim Industries (−1.11), Gravity (−0.57), Virtu Finance (−0.41), and American State Water (−0.10), just to list a few.

Returning to our key question—does a negative beta imply negative risk? First, let us reflect on the following quote:

> » A negative beta coefficient does not necessarily mean absence of risk. Instead, negative beta means your investment offers a hedge against serious market downturns. If the market continues rising, however, a negative-beta investment is losing money through opportunity risk—the loss of the chance to make higher returns—and inflation risk, in which a low rate of return does not keep pace with inflation. Because the stock market has historically produced a positive return in most years, the mere act of investing in negative-or low-beta stocks increases these risks over time (Streissguth and Cockerham,2019).

Dan Caplinger, in an article published in The Motley Fool on December 12, 2012, and updated on October 4, 2018, had the following question: "Negative-Beta Stocks: Worth Buying?", the analyst suggests that:

12

» Stocks that tend to move opposite the market can be useful and The key to investing in these unusual stocks is not to draw generalizations based on beta. Instead, you have to look at each stock to determine why the beta is negative, and then decide if it's a good fit for your portfolio (Caplinger 2018).

▶ Exhibit 12.10 summarizes some implications of a negative beta in selected stocks: it may not necessarily have anything to do with market risks.

Banner 12.19 Negative Beta

A negative beta does not necessarily imply higher risk and may have nothing to do with market risks. It should be carefully interpreted considering the specific circumstances of a company.

Exhibit 12.10 Stocks with Negative Betas and Implications

Selected Case Examples

Company and beta	Implication of a negative beta
Arena Pharmaceuticals NASDAQ (−0.32)	It has nothing to do with market risks but company-specific news. A negative beta does not imply low risk.
Ferrellgas Partners NYSE (−0.01)	The gas company is recession-resistant; its businesses tend to be more correlated with gas prices but has little or no correlation with the broad market.
Agnico-Eagle Mines NYSE (−0.33)	The nature of business (gold and other precious metals) tends to "attract safe-haven money when stocks start to decline," and, hence, it has a negative correlation with the market.
Dr Pepper Snapple NYSE (−0.11)	"As a distant third in the soft-drink wars, Dr. Pepper is understandably insulated from the moves of the overall market. With its own niche from its unique namesake beverage, Dr. Pepper has found ways to sustain its business regardless of the strategies of its larger competitors."

Source: Caplinger (2018)

12.5 Limitations of CAPM

The limitations of CAPM clearly arise from its assumptions, which allow it to focus on the relationship between returns and systematic risk. However, the idealized world created by assumptions is not the same because investment decisions are made by companies and individuals. As evidenced in the study by Fama and French (1997), the use of CAPM to estimate the cost of equity capital for specific industries is not precise, mainly because of the uncertainty about the true expected risk premia and the inaccuracy in the estimates of industry betas. Additionally, the inaccuracy is even higher for the estimates of the cost of equity for individual firms and projects. Let us look at the following limitations:

- **Markets Are Inefficient and Imperfect**

The perfect market assumption cannot truly apply to real-world capital markets. Even advanced and well-developed stock markets experience some imperfections despite exhibiting a high degree of efficiency (see Reilly and Brown 2003).

- **Disagreement over Sample Period to Estimate Beta**

The estimation of beta depends on the holding period sample that an analyst decides to use. While CAPM assumes that investors have a single-period transaction horizon, it may not be true in real-world practices. Investors' intention is not to rely only on returns generated at the end of a single period but rather to receive returns for a long investment period.

- **Historical Data**

Some CAPM inputs, like beta and risk-free rate, are estimated using historical data. However, investment analysis is based on expected returns on future cash flows. Although it is reasonable to use the past to predict the future, there may be significant deviations due to unexpected future events.

- **Disagreement over Proper Risk-Free Rate**

The assumption that all investors borrow at the risk-free rate is not realistic in the real world (see Black 1972). Investments carry risk, and, hence, the risk associated with individual investors tend to be much higher than that associated with government securities (proxies for risk-free rates). Moreover, as suggested by Friend and Blume (1970), there is inequality between borrowing and lending rates. Therefore, an apparent discrepancy exists between the observed ex post relationship between market returns and risks and the ex ante predications of the CAPM.

- **Reliance on a Single Risk Factor**

According to CAPM, beta is the only risk factor determining the estimated cost of equity. In the real world, however, several firms' internal factors and external macroconomic factors tend to influence investors' expected returns (see Fama and French 1992, 2004). Several studies suggest that the variability in expected returns is not related only to market beta (see, for example, Basu 1977; Banz 1981; Bhandari

1988; Chan et al. 1991). While CAPM considers only one-period risk and return, investors in the real world consider how their portfolio returns are linked to their income and future investment opportunities. The "arbitrage pricing theory (APT)" addresses CAPM limitations by introducing a multifactor model (see Appendix).

- **Variations in Beta**

Beta can shift over time due to being sensitive to the historical time horizon. Hence, the stability of beta is hard to sustain for a long future period to match investments' future risks and returns.

Think 12.9

According to CAPM, an asset with zero beta should have the same expected rate of return as that of a risk-free asset. Can the returns on that asset still have a positive standard deviation? Does it make sense for such a risky asset not offering a higher rate of return than a risk-free asset in a world in which investors are risk-averse?

12.6 CAPM in Real-World Applications

Despite several limitations, CAPM is still a prominent model in real-world applications for estimating the equity rate of return. There are theoretical and practical reasons to explain the prominence of CAPM, as outlined below.

- **Diversification**

CAPM is based on the diversification concept. In the real world, investors are assumed to be risk-averse, and they tend to manage their investment risks through portfolio diversification. The assumption that investors hold diversified portfolios means that all investors prefer to hold a portfolio that reflects the stock market. Realistically, it is almost impossible for an investor to own the market portfolio itself. However, an investor can diversify unsystematic risk and construct portfolios that align with the stock market. Therefore, it is quite reasonable to assume that investors are concerned only with returns providing compensation for only systematic risk. According to CAPM, investors diversify their risk better than a firm does, and, hence, the cost of equity is expected to be higher than the risk-free rates.

- **Beliefs**

Practical evidence in favor of CAPM is either weak or mixed. Hence, CAPM is applicable only based on the belief that it really works. After all, there is neither sufficient evidence against it nor a substitute model practically better than CAPM. For these reasons, CAPM serves as a standard (or benchmark) model for estimating stock expected returns. Financial analysts, managers, and investors apply it as a true standard model for investment analysis.

- **Usefulness**

CAPM is applicable in specific and suitable circumstances—not on every kind of analysis. Its application considers its practical suitability in estimating the cost of capital. As discussed earlier, some of the factors to be considered are availability of data, estimation accuracy, estimation purpose, and so on.

- **Objectivity and Simplicity**

Unlike several other alternative methods, the principal advantage of CAPM rests on its objectivity in estimating costs of equity. However, due to its simplicity in explaining the determinants of equity cost of capital, it should not be applied in isolation. Instead, it can be supplemented with other techniques (and even analysts' judgment) to arrive at realistic estimates.

12.7 Alternative Betas

Typically, CAPM is designated for actively trading public companies because beta requires stock prices. It is neither suitable for inactive public stocks nor private companies. To address these limitations, alternative approaches can be applied to estimations—comparable beta and accounting beta.

Banner 12.20 Alternative Betas' Application
Alternative betas are typically suitable for private firms but can be applied in public companies with market data limitations.

12.7.1 Comparative Beta

This approach allows beta to be estimated from comparable public firms to become a proxy beta for a comparable target firm (public or private). Companies are regarded as comparable if they possess similar financial and operating characteristics relative to value drivers—returns, risk, and growth (refer to ▶ Chap. 19). ▶ Exhibit 12.11 presents an illustrative case of Pemex (Mexico).

Think 12.10
Since comparable beta can be estimated from arithmetic or weighted average and on book or market DE, which beta should one choose? Explain.

12

Exhibit 12.11 Estimating Beta from Comparable Companies

Illustrative Case: Pemex (Mexico) (See Excel Workings—▶ Chap. 12, Sheet E.12.11)

About Pemex

Pemex, a Mexico City-based company, is owned by the Mexican government but does not trade publicly. This energy company was founded in 1938. Its beta can be estimated using the following steps:

Step 1: Identify the line of business

The energy industry is broad. Companies in this industry include energy producers, manufactures of energy equipment, energy logistics and supply, etc. Pemex is in the line of integrated oil and gas.

Step 2: Determine a group of comparable public firms (peers)

The following public companies are used: Suncor (Canada), Cenovus (Canada), Exxon Mobil (United States), Chevron (United States), Husky (Canada), and Imperial (Canada). Refer to ▶ Chap. 19 on how to determine peers. ◘ Exhibit 12.11.1 compares companies' key market and financial information for 2019, which include return on assets (ROA), debt to equity (DE), total assets, enterprise value (EV), market cap, growth of revenue and free cash flows (FCFs), beta, and credit ratings.

Step 3: Determine the average beta of the comparable public companies

◘ Exhibit 12.11.1 shows each company's stock beta. The average beta can be determined using two methods (1) arithmetic average and (2) weighted average based on enterprise value (EV). ◘ Exhibit 12.11.2 shows each company's average beta from the two approaches. An arithmetic average is just a simple average (0.99). A weighted average beta is calculated as follows: (a) calculate EV weights by dividing the company's EV by peers' total EV ($B733.3); (b) calculate the company's weighted beta as a product of its beta and EV weight; and (c) weighted average beta is the sum of all weighted betas (0.91)

Step 4: Determine unlevered beta for public peer companies

To determine unlevered beta, we need two additional pieces of information—average DE and average tax rate. ◘ Exhibit 12.11.2 shows each company's average DE from arithmetic average and weighted average based on EV. The arithmetic averages on book and market DE are 0.26 and 0.27, respectively. The weighted averages are 0.16 and 0.15, respectively. The energy sector's median tax rate in 2019 was 36.8% (▶ Forbes.com). Therefore, the asset beta for the group of public companies is calculated as follows:

$$\beta_U = \frac{\beta_L}{1+(1-T_c)\left(\frac{D}{E}\right)}$$

where βU and βL are the unlevered and levered betas, respectively. Tc is the average corporate tax rate, and D/E is the average debt-to-equity ratio. For example, from arithmetic and weighted averages on book metrics, unlevered betas are calculated as follows:

$$\beta_U = \frac{0.99}{1+(1-0.368)(0.26)} = 0.85$$

$$\beta_U = \frac{0.91}{1+(1-0.368)(0.16)} = 0.82$$

Estimated unlevered betas for each metric are presented in ◘ Exhibit 12.11.3.

Step 5: Calculate levered beta of the target firm (public or private)

To calculate the beta of the target firm, the formula is as follows:

$$\beta_{L(p)} = \beta_U\left[1+\left(1-T_{c(p)}\right)\left(\frac{D_P}{E_p}\right)\right]$$

where βU is the unlevered beta from comparable public firms; for the target company, $\beta L(p)$ is the beta to be estimated, $Tc(p)$ is the tax rate, and Dp/Ep is the DE ratio.

According to Form 6-K (► sec.gov), Pemex's tax rate was 65% for 2019. For different metrics, the estimated betas for Pemex are presented in ◘ Exhibit 12.11.4. For example, when the unlevered beta of public companies' peers is 0.85:

$$\beta_{L(p)} = 0.85\left[1+(1-0.65)(5.30)\right] = 2.43$$

Exhibit 12.11.1 Comparison of key variables for 2019

Company	ROA	Book DE	Market DE	Total asset ($B)	EV ($B)	Market cap ($B)	Growth		Beta	S&P Rating
							Revenue	FCF		
Pemex	**5.6%**	**5.3**	**NA**	**108**	**NA**	**NA**	**35.7%**	**27.7%**	**NA**	**BBB+**
Chevron	4.7%	0.2	0.2	260	252	228	23.1%	36.1%	0.93	AA
Cenovus	−1.3%	0.5	0.7	31	15	9.0	22.5%	347.3%	0.94	BBB
Exxon	6.1%	0.1	0.1	349	378	343	27.5%	25.3%	0.85	AA+
Husky	4.5%	0.3	0.3	26	13	10	38.1%	48.6%	1.27	BBB+
Imperial	2.3%	0.2	0.2	31	23	20	38.7%	77.1%	0.78	AA+
Suncor	4.9%	0.3	0.2	70	52	45	42.8%	−30.7%	1.17	A-

Note: Averages exclude Pemex

Source: Company Financials, Micro Trends, Bloomberg (2019)

Exhibit 12.11.2 Average beta and average D/E ratio

Company	Beta	Book DE	Market DE	Weights based on EV			
				EV weights	Beta	Book DE	Market DE
Chevron (United States)	0.93	0.19	0.15	34.38%	0.32	0.07	0.05
Cenovus (Canada)	0.94	0.49	0.71	2.05%	0.02	0.01	0.01
Exxon (United States)	0.85	0.10	0.11	51.55%	0.44	0.05	0.05
Husky (Canada)	1.27	0.25	0.29	1.79%	0.02	0.00	0.01
Imperial (Canada)	0.78	0.2	0.16	3.13%	0.02	0.01	0.00
Suncor (Canada)	1.17	0.3	0.2	7.11%	0.08	0.02	0.02
Average	*0.99*	*0.26*	*0.27*		*0.91*	*0.16*	*0.15*

Exhibit 12.11.3 Peers' unlevered beta

	Arithmetic		EV-weighted	
	Book DE	Market DE	Book DE	Market DE
Peers' DE	0.26	0.27	0.16	0.15
Peers' unlevered beta	0.85	0.85	0.82	0.83

Exhibit 12.11.4 Pemex' levered beta

	Arithmetic		EV-weighted	
	Book DE	Market DE	Book DE	Market DE
Peers' unlevered beta	0.85	0.85	0.82	0.83
Pemex's levered beta	2.43	2.43	2.34	2.37

12.7.2 Accounting Beta

Accounting beta is not popular but can be applied as a last resort when CAPM or comparable beta is practically impossible to determine. The process to estimate accounting beta is the same as that to estimate CAPM beta, but it uses financial data (earnings) instead of stock prices. It is the estimated coefficient from a regression of earnings growth against market returns, which are assumed to be proxies for average earnings growth within the market. This aspect is illustrated in ▶ Exhibit 12.12 using Jubilee Holdings, a Kenyan public company.

Exhibit 12.12 Estimating Accounting Beta

Illustrative Case: Jubilee Holdings (Kenya) Limited (See Excel Workings—▶ Chap. 12, Sheet E.12.12)

Jubilee Holdings Ltd. is incorporated in the Republic of Kenya under the Companies Act and is domiciled in Kenya. Its stocks are listed at the Nairobi Securities Exchange (NSE) in Kenya. This illustration is to estimate beta as of December 2016. To estimate the accounting beta, the following steps are used:

Step 1: Obtain the company's historical earnings and market index data

The type of beta determines the types of earnings to use—operating earnings for unlevered beta and net income for levered beta. ◘ Exhibit 12.12.1 displays a section of estimation data covering 15 years from 2000 to 2016. Jubilee's annual stock prices were obtained from Morningstar, whereas its after-tax earnings were obtained from its financial reports. Market prices represent NASI (Nairobi All Share Index) designed as a barometer of the Kenyan economy with a view that companies listed on the NSE are good representatives of the sectors to which they belong.

Step 2: Calculate returns or changes

From the data, calculate changes depending on data frequency. In this example, we use annual data and hence annual changes (◘ Exhibit 12.12.1).

Step 3: Calculate accounting beta

Use any of the three approaches covered in CAPM beta. A regression equation can be presented as follows:

$$ER_t = c + \beta MR_t + \varepsilon_t$$

where *ERt* and *MRt* represent a firm's earning returns and market returns at a given time (t), respectively, β is the accounting beta to be estimated, c is a constant, and *εt* is the error term. ◘ Exhibit 12.12.2 displays the estimated accounting beta (0.2532).

Step 4: Determine a forward-looking beta

The estimated accounting beta in step 3 (backward-looking) can be transformed into a forward-looking beta that reflects the expected future performance. Research suggests that beta is mean-reverting as it tends to adjust its state of equilibrium toward unit in the long run. One way to adjust beta is to use the following equation:

$$\beta_f = \alpha + (1 - \alpha)\beta$$

where βf is the estimated forward-looking beta, β is the historical accounting beta, and α is an adjustment factor carrying the value of 0.33 as a rule of thumb but can be derived from statistical analysis.

Thus, for Jubilee,

$$\beta_f = 0.33 + (1 - 0.33)\,0.2532 = 1.2532$$

Exhibit 12.12.3 compares Jubilee's accounting beta to CAPM beta.

Exhibit 12.12.1 Estimation data

Year	Company earnings				Stock price		Returns	
	Operating	Change	Net	Change	Market	Stock	Market	Stock
2016	4563	0.10	3297.00	0.17	3555.71	445.45	−0.23	0.01
2015	4145	0.05	2814.00	−0.02	4618.04	440.00	−0.08	0.19
…	…	…	…	…	…	…	…	…
2003	313	0.47	213.00	0.30	2079.76	37.57	0.79	2.22
2002	213	0.25	164.00	0.36	1162.66	11.65	−0.28	0.00
2001	170	0.45	121.00	0.55	1624.82	11.65	−0.22	−0.16
2000	117		78.00		2072.34	13.90		

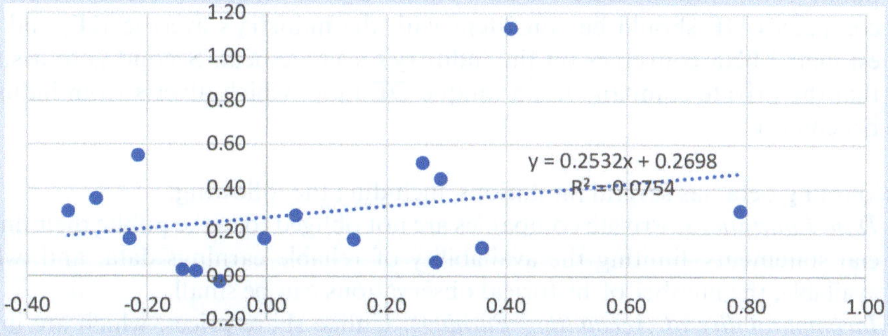

Exhibit 12.12.2 Estimation of accounting beta

Exhibit 12.12.3 Accounting beta Vs. CAPM beta (Jubilee)

Type of beta	Beta	Data frequency
Accounting beta	*0.2532*	*Annual*
Accounting beta (adjusted)	1.2532	Annual
CAPM beta	1.9088	Annual
CAPM beta	1.3311	Monthly

12.7.3 Limitations of Alternative Betas

Comparable beta faces several practical issues. Some of them are as follows:

- *Size Issue*: Comparable companies tend to have different sizes, and most private firms tend to be smaller than public firms. Comparing an extremely small company to huge private companies can cause estimate bias.
- *Comparable Public Companies*: Obtaining a group of comparable companies may be difficult or impossible in markets with few or zero listed stocks. This is likely in most infant and some emerging markets.
- *DE Ratio*: Usually, the target DE ratio is preferred, but the actual DE ratio tends to be practically used because the target may not be easily determined. Two major assumptions can be made to determine DE for a private firm. First is to assume that that a private firm belongs to an industry in which comparable public companies operate on an optimal capital structure. Hence, a private company's DE should be consistent with the industry's average DE, and the estimated beta converges on the industry's average beta. Second is to assume that the private company has a unique DE ratio, which diverts from industry benchmarks.

Accounting beta has several limitations, including the following:

- *Data Limitations:* Private companies are not obliged to make public their financial statements, limiting the availability of reliable earnings data, and, when available, the number of historical observations can be small.
- *Incomparability of Accounting Earnings*: Unlike share prices, which are influenced by market expectations, accounting earnings are mostly influenced by firms' internal factors—they can be subjected to accounting manipulations, thereby limiting comparability among companies.

Think 12.11

Is it possible to compare three companies' betas, each one estimated from a different approach—company A (CAPM beta), company B (comparable beta), and company C (accounting beta)?

Review Questions

1. What is the assumed risk factor according to CAPM? Why should it be the only concern to investors?
2. Define the following terms as applied in CAPM:
   (a) Risk-free interest rate
   (b) Market return
   (c) Beta
   (d) Market risk premium
3. Can assets be correctly priced under CAPM? What is the real-world implication?
4. The risk-free rate is 3%. The expected market return is 8%. Three stocks (A, B, and C) have betas of 1.5, 1, and 0.8, respectively.
   (a) What is the cost of each stock?
   (b) Rank the stocks according to the market risk (1 = highest risk and 3 = lowest risk).
   (c) Make a security market line (SML) graph for the three stocks.
   (d) Repeat (a)–(c) if the risk-free interest rate is 4% and the expected market return is 12%.
   (e) Compare graphs in (c) and (d) and comment on the influence of the risk-free rate and market return on the cost of equity.
5. The risk-free rate is 3%. The expected market rate of return is 8%. A company's stock beta is −2.0. What is the cost of equity capital? Does it make any economic sense? Explain.
6. Provide an intuitive and mathematical meaning of equity risk premium.
7. Why should we use government securities as a proxy for risk-free investments?
8. What are the practical considerations when determining a risk-free interest rate?
9. A 10-year government bond yield is 3.80%. The government sovereignty debt is rated AA by S&P and has a default spread of 1.02%. The inflation rate is 4.5%.
   (a) Calculate the nominal risk-free rate
   (b) Calculate the real risk-free rate
10. A 10-year government bond yield is 2.40%. The government sovereignty debt is rated AAA by S&P and has a default spread of 0.00%. The inflation rate is 3.8%.
    (a) Calculate the nominal risk-free rate
    (b) Calculate the real risk-free rate
11. Suppose that you have been asked to value three different investments in different lifetime horizons: 1-year investment, 10-year investment, and indefinite lifetime investment. Explain how investment lifetime will influence the choice of a risk-free interest rate for each of the three investments.
12. Two different analysts are estimating the stock market risk premium of the same market. Should they come up with the same estimate? Use examples to support your answer.
13. What type of information is required to estimate the expected stock market return?

14. Explain the practical circumstances in which you will apply each of the following methods when estimating market returns:
    (a) Arithmetic mean
    (b) Geometric mean
15. Outline the type of information required when estimating a company's stock beta. Explain how each of that information can be obtained.
16. Can you apply the beta of company A's stocks on company B's stocks? Explain.
17. Explain how you should overcome the following practical challenges in estimating beta:
    (a) Data frequency
    (b) Time coverage (sample size)
    (c) Choice of the market index
    (d) Outliers
18. Explain the possible circumstances in which the following betas can occur.
    (a) Beta is greater than one
    (b) Beta is less than one
    (c) Beta is one
    (d) Beta is zero
    (e) Beta is negative
19. Is there any similarity between the APT and CAPM? Explain.
20. In terms of theoretical reasoning, what is the difference between CAPM and the APT?
21. What is the difference between systematic risk and unsystematic risk, and how does each affect the expected investment return?
22. An investor is anticipating investing in an emerging market of Asia. You are an analyst trying to value some stocks in Malaysia. During the last 5 years, the Malaysian stock market has been 15% a year on average, whereas the government borrowing rate has been 5%, yielding an historical premium of 10%. Would you use this as the risk premium for the investor, looking into the future? Provide reasons.
23. The beta for ABC company is 1.10. The current 3-month treasury bill yield is 1.24%, whereas the 10-year bond rate is 4.25%. ABC's domicile country is rated BBB with a default spread of 0.95%. Estimate the cost of equity for ABC, based on:
    (a) The treasury bill rate to determine your risk-free rate.
    (b) The treasury bond rate to determine your risk-free rate.
    (c) Which one of these estimates would you use in valuation of the company? Provide reasons to support your answer.

24. You have been asked to estimate the beta of an energy company, which has three divisions with the following characteristics:

Divisions	Beta	Market value
Energy consulting	0.95	$180 million
Energy extraction	1.65	$550 million
Energy distribution	1.02	$520 million

Required:
(a) What is the company's equity beta?
(b) Assume that the company decides to diversify by establishing a new business in the technology sector. What would happen to its stock beta?

25. The total market value of DFS Company's stocks is $6 million, and the total value of its debt is $4 million. The company's finance manager estimates that the beta of the stock is currently 1.5 and that the expected risk premium on the market is 8.5%. The 10-year government bond yield is 6.5%, and the government credit is rated BBB with a default spread of 1.25%.
Required:
(a) What is the required rate of return on DFS stocks?
(b) Suppose that the company intends to diversity into manufacturing a new product in the transport sector. The beta of transporters is approximately 1.26 without debt. What is the required rate of return on DFS's new business?

26. The following table summarizes the market returns of a country based on the historical average of the stock market index.

Period	Arithmetic	Geometric
1950–2020	10.60	9.98
1990–2020	6.24	6.01
2010–2020	8.50	8.02

Required:
(a) Explain the difference between arithmetic and geometric measures.
(b) Explain why the geometric mean is lower than the arithmetic mean?
(c) If you were asked to estimate a company's cost of equity using CAPM, which sample period would you choose: the most recent data (2010–2020), a longer period (1990–2020), or the whole period (1950–2020)? Provide reasons to justify your decision.

27. The average required rate of return in the market is 6.8%. The risk-free rate is 2.2%. The following information is related to three stocks trading in the same market.

	Stock A	Stock B	Stock C	Stock D
Beta	0.45	0.98	1.67	−0.03

Required:
(a) Calculate the cost of equity for each stock.
(b) Explain the relationship between beta and the cost of equity.
(c) What is the possible reason for a negative beta on stock D?
(d) With other factors being equal, which stock's cost of equity will be the most affected if the market return changes? Provide reasons to support your answer.
(e) With other factors being equal, which stock's cost of equity will be the most affected if the risk-free rate changes? Provide reasons to support your answer.

28. The following information relates to three countries, the United Kingdom (UK), the United States (US), and Brazil on 27 July 2022.

Country	Credit rating	Default spread	Bond yield
United States	Aaa	0.00%	10-year = 2.76%
United Kingdom	Aa3	0.51%	10-year = 1.94%
Brazil	Ba2	2.56%	10-year = 13.49%
Japan	A1	0.60%	10-year = 0.20%
Japan	A1	0.60%	4-year = −0.046%

Required:
(a) What should be the risk-free rate applicable in each country?
(b) BP Plc, a UK-based oil company, is trading its stocks at the NYSE (the United States) at a price of US$20.36. What risk-free rate would you apply when estimating its cost of equity for the US investor?
(c) Petroleo Brasileiro S.A. is a Brazilian company whose stocks are trading in the US market with a beta of 1.94. Calculate its cost of equity using CAPM.
(d) What is the implication of a negative 4-year bond yield in Japan? Can it be used in CAPM to estimate the cost of equity?

29. The following information relates to two companies whose stocks are listed at the Colombian Stock Exchange (BVC) and New York Stock Exchange (NYSE).

    Company A is a Colombian-based company and is listed at the BVC. The covariance between its stock returns and the Colombian market returns is 15.5%, whereas the variance of market returns is 12.8%. The company has debt paying 10% interest. Its marginal tax rate is 34%.

    Company B is a US-based company and listed at the NYSE. The covariance between its stock returns and the US market returns is 32.4%, whereas the variance of market returns is 36.0%. The company has debt paying 8.5% interest. Its marginal tax rate is 40%.

    The following additional information is available:

	Colombia	United States
Expected market return	10.54%	12.65%
10-Year treasury bond yield	6.42%	2.54%
Country default spread	2.04%	0.00%

    Required:
    (a) Calculate the cost of equity for company A and company B.
    (b) Is it possible to use the beta of company A for estimating the cost of equity of company B? Explain.
    (c) Is it possible to use the US government bond yield to estimate the risk-free rate for Colombia? Explain.

30. The following information relates to three companies (A, B, and C) whose stocks are listed at the Colombian Stock Exchange (BVC). The 10-year treasury bond yield in Colombia is 6.42%. The BVC's average market return is 10.54%, and the variance or returns is 12.8%. The country's default spread is 2.04%.

	Company A	Company B	Company C
Covariance between stock and market returns	15.5%	12.2%	10.8%
Total debt (millions)	$120	$560	$340
Interest on debt	10%	8.5%	11.2%
Corporate tax rate	34.6%	34%	36%

    Use CAPM to calculate each company's cost of equity.

31. The following information relates to two companies whose stocks are listed at the NYSE in the United States. A 10-year treasury bond yield in the United States is 1.26%. The S&P 500 market index has an average return of 8.54% and a variance of 12.8%. According to Moody's credit ratings, the US government is rated Aaa (default spread is 0.00%). Companies' data are given as follows:

	Company A	Company B
Covariance of stock and market returns	15.5%	12.2%
Total debt ($ billions)	120	560
Pretax cost of debt	10%	8.5%
Corporate tax rate	38%	38%
Number of common shares outstanding (billions)	3.4	5.2
Current stock price ($) per share	12	159
Market value of debt ($ billions)	122	555

Required:
(a) Calculate each company's cost of equity using CAPM.
(b) Which of the two companies has a higher market risk? Why?

Appendix: Arbitrage Pricing Theory

Reflection on CAPM

Among CAPM critiques is its reliance on only one systematic risk factor—market risk—influencing investor's required rate of return. What about other factors? The arbitrage pricing theory (APT) by Ross (1976) considers several factors to determine security returns. It is an arbitrage-based theory positing a multilinear relationship between security returns and multiple factors. Its assumptions consider the following:

1. *Sources of systematic risk*: The uncertain world of investment is exposed to many sources of risks, which are inevitable regardless of diversification strategies, and they should be precisely priced in investment returns. Therefore, a multifactorial model can be used to describe the risk–return trade-off, whereby the expected return carries a multifactorial risk premium measured by a multifactorial beta.

2. *Unsystematic risk*: Like CAPM, investors do not bother about diversifiable risk (idiosyncratic or unsystematic risk). They have portfolio choices to suit their risk and return profiles—they tend to select investment portfolios with betas suitable to their own preference.
3. *Perfect and efficient markets*: Efficient capital markets eliminate persisting arbitrage opportunities, to imply the following: no security exists nor can it be created with a negative value and a nonnegative payoff; no security exists with a zero value and a strictly positive payoff; and two securities that always have the same payoff must be equally priced.

From these assumptions, the expected return on a financial asset depends on two aspects: (1) "systematic risk factors" and (2) "assets' sensitivity to those factors."

Investors' "expected returns," therefore, should incorporate the "anticipated" risk factors into their expected returns, although most of the "realized returns" tend to be influenced by "unanticipated" events. However, since systematic factors are the only primary source of risk, they are also the main determinants of both expected returns and actual returns on portfolios. Nevertheless, in the real world, the magnitude or direction of the unforeseen events cannot be anticipated, except the sensitivity of asset returns to those events—based on historical experience. Factor sensitivity is not equal to every investment: it depends on the investment's specific factors, including unsystematic factors.

The Factor Structure

Returns from each investment are sensitive to changes in factor returns. Therefore, realized asset returns can be estimated as:

$$r_j = a_j + b_{j1}F_1 + b_{j2}F_2 + b_{j3}F_3 + b_{j4}F_4 + \dots b_{jn}F_n + \varepsilon_j$$

where r_j is the actual return on an asset *j*, *ai* is a coefficient that can be interpreted as the expected return of security *j* and is denoted as *E(rj)*; *bj* is the sensitivity of an asset's return on a particular systematic factor, whereas *Fn* is the return associated with that factor, which is common to all securities; and *εj* is the random error term representing the return on unsystematic factors, carrying the value of zero.

To interpret this factor structure, the "actual return" on a security depends on the "expected return" and "factor returns" related to factor sensitivity (systematic risk). The expected return is consistently common for any portfolio and almost all securities, and it incorporates any anticipated change in factor returns. Therefore, *Fn* represents a deviation of the actual factor return from the expected return. Thus, *Fn* = *fn* − *E(fn)*, where *fn* is the actual factor value and *E(fn)* is the expected factor value. A zero *Fn* means that the respective expected factor has not changed—it did not have an impact on the actual portfolio return. If all the factor movements are zero, then the actual portfolio return on an asset will be the same as what investors expect: i.e., *rj* = *E(rj)*. Therefore, the return-generating equation can be restated as:

12

$$r_j = E(r_j) + b_{j1}F_1 + b_{j2}F_2 + b_{j3}F_3 + b_{j4}F_4 + \ldots b_{jn}F_n + \varepsilon_j$$

Thus, in a well-diversified economy with no arbitrage opportunities, if returns on an asset follow a factor structure, then the relationship between the expected return *E(rj)* and portfolio factor sensitivity can be expressed as:

$$E(r_j) = \lambda_0 + b_{j1}\lambda_1 + b_{j2}\lambda_2 + b_{j3}\lambda_3 + b_{j4}\lambda_4 + \ldots b_{jn}\lambda_n$$

where $\lambda 0$ is the intercept so that when each random factor variable has a zero value, $E(rj) = \lambda 0$; the rest of the λn are the risk premiums associated with each risk factor.

This equation represents a no-arbitrage condition, as a generalization of CAPM with allowance for multiple risk factors and holds for well-diversified portfolios and almost all individual securities. To consider return on risk-free security and specific portfolios, the corresponding expected return can be expressed as:

$$E(r_j) = r_f + b_{j1}\lambda_1 + b_{j2}\lambda_2 + b_{j3}\lambda_3 + b_{j4}\lambda_4 + \ldots b_{jn}\lambda_n$$

whereby the factor risk premium is the difference between the expected return and the risk-free rate, such that $\lambda n = E(rj) - rf$.

To illustrate the APT, we use a three-factor structure example in ▶ Exhibit 12.13 and a four-factor structure in ▶ Exhibit 12.14.

Exhibit 12.13 Arbitrage Pricing: A Three-Factor Structure

Illustrative Examples (See Excel Workings—▶ Chap. 12, Sheet E.12.13)

Consider a stock with an expected return of 14%. An investor believes that the stock's risk is influenced by three main systematic factors: economic industrial production (*FP*), inflation rate (*Ff*), and interest rates (*Fr*). The following table provides more information:

	Fp	*Ff*	*Fr*
Expected growth rate	5.0%	6.2%	9.0%
Actual growth rate	6.8%	7.6%	11.0%
Stock factor sensitivity (*bf*)	1.1	0.8	0.4

To determine a revised estimate of the stock's return (i.e., actual return), our three-factor model can be written as follows:

$$r_j = E(r_j) + b_p F_p + b_f F_f + b_r F_r + \varepsilon_j$$

where *rj* is the actual rate of return on the stock; *E(rj)* is the expected stock return; *bj* is the sensitivity of the stock' return on a particular systematic factor, *F* is the change in return associated with each factor; and ε is the random error term that represents the return on unsystematic (idiosyncratic) factors. The following two steps are followed:

Step 1: Determine factor changes (i.e., the deviation from expected factor returns) as follows:

$$F_p = 6.8\% - 5\% = 1.8\% F_f = 7.6\% - 6.2\% + 1.4\% F_r = 11.0\% - 9.0\% = 2.0\%$$

Step 2: Calculate the actual stock return as follows:

$$r_j = 14\% + 1.1(1.8\%) + 0.8(1.4\%) + 0.4(2.0\%) = 17.9\%$$

Note: The unsystematic risk is ignored due to the reasons explained earlier.

Exhibit 12.14 Arbitrage Pricing: A Three-Factor Structure

Illustrative Examples (See Excel Workings—▸ Chap. 12, Sheet E.12.14)

An investor has a portfolio investment in five stocks. He believes that each stock's return is primarily dependent upon four factors: economic growth as measured by the growth in industrial production, interest rates determined by the term structure, market size measured by market capitalization, and inflation measured by consumer price indices. ▪ Exhibit 12.14.1 provides information about the anticipated factor risk premia and the respective factor sensitivities applicable to all stocks in the portfolio.

Deviations from expected factor returns were realized as follows: growth (−0.60%), interest (2.00%), market size (1.50%), and inflation (0.50%). The stock portfolio with its estimated factor sensitivity (*bj*) is provided in ▪ Exhibit 12.14.2.

CAPM betas for each stock are as follows: A (1.06), B (1.04), C (0.95), D (0.54), and E (1.00). The risk-free interest rate is 2.40%.

To estimate the actual returns for each individual stock in the portfolio, we follow the following steps:

Step 1: Estimate the expected market return

This is the return that an investor expects from each stock considering the risk-free interest rate and factor risk premia as follows:

$$E(r_j) = r_f + b_{j1}\lambda_1 + b_{j2}\lambda_2 + b_{j3}\lambda_3 + b_{j4}\lambda_4 + \ldots b_{jn}\lambda_n$$

$$E(r_j) = 2.40\% + 0.51(2.00\%) + 0.25(3.10\%) + 0.10(0.60\%) + 0.57(1.60\%) = 5.17\%$$

Step 2: Calculate the actual returns

12

This is the revised estimate of the stock's return (i.e., actual return) using the following equation:

$$r_j = E(r_j) + b_{j1}F_1 + b_{j2}F_2 + b_{j3}F_3 + b_{j4}F_4 + \varepsilon_j$$

Using stock A as an example, the actual return is calculated as follows:

$$r_A = 5.17\% + 0.12(-0.60\%) + 1.13(2.00\%) + 0.30(1.50\%) - 0.44(0.50\%) = 8.03\%$$

The rest of the actual stock returns can be calculated in the same way—results are presented in Exhibit 12.14.3.

Comparison Between the APT and CAPM

To replicate the expected stock returns according to CAPM, we apply the following equation for each stock:

$$k_{ej} = r_f + \beta_j\left(E(r_j) - r_f\right)$$

For example, for stock A, we have:

$$k_{ej} = 2.40\% + 1.06(5.17\% - 2.40\%) = 5.34\%$$

The APT estimates and the respective CAPM comparisons are presented in Exhibit 12.14.3

Key aspects to note:

1. *When all factor sensitivities are zero* (case of stock D): (a) APT stock's actual return equals the expected market return (i.e., 5.17%) and (b) the difference between the expected market return from APT and the expected stock return from CAPM is 1.28%: this equals the difference between APT stock's actual return and CAPM's expected stock return.
2. *When CAPM beta is 1.00* (case of stock E): The expected stock return (form CAPM) equals the expected market return (i.e., 5.17%). Hence, the difference between APT's expected market return and CAPM's expected stock return is zero.

Exhibit 12.14.1 Factor risk premia and sensitivity

	Growth	Interest	Market size	Inflation
Factor risk premium	2.00%	3.10%	0.60%	1.60%
Factor sensitivity (*bj*)	0.51	0.25	0.10	0.57

Exhibit 12.14.2 Factor sensitivity for each stock

Portfolio		Factor sensitivity (Beta)			
Stocks	**Weights**	**Growth**	**Interest**	**Market size**	**Inflation**
Stock A	0.2	0.12	1.13	0.30	0.44
Stock B	0.1	0.67	0.70	0.90	0.58
Stock C	0.4	1.00	1.00	1.00	1.00
Stock D	0.2	0.00	0.00	0.00	0.00
Stock E	0.1	0.18	0.86	0.50	0.22

Exhibit 12.14.3 APT vs. CAPM

	APT		CAPM	APT–CAPM	
	E(rj)	*rj*	*kej*	*E(rj) − kej*	*rj − kej*
Stock A	5.17%	8.03%	5.34%	−0.17%	2.69%
Stock B	5.17%	7.81%	5.28%	−0.11%	2.53%
Stock C	5.17%	8.57%	5.03%	0.14%	3.54%
Stock D	**5.17%**	**5.17%**	3.90%	**1.28%**	**1.28%**
Stock E	5.17%	7.64%	**5.17%**	**0.00%**	2.47%

Application and Limitations of the APT

As a security pricing model, the APT possesses several benefits. Compared to CAPM, the main benefit of APT is the allowance for multiple risk factors affecting security returns and provision of flexibility regarding the requirement about individual portfolios. Hence, APT can be applicable in portfolio construction to suit the specific needs of an investor in the world of arbitrageurs and vendors of information. Nevertheless, these benefits are diluted by several drawbacks. The main limiting factor of the APT is how to identify the risk factors—since they are not determined in a priory, they tend to differ among analysts. Statistically, the larger the number of factor sensitivities, the more statistical noise on estimations.

Bibliography

Anspach, D., & Wohlner, R., (2020). 20 Years of Stock Market Returns, by Calendar Year, Available at The Balance, https://www.thebalance.com/stock-market-returns-by-year-2388543, Accessed June 29, 2020.

Banz, R. W. (1981). The relationship between return and market value of common stocks. *Journal of Financial Economics*, 9 (1), 3-18, https://doi.org/10.1016/0304-405X(81)90018-0

Bahcel, T. (2020). Euro zone bond yields edge down as inflation turns negative, Available at Reuters, https://www.reuters.com/article/eurozone-bonds/update-2-euro-zone-bond-yields-edge-down-as-inflation-turns-negative-idUSL8N2FY30H, Accessed September 1, 2020.

Basu, S. (1977). Investment performance of common stocks in relation to their price-earnings ratios: a test of the efficient market hypothesis, *Journal of Finance*, 12 (3), 129-156, https://doi.org/10.2307/2326304

Bhandari, L. C. (1988). Debt/Equity ratio and expected common stock returns: empirical evidence. *Journal of Finance*, 43 (2), 507-528, https://doi.org/10.2307/2328473

Black, F. (1972). Capital market equilibrium with restricted borrowing. *The Journal of Business*, 45 (3), 444-455, https://doi.org/10.1086/295472

Butler, J. S. & Schachter, B. (1989), The investment decision: estimating risk and the risk adjusted discount rates, *Financial Management,* 18(4), 13-22, https://doi.org/10.2307/3665793

Caplinger, D. (2018), Negative-Beta Stocks: Worth Buying? Available at The Montley Fool, https://www.fool.com/how-to-invest/2012/12/12/negative-beta-stocks-worth-buying.aspx. Accessed October 9, 2020.

Chan, L. C., Yasushi, H., & Josef, L. (1991). Fundamentals and stock returns in Japan. *Journal of Finance*, 46 (5),1739–1789, https://doi.org/10.2307/2328571

Cherowbrier, J (2020). Average market risk premium (MRP) in the United Kingdom (UK) from 2011 to 2020, Available at Statista, https://www.statista.com/statistics/664833/average-market-risk-premium-united-kingdom/ Accessed April 20, 2020.

Cohen, K.J., G.A. Hawawini, S.F. Maier, R.A. Schwartz and D.K. Whitcomb, (1983), Estimating and Adjusting for the Intervalling-Effect Bias in Beta, *Management Science*, 29(1), 135-148, https://www.jstor.org/stable/2631171

Cooper, Ian (1996) Arithmetic versus Geometric mean estimators: Setting discount rates for capital budgeting, *European Financial Management, 2(2), 157-167*, https://doi.org/10.1111/j.1468-036X.1996.tb00036.x

Damodaran, Aswath (2015), Country Risk—Determinants, Measures and Implications—The 2015 Edition, available at https://papers.ssrn.com/sol3/papers.cfm?abstract_id=2630871

Damodaran, Aswath (2019a), Country Risk—Determinants, Measures and Implications—The 2019 Edition, available at https://papers.ssrn.com/sol3/papers.cfm?abstract_id=3427863

Damodaran, Aswath (2019b), Equity Risk Premiums (ERP): Determinants, Estimation and Implications—The 2019 Edition, available at https://papers.ssrn.com/sol3/papers.cfm?abstract_id=3378246

Damodaran, A. (2020), Data file, available at https://pages.stern.nyu.edu/%7Eadamodar/New_Home_Page/datafile/ctryprem.html

Dimson, E., (1979), Risk Measurement when Shares are Subject to infrequent Trading, *Journal of Financial Economics,* 7(2), 197-226, https://doi.org/10.1016/0304-405X(79)90013-8

Ernest & Young Global Limited (2015), Estimating risk-free rates for valuation, EYGL Limited, EYG No. DE0583, 1593372.indd (UK) 02/15.

Fama, E. F., & French, K. R. (1992). The Cross-section of expected stock returns. *Journal of Finance*, 47 (2),427- 465, https://doi.org/10.2307/2329112

Fama, E., & French, K. (1997). Industry costs of equity. *Journal of Financial Economics*, 43(2), 153–193, https://doi.org/10.1016/S0304-405X(96)00896-3

Fama, E. F., & French, K. R. (2004). The Capital Asset Pricing Model: theory and evidence. *Journal of Economic Perspectives*, 18 (3), 25–46, https://doi.org/10.1257/0895330042162430

French, K. R., Schwert, G. W. & Stambaugh, R. F. (1987), Expected Stock Returns and Volatility. *Journal of Financial Economics*, 19 (1), 3-29. https://doi.org/10.1016/0304-405X(87)90026-2

Friend, I., & Blume, M. (1970). Measurement of portfolio performance under uncertainty. *American Economic Review*, 60(4), 561–575, https://www.jstor.org/stable/pdf/1818402.pdf

Investment Week (2002). Equity risk premium for UK falling, Available at Investment Week, https://www.investmentweek.co.uk/investment-week/news/1394405/equity-risk-premium-uk-falling. Accessed February 11, 2022.

Kolbe, L. A., Read, J. A., and Hall, G. R. (1984), The cost of capital: Estimating the rate of return for public *utilities*, Cambridge Mass, MIT Press.

Lintner, J. (1965), Security Prices, Risk, and Maximal Gains from Diversification, *Journal of Finance*, 20 (4), 587-615, https://doi.org/10.2307/2977249

Markowitz, H. (1959), Portfolio Selection: Efficient Diversification and Investments, New York, John Wiley & Sons.

Mullins, D. W. (1982, January), *Does the Capital Asset Pricing Model Work?* Harvard Business Review, January 1982 issue, https://hbr.org/1982/01/does-the-capital-asset-pricing-model-work

Oh, S. (2020). Here's how record negative 'real yields' are driving a crowded rally in stocks, gold and everything else, Available at Market Watch, https://www.marketwatch.com/story/heres-how-record-negative-real-yields-are-driving-a-crowded-rally-in-stocks-gold-and-everything-else-11597062332, Accessed August 10, 2020.

Reilly, F., & Brown, K. (2003). Investment analysis portfolio management (7th Ed.). Thomson, South-Western.

Ross, S. A. (1976), The arbitrage theory of capital asset pricing, *Journal of Economic Theory*, 13(3), 341–360, https://doi.org/10.1016/0022-0531(76)90046-6

Royal J., & O'Shea, A. (2020). What Is the Average Stock Market Return? Available at Nerd Wallet, https://www.nerdwallet.com/blog/investing/average-stock-market-return/, Accessed May 11, 2020.

Santoli, M., (2017). The S&P 500 has already met its average return for a full year, but don't expect it to stay here, Available at CNBC, https://www.cnbc.com/2017/06/18/the-sp-500-has-already-met-its-average-return-for-a-full-year.html, Accessed June 18, 2017.

Sharpe, W. F. (1964), Capital Asset Prices: A Theory of Market Equilibrium under Conditions of Risk, *The Journal of Finance*, 19(3), 425-442. https://doi.org/10.1111/j.1540-6261.1964.tb02865.x

Streissguth, T., & Cockerham, R. (2019). Is a Negative Beta Coefficient More Risky Than a Positive in the Stock Market? Available at Zacks, https://finance.zacks.com/negative-beta-coefficient-risky-positive-stock-market-7596.html, Accessed March 31, 2019.

Williams, J.T. (1977), Capital Asset Prices with Heterogeneous Beliefs. *Journal of Financial Economics*, 5, 219-239. https://doi.org/10.1016/0304-405X(77)90019-8

Zaccardi, M. (2020). Ripple Effects Of Low Interest Rates, Available at Investng.com, https://www.investing.com/analysis/ripple-effects-of-low-interest-rates-200535632, Accessed August 28, 2020.

Zenner, M., Hill, S., Clark, J., & Mago, N. (2008), Most Important Number in Finance: The Quest for the Market Risk Premium, Available at JP Morgan. https://files.pca-cpa.org/pcadocs/bi-c/2.%20Canada/3.%20Exhibits/R-0735.PDF. Accessed May 3, 2022.

The Cost of Debt

Contents

Supplementary Information The online version contains supplementary material available at https://doi.org/10.1007/978-3-031-28267-6_13.

B. Kulwizira Lukanima, *Corporate Valuation*, Classroom Companion: Business, https://doi.org/10.1007/978-3-031-28267-6_13

13.1 Introduction

Debt is one of the key components of a firm's capital structure. Like equity holders, lenders (debtholders) are investors too because they inject funds into a business, expecting returns from their investments. This chapter is about estimating the cost of debt using different approaches. The concept of the cost of debt, therefore, is defined according to the estimation approach and valuation implications.

Specifically, this chapter uses three estimation approaches to explain the cost of debt, hereafter referred to as the effective interest rate (EIR) approach, the corporate default spread (CDS) approach, and the yield-to-maturity (YTM) approach. Special emphasis is placed on the practical applications and limitations of each approach.

Learning Outcomes

- Define the cost of debt capital.
- Understand the different concepts of and approaches to estimating the cost of debt.
- Estimate the cost of debt using the effective interest rate approach.
- Estimate the cost of dent using the default spread approach.
- Estimate the cost of debt using the yield-to-maturity approach.
- Explain the practical applications and limitations of each estimation approach.
- Decide the best approach for a specific company.

13.2 Understanding the Cost of Debt

A debt generally refers to a company's short- and long-term financial obligations, which typically comprise all interest-bearing liabilities (such as bonds, notes payable, and other types of debts) and lease obligations. Considering the effect of interest expenses on corporate tax, the cost of debt can be explained as pretax and after-tax cost of debt.

13.2.1 Pretax Cost of Debt

The pretax cost of debt is the rate of return paid on the debt-financed portion of a company's capital structure without considering the impact of corporate tax. It therefore describes the rate of return that debtholders receive from the company's overall debt but not what the company effectively incurs. ▶ Exhibit 13.1 summarizes the cost of debt concept and classifies the estimation approaches into three categories: the effective interest rate (EIR) approach, the corporate default spread (CDS) approach, and the yield-to-maturity (YTM) approach. Each of them can be used to estimate the pretax cost of debt depending on the specific circumstances of a company. The EIR approach is probably the simplest concept, considering the cost of debt as an interest rate (IR) effectively paid on current outstanding debt—

the estimated cost of debt is basically "actual." The CDS and YTM approaches capture expectations directly through analysis of default risk and market interest rates—the estimated cost of debt is "expected" rather than "actual." Further details on each approach are provided in the subsequent sections.

Exhibit 13.1 Cost of Debt Concept and Estimation Approaches

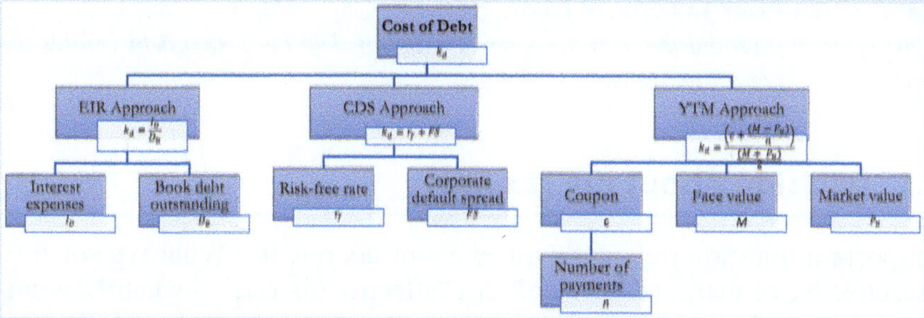

Estimation Variables

The EIR Approach: I_D is the current interest paid in total debt outstanding. D_B the current annual average of the total debt outstanding.

The CDS Approach: r_m is the risk-free interest rate, whereas *FS* is the corporate default spread.

The YTM Approach: *c* denotes bond coupon payments, whereas *n* represents the number of payment installments. *M* is the bond face value, whereas P_B is its trading market value.

Think 13.1

Why should we consider corporate income tax when estimating the cost of debt but not the cost of equity?

13.2.2 After-Tax Cost of Debt

To estimate weighted average cost of capital (WACC), the after-tax cost of debt, and not the pretax cost of debt, is used. This is because a debt creates tax savings due to interest tax deductibility, technically referred to as the "interest tax shield" (refer to ▶ Exhibit 11.3 in ▶ Chap. 11)—a firm with debts pays less taxes than that without debts. The implied effect of tax savings is to create a cash flow advantage to the firm and common equity holders, thereby generating additional value from the interest tax shield. Since the cost of capital is the discount rate used to estimate firm value, the after-tax cost of debt accounts for the value added from tax savings—the present value of interest-tax shield. Specific valuation applications of this concept are covered in ▶ Chaps. 15 and 16.

Overall, interest on debt reduces tax bills, thereby lowering the cost of debt by the corporate income tax rate, such that:

$$k_{dAT} = k_d\left(1 - T_c\right)$$

where r_d and r_{dAT} are the pre- and after-tax cost of debt, respectively. T_c is the corporate tax rate.

Banner 13.1 After-Tax Cost of Debt
Cost of capital estimation uses the after-tax cost of debt because a debt creates tax savings (i.e., interest tax shield).

13.2.3 Decision About the Tax Rate

An important question frequently asked about tax rate is: "What type of tax rate to use: effective or marginal tax rate?" An "effective tax rate" is what the company pays from all its income regardless of where they are generated, which is determined by simply dividing income tax by pretax income. A "marginal tax rate" is based on the statutory tax rate depending on the tax codes imposed by governments and thus differs across countries. Practically, the two types of tax rates tend to differ due to several reasons. For instance, an effective tax rate can be lower than a marginal tax rate due to operating losses, deferred taxes, and tax credits (or holidays). Moreover, companies with international operations can report lower or higher effective tax rates depending on the tax codes in foreign countries. Hence, for many companies, effective taxes are subject to periodical variations and never equal marginal taxes.

Banner 13.2 Effective or Marginal Tax Rate?
This is debatable. The tax rate should be decided by analyzing a company's expected tax profile.

Let use Amazon Inc. to clarify this point. Based on US statutory corporate tax, Amazon's marginal tax rate was 21% from 2019 to 2021, reduced from 24.5% in 2018 and 35% in 2017. These rates are higher than its effective tax rates: 12.6%, 11.8%, 17.0%, and 10.6% from 2021 backward to 2018, respectively—mainly from lower taxes paid outside the United States. The following quoted news insights from CNBC envisages a clearer picture regarding Amazon and other companies:

> » The current United States tax code allows some of the biggest company names in the country to not pay any federal corporate income tax. In fact, at least 55 of the largest corporations in America paid no federal corporate income taxes on their 2020 profits, according to the Institute on Taxation and Economic Policy. The companies include names like Whirlpool, FedEx, Nike, HP, and Salesforce (Miller 2022).
>
> The federal corporate tax rate is 21%, but as in the past, Amazon likely employed various tax credits and deductions to reduce its federal tax bill… The company also

came under fire for seeking huge tax incentives worth billions of dollars as part of its search for a second headquarters, or 'HQ2,' in 2018…In 2018, Amazon posted income of more than $11 billion, but the company paid $0 in federal taxes. In fact, thanks to tax credits and deductions, Amazon actually received a federal tax refund of $129 million. That was a year after Amazon received a $137 million refund from the federal government for 2017. (Huddleston 2020).

"So, which tax rate to use?" Analysts face a decision puzzle on which tax rate to apply. To unlock this puzzle, we need to reflect on two vital criteria. First, the purpose of the cost of capital is to discount future cash flows, and, therefore, the tax rate should reflect the future—it is more about expected tax rates rather than the type of tax rate. Second, the tax rate is deducted from the cost of debt to account for the interest tax shield, and, therefore, tax savings should be related to interest expenses and not other variables. A decision, therefore, should be made after careful analysis of a particular company's specific tax circumstances, considering its historical, current, and anticipated tax profiles. Some companies pay taxes that are relatively equal to the marginal tax rate—hence, a marginal tax rate can apply. However, some companies experience persistent significant differences between marginal and effective tax rates—thus, an effective tax rate can be sensibly applied. When the decision is to use an effective tax rate, it is vital to consider possible convergency to the marginal tax rate in the future because the causes of differences (like tax credits, incentives, losses, etc.) tend to be temporary—it is possible to allow the tax rate to vary from an effective rate now to a marginal rate at a later stage. Generally, an effective tax rate tends to be more realistic and practically reasonable.

► Exhibit 13.2 presents three cases (Amazon Inc., Ford Motor Co., and Ecopetrol SA) in which a decision to determine tax rate is required for each company. Overall, the decision can be straightforward in some cases but not always.

Exhibit 13.2 Decision About Tax Rate

Illustrative Cases: Amazon Inc., Ford Motor Co., Ecopetrol SA (See Excel Workings—► Chap. 13, Sheets E.13.2, D.13.1, D.13.2, and D.13.3)

Exhibits 13.2.1, 13.2.2, and 13.2.3 present three different cases in which an analyst has to decide on the tax rate. The three cases have international operations but are different in terms of actual tax payments compared to marginal tax rates.

Exhibit 13.2.1 Amazon Inc. (US$ millions, except rates)

Amazon	2021	2020	2019	2018
Pretax income	38,151	24,178	13,976	11,261
Income tax	4791	2863	2374	1197
Effective tax rate (Note 1)	12.6%	11.8%	17.0%	10.6%
Marginal tax rate	21.0%	21.0%	21.0%	24.5%

Exhibit 13.2.2 Ford Motor Co. (US$ millions, except rates)

Ford Motor	2021	2020	2019	2018
Pretax income (Note 2)	17,780	−1116	−640	4345
Income tax (Note 3)	−130	160	−724	650
Effective tax rate (Note 4)	−0.7%	−14.3%	113.1%	15.0%
Marginal tax rate	21.0%	21.0%	21.0%	24.5%

Exhibit 13.2.3 Ecopetrol SA (COP billions, except rates)

Ecopetrol	2021	2020	2019	2018
Pretax income	26,426	4777	19,724	26,426
Income tax	8795	2039	4718	8795
Effective tax rate (Note 5)	33.3%	42.7%	23.9%	40.1%
Marginal tax rate	31.0%	32.0%	33.0%	33.0%

Case of Amazon

Note 1: Historically and currently, Amazon has been paying taxes at lower effective tax rates than at marginal tax rates.

- *Question 1:* Which of the two rates (effective or marginal) is likely to persist in the future? Reasonably, effective tax rates will, at least soon.
- *Question 2:* Does the effective rate reflect the interest tax shield? Amazon's pretax earnings are positive; hence, the positive tax expenses reflect savings in interest expenses.
- *Decision*: The effective tax rate is practically sensible and hence applicable to reflect the reality of the company's tax profile soon. If a stage valuation model is applied, then it is reasonable to assume convergence to the marginal tax rate at a later stage.

Case of Ford Motor

Note 2: Historically, Ford Motor has experienced highly volatile pretax earnings, combining negative and positive performances. Negative pretax earnings simply imply no tax paid for that period (e.g., 2019 and 2020): an effective tax rate cannot be determined mathematically but reasonably—it should be 0%.

Note 3: Historically, Ford Motor's income tax profile has combined positive values (expenses) and negative values (benefits). In 2021 (current period), no tax was paid despite significant pretax income. In 2020, income tax was paid despite making a loss (negative pretax income). In 2019, negative pretax income was reflected in negative income tax (benefits). In 2018, positive income tax (expenses) reflected positive pretax income.

Note 4: In 2021, the negative tax rate (−0.7%) implied a tax advantage, but no tax was paid—the effective tax rate should be 0%. In 2020, the negative tax rate (−14.3) did not imply tax benefits because the company paid income taxes out of its operating loss, and, therefore, tax expenses had nothing to do with that period's income—the effective tax rate should be 0%. In 2019, the positive tax rate (113.1%) neither reflected the pretax income nor income tax because the company neither made pretax profits nor paid income tax—the effective tax rate should be 0%. In 2018, 15% was an effective tax rate related to income tax and pretax income.

- *Question 1:* Which of the two rates (effective or marginal) is likely to persist in the future? Reasonably, effective tax rates will, at least soon. However, the effective rate in this case is beyond mathematics because of no tax paid—it is simply 0%.
- *Question 2:* Does the effective rate reflect the interest tax shield? Based on reasoning rather than mathematics, the 0% effective tax rate makes sense—that is, there is no influence of interest expenses on tax benefits.
- *Decision*: The effective tax rate is practically sensible and hence applicable to reflect the reality of the company's tax profile soon. If a stage valuation model is applied, then it is reasonable to assume convergence to a marginal tax rate at a later stage.

Case of Ecopetrol

Note 5: Historically and currently, Ecopetrol has been paying taxes at effective tax rates relatively higher than marginal tax rates. The average effective tax rate is 35% (4-year) and 38% (2-year). The current effective and marginal tax rates are almost equal.

- *Question 1:* Which of the two rates (effective or marginal) is likely to persist in the future? Reasonably, both effective and marginal tax rates will.
- *Question 2:* Does the effective or marginal tax rate reflect the interest tax shield? Ecopetrol's pretax earnings, from which income tax is determined, are positive—that is, positive tax expenses reflect savings in interest expenses. The effective tax rate reflects the actual interest tax shield. Both the current effective and marginal rates reflect the expected interest tax shield.
- *Decision*: Both effective and marginal tax rates are practically sensible and hence applicable to reflect the reality of the company's tax profile soon. If a stage valuation model is applied, then it is reasonable to start with an effective tax rate, to be reach the marginal tax rate at a later stage.

13.3 Estimating the Cost of Debt

Estimating the cost of debt can be straightforward depending on the suitability of the estimation approach for a particular company. In this section, each approach is presented and illustrated with real case examples.

13.3.1 The Effective Interest Rate Approach

The concept behind the effective interest rate (EIR) approach is that the pretax cost of debt (k_d) can be captured from interest expenses relative to total debt outstanding, such that:

$$k_d = \frac{I_D}{D_B}$$

where I_D is the total amount of interest expenses in the current period and D_B is the total book value of debt outstanding. Clearly, this is the most simplified and commonly applied approach. Its simplicity is due to relying on historical financial data, which tend to be readily available without necessarily requiring further adjustments. For example, if a company paid US$120 million interest for the current year and the average total debt obligation is US$2.06 billion, then the pretax cost of debt is 5.83% (i.e., US$120 million divided by US$2.06 billion).

Consequently, two valuation issues arise. First, lenders provide funds and determine interest rates based on a profound analysis of the company's prospects and risks—hence, interest rates on debts are forward-looking. Second, interest expenses and book debt values are historical—hence, the estimated cost of debt seems backward-looking. A convergence point is that debt and interest should eventually be paid (lenders' expectations)—hence, the EIR approach is justifiable.

13

Think 13.2

How can you defend the use of the EIR approach to estimate the cost of debt despite relying upon historical data?

Practical case examples are presented in ▶ Exhibit 13.3. The estimation process is simple. First, interest expenses from the income statement are identified. Second, total debt from the balance sheet is determined. Third, the pretax cost of debt is calculated. Finally, the tax rate is determined and the after-tax cost of debt is calculated.

Banner 13.3 Effective Interest Rate Approach

EIR is the most applied approach due to its simplicity. It is based on historical data but is justifiable by lenders' expectations about a company's prospects.

Exhibit 13.3 Estimating the Cost of Deb: The EIR Approach

Illustrative Cases: Amazon Inc., Ford Motor Co., Ecopetrol SA (See Excel Workings—▶ Chap. 13, Sheets E.13.3, D.13.1, D.13.2, and D.13.3)

Exhibit 13.3.1 presents the financial and tax data of the three companies for 2021 (current year) and 2020. Exhibit 13.3.2 presents the calculations of pretax and after-tax cost of debt based on the EIR approach.

Note 1 (tax decision): The effective tax rate is used, in which 0% is applied for Ford Motor based on reasoning rather than mathematics (refer to ▶ Exhibit 13.2).

Note 2 (total debt): Depending on the company's debt portfolio, total debt should include any interest-bearing liabilities (short-term debts, current portion of long-term debts, and long-term debts) and any short- and long-term lease obligations (operating and capital).

Note 3: Total debt is applied as an average of the two most current years (2021 and 2020).

Note 4: Pretax is obtained by dividing the interest expenses of the most current year by the average total debt (Note 3).

Note 5: The effective tax rate is applied as a 2-year average to match the average total debt when calculating the pretax cost of debt.

Note 6: From Notes 4 and 5, the after-tax cost of debt is calculated as:

$$k_{dAT} = k_d \left(1 - T_c\right)$$

Exhibit 13.3.1 Financial data to apply the EIR approach (millions, except rates)

Variables	Amazon (US$)		Ford Motor (US$)		Ecopetrol SA (COP)	
	2021	**2020**	**2021**	**2020**	**2021**	**2020**
Interest expenses	1809	1647	1803	1649	4139	3257
Pretax income	38,151	24,178	17,780	−1116	26,426	4777
Income tax	4791	2863	−130	160	8795	2039
Effective tax rate (Note 1)	12.6%	11.8%	0.0%	0.0%	33.3%	42.7%
Marginal tax rate	21.0%	21.0%	21.0%	21.0%	31.0%	32.0%
Total debt (Note 2)	116,395	84,389	139,485	162,998	95,061	46,732

Exhibit 13.3.2 Cost of debt calculations: current period is 2021 (US$ millions, except rates)

	Amazon (US$)	**Ford Motor (US$)**	**Ecopetrol SA (COP)**
Interest expenses	1809	1803	4139
Total debt: 2-year average (Note 3)	100,392	151,242	70,896
Pretax cost of debt (Note 4)	1.8%	1.2%	5.8%
Tax rate: 2-year average (Note 5)	12.2%	0.0%	38.0%
After-tax cost of debt (Note 6)	1.6%	1.2%	3.6%

Apply 13.1

Objective: Estimate the cost of debt using the EIR approach.

Consider any two companies of your choice, one with international operations and the other with only domestic operations.

1. Collect data for estimating the pretax and after-tax cost of debt.
2. Analyze the company's tax profile, determine the tax rate, and calculate the cost of debt.

13.3.2 The Corporate Default Spread Approach

13

The corporate default spread (CDS) approach estimates the pretax cost of debt (k_d) as the sum of the risk-free rate (r_f) and a firm's default (risk) spread (*FS*), such that:

$$k_d = r_f + FS$$

Like the capital asset pricing model (CAPM) (to estimate the cost of equity), the CDS approach considers the risk-free interest rate as the minimum expected rate of return on debt (lenders' perspective)—hence, r_f should be the same as applied in CAPM. Then, the default spread (*FS*) is a risk premium on the firm's debt portfolio, depending on the company's overall credit rating. Hence, the cost of debt will differ across companies according to their differences in credit risk ratings and default spreads (also known as credit spread), which can be estimated as:

$$FS = DP(1 - RR)$$

where *DP* and *RR* denote default probability and recovery rate related to a particular company's credit rating, respectively. ▶ Exhibit 13.4 presents case examples using the same companies in ▶ Exhibit 13.3.

Banner 13.4 Corporate Default Spread Approach
The CDS approach considers the cost of debt as the rate of return that lenders expect from a risk-free investment adjusted for borrowers' specific default risk.

Exhibit 13.4 Estimating the Cost of Debt: The CDS Approach for Rated Companies

Case Examples: Amazon Inc., Ford Motor Co., Ecopetrol SA (See Excel Workings—▶ Chap. 13, Sheets E.13.4 and D.13.4)

Key steps to apply the CDS approach:
1. Collect data for determining the risk-free rate based on the company's domicile country.
2. Collect company data on credit rating and default spread.
3. Calculate the pretax and after-tax cost of debt.

Exhibit 13.4.1 contains information relating to the three companies and respective two countries (United States and Colombia) to calculate each company's cost of debt using the CDS approach as on 31 December 2021.

Solution:

Exhibit 13.4.2 presents the calculated cost of debt for each company and notes on workings.

W1 (risk-free rate): $r_f = GBY - GDS$. For example, a 10-year US government bond yield (GBY) is 1.51% and a government default spread with an Aaa rating is 0%. The risk-free rate is 1.51% (i.e., 1.51% – 0%).

W2 (pretax cost of debt): $k_d = r_f + FS$. For example, for Amazon, the risk-free rate is 1.51% and the corporate default spread (FS) is 0.9%: $k_d = 1.51\ \% + 0.9\ \% = 2.41\%$.

W3 (after-tax cost of debt): $k_{dAT} = k_d(1 - T_c)$. For example, for Amazon, the pretax cost of debt is 2.41% and the corporate tax rate is 12.2%: $r_{dAT} = 2.41\ \%\ (1 - 0.122) = 2.12\%$.

Exhibit 13.4.1 Data to apply the CDS approach

	Amazon	Ford Motor	Ecopetrol
Country	United States	United States	Colombia
Country credit rating	Aaa	Aaa	Baa2
10-Year bond yield (GBY)	1.51%	1.51%	8.12%
Government default spread (GDS)	0%	0%	1.62%
Company credit rating	AA–	BB+	BB+
Corporate default spread (*FS*)	0.9%	2.3%	2.3%
Corporate tax rate	12.2%	0.0%	38.0%

Exhibit 13.4.2 Cost of debt calculations

	Amazon	Ford Motor	Ecopetrol
Risk-free rate (r_f) (W1)	1.51%	1.51%	6.50%
Pretax cost of debt (W2)	2.41%	3.81%	8.80%
After-tax cost of debt (W3)	2.12%	3.81%	5.46%

Practical Considerations When Applying the CDS Approach: Rated Companies

A practical application of the CDS approach is limited to data availability and estimation methods. Overall, the following aspects should be considered regarding the two estimation variables: risk-free rate and corporate default spread.

13.3.2.1 Risk-Free Interest Rate

Details about determining the risk-free rate and related considerations have been discussed in ► Chap. 12 (CAPM estimation inputs). However, when estimating the cost of debt, it is recommended to aim at a long-term cost of debt. Therefore, it is more appropriate to use a yield of a long-term government bond (say 10-year) rather than short-term maturity (say months to a year).

Think 13.3

When determining the risk-free rate for the CDS approach, why is it not recommended to apply a government bond yield of short-term maturity?

13.3.2.2 Default Spreads for Rated Companies

13

A major constraint in the application of the CDS approach is the availability of data and estimation challenges (see Elton et al. 2001). To determine a firm's default spread, a credit rating is required: either from credit rating agencies or through synthetic rating. Among the useful sources of data are S&P Global Rating, Moody's, and FRED St. Louis Fed (for US companies). However, approaches to estimate default spreads tend to differ among analysts. Although when estimating default spreads, generally, the default risk is considered, only a fraction of it can be attributed to that risk because other factors also tend to contribute. For instance, the default probability of highly rated corporations (AAA quality) is low, and, therefore, their default spreads seem too large to be solely attributed to the default risk.

Moreover, credit ratings are subject to regular reviews and can differ across industries. They are susceptible to variations over time due to economic conditions—usually, higher spreads during bad economic conditions and lower spreads during good conditions.

Apply 13.2

Objective: Determine the default spread of a rated company.

Use companies in ► Apply 13.1 (if rated) or consider any two rated companies.

1. Obtain the company's credit ratings from any of the rating agencies (S&P, Moody's, or Fitch) and determine their default spreads.
2. Explain the challenges (if any) you encountered when implementing this task.

13.3.2.3 Default Spreads with Synthetic Rating

Synthetic rating is an alternative way to determine credit ratings, especially for companies unrated by credit rating agencies, such as private and small companies. The most applicable synthetic rating methods are (1) interest coverage (IC) and (2) Altman's Z-score.

The Interest Coverage Approach

An interest coverage ratio (refer to ► Chap. 8) can be used to estimate a company's default risk. The approach is basically straightforward. It requires calculating the interest cover and determining its appropriate credit rating and default spread. The respective credit rating becomes an approximate estimate of default spreads relating to rated companies with similar financial characteristics. Some analysts and valuation experts provide helpful default spread data for interest coverage. For example, Damodaran (2022) develops, maintains, and publicly shares typical ratings and default spreads for US-based companies, which can be modified and applied to non-US companies.

Exhibit 13.5 Estimating the Cost of Debt with Synthetic Rating: The Interest Coverage Approach

Case Examples: Amazon Inc., Ford Motor Co., Ecopetrol SA (See Excel Workings—► Chap. 13, Sheets E.13.5 and D.13.4).

This illustration utilizes interest coverage default ratings from Damodaran, which are based on US data (nonfinancial services). Modifications are required to apply the data for non-US companies like Ecopetrol. The following general steps can be used to determine the synthetic rating and estimate the cost of debt:

1. Collect the company's financial data to calculate the interest coverage.
2. Calculate the interest cover for the company.
3. Obtain the domicile country's interest rate for a non-US company and the US interest rate.
4. Determine the interest rate ratio by dividing the company's country interest rate by the US interest rate. The ratio is measured as the number of times, and is 1 for US-based companies.
5. Calculate the modified interest cover for a non-US company: divide the company's interest cover

(in step 2) by the interest rate ratio (in step 4).
6. Use the modified interest cover to determine the company's ratings and default spread (modified) based on a US-based synthetic rating scale.
7. Calculate the pretax cost of debt using the CDS approach.
8. Use an appropriate corporate tax rate to calculate the after-tax cost of debt.

Exhibit 13.5.1 contains information relating to the three companies and respective two countries (United States and Colombia) to estimate the cost of debt as on 31 December 2021. Calculations and estimated cost of debt are presented in Exhibit 13.5.2.

Solution:

W1: $r_f = GBY - GDS$. This is the same rate used in ▶ Exhibit 13.4.

W2: Interest coverage (IC) ratio = Earnings before interest and taxes (EBIT)/interest expenses. For example, for Ecopetrol, IC = COP 30,589/COP 4139 = 7.39 times.

W3: Country's interest rate (IR) ratio = Domicile's country rate/US rate. For example, for Ecopetrol, 3.00%/0.25% = 12 times.

W4: Interest coverage, modified = interest coverage/interest rate ratio. For example, for Ecopetrol, 7.39/12 = 0.62 times.

W5 and W6: Based on Damodaran's interest coverage default rating scale.

W7 (pretax cost of debt): $k_d = r_f + FS$. For example, for Amazon, the risk-free rate is 1.51% and the corporate default spread (FS) is 0.67%: $k_d = 1.51\,\% + 0.67\,\% = 2.18\%$.

W8 (after-tax cost of debt): $k_{dAT} = k_d(1 - T_c)$. For example, for Amazon, the pretax cost of debt is 2.18% and the corporate tax rate is 12.2%: $r_{dAT} = 2.18\,\%(1 - 0.122) = 1.91\,\%$.

Exhibit 13.5.1 Data to apply the CDS approach: synthetic rating with interest coverage

	Amazon	Ford Motor	Ecopetrol
Country	United States	United States	Colombia
Official interest rate (domicile country)	0.25%	0.25%	3.00%
Official interest rate (United States)	0.25%	0.25%	0.25%
EBIT (millions in local currency)	39,965	5033	30,589
Interest expenses (millions in local currency)	1809	1803	4139
Corporate tax rate	12.2%	0.0%	38.0%

13

Exhibit 13.5.2 Cost of debt calculations

	Amazon	Ford Motor	Ecopetrol
Risk-free rate (r_f) (W1)	1.51%	1.51%	6.50%
IC ratio (W2)	22.09	2.79	7.38
IR ratio: domicile/United States (W3)	1	1	12
IC ratio, modified (W4)	22.09	2.79	0.62
Synthetic credit rating (W5)	Aaa/AAA	B1/B+	C2/C
Corporate default spread, *FS* (W6)	0.67%	3.15%	10.76%
Pretax cost of debt (W7)	2.18%	4.66%	17.26%
After-tax cost of debt (W8)	1.91%	4.66%	10.70%

Practical Considerations When Applying the CDS Approach: Synthetic Rating with Interest Coverage

Using interest coverage to determine a company's credit rating is a basic way to quickly establish its default spread, but it has several limitations.

Rating Data: Although it is generally easy to obtain an interest coverage ratio from financial data, it is not the case for ratings and default spreads. Most of the ratings (e.g., Damodaran's) are based on US data and other developed markets, thereby limiting application for non-US companies and those from undeveloped countries. Although necessary adjustments can be made to suit other markets, accuracy can be easily compromised. ▶ Exhibit 13.6, for example, compares the cost of debt estimates from three approaches. While credit and synthetic rating estimates appear consistent for the US-based companies (Amazon and Ford Motor), a significant difference is evident for the non-US company (Ecopetrol).

Exhibit 13.6 Cost of Debt Using Different Approaches

Case Examples: Amazon Inc., Ford Motor Co., Ecopetrol SA (See ▶ Exhibits 13.3–13.5).

	Amazon	Ford Motor	Ecopetrol
EIR approach	1.6%	1.2%	3.6%
CDS approach: rated companies	2.12%	3.81%	5.46%
CDS approach: synthetic rating	1.91%	4.66%	10.70%

Realistic Value: The interest cover approach relies on the financial performance for a particular current period. Unlike credit rating agencies, this approach does not consider the outlook, a vital aspect of corporate valuation. To address this drawback, it may be appropriate to apply interest coverage as an historical average (say 5–10 years) or a normalized value.

Apply 13.3

Objective: Estimate the cost of debt using the default spread approach with the interest coverage ratio.

Use companies in ► Apply 13.2 (if rated) or consider any two (rated or unrated) companies.

1. Collect relevant data for estimating the interest coverage ratio for each company.
2. For non-US companies, collect relevant data to modify the interest coverage ratio.
3. Determine the synthetic ratings and default spread (use Damodaran's or any other acceptable scale).
4. Determine the cost of debt for each company.
5. Explain the challenges (if any) you encountered when implementing this task.

Altman's *Z*-Score

The aim of Altman's *Z*-score (hereafter referred to as a set of scores: *Z*-score, *Z'*-score, and *Z"*-score) is to estimate a score that can be compared with a particular credit rating for rated companies. The score was developed and published by Altman (1968) and advanced from time to time (Altman et al. 2017). The *Z*-score is a statistical measure applying multiple financial variables to determine the financial soundness of a company (see ► Exhibit 13.7).

13

Exhibit 13.7 Altman's *Z*-Score Approach

Altman's *Z*-scores are available in the following four categories: original score (*Z*-score) for US public manufacturing companies (PLCs), private companies' score (*Z'*-score) for US private manufacturing (PM) companies, nonmanufacturing (NM) score (*Z"*-score) for US companies, and nonmanufacturing f-score (*Z"*-score) for all companies (AC) companies in developed and emerging markets. These scores are summarized in ◘ Exhibit 13.7.1, and the respective credit risk categories are presented in ◘ Exhibit 13.7.2.

Exhibit 13.7.1 Altman's *Z*-scores

		Variable scores for company categories			
		PLC	PM	NM	AC
Variable	*Financial ratio*	*Z-score*	*Z'-score*	*Z''-score*	*Z''-score*
Constant		–	–	–	3.25
X_1	$\frac{Working\ capital}{Total\ assets}$	1.2	0.717	6.56	6.56
X_2	$\frac{Retained\ earnings}{Total\ assets}$	1.4	0.847	3.26	3.26
X_3	$\frac{EBIT}{Total\ assets}$	3.3	3.107	6.72	6.72
X_4	$\frac{Market\ value\ of\ equity}{Total\ liabilities}$	0.6			
	$\frac{Book\ value\ of\ equity}{Total\ liabilities}$		0.42	1.05	1.05
X_5	$\frac{Sales}{Total\ assets}$	0.999	0.998	-	-

Exhibit 13.7.2 Altman's creditworthy zones

Score category	Creditworthiness zones		
	Safe	Gray	Distress
Original: public manufacturing companies (Note 1)	$Z > 2.99$	$1.81 < Z < 2.99$	$Z < 1.81$
Private companies (Note 2)	$Z' > 2.9$	$1.23 < Z' < 2.9$	$Z' < 1.23$
Nonmanufacturing US companies (Note 3)	$Z'' > 2.6$	$1.1 < Z'' < 2.6$	$Z'' < 1.1$
Nonmanufacturing non-US companies (Note 4)	$Z'' > 2.6$	$1.1 < Z'' < 2.6$	$Z'' < 1.1$

Altman's Z-Score Variables

Working Capital to Total Assets: Working capital is calculated as a company's current assets minus its current liabilities. It measures a company's ability to meet its day-to-day (short-term) financial obligations. A positive working capital indicates that a company can meet its short-term obligations, whereas a negative working capital is an indication of liquidity problems that can lead to bankruptcy.

Retained Earnings to Total Assets: Retained earnings include beginning earnings and ending earnings of a company minus any dividend. The ratio measures the extent to which a company may rely on debts to finance its investments. The lower the ratio, the more a company's reliance on debts to fund its assets, thereby increasing the risk if financial distress or bankruptcy arises.

EBIT to Total Assets: EBIT denotes earnings before interest and taxes (operating income). The ratio measures a variation on ROA (return on assets), calculated as net income divided by total assets. This ratio assesses the efficiency of assets to generate income before interest and taxes.

Market Value of Equity to Total Liabilities: Market value can be determined from either market capitalization or calculated through multiplying share price by shares outstanding. The ratio measures how much a company's market value could decline before its liabilities exceed its assets. It indicates the ability to survive and investors' confidence over the company.

Sales to Total Assets: This ratio measures the efficiency of the assets to generate sales revenues (i.e., asset turnover). A high turnover is desirable, whereas a low or falling turnover sends a negative signal of possible failure to enhance the company's market share.

The scores are based on the following statistical equations:

- *Note 1* (original score): Z = 1.2X1 + 1.4X2 + 3.3X3 + 0.6X4 + 0.999X5
- Note 2 (private companies): Z′ = 0.717X1 + 0.847X2 + 3.107X3 + 0.420X4 + 0.998X5
- Note 3 (Nonmanufacturing US companies): Z″ = 6.56X1 + 3.26X2 + 6.72X3 + 1.05X4
- Note 4 (Nonmanufacturing companies—*developed and emerging markets*): $Z'' = 3.25 + 6.56X_1 + 3.26X_2 + 6.72X_3 + 1.05X_4$

13

Applying Altman's *Z*-scores generally involves the following key tasks: (1) obtaining the most current financial data of a respective company, (2) depending on the relevant *Z*-score model, calculating the relevant financial ratios presented, as suggested by Altman, and (3) applying the ratios to determine credit risk. To illustrate this point, ▶ Exhibit 13.8 uses the case of Ensco Plc as on 31 December 2016—the company was also rated B2 (Moody's).

Exhibit 13.8 Altman's *Z*-Score

Case Example: Ensco Plc. (See Excel Workings—▶ Chap. 13, Sheet E.13.8)

Ensco is incorporated in England. This company deals with the provision of grilling services in the oil industry globally—it is, therefore, a nonmanufacturing company. In this illustration, the company is categorized as nonmanufacturing (a non-US company) to determine the *Z*-score. The rating is estimated as on 31 December 2016.

Step 1: Collect data

Obtain financial data for the key Altman variables (see Exhibit 13.8.1). Share prices during the year 2016 were as follows: highest = US$16.10 and lowest = US$7.19. The closing price on 30 December 2016 = US$9.72. Common shares outstanding as of 31 December 2016 = 303.5 million. Hence, market capitalization = US$2950.02 million.

Step 2: Determine a relevant Z-score model and calculate ratios and respective scores.

Ensco is categorized as a nonmanufacturing (non-US) company in a developed economy. From the financial data in Exhibit 13.8.1, ratios are calculated and multiplied by respective *Z*-scores of the respective score model (AC), as presented in Exhibit 13.8.2. The overall *Z*-score is 6.63.

Step 3: Use Altman's Z-score table to establish a synthetic rating.

Using the *Z*-score model for nonmanufacturing companies, our estimated value of 6.63 is greater than 2.6: that is, $Z'' > 2.6$ is a safe ranking (unlikely to default).

Exhibit 13.8.1 Ensco's financial data as on 31 December 2016

Financial data	US$ (millions)
Sales	2776.4
EBIT	929.3
Interest expenses	228.8
Net income	890.2
Retained earnings	1864.1
Current assets	3279.3
Current liabilities	854.4
Total assets	14,374.5
Total liabilities	6123.9
Total equity (book value)	8250.6

Source: Bloomberg Terminal (2017)

Exhibit 13.8.2 Estimated Z-score for Ensco: a nonmanufacturing company

Variable	Z-score	Ratio	Score × ratio
Constant	3.25		*3.25*
X_1	6.56	16.87%	1.11
X_2	3.26	12.97%	0.42
X_3	6.72	6.46%	0.43
X_4	1.05	134.73%	1.41
Z-score total			6.63

Practical Considerations When Applying Altman's Z-Score

Practical Performance: The predictive power of Altman's Z-score is clear from practical evidence. The score is regarded as a useful tool for a quick check of the financial health of a company. The accuracy of the scores in predicting bankruptcy 2 years before an event was initially 72% (Altman 1968) but has since increased to 75–90% (Altman 2017).

Reviews and Updates: Altman's Z-score and the equivalent ratings are subject to reviews and updates from time to time. Applying outdated data may provide misleading estimates. Updates for Altman's Z-scores can be accessed from a dedicated online application (Z-score+).

Data Reliability: Altman's Z-score relies only on financial statement data, and, therefore, estimation accuracy depends on data availability, reliability, and accuracy.

13

Working Capital: Altman's Z-score uses working capital as a measure of a company's strength in a liquidity position: that is, the higher the working capital, the stronger the financial health of the company. This argument is ambiguous because high working could also imply an inefficient use of short-term financial resources. Moreover, the approach does not consider adjustment to address the issue of companies with a negative working capital.

New Developments: In an interview with Edward Altman, an analyst Larry Cao asked the following question: "Has the ranking changed from Z to Z?" The answer from Altman was "No, it has not changed, except that sales/total asset is no longer a factor in the revised Z-score model" (Cao 2016).

Banner 13.5 Altman's Z-Score

Altman's Z-score does not intend to provide a specific corporate credit rating but to indicate credit strength or weakness—predicting bankruptcy.

13.3.3 The Yield to Maturity Approach

Yield to maturity (YTM) is the return that an investor is expecting to receive by holding the bond to its redemption date. It is the rate at which the current market price of a bond is equated to the present value of the bond's coupon payments and par value. Consider the price of a bond as follows (refer to ► Chap. 4):

$$P_B = \sum_{t=1}^{n}\left[\frac{c}{\left(1+r_{YTM}\right)^t}\right] + \frac{M}{\left(1+r_{YTM}\right)^n}$$

where P_B is the market price of the bond, c is the fixed coupon payment, M is the par value, r_{YTM} is the yield to maturity to be estimated, and n is the number of interest payments. Working for r_{YTM} manually is not an easy task, but it has been simplified by computer applications. Nevertheless, the following formula can be used to determine an approximate value:

$$r_{YTM} = \frac{\left(c + \frac{\left(M - P_B\right)}{n}\right)}{\frac{\left(M + P_B\right)}{2}}$$

Typically, the YTM approach is more suitable for traded debts, especially straight corporate bonds. ► Exhibit 13.9 presents an illustration to calculate YTM.

Think 13.4

Under what circumstances is the YTM approach likely to be applicable to estimate the cost of debt?

Exhibit 13.9 Calculating the Cost of Debt: The Yield-to-Maturity Approach

Illustrative Example (See Excel Workings—► Chap. 13, Sheet E.13.9).

A company has \$400 million of total debt outstanding. The debt is based on a 6.5% fixed coupon bond with a face value of \$100.00, 10 years to maturity, and semiannual interest payments. It was issued under discount a year ago at \$98.25. It is currently trading at \$82.0. The corporate tax rate is 35%. Calculate the cost of debt.

Solution:

Let us use the following approximation formula.

$$r_{YTM} = \frac{\left(c + \frac{\left(M - P_B\right)}{n}\right)}{\frac{\left(M + P_B\right)}{2}}$$

where P_B is the market price of the bond (\$82), c is the coupon (\$6.5 annually = \$3.25 semiannually), M is the par value (\$100), and n is the number of interest payments (i.e., 10 years × 2 times = 20 installments).

$$r_{YTM} = \frac{\left(\$3.25 + \frac{\left(\$100 - \$82\right)}{20}\right)}{\frac{\left(\$100 + \$82\right)}{2}} = 4.56\%$$

Pretax cost of debt is the equivalent yield: Since, the corporate tax rate (35%) is annual, YTM should be annualized too to determine the equivalent yield by multiplying the semiannual yield (4.56%) by 2. For this case, it is 9.12%.

After-tax cost of debt: r_{dAT} = 9.12% (1 – 0.35) = 5.93%.

Practical Considerations When Applying the YTM Approach

From ▶ Exhibit 13.9, the YTM approach appears easy. The reality is different. It can be complicated because companies tend to have debt portfolios comprising not only a single bond but several bonds and untraded debts. To estimate a portfolio's YTM is a complex task, but it can be approximated using weighted average approaches based on (1) bond duration or (2) bond maturity, as illustrated below.

Banner 13.6 Yield-to-Maturity Approach
The YTM approach is more relevant for a traded debt portfolio but can be modified to include untraded debts.

13.3.3.1 The Duration Weighted Averaging (DWA) Approach

Bond duration is a measure of bond price sensitivity to a change in interest rates—it measures the interest rate risk: the higher the duration, the higher the risk, and vice versa. Technically, bond duration indicates time length (in years) an investment will recover bond price from the present value of expected cash inflows (coupon payments and face value)—that is, duration is the payback period. The longer the length, the more a bond's price will drop as interest rates rise. This section neither focuses on explaining the types of durations nor their calculations but instead focuses on estimating portfolio YTM. It works as follows:

13

$$r_{YTM_p} = \sum_{i=1}^{n} w_i r_{YTM_i}$$

where r_{YTMP} and r_{YTMi} represent portfolio and individual bond YTM, respectively, w_i is the duration weight of an individual bond i in the portfolio, and n is the number of bonds in the portfolio. To apply this approach, the general steps are as follows:

1. Determine YTM for each individual bond in a portfolio.
2. Determine the bond duration for each bond in the portfolio.
3. Use the bond duration to determine bond weightings.
4. Calculate weighted YTM for each bond.
5. Calculate weighted average YTM for the bond portfolio.

▶ Exhibit 13.10 presents an illustrative case of Ensco Plc as on 5 September 2017

Exhibit 13.10 Portfolio YTM: The Bond Duration Approach

Case Example: Ensco Plc. (See Excel Workings—▶ Chap. 13, Sheet E.13.10)

Exhibit 13.10.1 displays Ensco's debt profile as on 5 September 2017, comprising bonds and a bank loan. The loan is based on a bank's revolving loan facility worth US$1.2 billion till September 2022 (which can be increased up to US$1.5 billion). The interest rate on this loan facility is floating upon base rate (2.5%) or LIBOR plus an applicable margin of 3.5% per annum. The company's debt portfolio had an outstanding value of approximately US$5.27 billion.

Exhibit 13.10.1 Ensco's debt portfolio

Debt type	Issue date	Maturity date	Value (US$ millions)	Market price 09/05/2017	Coupon rate
Ensco 5.75%	09/29/14	10/01/44	1000.50	82.50	5.75%
Ensco 5.20%	03/12/15	03/15/25	669.30	74.25	5.20%
Ensco 3.00%	9/29/14	10/01/24	623.30	99.40	4.50%
Ensco 8.00%	01/09/17	01/31/24	332.00	95.75	8.00%
Ensco 4.70%	3/17/11	03/15/21	309.10	91.20	4.70%
Ensco 7.20%	11/25/97	11/15/27	150.00	95.00	7.20%
Ensco 144A 8.00%	07/12/16	01/31/24	0.85	98.20	3.00%
Ensco 8.5%	06/02/09	06/15/19	237.50	95.30	8.50%
Ensco 6.875%	08/06/10	08/15/20	450.90	93.50	6.88%
Ensco 7.875%	08/06/10	08/15/40	300.00	66.40	7.88%
Bank loan			1200.00		
Total			5273.45		

Sources: Bloomberg Terminal (2017)

Estimating Portfolio YTM

To estimate portfolio YTM based on duration weights, we exclude the bank loan facilities worth US$1.2 billion. Exhibit 13.10.2 presents calculations based on the following steps:

1. For each bond, YTM and durations have been estimated using the "Investopedia" online application. The total portfolio duration is the sum of all durations (i.e., 83.9).
2. To calculate the duration-based weights for each bond, divide the duration of an individual bond by the total portfolio duration. For example, for Ensco 5.75%, weight = 11.5/83.9 = 0.14 or 14%.
3. To calculate weighted YTM for each bond, multiply the bond's YTM by its duration weight. For example, for Ensco 5.75%, weighted YTM = 9.03% (0.14) = 1.24%.
4. To determine portfolio YTM, calculate the sum of duration weighted YTM: it is 7.73%.

Exhibit 13.10.2 Ensco's bond portfolio YTM

Bond type	YTM	Duration	Duration weights	Weighted YTM
Ensco 5.75%	9.03%	11.5	0.14	1.24%
Ensco 5.20%	7.78%	7.67	0.09	0.71%
Ensco 3.00%	8.75%	7.2	0.09	0.75%
Ensco 8.00%	8.12%	5.49	0.07	0.53%
Ensco 4.70%	5.26%	8.04	0.10	0.50%
Ensco 7.20%	7.98%	11.97	0.14	1.14%
Ensco 144A 8.00%	3.82%	6.35	0.08	0.29%
Ensco 8.5%	9.08%	6.86	0.08	0.74%
Ensco 6.875%	7.56%	7.32	0.09	0.66%
Ensco 7.875%	8.48%	11.5	0.14	1.16%
Portfolio total		83.9	1.00	7.73%

13

13.3.3.2 The Weighted Average Maturity (WAM) Approach

This approach uses weighted average maturity to determine a company's default spread based on the credit rating of its comparable bonds. The weights are derived from debt values such that:

$$M_p = \sum_{i=1}^{n} w_i M_i$$

where M_p and M_i represent portfolio and individual debt maturity, respectively, w_i is the value weight of an individual debt i in the portfolio, and n is the number of bonds in the portfolio.

This approach can be used to estimate the cost of debt through comparative analysis—that is, comparing credit ratings between a firm and other bonds of similar maturity. It works as follows:

1. Determine the firm's credit rating from rating agencies (if rated) or synthetic rating (if unrated).
2. Determine the average maturity of the firm's debt portfolio (M_p).
3. Determine the corporate default spread (*FS*) based on corporate debts with similar credit ratings and maturities.
4. Use the CDS approach ($k_d = r_f + FS$) to determine the average YTM of comparable debts, which becomes an approximated firm's cost of debt.

Unlike the DWA, this approach can be applicable even if a debt comprises bonds and untraded debts. ▶ Exhibit 13.11 presents an illustrative case of Ensco Plc.

Exhibit 13.11 Portfolio YTM: The Bond Maturity Approach

Case Example: Ensco Plc. (See Excel Workings—▶ Chap. 13, Sheet E.13.11)

Refer to ◘ Exhibit 13.10.1 regarding Ensco's debt profile as on 5 September 2017.

Estimating Portfolio YTM

In this approach, portfolio YTM is estimated from average maturity weights: hence, it includes the bank loan facilities facility worth US$1.2 billion commitment until 2022. ◘ Exhibit 13.11.1 presents debt data and calculated weights. The following steps are used to determine portfolio YTM:

1. Determine the firm's rating: the overall credit rating for Ensco (based on Moody's) was B2.
2. Determine the average maturity of the firm's debt portfolio (including the bank loan): (1) calculate the debt value weights through dividing the individual debt value by the total debt value (US$5273.45 million). For example, for Ensco 5.75%, it is US$1000.50 divided by US$5273.45 (weight = 0.19); (2) calculate the weighted average maturity through multiplying debt maturity by its value weight. For example, for Ensco 5.75%, it is 30 years times 0.19 (weighed maturity = 5.69 years); and (3), the portfolio weighted average maturity is the sum of all weighted maturities (approximately 14.06 years).
3. Determine the default spread of corporate debt with similar ratings: Ensco is rated B2, and, hence, comparable bonds with B2/B ratings and an average maturity of approximately 14 years are used. Based on various sources, B2/B-rated 10-year corporate bonds (approximately similar maturity) had a default spread of approximately 578 basis points (i.e., 5.78%).
4. Use the CDS approach to determine the average YTM of comparable debts: (1) determine the risk-free rate (it was 1.19% based on the UK 10-year government bond yield) and

(2) calculate portfolio YTM as a sum of the risk-free rate and the comparable corporate default spread (i.e., 1.19% + 5.78% = 6.77%.).

Ensco's estimated pretax cost of debt is presented in ◘ Exhibit 13.11.2. It should be noted that the DWA approach in ▶ Exhibit 13.10 does not include untraded debts (the bank loan). To include untraded debts in the DWA approach, the pretax cost of debt can be determined by applying value or maturity weights (see ◘ Exhibit 13.11.3). Overall, with the bank loan, the estimates from the DWA approach (7.16%) and the WAM approach (6.77%) differ but are consistent.

Notes: In ◘ Exhibit 13.11.3, portfolio YTM (7.73%) is based on the DWA approach (▶ Exhibit 13.10). The expected interest rate on bank loan (5.25%) is determined from the LIBOR forecast (1.75%) plus a margin of 3.50%. Maturity on the bank loan is determined from the company's projected debt commitment to 2022 (approximately 5 years). The average maturity on bond portfolio (16.72) is based on WAM value weights excluding the bank loan (◘ Exhibit 13.11.1). The pretax cost of debt can be calculated from both maturity and value weights, which is 7.157% and 7.164%, respectively (k_d is approximately 7.16%).

◘ **Exhibit 13.11.1** Ensco's debt portfolio data and weights

Debt type	Maturity (years)	Value (US$ millions)	With the bank loan		Without the bank loan	
			Value weight	Weighted average maturity	Value weight	Weighted average maturity
Ensco 5.75%	30	1000.50	0.19	5.69	0.25	7.37
Ensco 5.20%	10	669.30	0.13	1.27	0.16	1.64
Ensco 3.00%	9	623.30	0.12	1.06	0.15	1.38
Ensco 8.00%	7	332.00	0.06	0.44	0.08	0.57
Ensco 4.70%	10	309.10	0.06	0.59	0.08	0.76
Ensco 7.20%	30	150.00	0.03	0.85	0.04	1.10
Ensco 144A 8.00%	7	0.850	0.00	0.00	0.00	0.00
Ensco 8.5%	10	237.500	0.05	0.45	0.06	0.58
Ensco 6.875%	10	450.900	0.09	0.86	0.11	1.11
Ensco 7.875%	30	300.000	0.06	1.71	0.07	2.21
Bank loan	5	1200.000	0.23	1.14		
Total (excluding the bank loan)		4073.45				16.72
Total (with the bank loan)		5273.45		14.06		

13

Exhibit 13.11.2 Ensco's pretax cost of debt: the maturity approach

Estimation variables	Data and calculations
Risk-free rate (domicile country)	UK 10-year government bond yield = 1.19%
Corporate default spread for B2/B	Basis point spread = 578 (i.e., 5.58%)
Pretax cost of debt based on the CDS approach	$k_d = 1.19\% + 5.58\% = 6.77\%$

Exhibit 13.11.3 Ensco's pretax cost of debt: the duration approach

Debt type	YTM interest	Maturity (years)	Value (US$ millions)	Weight based on		Weighted YTM based on	
				Maturity	Value	Maturity	Value
Bond portfolio	7.73%	16.72	4073.45	0.74	0.77	5.95%	5.97%
Bank loan	5.25%	5	1200.00	0.26	0.23	1.21%	1.19%
Total		21.72	5273.45	1.00	1.00	7.16%	7.16%

Apply 13.4

Objective: Estimate the cost of debt using the YTM approach.

Use companies in ▶ Apply 13.2 or 13.3 or consider any two (rated or unrated) companies.

1. Collect relevant data to apply the bond duration approach.
2. Collect relevant data to apply the debt maturity approach.
3. Estimate the cost of debt for each company and compare the results of the two approaches.
4. Explain the challenges (if any) you encountered in implementing this task.

Think 13.5

If you were to recommend the most suitable approach to estimate the cost of debt, how would you respond? Why?

Review Questions

1. Explain the meaning of cost of debt and why it is different from interest rate?
2. Why should we consider corporate tax when estimating the cost of debt capital? Show an equation for the after-tax cost of debt.
3. What is the difference between effective and marginal tax rate? Which tax rate should be applied when estimating the cost of debt and why?
4. When estimating the cost of debt, why is the effective interest rate approach backward-looking?
5. What is the type and sources of information applicable for the effective interest rate approach?
6. Mention the main financial statement items to be considered or included when determining a company's total debt.
7. OPA company has just reported \$104 million interest and \$990 million total debt in its 2021 financial results (current period ended on 31 December). Its total debt as on 31 December 2020 was \$1500 million. The corporate tax rate was 32%. Calculate OPA's cost of debt.
8. The following information was extracted from the financial statements of two companies BIA and TAMU on 31 December 2021. Both companies are based in the same country where the statutory corporate tax rate is 28%.

	BIA ($ millions)		TAMU ($ millions)	
	2021	2020	2021	2020
Interest expenses	35	23	540	312
Pretax income	890	530	2004	1890
Income tax	245	198	812	268
Total debt	250	560	8903	7654

13

   (a) Calculate the pretax cost of debt for each company.
   (b) Determine the tax rate to be used for each company. Provide reasons to support your answer.
   (c) Calculate the after-tax cost of debt for each company.
9. What is corporate credit risk, and why is it important in the estimation of cost debt capital?
10. Explain the meaning of the following terms as applied in estimating the cost of debt:
    (a) Risk-free interest rate
    (b) Country default spread
    (c) Corporate default spread
11. When using the CDS approach to estimate the cost of debt, what factors would you consider in determining the following inputs:
    (a) Risk-free interest rate
    (b) Country default spread
    (c) Corporate default spread

12. DEF company is based in Tanzania: the appropriate risk-free rate is 8.07%. The company's default spread is 3.4% and corporate tax rate is 35%. Calculate the company's cost of debt capital.
13. F Co. is a Brazilian company financed by equity and debt. Its stocks are currently trading at the Sao Paulo Stock Exchange at BRL 2.5 with 5 million shares outstanding. The debt has an outstanding book value of BRL 10 million as on 31 December 2021: it was BRL 15 million at the year end of 2020. The income statements for the year end 31 December 2021 and 2020 indicate interest expenses of BRL 1.4 million and BRL 1.2 million, respectively. Income tax is currently 25%. The company is rated BBB with a corporate default spread of 1.7%. The Brazilian government's 10-year bond yield is currently at 11.90, whereas the sovereignty credit rating is Ba2 with a default spread of 2.56%.
    (a) Calculate the cost of debt using the EIR approach
    (b) Calculate the cost of debt using the CDS approach
14. Briefly explain the circumstances in which you would apply each of the following approaches for estimating the cost of debt:
    (a) YTM approach
    (b) CDS approach
    (c) EIR approach
15. Define the variables required to estimate the cost of debt under each of the following approaches and mention the respective sources of data:
    (a) YTM approach
    (b) CDS approach
    (c) EIR approach
16. ABC company has US$150 million of debt outstanding. This debt was raised from a 5.5% 5-year fixed coupon bond with a face value of US$100 and semi-annual interest payments. The current market price of the bond is US$102. The corporate tax rate is 38%. Calculate the after-tax cost of debt using the yield-to-maturity approach.
17. Four companies, A, B, C, and D, are based in the same country. The appropriate risk-free rate is 5.4%. The four companies pay corporate tax at the rate of 38%. Information about the companies' credit ratings and default spreads is provided below

Company	Rating	Default spread	Tax rate
A	AA	1.22%	38%
B	BB	3.71%	40%
C	B+	4.95%	25%
D	C	13.54%	32%

    (a) Calculate the cost of debt for each company.
    (b) What are the factors determining the cost of debt? Why do they differ across companies?

Bibliography

Altman, E. I. (1968). Financial Ratios, Discriminant Analysis and the Prediction of Corporate Bankruptcy. *The Journal of Finance*, 23(4), 589–609. https://doi.org/10.2307/2978933

Altman, E. I., Iwanicz-Drozdowska, M., Laitinen, E. K., and Suvas, A. (2017). Financial Distress Prediction in an International Context: A Review and Empirical Analysis of Altman's Z-Score Model, *Journal of International Financial Management and Accounting*, 28(2), 131–171, https://doi.org/10.1111/jifm.12053

Cao, L. (2016, February 14), The Altman Z-Score In Edward Altman's Own Words, Seeking Alpha. https://seekingalpha.com/article/3895266-altman-z-score-in-edward-altmans-own-words?

Damodaran, A., (2022 January), Ratings, Interest Coverage Ratios and Default Spread. https://pages.stern.nyu.edu/~adamodar/New_Home_Page/datafile/ratings.html

Dionne, G., Gauthier, G., Hammami, K., Maurice, M., & Simonato, J.-G. (2010). Default Risk in Corporate Yield Spreads. *Financial Management*, 39(2), 707–731. http://www.jstor.org/stable/40732454

Elton, E. J., Gruber, M. J., Agrawal, D., & Mann, C. (2001). Explaining the Rate Spread on Corporate Bonds. *The Journal of Finance*, 56(1), 247–277. http://www.jstor.org/stable/222468

Huddleston, T. (2020, February 4), *Amazon had to pay federal income taxes for the first time since 2016 — here's how much*, https://www.cnbc.com/2020/02/04/amazon-had-to-pay-federal-income-taxes-for-the-first-time-since-2016.html

Miller, A. (2022, April 14), How companies like Amazon, Nike and FedEx avoid paying federal taxes, https://www.cnbc.com/2022/04/14/how-companies-like-amazon-nike-and-fedex-avoid-paying-federal-taxes-.html

Intrinsic Valuation

Contents

Estimating Growth Rates

Contents

Supplementary Information The online version contains supplementary material available at https://doi.org/10.1007/978-3-031-28267-6_14.

B. Kulwizira Lukanima, *Corporate Valuation*, Classroom Companion: Business, https://doi.org/10.1007/978-3-031-28267-6_14

14.1 Introduction

Reflecting on ▶ Chap. 1, we know that intrinsic valuation is based on projected cash flows to determine firm value or equity value. To project cash flows, an expected growth rate is required. However, growth rate is probably the most complex to estimate compared to other valuation variables. There are several reasons for this: the existence of numerous estimation approaches based on different growth concepts, analysts' subjective decisions, which help determine an applicable growth rate, and the absence of an absolute growth rate for a particular company.

This chapter focuses on estimating growth rates, building on two growth concepts and approaches: historical growth and fundamental growth.

Learning Outcomes

- Understand growth concepts and assumptions.
- Understand growth estimation approaches.
- Estimate growth rate from historical extrapolation.
- Estimate growth rate from fundamentals.
- Address practical estimation challenges.
- Decide on the expected growth rate.

14.2 Growth Concept: The Past, Current, and Future

"What is corporate growth?" Let us consider the following quote from Ross Kernez, a Forbes council member:

> In the context of business economics, we can think of growth rate as an attempt to measure the overall growth of the company, or an attempt to measure a specific variable associated with growth (Kernez 2021).

From this quote, growth rate is a broad concept and not an absolute value—it is estimated from various approaches, which are illustrated in this chapter.

From valuation's point of view, the estimated growth rate should be forward-looking. However, forecasting methods typically rely on what is already known (historical performance), what is happening at present (current), and what is expected (future). Overall, growth rate estimation utilizes actual results (financial statements) to make projections (assumptions about the future).

Financial Information

In ▶ Chap. 5, financial statements are described as tools used to gauge a company's historical performance in a particular period. Cash flows (free cash flows and dividends) are derived from financial statements and supporting information. However, this information has a major valuation drawback—it is backward-looking.

■ **Assumptions**

To determine expected growth, a forward-looking picture should be depicted. Realistic assumptions help depict that picture—it should reflect known facts (both past and current), expectations (future), and other factors driving growth. Although financial statements, from which cash flows are determined, provide quantitative measures, they tend to be interpreted in conjunction with factors affecting a company's performance. Some of these factors are internal (company's own factors), whereas others are external (economic factors). Therefore, the basic consideration when estimating growth rates is to assume that historical growth or growth determinants will prevail in the future. However, other external factors should be considered. For example, from the following quote, expectations about the future of lithium-ion battery manufacturers are higher than historically ever seen:

» Lithium-Ion Battery Market to Witness High Growth Rate Of 11.5% due Increased Industrial Use... Exactitude Consultancy, the market research and consulting wing of Ameliorate Digital Consultancy Private Limited has completed and published the final copy of the detailed research report on the Lithium-Ion Battery Market...From 2020 to 2029, the global lithium-ion battery market is anticipated to expand at a CAGR of 11.5%. From USD 38 billion in 2020, it is anticipated to rise to over USD 101 billion by 2029...Everything from smartphones to power tools, electric automobiles to aerospace parts is powered by lithium ion batteries (Yahoo Finance, 2022).

Banner 14.1 Expected Growth

Expected growth is a function of backward-looking corporate performance and expectations about the future.

Think 14.1

Since financial statements are considered backward-looking, why should they form the basis for estimating the expected growth rate?

14.3 Growth Estimation Approaches

Several approaches to estimating growth rates exist, but they are based on two growth concepts: (1) "historical extrapolation" and (2) "fundamentals." One thing that these two have in common is they both rely on financial statement information ▶ (Exhibit 14.1).

Exhibit 14.1 Growth Estimation Approaches

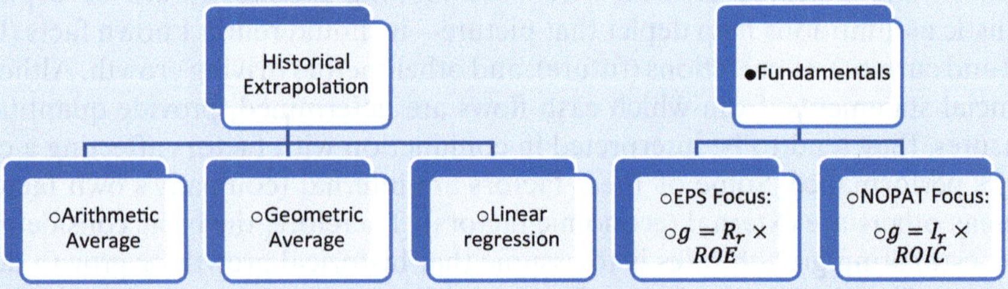

Estimation Variables

Historical Extrapolation: The expected growth rate (g) is the average of historical free cash flows (a direct approach) or proxies (an indirect approach).

Fundamentals: The expected growth rate (g) is estimated from growth determinants: return on investment (return on equity (ROE) or return on invested capital (ROIC)), retention ratio (R_r), or investment rate (I_r).

14.4 Historical Extrapolation

This approach involves calculating the historical growth of a company from financial statement variables (free cash flows, earnings, dividends, etc.). The main assumption is that the past growth fundamentals will persist and therefore the average historical growth will reflect future growth. The estimation process can be either direct or indirect depending on data availability and knowledge about cash flow drivers.

- **Direct Estimation**

Direct estimation first involves calculating free cash flows or obtaining cash dividend data (for dividend companies). Then, historical averages are estimated based on these free cash flows or dividends.

- **Indirect Estimation**

An indirect estimation involves using cash flow proxies—that is, financial performance items considered or assumed to drive or closely relate to free cash flows or dividends. The most applied proxies are earnings per share (EPS) (for free cash flow to equity (FCFE) and dividend growth) and earnings before interest, taxes, depreciation, and amortization (EBITDA) (for free cash flow to the firm (FCFF)).

Banner 14.2 Historical Extrapolation

Expected growth is estimated from observed historical growth, assuming that the past is a true reflection of the future.

14.4.1 Arithmetic and Geometric Averages

Average growth rates can be computed either arithmetically or geometrically based on historical extrapolation (refer to ▶ Chap. 12 for the two averaging concepts). There are no strict rules when it comes to choosing a sample historical period, but 5–10 years is generally suitable—it can also be somewhat more or less. ▶ Exhibit 14.2 presents an illustrative example, using dividend per share (DPS) and earnings per share (EPS). This example is simplified to avoid estimation challenges at this stage, but they are addressed in subsequent illustrative cases.

Exhibit 14.2 Historical Extrapolation: Arithmetic vs. Geometric Average

Illustrative Example (See Excel Workings—▶ Chap. 14, Sheet E.14.2)
This example shows how to determine growth rate based on historical extrapolation. The following key steps apply:

Step 1: Obtain historical data

◘ Exhibit 14.2.1 presents an example of a data sheet extracted from the financial reports of ABC Enterprises Ltd. for the most recent 6 years till 2016 (the current year).

◘ **Exhibit 14.2.1** Historical financial data of ABC Enterprises Ltd

Year	2011	2012	2013	2014	2015	2016
EPS (US$)	7.85	9.27	6.17	23.35	11.15	4.23
DPS (US$)	1.80	2.10	2.10	2.40	2.40	2.45

Step 2: Calculate the periodic growth or percentage changes

For annual data, it is the annual growth rate, such that:

$$\Delta D_t = \frac{D_t - D_{t-1}}{D_{t-1}} \times 100$$

where Δ denotes change and *D* is the financial variable (e.g., EPS, DPS, FCFE, FCFF, etc.) used in the current (t) and previous periods ($t - 1$). ◘ Exhibit 14.2.2 presents the calculated percentage changes. To calculate the geometric mean, negative values are avoided by adding 1 (or 100%) to each annual change.

◘ **Exhibit 14.2.2** Periodic growth rates (percentage changes)

Year	2011	2012	2013	2014	2015	2016
EPS growth		18.1%	−33.4%	278.4%	−52.2%	−62.1%
DPS growth		16.7%	0.0%	14.3%	0.0%	2.1%
EPS growth +1		118.1%	66.6%	378.4%	47.8%	37.9%
DPS growth +1		116.7%	100.0%	114.3%	100.0%	102.1%

Step 3: Calculate the average growth rate (g) for a sample period

In this example, three different samples are applied (5-year, 4-year, and 3-year). The average can be computed using either the "arithmetic" mean or the "geometric" mean (see Exhibit 14.2.3).

Exhibit 14.2.3 Average growth rates

Sample period	EPS growth		DPS growth	
	Arithmetic	Geometric	Arithmetic	Geometric
5 Years (2011–2016)	29.8%	−11.6%	6.6%	6.4%
4 Years (2012–2016)	32.7%	−17.8%	4.1%	3.9%
3 Years (2013–2016)	54.7%	−11.8%	5.5%	5.3%

14.4.2 Linear Regression

Linear regression can be used to estimate growth rate as a coefficient of the relationship between a financial variable (e.g., FCFE, FCFE, DPS, EPS, EBITDA, etc.) and a time trend. To determine dependent financial variables, original values or logarithmic values can be used. Like geometric averaging, this approach considers all observed data points in a sample period. The growth rate is, therefore, the estimated coefficient of linear regression, assuming continuous compounding. ▶ Exhibit 14.3 presents an illustrative example using the same data from ▶ Exhibit 14.2.

Exhibit 14.3 Historical Extrapolation: Linear Regression

Illustrative Example (See Excel Workings—▶ Chap. 14, Sheet E.14.3)

14

This example shows how to determine growth rate using linear regression with both original and log values (natural log and log10). The following key steps apply:

Step 1: Obtain historical data

See Exhibit 14.2.1.

Step 2: Generate dependent variables

These are financial variables like FCFE, FCFE, EPS, etc. They can be estimated as original values or transformed into natural log or log10 values using Excel functions (=LN) and (=Log10), respectively (see Exhibit 14.3.1).

Step 3: Determine the sample period and generate time trend values

The holding period determines the sample period in which periodic growth rates are estimated. For instance, a 6-year sample is required to estimate a 5-year growth rate, a 5-year sample is required to estimate a 4-year growth rate, and so on. Time trend values can be

Exhibit 14.3.1 Historical financial data of ABC Enterprises Ltd

Variables	Year	2011	2012	2013	2014	2015	2016
Dependent	EPS (US$)	7.85	9.27	6.17	23.35	11.15	4.23
	EPS log10	0.89	0.97	0.79	1.37	1.05	0.63
	EPS LN	2.06	2.23	1.82	3.15	2.41	1.44
	DPS (US$)	1.80	2.10	2.10	2.40	2.40	2.45
	DPS log10	0.26	0.32	0.32	0.38	0.38	0.39
	DPS LN	0.59	0.74	0.74	0.88	0.88	0.90
Independent	5-Year growth	0	1	2	3	4	5
	4-Year growth		0	1	2	3	4
	3-Year growth			0	1	2	3
	5-Year growth	1	2	3	4	5	6
	4-Year growth		1	2	3	4	5
	3-Year growth			1	2	3	4
	5-Year growth	*2011*	*2012*	*2013*	*2014*	*2015*	*2016*
	4-Year growth		*2012*	*2013*	*2014*	*2015*	*2016*
	3-Year growth			*2013*	*2014*	*2015*	*2016*

applied in three ways: (1) as original values like 2011, 2012, 2013, and so on; (2) as numbers from 0 (the initial period), increasing toward the current period; and (3) as numbers from 1 (the initial period), increasing toward the most current period (see Exhibit 14.3.1).

Step 4: Estimate regression

Run an ordinary least squares (OLS) regression of a dependent variable against the time trend (an independent variable) for a respective sample period. The general regression equation can be presented as:

$$Y_t = c + \alpha T + \varepsilon_t$$

where Y_t denotes the dependent variable, c is the constant, α is the coefficient to be estimated in the time trend (T), and ε_t is a random error term.

Step 5: Determine the growth rate (g)

Growth rate is determined from an estimated coefficient (α) depending on the estimation data as follows: (1) If the estimated coefficient (α) is based on a log10 value, then the growth rate is calculated as follows: $g = (10^{\alpha} - 1) \times 100$ (see Exhibit 14.3.2). (2) If the estimated coefficient (α) is based on a natural log (LN) value, then the growth rate is simply the estimated coefficient: $g = \alpha \times 100$ (see Exhibit 14.3.3). (3) If the estimated coefficient (α) is based on original values, then the growth rate can be determined by dividing the coefficient by the average of the original values (γ) in the sample period (an absolute value should be used if the average is negative): $g = (\alpha/\gamma) \times 100$ (see Exhibit 14.3.4). (4) If the estimated coefficient (α) is based on original values (but estimated with Excel's LOGEST function), then the growth rate is estimated by subtracting 1 from the estimated coefficient: $g = (\alpha - 1) \times 100$ (see Exhibit 14.3.5).

Notes: Growth variations are expected among estimation methods and variables: narrow variations for stable observations and wider variations for erratic observations. In this

Exhibit 14.3.2 Growth rates based on log10 values: $g = (10^{\alpha} - 1) \times 100$

Growth period and sample	EPS growth		DPS growth	
	Coefficient (α)	Growth rate	Coefficient (α)	Growth rate
5 Years (2011–2016)	−0.015	−3.4%	0.026	6.1%
4 Years (2012–2016)	−0.042	−9.3%	0.019	4.5%
3 Years (2013–2016)	−0.081	−17.1%	0.020	4.7%

Exhibit 14.3.3 Growth rates based on LN values: $g = \alpha \times 100$

Growth period and sample	EPS growth		DPS growth	
	Coefficient (α)	Growth rate	Coefficient (α)	Growth rate
5 Years (2011–2016)	−0.034	−3.4%	0.059	5.9%
4 Years (2012–2016)	−0.098	−9.8%	0.044	4.4%
3 Years (2013–2016)	−0.187	−18.7%	0.046	4.6%

14

Exhibit 14.3.4 Growth rates based on original values: $g = (\alpha/\gamma) \times 100$

Growth period	EPS growth			DPS growth		
	Coefficient (α)	Average (γ)	Growth rate	Coefficient (α)	Average (γ)	Growth rate
5 Years (2011–2016)	0.135	10.34	1.3%	0.127	2.21	5.8%
4 Years (2012–2016)	−0.510	10.83	−4.7%	0.100	2.29	4.4%
3 Years (2013–2016)	−1.802	11.23	−16.1%	0.105	2.34	4.5%

Exhibit 14.3.5 Growth rates based on original values (using the LOGEST function): $g = (\alpha - 1) \times 100$

Growth period and sample	EPS growth		DPS growth	
	Coefficient (α)	Growth rate	Coefficient (α)	Growth rate
5 Years (2011–2016)	0.966	−3.4%	1.061	6.1%
4 Years (2012–2016)	0.907	−9.3%	1.045	4.5%
3 Years (2013–2016)	0.829	−17.1%	1.047	4.7%

example, variations are narrow because both EPS and DPS are lowly volatile variables. It should be noted, however, that EPS growth estimates from original values vary significantly from those based on log values (logs tend to smoothen the variability of the observed variables). Hence, original values may not be suitable for highly volatile variables.

Think 14.2

Since different historical extrapolation methods produce different growth rates, which method should be used to decide about a suitable growth rate? Discuss.

14.4.3 Practical Considerations

Historical extrapolation is subject to estimation limitations and is sometimes inapplicable when certain technical conditions are not fulfilled. Illustrative cases are presented in ► Exhibit 14.5 to elaborate the common challenges and suggested solutions. Overall, the following issues should be considered: negative and zero values, abnormal values, historical patterns, sample period, and suitability of the estimation method.

Banner 14.3 Historical Extrapolation Challenges

Historical extrapolation should rely not only on mathematics but also on reasoning to make sense of the numbers and address estimation challenges.

- *Negative and Zero Values*: When variables include negative or zero values, percentage changes cannot be calculated using the generic formula presented in ► Exhibit 14.2 because the results will be meaningless and misleading (see ► Exhibit 14.4 for explanations).

Exhibit 14.4 Historical Extrapolation: Issues with Negative and Zero Values

Direction of value	Effect and clarifications
From 0 to 0	Any change from zero to zero is nothing: percentage change should be 0%. A generic formula produces an undefined result. For example, if DPS in 2021 and 2022 was \$0, then percentage change = (\$0 – \$0)/\$0 = undefined.
From 0 to +	Any change from zero (nothing) to any value (something) is a full change: percentage change should be 100%. However, according to the generic formula, percentage change is undefined. For example, Ecopetrol's DPS was \$0.16 and \$0 in 2017 and 2016, respectively: (\$0.16 – \$0)/\$0 = undefined. There is no problem when a change is from something to zero (i.e., current value = 0); it is a negative change by –100%. For example, in 2016, Ecopetrol's DPS was \$1.04: (\$0 – \$1.04)/\$1.04 = –100%.
From – to +	Any change from negative to positive is an increase, but the formula generates a negative percentage change. For example, Chevron's EPS in 2017 and 2016 was \$4.85 and \$–0.27: (\$4.85 – \$–0.27)/\$–0.27 = –1896%. There is no problem when the current value is negative: any change from positive to negative is a decline. For example, in 2015, Chevron's EPS was \$2.45: (\$–0.27 – \$2.45)/\$2.45 = –111%.
From – to – (small to big)	Any change from a smaller negative value to a bigger negative value is a decrease: percentage change should be negative and not positive from the formula. For example, if FCFF in 2021 and 2020 was \$–2.50 million and \$–2.0 million, respectively, then it decreased by \$–0.5 million. However (\$–2.5 – \$–2.0)/\$–2.0 = 25%.
From – to – (big to small)	Any change from a bigger negative value to a smaller negative value is an increase: percentage change should be positive and not negative from the formula. For example, if FCFF in 2021 and 2020 was \$–2.0 million and \$–2.5 million, respectively, then it increased by \$0.5 million. However (\$–2.0 – \$–2.5)/\$–2.5 = –20%.

Notes: The generic formula to calculate the periodic percentage change (presented in ▶ Exhibit 14.2) is only relevant when observed variables (e.g., FCFE, FCFF, EPS, DPS, etc.) do not include negative or zero values. Otherwise, custom formulas should be used (see Excel sheet 14.4).

14

- *Geometric Average and Log Regression:* To apply geometric average, negative and zero percentage changes should be eliminated by adding a common number (usually 1 or 100%). However, this problem cannot be solved when a negative percentage change is equal to or greater that –100%: otherwise, geometric averaging becomes redundant. To apply log values in regression, the observed values must be greater than 0 (neither negative nor zero): otherwise, regression can be performed with original values.
- *Abnormal Growth*: It is vital to identify any abnormal variables: extremely high or low values, which are unlikely to recur. When calculating average growth, these values tend to overweigh other observations, thus producing misleading results. Data should be carefully inspected before being applied to address any abnormality issues.

- *Historical Patterns*: The accuracy of historical extrapolation depends on the pattern of historical values: stable or erratic. Growth estimates can be misleading when patterns are erratic.
- *Sample Period*: There are no strict rules when it comes to determining a sample period for historical extrapolation, but sample selection can cause variations in the average growth rate. The magnitude of variations tends to be high for erratic patterns.
- *Suitability:* Based on points 1–5 above, historical extrapolation can be suitable in some but not every situation.
- *Arithmetic vs. Geometric Average:* Statistically, arithmetic mean tends to be misleading when the observed variables include outliers (abnormal values). Geometric mean tends to minimize the effect of abnormality by capturing the compounding effect of growth from one period to another. The greater the variability in the observed values, the greater the difference between arithmetic and geometric averages.

Exhibit 14.5 Historical Extrapolation: Estimation Challenges and Suggested Solutions

Illustrative Cases: Chevron Corp., Ecopetrol, and Boeing (See Excel Workings—▸ Chap. 14, Sheet E.14.5A–D)

▪ Exhibit 14.5.1 presents historical EPS and DPS data for Chevron, Ecopetrol, and Boeing to illustrate the practical challenges of historical extrapolation—the same clarifications apply to any other variables like FCFF and FCFE.

▪ Exhibit 14.5.2 plots EPS and DPS for a quick eyeball of trends over time to explain the possible limitations of historical extrapolation. Boeing experienced a stable upward trend on both EPS and DPS—we should expect historical extrapolation to be suitable. The same applies to Chevron's DPS (stable growth) but not EPS (erratic pattern).

▪ **Exhibit 14.5.1** Chevron, Ecopetrol, and Boeing: historical EPS and DPS

Company	Variable	2018	2017	2016	2015	2014	2013	2012
Chevron	EPS (US$)	7.81	4.88	−0.27	2.46	10.21	11.18	13.42
	DPS (US$)	4.48	4.32	4.29	4.28	4.21	3.90	3.51
Ecopetrol	EPS (US$)	0.10	0.05	0.01	−0.04	0.07	0.17	0.20
	DPS (US$)	0.03	0.03	0.01	0.00	0.13	0.16	0.17
Boeing	EPS (US$)	18.05	14.03	7.92	7.52	7.47	6.03	5.15
	DPS (US$)	7.19	5.97	4.69	3.64	2.92	2.19	1.81

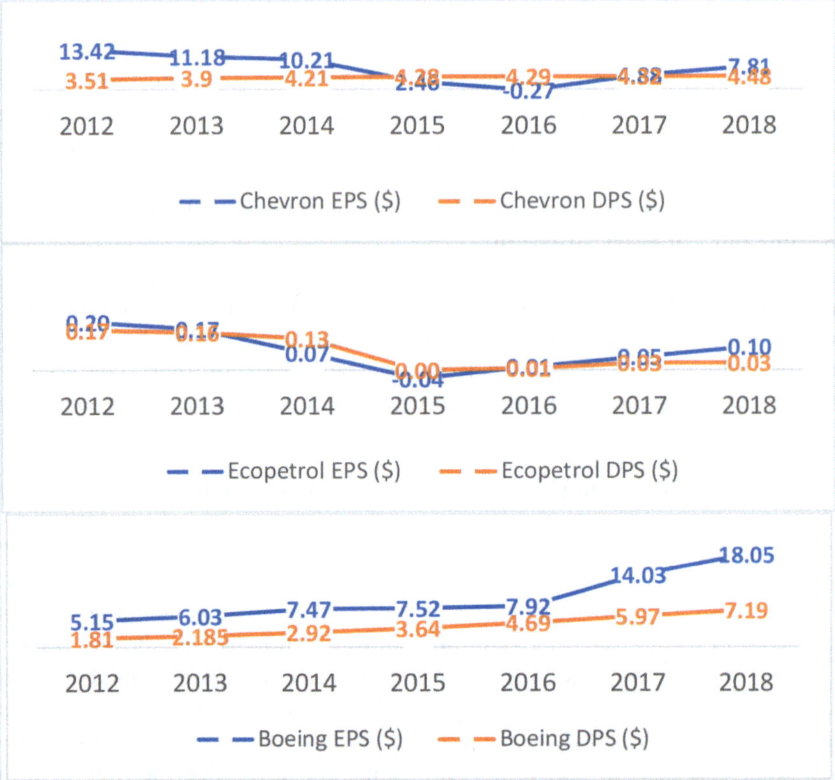

Exhibit 14.5.2 EPS and DPS patterns

Ecopetrol experienced erratic patterns on both EPS and DPS. With erratic values, historical extrapolation should be applied with a careful selection of the sample period to avoid significant variability of values. Details about possible challenges are explained below.

Estimation Challenges

1. *Negative and Zero Values:* The following are typical practical issues related to negative and zero values.
   (a) *Misleading Percentage Changes:* The generic formula to calculate percentage change, $\Delta D_t = \frac{D_t - D_{t-1}}{D_{t-1}} \times 100$, is misleading. For example, using this formula, Chevron's EPS in 2016 ($–0.27) would have shown a negative growth rate for 2017, whereas EPS would have increased to $4.88. The same applies to Ecopetrol's EPS in 2015 ($–0.04) for the 2016 percentage change. Ecopetrol's DPS in 2015 ($0) would have generated an undefined growth rate for 2016: it should have been 100%. Exhibit 14.5.3 presents the annual percentage changes based on custom formulas to address negative and zero values (refer to Excel workings).

(b) *Geometric Average:* To use geometric averaging, negative and zero percentage changes tend to be removed by adding 1 or 100% to each percentage value. However, this works only if the negative value is not equal to or greater than −100%. For example, Chevron's and Ecopetrol's EPS growth rates in 2016 and 2015 were −111.0% and −151.1%, respectively, and Ecopetrol's DPS growth in 2015 was −100%: in these situations, geometric averaging is inapplicable.

(c) *Log-Linear Regression*: Negative and zero values cannot be transformed into log values. This applies to Chevron's EPS in 2016 ($−0.27) and Ecopetrol's EPS in 2015 ($−1.4) and DPS in 2016 ($0). Regression for these cases is applicable with original values (see Exhibit 14.5.4). Log regression is applicable for Chevron's DPS and Boeing's EPS and DPS (see Exhibit 14.5.5).

2. *Abnormal Growth*: A percentage change can be regarded as abnormal if it is too high or low relative to other historical growth rates. For example, in Exhibit 14.5.3, Chevron's EPS in 2017 (1907.4%) is too high compared to other values: its effect is reflected in abnormally high growth rates, especially with arithmetic average, which can be misleading (see Exhibit 14.5.4).
3. *Historical Patterns*: Historical values can either be stable or erratic. From Exhibit 14.5.2, it is easy to identify a stable pattern on Boeing (EPS and DPS) and Chevron (DPS). However, Chevron (EPS) and Ecopetrol (EPS and DPS) are erratic—they change direction from downward to upward trends. Growth rate estimates from erratic patterns tend to be misleading.
4. *Sensitivity to the Sample Period*: Sensitivity of growth rate estimates to change in the sample period is a quick way to determine whether they can predict future growth: low sensitivity is preferable. Erratic patterns (point 3 above) tend to cause high sensitivity (see Exhibits 14.5.4 and 14.5.5). Sample periods vary

Exhibit 14.5.3 Percentage changes: historical EPS and DPS

Company	Variable	2018	2017	2016	2015	2014	2013
Chevron	EPS (US$)	60.0%	1907.4%	−111.0%	−75.9%	−8.7%	−16.7%
	DPS (US$)	3.7%	0.7%	0.2%	1.7%	7.9%	11.1%
Ecopetrol	EPS (US$)	74.5%	336.8%	135.0%	−151.1%	−59.1%	−14.7%
	DPS (US$)	0.0%	297.4%	100.0%	−100.0%	−16.3%	-6.7%
Boeing	EPS (US$)	28.7%	77.1%	5.3%	0.7%	23.9%	17.1%
	DPS (US$)	20.4%	27.3%	28.8%	24.7%	33.6%	20.7%

Exhibit 14.5.4 EPS growth estimates: arithmetic, geometric, and regression

Sample	Chevron EPS			Ecopetrol EPS			Boeing EPS		
	ARITH	GEOM[a]	REGR[b]	ARITH	GEOM[a]	REGR[b]	ARITH	GEOM[c]	REGR[b]
6-Year	292.5%	NA	−20.1%	53.6%	NA	−26.6%	25.5%	23.2%	20.8%
5-Year	354.4%	NA	−16.8%	67.2%	NA	−17.5%	27.1%	24.5%	22.5%
4-Year	445.1%	NA	−4.7%	98.8%	NA	36.0%	27.9%	24.7%	25.2%
3-Year	618.8%	NA	57.0%	182.1%	161.7%	137.4%	37.0%	33.9%	31.7%
Sample	**Chevron DPS**			**Ecopetrol DPS**			**Boeing DPS**		
	ARITH	GEOM[c]	REGR[b]	ARITH	GEOM[a]	REGR[b]	ARITH	GEOM[c]	REGR[b]
6-Year	4.2%	4.2%	3.3%	45.7%	NA	−37.6%	25.9%	25.8%	22.4%
5-Year	2.8%	2.8%	2.2%	56.2%	NA	−44.6%	27.0%	26.9%	22.7%
4-Year	1.6%	1.6%	1.3%	74.3%	NA	−42.9%	25.3%	25.3%	22.3%
3-Year	1.5%	1.5%	1.5%	132.5%	99.6%	66.6%	25.5%	25.5%	22.2%

[a] Geometric average is inapplicable because negative percentage changes cannot be adjusted to positive by adding 1 or 100% throughout

[b] Regression is based on original values

[c] Negative percentage changes were adjusted by adding 100% throughout, which was then subtracted from the geometric average. For example, Boeing's 6-year EPS geometric average was 123%%: subtracting 100% gives 23.0%

Exhibit 14.5.5 EPS and DPS growth estimates: regression (log values)

Sample	Chevron DPS			Boeing EPS			Boeing DPS		
	Log10	**LN**	**LOGEST**	**Log10**	**LN**	**LOGEST**	**Log10**	**LN**	**LOGEST**
6-Year	3.7%	3.7%	3.7%	22.3%	20.1%	22.3%	26.7%	23.6%	26.7%
5-Year	−1.7%	−1.7%	−1.7%	23.7%	21.3%	23.7%	27.4%	24.2%	27.4%
4-Year	−4.1%	−4.2%	−4.1%	25.6%	22.8%	25.6%	24.0%	21.5%	24.0%
3-Year	−6.7%	−7.0%	−6.7%	32.9%	28.5%	32.9%	24.1%	21.6%	24.1%

Notes: LOGEST is an alternative Excel function to estimate log10: the estimates are the same. LN denotes natural log. There is no log-linear regression for Chevron's EPS and Ecopetrol's EPS and DPS because of negative or zero values

from 4 to 7 years to allow 3–6-year growth estimations. Boeing's estimates are almost insensitive to variations in samples, but high sensitivity is vivid for Chevron's and Ecopetrol's variables.

5. *Selection of the Sample Period*: To determine a good sample, without compromising sample size, several factors can be considered, including the following.
   (a) *A significant shift in pattern or direction*: A sample can be truncated from the shift point if we can expect the same trend in the future. For example, Chevron's EPS shows a direction change from 2016. Similarly, there is a noticeable shift in Ecopetrol's EPS and DPS from 2015.
   (b) *Abnormal percentage change*: Any abnormal growth rate that significantly overpowers other periods' growth rates should be avoided. For example, Chevron's EPS growth estimates are extremely high only because of an extremely high percentage change in 2017 (1907.4%). Otherwise, negative percentage changes were dominant until 2016 (see Exhibits 14.5.3 and 14.5.4).
6. *Variation Between Approaches*: As indicated in Exhibits 14.5.4 and 14.5.5, there are always variations between different estimation approaches (arithmetic, geometric, and regression) and between methods in the same approach (e.g., regression with log10, natural log, and original values). The greater the variation, the higher the possibility that the estimated growth rates can be misleading: it is difficult to tell what the growth rate is as in the cases of Chevron's EPS growth rates and Ecopetrol's EPS and DPS both. There is no problem regarding Boeing's estimates because variations are almost negligible.
7. *Suitability:* From the six points above, historical extrapolation can be suitable in some but not every situation.
   (a) On Boeing's EPS and DPS, sample variations keep average growth rates stable regardless of the sample period and estimation approach: historical estimates can be considered forward-looking and suitable.
   (b) On Chevron's EPS, a decision about growth cannot be easily reached: the estimates can be misleading. In contrast, DPS growth rates are consistent across estimation approaches and within the same sample period—historical extrapolation is suitable.
   (c) On Ecopetrol, a decision on both EPS and DPS growth estimates is difficult due to significant variations between the approaches and across the sample periods.

14

Think 14.3

In linear regression, is there any advantage of using logs over original values? Discuss.

Apply 14.1

Objective: Estimate expected growth rate using historical extrapolation.

Choose any two companies to estimate growth based on any of the following variables: EPS, DPS, FCFF, or FCFE.

1. Collect relevant historical data for at least 6 years.
2. Calculate growth rates based on the following methods (vary your sample periods to a minimum of 3 years):
   (a) Arithmetic and geometric averages.
   (b) Regression with original values.
   (c) Regression with logs where appliable (log10 and LN).
3. Compare and contrast estimates from the different methods and comment on their suitability.
4. Explain estimation challenges (if any) and suggested solutions.

14.5 The Fundamentals

Unlike historical extrapolation approaches, estimating growth from fundamentals is not based on historical events. Instead, growth is expected to come from fundamental determinants: the rate at which earnings are reinvested and returns are generated from investments (both existing and new). That is, when a firm plows back its earnings for reinvestment, and, when such investments produce positive returns, growth should accelerate. Although various growth determinants can be used (e.g., revenues, net income, operating, and equity), the most relevant are EPS and operating earnings—EPS growth is more relevant for equity valuation, whereas operating growth applies to firm valuation. These two aspects are explained and illustrated in this section.

Banner 14.4 Fundamental Growth

Expected growth is estimated from fundamental growth determinants—the rate at which earnings are reinvested and returns are generated from investments.

14.5.1 Equity Value Determinants

The ability of a firm to increase owners' equity is reflected in net income or EAC (earnings available to common shareholders) or EPS (considering the number of common shares outstanding). Depending on dividend policy, companies can use EAC to pay dividends (not mandatory) and retain the rest (addition to owners' equity). If retained earnings are effectively reinvested, then they should generate more earnings in future to accelerate growth. EPS growth rate can be explained through two concepts: (1) internal growth rate (IGR) and (2) sustainable growth rate (SGR).

Banner 14.5 IGR vs. SGR

IGR is growth that is solely driven by internal funding: the rate at which a business can grow with only existing resources.

SGR is growth driven by both internal and external funding: the rate at which a business can grow in its life cycle.

IGR is the maximum rate at which growth can be achieved by only relying on internal funding (i.e., reinvested retained earnings)—if new investments are not financed by external funds (e.g., issue of new equity or debt). Thus, IGR is expressed as growth of EPS (g_{EPS}) as follows:

$$g_{\text{IRG}} = g_{\text{EPS}} = R_r \times \text{ROA}$$

where R_r is the retention ratio (i.e., plowback) and ROA is the return on assets. The retention ratio is based on a company' dividend policy, such that $R_r = (\text{EPS} - \text{DPS})/\text{EPS}$. This can also be expressed as $R_r = 1 - P_r$, where P_r is the payout ratio, such that $P_r = \text{DPS}/\text{EPS}$. The concept is that ROA measures an asset's ability to generate net earnings, which can be reinvested to generate the same ROA (on "unlevered assets").

SGR, on the other hand, is driven by both internal and external funding (a new issue of debt), assuming a constant capital structure. That is, a new issue of debt will not affect the leverage ratio because equity should also increase as retained earnings increase. For instance, to fund a $2 investment, a company issues $1 debt, whereas $1 of retained earnings increases equity by the same amount to maintain the same leverage ratio. Thus, SGR is expressed as the growth of EPS (g_{EPS}) as follows:

$$g_{\text{SRG}} = g_{\text{EPS}} = R_r \times \text{ROE}$$

where ROE is the return on equity, which measures the ability of "levered assets" to generate net earnings and be reinvested to generate the same ROE. If the payout ratio is constant, then dividends should grow faster than earnings. Moreover, if the growth rate is constant, and a firm pays a fixed rate of earnings as dividends, then both the earnings and dividends should grow at the same rate.

14

For a profitable company, SGR (with levered assets) should be greater than IGR (with unlevered assets). Hence, SGR is considered a more realistic growth rate and a good proxy for dividend or FCFE growth. ▶ Exhibit 14.6 clarifies the two growth concepts—growth in ABC Company is internally driven (IGR), whereas XYZ Company is both internally and externally funded (SGR).

Exhibit 14.6 IGR vs. SGR

Illustrative Examples: ABC and XYZ (See Excel Workings—▶ Chap. 14, Sheet E.14.6)

This illustration compares two situations: (1) ABC Company growing with internal funding and (2) XYZ Company growing with both internal and external funding.

▪ Exhibits 14.6.1 and 14.6.2 present their respective historical financial data.

Exhibit 14.6.1 ABC Company: IGR ($ millions, except rates)

Financials	Section	Variable	2021	2020	2019	2018	2017
Balance sheet	Assets	Total assets	606	558	514	472	432
	Liabilities	Total debt	190	190	190	190	190
		Other liabilities	312	289	282	260	214
	Equity	Common equity	210	210	210	210	210
		Retained earnings	206	158	114	72	32
Income statement		Revenues	520	490	440	402	386
		Net income	80	74	70	66	54
Dividend policy		Dividends	32	30	28	26	22
		Retained earnings	48	44	42	40	32
Ratios		Retention ratio (R_r)	60.0%	60.0%	60.0%	60.0%	60.0%
		ROA	13.7%	13.8%	14.2%	14.6%	
		ROE	19.2%	18.9%	20.2%	21.8%	
		Debt/equity	45.6%	51.6%	58.6%	67.4%	78.4%
		Debt/asset	31.3%	34.0%	37.0%	40.3%	43.9%
Growth rate		IGR (EPS)	8.2%	8.3%	8.5%	8.8%	
		SGR (EPS)	11.5%	11.3%	12.1%	13.1%	

Exhibit 14.6.2 XYZ Company: SGR ($ millions, except rates)

Financials	Section	Variable	2021	2020	2019	2018	2017
Balance sheet	Assets	Total assets	650	548	523	509	432
	Liabilities	Total debt	286	241	230	224	190
		Other liabilities	401	397	365	286	280
	Equity	Common equity	210	210	210	210	210
		Retained earnings	155	97	83	75	32

(continued)

Exhibit 14.6.2 (continued)

Financials	Section	Variable	2021	2020	2019	2018	2017
Income statement		Revenues	880	850	796	720	610
		Net income	102	98	92	89	70
Dividend policy		Dividends	44	84	85	46	38
		Retained earnings	58	14	8	43	32
Ratios		Retention ratio (R_r)	56.9%	14.3%	8.2%	48.3%	46.3%
		ROA	17.0%	18.3%	17.8%	18.9%	
		ROE	28.0%	29.2%	30.7%	30.8%	
		Debt/equity	78.4%	78.5%	78.5%	78.5%	78.4%
		Debt/asset	44.0%	44.0%	44.0%	44.0%	43.9%
Growth rate		IGR (EPS)	9.7%	2.6%	1.5%	9.1%	
		SGR (EPS)	15.9%	4.2%	2.5%	14.9%	

General observation: Both companies are growing in terms of revenues, profitability, and assets. SGR is higher than IGR in both cases. However, the two companies differ on growth funding.

ABC: Growth is solely financed internally by incremental retained earnings. There is no new debt nor equity. Dividend policy maintains a constant retention ratio—this is reflected in stable IGR. The capital structure (leverage ratio) is not constant—as retained earnings add equity, debt remains constant. SGR does not rely only on the retention ratio.

14

XYX: Growth is financed internally and externally by retained earnings and debts, respectively. A new issue of debt is associated with a change in retention ratio (dividend policy) to maintain a constant capital structure (leverage ratio). A stable ROA implies that IGR is mainly driven by retained earnings, which vary from time to time. SGR relies on both leverage and retained earnings, keeping the capital structure constant.

14.5.2 Firm Value Determinants

Firm valuation focuses on after-tax earnings attributed to all investors (net operating profit after tax (NOPAT)) and the ability of invested capital to generate returns (ROIC). Refer to ► Chap. 7 for details about ROIC and NOPAT. Overall, ROIC measures efficient use of injected capital to generate after-tax operating earnings.

A higher ROIC implies that higher growth should be achieved by larger reinvestment of earnings or free cash flows. Hence, operating SGR is expressed as growth of operating earnings (g_{NOPAT}) as follows:

$$g_{SRG} = g_{NOPAT} = I_r \times \text{ROIC}$$

where I_r is the reinvestment rate, a percentage of after-tax operating earnings allocated to reinvestments (fixed capital and working capital expenditure), such that:

$$I_r = (\text{NCE} + \Delta\text{WC}) / \text{NOPAT}$$

$$\text{NCE} = \text{CE} - \text{DFA} - \text{DEP}$$

where NCE denotes the net capital expenditure determined by fixed capital expenditure (CE) after deducting proceedings from disposal of fixed assets (DFA) and depreciation (DEP). ΔWC denotes change in noncash working capital. The assumption is that reinvestments (NCE + ΔWC) are efficiently used to generate future NOPAT to impact free cash flows. That is, reinvestments reduce current free cash flows but are potentially expected to increase operating earnings upon generating positive investment returns (ROIC)—hence, free cash flows are expected to grow in future.

To illustrate these three growth concepts, we use the same three cases from ► Exhibit 14.5. Estimations and explanations are presented in ► Exhibit 14.7.

Think 14.4

Can EPS growth be used in firm valuation and can NOPAT growth be used in equity valuation? Discuss.

Exhibit 14.7 Fundamental Determinants of Growth

Illustrative Cases: Chevron Corp., Ecopetrol, and Boeing (See Excel Workings—► Chap. 14, Sheet E.14.7)

These three cases illustrate how to estimate growth rate based on fundamental determinants. The key steps are as follows:

Step 1: Obtain data

◘ Exhibits 14.7.1, 14.7.2, and 14.7.3 present historical data for the three companies for all the required variables. The most current period was 2018. Negative values that tend to cause estimation challenges should always be noted.

Step 2: Calculate investment rates and return on investments

The rates to be calculated are retention ratio (R_r), reinvestment rate (I_r), ROA, ROE, and ROIC. These variables can be calculated for the current period (refer to ◘ Exhibit 14.7.4) and for the average per selected sample period (refer to ◘ Exhibit 14.7.5).

Step 3: Calculate growth rates

Depending on the growth concept, growth rates can be calculated for the current period (refer to ◘ Exhibit 14.7.4) and for the average per sample period (refer to ◘ Exhibit 14.7.6).

Step 4: Analyze the estimated growth rates

The purpose of analyzing the estimated growth rates is to make decisions about expected growth. This is probably the most complicated task. It is discussed in the "Practical Considerations" section.

Exhibit 14.7.1 Financial data: Chevron

Variable	2012	2013	2014	2015	2016	2017	2018
EPS ($)	13.42	11.18	10.21	2.46	−0.27	4.88	7.81
DPS ($)	3.51	3.90	4.21	4.28	4.29	4.32	4.48
Net income ($ millions)	26,179	21,423	19,241	4587	(497)	9195	14,824
NOPAT ($ millions)	20,191	19,000	12,316	(1236)	(4739)	1685	13,612
Total equity ($ millions)	137,832	150,427	156,191	153,886	146,722	149,319	155,642
Total assets ($ millions)	232,982	253,753	266,026	264,540	260,078	253,806	253,863
Invested capital ($ millions)	169,004	193,473	203,237	209,861	206,881	199,179	202,711
Net capital expenditure ($ millions)	14,748	22,656	12,885	2728	(4824)	(11,041)	(8019)
Change in noncash working capital ($ millions)	363	(1331)	(540)	(1979)	(327)	520	(718)

Exhibit 14.7.2 Financial data: Ecopetrol

Variable	2012	2013	2014	2015	2016	2017	2018
EPS ($)	0.20	0.17	0.07	−0.04	0.01	0.05	0.10
DPS ($)	0.17	0.16	0.13	0.00	0.01	0.03	0.03
FCF ($ millions)	3219	1871	3815	754	2963	3195	4097
Net income ($ millions)	8225	7017	2871	(1467)	514	2243	3917
NOPAT ($ millions)	8578	7338	4547	5332	916	1732	4506
Total equity ($ millions)	36,636	36,983	19,786	13,658	14,555	16,040	17,614
Total assets ($ millions)	64,442	68,865	46,675	38,745	40,426	39,813	38,865

14

Exhibit 14.7.2 (continued)

Variable	2012	2013	2014	2015	2016	2017	2018
Invested capital ($ millions)	47,608	51,332	33,788	26,130	27,879	27,989	25,853
Net capital expenditure ($ millions)	7538	6502	3028	2001	(79)	521	1442
Change in noncash working capital ($ millions)	(554)	(1695)	(1197)	(1239)	(67)	(900)	(1029)

Exhibit 14.7.3 Financial data: Boeing

Variable	2012	2013	2014	2015	2016	2017	2018
EPS ($)	5.15	6.03	7.47	7.52	7.92	14.03	18.05
DPS ($)	1.81	2.19	2.92	3.64	4.69	5.97	7.19
Net income ($ millions)	3900	4585	5446	5176	5034	8458	10,460
NOPAT ($ millions)	4518	5432	6340	6534	8519	7526	9479
Total equity ($ millions)	5867	14,875	8665	6335	817	1656	339
Total assets ($ millions)	88,896	92,663	92,921	94,408	89,997	112,362	117,359
Invested capital ($ millions)	9595	21,679	19,750	18,488	11,835	14,697	15,709
Net capital expenditure ($ millions)	552	811	856	1135	1233	283	286
Change in noncash working capital ($ millions)	(926)	(1058)	(937)	(746)	3760	1959	1620

Exhibit 14.7.4 Growth estimation: current (2018) compared to previous years

Company	Variable	2012	2013	2014	2015	2016	2017	2018
Chevron	ROA	11.2%	8.8%	7.4%	1.7%	−0.2%	3.6%	5.8%
	ROE	18.99%	14.86%	12.55%	2.96%	−0.33%	6.21%	9.72%
	ROIC	11.9%	10.5%	6.2%	−0.6%	−2.3%	0.8%	6.8%
	Retention ratio (R_r)	73.8%	65.1%	58.8%	−74.0%	−1688.9%	11.5%	42.6%
	Reinvestment rate (I_r)	74.8%	112.2%	100.2%	−60.6%	−108.7%	−624.3%	−64.2%
	IGR (EPS)	8.3%	5.7%	4.4%	−1.3%	−3.2%	0.4%	2.5%
	SGR (EPS)	14.0%	9.7%	7.4%	−2.2%	−5.6%	0.7%	4.1%
	SGR (NOPAT)	8.9%	11.8%	6.2%	−0.4%	−2.5%	−5.2%	−4.3%
Ecopetrol	ROA	12.8%	10.5%	5.0%	−3.4%	1.3%	5.6%	10.0%
	ROE	22.45%	19.06%	10.11%	−8.77%	3.64%	14.67%	23.28%
	ROIC	18.0%	14.8%	10.7%	17.8%	3.4%	6.2%	16.7%
	Retention ratio (R_r)	16.5%	8.7%	−86.8%	−100.0%	39.2%	44.7%	68.3%
	Reinvestment rate (I_r)	81.4%	65.5%	40.3%	14.3%	−15.9%	−21.9%	9.2%
	IGR (EPS)	2.1%	0.9%	−4.3%	3.4%	0.5%	2.5%	6.8%
	SGR (EPS)	3.7%	1.7%	−8.8%	−8.8%	1.4%	6.6%	15.9%
	SGR (NOPAT)	14.7%	9.7%	4.3%	2.5%	−0.5%	−1.4%	1.5%

Company	Variable	2012	2013	2014	2015	2016	2017	2018
Boeing	ROA	4.4%	5.1%	5.9%	5.5%	5.5%	8.4%	9.1%
	ROE	66.47%	44.21%	46.27%	69.01%	140.77%	684.03%	1048.62%
	ROIC	47.1%	34.7%	30.6%	34.2%	56.2%	56.7%	62.3%
	Retention ratio (R_r)	64.9%	63.8%	60.9%	51.6%	40.8%	57.4%	60.2%
	Reinvestment rate (I_r)	−8.3%	−4.5%	−1.3%	6.0%	58.6%	29.8%	20.1%
	IGR (EPS)	2.8%	3.2%	3.6%	2.9%	2.2%	4.8%	5.5%
	SGR (EPS)	43.1%	28.2%	28.2%	35.6%	57.4%	393.0%	630.9%
	SGR (NOPAT)	−3.9%	−1.6%	−0.4%	2.0%	32.9%	16.9%	12.5%

Exhibit 14.7.5 Average rates per sample period

Company	Variable	7-Year	6-Year	5-Year	4-Year	3-Year
Chevron	ROA	5.3%	4.4%	3.6%	2.7%	3.1%
	ROE	9.0%	7.5%	6.2%	4.6%	5.2%
	ROIC	4.4%	3.3%	2.1%	1.1%	1.7%
	Retention ratio (R_r)	41.7%	29.7%	14.0%	−16.7%	−5.4%
	Reinvestment rate (I_r)	41.3%	24.6%	−52.3%	−253.8%	−231.2%
Ecopetrol	ROA	6.9%	5.5%	3.9%	3.3%	5.6%
	ROE	15.0%	12.7%	9.9%	8.4%	13.8%
	ROIC	13.7%	12.6%	12.0%	11.6%	8.8%
	Retention ratio (R_r)	8.1%	3.5%	−1.0%	46.3%	58.1%
	Reinvestment rate (I_r)	43.3%	29.9%	14.6%	5.2%	−1.6%
Boeing	ROA	6.3%	6.5%	6.8%	7.0%	7.5%
	ROE	111.7%	119.8%	194.1%	318.4%	851.8%
	ROIC	43.3%	42.9%	47.7%	52.8%	60.4%
	Retention ratio (R_r)	57.1%	56.4%	55.6%	54.8%	55.4%
	Reinvestment rate (I_r)	18.3%	21.0%	24.6%	29.7%	35.8%

Notes:

Investment Rates: (1) R_r = (EPS − DPS)/EPS; (2) I_r = NCE + ΔWC)/NOPAT. The following aspects should be noted regarding negative values.

(a) The retention ratio can be negative if DPS > EPS. For example, Chevron's retention ratio in 2015 was ($2.46 − $4.28)/$2.46 = −0.74%. When EPS is negative, an absolute value should be applied in the denominator to avoid misleading results (that the retention ratio is positive). For example, Chevron's retention ratio in 2016 is calculated as (−$0.27 − $4.29)/ABS ($−0.27) = −1.688.9%.

(b) Reinvestment rates can be negative under the following conditions: (1) if the investment in working capital falls significantly compared to fixed capital expenditure (see Boeing's case from 2012 to 2014); (2) if NOPAT is negative (see Chevron's case

Exhibit 14.7.6 Average growth rate estimates per sample period vs. current-year growth rate

Company	Growth type	7-Year	6-Year	5-Year	4-Year	3-Year	Current (2018)
Chevron	IGR (EPS)	2.2%	1.3%	0.5%	−0.5%	−0.2%	2.5%
	SGR (EPS)	3.8%	2.2%	0.9%	−0.8%	−0.3%	4.1%
	SGR (NOPAT)	1.8%	0.8%	−1.1%	−2.9%	−4.0%	−4.3%
Ecopetrol	IGR (EPS)	0.6%	0.2%	0.0%	1.5%	3.3%	6.8%
	SGR (EPS)	1.2%	0.5%	−0.1%	3.9%	8.0%	15.9%
	SGR (NOPAT)	5.9%	3.8%	1.8%	0.6%	−0.1%	1.5%
Boeing	IGR (EPS)	3.6%	3.7%	3.8%	3.9%	4.1%	5.5%
	SGR (EPS)	63.7%	67.6%	107.9%	174.4%	471.7%	630.9%
	SGR (NOPAT)	7.9%	9.0%	11.7%	15.7%	21.6%	12.5%

in 2015, where I_r = 60.6%); and (3) if both reinvestments and NOPAT are negative—in this situation, use an absolute value in the denominator to avoid misleading calculations (see Chevron's case in 2016, where I_r = −108.7%).

Return on Investments: (1) ROA = Net income/Average total assets. (2) ROE = Net income/Average total equity. (3) ROIC = NOPAT/Average invested capital. The average in the denominator is a 2-year average. It should be noted that returns are negative due to negative earnings (net income or NOPAT).

Growth Rates: The following calculation issues should be noted regarding negative values:

(a) When one of the variables (investment rate or investment return) is negative. This is a straightforward calculation (see the Chevron case in 2015 for IGR (EPS) and SGR (EPS) where ROA and ROE are positive but R_r is negative).
(b) When both investment rate and investment return are negative. In this case, an absolute value should be used on one of them to avoid a misleading positive result (see the case of Ecopetrol's SGR (EPS) in 2015 or Chevron in 2016, where both investment returns (ROA, ROE, or ROIC) and investment rates (R_r or I_r) are negative.

Notes:

The following steps are applied to estimate average growth rates:

1. Determine the sample period from which averages will be calculated. For example, in our illustration, we use 7-year to 3-year samples.
2. For each sample, calculate the total for each variable item in the data sheets (Exhibits 14.7.1, 14.7.2, and 14.7.3). For example (in Ecopetrol's case), totals for a 7-year sample are as follows: EPS ($0.6), DPS ($0.5), net income ($23,356 millions), NOPAT ($32,949 million), total equity ($155,271 million), total asset ($337,831 million), invested capital ($20,954 million), and change in working capital (–$6681 million).
3. Use the totals to calculate the average growth variables (ROA, ROE, ROIC, R_r, and I_r) for the sample period. For example (in Ecopetrol's case), 7-year averages are as follows: ROA = $23,356/$337,831 = 6.9%; R_r = ($0.06 – $0.05)/$0.06 = 8.1%.
4. Calculate growth rates based on averages from (3) above. For example (in Ecopetrol's case), 7-year IGR (EPS) = 6.9% (8.1%) = 0.6%. All the results (including the current period) are presented in Exhibit 14.7.6.

Analysis of Estimates

Like in historical extrapolation, the main challenge is not to calculate but to determine growth rate. The main decision criteria are as follows: (1) Is the estimation approach suitable considering the specific circumstances of the company? (2) Which growth rate is expected in the future? Let us examine these aspects for each of the three companies in our case:

Chevron

- Exhibit 14.7.7 depicts Chevron's growth determinants and growth estimates historically. There is a clear change in growth direction for IGR(EPS) and SGR (EPS) from 2016, following the same direction on ROA, ROE, and R_r. In contrast, SRG (NOPAT) continues to decline until a slight increase from 2017, mainly due to an increase in I_r in 2018 (but still negative).
- *Suitability:* There are no estimation issues relating to abnormal values. The estimates do not show significant variations across the samples and within the same type of growth. Overall, the estimation approach seems suitable for all the three growth types: that is, IGR (EPS), SGR (EPS), and SGR (NOPAT).
- *Decision*: There is no straightforward answer to what growth rate should be applied. Nevertheless, a more likely expected growth can be determined by considering the direction change from 2016 for IGR (EPS) and SGR (EPS). If we expect the current growth to persist, then IGR (EPS) and SGR (EPS) should be 2.5% and 4.1%, respectively. If we expect the future to reflect the change in direction from 2016, and that R_r and I_r will continue to be negative, then a 3-year average growth can be used: that is, negative growth for both IGR (EPS) and SGR (EPS, –0.2% and –0.3%, respectively). If we consider that a 3-year sample does not reflect the future, then decisions can be made using larger samples (say 5-year, 6-year, 7-year, or more). Regarding

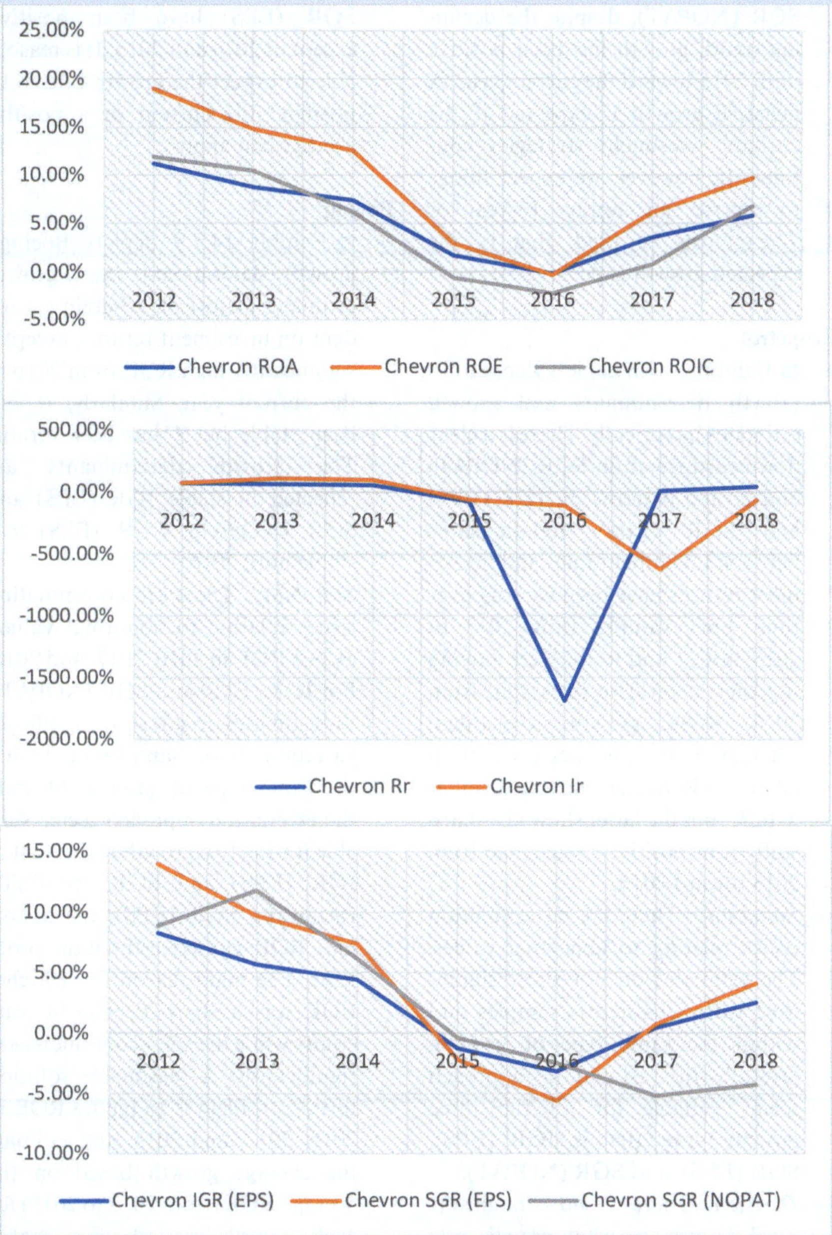

Exhibit 14.7.7 Chevron's growth determinants and growth rates

SGR (NOPAT), despite the declining trend, growth has been positive until 2015 toward the current year. A negative growth is expected if the current investment strategies continue. If, however, we expect things to reverse, an average (6-year or 7-year) can be used: that is, the expected growth is positive.

Ecopetrol

- Exhibit 14.7.8 depicts Ecopetrol's growth determinants and growth estimates historically. There is a clear downward trend on SGR (NOPAT) and erratic patterns on IGR (EPS) and SGR (EPS). Relationships between investment rates and investment returns have been varying over time. For example, from 2012 to 2015, both I_r and ROIC were moving together at positive rates, but, from 2016, ROIC growth accelerated, whereas I_r became negative. Both ROA and ROE were moving together with R_r, but the latter showed a sharp shift from positive to negative from 2013 toward 2016.
- *Suitability*: There are no estimation issues relating to abnormal values. The estimates do not show significant variations across samples and within the same type of growth. Overall, the estimation approach seems suitable for all the three growth types: that is, IGR (EPS), SGR (EPS), and SGR (NOPAT).
- *Decision*: There is no straightforward answer to what growth rate should be applied. SGR (NOPAT) shows a declining trend but is positive throughout, except in 2016 and 2017. Similarly, both IGR (EPS) and SGR (EPS) have been positive, except in 2014 and 2015. It is reasonable to expect the growth rate to be positive: the current or a positive average can apply.

Boeing

- Exhibit 14.7.9 depicts Boeing's growth determinants and growth estimates historically. Stability is evident on investment returns, except a significantly high ROE from 2016 to the current year. Similarly, R_r has been stable but I_r has been erratic. The growth determinants are reflected in stable IGR (EPS) and SGR (NOPAT): SGR (EPS) was stable until 2016.
- *Suitability*: There are no estimation issues relating to abnormal values, except ROE in 2016, 2017, and 2018. For IGR (EPS) and SGR (NOPAT), the estimates do not show significant variations across samples and within the same type of growth. Overall, the estimation approach seems suitable for the two growth types: that is, IGR (EPS) and SGR (NOPAT). Regarding SGR (EPS), the abnormal ROE caused estimation problems. The main reason for a higher ROE was a sharp decline in total equity while the net income increased significantly. A reasonable solution to this problem is to ignore ROE in 2016, 2017, and 2018, and estimate the average growth based on the average ROE (from 2012 to 2015) for each sample period—this makes sense because ROE has been stable within that average level (53.3%). Growth estimates will be as presented in Exhibit 14.7.10.

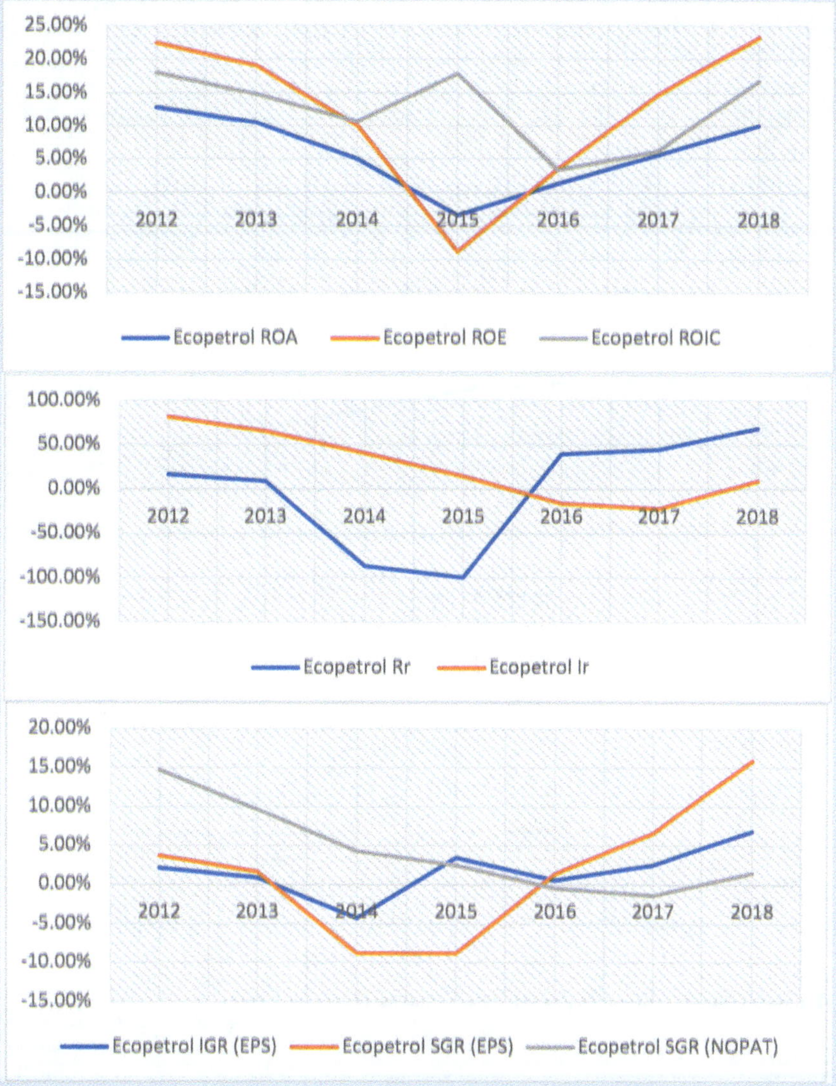

Exhibit 14.7.8 Ecopetrol's growth determinants and growth rates

- *Decision*: There is no straightforward answer to what growth rate should be applied. However, SGR (EPS) should be determined from Exhibit 14.7.10. Overall, there are no significant variations across sample periods and within the same growth type. Due to stable growth rates, decision can be easy for this company: any of them, current or average can apply.

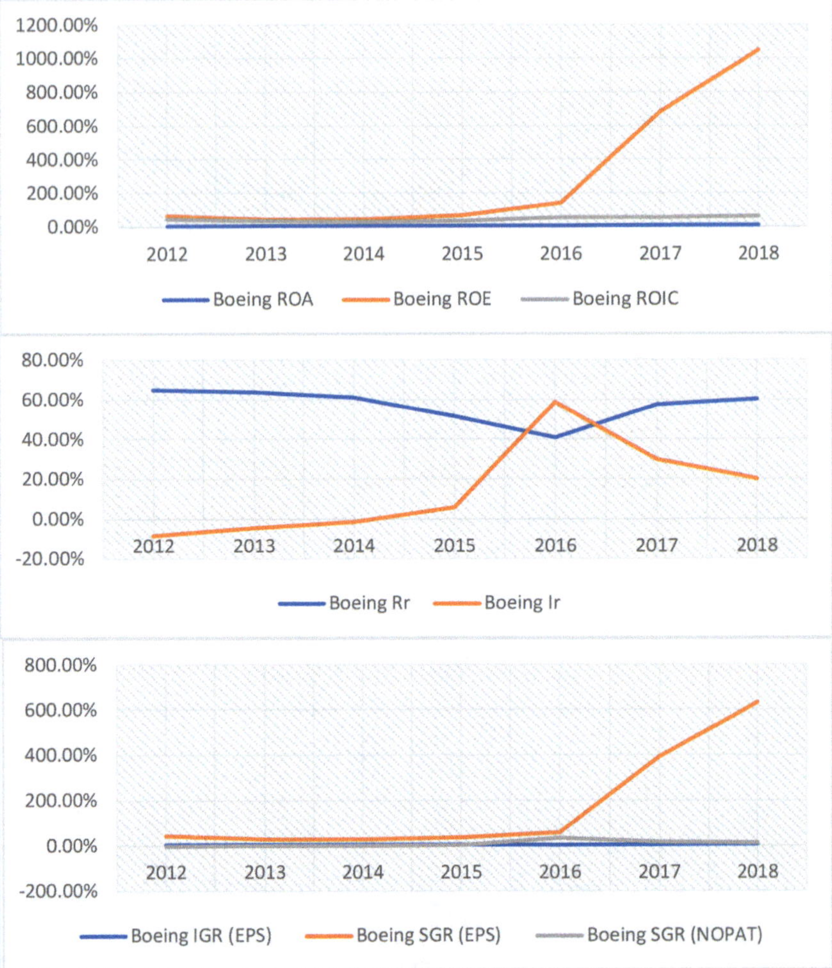

Exhibit 14.7.9 Boeing's growth determinants and growth rates

Exhibit 14.7.10 Boeing's stable ROE and growth rates

Variable	7-Year	6-Year	5-Year	4-Year	3-Year	Current (2018)
ROE	53.5%	53.5%	53.5%	53.5%	53.5%	53.5%
Retention ratio (R_r)	57.1%	56.4%	55.6%	54.8%	55.4%	60.2%
SGR (EPS)	30.5%	30.2%	29.7%	29.3%	29.6%	30.7%

Apply 14.2

Objective: Estimate expected growth rate using fundamentals.

Use the two companies in ► Apply 14.1 to estimate growth based on fundamental determinants.

1. Collect relevant historical data for at least 6 years.
2. Calculate growth rates for the current period and historical averages (vary your sample periods to a minimum of 3 years):
   (a) IGR (EPS)
   (b) SGR (EPS)
   (c) SGR (NOPAT)
3. Critically analyze the estimates and make interpretations.
4. Explain the estimation challenges (if any) and suggested solutions.

14.5.3 Practical Considerations

Like historical extrapolation, estimating growth with fundamentals has several limitations as discussed below.

1. *Stability:* The fundamental approach assumes stability in growth determinants and capital structure. However, practically, they can change over time depending on several firms' specific factors. It is, therefore, important to perform further analysis to address this assumption. The following aspects should be considered:
   (a) *Retention Ratio*: This ratio is sensitive to earnings and dividend policy. Some companies tend to have highly volatile EPS and dividend payout ratios.
   (b) *Reinvestment Rate*: The assumption that invested capital will generate the same NOPAT in the future only applies for companies with recurring capital expenditure and depends on whether operating earnings arise from such investments. Some companies, especially in capital-intensive industries, tend to have huge nonrecurring capital investments, and operating earnings from those investments may not be realized soon: the reported earnings are not related to such investments.
   (c) *Investment Returns*: The generic fundamental approach assumes constant returns (ROE, ROA, ROIC). However, these variables tend to change due to several operational factors affecting profitability.
   (d) *Capital Structure*: A constant capital structure is a reasonable assumption for most companies, but some of them tend to change their capital structure for several reasons, like for reducing financing cost.
2. *Negativity:* Applying fundamentals to estimate growth rate can be challenging when dealing with negative values (refer to ► Exhibit 14.7). Things should not be handled mathematically but sensibly. For instance, a negative payout ratio

means paying dividends out of negative earnings—it is a red flag threatening both the company's ability to grow (from reinvesting earnings) and to continue paying dividends in the future.

3. *Research and Development (R&D) Expenses*: Although R&D tends to be treated as expenses, they are expected to improve earnings in the future. It is, therefore, recommended to capitalize such expenses and be included in calculating the capital expenditure.
4. *Average Growth:* The use of average growth rates has two major advantages: to address negativity and to estimate forward-looking growth. The main challenge, however, is to determine an appropriate sample period (see ▶ Exhibit 14.7). There is no standard for sample period, but it should be carefully selected to reflect the expected growth. Complications arise when average growth rates are highly sensitive to change in the sample period, suggesting erratic patterns in growth determinants. Under such conditions, critical analysis is required to determine the most appropriate sample.

Think 14.5

Why is it reasonable to assume that a company's growth rate should not exceed economic growth?

14.6 Decision Challenge: Which Growth Rate to Use?

Estimation of growth rates is considered one of the challenging tasks in corporate valuation. As seen in ▶ Exhibits 14.5 and 14.7, there is no absolute growth rate for a company: variations are evident between estimation approaches. Here, we outline some of the challenges and the proposed measures on how to addresses those challenges.

Historical Extrapolation vs. Fundamentals

14 Generally, there is no consensus about which approach is practically superior and more appropriate. Each of the estimation approaches has pros and cons. Historical extrapolation is merely based on historical events rather than factors affecting growth. In contrast, fundamental growth determinants are based on a company's efficiency to drive growth through earnings and investments. ▶ Exhibit 14.8 compares EPS and operating growth estimates from different estimation approaches—differences are noticeable.

Exhibit 14.8 Growth Rate Variations

Illustrative Cases: Chevron Corp., Ecopetrol, and Boeing (See Excel Workings—► Chap. 14, Sheet E.14.7)

	Period	Historical extrapolation			Fundamentals		
	Sample	ARITH	GEOM	REGR	IGR (EPS)	SGR (EPS)	SGR(NOPAT)
Chevron	6-Year	292.5%	44.2%	−20.1%	1.3%	2.2%	0.8%
	5-Year	354.4%	58.7%	−16.8%	0.5%	0.9%	−1.1%
	4-Year	445.1%	78.9%	−4.7%	−0.5%	−0.8%	−2.9%
	3-Year	618.8%	165.4%	57.0%	−0.2%	−0.3%	−4.0%
	Current				2.5%	4.1%	−4.3%
Ecopetrol	6-Year	53.6%	−0.5%	−26.6%	0.2%	0.5%	3.8%
	5-Year	67.2%	2.4%	−17.5%	0.0%	−0.1%	1.8%
	4-Year	98.8%	21.6%	36.0%	1.5%	3.9%	0.6%
	3-Year	182.1%	166.9%	137.4%	3.3%	8.0%	−0.1%
	Current				6.8%	15.9%	1.5%
Boeing	6-Year	25.5%	23.2%	20.8%	3.7%	30.2%	9.0%
	5-Year	27.1%	24.5%	22.5%	3.8%	29.7%	11.7%
	4-Year	27.9%	24.7%	25.2%	3.9%	29.3%	15.7%
	3-Year	37.0%	33.9%	31.7%	4.1%	29.6%	21.6%
	Current				5.5%	30.7%	12.5%

Observations

Historical vs. Fundamental: There is significant variation between historical extrapolation and fundamentals.

Chevron: Historically extrapolated growth rates vary significantly between estimation methods and across sample periods. Fundamental growth rates (IGR and SGR) are consistent because of small differences between ROA and ROE.

Ecopetrol: Historically extrapolated growth rates vary significantly between estimation methods and across sample periods. Fundamental growth rates (IGR and SGR) are consistent because of small differences between ROA and ROE.

Boeing: Historically extrapolated growth rates are consistent between estimation methods and across sample periods. Fundamental growth rates (IGR and SGR) vary significantly because of big differences between ROA and ROE. However, SGR and historically extrapolated growth rates are consistent.

Decision-Making

Judgment about growth is complex and should be reached by combining facts and reasoning—that is, quantitative and qualitative analysis. Chevron's and Ecopetrol's cases demonstrate the complex nature of growth rate decisions: numbers do not provide a direct answer. This is another example where the "art and science" of valuation apply (refer to ► Chap. 1). To arrive at a realistic expected growth rate, decision-making cannot rely solely on numbers. Instead, it requires critical scrutiny of the numbers and reasoning.

Usually, high growth forecasts tend to be problematic as they cannot be sustained for a long term, and it is extremely difficult to predict when growth will stall. It is, therefore, reasonable to take a conservative stance and avoid assuming that growth will be maintained at a high rate for a long period in the future. Moreover, it is unreasonable to assume that companies can maintain growth rates at higher rates than the overall economic growth. That is, if the average economic growth (gross domestic product (GDP)) is around 5.7%, then any corporate growth rate above GDP can only be temporary. Other specific growth decision-making criteria are discussed and illustrated in ► Chap. 15—that is, growth rate cannot exceed the cost of capital when valuation is based on a constant cash flow growth model. ► Exhibit 14.9 summarizes some of other factors to consider, such as a firm's specific and external factors, when determining on an appropriate growth rate.

Exhibit 14.9 Growth Rate Decision: Additional Factors to Consider

Firm-Specific Factors. The following firm-specific circumstances may be helpful in determining the most appropriate (no necessarily correct) growth rate:

Nature of business	Past and current performance	Expectations
Cyclical	Significant fall in earnings due to economic recession	The firm is heading toward recovery from recession—an expected increase in earnings
Troubled	Significant fall in earnings due to management inefficiency. New management has been imposed	The firm is likely to undergo internal restructuring. The new management is expected to turn things around, thereby improving performance and earnings
Stable	Stable earnings growth in both historical measures and fundamentals	The firm is expected to maintain its performance trend

14

Nature of business	Past and current performance	Expectations
Transforming	Constant growth in earnings with consistent growth estimates from history and fundamentals. However, the firm is in the process of transformation (e.g., selling some of its subsidiaries, product diversification, etc.)	Growth is likely to slow initially but temporality. Transformation can speed up growth in the long-term future
Competitive	Volatile earnings due to high competition in the industry. New competitors have emerged with more attractive products or services	Growth is likely to slow initially: it can return to normal if the company is expected to adjust its competitive strength or continue to slow if competitiveness is expected to weaken
Mature	Positive earnings but growth is at the peak. Two scenarios: (1) No heavy reinvestment. Most of the earnings are returned to shareholders through share repurchases and (or) dividends. (2) Investment into new attractive markets or business acquisitions	Scenario 1: growth is likely to be slow but steady. Scenario 2: growth will depend on the nature of new markets or acquisitions. It can be stable if the company expects to maintain its historical growth (ROE, ROIC). Otherwise, growth can be volatile at either a high or low pace
New	New company entering a mature competitive industry for the same product or service. Two scenarios: (1) New brand but positive market perception. Encouraging earning performance from the outset. (2) New brand but negative market perception. Deteriorating earnings from the outset	Scenario 1: expected volatile but growing earnings in the short term, followed by high growth in the long term. Scenario 2: expected volatile and slow or negative growth
Industry	Scenarios: (1) high-growth industry, (2) moderate-growth industry, (3) low-growth industry, (4) volatile-growth industry, and (5) stable-growth industry	Growth is not expected to deviate significantly from the industry

Review Questions

1. What is the role of financial statement information in estimating cash flow growth rate?
2. How can backward-looking financial information be made forward-looking?
3. Since financial statements are backward-looking, why should they form the basis for estimating the expected growth rate?
4. Explain the concepts behind the following growth estimation approaches:
   (a) Historical extrapolation
   (b) Fundamentals
5. Describe the following terms relating to historical extrapolation growth estimation:
   (a) Direct estimation
   (b) Indirect estimation
6. The following information relate to YUI Company's FCFF and DPS over the past 7 years.

Year	2015	2016	2017	2018	2019	2020	2021
FCFF ($ millions)	1.85	2.27	2.34	−0.56	1.67	4.03	3.45
DPS ($)	1.20	2.40	2.20	0.00	3.40	2.55	2.45

   (a) Use historical extrapolation to estimate growth rates under the following methods:
      - Arithmetic and geometric averages
      - Regression with original values, log10, and natural log
   (b) Compare growth estimates from the different methods and provide comments about the suitability of the estimates.
   (c) Explain any estimation challenges or limitations.
7. What are the common estimation challenges and limitations of the historical extrapolation approach?

14

8. Explain how the following practical issues effect growth estimates when using historical extrapolation:
   (a) Negative values
   (b) Stable vs. erratic historical values
   (c) Abnormal values
   (d) Sample period
9. According to fundamentals, what are the key determinants of growth under the following aspects:
   (a) Internal growth
   (b) Sustainable growth

10. Explain a situation in which a company's growth is solely driven by internal funding.
11. Explain a situation in which a company's growth is driven by both internal funding and external funding.
12. Why should SGR be higher than IGR?
13. BNM Company has just reported the following financial snapshots: ROE = 27.46%, ROA = 16.0%, EPS = \$3.0, and DPS = \$1.6. Calculate IGR and SGR.
14. SDF Company's performance for the current financial period indicates the following: ROE = 26.82%, ROA = 16.6%, ROIC = 34.1%, EPS = \$2.3, DPS = \$1.6, net capital expenditure = \$0.8 million, and change in noncash working capital = –\$0.76 million. Calculate the following: IGR (EPS), SGR (EPS), and SGR (NOPAT).
15. The following information relates to the financial statements of LAS Company over the past 5 years.

Variable	2012	2013	2014	2015	2016
EPS (\$)	1.50	2.40	2.50	1.60	1.40
DPS (\$)	0.70	1.20	1.20	1.20	1.30
Net income (\$ millions)	9.2	8.4	8.6	7.3	6.8
NOPAT (\$ millions)	12.6	14.2	12.8	11.7	13.6
Total equity (\$ millions)	26.0	27.4	28.5	29.1	30.0
Total assets (\$ millions)	66.0	70.0	54.0	48.0	45.0
Invested capital (\$ millions)	56.0	63.0	34.7	32.0	39.0
Net capital expenditure (\$ millions)	9.2	8.3	4.6	2.9	1.2
Change in noncash working capital (\$ millions)	(0.8)	1.0	(1.9)	(1.4)	1.3

16. Calculate the following growth rates:
    (a) IGR (EPS)
    (b) SGR (EPS)
    (c) SGR (NOPAT)
    (d) Repeat (a)–(c) for the following averages: 3-year, 4-year, and 5-year
17. Outline the key decision criteria for expected growth rate.

Bibliography

Exactitude Consultancy (2022), Lithium Ion Battery Market Analysis by ROI, Cash Flow, Revenue, Demand, Growth Factors, Key Segmentations and Forecast By 2029, Luton, Bedfordshire, United Kingdom, Available at GLOBE NEWSWIRE, https://finance.yahoo.com/news/lithium-ion-battery-market-analysis-130900100.html, Accessed August 18, 2022.

Kernez, R. (2021). Calculating Your Company's Growth Rate (And Other Important Business Indicators), Available at Forbes, https://www.forbes.com/sites/forbescommunicationscouncil/2021/08/31/calculating-your-companys-growth-rate-and-other-important-business-indicators/?sh=369a0271add9, Accessed August 31, 2021.

Yahoo Finance (2022), With 11.5% CAGR, Lithium-Ion Battery Market Size to Reach USD 101 billion by 2029, available at https://finance.yahoo.com/news/11-5-cagr-lithium-ion-085500586.html?guccounter=1&guce_referrer=aHR0cHM6Ly93d3cuZ29vZ2xlLmNvbS8&guce_referrer_sig=AQAAAACDzveYZ42GmCOY08frue9ZHVxnbBZYTA_NRAz1ZdYB5e_1P6HBtY_MVxzcXaXO2T2SE-f0jy-eVhoOv7YT8amr1gila3ABc9Na0aEgnas0oQOBNww1t3K5fB2i2fQ6xtSazx8vxrLoTt5oM2hbkbHiugL4peE-PFxMjg-rQoj, accessed on November 2nd 2022.

Free Cash Flow Discount Models: Cost of Capital Approach

Contents

Supplementary Information The online version contains supplementary material available at https://doi.org/10.1007/978-3-031-28267-6_15.

B. Kulwizira Lukanima, *Corporate Valuation*, Classroom Companion: Business, https://doi.org/10.1007/978-3-031-28267-6_15

15.1 Introduction

This chapter is about performing corporate valuation using free cash flow discount models. It builds on the knowledge and information from the preceding chapters. Indeed, this chapter covers the valuation stage in which the "art" side is more applicable than the "science" side. Issues covered in the preceding chapters are mainly "objective" (e.g., estimating the cost of capital and calculating free cash flows and growth rates); they form the basis on which basic preparations to accomplish the remaining valuation process are made: discounted future cash flows. At this stage, analysts make "subjective" judgments depending on the company's specific circumstances. The most challenging aspect is deciding on an appropriate variable that suits the specific valuation circumstances of the company. This chapter endeavors to illustrate how to navigate a typically complex path toward reaching reasonably acceptable decisions.

In particular, the cost of capital approach is designed to estimate firm value using free cash flow to the firm (FCFF) (a direct approach) and equity value from firm value (an indirect approach). Although this chapter focuses on the cost of capital approach, it also covers equity valuation using free cash flow to equity (FCFE) (a direct approach)—these two equity valuation methods are compared and discussed.

Learning Outcomes

- Relate free cash flows to a firm's main objective of value maximization.
- Explain the usefulness of free cash flows as a valuation input.
- Determine intrinsic valuation inputs.
- Understand the different valuation models and approaches.
- Understand the basic criteria for making valuation decisions.
- Decide about valuation inputs that suit a specific company's circumstances.
- Apply single-stage and multiple stage models to perform valuation.
- Apply the cost of capital approach and direct approach to estimate intrinsic value.

15.2 Valuation Role of Free Cash Flows

According to Warren Buffett, intrinsic valuation is vital for ascertaining business attractiveness.

> Intrinsic value is an all-important concept that offers the only logical approach to evaluating the relative attractiveness of investments and businesses. Intrinsic value can be defined simply: It is the discounted value of the cash that can be taken out of a business during its remaining life. (Warren Buffett 1996)

Cash flow is, therefore, an important measure of value because it is linked to the perceived main objective of a firm—maximization of shareholders' value (refer to

▶ Chap. 1). Unlike accounting income, cash flows can be used to determine whether managers create or destroy value.

The use of cash flows to value equity is noteworthy. For example, a survey conducted on a professional practice (Pinto et al. 2019) with 1980 respondents shows that approximately 79% use cash flow discounting models. Specifically, cash flows applicable in valuation are free cash flows to the firm (FCFFs), free cash flows to equity (FCFEs), and dividends. Nevertheless, cash dividends have limited applications because paying dividends is not mandatory (see ▶ Chap. 17)—but FCFE is cash available to equity holders. A survey by Bancel and Mittoo (2014) on European valuation practitioners shows an 80% use of FCFFs compared to about 40% FCFEs and 20% dividends. Overall, free cash flow is a more logical way to determine a company's economic value compared to other variables like earnings and dividends.

Banner 15.1 Valuation Role of Free Cash Flows
Both FCFF and FCFE have vital valuation roles in determining a company's economic value and are more applicable than measures like earnings and dividends.

Think 15.1
Since FCFEs and dividends represent cash available and cash paid to equity holders, respectively, should they achieve consistent equity valuation?

15.3 The Cost of Capital Approach

The cost of capital approach (hereafter the CC approach) is a valuation approach that involves discounting the expected FCFF at weighted average cost of capital (WACC). Recall from ▶ Chap. 10 that FCFF is computed by deducting operating capital expenditure (i.e., both net capital expenditure and working capital expenditure) from earnings before interest and taxes (EBIT) (1 − tax rate). Hence, the appropriate discount rate is WACC because it considers a firm's operating risk. Consequently, the present value of FCFF is the present value of the firm's operating assets (PV_{OA}). Therefore, total firm value (V_F) should include nonoperating assets (NonOA) as follows:

15

$$V_F = PV_{OA} + NonOA$$

The estimated firm value can then be used to determine equity value (V_E) by deducting non-equity claims (NECs) such as debts outstanding (an indirect approach), such that:

$$V_E = V_F - NEC$$

Alternatively, equity valuation can be performed using FCFE discounted at the cost of equity (a direct approach), such that:

$$V_E = PV_{FCFE}$$

▶ Exhibit 15.1 summarizes the key features of intrinsic valuation with both the cost of capital approach and direct approach.

Exhibit 15.1 Equity Valuation: Cost of Capital Approach vs. Direct Approach

Cost of Capital Approach				Direct Approach		
Variables		Firm Value	Equity Value	Variables		Equity Value
FCFF	WACC	PV_{OA} + *NonOA*	Firm Value – NEC	FCFE	Cost of Equity	PV_{FCFE}

Estimation Variables

1. *Free Cash Flows*: FCFF and FCFE are expected free cash flows.
2. *Discount Rates*: WACC reflects all sources of firm's financing (equity and debt) and related risks: the cost of equity includes leverage risk captured through levered beta; the pre-tax cost of debt includes leverage risk (bankruptcy cost) whereas pre-tax cost of debt captures interest-tax-shield (tax benefits of debt).
3. *Non-operating Assets*: Some companies tend to have significant non-operating assets (NonOA) such as cash and marketable securities, land held for investments, etc.

15.3.1 Valuation Process and Considerations

As discussed in ▶ Chap. 14, valuation is a forward-looking process: it requires forecasted free cash flows to be discounted at an appropriate cost of capital or equity (refer to ▶ Chaps. 11–13). As discussed in ▶ Chap. 1, valuation involves both objective and subjective aspects to reflect the so-called "science and art" of valuation. ▶ Exhibit 15.2 presents a typical intrinsic valuation process considering its objectivity and subjectivity. Generally, objectivity is dominant in processes relating to financial information (such as earnings, free cash flows, and cost of capital) and calculating valuation variables, whereas subjectivity dominates decisions relating to forecasting future cash flows and determining valuation models. Hence, even with the same set of valuation data, different analysts tend to achieve different valuation results for the same company: subjective decisions have more influence than universal approaches, methods, and techniques.

Banner 15.2 The Science and Art of Valuation

Intrinsic valuation utilizes both objective and subjective aspects, but analysts' subjective aspects are more influential.

Consider valuation as a goal to arrive at a "destination" (an intrinsic value). To reach that destination, analysts make different decisions about "routes and means of transport" (subjective judgments). According to Booth (2007:29), the main criteria to make judgments is to ask "… which valuation technique offers the most direct route, that is, the easiest and most accurate implementation and how can you check the resulting value against other models." Eventually, correct valuation decisions among different analysts should achieve consistent, but not necessarily equal, results. As stated by Warren Buffett (1996),

> The calculation of intrinsic value, though, is not so simple. As our definition suggests, intrinsic value is an estimate rather than a precise figure…Two people looking at the same set of facts, moreover – and this would apply even to Charlie and me – will almost inevitably come up with at least slightly different intrinsic value figures. That is one reason we never give you our estimates of intrinsic value. What our annual reports do supply, though, are the facts that we ourselves use to calculate this value. (Warren Buffett 1996)

Exhibit 15.2 Valuation Objectivity vs. Subjectivity (Exhibits 15.2.1 and 15.2.2)

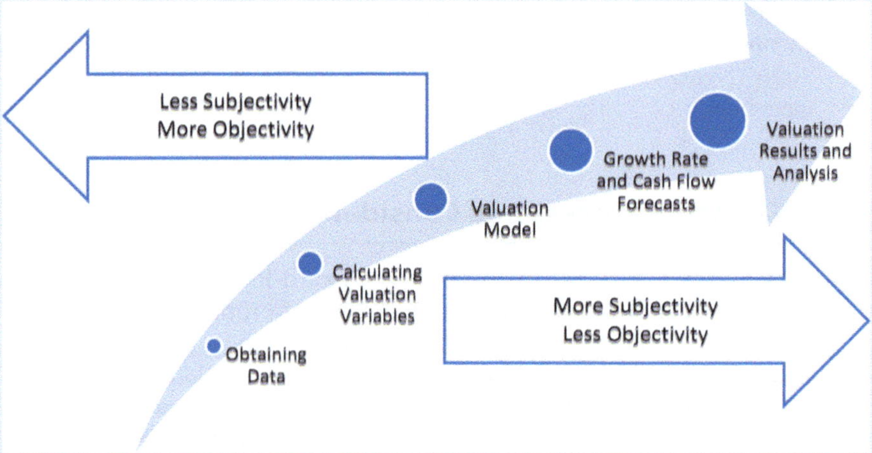

Exhibit 15.2.1 Valuation process: cash flow discount models

Exhibit 15.2.2 Valuation objectivity vs. subjectivity

Process	Objectivity	Subjectivity
Obtaining data	Valuation data such as financial statements and market values represent actual measures about a company's financial and market performance	Almost none
Calculating valuation variables	Valuation variables (e.g., cost of capital, earnings, returns, free cash flows, growth rates, etc.) are calculated from universal methods (i.e., standard formulas or models)	Analysts make assumptions and choices about several aspects (e.g., sample selection, specific methods, approaches to apply, etc.)
Valuation model	Intrinsic valuation is based on universal cash flow growth models: single-stage constant growth or multiple stage growth	Analysts make assumptions and chose the valuation model
Forecasting growth rates and cash flows	Growth rates are calculated using universal approaches: historical average, linear regression, and fundamentals	Analysts determine criteria to make decisions about the expected growth rate, depending on the valuation model and assumptions
Valuation results	Values are calculated using standard mathematics: discounted expected future cash flows	Values are estimates based on analysts' assumptions and judgments

Think 15.2

In valuation, why is subjectivity more influential than objectivity?

15.3.2 Valuation Variables

Intrinsic valuation utilizes the following key variables: free cash flows, cost of capital, expected growth rate, nonoperating assets, and non-equity claims. They are described as follows:

- *Discount Rates*: WACC represents the required rate of return for a firm's overall finance providers, considering the risk of FCFF streams. An important consideration is that WACC variables (cost of debt and cost of equity) address respective risks. The pretax cost of debt captures leverage (financial risk), whereas the after-tax cost of debt captures leverage benefit (interest tax shield). The cost of equity for a levered firm is based on levered beta to capture the market risks.
- *Free Cash Flows*: Free cash flows are derived from a company's historical data (backward-looking), but valuation applies expected cash flows based on the expected growth rate (forward-looking). Individual decisions about take-off

free cash flows and growth assumptions are vital as they influence valuation. Historical average metrics tend to provide better forward-looking measures than current metrics. This aspect is illustrated in ▶ Exhibits 15.5A–15.7A.

- *Growth Rate*: A decision about the most appropriate growth rate to apply is probably the most challenging valuation task—as seen in ▶ Chap. 14, growth rates differ according to estimation approaches and techniques. Growth decision criteria should consider the specific circumstances of a company, namely, values, valuation model, and approach to be applied. For instance, FCFF and FCFE growth rates are not necessarily equal: FCFE should be equal or greater than FCFF. This aspect is explained and illustrated in subsequent sections.
- *Nonoperating Assets*: As indicated in Exhibit 15.1, some companies tend to have a significant amount of nonoperating assets—usually, cash and marketable securities, value of minority holdings in other companies, and value of idle or unutilized assets. Their values can be quite significant.
- *Non-equity Claims*: An interest-bearing debt is the most common non-equity claim on a firm. However, adjustments may be required to consider other items like values of operating lease commitments, minority interests, unfunded health care or pension obligations, and expected litigation payouts. These claims reduce equity holders' value: lease commitments are treated as the equivalent of debt to estimate the cost of capital; valuation of parent companies tends to be based on consolidated operating income and cash flows, which include the value of minority interests in the subsidiaries; some companies tend to have other significant potential claims such as unfunded pension plans and health care obligations; and some companies tend to have outstanding lawsuits that may have the potential for significant payouts, constituting expected liabilities. To determine equity value, non-equity claims should be deducted from the total firm value.

Think 15.3

If the valuation process is 100% objective, then should valuation results be equal among different analysts? Why?

15.4 Valuation Models

There are several intrinsic valuation models, generally described as growth stage models. A stage represents a period (fixed or indefinite) wherein free cash flows are expected to exhibit similar behavior. The two main modeling categories are single-stage growth and multiple stage growth. ▶ Exhibit 15.3 describes and depicts ideal patterns of single-stage, two-stage, and three-stage growth models. Overall, the models are built around growth rates to forecast cash flows and therefore growth assumptions relate to three variables: take-off cash flow, expected growth rate, and stage period coverage.

The choice and application of a model depends on various factors like the nature of industry, the company's business cycle, historical cash flow patterns, and investment and capital expenditure. This aspect is explained and illustrated with cases in ▶ Exhibits 15.5A–15.7A and 15.8.

15.4.1 Single-Stage Models

A single-stage growth model is simply a constant growth model, assuming stable growth of cash flows indefinitely. It is analogous to Gordon' constant dividend growth model, which can be expressed as follows:

$$Value = \frac{CF_0(1+g)}{(r-g)}$$

where CF_0 is the initial free cash flow (FCFF or FCFE), g denotes the expected growth rate of free cash flow (FCFF or FCFE), and r is a discount rate (WACC or cost of equity).

Pros and Cons: The model is highly simplified and easy to apply, but the assumption that growth will remain unchanged forever is difficult to justify. Companies can experience business cycles as they implement strategies to improve performance, thereby reinitiating high growth.

15.4.2 Multiple Stage Models

Multiple growth models assume that free cash flows are expected to experience different growth stages or phases: usually two-stage or three-stage growth models. It should be noted that although the patterns in ▶ Exhibit 15.3 only depict long-term growth trends, short-term variations are also expected within a growth stage and that a true transition between stages tends to be gradual rather than drastic or abrupt.

Pros and Cons: The models provide flexibility to adjust growth rate patterns from one stage to another, depending on expectations and the nature of business. However, there is more room for an analyst's subjective influence on vital valuation variables like take-off growth rate and projecting the time limit for a high or transitional growth stage.

15.4.2.1 Two-Stage Models

A two-stage growth model assumes that cash flows will go through two stages of growth. Usually, stage 1 has a limited short period of moderate or high growth, whereas stage 2 is expected to experience steady growth indefinitely. A general model for the value of operating assets (PV_{OA}) can be presented as follows:

$$PV_{OA} = \sum_{t=1}^{n} \frac{CF_t(1+g_{t+1})}{(1+r)^t} + \frac{CF_{n+1}/(r-g_S)}{(1+r)^n}$$

where $\sum_{t=1}^{n} \frac{CF_t(1+g_{t+1})}{(1+r)^t}$ is the present value of free cash flows in stage 1 and the terminal value $CF_{t+n}/(r-g_S)$ represents the stable stage 2 at a constant growth rate g_S.

15.4.2.2 Three-Stage Models

A three-stage growth model assumes that cash flows will go through three different phases of growth. Stage 1 is usually a fixed short period of high growth, whereas stage 2 is transitional with fading growth, approaching stage 3 of low but stable growth. The model can be expressed as follows:

$$PV_{OA} = \sum_{t=1}^{T} \frac{CF_t(1+g_{t+1})}{(1+r)^t} + \sum_{t*T+1}^{n} \frac{CF_t}{(1+r)^t} + \frac{CF_{n+1}/(r-g_S)}{(1+r)^n}$$

where $\sum_{t=1}^{n} \frac{CF_t(1+g_{t+1})}{(1+r)^t}$ and $\sum_{t*T+1}^{n} \frac{CF_t}{(1+r)^t}$ are the present value of free cash flows in stage 1 and stage 2, respectively and $CF_{t+n}/(r-g_S)$ is the terminal value.

Banner 15.3 Reality of Growth Models

Growth models have been simplified to make valuation practically possible. The reality is that variations are possible within a particular growth stage.

Exhibit 15.3 Valuation Models (See Excel Workings—▸ Chap. 15, Sheet E.15.3)

This exhibit presents three different types of valuation models: single-stage, two-stage, and three-stage growth models. The choice and application of a model depends on the general criteria (considerations) outlined below. Specific criteria should reflect the specific characteristics of a company being valued.

Notes

Percentages (vertical axis) indicate variations in growth rates within a growth stage. Numbers on the horizonal axis represent the period from now to future (0, 1, 2, 3, …, *n*). Therefore, g_n is the growth rate for period *n*, 1 and T denote period 1 and terminal period, respectively, and g_1 and g_T denote take-off growth rate (in period 1) and terminal growth, respectively. A stable growth rate can be assumed to be either equal to the terminal growth rate (▫ Exhibit 15.3.1) or less than the terminal growth rate (▫ Exhibit 15.3.2).

Single-Stage Model

- *Application*: This model can be applied in the valuation of a mature company that has passed the transitional stage, experiencing extremely stable free cash flows, and does not have the potential for moderate or high growth.

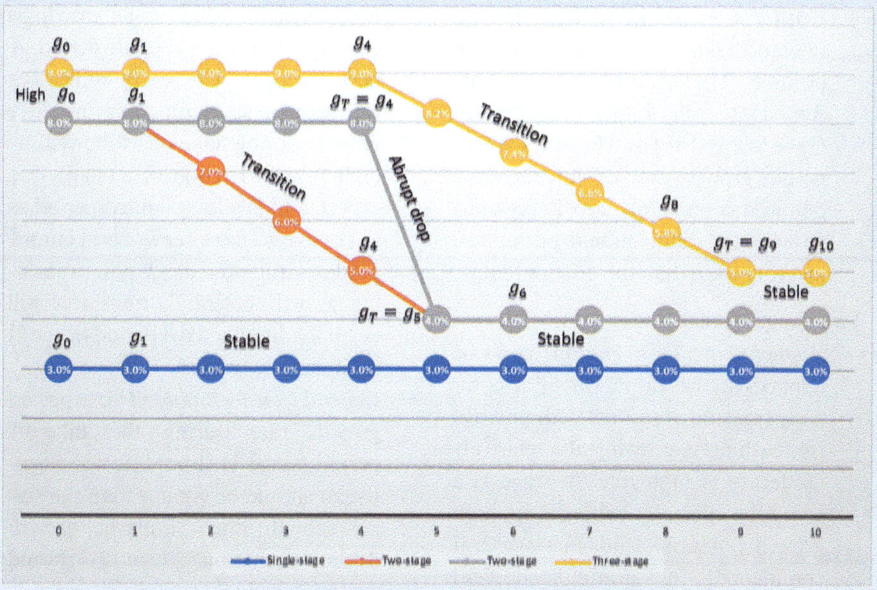

Exhibit 15.3.1 Valuation models: if stable growth equals terminal growth

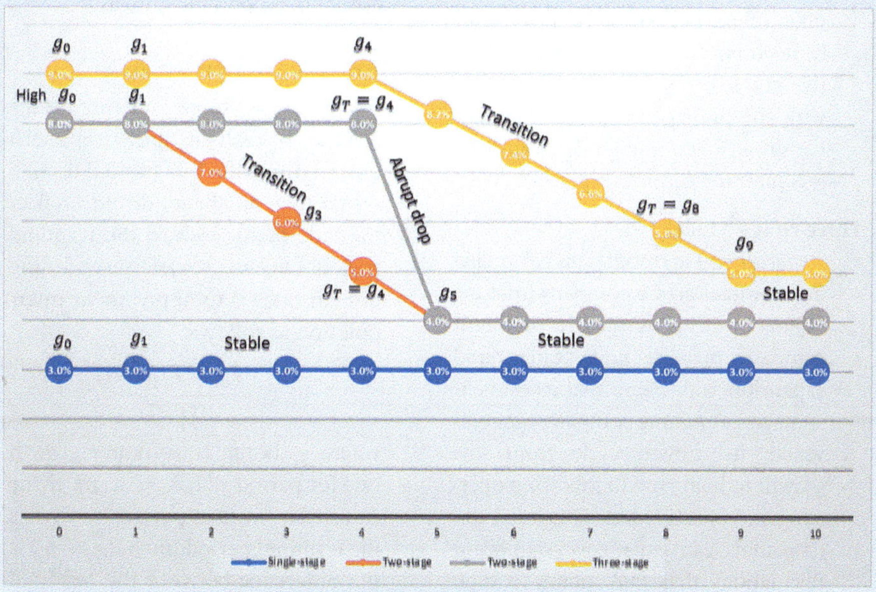

Exhibit 15.3.2 Valuation models: if stable growth is lower than terminal growth

- *General Considerations*: Both growth rate and take-off cash flows must be positive. The expected growth rate should satisfy the following conditions: (1) be low and not outperform the economic growth rate of a company's domicile country or global economic growth (for multinational businesses) and (2) be less than the discount rate.

Two-Stage Model

- *Application*: This model can be applied in the valuation of a company (mature or infant) with positive free cash flows growing at a relatively moderate to high rate. In stage 1, a company typically exhausts its high growth potential, and, in stage 2, it commences a gradual descent toward stability for a fixed period.
- *General Considerations*: The expected growth rate during the take-off period (stage 1) should not be negative: it should be greater than the stable growth rate to comply with the fading-out factor. The stable growth rate (stage 2) should be less than the economic growth.

Three-Stage Model

- *Application*: This model can be applied in the valuation of a company (mature, infant, or new). A mature or infant company may be undergoing rapid expansion with aggressive investment strategies. A mature company can rejuvenate its growth cycle from low growth to high growth following operating and financial restructuring. Fundamentals can experience significant fluctuations that may point to high growth. A new company can experience strong market entry and competitive power, in which high growth is expected during the take-off period. A new company with entry difficulties can experience temporary negative growth during take-off, followed by high growth. High growth (stage 1) is expected to last for a limited period as a company faces new competitors, market saturation, etc. Upon exhausting growth potential, transition will begin for another fixed period (stage 2) until stability (stage 3).
- *General Considerations*: The expected growth rate during the take-off period (stage 1) should not be negative: it should be greater than the stable growth rate. Similarly, growth during transition (stage 2) should exceed terminal growth to comply with the fading-out factor. The stable growth rate (stage 3) should not exceed the economic growth.

Transitional Growth Rates

For both two-stage and three-stage models, a realistic growth pattern during transition is a gradual decline rather than an abrupt drop to reflect the fade factor toward the terminal period. One way to determine fading growth rates is to apply linear interpolation as follows:

$$g_n = g_1 + \frac{\left(g_T - g_{1)}\right)(n-1)}{(T-1)}$$

where g_n is the transitional growth rate for period n (1, 2, 3, …, n). If the transition starts in period 1 and T is the terminal period, then, $(g_T - g_1)$ is the difference between the terminal growth and growth rates in period 1, $(n - 1)$ is the difference between the transitional period n and period 1, and $(T-1)$ is the difference between the terminal period and period 1.

Examples (Refer to Exhibit 15.3.1):

For a two-stage model, transition starts at stage 1 (period 1):

$T = 5$; $g_1 = 8\%$ and $g_T = g_5 = 4\%$. If $n = 2$:

$$g_2 = g_1 + \frac{(g_5 - g_{1)})(2-1)}{(5-1)}$$

$$= 8\% + \frac{(4\% - 8\%)(2-1)}{(5-1)} = 7.0\%$$

For a three-stage model, transition starts at stage 2. If transition starts at period 5 and the terminal period is 9:

$T = 9$; $g_4 = 9\%$; and $g_T = g_9 = 5\%$. If $n = 5$:

$$g_5 = g_4 + \frac{(g_9 - g_{4)})(5-4)}{(9-4)}$$

$$= 9\% + \frac{(5\% - 9\%)(5-4)}{(9-4)} = 8.2\%\%$$

15.4.3 Practical Considerations

Analysts' subjective judgments are vital at this valuation stage. Among others, the following practical aspects should be considered (refer to ► Exhibits 15.5A–15.7A and 15.8 for illustrative cases):

1. *Valuation Model:* The choice of a valuation model depends on analysts' views about the characteristics of the company being valued. It involves a profound analysis of the company's historical performance and current position and how they are expected to influence future growth. Generally, the CC approach better suits companies with significant leverage, whereas the direct approach is more applicable for low-leverage companies.
2. *Take-Off Cash Flow:* A decision should be made about the initial (take-off) cash flow (FCFF or FCFE) to commence stage 1—it should be positive and forward-looking. Free cash flows of the current period can be chosen, but these tend be misleading due to abnormalities (extremely high or extremely low) and are thus not forward-looking. The use of a historical average of a correctly selected sample period addresses several issues, including negativity problems, normalization of erratic cash flow patterns, and improved forward-looking measures.
3. *Take-Off Growth Rate*: A decision about the take-off growth rate has a great impact on valuation. It should be reasonably justified to reflect the company's characteristics and valuation model. Conservative analysts tend to avoid over-valuation—they aim at a moderate growth rate. Aggressive analysts tend to avoid undervaluation—they aim at a high growth rate.
4. *Terminal Growth:* A decision about terminal growth rate should satisfy stability characteristics. A stable growth rate should not outperform an economic growth rate but can be slightly higher for high-growth industries. Typical proxies for

terminal growth rates tend to be gross domestic product (GDP) growth rate, risk-free interest rate, or mature industry growth rate.

5. *Discount Rate*: Depending on free cash flows (FCFF or FCFE), the discount rate is either WACC or cost of equity. These variables can vary according to variations in the target capital structure and respective financing costs. In practice, however, analysts tend to assume a constant discount rate for simplicity (see Bancel and Mittoo 2014). This assumption is justifiable and acceptable because of the complexities involved in determining continuous WACC (or cost of equity) adjustments, which may be practically inaccurate and unjustifiable. Should there be a need to vary discount rates, then several adjustments can be made, including, but not limited to, the following:
   (a) If expecting a change in the capital structure (debt ratio), then an increase (decrease) in leverage should be associated with an increase (decrease) in pretax cost of debt to reflect credit risk. Use the current cost of debt at take-off, then allow variations in each growth stage following the target debt ratio. A market or industry average debt ratio can be used to determine the stability of the capital structure.
   (b) Allow beta variations of each period to approach 1.00 or the industry average in the terminal period (stable beta).
   (c) To vary the risk-free rate, you can consider the government's credit rating projections or the term structure of interest rates.
   (d) The market risk premium can also vary if information is available about expected country default spreads and capital market volatility.
   (e) Varying variables in (a) above will affect WACC, whereas varying variables in (b) and (c) will affect both cost of equity and WACC.
6. *Projection Period*: There is no universal rule about fixing time projections for stages 1 and 2. A decision is challenging and highly subjective because it is difficult to predict when a company will reach transition or maturity (stability). Generally, before reaching stability, a new or infant company should expect a longer fixed period than a mature business: the former tends to have higher growth expectations than the latter. A 3- to 5-year period is commonly applicable for fixed growth phases, although it can be longer depending on analysts' ability to provide accurate forecasts. The longer the forecast time horizon, the higher the possibility of valuation inaccuracy.

7. *Growth Stages*: Several factors can be considered to determine growth stages:
8. *Stable Stage*: Stability can be characterized by several factors. However, a quick indication is low investments and a narrower gap between capital expenditure and depreciation. Usually, the gap between capital expenditure and depreciation is wide during high growth and should be narrowing when approaching stability. An almost constant gap over a long historical period signifies maturity or stability.
9. *Transitional Stage*: An abrupt change from one stage to another is not realistic. The fade factor should be considered when approaching the terminal period. It is generally reasonable to assume a gradual decline of growth in a stage preceding stable growth.

Exhibit 15.4 Case Companies

Ecopetrol SA (See Excel Workings—▶ Chap. 15 Sheets E.15.4A, E.15.4D, E.15.4G, E.15.4H, and E.15.4K)

Ecopetrol SA (hereafter EC) is an oil company operating in "Colombia, Peru, Brazil, and the United States Gulf Coast. The Company's segments include Exploration and Production, Transportation and Logistics, and Refining, Petrochemicals and Biofuels. The Company's Exploration and Production segment includes exploration, development, and production activities in Colombia and abroad. The Company's Transportation and Logistics segment includes the transportation of crude oil, motor fuels, fuel oil and other refined products, including diesel and biofuels" (Reuters 2022). Its "Baa3 ratings continue to reflect the company's status as Colombia's leading oil and gas producer, accounting for over 60% of the country's production and close to 100% of the supply of oil products, as well its large power transmission business in Colombia and other countries in Latin America" (Moody's 2022).

Exhibit 15.4.1 presents EC's free cash patterns and key fundamentals over the past 13 years to the current year 2021. Exhibit 15.4.2 depicts its fundamental growth determinants. The following key points should be noted and reflected on during valuation decisions:

1. Both FCFF and FCFE have been generally highly volatile (including negative moments). Their fundamentals have been generally stable. The year 2009 marked the end of the global financial crisis (2007–2008). Upward trending performance (free cash flows and fundamentals) after 2009 may imply a recovery process.
2. Using total assets as a measure of size, the company grew at a higher pace until 2013. Thereafter, it slowed down until 2020. The year 2019 marked the beginning of the coronavirus disease of 2019 (COVID-19) crisis, the effect of which was reflected in the company's dropping performance (of all variables) in 2020; this can be considered abnormal; the reverse in 2021 may imply a recovery process, associated with heavy investments during that year.
3. Return on assets (ROA), return on equity (ROE), and return on invested capital (ROIC) have all changed direction twice over the last 10 years: dropping from 2011 to 2015 and rising afterward to 2021 (the 2020 decline was likely to have been temporary). An increase from 2009 to 2011 may have been related to recovery from the financial crisis.
4. The retention ratio was highly volatile, a typical feature of the industry attributed by volatile earnings. The sharp decline in 2020 reflected the effect of the COVID-19 crisis (abnormal). The reinvestment rate dropped steadily but improved between 2017 and 2020: the 2021 drop could have been temporary.

Cost of Capital: The valuation date was 31 December 2021. WACC and cost of equity were 8.3% and 12.8%, respectively. The risk-free rate was 6.5%, proxied by a 10-year Colombian government bond yield (8.14%) adjusted for country risk spread (1.62%). The expected market return was 11. 53% based on the

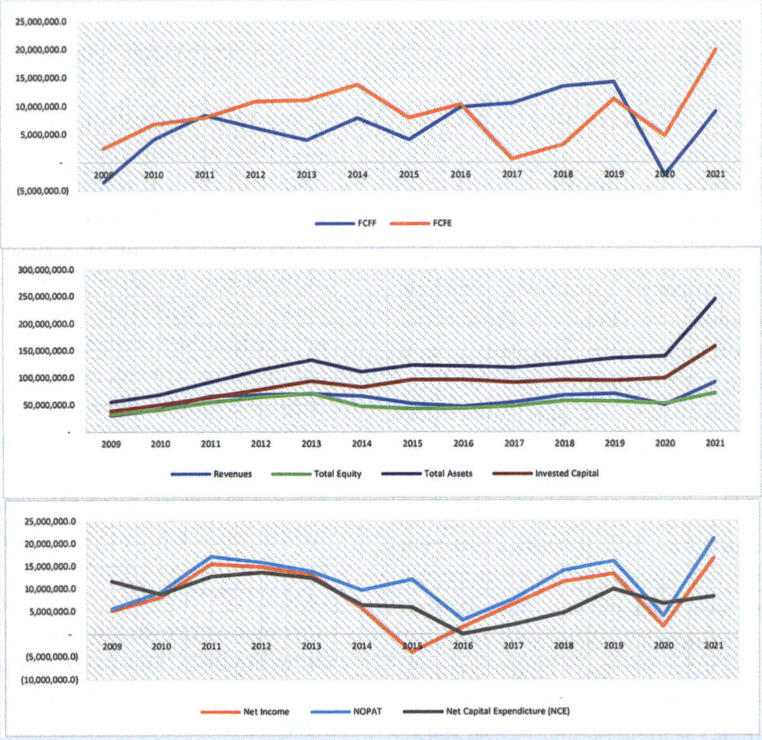

Exhibit 15.4.1 EC's historical free cash flows and fundamentals

Exhibit 15.4.2 EC's fundamental growth determinants

Exhibit 15.4.3 EC's growth rate estimates: average and current

Approach	Method	Sample period						
		10-Year	8-Year	6-Year	5-Year	4-Year	3-Year	Current (2021)
Historical extrapolation (FCFF)	Arithmetic	55.4%	77.0%	94.3%	84.7%	104.3%	129.8%	
	Geometric							
	Regression	2.1%	2.9%	−2.4%	−13.0%	−20.8%	−34.5%	
Historical extrapolation (FCFE)	Arithmetic	90.3%	108.1%	147.1%	170.5%	236.7%	139.9%	
	Geometric	9.5%	7.6%	16.5%	13.9%	173.0%	84.5%	
	Regression	0.7%	1.3%	15.2%	23.3%	50.6%	44.7%	
Fundamentals	IGR_{EPS}	1.0%	0.9%	2.1%	2.4%	2.4%	1.4%	3.5%
	SGR_{EPS}	2.4%	2.3%	5.7%	6.4%	6.4%	4.0%	10.8%
	SGR_{NOPAT}	4.0%	2.2%	1.8%	2.1%	2.7%	3.0%	−3.5%

Note: The average GDP growth rate (Colombia): 10 years (3.3%) and 5 years (2.1%)

COLCAP market index. Beta was 1.2484 based on a 5-year sample period. The after-tax cost of debt was 2.9%, based on an effective interest rate of 4.4% and a corporate tax rate of 33.6%. Market capitalization on valuation data was COP 110,603,909 million from 41,116.7 million shares outstanding, trading at COP 2690 per share. The market value of debt was COP 95,060,928 million, simplified by assuming that it equaled the book value on the valuation date.

Growth Rate Estimates: Exhibit 15.4.3 summarizes the growth estimates from various approaches. Analysts should decide on a suitable estimation approach and growth rate to apply.

Harley-Davidson (See Excel Workings—► Chap. 15, Sheets E.15.4B, E.15.4E, E.15.4G, E.15.4I, and E.15.4L)

Harley-Davidson, Inc. (hereafter HD) is a US-based company "engaged in the manufacture and sale of custom, cruiser, and touring motorcycles. It operates through the following segments: Motorcycles & Related Products and Financial Services. The Motorcycles & Related Products segment manufactures, designs, and sells at wholesale on-road Harley-Davidson motorcycles as well as motorcycle parts, accessories, general merchandise, and related services. The Financial Services segment consists of financing and servicing wholesale inventory receivables and retail consumer loans, primarily for the purchase of Harley-Davidson motorcycles" (CNN Business 2022).

Exhibit 15.4.4 presents HD's free cash patterns and key fundamentals over the past 20 years to the current year 2022. Exhibit 15.4.5 depicts its fundamental growth determinants. The following key points should be noted and reflected on during valuation decisions:

1. FCFFs have been generally highly volatile (including negative moments). They have remained stable, except during a sharp drop in 2008, coincid-

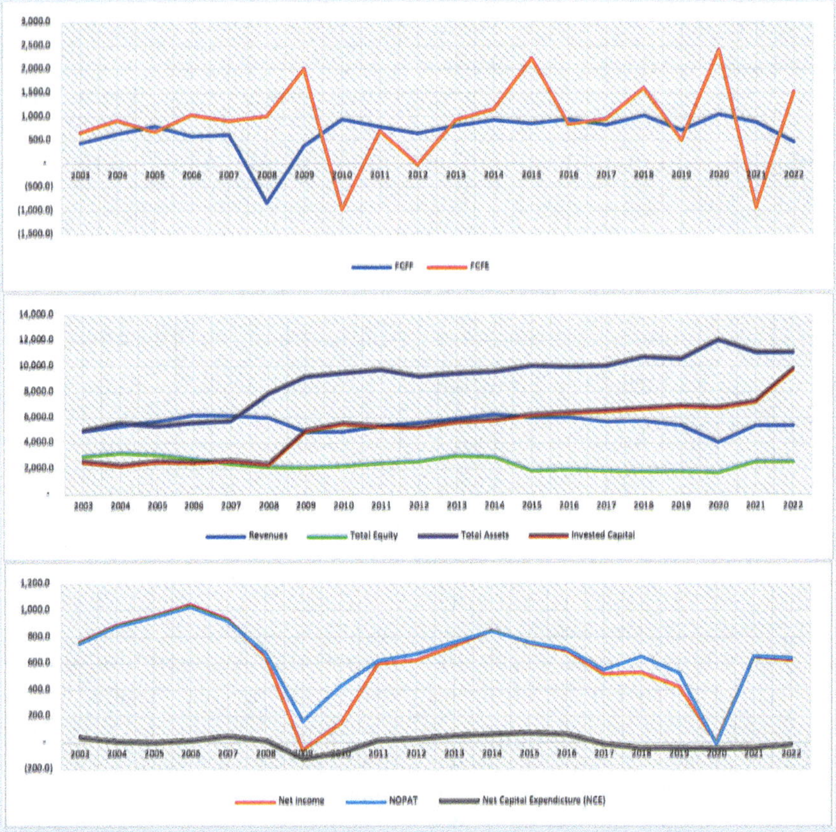

Exhibit 15.4.4 HD's historical free cash flows and fundamentals

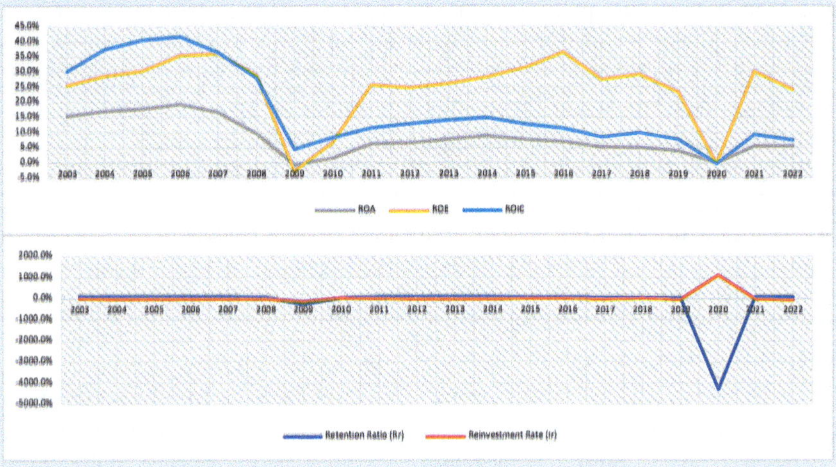

Exhibit 15.4.5 HD's fundamental growth determinants

Exhibit 15.4.6 HD's growth rate estimates: average and current

Approach	Method	Sample period					
		15-Year	10-Year	5-Year	4-Year	3-Year	Current (2022)
Historical extrapolation (FCFF)	Arithmetic	2.1%	0.8%	−4.4%	−11.6%	−5.4%	
	Geometric		−3.2%	−10.7%	−17.8%	−13.3%	
	Regression	6.1%	−0.4%	−6.4%	−11.4%	−11.7%	
Historical extrapolation (FCFE)	Arithmetic	294.8%	439.1%	101.1%	109.2%	168.5%	
	Geometric						
	Regression	2.2%	1.3%	−7.9%	−15.5%	−3.0%	
Fundamentals	IGR_{EPS}	3.4%	3.7%	2.7%	2.7%	3.0%	4.8%
	SGR_{EPS}	15.3%	17.6%	14.5%	14.1%	15.0%	20.8%
	SGR_{NOPAT}	−0.5%	−0.5%	−1.0%	−1.7%	−1.7%	−4.8%

Note: The average GDP growth rate (United States): 10 years (2.0%) and 5 years (1.9%)

ing with the global financial crisis of 2007–2008: this can be considered abnormal. Fundamentals have been generally stable with a gradual upward trend in total assets and invested capital despite flat earnings.

2. The aftermath of the global financial crisis resulted in a sharp shift in company size (total assets and invested capital). The slight fall of earnings in 2020 reflected a moderate effect of the COVID-19 crisis.
3. ROA, ROE, and ROIC dropped sharply during the global financial crisis (2007–2009). Recovery from 2010 was followed by a relatively stable performance until a sudden decline in 2020, reflecting the COVID-19 crisis (considered to be abnormal): the reverse in 2021 indicates the company's recovery.
4. Both retention ratio and reinvestment rate have been stable. Variations in 2009 and 2020 seemed to respond abnormally to crises.

Cost of Capital: The valuation date was 16 August 2022. WACC and cost of equity were 4.5% and 9.4%, respectively. The risk-free rate was 2.79%, proxied by a 10-year US government bond yield: country risk spread was 0%. The expected market return was 7.6% based on Standard and Poor's 500 (S&P 500's) market index. Beta was 1.3780 based on a 5-year sample period. The after-tax cost of debt was 0.35%, based on an effective interest rate of 0.43% and a corporate tax rate of 19.9%. Market capitalization on valuation data was US$ 6128.61 million from 145.40 million shares outstanding, trading at US$ 42.15 per share. The market value of debt was US$ 7154.85 million, simplified by assuming that it equaled the book value on the valuation date.

Growth Rate Estimates: Exhibit 15.4.6 summarizes the growth estimates from various approaches. Analysts should decide on a suitable estimation approach and growth rate to apply.

Tanzania Breweries Ltd. (See Excel Workings—▶ Chap. 15, Sheets E.15.4C, E.15.4F, E.15.4G, E.15.4J, and E.15.4M)

Tanzania Breweries Ltd. (hereafter TBL) "is a Tanzania-based company. The Company's principal activities are the production, distribution and sale of malt beer, non-alcoholic malt beverages and alcoholic fruit beverages (AFB's) in Tanzania. It operates breweries in Dar es Salaam, Arusha, Mwanza and Mbeya and depots throughout the country. The Company has a controlling interest in Tanzania Distilleries Limited, a spirituous liquor company that is situated in Dar es Salaam located in Dar es Salaam. It also fully owns Kibo Breweries Limited, a property management company domiciled in Moshi. The Company also produces and distributes Castle Lager, Castle Milk Stout, Castle Lite, and Redds Premium Cold under license from ABInbev International BV. In addition, it distributes ABInbev beer brands Budweiser and Corona." (Reuters 2022).

Exhibit 15.4.7 presents TBL's free cash patterns and key fundamentals over the past 18 years to the current year 2021. Exhibit 15.4.8 depicts its fundamental growth determinants. The following key points should be noted and reflected on during valuation decisions:

1. Both FCFF and FCFE have been almost equal and follow identical patterns because the company has an extremely low debt ratio (the debt-to-equity ratio is about 20% on average): the narrower the gap between FCFF and FCFE, the lower the leverage ratio during the respective period, and vice versa. A wider gap in 2010 followed the withdrawal of 20% stock stake by EABL (East African Breweries Ltd.) through public offerings (not repurchases), forcing the company to borrow heavily (TZS 87 billion compared to just TZS 1.8 billion in 2009). A wider gap in 2014 was due to heavy debt repayment (TZS 53 billion compared to TZS 10 billion in 2013).
2. The company can be considered as fast-growing between 2004 and 2016. Overall, free cash flows and company size have been growing at a high speed since 2009 (after the global financial crisis). A sharp downward free cash flow trend from 2017 onward coincides with dropping investments, revenues, and earnings during the same period. While the growth of total assets, invested capital, and revenues has been widening, net capital expenditure has been relatively stable but low. Net income and net operating profit after tax (NOPAT) have been almost equal and identical due to low leverage: they have been growing at a moderate but stable rate.
3. The COVID-19 crisis (2020) had a negligible impact on company performance because the Tanzanian government did not implement lockdown measures.
4. ROA, ROE, and ROIC have been dropping gradually since 2009, implying a slower pace of earnings growth than company size.
5. Retention ratio and reinvestment rate have been moving together in the long term. A shift in direction was evident from 2011 onward: from an upward trend prior to the downward trend until recent years. The sharp drop in the retention ratio to

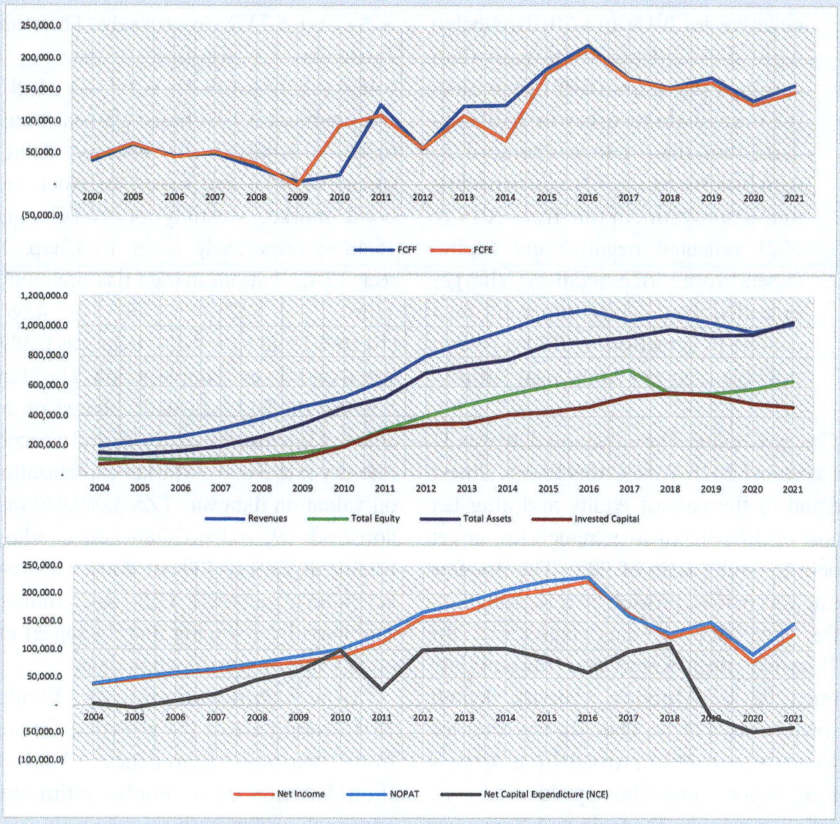

Exhibit 15.4.7 TBL's historical free cash flows and fundamentals

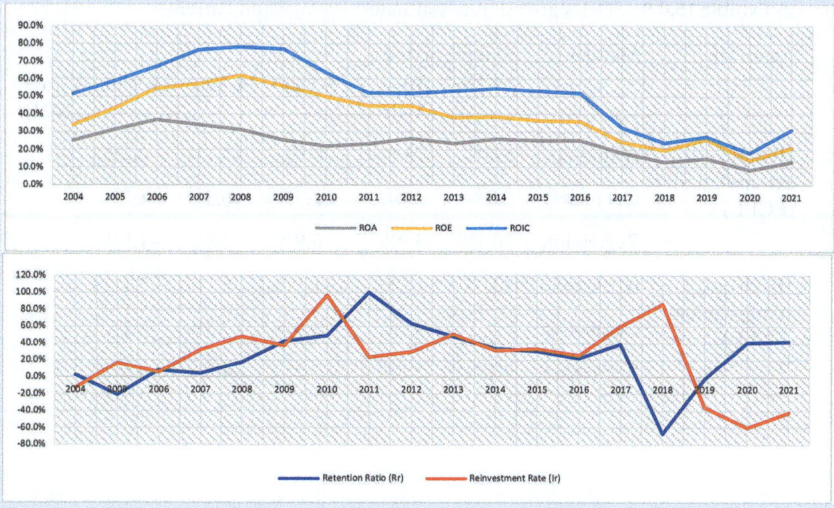

Exhibit 15.4.8 TBL's fundamental growth determinants

negative in 2018 and 2019 reflected more dividend per share paid than earnings per share (EPS) generated: the immediate recovery in 2020 suggests that the event was temporary (can be abnormal). The sharp decline in the reinvestment rate from 2019 to 2021 reflected negative net capital expenditure: depreciation charges exceeded fixed capital expenditure; a change in direction in 2021 signified possible recovery in the near future.

Cost of Capital: The valuation date was 31 December 2021. WACC was 10.0%, almost equal to the cost of equity and after-tax cost of debt due to an extremely low target debt-to-equity ratio of 20%. The risk-free rate was 6.46%, proxied by a Kenyan risk-free rate due to data limitations for Tanzania. Both Kenya and Tanzania are rated B2 by Moody's. Country default spread was 4.68%. The risk-free rate for Kenya was 8.49%, proxied by a 10-year Kenyan government bond yield of 13.17%. Inflation rates in Tanzania and Kenya are 3.7% and 5.73%, respectively. Therefore, Tanzanian risk-free rate is 6.46% = 8.49% + (3.7% – 5.73%). Market risk premium is 9.4% based US benchmark (6.32%): adjusted for country default spread (4.68%) and scaled for stock and bond market volatility of 10.16% and 15.48%, respectively (refer to Chap. 12 sect. 12.4.3.3 about market risk premium). Thus, 6.32% + 4.68% (10.16%/15.48%) = 9.4%. Beta was 0.3891 based on a 5-year sample period. The after-tax cost of debt was 10.0%, based on an effective interest rate of 15.3% and a corporate tax rate 34.3%. Market capitalization on valuation data was TZS 3,069,040 million from 295 million shares outstanding, trading at TZS 10,400 per share. The market value of debt was TZS 14,423 million, simplified by assuming that it equaled the book value on the valuation date.

Growth Rate Estimates: Exhibit 15.4.9 summarizes the growth estimates from various approaches. Analysts should decide on a suitable estimation approach and growth rate to apply.

Exhibit 15.4.9 TBL's growth rate estimates: average and current

Approach	Method	Sample period					
		15-Year	10-Year	5-Year	4-Year	3-Year	Current (2021)
Historical extrapolation (FCFF)	Arithmetic	57.4%	74.6%	–0.9%	–5.1%	–0.5%	
	Geometric	5.8%	23.4%	–2.5%	–6.5%	–1.7%	
	Regression	10.1%	3.9%	–6.9%	–2.8%	–1.8%	
Historical extrapolation (FCFE)	Arithmetic	926.3%	15.1%	–1.5%	–6.1%	–2.1%	
	Geometric		4.2%	–3.0%	–7.3%	–3.2%	
	Regression	9.1%	5.2%	–7.9%	–4.3%	–3.5%	

15

Exhibit 15.4.9 (continued)

Approach	Method	Sample period					
		15-Year	10-Year	5-Year	4-Year	3-Year	Current (2021)
Fundamentals	IGR_{EPS}	6.0%	4.8%	1.3%	0.0%	2.8%	5.4%
	SGR_{EPS}	9.6%	7.5%	2.1%	0.0%	4.7%	8.8%
	SGR_{NOPAT}	11.1%	8.3%	1.4%	−2.9%	−11.5%	−13.1%

Note: The average GDP growth rate (Tanzania): 20 years (6.1%), 10 years (5.5%), and 5 years (4.9%)

Think 15.4

From ▶ Exhibit 15.4, *(a) How would you determine whether a company's expected growth is stable, moderate, or growth? (b) What are the decision challenges facing growth rates and take-off free cash flows?*

15.5 Valuation: Single-Stage, Two-Stage, and Three-Stage Models

15.5.1 Analysts' Judgments and Practical Applications

▶ Exhibits 15.5A–15.7A apply real company cases to illustrate intrinsic valuation. The three case companies are Ecopetrol SA (Colombia), Harley-Davidson (United States), and Tanzania Breweries Ltd. (Tanzania), selected to reflect different business characteristics and enable envisage various decision challenges from analysts' point of view. Suppose that three different analysts value the same company using the same information described in ▶ Exhibit 15.4 but have conflicting decisions about valuation models, growth rates, and take-off free cash flows. Each analyst provides justification to back his/her judgments. The aim is to demonstrate the valuation influence of analysts' subjective judgments. One must pay attention to their decision criteria and reasoning to justify their key decisions. They can be correct or wrong— ▶ Exhibit 15.8 provides counteractive views (by a different analyst) to point out the possible wrong decisions.

Overall, both valuation decisions and results should make sense. It is not only about numbers but also the story behind the numbers. ▶ Exhibit 15.4 illustrates a typical way to make sense of the numbers by reflecting on a company's profile and financial characteristics: examining historical patterns of free cash flows and fundamentals to identify the key events, cycles, trends, direction, and magnitude of change, among others. Historical patterns give quick indications of growth directions and help analysts make key decisions such as growth assumptions, estimation methods, and sample selection. For instance, highly volatile historical free cash flows may suggest a limited application of historically extrapolated growth estimates and may call for the use of average rather than current metrics: they tend to be misleading. A sharp (gentle) upward trend implies high (moderate) growth, whereas a flat (downward) trend suggests stable (declining) growth. Structural shifts or outliers can help determine the cutoff points for sample period selection.

Banner 15.4 Sense-Making of Valuation Judgments

Subjective judgments are inevitable, but they should be backed by the reality of the company and other factors influencing value.

Generally, the following key steps can guide valuation (see ► Exhibits 15.5A–15.7A):

1. Know the story of the company (refer to ► Exhibit 15.4).
2. Prepare a data sheet comprising all valuation variables determined earlier:
   - (a) Cost of capital, free cash flows, growth rate estimates.
   - (b) Others: market cap, current stock price, shares outstanding, debts outstanding, nonoperating assets, etc.
3. Decide about the following valuation aspects and provide reasons to justify your judgments based on your knowledge about the company in (1).
   - (a) Valuation approach and model.
   - (b) Expected growth rates: take-off, terminal, stable.
   - (c) Take-off free cash flow for the initial growth stage.
4. Estimate value based on information in (2) and (3):
   - (a) *If a Single-Stage Model*: Discount the expected cash flows with a constant growth model.
   - (b) *If a Multiple stage Model*: Forecast future cash flows, determine the terminal value, discount the expected free cash flows (and terminal value), and calculate the total present value.
5. Calculate value based on estimates in (4) and other variables in (2).
   - (a) *If the CC Approach*: Calculate the total firm value by adding nonoperating assets. Calculate equity value by subtracting the debts outstanding from the total firm value.
   - (b) *If the Direct Approach*: Equity value is the sum of FCFE present values.
6. Calculate value per share based on the results in (5) and information in (2):
   - (a) Divide equity value by the number of common shares outstanding.
   - (b) Determine whether the stock is overvalued or undervalued.
7. Consider valuation sense-making
   - (a) Compare intrinsic value per share to market price per share. Rarely will the market value be equal to the intrinsic value, but the difference should be within a reasonable range. An extremely large difference gives a quick indication that valuation can be misleading.
   - (b) If valuation does not make sense, then it may be due to several reasons relating to quantitative errors and analysts' subjective decisions. Consider corrective measures—a sense-making valuation should always be achieved.

Exhibit 15.5A Intrinsic Valuation

Illustrative Case: Ecopetrol SA (See Excel Workings—► Chap. 15, Sheet E.15.5A)

Exhibit 15.5A.1 presents a data sheet summary using which valuation is performed. Decisions about the valuation model and specific variable choices depend on the individual judgments of each of the three analysts: Joseph, Josephine, and Joseline.

Valuation by Joseph: A Single-Stage Growth Model

Why a Single-Stage Constant Model? Ecopetrol is a mature company with limited growth potential. Free cash flows will grow at a positive constant rate indefinitely. Its total assets and invested capital have been rising at a relatively low rate over time (see Exhibit 15.4.1).

General Considerations: Constant growth rate should neither be negative nor greater than the country's 10-year average economic growth (3.3%) and cost of capital. However, having global operations, Ecopetrol's growth should not solely depend on domestic economic growth: it can be slightly higher. Ecopetrol's free cash flows (see Exhibit 15.4.1) are highly volatile and do not show a clear long-term trend. Historically extrapolated growth rates can be misleading (they are negative or

Exhibit 15.5A.1 Valuation data sheet (all in COP millions, except per share and percentages)

Variables	Sample period and averages						
	Current (2021)	10-Year	8-Year	6-Year	5-Year	4-Year	3-Year
$FCFF_0$	9,028,866	7,685,395	8,342,645	9,136,436	8,992,520	8,611,313	7,003,617
$FCFE_0$	19,887,236	9,372,423	8,972,244	8,333,985	7,928,964	9,761,169	11,959,133
SGR_{NOPAT}	−3.5%	4.0%	2.2%	1.8%	2.1%	2.7%	3.0%
SGR_{EPS}	10.8%	2.4%	2.3%	5.7%	6.4%	6.4%	4.0%
Nonoperating assets	14,549,906						
Market cap	110,603,909						
Debts outstanding	95,060,928						
WACC	8.3%						
Cost of equity	12.8%						
Shares outstanding	41,117						
Market price	2690						

extremely high or extremely small): decisions about growth rates are therefore based on fundamentals. The initial values (both growth rates and free cash flows) are based on average estimates to ensure a forward-looking valuation.

Valuation Judgments: The Cost of Capital Approach

Expected Growth Rate

- *Decision*: FCFFs are expected to grow constantly at 2.7% (a 4-year average).
- *Justification*: A 4-year average growth fulfills the general considerations. Average estimates from other sample periods can also be used, except a 10-year average growth rate (4.0%) because it exceeds Colombia's average GDP growth rate.

Initial FCFF

- *Decision*: The initial free cash flow is COP 8,611,313 (millions) based on a 4-year average.
- *Justification*: FCFF is highly volatile: the current position cannot be a better reflection of the future. Average estimates from other samples could also be used depending on analysts' judgment.

Valuation Judgments: The Direct Approach

Expected Growth Rate

- *Decision*: FCFE will grow constantly at 2.7% (a 4-year average).
- *Justification*: The selected growth rate satisfies the general considerations. As a rule (generally), the FCFE growth rate should not be lower than the FCFF growth rate. Estimated sustainable growth rates on EPS (SGR) are either greater than GDP growth or lower than the assumed FCFF growth (2.7%). Hence, a reasonable decision is to assume that both FCFE and FCFF will grow at the same rate.

Initial FCFE

- *Decision*: The initial free cash flow is COP 9,761,169 (millions) based on a 3-year average.
- *Justification*: This is the same as FCFF.

Valuation Results

The results are presented in Exhibit 15.5A.2.

Valuation by Josephine: A Two-Stage Growth Model

Why a Two-Stage Model? Ecopetrol is a mature company, but its recent performance points to potential high or moderate growth. From Exhibit 15.4.1, net income, NOPAT, and net capital expenditure, which were declining until 2016, have started a sharp upward trend recently. The gap between capital expenditure and depreciation (reflected in net capital expenditure) has been widening since 2016. These features signify potential high growth, which should last for a limited period while on transition to regain steady growth. Global events like the COVID-19 pandemic might have affected its growth pace over the last 3 years (especially in 2020).

General Considerations: Growth rate decisions are based on fundamentals: historically extrapolated estimates are highly sensitive to the sample period and can be misleading. The expected initial growth rate is determined by average estimates and assumed to be higher than a country's GDP growth rate (a 10-year average), which is 3.3%. Growth in stage 1 is expected to last for 5 years at a fading rate toward the terminal period to

Exhibit 15.5A.2 Joseph's valuation model and results (all in COP millions, except per share and percentages)

CC approach		Direct approach	
	Take-off		Take-off
Period	0	Period	0
Year	2021	Year	2021
g_{FCFF}	2.7%	g_{FCFE}	2.7%
FCFF	8,611,313	FCFE	9,761,169
PV_{OA}	160,869,572	PV_{FCFE}	99,619,748
Total firm value	175,419,478		
Equity value	80,358,550	Equity value	99,619,748
Value per share	1954	Value per share	2423
Market price	2690	Market price	2690
Status	Overvalued	Status	Overvalued

converge economic growth. Both FCFF and FCFE can grow at the same rate, but, generally, FCFF growth should not be higher than FCFE growth. WACC and cost of equity are assumed to be constant.

Valuation Judgments: The Cost of Capital Approach

Expected Growth Rates

- *Decision*: The initial growth rate in stage 1 is 4.0% (a 10-year average).
- *Justification*: A growth rate decision aims at complying with the general considerations. Estimates from the current period (2021) and lower sample periods (3- to 8-year) are either negative or lower than the expected terminal growth rate.

Initial FCFF

- *Decision*: The initial FCFF in stage 1 is COP 7,685,395 (millions) based on a 10-year average.
- *Justification*: A highly volatile FCFF implies that the current measures may not be a better reflection of the future. Average estimates on shorter sample periods (e.g., 3- to 8-year) can be used as they are consistent.

Valuation Judgments: The Direct Approach

Expected Growth Rate

- *Decision*: The initial growth rate in stage 1 is 6.4% (a 5-year average).
- *Justification*: To satisfy the general considerations, the FCFE growth rate should not be lower than the FCFF growth rate. Estimated SGR (EPS) on larger sample periods (8- and 10-year) are lower than the assumed initial FCFF growth rate (4.0%). Growth rate estimates from other samples (3-, 4- to 6-year) could be applied for the same decision criteria.

Initial FCFE

- *Decision*: The initial FCFE in stage 1 is COP 7,928,964 (millions) based on a 5-year average.
- *Justification*: This is the same as FCFF. Average estimates from other sample periods can be used: an aggressive analyst could choose a higher average.

Valuation Results

Exhibit 15.5A.3 depicts the growth rate projections: refer to ► Exhibit 15.3 for transitional growth rates. Valuation results are presented in Exhibits 15.5A.4 and 15.5A.5.

Valuation by Joseline: A Three-Stage Growth Model

Why a Three-Stage Model? Ecopetrol is a mature company but recent performance points to potential growth for a long fixed period. The company has significant fixed capital expenditure in the last 5 years from COP 3.6 trillion in 2016 to COP 12.9 trillion in 2021, which is reflected in an increase in their revenues, earnings, and current free cash flows. These investments are expected to boost productive operations for a long future. The company is also recovering from the COVID-19 pandemic and adjusting to the Russia–Ukraine crisis. Recovery strategies are expected to rejuvenate growth at a high rate for a limited period, followed by the transitional phase before reverting to stability.

General Considerations: To determine the expected growth rates, we focus on growth fundamentals: the erratic nature of historical free cash flows limit the use of historical extrapolation. An average estimate is the basis for determining forward-looking growth rate estimates. A 10-year GDP growth rate (3.3%) is used to benchmark economic growth. Free cash flows are expected to grow at a rate higher than economic growth during stages 1 and 2. Growth in stage 1 is expected to last for 5 years. Thereafter, fading will begin during transition at stage 2, lasting for 5 years toward the terminal period. Terminal growth rate is proxied by economic

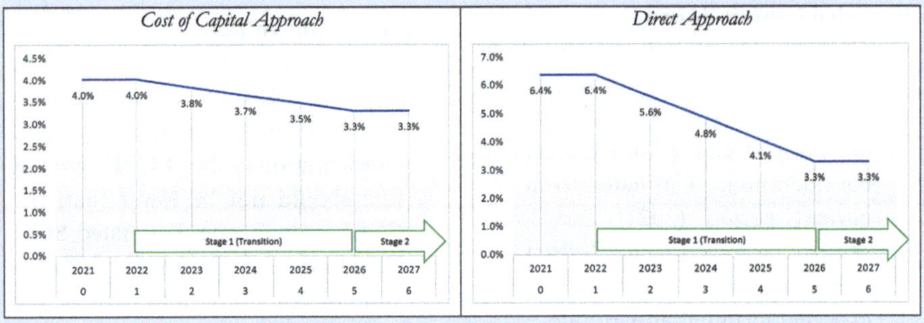

Exhibit 15.5A.3 Josephine's growth projections

Exhibit 15.5A.4 Josephine's valuation model and results (all in COP millions, except per share and percentages)

Cost of capital approach						
Stages	**Period**	**Year**	g_{FCFF}	**FCFF**	**Terminal value**	**Present value**
Take-off	0	2021	4.0%	7,685,395		
Stage 1	1	2022	4.0%	7,993,855		7,387,297
	2	2023	3.8%	8,300,180		7,088,366
	3	2024	3.7%	8,603,172		6,789,637
	4	2025	3.5%	8,901,604		6,492,105
	5	2026	3.3%	9,194,223	192,878,507	136,192,844
Stage 2	6	2027	3.3%			
PV_{OA}						163,950,249
Nonoperating assets						14,549,906
Firm value						178,500,155
Equity value						83,439,227
Value per share						2029
Market price						2690
Status						Overvalued

Exhibit 15.5A.5 Josephine's valuation model and results (all in COP millions, except per share and percentages)

Direct approach						
Stages	**Period**	**Year**	g_{FCFE}	**FCFE**	**Terminal value**	**Present value**
Take-off	0	2021	6.4%	7,928,964		
Stage 1	1	2022	6.4%	8,433,346		7,477,905
	2	2023	5.6%	8,905,003		7,001,548
	3	2024	4.8%	9,334,604		6,507,826
	4	2025	4.1%	9,713,194		6,004,573
	5	2026	3.3%	10,032,493	109,196,440	65,355,436
Stage 2	6	2027	3.3%			
PV_{FCFE}						92,347,288
Value per share						2246
Market price						2690
Status						Overvalued

growth rate, which will prevail indefinitely during the stable phase. FCFE growth is expected to outperform FCFF growth. WACC and cost of equity are assumed to be constant.

Valuation Judgments: The Cost of Capital Approach

Expected Growth Rate

- *Decision*: The initial growth rate is 4.0% (a 10-year average).
- *Justification*: Stage 1 and stage 2 growth should neither be negative nor lower than the country's GDP growth. Stage 3 growth should not exceed the GDP growth. The average growth estimated from smaller sample periods does not satisfy the general considerations.

Initial FCFF

- *Decision*: The initial FCFF in stage 1 is COP 7,685,395 (millions) based on a 10-year average.
- *Justification*: FCFF is highly volatile: using the current position at the initial stage may not be a better reflection of the future. Average estimates from shorter sample periods could be used as they are relatively consistent.

Valuation Judgments: The Direct Approach

Expected Growth Rate

- *Decision*: The initial growth rate is 6.4% (a 5-year average).
- *Justification*: This is the same as FCFF. To comply with the general considerations, the FCFE growth rate is set higher than the FCFF growth rate. Estimated SGR (EPS) on larger sample periods (8- and 10-year) are lower than the assumed initial FCFF growth (4.0%), whereas those from other samples (3-, 4-, and 6-year) also meet the criteria.

Initial and Terminal FCFE

- *Decision*: The initial FCFE in stage 1 is COP 7,928,964 (millions) based on a 10-year average.
- *Justification*: This is the same as FCFF. Nevertheless, depending on analysts' discretion, average estimates from other sample periods can be used.

Valuation Results

Exhibit 15.5A.6 depicts the growth rate projections: refer to Exhibit 15.3 for transitional growth rates. Valuation results are presented in Exhibits 15.5A.7 and 15.5A.8.

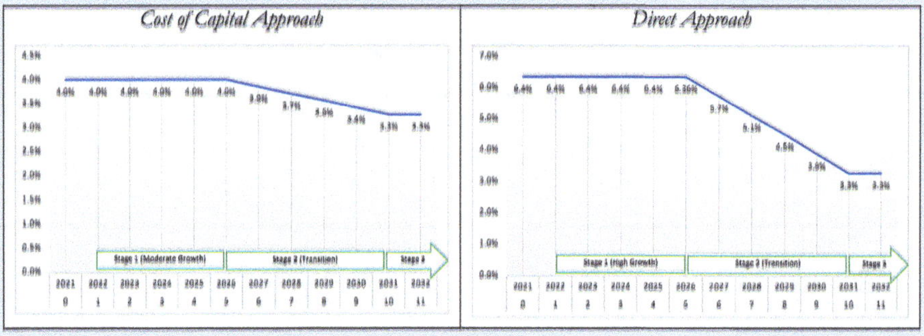

Exhibit 15.5A.6 Joseline's growth projections

Exhibit 15.5A.7 Joseline's valuation model and results (all in COP millions, except per share and percentages)

Cost of capital approach						
Stages	**Period**	**Year**	g_{FCFF}	**FCFF**	**Terminal value**	**Present value**
Take-off	0	2021	4.0%	7,685,395		
Stage 1	1	2022	4.0%	7,993,855		7,387,297
	2	2023	4.0%	8,314,695		7,100,762
	3	2024	4.0%	8,648,413		6,825,341
	4	2025	4.0%	8,995,524		6,560,603
	5	2026	4.0%	9,356,567		6,306,133
Stage 2	6	2027	3.9%	9,718,509		6,053,068
	7	2028	3.7%	10,080,335		5,802,033
	8	2029	3.6%	10,440,989		5,553,620
	9	2030	3.4%	10,799,380		5,308,388
	10	2031	3.3%	11,154,385	233,999,219	111,360,568
Stage 3	11	2032	3.3%			
PV_{OA}						168,257,813
Nonoperating assets						14,549,906
Firm value						182,807,719
Equity value						87,746,791
Value per share						2134
Market price						2690
Status						Overvalued

Exhibit 15.5A.8 Joseline's valuation model and results (all in COP millions, except per share and percentages)

Direct approach						
Stages	**Period**	**Year**	g_{FCFE}	**FCFE**	**Terminal value**	**Present value**
Take-off	0	2021	6.4%	7,928,964		
Stage 1	1	2022	6.4%	8,433,346		7,477,905
	2	2023	6.4%	8,969,813		7,052,505
	3	2024	6.4%	9,540,406		6,651,306
	4	2025	6.4%	10,147,296		6,272,929
	5	2026	6.4%	10,792,792		5,916,078
Stage 2	6	2027	5.7%	11,412,996		5,547,275
	7	2028	5.1%	11,998,672		5,171,223
	8	2029	4.5%	12,540,637		4,792,473
	9	2030	3.9%	13,029,981		4,415,337
	10	2031	3.3%	13,458,312	146,484,001	48,057,756
Stage 3	11	2032	3.3%			
PV_{FCFE}						101,354,787
Value per share						2465
Market price						2690
Status						Overvalued

Exhibit 15.6A Intrinsic Valuation

15

Illustrative Case: Harley-Davidson (See Excel Workings—▶ Chap. 15, Sheet E.15.6A).

Exhibit 15.6A.1 presents a data sheet summary using which valuation is performed. Decisions about the valuation model and specific variable choices depend on the individual judgments of each of the three analysts: Verediana, Valentina, and Valeriana.

Valuation by Verediana: A Single-Stage Constant Growth Model

Why a Single-Stage Constant Model? The company is mature with limited growth potential in its business segment. As depicted in Exhibit 15.4.4, historical revenues and net capital expenditure have been generally stable for a long period, whereas total assets have been increasing slowly. Cash flows are expected to grow indefinitely at a positive constant rate.

General Considerations: Decisions about growth rates are based on historical extrapolation: growth estimates from fundamentals are either negative or higher than the economic growth or cost of capital. The initial FCFF is based on the current year because the historical FCFF pattern has been stable. The initial FCFE is based on the average estimates due to the erratic nature of historical patterns. The expected growth rates for both FCFF and FCFE are determined by average estimates. The constant growth rate should neither be negative nor greater than the average of a country's 10-year GDP growth rate (2.0%) and cost of capital. FCFE growth is expected be higher than FCFF growth.

Valuation Judgments: The Cost of Capital Approach

Expected Growth Rate

- *Decision*: Stable growth is expected to be 0.8% based on a 10-year arithmetic average.
- *Justification*: Fundamentals suggest that this is a low-growth company. The applicable growth rate is lower than the GDP growth rate to satisfy the general considerations.

Initial FCFF

- *Decision*: The initial FCFF is $463 million (current year).
- *Justification*: Historical FCFFs have shown stability. However, the past 3 years (2020–2022) point toward a declining direction. Historical averages are relatively high for a conservative position but can be applied by an aggressive analyst.

Valuation Judgments: The Direct Approach

Expected Growth Rate

- *Decision*: The expected growth is 1.3% based on a 10-year average (linear regression).
- *Justification*: Historical FCFEs are highly volatile: linear regression provides compounded growth estimates, which capture long-term effects on FCFE within a larger sample period. An aggressive analyst could apply estimates from a 15-year sample (2.2%) as they are nearly equal to the economic growth rate.

Initial FCFE

- *Decision:* The initial FCFE is US$ 1125.6 million (a 10-year average).
- *Justification*: Unlike FCFF, historical FCFEs have been highly volatile. Average estimates on other sample periods can be applied depending on analysts' decision.

Valuation Results

The results are presented in ▫ Exhibit 15.6A.2.

Valuation by Valentine: A Two-Stage Growth Model

Why a Two-Stage Model? The company is mature but not yet to exhaust all growth opportunities. It is still transiting toward potential stability. It is, therefore, expected to go through two growth phases. The current capital structure will be maintained in the future.

General Considerations: Decisions about growth rates are based on historical extrapolation. Growth estimates from fundamentals are disregarded because they are either negative or significantly outperform economic growth. The initial FCFF is based on the current year because the historical FCFF pattern has been stable. The initial FCFE is based on average estimates due to the erratic nature

Exhibit 15.6A.1 Valuation data sheet (all in US$ millions, except per share and percentages)

Variables	Sample period and averages				
	Current (2022)	15-Year	10-Year	5-Year	3-Year
$FCFF_0$	463.0	689.0	843.4	822.8	795.8
$FCFE_0$	1531.4	932.1	1125.6	1027.1	1006.8
g_{FCFF} [a]	−4.8%	2.1%	0.8%	−4.4%	−5.4%
g_{FCFE} [b]	20.8%	2.2%	1.3%	−7.9%	−3.0%
Nonoperating assets	1874.7				
Market cap	6128.6				
Debts outstanding	7154.9				
WACC	4.5%				
Cost of equity	9.4%				
Shares outstanding	145.4				
Market price	42.2				

[a] Based on the arithmetic average, except the current year (fundamentals)
[b] Based on linear regression, except the current (fundamentals)

Exhibit 15.6A.2 Verediana's valuation model and results (all in US$ millions, except per share and percentages)

CC approach		Direct approach	
	Take-off		Take-off
Period	0	Period	0
Year	2022	Year	2022
g_{FCFF}	0.8%	g_{FCFE}	1.3%
FCFF	463	FCFE	1125.6
PV_{OA}	12,315.7	PV_{FCFE}	13,976.3
Total firm value	14,190.5		
Equity value	7035.6	Equity value	13,976.3
Value per share	48.4	Value per share	96.1
Market price	42.2	Market price	42.2
Status	Undervalued	Status	Undervalued

15

of historical patterns. The expected growth rates for both FCFF and FCFE are determined by average estimates. Growth rates in the initial year are set higher than the 10-year average economic growth (2.0%). Stage 1 will last for 5 years in which growth is expected to fade out toward the terminal growth rate: GDP growth is assumed to be the terminal growth rate. FCFE growth is expected to be equal to or higher than FCFF. We assume stable WACC and cost of equity.

Valuation Judgments: The Cost of Capital Approach

Expected Growth Rate

- *Decision*: The initial growth rate is expected to be 2.1% based on a 15-year arithmetic average.
- *Justification*: To satisfy the general considerations, stage 1 growth is higher than the country's GDP growth. The average growth estimates from other samples do not satisfy the general criteria.

Initial FCFF

- *Decision*: The initial FCFF is $463 million (current year).
- *Justification*: FCFFs have been stable and a conservative position is taken to keep FCFFs relatively low. Historical averages are higher but can be applied by an aggressive analyst.

Valuation Judgments: The Direct Approach

Expected Growth Rate

- *Decision*: The initial growth rate is 2.2% based on a 15-year linear regression.
- *Justification*: This is the same as FCFF. Moreover, the FCFE growth rate is assumed to be slightly higher than the FCFF growth rate.

Initial FCFE

- *Choice*: The initial FCFE is US$ 932.1 million (a 15-year average).
- *Justification*: Unlike FCFFs, historical FCFEs have been highly volatile: an average from a large sample period is preferable. Averages on smaller sample periods can be applied depending on analysts' reasoning and judgment.

Valuation Results

Exhibit 15.6A.3 depicts the growth rate projections: refer to ▶ Exhibit 15.3 for transitional growth rates. Valuation results are presented in Exhibits 15.6A.4 and 15.6A.5.

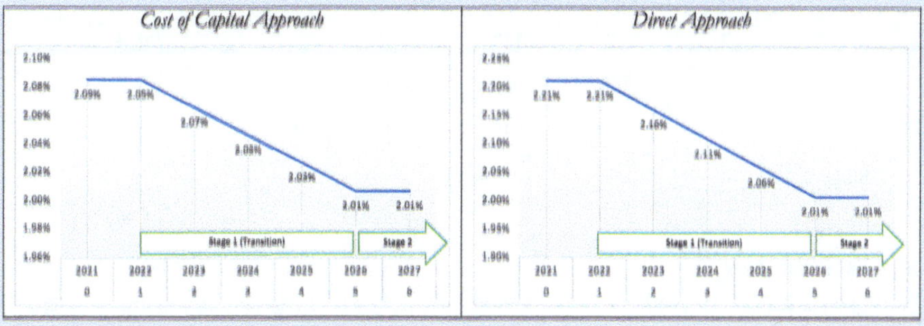

Exhibit 15.6A.3 Valentine's growth projections

Exhibit 15.6A.4 Valentine's valuation model and results (all in US$ millions, except per share and percentages)

Cost of capital approach						
Stages	**Period**	**Year**	g_{FCFF}	**FCFF**	**Terminal value**	**Present value**
Take-off	0	2022	2.09%	463.0		
Stage 1	1	2023	2.09%	472.7		452.2
	2	2024	2.07%	482.4		441.5
	3	2025	2.05%	492.3		430.9
	4	2026	2.03%	502.3		420.6
	5	2027	2.01%	512.4	20,653.7	16,954.0
Stage 2	6	2028	2.01%			
PV_{OA}						18,699.2
Nonoperating assets						1874.7
Firm value						20,573.9
Equity value						13,419.1
Value per share						92.3
Market price						42.2
Status						Undervalued

Exhibit 15.6A.5 Valentine's valuation model and results (all in US$ millions, except per share and percentages)

Direct approach						
Stages	**Period**	**Year**	g_{FCFE}	**FCFE**	**Terminal value**	**Present value**
Take-off	0	2022	2.21%	932.1		
Stage 1	1	2023	2.21%	952.7		870.6
	2	2024	2.16%	973.3		812.7
	3	2025	2.11%	993.8		758.4
	4	2026	2.06%	1014.2		707.3
	5	2027	2.01%	1034.6	14,217.0	9719.0
Stage 2	6	2028	2.01%			
PV_{FCFE}						12,867.9
Value per share						88.5
Market price						42.2
Status						Undervalued

15

Valuation by Valeriana: A Three-Stage Growth Model

Why a Three-Stage Model? The company is mature and operates in a specialty business (customized products). It is still exploring potential growth opportunities from strong fundamentals: total assets and invested capital show an upward trend despite flat earnings, reflecting the nature of the business. Recovery from the COVID-19 pandemic is likely to reignite the business cycle while adjusting to global events until stability. Growth in stage 1 is expected to commence with a high growth rate reflecting the take-off pace from recovery strategies. Stage 2 will experience fading growth and the company will restabilize in stage 3.

General Considerations: The take-off face (stage 1) is expected to be slightly higher than the economic growth rate (2.0%). Estimates from fundamentals do not fulfill these criteria, and, therefore, historical extrapolation is the basis for determining expected growth rates. The initial FCFF is based on the current year to reflect the most current fundamentals, considering historical FCFF stability. The initial FCFE is based on average estimates due to the erratic nature of historical patterns. The expected growth rates for both FCFF and FCFE are determined by the average estimates to reflect forward-looking valuation. FCFE growth is expected to be higher than FCFF growth. The growth rate in stage 2 will begin fading out toward the terminal growth (lower than the GDP growth rate by half). WACC and cost of equity are assumed to be constant.

Valuation Judgments: The Cost of Capital Approach

Expected Growth Rate

- *Decision*: The initial growth rate in stage 1 is 2.1% based on a 15-year arithmetic average.
- *Justification*: Harley-Davidson is generally a low-growth business. However, growth in stage 1 and stage 2 is expected at a slightly higher pace than the country's GDP growth. Growth will be lower than economic growth during stage 3 of stability.

Initial FCFF

- *Decision*: The initial FCFF is $463 million (current year).
- *Justification*: A conservative position is taken to avoid overestimation: the initial FCFF is kept relatively low, considering the stable nature of historical FCFF. An aggressive analyst can consider the average values, which are relatively higher.

Valuation Judgments: The Direct Approach

Expected Growth Rate

- *Decision*: Stage 1 is expected to take off with an initial growth rate of 2.2% based on a 15-year linear regression.
- *Justification*: This is the same as FCFF. Moreover, FCFE growth is kept higher than FCFF growth to satisfy the general considerations.

Initial FCFE

- *Decision*: The initial FCFE is US$ 932.1 million (a 15-year average).
- *Justification*: Historical FCFEs have been highly volatile to justify the use of average estimates. Other analysts can consider average estimates from other sample periods.

Valuation Results

◘ Exhibit 15.6A.6 depicts the growth rate projections: refer to ▶ Exhibit 15.3 for transitional growth rates. Valuation results are presented in ◘ Exhibits 15.6A.7 and 15.6A.8.

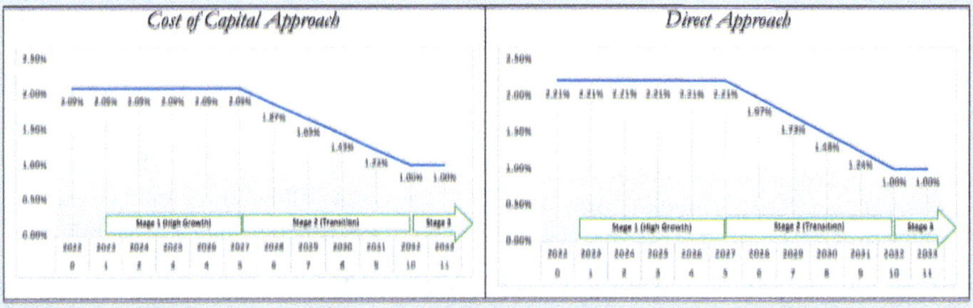

Exhibit 15.6A.6 Valeriana's growth projections

Exhibit 15.6A.7 Valeriana's valuation model and results (all in US$ millions, except per share and percentages)

Cost of capital approach						
Stages	**Period**	**Year**	g_{FCFF}	**FCFF**	**Terminal value**	**Present value**
Take-off	0	2022	2.09%	463.0		
Stage 1	1	2023	2.09%	472.7		452.2
	2	2024	2.09%	482.5		441.5
	3	2025	2.09%	492.6		431.2
	4	2026	2.09%	502.9		421.1
	5	2027	2.09%	513.4		411.2
Stage 2	6	2028	1.87%	522.9		400.7
	7	2029	1.65%	531.6		389.6
	8	2030	1.43%	539.2		378.1
	9	2031	1.22%	545.8		366.1
	10	2032	1.00%	551.2	15,736.6	10,450.3
Stage 3	11	2033	1.00%			
PV_{OA}						14,141.9
Nonoperating assets						1874.7
Firm value						16,016.7
Equity value						8861.8
Value per share						60.9
Market price						42.2
Status						Undervalued

Exhibit 15.6A.8 Valeriana's valuation model and results (all in US$ millions, except per share and percentages)

Direct approach						
Stages	**Period**	**Year**	g_{FCFE}	**FCFE**	**Terminal value**	**Present value**
Take-off	0	2022	2.21%	932.1		
Stage 1	1	2023	2.21%	952.7		870.6
	2	2024	2.21%	973.7		813.1
	3	2025	2.21%	995.3		759.5
	4	2026	2.21%	1017.3		709.4
	5	2027	2.21%	1039.8		662.6
Stage 2	6	2028	1.97%	1060.3		617.4
	7	2029	1.73%	1078.6		574.0
	8	2030	1.48%	1094.6		532.3
	9	2031	1.24%	1108.2		492.5
	10	2032	1.00%	1119.3	13,409.42	5899.8
Stage 3	11	2033	1.00%			
PV_{FCFE}						11,931.2
Value per share						82.1
Market price						42.2
Status						Undervalued

Exhibit 15.7A Intrinsic Valuation

Illustrative Case: Tanzania Breweries Ltd. (TBL) (See Excel Workings—▶ Chap. 15, Sheet E.15.7A)

Exhibit 15.7A.1 presents a data sheet summary using which valuation is performed. Decisions about the valuation model and specific variable choices depend on the individual judgments of each of the three analysts: Costancia, Leparata, and Asela.

Valuation by Costancia: A Single-Stage Constant Growth Model

Why a Single-Stage Constant Model? Founded in 1933, TBL is a mature company with limited growth potential in the East African region. From Exhibit 15.4.7, the company has grown significantly since 2004 in terms of its operations and financial position. However, revenues, earnings, net capital expendi-

Exhibit 15.7A.1 Valuation data sheet (all in TZS millions, except per share and percentages)

Variables	Sample period and averages				
	Current (2021)	15-Year	10-Year	5-Year	3-Year
$FCFF_0$	157,453	114,724	149,640	156,931	153,722
$FCFE_0$	147,150	111,803	138,787	151,544	145,870
SGR_{NOPAT}	−13.1%	11.1%	8.3%	1.4%	−11.5%
SGR_{EPS}	8.8%	9.6%	7.5%	2.1%	4.7%
Nonoperating assets	224,635				
Market cap	3,069,040				
Debts outstanding	14,423				
WACC	10.0%				
Cost of equity	10.0%				
Shares outstanding	295.1				
Market price	10,400				

ture, and free cash flows have declined over the past 5 years. We assume that free cash flows will grow indefinitely at a constant rate.

General Considerations: Decisions about growth rates are based on fundamentals: estimates from SGR (EPS) are considered more appropriate due to low leverage. Historically extrapolated growth rates are either negative or extremely high. Average growth rates and free cash flows are desirable (where necessary) to improve forward-looking valuation. A stable growth rate is not expected to outperform the country's 10-year average economic growth (5.5%). Both FCFF and FCFE are expected to grow at the same rate as they experience identical patterns, reflecting low leverage.

Valuation Judgments: The Cost of Capital Approach

Expected Growth Rate

- *Decision*: FCFF will grow constantly at 4.7% (a 3-year average).
- *Justification*: A 3-year average growth rate reflects the most current growth trend and fulfills the general considerations: it is lower than both the GDP growth rate and WACC.

Initial FCFF

- *Decision*: The initial free cash flow is TZS 153,722 (millions) based on a 3-year average.
- *Justification*: The past 5 years (2016–2021) suggest a declining FCFF trend. A 3-year average is almost equal to the current FCFF and can capture the most current trend to reflect the future. The current or average estimates from other sample periods can also be used since they are consistent.

15

Exhibit 15.7A.2 Costancia's valuation model and results (all in TZS millions, except per share and percentages)

CC approach		Direct approach	
	Take-off		Take-off
Period	0	Period	0
Year	2021	Year	2021
g_{FCFF}	4.7%	g_{FCFE}	4.7%
FCFF	153,722	FCFE	145,870
PV_{OA}	2,984,186	PV_{FCFE}	2,831,745
Total firm value	3,208,821		
Equity value	3,194,398	Equity value	2,831,745
Value per share	10,826	Value per share	9596
Market price	10,400	Market price	10,400
Status	Undervalued	Status	Overvalued

Valuation Judgments: The Direct Approach

Expected Growth Rate

- *Decision*: FCFE will grow constantly at 4.7% (a 3-year average).
- *Justification*: This is the same as FCFF.

Initial FCFE

- *Decision*: The initial free cash flow is TZS 145,870 (millions) based on a 3-year average.
- *Justification*: This is the same as FCFF.

Valuation Results

The results are presented in Exhibit 15.7A.2.

Valuation by Leparata: A Two-Stage Growth Model

Why a Two-Stage Model? TBL is a mature company but was growing at a high pace. From 2016, growth seems to have slowed down regarding key fundamentals: revenues, earnings, invested capital, net capital expenditure, and free cash flows (see Exhibit 15.4.7). This suggests that the company may be in transition toward stability.

General Considerations: Decisions about growth rates are based on fundamentals: estimates from shareholder earnings are considered more appropriate due to the extremely low leverage. Expected growth rates are determined by average estimates (forward-looking). The growth rate in the initial year is expected to be higher than a 5-year average economic growth (4.9%) to provide for the fading-out effect. Growth in stage 1 is fixed to 5 years: free cash flow will grow at a decreasing rate toward the terminal period to converge with economic growth. Generally, FCFE growth should be higher than or equal to FCFF growth, but we consider them to be equal. WACC and cost of equity are assumed to be constant and applicable in the two growth phases.

Valuation Judgments: The Cost of Capital Approach

Expected Growth Rates

- *Decision*: The initial growth rate in stage 1 is expected to be 7.5% (a 10-year average).
- *Justification*: The expected initial growth rate in stage 1 is higher than stable growth to comply with the general criteria. An aggressive analyst can consider a higher growth estimate (9.6%) from a 15-year sample period or 8.8% on the current year.

Initial FCFF

- *Decision*: The initial FCFF in stage 1 is TZS 149,640 (millions) based on a 10-year average.
- *Justification*: Averages provide a more forward-looking picture. The current FCFF and average estimates from other sample periods are consistent and can be alternatives.

Valuation Judgments: The Direct Approach

Expected Growth Rates

- *Decision*: The initial growth rate in stage 1 is expected to be 7.5% (a 10-year average).
- *Justification*: This is the same as FCFF growth. A higher rate from the current year (8.8%) or a 15-year average (9.6%) can also apply.

Initial FCFE

- *Decision*: The initial FCFE in stage 1 is TZS 138,787 (millions) based on a 10-year average.
- *Justification*: This is the same as FCFF.

Valuation Results

Exhibit 15.7A.3 depicts the growth rate projections: refer to Exhibit 15.3 for transitional growth rates. Valuation results are presented in Exhibit 15.7A.4 and Exhibit 15.7A.5.

Valuation by Asela: A Three-Stage Growth Model

Why a Three-Stage Model? TBL is a mature company but recent performance points to potential growth for a limited period. Over the past 5 years, the key growth fundamentals (net capital expenditure, invested capital, and earn-

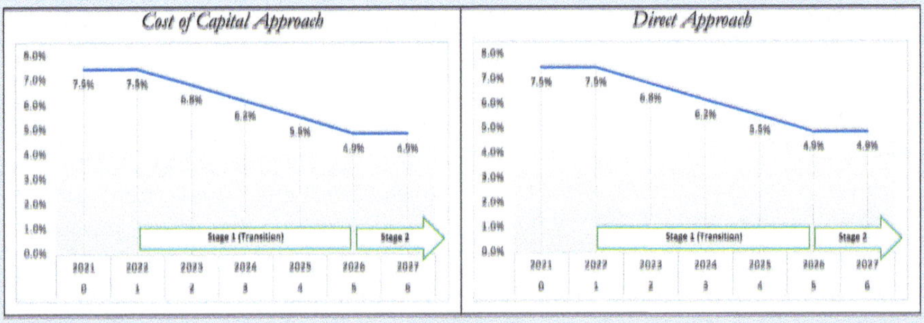

Exhibit 15.7A.3 Leparata's growth projections

Exhibit 15.7A.4 Leparata's valuation model and results (all in TZS millions, except per share and percentages)

Cost of capital approach						
Stages	**Period**	**Year**	g_{FCFF}	**FCFF**	**Terminal value**	**Present value**
Take-off	0	2021	7.5%	149,640		
Stage 1	1	2022	7.5%	160,806		146,130
	2	2023	6.8%	171,760		141,840
	3	2024	6.2%	182,345		136,839
	4	2025	5.5%	192,399		131,206
	5	2026	4.9%	201,757	4,085,277	2,656,733
Stage 2	6	2027	4.9%			
PV_{OA}						3,212,748
Nonoperating assets						224,635
Firm value						3,437,383
Equity value						3,422,960
Value per share						11,599
Market price						10,400
Status						Undervalued

Exhibit 15.7A.5 Leparata's valuation model and results (all in TZS millions, except per share and percentages)

Direct approach						
Stages	**Period**	**Year**	g_{FCFE}	**FCFE**	**Terminal value**	**Present value**
Take-off	0	2021	7.5%	138,787		
Stage 1	1	2022	7.5%	149,143		135,530
	2	2023	6.8%	159,302		131,550
	3	2024	6.2%	169,120		126,911
	4	2025	5.5%	178,444		121,686
	5	2026	4.9%	187,123	3,788,383	2,463,584
Stage 2	6	2027	4.9%			
PV_{FCFE}						2,979,262
Value per share						10,096
Market price						10,400
Status						Overvalued

ings) have shown a steady decline, but total assets have maintained a steady increase (see ◘ Exhibit 15.4.7). The current fundamentals are strong: retention ratio and ROE show an increase over the past 3 years. High growth is expected over the next 5 years (stage 1) before transitioning for another 5 years (stage 2) toward steady growth (stage 3).

General Considerations: Decisions about growth rates are based on fundamentals. Considering the extremely low debt ratio, both FCFF and FCFE are expected to grow at the same rate based on shareholders' earnings. Expected growth rates are determined by average estimates (forward-looking). Growth in stage 1 is expected to be higher than the 5-year average economic growth (4.9%). To capture the fading effect, growth rate in stage 2 will descend toward the terminal period to converge with economic growth. WACC and cost of equity are assumed to be constant.

Valuation Judgments: The Cost of Capital Approach

Expected Growth Rates

- *Decision*: The initial growth rate in stage 1 is 7.5% (a 10-year average).
- *Justification*: To satisfy the general considerations, growth in stage 1 and stage 2 is greater than the country's GDP growth. Growth in a stable phase does not exceed the GDP growth. An aggressive position can consider a higher growth rate in stages 1 and 2.

Initial FCFF

- *Decision*: The initial FCFF in stage 1 is TZS 149,640 (millions) based on a 10-year average.
- *Justification*: A 10-year average coincides with growth decisions to consider forward-looking valuation. Nevertheless, the current or average estimates from other sample periods can be applied depending on analysts' subjective judgments.

Valuation Judgments: The Direct Approach

Expected Growth Rates

- *Decision*: The initial growth rate in stage 1 is 7.5% (a 10-year average).
- *Justification*: This is the same as FCFF. To satisfy the general considerations, FCFE growth is equal to FCFF growth.

Initial FCFF

- *Decision*: The initial FCFE in stage 1 is TZS 138,787 (millions) based on a 10-year average.
- *Justification*: This is the same as FCFF.

Valuation Results

◘ Exhibit 15.7A.6 depicts the growth rate projections: refer to ► Exhibit 15.3 for transitional growth rates. Valuation results are presented in ◘ Exhibits 15.7A.7 and 15.7A.8.

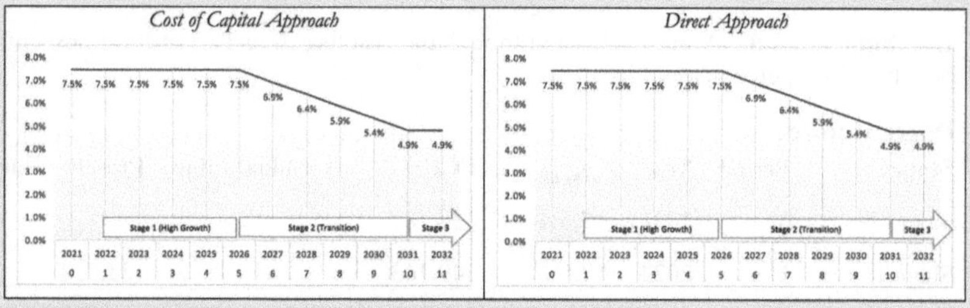

Exhibit 15.7A.6 Asela's growth projections

Exhibit 15.7A.7 Asela's valuation model and results (all in TZS millions, except per share and percentages)

Cost of capital approach						
Stages	**Period**	**Year**	g_{FCFF}	**FCFF**	**Terminal value**	**Present value**
Take-off	0	2021	7.5%	149,640		
Stage 1	1	2022	7.5%	160,806		146,130
	2	2023	7.5%	172,804		142,702
	3	2024	7.5%	185,698		139,355
	4	2025	7.5%	199,554		136,086
	5	2026	7.5%	214,443		132,893
Stage 2	6	2027	6.9%	229,330		129,149
	7	2028	6.4%	244,059		124,900
	8	2029	5.9%	258,465		120,201
	9	2030	5.4%	272,380		115,111
	10	2031	4.9%	285,628	5,783,552	2,330,837
Stage 3	11	2032	4.9%			
PV_{OA}						3,517,364
Nonoperating assets						224,635
Firm value						3,741,999
Equity value						3,727,576
Value per share						12,632
Price per share						10,400
Status						Undervalued

Exhibit 15.7A.8 Asela's valuation model and results (all in TZS millions, except per share and percentages)

Direct approach						
Stages	**Period**	**Year**	g_{FCFE}	**FCFE**	**Terminal value**	**Present value**
Take-off	0	2021	7.5%	138,787		
Stage 1	1	2022	7.5%	149,143		135,530
	2	2023	7.5%	160,271		132,350
	3	2024	7.5%	172,229		129,244
	4	2025	7.5%	185,080		126,212
	5	2026	7.5%	198,890		123,250
Stage 2	6	2027	6.9%	212,697		119,776
	7	2028	6.4%	226,357		115,835
	8	2029	5.9%	239,719		111,476
	9	2030	5.4%	252,624		106,755
	10	2031	4.9%	264,912	5,363,236	2,161,303
Stage 3	11	2032	4.9%			
PV_{FCFE}						3,261,732
Value per share						11,053
Price per share						10,400
Status						Undervalued

15.5.2 Are the Valuation Models Appropriate?

15

In ▶ Exhibits 15.5A–15.7A, three different analysts have presented their valuations for a particular company based on their assumptions and justifications. They have generally produced consistent results for the same company regardless of the models and approaches used. Does this suggest the use of proper valuation models by each of the analysts? Not necessarily.

Key Question: Which analyst's approach and model are reasonably the most suitable for the company? To answer this question, consider the following key issues: (1) whether growth assumptions realistically reflect a company's specific behavior—maturity or stability, high or low growth, or industry behavior; (2) whether there is a noticeable difference between one growth stage to another—for multiple stages, the differences between each stage, and the range between high growth and stable growth, should be reasonably sufficient; and (3) whether valuation should apply the cost of capital or the direct approach. Generally, the cost of capital approach is more suitable for companies with high leverage. The direct approach is more appropriate for low-leverage companies—leverage tends to cause FCFE volatility due to debt repayments. The effect of leverage is clarified in ▶ Exhibit 15.9.

Now, let us focus on our three cases. Suppose that investors are interested to know whether they should rely on the valuation results presented in ▶ Exhibits 15.5A–15.7A. They have decided to hire Jordan, an independent valuation expert, to give his views on each the three cases. To do so, Jordan focused on analysts' valuation assumptions and judgments. He also performed alternative valuation for Ecopetrol and Tanzania Breweries using the same variables but allowing variations in discount rates. His alternative reviews and valuation results are summarized in ▶ Exhibit 15.8, from which the following key issues should be noted:

1. The cost of capital approach and direct approach can arrive at consistent but different valuation results. Consider the leverage ratio to determine a better approach on which to rely.
2. The best model is never universal. Valuation is more sensitive to individual decisions than to quantitative metrics.
3. Valuation results should make sense when both valuation variables and individual judgments are correct. However, in some cases, even wrong judgments can end up with sensible results but should not be trusted.
4. Wrong valuation decisions should lead to wrong valuation—an overvalued stock can be undervalued, and vice versa, and thereby be misleading. Since there is no perfect valuation, Benjamin Graham advises investors to consider a "margin of safety": buy as cheap as possible to avoid losing money in case of wrong expectations founded by wrong valuation (Graham, 2006).

Banner 15.5 Caution: Sensible Results vs. Sensible Judgments

Valuation results can be consistent (and make sense) even if some of them were determined by improper approaches. To be reasonably acceptable, valuation should not only produce sensible results but also be based on correct judgments.

Exhibit 15.8 Valuation Cases (See ▶ Exhibits 15.5A, 15.6A, and E.15.7A)

Valuation Review by Jordan

Jordan, an independent analyst, has reviewed the valuation models and results in ◘ Exhibit 15.5A, 15.6A and 15.7A. The aim is to give an alternative opinion to help investors' decisions. ◘ Exhibits 15.8.1, 15.8.2, and 15.8.3 show the views of Jordan about each of the three models and the approaches applied by each of the three analysts for each case company. Generally, he agrees and disagrees with some analysts' judgments.

Valuation with Variable Discount Rates (See Excel Workings—▶ Chap. 15, Sheets E.15.5B, E.15.6B, and E.15.7B)

Jordan agrees with the assumption of constant discount rates applied by other analysts. However, he decides to perform alternative valuations with variable dis-

Exhibit 15.8.1 Ecopetrol SA (see ▶ Exhibits 15.5A) (market price = COP 2690 per share)

Model	Approach	Original valuation: constant discount rates			Jordan's valuation: variable discount rates	
		Is the model appropriate?	Value (COP)	Status	Value (COP)	Status
Single-stage	CC	Yes	1954	Overvalued		
	Direct	Yes	2423	Overvalued		
Two-stage	CC	Yes	2029	Overvalued	2577	Overvalued
	Direct	Yes	2246	Overvalued	2510	Overvalued
Three-stage	CC[a]	No	2134	Overvalued	2592	Overvalued
	Direct	Yes	2465	Overvalued	2668	Overvalued

[a] Despite sensible results, the valuation model is considered unsuitable as per comment (c)

Exhibit 15.8.2 Harley-Davidson (see E.15.6A) (market price = US$ 42.2 per share)

Model	Approach	Original valuation: constant discount rates			Jordan's valuation: variable discount rates	
		Is the model appropriate?	Value (US$)	Status	Value (US$)	Status
Single-stage	CC	Yes	48.4	Undervalued		
	Direct	Yes	96.1	Undervalued		
Two-stage[a]	CC	No	92.3	Undervalued	73.5	Undervalued
	Direct	No	88.5	Undervalued	93.0	Undervalued

15

Exhibit 15.8.2 (continued)

Model	Approach	Original valuation: constant discount rates			Jordan's valuation: variable discount rates	
		Is the model appropriate?	Value (US$)	Status	Value (US$)	Status
Three-stage[a]	CC	No	60.9	Undervalued		
	Direct	No	82.1	Undervalued		

[a] Despite sensible results, the valuation model is considered unsuitable as per comment (b). However, an alternative valuation with a lower terminal growth rate is applied to a two-stage model

Exhibit 15.8.3 Tanzania Breweries Ltd. (see E.15.7) (market price = TZS 10,400 per share)

Model	Approach	Original valuation: constant discount rates			Jordan's valuation: variable discount rates	
		Is the model appropriate?	Value (TZS)	Status	Value (TZS)	Status
Single-stage	CC	Yes	10,826	Undervalued		
	Direct	Yes	9596	Overvalued		
Two-stage	CC	Yes	11,599	Undervalued	8871	Overvalued
	Direct	Yes	10,096	Overvalued	7220	Overvalued
Three-stage[a]	CC	Somehow	12,632	Undervalued	10,176	Overvalued
	Direct	Somehow	11,053	Undervalued	8464	Overvalued

[a] The valuation model can be questionable as per comment (b). To determine stable growth for the three-stage model, Jordan uses a 5-year average GDP growth rate (4.9%) instead of a 10-year average (5.5%) applied by other analysts

count rates. He applies the same variables as the other analysts, except he allows the betas to vary. For Ecopetrol and Harley-Davidson, whose betas are greater than the market beta, he lowers them to 1.000 in the stable stage. For Tanzania Breweries, whose current beta is just 0.3819, he increases them to 0.65 in the stable stage to approach the company's long-term beta—from historical analysis, the company's beta is unlikely to reach the market beta. To determine beta variations, he applies linear interpolation—it is the same process applied to determine transitional growth rates (see ▶ Exhibit 15.3). Then, both the cost of equity and WACC vary with beta in each period until stability (see ◘ Exhibits 15.8.4, 15.8.5, and 15.8.6). Based on his review, a three-stage growth model is not suitable for Harley-Davidson.

His specific views are as follows:

On Ecopetrol

(a) Joseph's assumptions on single-stage models are generally acceptable.

(b) Josephine's assumptions and justifications for a two-stage model are reasonable and acceptable. They reflect free cash flow patterns for the most current 5 years: FCFE grows at a higher rate than FCFF.

(c) Joseline's assumptions and justifications for a three-stage model are reasonable and acceptable. However, a low take-off growth rate of FCFF does not justify the three stages: that is, the CC approach does not seem to be realistic.

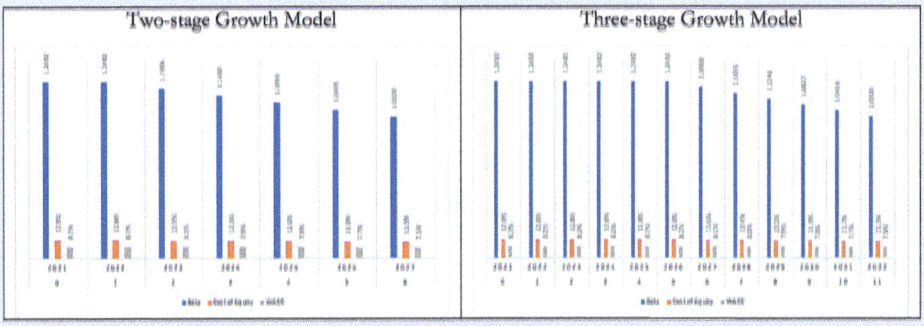

◘ **Exhibit 15.8.4** Ecopetrol SA: variable cost of capital

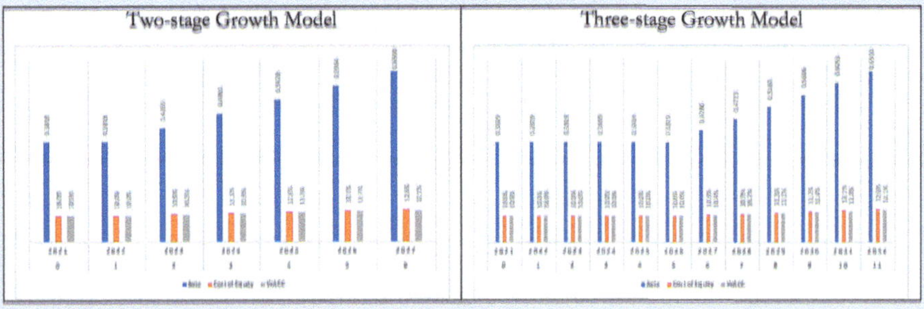

◘ **Exhibit 15.8.5** Tanzania Breweries Ltd.: variable cost of capital

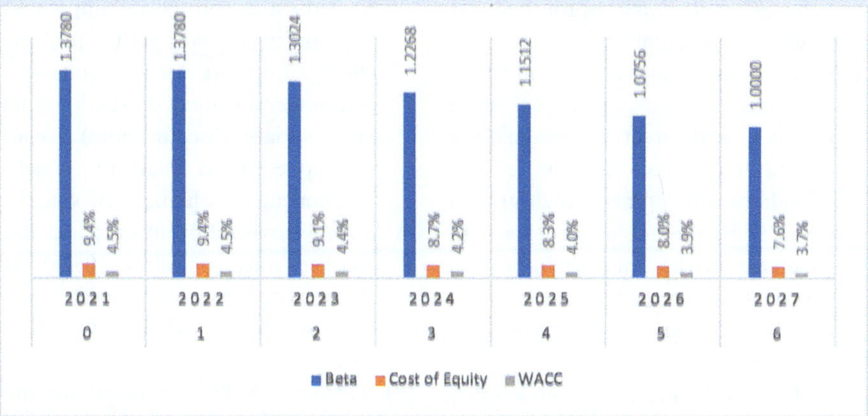

Exhibit 15.8.6 Harley-Davidson: variable cost of capital (two-stage model)

(d) Based on the acceptable models and approaches, Ecopetrol's stocks were overvalued at a market price of COP 2690.

(e) *Approach*: Both CC and direct approaches are applicable, but valuation based on the former should be preferred to the latter because Ecopetrol has significant leverage.

On Harley-Davidson

(a) Valentine's assumptions and justifications on single-stage models are generally acceptable.

(b) Verediana's and Valeriana's assumptions and justifications on two-stage and three-stage models (both the CC approach and direct approach) do not seem to reflect the company's characteristics depicted in Exhibits 15.4.4 and 15.4.5. Both retention ratio and reinvestment rates have been stable over a long historical period, except in 2020: indeed, negative reinvestment rates have been dominant in recent years due to the negative net capital expenditure. Take-off growth rates (2.09% for FCFF and 2.21% for FCFE) are relatively equal to terminal growth (2.01% GDP)—basically, multiple stage growth is unrealistic. Nevertheless, if the take-off growth rates are regarded as moderate for the company (based on its specific characteristics), then then terminal growth rates should be much lower than the GDP growth: hence, Jordan uses 0.75% as the terminal growth rate for both FCFF and FCFE for alternative valuation on a two-stage model.

(c) Based on single-stage and two-stage models, HD's stocks were undervalued at a market price of US$ 42.2.

(d) *Approach*: Valuation based on the CC approach should be preferred to the direct approach because Harley-Davidson has a significant leverage ratio.

On Tanzania Breweries

(a) Costancia's and Leparata's assumptions and justifications for single-stage and two-stage models (both the CC and direct approaches) are generally acceptable.

(b) Asela's assumptions and justifications for a three-stage model (both the CC and direct approaches) are questionable because none of the fundamentals point to high growth (see Exhibit 15.4.5): despite an increase in the retention ratio and ROE in recent years, the long-term trend has been a decline over the past 10 years.

(c) Based on the acceptable models and approaches, Jordan's valuation is in contrast to those of other analysts on the CC approach. Both Constancia's and Leparata's results give an undervalued status (on the CC approach) but an overvalued status (on the direct approach). Asela's results suggest undervaluation. Jordan's results (with variable discount rates) give an overvalued status. There was no definite conclusion whether TBL's stocks were overvalued or undervalued at a market price of TZS 10,400: it depends on the decision-maker's perspective about whose valuation results to rely on.

(d) *Approach*: Valuation based on the direct approach should be preferred to the CC approach because Tanzania Breweries has extremely low leverage.

Think 15.5

From ► Exhibit 15.8, *do you agree with Jordan's comments? Are there any alternative views? Give your comments.*

15.6 The Cost of Capital Approach vs. the Direct Approach

A major drawback of the cost of capital approach is its insensitivity to changes in the capital structure because FCFF, unlike FCFE, is not affected by pretax net borrowing. Hence, the cost of capital approach tends to simplify valuation for companies experiencing significant variations in their capital structure over time. In this context, capital structure is the main determinant of whether estimating the equity value with the CC approach will be consistent with the direct approach. To obtain consistent valuation results (not equal), the following conditions should be satisfied:

1. *Discount Rate*: WACC is sensitive to capital structure (market values of equity and debt). The two approaches should produce consistent (not equal) valuation results if the capital structure is fairly priced.
2. *Nonoperating Assets*: Nonoperating or extraordinary items, which effect net income, should not be significant—net income is determined by simply subtracting interest expenses and taxes from EBIT.
3. *Interest Expenses*: If the debt is fairly priced, then interest expenses should be equal to the product of the pretax cost of debt and the market value of the debt.

15

▶ Exhibit 15.9 illustrates these conditions using a simple example of a firm without growth potential and perpetual cash flows. In complex cases, firms tend to grow through reinvesting cash flows. Complexity arises when attempting to maintain the capital structure to satisfy the necessary conditions for an ideal cost of capital. This example shows 11 scenarios in which leverage is allowed to vary from 0% to approach 100%. The following key issues regarding the valuation effect of leverage should be noted:

1. The gap between WACC and cost of equity tends to widen as leverage increases, and vice versa.
2. Considering Modigliani and Miller's propositions (with corporate tax), as leverage increases, the cost of equity increases to reflect financial risk while WACC declines to reflect the interest tax shield.
3. The valuation gap between the CC approach and direct approach tends to widen as leverage increases. In the absence of debt, both approaches produce equal results and firm value equals equity value.

Exhibit 15.9 Comparison of Valuation Models

Illustrative Example (See Excel Workings—▶ Chap. 15, Sheet E.15.9)

Consider a firm in different capital structure scenarios as indicated in ◘ Exhibit 15.9.1. The following assumptions are made: no growth and perpetual cash flows. The following variables are constant: the firm's total market value (V_F), EBIT, pretax cost of debt (k_d), and corporate tax rate (T_c). The following variables are allowed to vary due to variations in the market value of debt (V_D) and equity (V_E): levered cost of equity (k_e) from unlevered cost of equity (k_u), debt interest expenses (I_D), and shareholders' net income (NI).

Notes

$$I_D = k_d(V_D)$$

$$NI = (EBIT - I_D)(1 - T_c)$$

$$k_e = k_u + \frac{V_D}{V_E}(1 - T_c)(k_u - k_d)$$

$$NOPAT = EBIT(1 - T_c)$$

Valuation

NOPAT and NI are used as proxies for FCFF and FCFE, respectively.

The Cost of Capital (CC) Approach

Firm value (V_F) with perpetual cash flows is calculated as follows:

$$V_F = \frac{EBIT(1 - T_c)}{WACC}$$

$$V_E = V_F - V_D$$

The Direct Approach

Equity value is estimated by discounting the net income with the cost of equity as follows:

$$V_E = \frac{NI}{k_e}$$

Key Observations

◘ Exhibit 15.9.2A and 15.9.2B present the valuation results.

Cost of Capital

From ◘ Exhibit 15.9.1, the gap between WACC and the cost of equity tends to widen as leverage increases, and vice versa. In the absence of debt (sce-

Exhibit 15.9.1 Company data sheet (all US$ millions, except percentages)

Variables	Leverage scenarios 1	2	3	4	5	6	7	8	9	10	11
V_D	0	200	400	600	800	1000	1200	1400	1600	1800	2000
V_E	2000	1800	1600	1400	1200	1000	800	600	400	200	0
V_F	2000	2000	2000	2000	2000	2000	2000	2000	2000	2000	2000
k_d	7.0%	7.0%	7.0%	7.0%	7.0%	7.0%	7.0%	7.0%	7.0%	7.0%	7.0%
T_c	35.0%	35.0%	35.0%	35.0%	35.0%	35.0%	35.0%	35.0%	35.0%	35.0%	35.0%
k_{dT}	4.6%	4.6%	4.6%	4.6%	4.6%	4.6%	4.6%	4.6%	4.6%	4.6%	4.6%
k_e	10.0%	10.2%	10.5%	10.8%	11.3%	12.0%	12.9%	14.6%	17.8%	27.6%	12.0%
WACC	10.0%	9.7%	9.3%	9.0%	8.6%	8.3%	7.9%	7.6%	7.2%	6.9%	4.6%
EBIT	334	334	334	334	334	334	334	334	334	334	334
I_D	0	14	28	42	56	70	84	98	112	126	140
NI	217	208	199	190	181	172	163	153	144	135	126

Exhibit 15.9.2A Valuation effect of leverage (all US$ millions, except percentages)

	Leverage scenarios 1	2	3	4	5	6	7	8	9	10	11
Leverage	0%	10%	20%	30%	40%	50%	60%	70%	80%	90%	100%
V_F (CC)	2171	2250	2334	2426	2524	2632	2748	2875	3015	3169	4771
V_E (CC)	2171	2050	1934	1826	1724	1632	1548	1475	1415	1369	2771
V_E (direct)	2171	2036	1897	1752	1599	1436	1257	1054	811	491	1055

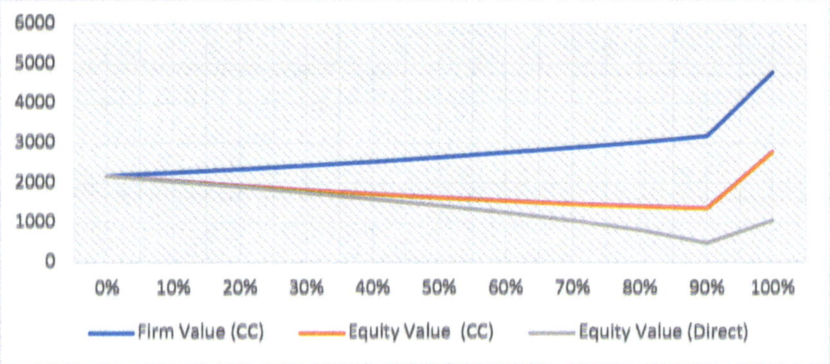

Exhibit 15.9.2B Valuation effect of leverage

nario 1, the leverage is 0%), WACC equals the cost of equity. At 90% leverage (scenario 10) WACC is 6.9%, whereas the cost of equity is 27.6%. However, at 100% leverage (scenario 11), WACC equals after-tax cost of debt and the cost of equity declines to 12.0% to equal that in scenario 6 (leverage 50%).

Considering Modigliani and Miller's propositions (with corporate tax), as leverage increases, the cost of equity increases to reflect financial risk while WACC declines to reflect the interest tax shield.

The Cost of Capital Approach vs. the Direct Approach (see Exhibit 15.9.2A and 15.9.2B).

The valuation gap between the CC approach and direct approach widens as leverage increases. In the absence of debt (0% leverage), both approaches produce equal results and firm value equals equity value.

Apply 15.1

Objective: Perform valuation using various models and approaches.

Use any three companies. Determine all the valuation variables (data) to apply both the cost of capital and direct approaches: free cash flows, growth estimates, cost of capital, etc.

1. Determine the suitable valuation model (s) for each company. Provide reasons to justify your decisions.
2. Make decisions about valuation variables. Provide reasons to justify your decisions.
3. Use Excel to perform valuation and present your results. Do they make sense?
4. Comment on valuation challenges (if any) and limitations.

Review Questions

1. Why are free cash flows preferred to other variables when performing equity valuation?
2. Define and compare the following terms as applied in valuation:
   (a) Objectivity vs. subjectivity
   (b) Forward-looking vs. backward-looking
   (c) Nonoperating assets vs. non-equity claims
3. What is the difference between the cost of capital approach and direct approach of equity valuation?
4. Why should two analysts valuing the same company and using the same data not arrive at equal results?
5. What are the key points to consider when deciding whether to apply the cost of capital approach or direct approach to value equity?
6. Describe the key assumptions and main criteria to justify a decision to apply each of the following valuation models:
   (a) Single-stage growth model

(b) Two-stage growth model
(c) Three-stage growth model

7. Explain the valuation criteria to consider when making decisions about the following:
   (a) Valuation model
   (b) Take-off cash flow and growth rate
   (c) Terminal growth rate
   (d) Discount rate
   (e) Projection period
   (f) Stable stage
8. Why is the history behind numbers vital during valuation?
9. With examples, explain how leverage affects the following valuation aspects:
   (a) Free cash flows
   (b) Discount rates
   (c) Valuation approach
10. Tengule Ltd. has provided its current FCFF and FCFE as US$ 3.2 million and US$ 4.8 million, respectively. These cash flows are expected to grow constantly and indefinitely at the rate of 5% and 5.2% for FCFF and FCFE, respectively. The company maintains its capital structure with a target debt-to-equity ratio of approximately 0.40. The market values of debt and equity are US$ 27 million and US$ 66 million, respectively. There are 4.1 million shares outstanding, currently trading at a market price of US$ 16.5 per share. Its stock beta is 0.9232. The risk-free rate is 2.5%, whereas the expected market return is 12.85%. The pretax cost of debt is 4%. The corporate tax rate is 40%. Cash and marketable securities amount to US$ 18.6 million. The total book debt outstanding is US$ 25.2 million.
    (a) Calculate the firm value and equity value using the cost of capital approach.
    (b) Calculate the equity value using the direct approach.
    (c) Which approach is more suitable for the company?
    (d) Provide comments on whether equity is overvalued or undervalued.

    (See Excel workings—► Chap. 15, Sheet R15.1).
11. Mulenga is a manufacturing company with a current FCFF of US$ 4.5 million. You have been assigned to value the company under the following assumptions: FCFF will grow in two stages, starting with 6% annually in the next 5 years, followed by 3.5% indefinitely. The company's capital structure comprises 5 million shares of common shares outstanding, currently trading at US$ 22.5 per share. The debt is paying 6.4% interest and is currently trading at a par value of US$ 50 million. The firm's WACC is 8% during high growth and 7% during stable growth. The company's tax rate is 34%. Cash and marketable securities are considered insignificant. Calculate the value of the firm and its equity using the cost of capital approach.

    (See Excel workings—► Chap. 15, Sheet R15.2).

12. Grace & Vero Ltd. is expected to experience growth of its FCFE in three distinctive stages. The first phase of high growth will last for 3 years from the current year, driven by the introduction of new products, commanding market shares, and a strong competitive stance. The second phase is expected to be transitional for another 3 years, where growth will decline annually due to new entries in the market and more competition. Thereafter, there will be a steady, but slow, growth indefinitely. The firm has just estimated its current FCFE to be US$ 4 million. The firm's capital structure comprises a bond at a par value of US$ 45 million paying 8% interest, whereas common shares outstanding are 2 million. Details about the three growth phases are summarized in the table below. Calculate the firm value.

	Phase 1: high growth	**Phase 2: declining growth**	**Phase 3: steady growth**
Duration	3 Years	3 Years	Infinity
FCFE growth rate	18% Annually	Declining by 5% annually until the beginning of phase 3	Maintaining the growth rate from the end of phase 2 constantly, forever
Cost of equity	16%	12%	10%

(See Excel workings—► Chap. 15, Sheet R15.3).

13. BKL company has currently reported its free cash flow to equity as $5 million and is expected to grow at a constant rate of 2.8% indefinitely, consistent with the country's GDP growth. BKL has 4 million shares outstanding and is currently trading at $25 per share, whereas the beta is 0.768. The expected market return and risk-free rate are 10.67% and 1.55%, respectively. Determine the appropriate valuation model, estimate BKL's equity value, and recommend whether it is better to buy or sell.

    (See Excel workings—► Chap. 15, Sheet R15.4).

14. VML Plc has currently reported its free cash flow to the firm as $4 million. Growth is expected to be constant at 2.8% indefinitely and consistent with the country's GDP growth. VML has 2 million shares outstanding and is currently trading at $38 per share, whereas the beta is 0.852. The expected market return and risk-free rate are 10.6% and 1.55%, respectively. WACC is 6.8%. Corporate tax rate is 34%. Debt outstanding is $28.0 million. Cash and cash equivalents amount to $6.8 million. Determine the appropriate valuation model, estimate VML's equity value, and recommend whether it is better to buy or sell.

    (See Excel Workings—► Chap. 15, Sheet R15.5).

Bibliography

Bancel, F. & Mittoo, U. R. (2014), The Gap between the Theory and Practice of Corporate Valuation: Survey of European Experts, *Journal of Applied Corporate Finance*, 26(4), 106-117. https://doi.org/10.1111/jacf.12095

Booth, L. (2007), Capital Cash Flows, APV and Valuation, *European Financial Management*, 13(1), 29–48. https://doi.org/10.1111/j.1468-036X.2006.00284.x

Buffett, W. (1996). An Owner's Manual, https://www.berkshirehathaway.com/ownman.pdf?_ga=2.120655688.1723902071.1662640534-1776864826.1661803154

CNN Business (2022), Harley-Davidson Inc (NYSE:HOG), available at https://money.cnn.com/quote/profile/profile.html?symb=HOG

Graham, B. (2006), *The Intelligent Investor Rev Ed.: The Definitive Book on Value Investing*, Harper Business Essentials

Pinto, J. E., Robinson, T. R., & Stowe, J. D. (2019), Equity valuation: A survey of professional practice, *Review of Financial Economics,* 37, 219-233. https://doi.org/10.1002/rfe.1040

Reuters (2022), About Tanzania Breweries PLC (TBL.TZ), available at https://www.reuters.com/markets/companies/TBL.TZ

Free Cash Flow Discount Models: The Adjusted Present Value Approach

Contents

Supplementary Information The online version contains supplementary material available at https://doi.org/10.1007/978-3-031-28267-6_16.

B. Kulwizira Lukanima, *Corporate Valuation*, Classroom Companion: Business, https://doi.org/10.1007/978-3-031-28267-6_16

16.1 Introduction

This chapter extends ► Chap. 15 by considering a different valuation approach—the adjusted present value (APV). Unlike the cost of capital (CC) approach, the APV approach determines firm value by splitting it into two components: value of the unlevered firm and value of the leverage effect. Except for considering leverage separately, other valuation aspects are not different from the CC approach: single-stage or multiple stage models can be applied in the same way on free cash flow to the firm (FCFF).

This chapter, therefore, focuses on issues distinguishing the CC approach from the APV approach. To illustrate the APV application, the same cases in ► Chap. 15 are used for the purpose of explaining the differences and comparing the valuation results.

Learning Outcomes

- Understand the meaning of the APV approach and its difference from the CC approach.
- Determine APV valuation variables.
- Apply APV to value firms with single-stage and multiple stage models.
- Compare the valuation results between the APV and CC approaches.
- Understand the practical limitations of the APV approach.

16.2 The Adjusted Present Value Approach

The APV and CC approaches share the same goal, i.e., to estimate the present value of operating assets, but they differ in valuation philosophy. The APV treats the effect of leverage separately by splitting value into two categories as follows:

- *Value of the Unlevered Firm* (V_U): Assume no leverage to estimate the value of the unlevered firm by discounting FCFF at an unlevered cost of equity (k_u). The estimated value is not the firm's operating assets because it excludes the leverage effect.
- *Value of the Leverage Effect*: Consider the positive and negative leverage effects separately, which relate to the amount of debt capital (V_D):
  - *The Debt Positive Effect*: A debt creates tax savings on interest expenses. Therefore, the present value of the "interest tax shield" (V_{TS}) is estimated depending on the benefits arising from corporate tax (T_c) savings on debt interest expenses (I_D). The expected tax savings are discounted at the cost of debt (k_d) to reflect the risk of the respective cash flows.
  - *The Debt Negative Effect*: A debt creates financial distress. The expected negative value of financial distress (V_{BC}) is estimated by considering the default probability (d) and bankruptcy costs (B).

16

Therefore, the general equation to estimate the present value of a firm's operating assets (PV_{OA}) can be presented as follows:

$$PV_{OA} = V_U + V_{TS} - V_{BC}$$

Then, like the CC approach, total firm value (V_F) and equity value (V_E) are calculated by considering nonoperating assets (NonOA) and non-equity claims (NECs) as follows:

$$V_F = PV_{OS} + NonOA$$

$$V_E = V_F - NEC$$

▶ Exhibit 16.1 summarizes the key features of intrinsic valuation with both the cost of capital approach and the direct approach.

Exhibit 16.1 Present Value of Operating Assets: The APV Approach

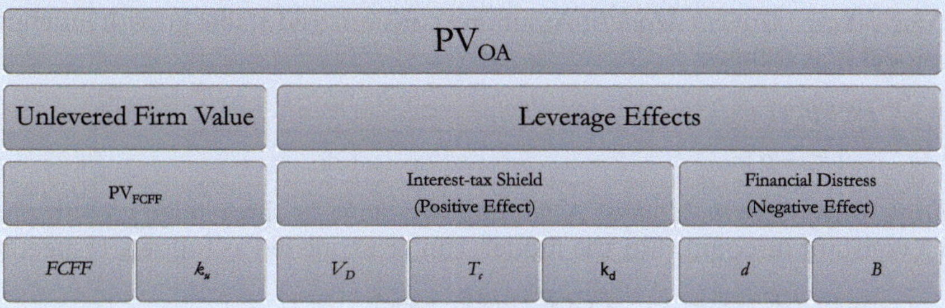

Estimation Variables

1. *Unlevered firm value*: FCFF discounted at unlevered cost of capital (k_u).
2. *Positive debt effects*: Tax savings are determined by debt value (V_D), pre-tax cost of debt (k_d), and corporate tax rate (T_c): they are discounted at pre-tax cost of debt (k_d).
3. *Negative debt effects*: expected bankruptcy costs depend on default probability (d) and expected bankruptcy costs (B).

16.2.1 Value of an Unlevered Firm

Like the CC approach, FCFF is used to estimate the value of an unlevered firm. However, instead of weighted average cost of capital (WACC), the discount rate is unlevered cost of equity (k_u). This discount rate is just an implied rate of return that a company expects to earn on its assets, without the effect of debt—that is, it is a theoretical value based on assumptions because the real value cannot be observed. To estimate the unlevered cost of equity, the capital asset pricing model (CAPM) equation is modified to substitute the standard (levered) beta (β_L) by unlevered beta (β_U) as follows:

$$k_u = r_f + \beta_u \left(r_m - r_f \right)$$

where the unlevered beta is determined by excusing the leverage effects as follows:

$$\beta_u = \frac{\beta_L}{1 + \left(1 - T_c\right)\left(\frac{V_D}{V_E}\right)}$$

where V_D and V_E are the market values of debt and equity, respectively, and T_c is the corporate tax rate.

The value on an unlevered firm (V_U) can then be estimated depending on the valuation model—single-stage or multiple stage growth models just like the CC approach, except that the discount rate is now k_u.

Single-Stage Growth Models: Assuming constant and stable growth indefinitely, the model is as follows:

$$V_U = \frac{FCFF_0 \left(1 + g\right)}{\left(k_u - g\right)}$$

Multiple stage Growth Models: Assuming two-stage or three-stage growth phases, and a constant discount rate, the models can be expressed as follows, respectively:

$$V_U = \sum_{t=1}^{n} \frac{FCFF_t \left(1 + g_{t+1}\right)}{\left(1 + k_u\right)^t} + \frac{FCFF_{n+1} / \left(k_u - g_S\right)}{\left(1 + k_u\right)^n}$$

$$V_U = \sum_{t=1}^{T} \frac{FCFF_t \left(1 + g_{t+1}\right)}{\left(1 + k_u\right)^t} + \sum_{t*T+1}^{n} \frac{FCFF_t}{\left(1 + k_u\right)^t} + \frac{FCFF_{n+1} / \left(k_u - g_S\right)}{\left(1 + k_u\right)^n}$$

where g_s is the expected stable growth rate in the final phase of constant growth indefinitely. In case discount rates vary over time (in fixed-period stages), they should be reflected in the models accordingly.

16

Banner 16.1 Value of an Unlevered Firm
APV determines the value of an unlevered firm by discounting FCFF at an unlevered cost of equity instead of WACC.

Think 16.1
Why does APV use an unlevered cost of equity to discount FCFF?

16.2.2 Value of the Interest Tax Shield

The present value of the interest tax shield depends on three key variables: debt value (V_D), pretax cost of debt (k_d), and corporate tax rate (T_c)—these three variables determine interest expenses, interest tax shield, and discount rate. Like V_U, the present value of tax savings depends on model assumptions: single-stage or multiple stage models.

▪ Single-Stage Perpetual Models

If the valuation model assumes perpetual tax savings, the present value of the interest tax shield (V_{TS}) is estimated as follows:

$$V_{TS} = \frac{I_D T_c}{k_d} = \frac{V_D k_d T_c}{k_d} = V_D T_c$$

where I_D or $V_D k_d$ denotes interest expenses, $I_D T_c$ or $V_D k_d T_c$ is the interest tax shield, and pretax cost of debt (k_d) is the discount rate.

▪ Multiple Stage Models

If valuation projected tax savings are expected to vary from time to time, then multiple stage models can be applied. Typically, different stages should reflect changes due to variations in any of the determinants of the interest tax shield (debt value, interest rate, and tax rate). For instance, if the current debt value does not represent target debt ratio, a model can consider a defined period (in early stages) where debt is assumed to vary over time so as to converge the target debt at terminal period, followed by perpetuity indefinity (during stable stage). The present value of tax savings can therefore be estimated using the following general equation:

$$V_{TS} = \sum_{t=1}^{n} \frac{(V_D k_d T_c)_t}{(1+k_d)^t} + \frac{(V_D T_c)_{n+1}}{(1+k_d)^n}$$

where $\sum_{t=1}^{n} \frac{(V_D k_d T_c)_t}{(1+k_d)^t}$ is the present value of tax savings during early stages (fixed period) and $(V_D T_c)_{n+1}$ is the terminal value depending on the expected debt in the stable stage.

Banner 16.2 Value of the Interest Tax Shield

APV determines the value of the interest tax shield by discounting tax savings at a pretax cost of debt.

Think 16.2

Why should tax savings be discounted at a pretax cost of debt to determine the present value of the interest tax shield?

16.2.3 Value of Financial Distress

Financial distress relates to negative leverage effects caused by default probability (d) and bankruptcy costs (B). The expected bankruptcy cost (V_{BC}) can therefore be estimated as follows:

$$V_{BC} = dB$$

Estimation of the value of financial distress is not straightforward because both default probability and bankruptcy costs are difficult to determine directly—estimations tend to be indirect and are based on proxies. Let us look at each of them.

- **Default Probability** (*d*)

Default probability reflects the possibility that a firm will default due to an increased risk of financial distress. Default probability, therefore, depends on a firm's credit rating (refer to ▸ Chap. 13). One way to determine default is to use default rate estimates, usually published by rating agents (see, for example, Standards and Poor's (S&P) Global 2021; Moody's Global 2009), or through empirical research (e.g., Altman and Kishore 1998; Altman et al. 2000). Nevertheless, accurate default probability is difficult to achieve because different estimation methods tend to produce inconsistent estimates (see Ensher and Jones 2008).

- **Bankruptcy Costs** (*B*)

Bankruptcy costs can be categorized as direct costs and indirect costs. Direct costs are measurable and mainly include professional fees relating to bankruptcy filing (e.g., legal fees and accounting fees) and other administrative costs. Indirect costs relate to negative perceptions, leading to loses (e.g., falling sales, earnings, and market value) and an inability to raise additional capital or raise at a higher cost. According to Warner (1977) "because the indirect costs of bankruptcy are mainly 'lost opportunities,' they are inevitably difficult, if not impossible to measure."

Due to measurement difficulties, determining these costs is complicated. For simplicity, valuation judgments tend to be commonly guided by research despite conflicting results among studies. Overall, as a percentage of firm value, direct costs are a smaller fraction than indirect costs. For example, Warner (1977), referring to direct costs on the railroad industry, found that a "firm's expected cost of bankruptcy is equal to fifteen one-hundredths of one percent of its now current market value. If the cost of bankruptcy is doubled to 6 percent and the probability of bankruptcy increased to 10 percent, the expected costs would still be only six-tenths of one percent of the current value of the firm." Consistently, other studies suggest that direct costs range between approximately 3–6.5% (Weiss, 1990; Betker, 1997; and Branch, 2002). Indirect costs, on the other hand, as a percentage of firm value, range between 10−30%. For example, on Australian data, the bankruptcy cost is about 20% of the firm value (Pham and Chow 1989), and, according to other studies they could be as large as 25−30% (Shapiro and Titman, 1994), 12−20% (Branch, 2002) and 12−28% (Kortweg, 2007). Overall, bankruptcy costs vary across firms and according to their geographical locations—there is no universal measure.

Banner 16.3 Value of Financial Distress
The expected value of financial distress is negative due to default probability and bankruptcy costs.

16.3 Practical Application

To illustrate the application of APV, let us use the same cases applied in the CC approach (refer to ▸ Chap. 15, ▸ Exhibits 15.5A–15.7A and 15.8). The three case companies are Ecopetrol SA (Colombia), Harley-Davidson (United States), and Tanzania Breweries Ltd. (Tanzania). Suppose that the same analysts use the same growth assumptions and judgments, except the following APV aspects:

1. The unlevered cost of equity replaces WACC to discount FCFF.
2. The present value of the interest tax shield.
3. The expected value of bankruptcy costs.

To determine the expected default, analysts have decided to use default rate data from S&P Global, which categorize default rates according to rating levels. To determine bankruptcy costs, they make judgments based on research, assuming that bankruptcy costs' range is between 20% and 35% of an unlevered firm's value. For simplicity, suppose that, for a particular company, the three analysts have the same assumptions about default probability and bankruptcy costs—the reality could be different. Regarding variable discount rates, Jordan (analyst 4) lets unlevered beta vary with levered beta and be reflected in the unlevered cost of equity. ▸ Exhibits 16.2–16.4 present valuation data sheets and results for the three cases.

Exhibit 16.2 Intrinsic Valuation: The APV Approach

Illustrative Case: Ecopetrol SA (See Excel Workings—▸ Chap. 16, Sheet E.16.2A–E)

◘ Exhibit 16.2.1 presents a data sheet summary from which the APV approach is used by four analysts: Joseph, Josephine, Joseline, and Jordan.

Valuation

To estimate the unlevered firm value, single-stage, two-stage, and three-stage models are applied for the company based on assumptions presented in ▸ Chap. 15 (see ▸ Exhibit 15.5A). Analyst 4 (Jordan) applies the same assumption with variable discount rates (see ◘ Exhibit 16.2.2). To estimate the present value of the interest tax shield, analysts assume perpetuity: the company is generally highly levered, and the current debt is considered a reasonable reflection of the expected debt. Regarding negative leverage effects, the company is rated BB+ according to S&P. All four analysts make the same judgments about default probability (a 10-year default rate from S&P Global) and assume that bankruptcy cost is 25% of the unlevered firm value (depending on the FCFF discount model). Valuation model results are presented in ◘ Exhibit 16.2.3.

16

Exhibit 16.2.1 Valuation data sheet (all in COP millions, except per share and percentages)

Variables	Sample periods and averages						
	Current (2021)	10-Year	8-Year	6-Year	5-Year	4-Year	3-Year
$FCFF_0$	9,028,866	7,685,395[a]	8,342,645	9,136,436	8,992,520	8,611,313[b]	7,003,617
$FCFE_0$	19,887,236	9,372,423	8,972,244	8,333,985	7,928,964	9,761,169	11,959,133
SGR_{NOPAT}	−3.5%	4.0%[a]	2.2%	1.8%	2.1%	2.7%[b]	3.0%
SGR_{EPS}	10.8%	2.4%	2.3%	5.7%	6.4%	6.4%	4.0%
Nonoperating assets	14,549,906						
Market cap	110,603,909						
Debts outstanding	95,060,928						
After-tax cost of debt	2.9%						
Unlevered cost of equity	10.5%						
Risk-free rate	6.5%						
Expected market returns	11.5%						
Unlevered beta	0.7948						

Variables	Sample periods and averages						
	Current (2021)	10-Year	8-Year	6-Year	5-Year	4-Year	3-Year
Levered cost of equity	12.8%						
Shares outstanding	41,117						
Market price	2690						
Tax rate	33.6%						
Credit rating	BB+						
Default probability (10-year)	6.18%						
Bankruptcy cost	25%						

Notes: Judgements about take-off variables are as follows: [a]Two-stage model (Josephine and Jordan) and Three-stage model (Joseline and Jordan), and [b]Single-stage model (Joseph)

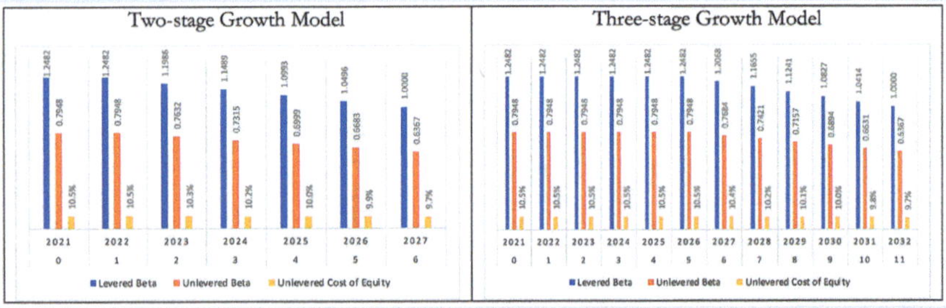

Exhibit 16.2.2 Ecopetrol SA: variable cost of capital

Exhibit 16.2.3 Ecopetrol SA: APV valuation models and results (all in COP millions, except per share)

Valuation	Joseph	Josephine vs. Jordan	Joseline vs. Jordan
Model	Single-stage	Two-stage	Three-stage
V_U	113,550,317	111,847,174	130,383,931
		123,180,171	123,188,039
$V_D T_C$	31,955,981	31,955,981	31,955,981
		31,955,981	31,955,981
dB	1,754,352	1,728,039	2,014,432
		1,903,134	1,903,255
PV_{OA}	143,751,946	142,075,116	160,325,480
		153,233,018	153,240,764
Firm value	158,301,852	156,625,022	174,875,386
		167,782,924	167,790,670
Equity value	63,240,924	61,564,094	79,814,458
		72,721,996	72,729,742
Value per share	1538	1497	1941
		1769	1769

Note: For multiple stage models, the bottom results for each variable relate to Jordan's valuation with varying discount rates

16

Exhibit 16.3 Intrinsic Valuation: The APV Approach

Illustrative Case: Harley-Davidson (See Excel Workings—► Chap. 16, Sheet E.16.3A–E)

Exhibit 16.3.1 presents a data sheet summary from which the APV approach is used by four analysts: Verediana, Valentina, Valeriana, and Jordan.

Exhibit 16.3.1 Valuation data sheet (all in US$ millions, except per share and percentages)

Variables	Sample period and averages				
	Current (2022)	15-Year	10-Year	5-Year	3-Year
$FCFF_0$	463.0[a,b]	689.0	843.4	822.8	795.8
$FCFE_0$	1531.4	932.1	1125.6	1027.1	1006.8
g_{FCFF}	−4.8%	2.1%[c]	0.8%[a]	−4.4%	−5.4%
g_{FCFE}	20.8%	2.2%	1.3%	−7.9%	−3.0%
Nonoperating assets	1874.7				
Market cap	6128.6				
Debts outstanding	7154.9				
After-tax cost of debt	0.35%				
Unlevered cost of equity	6.2%				
Risk-free rate	2.8%				
Expected market returns	7.6%				
Unlevered beta	0.7120				
Levered cost of equity	9.4%				
Shares outstanding	145.4				
Market price	42.2				
Tax rate	19.9%				
Credit rating	BBB+				
Default probability (10-year)	1.99%				
Bankruptcy cost	20.0%				

Note: Judgments about take-off variables are as follows: [a]a single-stage model (Verediana); [b,c]a two-stage model (Valentine and Jordan) and a three-stage model (Valeriana)

Valuation

To estimate the unlevered firm value, single-stage, two-stage, and three-stage models are applied for the company based on assumptions presented in ▶ Chap. 15 (see ▶ Exhibit 15.6A). Analyst 4 (Jordan) applies the same assumption with variable discount rates (see ◘ Exhibit 16.3.2). To estimate the present value of the interest tax shield, analysts rely on the current debt: historical data suggest that the company is highly levered and that the current debt is a reasonable reflection of expectations. Regarding negative leverage effects, the company is rated BBB+ according to Fitch. All four analysts make the same judgments about default probability (a 10-year default rate from S&P Global) and assume that the bankruptcy cost is 20% of the unlevered firm value (depending on the FCFF discount model). Valuation model results are presented in ◘ Exhibit 16.3.3.

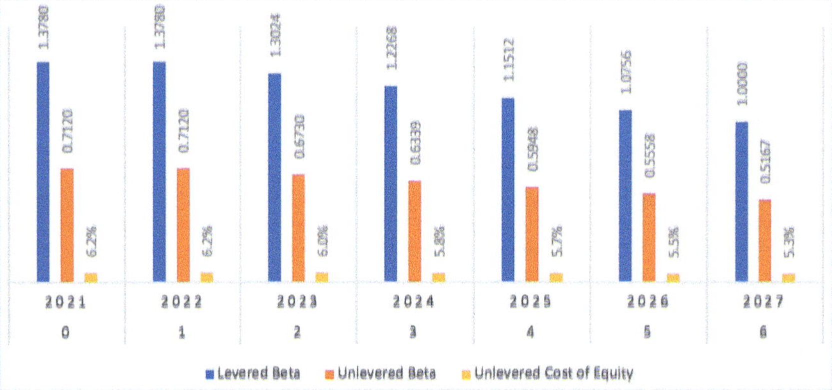

◘ **Exhibit 16.3.2** Harley-Davidson: variable cost of capital (a two-stage model)

◘ **Exhibit 16.3.3** Harley-Davidson: APV valuation models and results (all in US$ millions, except per share)

Valuation	Valentine	Verediana vs. Jordan	Valeriana
Model	Single-stage	Two-stage	Three-stage
V_U	8526	11,229	9553
		10,363	
$V_D T_C$	1422	1422	1422
		1422	
dB	34	45	38
		41	
PV_{OA}	9915	12,607	10,938
		11,745	

16

Exhibit 16.3.3 (continued)

Valuation	Valentine	Verediana vs. Jordan	Valeriana
Firm value	11,790	14,482	12,813
		13,619	
Equity value	4635	7327	5658
		6465	
Value per share	31.9	50.4	38.9
		44.5	

Note: For two-stage models, the bottom values for each variable relate to Jordan's valuation with varying discount rates—he did not apply a three-stage model because he considers it unsuitable for the company

Exhibit 16.4 Intrinsic Valuation: The APV Approach

Illustrative Case: Tanzania Breweries Ltd (TBL) (See Excel Workings—▶ Chap. 16, Sheet E.16.4A–H)

Exhibit 16.4.1 presents a data sheet summary from which the APV approach is used by four analysts: Costancia, Leparata, Asela, and Jordan.

Valuation

To estimate the unlevered firm value, single-stage, two-stage, and three-stage models are applied for the company based on assumptions presented in ▶ Chap. 15 (see ▶ Exhibit 15.7A). Analyst 4 (Jordan) applies the same assumption with variable discount rates (see Exhibit 16.4.2). To determine the present value of the interest tax shield, analysts decided to use projected debt instead of debt outstanding to reflect the target debt ratio of about 20%: the target debt equity ratio is based on the overall historical average. Regarding negative leverage effects, the company is not rated by any credit agency. To determine its creditworthiness, two methods are applied for the 5-year average data: (1) its interest coverage is 54 times and (2) Altman's *Z*-score is 7.3. Generally, the two measures suggest an extremely low default probability and should be rated at a premium level—AAA is reasonable. All four analysts make the same judgments about default probability (a 10-year default rate from S&P Global) and assume that the bankruptcy cost is 20% of the unlevered firm value (depending on the FCFF discount model). Valuation model results are presented in Exhibit 16.4.3.

Exhibit 16.4.1 Valuation data sheet (all in TZS millions, except per share and percentages)

Variables	Sample period and averages				
	Current (2021)	15-Year	10-Year	5-Year	3-Year
$FCFF_0$	157,453	114,724	149,640[a]	156,931	153,722[b]
$FCFE_0$	147,150	111,803	138,787	151,544	145,870
SGR_{NOPAT}	−13.1%	11.1%	8.3%	1.4%	−11.5%
SGR_{EPS}	8.8%	9.6%	7.5%[a]	2.1%	4.7%[b]
Nonoperating assets	224,635				
Market cap	3,069,040				
Debts outstanding	14,423				
Target debt-to-equity ratio	20.3%				
Projected debt	46,090				
After-tax cost of debt	10.0%				
Unlevered cost of equity	9.6%				
Risk-free rate	6.5%				
Market premium	9.4%				
Unlevered beta	0.3370				
Levered cost of equity	10.0%				
Shares outstanding	295.1				
Market price	10,400				
Tax rate	34.3%				
Credit rating (synthetic)	AAA				
Default probability (10-year)	0.69%				
Bankruptcy cost	20.0%				

Notes: Judgements about take-off variables are as follows: [a]Two-stage model (Leparata and Jordan) and Three-stage model (Asela and Jordan), and [b]Single-stage model (Costancia)

16

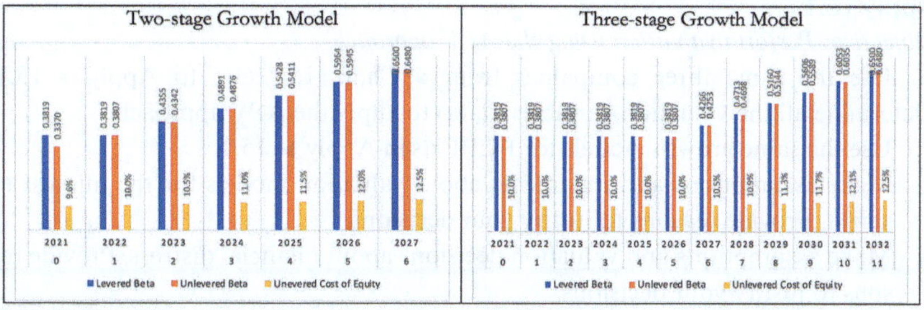

Exhibit 16.4.2 Tanzania Breweries Ltd.: variable cost of capital

Exhibit 16.4.3 Tanzania Breweries Ltd.: APV valuation models and results (all in TZS millions, except per share)

Valuation	Joseph	Josephine vs. Jordan	Joseline vs. Jordan
Model	Single-stage	Two-stage	Three-stage
V_U	3,237,620	3,497,923	3,834,958
		2,302,424	2,706,697
$V_D T_C$	15,813	15,813	15,813
		15,813	15,813
dB	4468	4827	5292
		3177	3735
PV_{OA}	3,248,965	3,508,909	3,845,479
		2,315,060	2,718,775
Firm value	3,473,600	3,733,544	4,070,114
		2,539,695	2,943,410
Equity value	3,459,177	3,719,121	4,055,691
		2,525,272	2,928,987
Value per share	11,722	12,603	13,743
		8557	9925

Note: For multiple stage models, the bottom values for each variable relate to Jordan's valuation with varying discount rates

Apply 16.1

Objective: Perform valuation using the APV approach.

Use the same three companies from ▶ Chap. 15 (refer to Apply ▶ 15.1). Determine all the valuation variables (data) to apply the APV approach.

1. Use the same growth models for FCFF as in Apply ▶ 15.1.
2. Make assumptions and judgments about valuation models for the interest tax shield. Provide reasons to justify your decisions.
3. Make assumptions and valuation decisions about financial distress. Provide reasons to justify your decisions.
4. Use Excel to perform valuation and present your results. Do they make sense?
5. Compare the results to those from the CC approach (Apply ▶ 15.1).
6. Recommend a more suitable approach for each company. Provide reasons to support recommendations.

Review Questions

1. What is the meaning of the following terms as applied in the APV approach:
   (a) Unlevered firm value
   (b) Value of the leverage effects
2. What are the key determinants of the following APV components?
   (a) Unlevered firm value
   (b) Expected value of the interest tax shield
   (c) Expected value of financial distress
3. Why does the APV determine the unlevered firm value by discounting FCFF at an unlevered cost of equity instead of WACC or cost of equity?
4. Why does the APV determine the value interest tax shield by discounting tax savings at a pretax cost of debt?
5. Tengule Ltd. has provided its current FCFF and FCFE as US$3.2 million and US$4.8 million, respectively. These cash flows are expected to grow constantly and indefinitely at the rate of 5% and 5.2% for FCFF and FCFE, respectively. The company maintains its capital structure with a target debt-to-equity ratio of approximately 0.40. The market values of debt and equity are US$27 million and US$66 million, respectively. There are 4.1 million shares outstanding, currently trading at a market price of US$16.5 per share. Its stock beta is 0.9232. The risk-free rate is 2.5%, whereas the expected market return is 12.85%. The pretax cost of debt is 4%. Corporate tax rate is 40%. Cash and marketable securities amount to US$18.6 million. Total book debt outstanding is US$25.2 million. The company's credit rating is A with a default probability of 1.27%. Bankruptcy costs are expected to be 35% of the unlevered firm value.
   (a) Calculate the firm value and equity value using the CC and APV approaches.
   (b) Which approach is more suitable for the company?
   (c) Provide comments on whether equity is overvalued or undervalued.
   (See Excel workings—▶ Chap. 15, Sheet R16.1).

16

6. Mulenga is a manufacturing company with a current FCFF of US$4.5 million. You have been assigned to value the company under the following assumptions: FCFF will grow in two stages, starting with 6% annually in the next 5 years, followed by 3.5% indefinitely. The company's capital structure comprises five million shares of common stock outstanding, currently trading at 22.5 per share. The debt is paying 6.4% interest and is currently trading at a par value of US$50 million. The firm's WACC is 8% during high growth and 7% during stable growth. The unlevered cost of equity is expected to be 8.8% during high growth and 7.6% during stability. The company's tax rate is 34%. Cash and marketable securities are considered insignificant. The company's default probability is 1.8%, whereas bankruptcy cost is expected to be 40% of the unlevered firm value. Calculate the value of the firm and its equity using the CC approach and APV approach.
(See Excel workings—▶ Chap. 15, Sheet R16.2).

Bibliography

Altman E. I., & Kishore, V. M. (1998). Defaults and returns on high-yield bonds: Analysis through 1997. Working paper, New York University, New York.

Altman E. I., Hukkawala, N., & Kishore, V. M. (2000). Defaults & Returns on High Yield Bonds: Analysis Through 1999 and Default Outlook for 2000-2002, Working paper No. FIN 99-005, New York University, New York.

Betker, B. L. (1997). The Administrative Costs of Debt Restructurings: Some Recent Evidence. Financial Management, 26(4), 56–68. https://doi.org/10.2307/3666127

Branch, B. (2002). The costs of bankruptcy A review. *International Review of Financial Analysis*, 11(1), 39–57. https://doi.org/10.1016/S1057-5219(01)00068-0

Ensher, D. A. & Jones, S. (2008) *Advances in Credit Risk Modelling and Corporate Bankruptcy Prediction*. Cambridge, UK: Cambridge University Press. ISBN 9780521869287.

Korteweg, A. G. (2007). The Costs of Financial Distress across Industries. University of Southern California - Marshall School of Business.

Moody's Global (2009), Credit Policy: Corporate Default and Recovery Rates, 1920-2008. https://www.moodys.com/uploadpage/MiscAnon/default_and_recovery_rates_02_09.pdf

Pham, T., & Chow, D. (1989). Some Estimates of Direct and Indirect Bankruptcy Costs in Australia: September 1978–May 1983. *Australian Journal of Management*, 14(1), 75–95. https://doi.org/10.1177/031289628901400105

Shapiro, A. C. & Titman, S. (1994): An Integrated Approach to Corporate Risk Management. In: Stern, J. M. & Chew, D., Jr. (Ed): The revolution in corporate finance. Cambridge, pp.331–345.

S&P Global (2021), Default, Transition, and Recovery: 2021 Annual Global Corporate Default And Rating Transition Study, https://www.spglobal.com/ratings/en/research/articles/220413-default-transition-and-recovery-2021-annual-global-corporate-default-and-rating-transition-study-12336975

Warner, J. B. (1977). Bankruptcy Costs: Some Evidence. *The Journal of Finance*, 32(2), 337–347. https://doi.org/10.2307/2326766

Weiss, L. A. (1990). Bankruptcy resolution: Direct costs and violation of priority claims. Journal of Financial Economics, 27(2), 285-314. https://doi.org/10.1016/0304-405X(90)90058-8

Dividend Discount Models

Contents

Supplementary Information The online version contains supplementary material available at https://doi.org/10.1007/978-3-031-28267-6_17.

B. Kulwizira Lukanima, *Corporate Valuation*, Classroom Companion: Business, https://doi.org/10.1007/978-3-031-28267-6_17

17.1 Introduction

This chapter presents an alternative equity valuation approach in which dividend cash flows are used instead of free cash flows to equity (FCFEs) (refer to ▶ Chap. 15). This approach utilizes several valuation models commonly known as dividend discount models (DDMs). Since dividend payment is not mandatory, this approach is only suitable for companies with a consistent track record of regular and predictable dividends.

This chapter focuses on explaining the approach and practical limitations to guide analysts' judgments on model suitability for specific valuation needs. More attention is paid to estimating valuation variables from the original data and deciding an appropriate model.

Learning Outcomes

- Explain corporate dividend decisions and valuation implications.
- Describe the application of dividend discount models to equity valuation.
- Compare dividends with free cash flows to equity.
- Estimate DDM variables from the original data.
- Apply different dividend discount models to value equity.
- Understand the limitations of DDMs for equity valuation.

17.2 Dividend Decisions

In ▶ Chap. 2, the concept of dividend decisions is described as one of the key managerial decisions. Nevertheless, companies are not obliged to pay common dividends—dividend payments are based on a company's dividend policy and are left to the discretion of its directors. Therefore, for non-dividend companies (e.g., Adobe, Biogen Inc., Amazon, etc.), a DDM is redundant. For dividend companies (e.g., McDonald's, Maruti Suzuki, Exxon, etc.), cash dividends are an alternative reward to equity holders, and, therefore, DDMs can be used to estimate equity value. Overall, the issue of dividend decisions is both controversial and debatable. Miller and Modigliani (1961) describe dividends as irrelevant to shareholders because it does not matter whether profits are paid out or retained—it all belongs to owners, except decisions regarding how profits should be split for reinvention. While dividend payments give shareholders an alternative way for self-reinvestment, retained earnings are reinvested on their behalf by the company. A general argument is that dividend payouts add value to shareholders only if they can generate a net present value higher than retained cash.

17.3 Why Use Dividends to Value Equity?

Dividends vs. FCFEs

While FCFE is cash available (not paid) to equity holders, cash dividends represent true cash returned (paid) to common shareholders. DDMs are, therefore, relevant if all expected dividends represent all expected FCFEs. Unlike FCFEs, dividends provide a focused valuation to investors preferring companies with regular dividends—these companies are generally characterized by maturity and stability in earnings and dividend growth. Moreover, unlike FCFEs, cash dividends are not susceptible to computational challenges and manipulations—FCFE application can be impossible due to it being negative or highly volatile.

Investor Expectations

Dividends have direct implication in investors' expected returns. Normally, investors expect two types of returns from stocks—dividend yield (DY) and capital gain rate—which represent the expected equity return (r_e) relative to stock market performance. A dividend yield (DY) is a return from a cash dividend per share, whereas a capital gain is a return from appreciation of the stock market value, such that:

$$r_e = \frac{D_1 + (P_1 - P_0)}{P_0} = \frac{D_1}{P_0} + \frac{P_1 - P_0}{P_0}$$

where D_1 is the expected dividend per share. Some companies tend to announce dividends in advance, which can be used as a proxy for expected dividends. Alternatively, for growing dividends, D_1 can be expressed as $D_0(1 - g)$ for the growth rate g; P_1 and P_0 are the expected and current stock market prices, respectively. P_1 can be projected for the terminal period as the present value of the expected dividend in that period. It is noteworthy that the appropriate stock price P_0 is the "ex-dividend" share price ($P_{0,Ex}$), which is determined by subtracting the cash dividends from the "cum-dividend" share price ($P_{0,Cum}$) such that $P_{0,Ex} = P_{0,Cum} - D_0$. The ex-dividend share price (also known as the adjusted stock price) is regarded as more accurate than the cum-dividend price because it considers market perception of dividends.

For example, suppose that an investor buys stocks that are currently trading at \$120 per share cum-dividend. The annual dividend per share is \$2.4 and is expected to grow at 4% annually. What is the expected return if the investor expects to sell stocks at \$135 per share next year? The ex-dividend price is \$117.6 (i.e., \$120 – \$2.4). The expected return from the dividend yield and capital gain rate is 16.9%, estimated as follows:

$$r_e = \frac{\$2.4(1+4\%)}{\$117.6} + \frac{\$135 - \$117.6}{\$117.6} = 16.9\%$$

where the dividend yield is 2.12% and the capital gain rate is 14.8%.

If, instead, the cum-dividend price is used, then the expected return will be just 14.6% as follows:

$$r_e = \frac{\$2.4(1+4\%)}{\$120} + \frac{\$135-\$120}{\$120} = 14.6\%$$

where the dividend yield is 2.08% and the capital gain rate is 12.5%.

Dividend investors like Warren Buffet would prefer dividends to FCFEs because actual cash matters most than available cash. "Dividend Kings" like Coca-Cola provide attractive investment opportunities to Buffet and others.

» With 400 million shares of Coke stock, the quarterly dividend payment of $0.44 per share means Buffett is making $176 million every three months, or almost three-quarters of a billion dollars every year. That's just on dividends alone and not including any capital appreciation (Duprey 2022).

Banner 17.1 Why Use Dividends to Value Equity?
Dividend investors prefer cash dividends as a measure of value, and it addresses some of the FCFE limitations such as negativity and volatility.

Think 17.1
Why should it be assumed that a cash dividend is equal to FCFE to use a DDM?

17.4 Dividend Discount Models

Using DDMs to value equity simply means discounting the expected cash dividends. Since valuation focuses on equity holders, the appropriate discount rate is the required rate of return on equity (ROE) or cost of equity (k_e). Depending on model assumptions, DDMs can be categorized into no-growth models (NGMs) and growth models, whereby growth models include constant growth models (CGMs) and nonconstant growth models (NCGMs).

▪ No-Growth Models (NGMs)

An NGM assumes that the expected dividends will not change indefinitely. It is applicable for stocks with fixed dividend streams, a typical situation of preference dividends. Equity value per share (V_E), therefore, is estimated as follows:

17

$$V_E = \frac{D_1}{k_e}$$

where D_1 and k_e denote expected dividend per share and cost of equity, respectively.

- **Constant Growth Models (CGMs)**

A CGM assumes that dividends will grow at a constant rate indefinitely. Generally, this model can be applied to the value stocks of high-yielding mature companies that have stable dividend payments but relatively low growth rates. The model is presented as follows:

$$V_E = \frac{D_0(1+g_s)}{(k_e - g_s)}$$

where D_0 and g_s denote current dividend per share and stable growth rate, respectively.

The key assumptions are, therefore, as follows:

1. *Business Stability*: No significant changes are expected in the firm's business operations. The current business status reflects the future.
2. *Steady Dividend Growth*: Cash dividends (equal to FCFEs) are expected to grow at a constant rate indefinitely.
3. *Stable Capital Structure*: The firm is expected to maintain stable financial leverage to keep the cost of equity constant.

These assumptions imply serious practical limitations of this model type. Generally, to determine suitability for a CGM, the correlation between dividend growth and earnings growth should be considered—historical dividend growth should be consistent with sustainable growth of earnings per share (EPS). The main condition, however, is that such growth should not exceed economic growth even by a small margin. These conditions dilute the reality of dividend growth because true growth rates can be higher than economic growth. Although applying a high growth rate violates model assumptions, a low growth rate for high-growing dividends can significantly cause undervaluation.

Banner 17.2 Constant Growth Model

A CGM assumption of low growth tends to contradict the reality of actual dividend growth, thereby limiting its application.

Think 17.2

Is there any problem applying a CGM with a high growth rate? Discuss.

- **Nonconstant Growth Models (NCGMs)**

NCGMs assume that dividends will grow at multiple stages (normally two-stage or three-stage), with each stage representing a different growth stage. These models are generally suitable for valuing equity in companies experiencing moderate or high growth and high payout ratios.

Assuming a constant discount rate, a two-stage NCGM can be presented as follows:

$$V_E = \sum_{t=1}^{n} \frac{D_t\left(1+g_{t+1}\right)}{\left(1+k_e\right)^t} + \frac{D_{n+1}/\left(k_e - g_S\right)}{\left(1+k_e\right)^n}$$

Assuming a constant discount rate, a three-stage NCGM can be presented as follows:

$$V_E = \sum_{t=1}^{T} \frac{D_t\left(1+g_{t+1}\right)}{\left(1+k_e\right)^t} + \sum_{t*T+1}^{n} \frac{D_t}{\left(1+k_e\right)^t} + \frac{D_{n+1}/\left(k_e - g_S\right)}{\left(1+k_e\right)^n}$$

where D_t is dividend per share in a specific period for a growth stage with a limited number of periods (n), g_s is the expected stable growth rate in the final phase of constant growth indefinitely, and k_e is the discount rate assumed to be constant. If variable discount rates are applied, then they should be reflected in the models accordingly.

Banner 17.3 Nonconstant Growth Models

NCGMs are not restricted to growth rates, thereby providing realistic and flexible valuation, subject to correct analysts' judgments.

17.5 DDM Valuation Variables

A DDM utilizes three key variables: dividend per share, discount rate, and growth rate (where applicable).

▪ Dividend Per Share

Dividend per share refers to cash dividend. This approach ignores other types of dividends like stock splits and repurchases. Since the main condition to apply a DDM is predictable cash dividends, the take-off dividend D_0 is generally the current dividend rather than normalized values (e.g., average estimates), which are common in the FCFE approach.

▪ Growth Rates

Like other valuation models, analysts' subjective judgments about growth have vital consequences on valuation results. Dividend growth rates can be determined using different methods like historical extrapolation and fundamentals (refer to ▶ Chap. 14). Considering the main condition to apply DDM—predictability of cash dividends—historically extrapolated growth rates reflect the true dividend growth, whereas fundamentals reflect EPS growth (form which dividends should grow). If dividend payments are consistent with fundamentals (stable earnings, stable capital structure), and if cash dividends are consistent with FCFEs, then fundamental growth rates are more appropriate. Otherwise, there are no strict rules about which approach to rely on when determining growth rates. Depending on the valuation model, decisions should be made about two growth aspects: take-off growth rate and terminal (or stable) growth rate.

Take-Off Growth Rates

Based on growth estimation approaches, decisions about take-off growth should depend on a valuation model as follows:

1. Low growth rates for a constant growth model.
2. Moderate growth rates for a two-stage growth model.
3. High growth rates for a three-stage growth model.

Terminal (Stable) Growth Rates

Terminal or stable growth rates should be consistent with a company's stability (generally low growth) and can be determined as follows:

- *Use proxies*: Like free cash flow valuation approaches, the common proxies for stable growth rates are gross domestic product (GDP) growth and risk-free rate.
- *Use Gordon's growth model (GGM)*: Stable growth can be implied by Gordon's growth model (GGM) assumptions as follows:

$$g_s = \frac{P_0(k_e) - D_0}{P_0 + D_0}$$

where g_s is the stable growth rate, which should not outperform the economic growth rate.
- *Limitations*: If the estimated GGM's growth rate is high, then it cannot be considered as stable growth. Moreover, the GGM approach should not be used to determine the growth rate for a constant growth model because the current trading price (P_0) will be equal to the estimated intrinsic value (V_E)—it will simply be reversing: $V_E = \frac{D_0(1+g_s)}{(k_e - g_s)}$.

Think 17.3

How low (high) should dividend growth be to apply a particular growth model—constant or nonconstant model?

Discount Rate

The required rate of return on equity or cost of equity (k_e) is commonly estimated using the capital asset pricing model (CAPM) (refer to ▶ Chap. 12), such that:

$$k_e = r_f + \beta(r_m - r_f)$$

where r_f and r_m denote the risk-free rate and market return, respectively and β is levered beta. Alternatively, the cost of equity can be estimated from the expected dividend yield and growth implied by GGM as follows:

$$k_e = \frac{D_0(1+g_s)}{P_0} + g_s$$

where g_s is the dividend growth rate implied by GGM. The cost of equity from CAPM and GGM should be exactly equal since $g_s = \dfrac{P_0(k_e) - D_0}{P_0 + D_0}$.

Think 17.4

Under what circumstances should the CAPM's cost of equity differ from the GGM's cost of equity.

17.6 Valuation Considerations

Cash dividend is not the only condition to apply DDMs—not every stock can be valued with a DDM. These models are practically challenging even if the basic condition is regular and cash dividend payments are predictable.

17.6.1 Regular and Predictable Dividends

▶ Exhibit 17.1 presents examples of different companies with a dividend payment history, but not all of them can be valued with DDMs—is it possible to determine their eligibility for DDMs? Based on their track records, their dividend payments can be considered regular. However, regarding dividend predictability, they can be categorized as follows: (1) predictable (McDonald's, Chevron, Exxon, Paramount, and HP)—companies with a complete stable dividend trend (see ▫ Exhibit 17.1.1); (2) somehow predictable (Harley-Davidson, Boeing, Maruti Suzuki, and General Motors)—companies with stable dividends but can be vulnerable in some periods (see ▫ Exhibit 17.1.2); and (3) unpredictable (Ecopetrol and Tanzania Breweries)—companies with unstable dividends (see ▫ Exhibit 17.1.2). Clearly, companies in category 3 should be ruled out of DDM valuation.

Exhibit 17.1 Dividend Payments and Eligibility for DDMs

Illustrative Cases: Ecopetrol, Harley-Davidson, Tanzania Breweries, Boeing, Chevron, Exxon, General Motors, HP, McDonald's, Paramount, Maruti Suzuki (See Excel Workings—▶ Chap. 17, Sheet E.17.1)

This exhibit presents case examples of historical dividend per share, earnings per share, and FCFE per share from 2009 to 2021 (current). ▫ Exhibit 17.1.1 is for companies with clearly predictable dividend trends. ▫ Exhibit 17.1.2 is for companies with somehow predictable dividends. ▫ Exhibit 17.1.3 is for companies with unpredictable dividends.

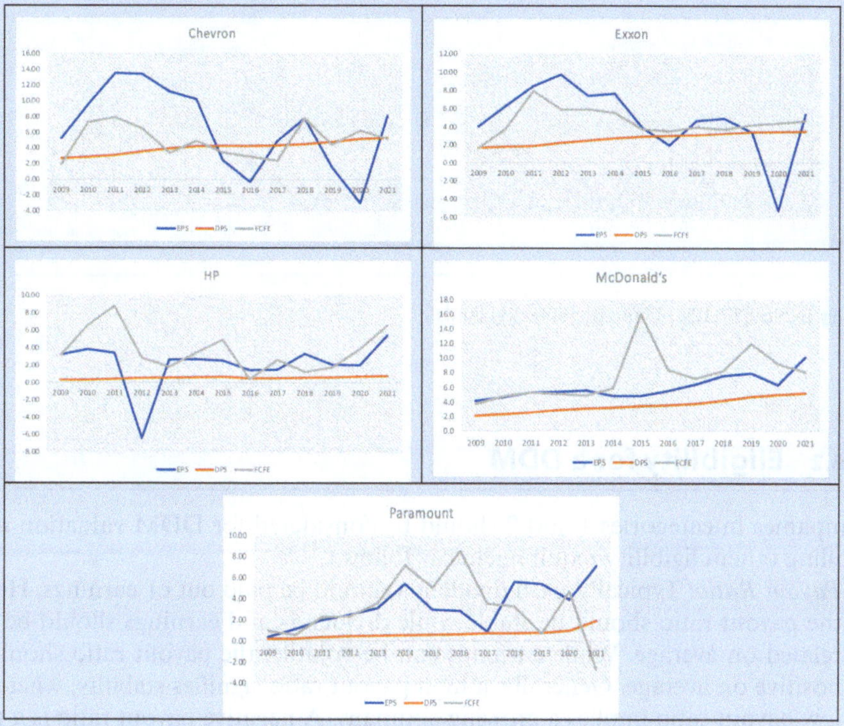

Exhibit 17.1.1 Predictable dividends

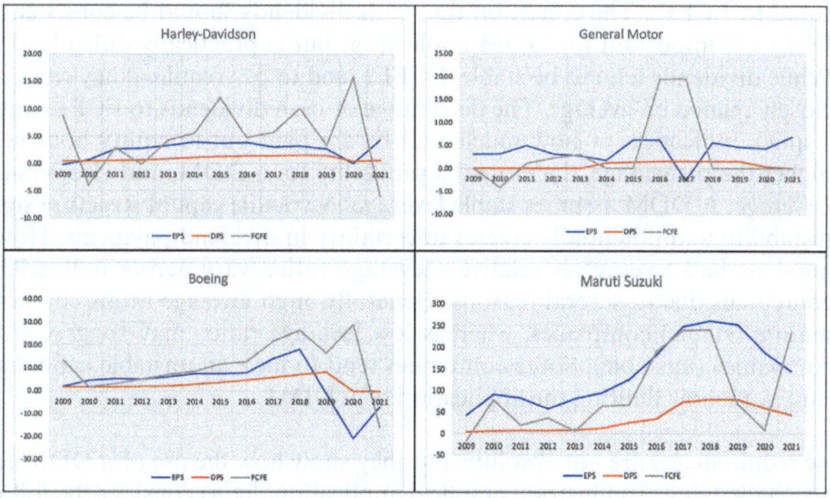

Exhibit 17.1.2 Somehow predictable dividends

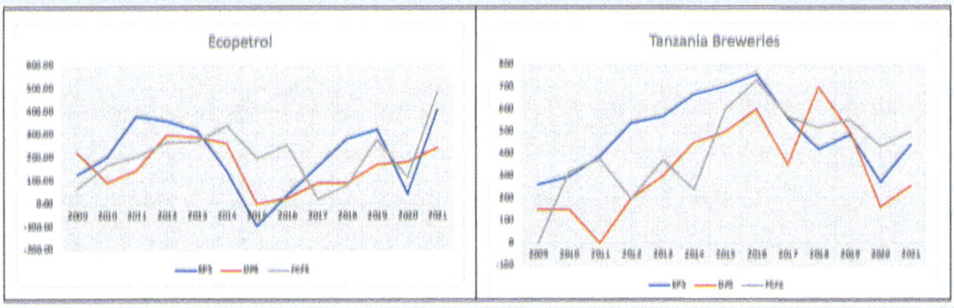

Exhibit 17.1.3 Unpredictable dividends

17.6.2 Eligibility for a DDM

Companies in categories 1 and 2 should be considered for DDM valuation upon fulfilling other eligibility requirements as follows:

1. *Payout Ratio*: Typically, cash dividends should be paid out of earnings. Hence, the payout ratio should be stable while dividends and earnings should be correlated on average. While earnings can be volatile, the payout ratio should be positive on average. Generally, a high payout ratio signifies stability, whereas a low payout ratio implies a growing company. A negative payout ratio is a typical situation of companies striving to maintain dividends through borrowing—hence, a negative retention ratio and declining long-term growth.
2. *Dividends vs. FCFEs*: A DDM assumes that dividend payments are relatively equal to FCFEs. The condition that cash dividends should be consistent with FCFEs is important for DDM application but is practically difficult to hold. While dividends tend to be stable, FCFEs tend to be volatile—they can only be closely related on average. The percentage of cash dividends to FCFEs can give a quick indication of how much FCFEs are paid out to equity holders—the higher the percentage, the more the suitability for a DDM, and vice versa.
3. *Leverage*: A DDM assumes stable leverage. A volatile capital structure signifies instability and potentially creates uncertainty in dividend payments. However, good or bad leverage is relative—leverage ratios vary across industries and companies due to several reasons. Generally, high leverage ratios characterize mature (stable) companies, whereas low leverage ratios may suggest growing companies (unstable). Some companies tend to have an unstable capital structure, somehow limiting the application of a DDM.

These requirements are not absolute, but they show how the use of a DDM can be highly challenging. To illustrate practical application, let us consider the following companies in categories 1 and 2 from ▶ Exhibit 17.1: Harley-Davidson (Harley), Chevron Corporation (Chevron), Exxon Mobil (Exxon), HP Inc. (HP), Paramount Global (Paramount), Maruti Suzuki India (Maruti), and McDonald's Corporation (McDonald's). They are consistent in their dividend payments, but do they qualify for DDM application? Based on information in ▶ Exhibits 17.1 and 17.2, DDM determination for each company can be briefly analyzed as follows.

- **Harley-Davidson**
  - *Acceptable:* The company has a strong dividend record with consistent growth both historically and fundamentally. A 5-year average growth is negative simply due to a 71% dividend decline in 2020. Dividend payments have been solely financed by earnings, except in 2020 when the earnings were negative—since this was a one-time variation, it is considered abnormal. The payout ratio is generally low (less than 50%) but stable. Leverage is high (greater than 1) and somehow stable.
  - *Limitations*: There is no sufficient information to predict whether the recovery in 2021 from declining dividends in 2020 is permanent. Less than 50% FCFE are paid out as cash dividends.
  - *Suitability*: A DDM is generally not suitable.

- **Maruti Suzuki**
  - *Acceptable:* The company maintains regular dividend payments with a high growth record on both measurements (historical extrapolation and fundamentals). Cash dividends arise completely from earnings—the payout ratio is low on average (less than 35%) but stable. Leverage is extremely low (less than 0.1 on average) but maintains a stable range between 0.01 and 0.09.
  - *Limitations:* Dividend payment history fails the basic condition of predictability. There has been a downward trending dividend growth in recent years. Less than 50% FCFEs are paid out as cash dividends.
  - *Suitability*: A DDM is generally not suitable.

- **HP Inc.**
  - *Acceptable*: The company has a stable dividend payment history—the decline in 2016 can be considered abnormal. The payout ratio is generally low on average (less than 36%) but stable. Dividends are consistent with earnings, except in 2012 when the company paid dividends despite negative earnings—since this was a one-time variation, it can be considered abnormal. Leverage has been generally normal prior to 2017 (0.7 on average). The overall negative average debt-to-equity (DE) ratio reflects negative retained earnings (significant deduction of shareholder equity) from 2017.
  - *Limitations*: The percentage of FCFE paid out to equity holders is generally low (less than 25%).
  - *Suitability*: A DDM may not be suitable.

- **Paramount Global**
  - *Acceptable*: The company has a strong dividend history, with consistently stable growth. The payout ratio is generally low (less than 25% on average) but stable—cash dividends are consistent with earnings. Leverage ratio is high on average (greater than 1).
  - *Limitations*: Its current FCFE is negative but has been positive on average. The percentage of FCFE paid out to shareholders has been low but has increased in recent years (above 50% on one 5-year average).
  - *Suitability*: A DDM can be applied.

- **Chevron**
  - *Acceptable*: The dividend payment record is stable and consistent despite volatile earnings. The payout ratio is above 60% on average. The percentage of FCFE paid to equity holders as dividend is high (approaching 100%). Leverage has been maintained low, consistent with the industry (less than 0.3).
  - *Limitations*: Dividend growth is supported by volatile earnings (EPS). However, highly volatile earnings typically characterize the energy industry due to a high influence of global factors like oil supply and price volatility.
  - *Suitability*: A DDM can be applied.

- **Exxon**
  - *Acceptable*: Like Chevron, the dividend payment record is stable and consistent despite volatile earnings. The payout ratio is above 60% on average. The percentage of FCFE paid to equity holders as dividends has been increasing over time (approaching 100% in recent years). Leverage has been maintained low, consistent with the industry (less than 0.3).
  - *Limitations*: Dividend growth is supported by volatile earnings (EPS). However, highly volatile earnings typically characterize the energy industry due to a high influence of global factors like oil supply and price volatility.
  - *Suitability*: A DDM can be applied.

- **McDonald's**
  - *Acceptable*: The company has a strong dividend history, with consistently stable growth. Earnings have been the sole source of dividends with a stable payout ratio of about 60% on average. Its percentage of FCFE paid out to shareholders has been above 50% on average.
  - *Limitations*: McDonald's has a negative leverage ratio on average but is related to treasury stocks from 2017. Prior to 2017, the company maintained positive total equity but relatively high leverage (greater than 1)—negative leverage from 2017 reflects treasury stocks (significant deduction of shareholder equity) during the same period.
  - *Suitability*: A DDM can be applied.

Exhibit 17.2 Background Analysis for DDM Eligibility

Illustrative Cases: Harley-Davidson, Maruti Suzuki, HP, Paramount, Chevron, Exxon, McDonald's (See Excel Workings—▶ Chap. 17, Sheet E.17.2A–G)

Exhibits 17.2.1A, 17.2.1B, 17.2.2A, 17.2.2B, 17.2.3A, 17.2.3B, 17.2.4A, 17.2.4B, 17.2.5A, 17.2.5B, 17.2.6A, 17.2.6B, 17.2.7A, 17.2.7B summarize the key background data and estimated growth rates (average and current year) for DDM determination. The debt-to-equity (DE) ratio is a measure of leverage. D/FCFE is the percentage of cash dividend per share to FCFE per share—it shows dividend payout as a percentage of FCFE.

Exhibit 17.2.1A Harley-Davidson

Item	Variable	Average and current (2021)			
		12-Year	10-Year	5-Year	Current
Reference	Dividend per share	0.96	1.07	1.10	0.60
	FCFE per share	4.52	5.53	5.77	−6.04
	Dividend/FCFE	21.3%	19.3%	19.0%	−9.9%
	Dividend yield	2.1%	2.2%	2.7%	1.6%
	Payout ratio	35.5%	34.8%	41.6%	14.2%
	Debt-to-equity ratio	3.2	3.3	4.1	2.8
Growth	SGR_{EPS}	17.3%	18.3%	15.1%	31.8%
	Dividend (arithmetic)	9.5%	9.5%	−5.5%	
	Dividend (geometric)	3.4%	2.4%	−15.6%	

Note: Harley-Davidson's negative 5-year average is due to the 71% dividend decline in 2020 (abnormal)

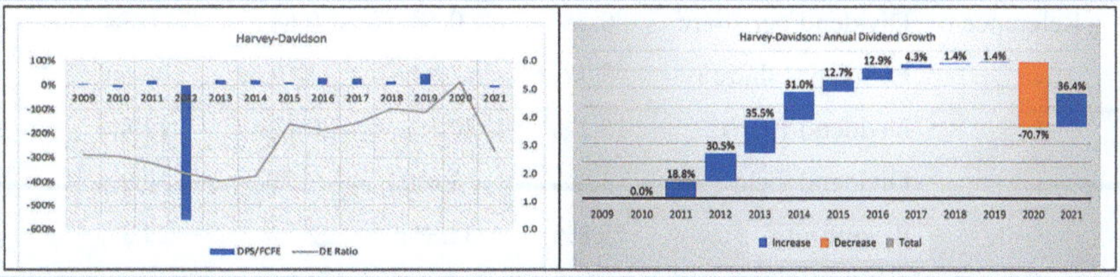

Exhibit 17.2.1B Harley-Davidson

Exhibit 17.2.2A Maruti Suzuki

Item	Variable	Average and current (2021)			
		12-Year	10-Year	5-Year	Current
Reference	Dividend per share	36.8	42.8	68.0	45.00
	FCFE per share	104.7	115.8	158.8	235.15
	Dividend/FCFE	35.1%	36.9%	42.8%	19.1%
	Dividend yield	0.8%	0.9%	1.1%	0.7%
	Payout ratio	24.0%	26.1%	31.0%	31.0%
	Debt-to-equity ratio	0.04	0.03	0.01	0.0
Growth	SGR_{EPS}	9.1%	8.4%	7.4%	3.2%
	Dividend (arithmetic)	31.0%	27.6%	14.2%	
	Dividend (geometric)	23.7%	19.6%	5.2%	

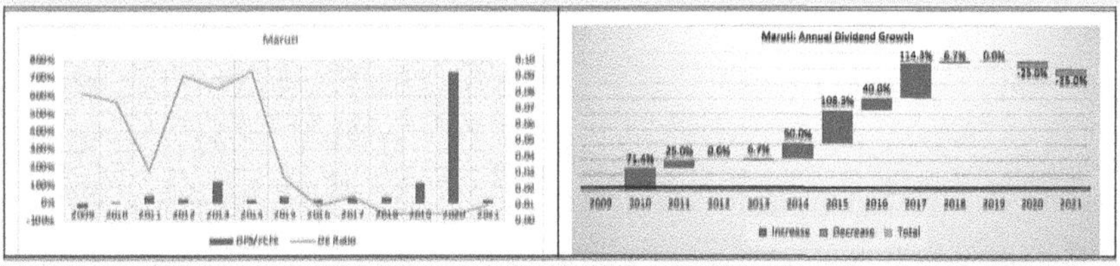

Exhibit 17.2.2B Maruti Suzuki

Exhibit 17.2.3A HP

Item	Variable	Average and current (2021)			
		12-Year	10-Year	5-Year	Current
Reference	Dividend per share	0.56	0.60	0.64	0.78
	FCFE per share	3.72	2.93	3.19	6.50
	Dividend/FCFE	15.2%	20.6%	20.1%	12.0%
	Dividend yield	3.6%	3.8%	2.7%	2.2%
	Payout ratio	25.8%	35.3%	22.5%	29.3%
	Debt-to-equity ratio	−1.8	−2.3	−4.9	−5.3
Growth	SGR_{EPS}	24.4%	27.6%	−150.1%	−203.7%
	Dividend (arithmetic)	8.5%	7.7%	9.4%	
	Dividend (geometric)	7.7%	6.9%	9.3%	

Notes: HP's negative average DE ratio is due to its negative retained earnings from 2017 to 2021. The pre-2017 average was 0.7

17

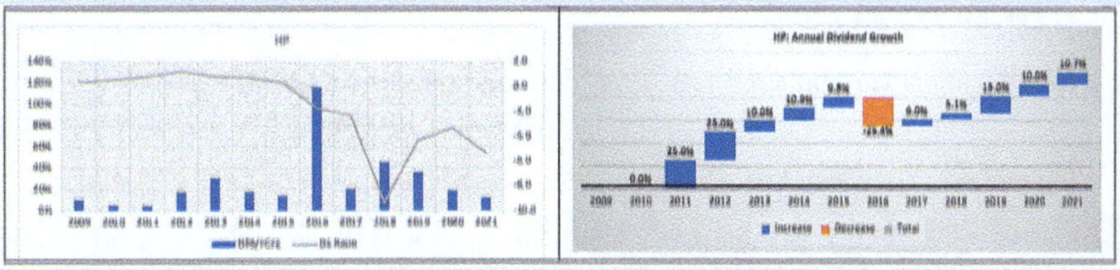

Exhibit 17.2.3B HP

Exhibit 17.2.4A Paramount Global

Item	Variable	Average and current (2021)			
		12-Year	10-Year	5-Year	Current
Reference	Dividend per share	0.70	0.78	1.02	1.92
	FCFE per share	3.24	3.61	1.90	−2.70
	Dividend/FCFE	21.5%	21.7%	53.7%	−71.1%
	Dividend yield	1.8%	1.9%	2.7%	6.2%
	Payout ratio	20.0%	19.8%	22.3%	27.1%
	Debt-to-equity ratio	1.52	1.71	2.14	0.9
Growth	SGR_{EPS}	16.0%	17.4%	16.2%	8.7%
	Dividend (arithmetic)	23.7%	20.9%	28.1%	
	Dividend (geometric)	20.7%	18.6%	23.8%	

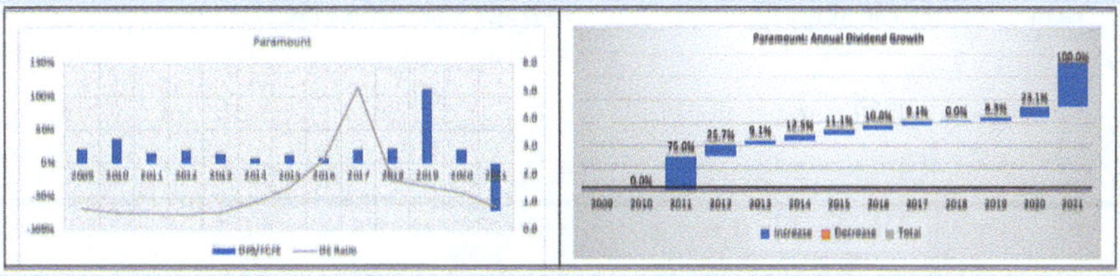

Exhibit 17.2.4B Paramount Global

Exhibit 17.2.5A Chevron

Item	Variable	Average and current (2021)			
		12-Year	10-Year	5-Year	Current
Reference	Dividend per share	4.18	4.42	4.81	5.31
	FCFE per share	5.20	4.72	5.22	5.17
	Dividend/FCFE	80.4%	93.7%	92.1%	102.6%
	Dividend yield	3.9%	4.1%	4.3%	4.6%
	Payout ratio	62.3%	78.4%	123.7%	65.2%
	Debt-to-equity ratio	0.21	0.23	0.26	0.2
Growth	SGR_{EPS}	3.6%	1.8%	−1.7%	4.3%
	Dividend (arithmetic)	6.0%	5.7%	4.4%	
	Dividend (geometric)	5.9%	5.6%	4.4%	

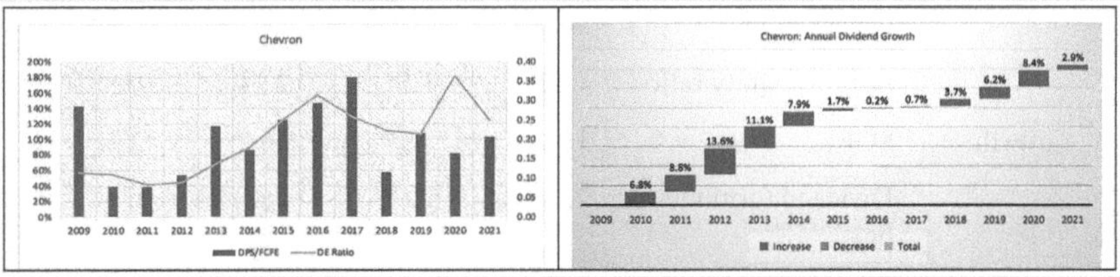

Exhibit 17.2.5B Chevron

Exhibit 17.2.6A Exxon

Item	Variable	Average and current (2021)			
		12-Year	10-Year	5-Year	Current
Reference	Dividend per share	2.79	2.99	3.34	3.49
	FCFE per share	4.75	4.54	4.16	4.62
	Dividend/FCFE	58.7%	65.9%	80.2%	75.6%
	Dividend yield	3.9%	4.2%	5.5%	5.7%
	Payout ratio	56.6%	68.9%	128.3%	64.7%
	Debt-to-equity ratio	0.20	0.22	0.28	0.3
Growth	SGR_{EPS}	5.7%	3.5%	−2.1%	4.6%
	Dividend (arithmetic)	6.5%	6.7%	3.2%	
	Dividend (geometric)	6.4%	6.6%	3.2%	

17

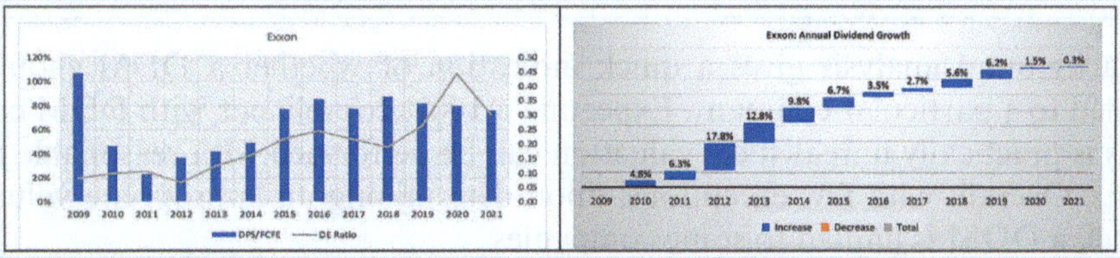

Exhibit 17.2.6B Exxon

Exhibit 17.2.7A McDonald's

Item	Variable	Average and current (2021)			
		12-Year	10-Year	5-Year	Current
Reference	Dividend per share	3.68	3.94	4.61	5.25
	FCFE per share	7.93	8.51	8.96	8.10
	Dividend/FCFE	46.4%	46.3%	51.4%	64.9%
	Dividend yield	2.7%	2.7%	2.3%	2.0%
	Payout ratio	58.7%	60.9%	59.9%	51.9%
	Debt-to-equity ratio	−3.4	−4.3	−7.4	−10.7
Growth	SGR_{EPS}	56.1%	113.0%	−39.0%	−56.5%
	Dividend (arithmetic)	8.2%	7.6%	7.8%	
	Dividend (geometric)	8.2%	7.6%	7.8%	

Notes: McDonald's negative average DE ratio is due to its treasury stocks from 2017 to 2021. The pre-2017 average was 1.3

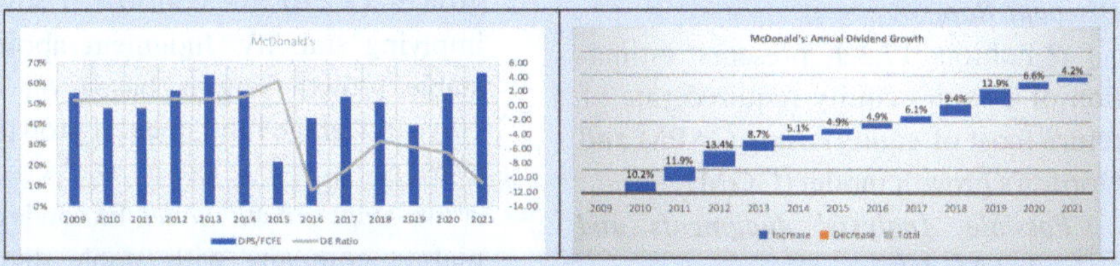

Exhibit 17.2.7B McDonald's

17.6.3 Valuation

A background analysis gives a quick indication of whether a DDM should be applied to a particular company. Expecting a 100% compliance with DDM conditions is practically unrealistic—valuation can be performed with reasonable judgments. Overall, with few exceptions, upon determining an appropriate valuation model, a DDM is limited to some companies.

▶ Exhibits 17.3–17.5 present equity valuation with DDMs for selected cases: Exxon, Paramount, and McDonald's. Analysts' subjective judgments are vital as they influence valuation. The following general aspects are observed:

1. *Valuation Models*: None of the selected cases can be valued with a no-growth model. A constant growth model can be applied, but valuation results should be interpreted with caution. Nonconstant growth models are more realistic, but analysts' subjective judgments influence results.
2. *Growth Rates*: Take-off growth decisions can be based on historical extrapolation of dividend per share—they focus on true dividend growth. Fundamentals can be used if not significantly high or negative—to reflect the realistic dividend stability. Terminal growth rates can slightly deviate from economic growth to reflect the reality of a company's high dividend growth.
3. *Discount Rate*: For simplicity, the cost of equity is assumed to be constant—it could be variable.
4. *Valuation Results*: Results are not absolute—other analysts can have conflicting judgments.

Exhibit 17.3 Equity Valuation with a DDM

Illustrative Case: Exxon (See Excel Workings—▶ Chap. 17, Sheet E.17.2A)

Discount Rate

▫ Exhibit 17.3.1 presents estimation of Exxon's equity required rate of return (cost of equity) using CAPM and Gordon's growth model (GGM).

Possible Analysts' Judgments and Valuation Models

Suppose that there are three different analysts with different valuation judgments. They could consider the following aspects to decide about models and growth rates:

17

- *A constant growth model*: Exxon is a mature company with stable dividend growth. Beta is close to 1. On average (10-year), both the fundamental EPS growth rate (3.5%) and extrapolated 5-year average dividend growth (3.2%) are considered low, implying stability. Judgment about stable growth rate is based on a 10-year average fundamental growth (3.5%).
- *A two-stage growth model*: Exxon is a mature company with stable dividends, but the current fundamental EPS growth (4.6%) is twice the average economic growth, and Gordon's implied growth rate is 5.3%—these rates suggest that the company could be in transition toward stability. Expected take-off dividend growth is assumed to be moderate (4.6% fundamental) and will last for

5 years. Terminal growth is assumed to be 3.5% (10-year average fundamental growth), which is expected to be indefinitely stable in stage 2.

- *A three-stage growth model*: Exxon is a mature company with stable dividends, but a 10-year extrapolated average growth is relatively high (6.7%). Fundamental average EPS growth rates appear low simply due to a one-time negative EPS in 2020 (considered abnormal)—disregarding 2020 makes a 10-year average EPS growth of about 10%. Taking a conservative position, the expected dividend growth at take-off is assumed to be 6.7% in stage 1 for 5 years, followed by transition for another 5 years. Terminal growth is assumed to be 3.5%, which is expected to be indefinitely stable in stage 3.

Valuation Results

Exhibit 17.3.2 summarizes Exxon's valuation results from three different models. Detailed information is available in Excel workings.

Exhibit 17.3.1 Exxon: cost of equity

CAPM		GGM	
Risk-free rate (r_f)	1.45%	Current dividend (D_0)	3.49
Beta (β)	1.068	Current stock price (P_0)	60.90
Expected market return (r_m)	10.67%	GGM growth (g_s)	5.27%
Cost of equity (k_e)	11.30%	Cost of equity (k_e)	11.30%

Notes: Dividend per share (D_0) and current stock price (P_0) are in US$. The stock price is as on 31 December 2021. The risk-free rate is based on a 10-year US treasury bond yield. The expected market return is according to Standards and Poor's 500 (S&P 500) long-term estimates. Beta is based on 3-year daily stock returns relative to S&P 500. GGM growth is implied by Gordon's model

Exhibit 17.3.2 Exxon's stock valuation results

	Constant growth	Two-stage	Three-stage
Valuation: price per share (US$)	46.3	47.4	55.0
Market: price per share (US$)	60.9	60.9	60.9
Status	Overvalued	Overvalued	Overvalued

Exhibit 17.4 Equity Valuation with a DDM

Illustrative Case: Paramount (See Excel Workings—▶ Chap. 17, Sheet E.17.2B)

Discount Rate

Exhibit 17.4.1 presents an estimation of Paramount's equity required rate of return (cost of equity) using CAPM and Gordon's growth model (GGM).

Possible Analysts' Judgments and Valuation Models

Suppose that there are three different analysts with different valuation judgments. They could consider the following aspects to decide about models and growth rates:

- *A Constant Growth Model*: Paramount is a mature company with stable dividend growth. Company stability can be reflected by a high leverage ratio (above 1 on average). However, the following reality violates CGM's basic requirements: GGM's implied growth is not consistent with the economic growth rate (2.1% on average); EPS fundamental growth is high (17.4% on a 10-year average and 8.7% currently), and true dividend growth from historical extrapolation is high (about 21% on a 10-year average). Using a lower growth rate to justify CGM is unrealistic and will cause significant undervaluation. Out of curiosity (not realistic), suppose that an analyst takes an aggressive position to assume a stable growth rate based on current-year GDP growth rate (5.7%).
- *A Two-Stage Growth Model*: Paramount is a mature company with stable dividends. On average, EPS fundamental growth is generally high (17.4% on a 10-year average) but moderate in the current year (8.7%). The company maintains a stable but relatively low payout ratio (about 20% on a 10-year average). A high leverage ratio (above 1) suggests that the company is generally stable. Beta is slightly above market (1.118) suggesting moderate risk. Taking a conservative position, it is reasonable to assume moderate divi-

Exhibit 17.4.1 Paramount: cost of equity

CAPM		GGM	
Risk-free rate (r_f)	1.45%	Current dividend (D_0)	1.92
Beta (β)	1.118	Current stock price (P_0)	31.00
Expected market return (r_m)	10.67%	GGM growth (g_s)	5.24%
Cost of equity (k_e)	11.76%	Cost of equity (k_e)	11.76%

Notes: Dividend per share (D_0) and current stock price (P_0) are in US$. The stock price is as on 31 December 2021. The risk-free rate is based on a 10-year US treasury bond yield. The expected market return is according to S&P 500's long-term estimates. Beta is based on 3-year daily stock returns relative to S&P 500. GGM growth is implied by Gordon's model

17

dend growth at take-off 8.7%, which will last for 5 years of transition to complete stability. Considering high EPS fundamentals and realistic dividend growth, terminal growth is assumed to be slightly higher than average economic growth—it is determined by GGM's assumptions (5.24%).

- *A Three-Stage Growth Model*: Paramount is a mature company with stable dividends and high growth performance in both aspects, i.e., EPS fundamentals ((17.4% on a 10-year average) and historical cash dividends ((about 21% on a 10-year average). Taking a conservative position, the take-off growth rate is assumed to be the current fundamental growth rate (8.7%), which will last for 5 years, followed by another 5 years of gradual transition to stability. Terminal growth is expected to be 4%, and is slightly higher than economic growth (by 2%) to reflect the reality that the company's dividend growth will continue to outperfom economic growth.

Valuation Results

▣ Exhibit 17.4.2 summarizes Exxon's valuation results from three different models. Detailed information is available in Excel workings.

▣ Exhibit 17.4.2 Paramount's stock valuation results

	Constant growth	Two-stage	Three-stage
Valuation: price per share (US$)	33.34	33.48	33.23
Market: price per share (US$)	31.00	31.00	31.00
Status	Undervalued	Undervalued	Undervalued

Exhibit 17.5 Equity Valuation with a DDM

Illustrative Case: McDonald's (See Excel Workings—► Chap. 17, Sheet E.17.2C)

Discount Rate

▣ Exhibit 17.5.1 presents estimation of McDonald's equity required rate of return (cost of equity) using CAPM and Gordon's growth model (GGM).

Possible Analysts' Judgments and Valuation Models

Suppose that there are three different analysts with different valuation judgments. They could consider the following aspects to decide about models and growth rates:

- *A Constant Growth Model*: McDonald's is a mature company with stable dividend growth and dividend yield—the stability of dividend growth can be reflected by almost equal arithmetic and geometric averages (7.6% on a 10-year average). Beta is below market, suggesting low risk. The payout ratio is about 60%

Exhibit 17.5.1 McDonald's: cost of equity

CAPM		GGM	
Risk-free rate (r_f)	1.45%	Current dividend (D_0)	5.25
Beta (β)	0.6100	Current stock price (P_0)	259.45
Expected market return (r_m)	10.7%	GGM growth (g_s)	5.0%
Cost of equity (k_e)	7.1%	Cost of equity (k_e)	7.1%

Notes: Dividend per share (D_0) and current stock price (P_0) are in US$. The stock price is as on 31 December 2021. The risk-free rate is based on a 10-year US treasury bond yield. The expected market return is according to S&P 500's long-term estimates. Beta is based on Zack's estimates (5-year data) as on 31 December 2021—median beta for the consumer discretionary sector is approximately 0.95. GGM's growth is implied by Gordon's model

on average. Excluding the effect of treasury stocks from 2017, leverage has been generally above 1 and EPS fundamentals are strong to maintain a high payout ratio. These features characterize a stable company. Considering strong EPS fundamentals and high dividend growth, judgment of stable growth rate faces challenges: a lower growth rate (to reflect economic growth) may not be realistic, whereas a relatively moderate growth violates model requirements. Based on reasonable judgment, stable growth rate is expected to be slightly lower than GGM's implied growth of 5.0% but slightly higher than the average GDP growth—we assume 4.5%.

- *A Two-Stage Growth Model*: McDonald's is a mature company with stable dividends and a strong track record of a high payout ratio (about 60% on average). True cash dividends have been stable at a moderate rate (7.6% on a 10-year average). EPS fundamental growth is generally strong despite recent negative equity due to stock repurchases (treasury stocks). Dividends are assumed to continue growing at a take-off rate of 7.6% for the next 5 years but fading toward stability. Stable growth rate is assumed to be consistent with GGM's assumptions (5.0%)—although this is higher than the average economic growth, it aligns the current economic growth (5.7%). Overall, McDonald's dividend growth is expected to outperform economic growth indefinitely—we assume 4.5%.
- *A Three-Stage Growth Model*: McDonald's is a mature company with stable dividends. Long-term EPS growth is extremely high (113% on a 10-year average), despite the effect of stock repurchases from 2017 (negative equity). True EPS historical growth is high and is highly correlated with a high payout ratio. An average reinvestment rate of about 40% has been effective enough to generate a high ROE (298% on a 10-year average). Overall, the company is expected to maintain strong

Exhibit 17.5.2 McDonald's stock valuation results

	Constant growth	Two-stage	Three-stage
Valuation: price per share (US$)	213.12	229.06	258.27
Market: price per share (US$)	259.45	259.45	259.45
Status	Overvalued	Overvalued	Overvalued

fundamentals to keep dividend growth relatively high. Taking a conservative position, the take-off growth in year 1 is expected to be 7.6% and will last for 5 years. Thereafter, transition to stability will follow for another 5 years. Stable growth rate is assumed to follow GGM assumptions and somehow outperform the average GDP growth rate but slightly less than the current economic growth: stable growth is assumed to be 4.5%.

Valuation Results

Exhibit 17.5.2 summarizes Exxon's valuation results from three different models. Detailed information is available in Excel workings.

Apply 17.1

Objective: Perform valuation using dividend discount models.

Determine any company that meets the DDM valuation criteria.

1. Collect valuation data.
2. Make assumptions and judgments about valuation models. Provide reasons to justify your decisions.
3. Use Excel to perform valuation and present your results. Do they make sense?

Review Questions

1. Comparing to FCFEs, why should dividends be used to value equity?
2. Outline the key requirements for a DDM be applied to value equity.
3. What is the difference between "cum-dividend" and "ex-dividend" stock price, and what is their application in equity valuation?
4. Mr. Bahati has purchased Exxon stocks at $60.5 per share cum-dividend. Exxon pays an annual dividend per share of $4.4, which is expected to grow at 3.2% annually. Bahati expects to liquidate his stocks next year at $62.2 per share. What is his expected return ex-dividend and cum-dividend? (see Excel workings R17.1).

5. According to Gordon's dividend growth model (GGM), what are the factors determining the cost of equity?
6. Define the following GGM variables and explain how they affect the cost of equity:
   (a) Dividend per share
   (b) Stock price
   (c) Dividend yield
   (d) Dividend growth
7. What are the GGM assumptions and how do they limit the application of the model in the real world?
8. A company has just announced \$5.2 annual cash dividend to common shareholders. Its stocks are currently quoted at \$34 per share ex-dividend. Dividends are expected to grow at 3.5% constantly and indefinitely. Calculate the cost of equity.
9. BKL is a company currently paying a cash dividend of \$4.9 per share, reflecting its stable historical record. Investors expect dividends to grow at a stable rate of 2.8% indefinitely and consistently with the country's GDP growth. BKL stocks are currently trading at \$100.6 per share, whereas beta is 0.768. The expected market return and risk-free rate are 10.67% and 1.55%, respectively. Estimate BKL's equity value and recommend whether it is better to buy or sell (see Excel workings R17.2).
10. Rusuyu Investments is a growing company with a strong dividend record. The current dividend per share is \$2.4 with an average growth of 7.2% annually. The company's stocks have a beta of 0.58 and are currently trading at \$55 per share. Market portfolio expected return is 11.8%, whereas risk-free interest rate is 2.55%. Average economic growth is 2.8%. An analyst believes that Rusuyu's equity should be valued using dividends with a two-stage growth model. The first stage is expected to last for 5 years in which growth will be transitional as follows: 7.2% in year 1, 6.3% in year 2, 5.3% in year 3, and 4.4% in year 4. Growth in terminal year 5 is implied by Gordon's constant growth assumptions (GGM) and will apply in stage 2 indefinitely.

    Required:
    (a) What is the terminal growth rate as implied by GGM?
    (b) What is the equity required rate of return based on CAPM?
    (c) Demonstrate that CAPM-based cost of equity is equal to GGM-implied cost of equity.
    (d) What is the expected stock price in year 5 and capital gain, assuming no transaction costs?
    (e) What is equity intrinsic value per share if the assumption of a two-stage growth model is correct?
    (f) Comment on the market perception of Rusuyu's stocks.
    (See Excel workings R17.2).

Bibliography

Duprey, R. (2022). Why Warren Buffett Loves Coca-Cola's Stock. Available at Fool, https://www.fool.com/investing/2022/10/06/why-warren-buffett-loves-coca-colas-stock/. Accessed October 6, 2022.

Lal C. Chugh, & Meador, J. W. (1984). The Stock Valuation Process: The Analysts' View. *Financial Analysts Journal*, 40(6), 41–48. http://www.jstor.org/stable/4478786

Miller, M. H., & Modigliani, F. (1961). Dividend Policy, Growth, and the Valuation of Shares. *The Journal of Business*, 34(4), 411–433. http://www.jstor.org/stable/2351143

Pinto, J. E., Robinson, T. R., & Stowe, J. D., (2019). Equity Valuation: A Survey of Professional Practice, *Review of Financial Economics*, 37, 219-233. https://doi.org/10.1002/rfe.1040

Further Issues with Cash Flow Discount Models

Contents

Supplementary Information The online version contains supplementary material available at https://doi.org/10.1007/978-3-031-28267-6_18.

B. Kulwizira Lukanima, *Corporate Valuation*, Classroom Companion: Business, https://doi.org/10.1007/978-3-031-28267-6_18

18.1 Introduction

In ► Chaps. 14–17, several valuation models and approaches have been presented, focusing on conceptual and technical issues. To expand learners' knowledge, this chapter provides additional explanations, focusing on valuation application, decision, and limitations.

Learning Outcomes

- Explain the key differences between the cost of capital (CC) approach and the adjusted present value (APV) approach.
- Explain shareholders' cash flows (CFs): dividends vs. free cash flows to equity (FCFEs).
- Understand the concepts of the relative value of growth (RVG) and the present value of growth.
- Estimate and apply the relative value of growth as a tool for value performance analysis.
- Estimate and apply present value of growth opportunities (PVGOs) for value analysis.
- Understand the general limitations of intrinsic valuation.
- Understand how to determine an appropriate valuation model.
- Estimate the cost of preference equity.

18.2 The Cost of Capital Approach vs. the Adjusted Present Value Approach

18.2.1 Estimation Issues

As presented in ► Chaps. 15 and 16, the CC and APV approaches are two different ways of estimating firm value. ► Exhibit 18.1 depicts a comparison between the CC and APV approaches. Overall, the two approaches share the same valuation purpose and variables but differ in terms of application, as follows:

1. *Treatment of Benefits from Debt Finance:* There are two differences to be explained in this aspect. First, whereas in the cost of capital approach, the interest tax benefits are included in future debt issues (through weighted average cost of capital (WACC)), the APV approach only considers these benefits in current debts. Second, the APV approach, in the treatment of tax benefits, considers an absolute debt value in monetary terms (e.g., dollars) of the existing debt. In the cost of capital approach, tax benefits are estimated based on a debt ratio, which depends on capital structure—hence, the current value incorporates the tax benefits from expected future borrowings.
2. *Consideration of Bankruptcy Costs*: The APV approach provides a more reasonable and flexible picture of bankruptcy costs—it can account for both direct

and direct costs. In contrast, WACC, despite considering the risks (in the pretax cost of debt), does not provide a clear account of bankruptcy costs.

Banner 18.1 CC vs. APV

Both the CC and APV approaches use free cash flows to the firm (FCFFs) but different discount rates: CC uses WACC, whereas APV uses unlevered cost of equity.

Exhibit 18.1 The CC Approach vs. APV Approach: Similarities and Differences

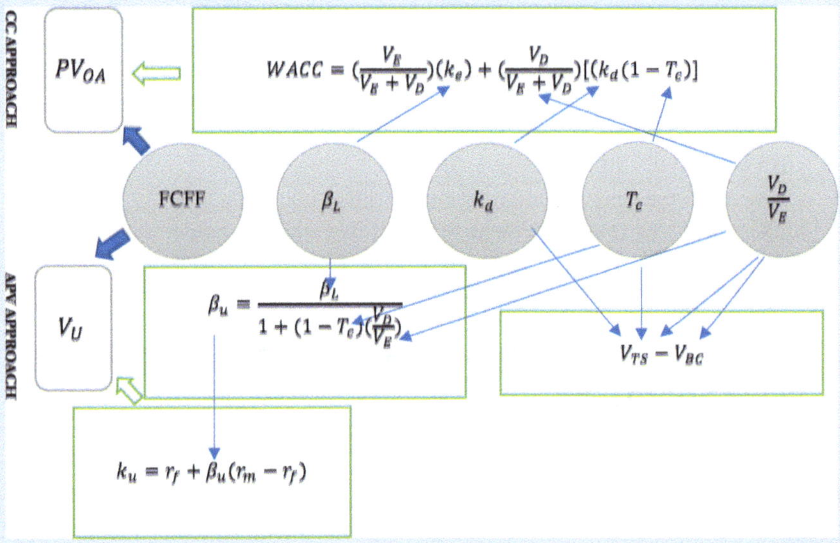

The CC Approach

1. The interest tax shield is reflected in WACC through debt value (V_D) and after-tax cost of debt: $k_d(1 - T_c)$.
2. Financial risk is reflected in WACC: the cost of equity (k_e) captures the financial risk through levered beta (β_L), whereas the pretax cost of debt (k_d) captures the financial risk through the debt ratio.
3. FCFF is discounted at WACC to determine the value of operating assets (PV_{OA}).

The APV Approach

1. The interest tax shield is reflected in debt value, interest rate, and tax rate ($V_D k_d T_c$).

18

2. Financial risk is reflected in default probability and bankruptcy costs (dB): unlevered beta (β_U) excludes the financial risk.
3. FCFF is discounted at an unlevered cost of equity (k_u) to determine only the unlevered firm value (V_U). The value of operating assets (PV_{OA}) is determined by adding debt effects separately ($V_{TS} - V_{BC}$).

18.2.2 Which Approach to Apply?

Both the CC and APV approaches tend to arrive at slightly different but consistent valuation results—a comparison is summarized in ▶ Exhibit 18.2. An important question, therefore, is "which approach to apply and why?" The answer is not straightforward, but the following aspects can guide decisions:

- *Capital Structure Stability*: The main assumption applicable to both CC and APV is that the leverage ratio is constant. However, financial risk can change if a company undertakes a new project (or acquires a business), which will change the overall company's capital structure. The CC approach can capture this effect in WACC, but adjustments tend to be complex. The APV is, therefore, more flexible because changes in financial risk can be separately quantified with default probability and bankruptcy costs.
- *Debt Ratio*: The size of a debt relative to equity is a vital element affecting valuation decisions and results between the CC and APV approaches—the higher the debt ratio, the wider the difference between the valuation results from the two approaches. ◘ Exhibits 18.2.1 and 18.2.2 show case examples of Ecopetrol and Harley-Davidson, both with a significant debt ratio—despite consistent valuation (overvalued or undervalued), the percentage differences between the CC and APV results are quite significant. ◘ Exhibit 18.2.3 presents an example of Tanzania Breweries: in contrast, differences are smaller due to an extremely low debt ratio.
- *Unusual Funding*: Some companies tend to have unusual funding arrangements like loan subsidies. For both CC and APV, debt financing cost is reflected in two variables, i.e., interest expenses and tax savings. A cheaper (expensive) debt, therefore, reduces (increases) both interest expenses and tax savings simultaneously. Both CC and APV capture this effect through WACC and $V_D T_C$, respectively.
- *Discount Rate*: To determine the present value of the interest tax shield, APV discounts tax savings at the pretax cost of debt assuming that it is risk-free rate—this assumption is not realistic considering the practical truth. Both WACC and unlevered cost of equity are more realistic when it comes to discounting FCFF.
- *Limitations*: The choice and application of a valuation approach should consider its main limitations, among other factors. One of the limitations of APV is the estimation of default probability and bankruptcy costs: some companies are not credit-rated by rating agencies, and synthetic ratings tend to be backward-looking; bankruptcy costs tend to be determined indirectly through

empirical research, the findings of which are inconclusive and vary across companies and countries; and decisions about default rates and bankruptcy costs depend on analysts' subjective judgments. Hence, some analysts tend to ignore bankruptcy costs due to estimation challenges or simply assume these as zero. Regarding CC, despite reflecting leverage effects, it does so indirectly and unconvincingly. Consider the following quote (Luehrman 1997):

> WACC has never been that good at handling financial side effects. In its most common formulations, it addresses tax effects only—and not very convincingly, except for simple capital structures.

- *Usefulness*: Although both CC and APV are used to determine the value of a firm's operating assets, APV can be more useful for managers intending to break down different sources of value according to financing decisions.

Think 18.1

How would you determine the suitability of either CC or APV for valuing a particular company?

Exhibit 18.2 The CC vs. APV Approach: Valuation Results

Illustrative Cases: Ecopetrol SA, Harley-Davidson, and Tanzania Breweries Ltd (Refer to Valuation Results in ▸ Chaps. 15 and 16)

Exhibit 18.2.1 Ecopetrol SA: the APV approach vs. CC approach (market price = COP 2690 per share)

Model	Approach	Original valuation: constant discount rates			Jordan's valuation: variable discount rates	
		Is the model appropriate?	Value (COP)	Status	Value (COP)	Status
Single-stage	CC	Yes	1954	Overvalued		
	APV	Yes	1538	Overvalued		
Two-stage	CC	Yes	2029	Overvalued	2577	Overvalued
	APV	Yes	1497	Overvalued	1769	Overvalued
Three-stage[a]	CC	No	2134	Overvalued	2592	Overvalued
	APV	No	1941	Overvalued	1769	Overvalued

[a] Despite sensible results, the valuation model is considered unsuitable as per the comments in ▸ Chap. 15 (see ▸ Exhibit 15.8.1)

Exhibit 18.2.2 Harley-Davidson: the APV approach vs. the CC approach (market price = US$42.2 per share)

Model	Approach	Original valuation: constant discount rates			Jordan's valuation: variable discount rates	
		Is the model appropriate?	Value (US$)	Status	Value (US$)	Status
Single-stage	CC	Yes	48.4	Undervalued		
	APV	Yes	31.9	Overvalued		
Two-stage[a]	CC	No[a]/Yes[b]	92.3	Undervalued	73.5	Undervalued
	APV	No[a]/Yes[b]	50.4	Undervalued	44.5	Undervalued
Three-stage[a]	CC	No	60.9	Undervalued		
	APV	No	38.9	Overvalued		

[a] Despite sensible results, the valuation model is considered unsuitable as per the comments in ► Chap. 15 (see ► Exhibit 15.8.2)
[b] However, an alternative valuation with a lower terminal growth rate (0.75%) is applied to a two-stage model

Exhibit 18.2.3 Tanzania Breweries Ltd.: the APV approach vs. the CC approach (market price = TZS 10,400 per share)

Model	Approach	Original valuation: constant discount rates			Jordan's valuation: variable discount rates	
		Is the model appropriate?	Value (TZS)	Status	Value (TZS)	Status
Single-stage	CC	Yes	10,826	Undervalued		
	APV	Yes	11,722	Undervalued		
Two-stage	CC	Yes	8871	Overvalued	8871	Overvalued
	APV	Yes	12,603	Undervalued	8557	Overvalued

(continued)

Exhibit 18.3.2 (continued)

Model	Approach	Original valuation: constant discount rates			Jordan's valuation: variable discount rates	
		Is the model appropriate?	Value (TZS)	Status	Value (TZS)	Status
Three-stage[a]	CC	Somehow	10,176	Overvalued	10,176	Overvalued
	APV	Somehow	13,743	Undervalued	9925	Overvalued

[a] The valuation model can be questionable as per the comments in ▶ Chap. 15 (see ▶ Exhibit 15.8.3). To determine stable growth for the three-stage model, Jordan uses a 5-year average gross domestic product (GDP) growth rate (4.9%) instead of a 10-year average (5.5%) as applied by other analysts

18.3 Issues with Equity Holders' Cash Flows

Intrinsic valuation uses cash flows as a measure of performance, which influences value, depending on the opportunity cost (the required rate of return) and the timing of the cash flows. Both cash dividends and free cash flows to equity (FCFEs) are drivers of equity holders' value, but several issues ought to be noted.

Think 18.2

Why should cash dividends and FCFEs have different valuation implications, despite being linked to equity holders' cash flows?

Value Creation

Dividend-based models are only suitable for companies with stable dividends, assuming that this stability will persist throughout the business lifetime. Its application is, therefore, limited to few companies with a strong track record of stable and prosperous profitability. However, to justify dividend stability, some companies tend to mask their poor performance using debts to finance cash dividends—such dividends can destroy value if persisting for a long run due to financial risks. Therefore, stable dividend payments do not necessarily imply value creation—it simply means wealth distribution in a particular period. Moreover, dividend discount models typically focus on cash dividends, thereby ignoring share repurchases, which are alternative ways to bring back cash to the investors.

In contrast, free cash flow to equity (FCFE) signifies shareholders' value creation because it reflects a company's good financial health. Since FCFE is levered, it has already accounted for all business cash flows from operations, investments, and financing. Hence, a positive FCFE truly signifies efficiency and potential value creation. A negative FCFE, however, does not necessarily imply value destruction if more cash has been injected into value-creating investments whose benefits will be realized in the future. The only limitation is that valuation cannot be performed with a negative FCFE.

- **Relevance**

Dividend relevance is questionable and debatable. It is, therefore, not mandatory to pay dividends. Some investors (especially large shareholders) do not rely on cash dividends as a value-generating reward—they prefer stock value appreciation associated with growth opportunities. Therefore, valuation with dividend discount models only makes sense to dividend-preferring investors. In contrast, FCFE models provide more meaningful valuation regardless of dividend preferences. Some studies suggest that analysts prefer earnings-based proxies to dividends for equity valuation (e.g., Chugh and Meador 1984; Pinto et al. 2019).

- **Consistency**

Dividend discount models (DDMs) assume that cash dividends are expected to be equal to or approaching FCFEs. Similarly, FCFE models assume that all FCFEs are paid out as dividends. Practically, this equality assumption is either difficult or impossible to fulfill, and, therefore, dividend and FCFE valuation results may be inconsistent.

- **Predictability**

Dividend policy and payment decisions are in the hands of companies' management and are hence controllable even if they depend on profitability performance. In contrast, FCFE is merely an outcome of business performance in its various aspects, which tends to experience both ups and downs, and is difficult to control. Hence, dividends are usually less volatile than FCFEs and therefore being forward-looking is more justified in the case of dividends than FCFE valuation models.

Banner 18.2 Dividends vs. FCFEs
Both dividends and FCFEs are equity valuation cash flows but have different implications in performance measurement and as value drivers.

18.4 The Relative Value of Growth

The concept of the relative value of growth (RVG) was invented by Mass (2005). It is a managerial performance measurement and decision-making multiple, which helps evaluate the extent to which revenue growth or profit margins reflect shareholders' value.

» The RVG metric expresses the value of an extra percentage point of growth as a multiple of the value of a percentage point increase in a company's operating profit margin. The higher the multiple, the more valuable growth is to a company (Mass 2005).

RVG is determined as follows:

$$\mathrm{RVG} = \frac{V_{\mathrm{RG}}}{V_{\mathrm{MI}}}$$

where V_{RG} is the value of revenue growth, measuring the percentage increase in the shareholder value to a 1% increase in revenue. V_{MI} is the value of margin improvement, measuring the increase in shareholder value with a 1% improvement in margin.

Banner 18.3 Relative Value of Growth

RVG is a multiple that expresses the value of revenue growth relative to the value of margin improvements. It helps determine which of the two values improves shareholder value.

18.4.1 Managerial Implications

Generally, the higher the RVG, the more the value of a company's growth.

- If RVG < 1, then margin improvements contribute more to shareholder value creation than to revenue growth—managers should put more emphasis on margin improvement than on revenue growth.
- If RVG > 1, then revenue growth contributes more to shareholder value creation than to margin improvements—managers should put more emphasis on revenue growth than on margin improvement.

18.4.2 Value Estimation

V_{RG} can be influenced by factors like sustainable cash flow (CF), cost of capital (WACC), and investors' growth expectations (g). Considering the value of a 1% increase in growth, V_{RG} can be estimated as follows:

$$V_{\mathrm{RG}} = \frac{\mathrm{CF}}{(\mathrm{WACC} - g - 1\%)} - V_F$$

18

where V_F is the current enterprise value. Hence, V_{RG} is the gain in shareholder value due to a 1% increase in growth rate.

V_{MI} depends on factors like current revenue (R), corporate tax rate (T_c), cost of capital (WACC), and investors' growth expectations (g). Considering the value of a 1% increase in growth, V_{MI} can be estimated as follows:

$$V_{MI} = \frac{R \times 1\%(1 - T_c)}{\text{WACC} - g}$$

Estimation variables can be determined as follows:

1. *WACC*: Use the normal estimation approaches covered in previous chapters.
2. *Sustainable Cash Flow (CF):* This is a free cash flow reflecting the earning power of a company. It should not be distorted by temporary performance—a normalized FCFF (e.g., average) can be used.
3. *Firm Value (V_F):* This is the current enterprise value that reflects market valuation (market cap and total debt). Refer to ▶ Chap. 21 for details on enterprise value.
4. *Growth Expectations (g)*: These reflect market expectations and therefore can be estimated by building a valuation model capturing the current enterprise value (market value), expected free cash flow, and WACC. Using a stable cash flow growth model, the following equation is applicable:

   $$g = \frac{V_F(\text{WACC}) - \text{FCFF}}{V_F + \text{FCFF}}$$

   It should be noted that complex models (multiple stage growth) can be used depending on specific valuation requirements.
5. *Current Revenue (R):* This is the revenue from the most current reporting period. It can be based on trailing 12 months (TTM) across 4 quarters.
6. *Tax Rate (T_c):* This is a corporate tax rate that captures tax expenses and interest tax shield on WACC.

▶ Exhibit 18.3 presents a simple case example using Ecopetrol SA.

Exhibit 18.3 Estimating the Relative Value of Growth

Illustrative Cases: Ecopetrol SA (Refer to Excel Workings ▶ Chap. 18, Sheet E18.3)

Estimation Data

- Exhibit 18.3.1 presents and clarifies Ecopetrol's valuation data for estimating the relative value of growth as on 17 November 2022.

Estimation Results

- Exhibit 18.3.2 presents Ecopetrol's RVG estimation results. Based on investors' growth expectations, and since RVG > 1, Ecopetrol's revenue growth contributes more to shareholders' value creation than to margin improvement.

Exhibit 18.3.1 Ecopetrol SA: data for relative value of growth (all in COP millions, except percentages)

Variable	Amount
Firm value: current enterprise value as on 17 November 2022	219,887,234
Revenue: current quarter (2022 Q3)	151,557,080
Sustainable cash flow: 5-year average FCFF	10,465,816
WACC[a]	5.1%
Tax rate[b]	29.5%
Investors' growth expectations[c]	0.3%

[a] WACC was obtained from Bloomberg based on the current financials (2022 Q3) and current market values (capital structure)
[b] Tax rate is a 2-year average effective tax rate for Ecopetrol
[c] Investors' growth expectations are estimated from a simple valuation model, assuming stable growth expectations, such that: $g = \frac{V_F(\mathrm{WACC}) - \mathrm{FCF}}{V_F + \mathrm{FCF}}$
The expected growth rate (0.3%) is below Colombia's GDP growth rate (the 5-year average is 2.1%)

Exhibit 18.3.2 Calculation of RVG (all in COP millions, except percentages)

Formula	Value	Implication
$V_{\mathrm{RG}} = \frac{10,465,816}{(5.1\% - 0.3\% - 1\%)} - 219,887,234$	57,346,085	A 1% increase in revenue will cause a COP 57,346,085 increase in shareholders' value
$V_{\mathrm{MI}} = \frac{151,557,080 \times 1\%(1 - 29.5\%)}{(5.1\% - 0.3\%)}$	22,383,246	A 1% increase in operating margin will cause a COP 22,383,246 increase in shareholder value
$\mathrm{RVG} = \frac{57,346,085}{22,383,246}$	2.6	Revenue growth contributes to shareholders' value creation 2.6 times more than margin improvement

Managerial Implications

1. Ecopetrol's management can use RVG to undertake operating strategies, which encourage more revenue growth than cost reduction (to improve operating margins).
2. Comparison with peers can help understand a company's value creation performance of its business operations.

Apply 18.1

Objective: Estimate the relative value of growth.

Use any company data from previous chapters (refer to Excel data sheets).

1. Identify all the variables for estimating RVG.
2. Determine investors' growth expectations. Provide reasons to justify your judgment.
3. Calculate RVG and interpret the results.

18.5 The Present Value of Growth Opportunity

The present value of growth opportunity (PVGO) or net PVGO (NPVGO) can be defined as an additional equity value caused by growth potential: it is the difference between value with growth and value without growth, such that:

$$\text{PVGO} = P_{0,g+} - P_{0,g0}$$

where $P_{0,g+}$ is the current stock price with growth expectations and $P_{0,g0}$ is the expected stock value in the absence of growth.

The assumption is that more value should be created by reinvesting earnings, whereby the return on equity (ROE) should be greater than the cost of equity. To determine PVGO, valuation considers market growth expectations and fundamentals. As presented in ▶ Chap. 14, a sustainable growth rate is determined as follows:

$$g = g_{\text{EPS}} = R_r \times \text{ROE}$$

where R_r is the retention ratio (i.e., plowback) and ROE is the return on equity, which measures the ability of "levered assets" to generate net earnings and be reinvested to generate the same ROE. If all earnings are reinvested, then R_r is 100%. If all earnings are distributed as dividends, then R_r is 0%. Hence, the higher the plowback ratio, the higher the growth potential, and vice versa.

18.5.1 Market Value vs. Intrinsic Value

PVGO can be analyzed under two contexts: market value and intrinsic value. The market context is generally applicable to public companies, whereby $P_{0,g+}$ is the current stock price. Regarding intrinsic value, $P_{0,g+}$ is estimated from discounting cash flows with a growth model.

A no-growth model assumes that a company is unable to generate a positive present value by reinvesting earnings—investors can gain more value from dividend distribution. Since earnings per share (EPS) equals dividend, $P_{0,g0}$ can be estimated with a perpetual model as follows:

$$P_{0,g0} = \frac{\text{EPS}_1}{k_e}$$

where EPS_1 denotes the expected earnings per share and k_e is the cost of equity.

A growth model assumes that more shareholder value will be created by reinvesting some of the earnings: hence, EPS is not equal to dividend. Assuming a constant growth model, $P_{0,g+}$ can be estimated as follows:

$$P_{0,g+} = \frac{D_0(1+g)}{k_e - g}$$

where D_0 is the current dividend per share. Hence, both market and intrinsic values carry information about growth expectations as follows:

$$P_{0,g+} = P_{0,g0} + \text{PVGO}$$

18.5.2 Managerial Implications

PVGO is an important decision-making tool for managers: the higher the PVGO, the more the value from reinvestment of earnings, and vice versa. More specifically, the managerial implications of PVGO are as follows:

- *PVGO < 0*: Reinvestment of earnings destroys shareholders' value—a higher payout ratio should be more favorable.
- *PVGO > 0*: Reinvestment of earnings creates more shareholders' value than dividend distribution—a higher retention ratio should be more favorable.
- *PVGO = 0*: It does not matter whether earnings are reinvested or not—reinvestment and dividend payment have the same impact on shareholders' value creation.

PVGO tends to be analyzed as a multiple of market price ($\text{PVGO}/P_{0,g+}$). The higher the multiple, the more the contribution of growth expectations.

▶ Exhibit 18.4 presents a simple example to explain both market value and intrinsic value contexts. ▶ Exhibit 18.5 presents a case example using Ecopetrol SA: the valuation results are consistent with those of previous models, as summarized in ▶ Exhibit 18.2.

Exhibit 18.4 Present Value of Growth Opportunity

Illustrative Example: RTY (Refer to Excel Workings ▶ Chap. 18, Sheet E18.4)

RTY company's stocks are currently trading at \$60 per share. The expected EPS is \$5. The cost of equity is 10.5%, whereas the ROE is 22%. Use PVGO to analyze the following:

1. What is RTY's stock value in the absence of growth opportunities?

18

2. What is the proportion of RTY's market price that is attributable to growth opportunities. Interpret the results.
3. Based on the intrinsic equity value (constant growth model), estimate PVGO under different retention ratios from 0% (increase in 10% intervals) to the point where the expected growth does not exceed the cost of equity.

Solution:

1. Stock value in the absence of growth:

$$P_{0,g0} = \frac{\text{EPS}_1}{k_e} = \frac{\$5}{10.5\%} = \$47.6$$

2. The proportion of RTY's market price that is attributable to growth opportunities:

$$\text{PVGO} = P_{0,g+} - P_{0,g0} = \$60 - \$47.6 = \$12.4$$

$$\frac{\text{PVGO}}{P_{0,g+}} = \frac{\$12.4}{\$60} = 0.206 = 20.6\%$$

Implication: 20.6% of the market price is attributable to the expected growth.

3. Intrinsic valuation with growth:

$$P_{0,g+} = \frac{D_0(1+g)}{k_e - g}$$

$$g = g_{\text{EPS}} = R_r \times \text{ROE}$$

Exhibit 18.4.1 presents variation in growth expectations depending on variations in retention ratio, with constant EPS and ROE. Exhibit 18.4.2 presents the intrinsic value without growth ($47.6) and variations in PVGO relative to growth variations. PVGO declines as retention ratio declines—more shareholders' value is created with more reinvestment of earnings to the extent that the growth rate is not equal to or greater than the cost of equity: for example, the value is negative if the retention ratio is 50% because $g > k_e$.

Exhibit 18.4.1 Retention ratio vs. growth

EPS ($)	**5.0**	**5.0**	**5.0**	**5.0**	**5.0**	**5.0**
Retention ratio	50.0%	40.0%	30.0%	20.0%	10.0%	0.0%
Payout ratio	50.0%	60.0%	70.0%	80.0%	90.0%	100.0%
Dividend per share ($)	2.5	3.0	3.5	4.0	4.5	5.0
ROE	22.0%	22.0%	22.0%	22.0%	22.0%	22.0%
Growth	11.0%	8.8%	6.6%	4.4%	2.2%	0.0%

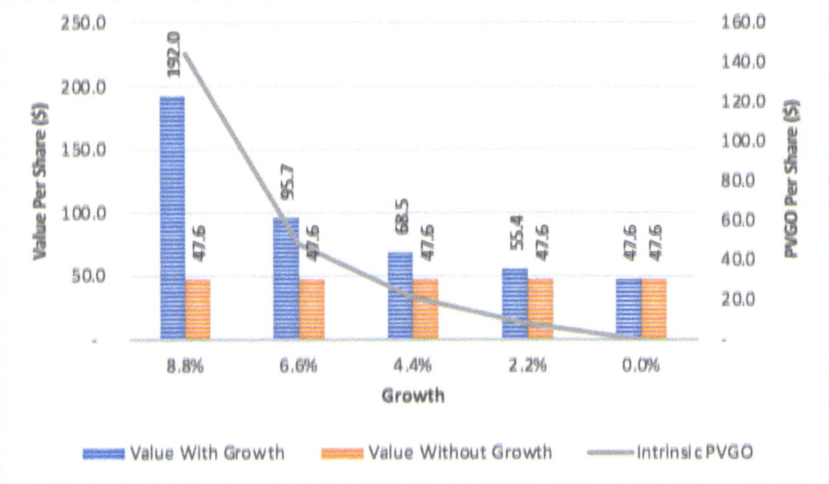

Exhibit 18.4.2 Variations in PVGO relative to growth

Banner 18.4 PVGO Implication

The higher the PVGO, the more the value from reinvestment of earnings, and vice versa.

Exhibit 18.5 Present Value of Growth Opportunity

Illustrative Cases: Ecopetrol SA (Refer to Excel Workings ▶ Chap. 18, Sheet E18.5)

Estimation Data

Ecopetrol's valuation data as on 31 December 2021 are as follows: stocks were trading at COP 2690 per share; EPS (a 5-year average) was COP 242.3 to reflect expectations; the cost of equity was 12.8%; normalized ROE was 17.5% (a 5-year average). The retention ratio is currently 59.8% but is subject to variations.

PVGO Analysis

1. Stock value in the absence of growth:

$$P_{0,g0} = \frac{\text{EPS}_1}{k_e} = \frac{\text{COP } 242.3}{12.8\%} = \text{COP } 1896$$

2. The proportion of Ecopetrol's market price that is attributable to growth opportunities:

$$\text{PVGO} = P_{0,g+} - P_{0,g0} = \text{COP } 2690 - \text{COP } 1896 = \text{COP } 794$$

18

$$\frac{\text{PVGO}}{P_{0,g+}} = \frac{\text{COP } 794}{\text{COP } 2690} = 0.295 = 29.5\%$$

3. Intrinsic valuation with growth:

   Exhibit 18.5.1 presents the intrinsic value without growth (COP 1896) and variations in PVGO relative to growth variations. PVGO increases as the retention ratio increases to the extent where the growth rate does not exceed the cost of equity.

Implications

1. Based on the market price, PVGO is positive (COP 794). At COP 2690, Ecopetrol's market pricing reflects 29.5% of the value attributed to growth opportunities.
2. Investors believe that reinvesting earnings creates more value—more value is created with an increase in the retention ratio.
3. From Exhibit 18.5.1, the sensitivity of value to growth increases as the growth rate approaches the cost of equity. Since the intrinsic value is estimated with a stable cash flow model, growth assumption should be consistent with economic growth. Considering GDP average growth (the 5-year and 10-year averages are 2.1% and 3.3%, respectively), a suitable growth rate should be between 1.7% and 3.5% and a realistic intrinsic value should range from COP 2011 to COP 2160: hence, intrinsic PVGO is between COP 115 and COP 265.
4. Assuming a stable growth model, at COP 2690, Ecopetrol's stocks were potentially overvalued.

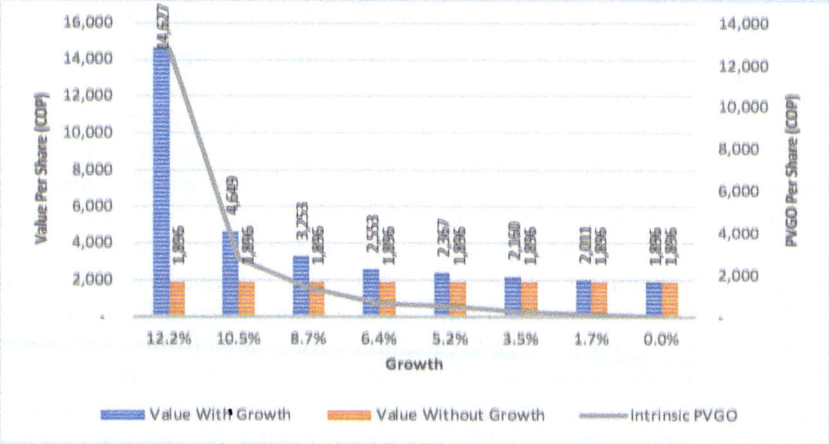

Exhibit 18.5.1 Retention ratio vs. PVGO

Apply 18.2

Objective: Estimate the present value of growth opportunities.

Use any company data from previous chapters (refer to Excel data sheets).

1. Identify all the variables for estimating PVGO.
2. Estimate the stock value without growth.
3. Determine the proportion of market price that is attributable to growth opportunities. Interpret the results.
4. Analyze PVGO based on intrinsic valuation with growth. Interpret the results.

18.6 Limitations of Intrinsic Valuation

So far, several valuation approaches and models have been presented and discussed, including practical limitations specific to each model and approach. The following general limitations should also be considered.

- *Cyclical Firms:* One of the assumptions in intrinsic valuation is that forecasted cash flows follow a particular pattern during the life horizon of a firm. This assumption is not appropriate for cyclical firms, the earnings of which tend to vary with external shocks that are uncontrollable by the firms (e.g., macroeconomic factors such as boom, recession, and recovery). Valuation models, which do not capture business cycles, tend to cause misleading value estimates, usually leading to systematic overvaluation during peak years and undervaluation during trough years (de Heer et al. 2000). Therefore, there should be alternative approaches to valuing cyclical firms (see, for example, Damodaran 2009; McKinsey & Company et al. 2010).
- *Troubled Firms*: The assumption of positive earnings has dominated free cash flow valuation so far. However, there are numerous complexities that free cash flow valuation faces when dealing with troubled firms experiencing negative earnings. As we have seen in previous chapters, negative earnings or cash flows cause several valuation limitations. The first and most common challenge is the estimation of growth rate, which tends to be more negative as we apply negative earnings. Second, the implication of tax rates tends to be difficult—computing taxes is a difficult task because tax liabilities are created from positive earnings rather than negative earnings. Third, the going-concern assumption becomes irrelevant in cases of high or abnormal negative earnings—persistence in operating losses signifies financial difficulties that threaten the survival of a firm.
- *Private Firms*: Parameters that are used in estimating risk during free cash valuation are based on historical records of past prices. Such risk measures are the key inputs for estimating appropriate discount rates (cost of equity and WACC). Since private firms are not traded, they do not have past prices. The difficulty of valuing private firms arises since their valuation may rely on proxy inputs from comparable public firms. A practical challenge is always on getting a proxy firm of similar characteristics.

18.7 Choosing an Appropriate Approach

Intrinsic valuation approaches share one common aspect: discounting of cash flows. However, they differ in several specific aspects such as the type of cash flow (e.g., FCFFs, FCFEs, or dividends), discount rate (e.g., WACC, levered cost of equity, or unlevered cost of equity), and valuation model (e.g., constant growth or multiple stage growth). Overall, there is no standard way to determine the most suitable valuation approach or model: it depends on specific valuation circumstances explained earlier in ▶ Chaps. 14–17. In this section, let us look at some issues relating to the cost of capital (CC) approach and the adjusted present value (APV) approach. The following factors can help determine an appropriate approach or valuation variable to suit specific circumstances of a company or equity to be valued.

1. *Ownership Perspective*: When considering the business ownership perspective, the appropriate cash flow is FCFE since it accounts for the effect of capital structure or leverage (i.e., interest payments and the repayment of debts). Equity value is, therefore, better estimated directly using FCFE and cost of equity.
2. *Consideration of Financial Risk*: By reckoning debt in cash flows, FCFF may be misleading in terms of how we view the potential financial risk to a firm, potentially caused by a high debt ratio without sufficient cash flows to cover it: an extremely high FCFF can be associated with a negative or extremely low FCFE due to high debt obligations. A prolonged negative or extremely low FCFE can have detrimental effects on shareholders' value and the firm's survival—it may be necessary to issue new equity to rectify the problem. Valuation with FCFE will focus attention on any danger caused by significant debt obligations: a FCFF model may help hide the problem.
3. *Considering the Target Capital Structure*: Some firms tend to determine the target capital structure, a vital input for estimating the cost of capital. Generally, the CC approach assumes a constant cost of capital, which might not be feasible and reasonable, especially for growing firms where maintaining a target capital structure may be difficult: the APV approach may be more suitable under such circumstances.

From these considerations, when choosing the appropriate type of cash flow, FCFE would be more appropriate for firms whose capital structures are stable or less volatile. In case of a negative FCFE and significant debt outstanding, it would be appropriate to use FCFF. To choose the appropriate valuation model, it is also important to weigh out their strengths and limitations.

18.8 The Cost of Preference Equity

In ▶ Chap. 12, attention was paid to the cost of common equity because it is the most applicable to every company. Some companies, however, tend to include preference equity in their financing structure. It is, therefore, important to be knowledgeable about the cost of preference equity, the rate of return required by the preference stockholders. It is basically a dividend yield derived as follows:

$$K_p = \frac{D_p}{P_n}$$

where K_p is the cost of preference equity and D_p is the preferred dividend, which can be determined as follows:

$$D_p = F_p(d)$$

F_p is the face value (par value) of the preferred stock and d is the fixed dividend rate. P_n is the market value ("ex-dividend") for outstanding stocks or net proceedings for new issuance.

For a new issue of preference stocks, adjustments should be made on P_n to consider issuance features—floatation costs (costs relating to issuing new stocks)—and whether the issue lies in the discount or the premium, such that:

$$P_n = P_p\left(1 - C_f\right)$$

where P_p is the issued stock value, which can be at par, discount, or premium. C_f represents floatation costs. Hence, the cost of preferred stock can be generally presented as:

$$K_p = \frac{F_p(d)}{P_p\left(1 - C_f\right)}$$

This estimation is applicable under basic assumptions that the stock is perpetual and so is the respective dividend; the stock is inconvertible and irredeemable; and the dividend payment is constant and regular.

For redeemable preference stocks, modifications are required in the formula, as follows:

$$K_p = \frac{D_p + (P_v - P_n)/N}{(P_v + P_n)/2}$$

where P_v is the redemption value and N is the number of years to redemption.

18

Think 18.3

Based on dividend models, what are the differences between estimating the cost of common equity and estimating preference equity?

▶ Exhibit 18.6 presents examples to illustrate estimation of preference cost of capital under three scenarios: (1) dealing with preferred stocks outstanding, (2) dealing with new issues in discount or premium, and (3) dealing with redeemable stocks.

Exhibit 18.6 Estimating Cost of Preference Equity

Illustrative Examples (See Excel Workings—▶ Chap. 18, Sheet E.18.6)

Scenario 1. Stocks outstanding: ABC company has 50,000 irredeemable and inconvertible preference stocks outstanding, paying dividend at 8.5% on its face value of $400.00. Its current market value is $380.50 per share. Calculate the cost of ABC's preference stock.

Solution:

$$D_p = F_p(d) = \$400(8.5\%) = \$34$$

$$K_p = \frac{D_p}{P_n} = \frac{\$34}{\$380.50} = 8.94\%$$

Scenario 2A. New stock issuance (at par): XYX company has decided to issue new irredeemable and inconvertible preference stocks, paying dividend at 6.4% on the stock's face value of $350.00 each at par. The floatation cost of the new issue is 4.6% of the issue price. Calculate the cost of XYZ's preference stock.

Solution:

$$D_p = F_p(d) = \$350(6.4\%) = \$22.4$$

$$P_p(at\ par) = F_p = \$350$$

$$P_n = P_p(1 - C_f) = \$350(1 - 4.6\%) = \$333.90$$

$$K_p = \frac{D_p}{P_n} = \frac{\$22.4}{\$333.90} = 6.71\%$$

Scenario 2B. New stock issuance (at discount): BKL company has decided to issue new irredeemable and inconvertible preference stocks, paying dividend at 10.5% on the stock's face value of $200.00 each at 2% discount. The floatation cost for the new issue is 3.2% of the issue price. Calculate the cost of BKL's preference stock.

Solution:

$$D_p = F_p(d) = \$200(10.5\%) = \$21.0$$

$$P_p(\text{at } 2\% \text{ discount}) = \$200(1 - 2\%) = \$196.0$$

$$P_n = P_p(1 - C_f) = \$196(1 - 3.2\%) = \$189.73$$

$$K_p = \frac{D_p}{P_n} = \frac{\$21.0}{\$189.73} = 11.07\%$$

Scenario 2C. New stock issuance (at premium): JJJ company has decided to issue new irredeemable and inconvertible preference stocks, paying dividend at 7.0% on the stock's face value of $500.00 each at 1.5% premium. The floatation cost for the new issue is 5% of the issue price. Calculate the cost of JJJ's preference stock.

Solution:

$$D_p = F_p(d) = \$500(7\%) = \$35.0$$

$$P_p(\text{at } 1.5\% \text{ premium}) = \$500(1+1.5\%) = \$507.5$$

$$P_n = P_p(1-C_f) = \$507.5(1-5\%) = \$482.13$$

$$K_p = \frac{D_p}{P_n} = \frac{\$35.0}{\$482.13} = 11.07\%$$

Scenario 3. New stock issuance (redeemable): BKL company has decided to issue new preference stocks, paying dividend at 10.5% on the stock's face value of $200.00 each at 2% discount. The floatation cost for the new issue is 3.2% of the issue price. The stock is inconvertible but redeemable at 6% premium after 5 years. Calculate the cost of BKL's preference stock. Compare this with scenario 2B and comment which stock alternative is more beneficial to the company.

Solution:

$$D_p = F_p(d) = \$200(10.5\%) = \$21.0$$

$$P_p(\text{at } 2\% \text{ discount}) = \$200(1-2\%) = \$196.0$$

$$P_n = P_p(1-C_f) = \$196(1-3.2\%) = \$189.73$$

$$P_v(\text{at } 6\% \text{ premium}) = \$200(1+6\%) = \$212.0$$

$$K_p = \frac{D_p + (P_v - P_n)/N}{(P_v + P_n)/2} = K_p = \frac{21 + (212.0 - 189.73)/5}{(212.0 + 189.73)/2} = 12.67\%$$

Comment: The cost of equity is lower with irredeemable stocks (scenario 2B) than with redeemable stocks (scenario 3). Therefore, scenario 2B is more beneficial to the company, whereas scenario 3 is more advantageous to the stockholders.

Banner 18.5 Cost of Preference Equity

The cost of preference equity is simply its dividend yield.

Review Questions

1. What is the conceptual difference between the APV and CC approaches of valuation?
2. Explain how the following valuation aspects are reflected in the CC and APV approaches:
   (a) Interest tax shield
   (b) Financial risk

18

3. Explain why FCFFs are discounted at WACC in the CC approach but at the unlevered cost of equity in the APV approach.
4. What factors would you consider when choosing between the following valuation approaches or variables?
   (a) CC approach or APV approach
   (b) Dividends or FCFEs
   (c) FCFFs or FCFFs
5. Regarding the relative value of growth, define the following terms:
   (a) Value of revenue growth
   (b) Value of margin improvements
6. Explain the difference between the relative value of growth (RVG) and the present value of growth opportunities (PVGOs) under the following aspects:
   (a) Meaning
   (b) Application
7. What is the main assumption when using the present value of growth opportunities to analyze value?
8. How would you interpret value performance under the following RVG conditions?
   (a) A company's RVG is 6.5
   (b) A company's RVG is 0.8
9. Adive company's current data show its enterprise value is $540 million, whereas revenue is $135 million. Sustainable cash flow is estimated to be $18 million. The cost of capital and corporate tax rate is 8.6% and 35%, respectively.
   Required:
   (a) Estimate the expected growth rate implied by a cash flow constant growth model.
   (b) Determine the relative value of growth and interpret the results.
   (Refer to Excel workings ▶ Chap. 18, Sheet R18.1)
10. How would you interpret valuation implications of the following PVGO conditions?
   (a) A company with a $245 stock price has a negative PVGO of $–60.
   (b) A company with a $90 stock price has a positive PVGO of $30.
11. La Vida company's stocks are currently trading at $150 per share. Its expected EPS is $12. The cost of equity is 14.0%, whereas ROE is 20%. Use PVGOs to analyze the following:
   (a) Stock value in the absence of growth opportunities.
   (b) The proportion of stock market price that is attributable to growth opportunities. Interpret the results.
   (c) Based on intrinsic equity value (a constant growth model), estimate PVGOs under different retention ratios (start from 0% with 10% intervals) to the point where equity value is not infinity. Use a graph to explain the relationship between growth and value.
   (Refer to Excel workings ▶ Chap. 18, Sheet R18.2)

12. Two companies X and Y have just announced cash dividends to common shareholders, with both paying $1.2 per share. Stock prices are currently trading at $12.5 and $20.4, respectively.
    (a) Calculate each company's cost of equity under each of the following growth assumptions: 1.5%, 4.2%, 8.0%, and 12.6%.
    (b) Use your results in (a) to explain the relationship between: (1) dividend yield and cost of equity and (2) dividend growth and cost of equity.
13. What are the basic assumptions when estimating the cost of preferred stocks? What are the practical limitations of those assumptions?
14. Define the following terms and explain their application in estimating the cost of preference stocks:
    (a) Face value
    (b) Market value
    (c) Issue value
    (d) Floatation costs
    (e) Price at discount
    (f) Price at premium
    (g) Price at par
    (h) Redeemable stocks
    (i) Irredeemable stocks
15. Considering the basic assumptions, mention and define the factors determining the cost of preferred stocks under the additional conditions:
    (a) Preference stocks are irredeemable
    (b) Preference stocks are redeemable
16. When estimating the cost of preferred stocks, what is the key practical consideration on the following two scenarios:
    (a) When dealing with stocks outstanding
    (b) When dealing with new issuance of stocks
17. UVW company has 1 million irredeemable and inconvertible preference stocks outstanding, paying dividend at 6.0% on its face value of $1000.00. Its current market value is $990.00 per share. Calculate the cost of UVW's preferred stock.
18. EFG company is considering issuing new irredeemable and inconvertible preference stocks at a face value $500.00, paying dividend at 10.0%. The floatation cost for the new issue is expected to be 4.5% of the face value. Calculate the cost of EFG's preference stock under the following issuance conditions:
    (a) If issued at a premium of 2.2%
    (b) If issued at a discount of 2.2%
    (c) If issued at par
19. HIJ company is considering issuing new preference stocks, paying dividend at 10.5% on the stock's face value of $200.00 each at 2% discount. The floatation cost for the new issue is 3.2% of the issue price. Calculate the cost of HIJ's preference stock under the following issue conditions:
    (a) If the stocks are inconvertible and irredeemable.

18

(b) If the stocks are inconvertible but redeemable at a 2% premium after 5 years.
(c) If the stocks are inconvertible but redeemable at a 2% discount after 5 years.
(d) If the stocks are inconvertible but redeemable at par after 5 years.
(e) Compare your answers in (a)–(d) and suggest the most advantageous issuance condition to the company.

Bibliography

Damodaran, A. (2009), Ups and Downs: valuing cyclical and commodity companies, Stern School of Business, New York University, (September 1) https://doi.org/10.2139/ssrn.1466041

de Heer, Marco; Koller, Tim; Schauten, Marc B J; Steenbeek, Onno W. (2000), The valuation of cyclical companies, McKinsey & Company, Erasmus University, Rotterdam

Lal C. Chugh, & Meador, J. W. (1984). The Stock Valuation Process: The Analysts' View. *Financial Analysts Journal*, 40(6), 41–48. http://www.jstor.org/stable/4478786

Luehrman, T. A., (1997), Using APV: A Better Tool for Valuing Operations, Harvard Business Review, May–June 1997. https://hbr.org/1997/05/using-apv-a-better-tool-for-valuing-operations

Mass, N. J. (2005), Valuation Relevance of Operating Profit Margin: The Relative Value of Growth, Harvard Business Review (April 2005), https://hbr.org/2005/04/the-relative-value-of-growth

McKinsey & Company; Koller, Tim; Goedhart, Marc; and Wessels, David (2010), Valuation: Measuring and managing the value of companies, John Wiley & Sons

Pinto, J. E., Robinson, T. R., & Stowe, J. D., (2019). Equity Valuation: A Survey of Professional Practice, *Review of Financial Economics*, 37, 219-233. https://doi.org/10.1002/rfe.1040

Relative Valuation

Contents

An Overview of Relative Valuation

Contents

Supplementary Information The online version contains supplementary material available at https://doi.org/10.1007/978-3-031-28267-6_19.

B. Kulwizira Lukanima, *Corporate Valuation*, Classroom Companion: Business, https://doi.org/10.1007/978-3-031-28267-6_19

19.1 Introduction

In previous chapters, valuation is referred to as "absolute valuation" because it is based on discounted cash flows—an income-based approach. This chapter presents a different valuation process known as "relative valuation"—a market-based approach. The general concept of relative valuation is comparability of companies operating in the same business environment in which market perceptions drive value. Comparable companies (known as peers) create a common benchmark from which a target company (in the peer group) is valued depending on performance indicators (known as value drivers). Relative valuation is more applicable for public firms because market values are observable. Nevertheless, private firms can be valued upon determining comparable public firms.

The focus of this chapter is to prepare learners apply relative valuation effectively. It introduces the overall concept of relative valuation, its fundamental principles, and its significance in corporate valuation.

Learning Outcomes

- Understand the concept and meaning of relative valuation
- Perform simple calculation of relative value from given information
- Understand the basic principles of relative valuation
- Understand the relative valuation process
- Determine the peer group for relative valuation
- Describe the goal of relative valuation

19.2 Relative Value

Let us begin with a normal-life definition of the term "relative." The Cambridge Dictionary defines relative as "a member of your family" and to be relative as "being judged or measured in comparison with something else" or "true to a particular degree when compared with other things" or "having a particular characteristic or value compared to other things of a similar type."

Valuation applies the same definitions—"relative value" is the value of a security or asset determined by comparing the valuation metrics of other similar securities or assets. Analogously, similar securities or assets represent a "family" or "things with particular characteristics"—a common technical term is a "peer." Relative value is, therefore, different from "absolute value"—the value of an asset solely derived from its unique features like cash flows, growth rates. and discount rates.

Think 19.1

Should relative value be consistent with intrinsic value?

19.2.1 Relative Valuation

From the definition of relative value, "relative valuation" is a process in which equity value or firm value is estimated by comparing the valuation multiples of similar companies. Valuation, therefore, is based on "value drivers," which are firms' specific financial performance measures (e.g., sales, earnings, book value of equity, cash flows, etc.) and market perception measures (market value). The two measures (financial and market) form ratios of market values to value drivers technically known as valuation multiples. Peer benchmarks are then derived from multiples for comparing the target company to the peer group. A company is considered undervalued if its multiples are below the peer benchmark and overvalued if above.

Banner 19.1 Relative Valuation
Relative valuation is the process of valuing equity or a firm by comparing the performance indicators (value drivers) of similar companies (peers) relative to market perception.

19.2.2 Valuation Multiples

Valuation multiples are generally categorized into two: "equity value multiples" and "enterprise value multiples." ▶ Exhibit 19.1 provides a breakdown of the composition of equity value and enterprise value to elaborate the two valuation categories and their multiples.

An "enterprise value (EV)" is the total value of a company, which incorporates all components of the capital structure such as equity and debt—EV multiples are referred to as operating multiples because they relate to unlevered value drivers such as sales, earnings before interest, taxes, depreciation, and amortization (EBITDA), earnings before interest and taxes (EBIT), and free cash flow to the firm (FCFF). Since EV includes both equity value and net debt, the value drivers are relevant to both equity holders and debtholders—that is, "before" the interest expenses, preferred dividends, and minority interest expenses. They are, therefore, immune from subjective accounting manipulations—and by ignoring financial leverage, EV multiples allow direct comparison of different firms regardless of capital structure differences. Hence, operating multiples are particularly more applicable in decisions relating to mergers and acquisitions.

An "equity value" reflects only the equity-financed portion of a firm (the difference between enterprise value and net debt)—relative valuation multiples should be related to levered value drivers such as earnings available to common equity holders, free cash flow to equity (FCFE), and book value of equity. Because of leverage, highly levered firms are expected to have high expected returns (to compensate for financial risk). For example, if earnings per share (EPS) is used as a value driver and the multiple is the price–earnings (P/E) ratio, then firms with high leverage are expected to have higher P/E multiples than those with low leverage.

Exhibit 19.1 Relative Valuation Concept

See Exhibit 19.1.1.

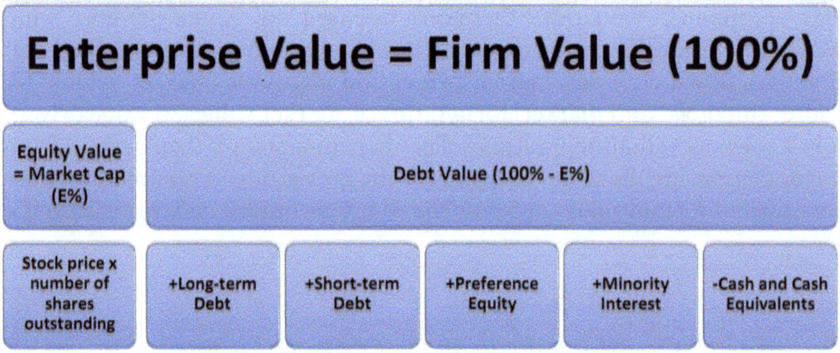

Exhibit 19.1.1 Breaking down equity value and enterprise value

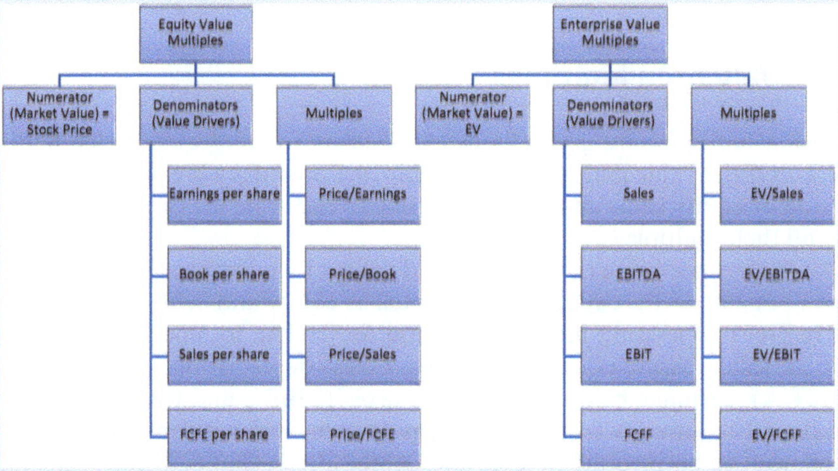

Exhibit 19.1.2 Value drivers and valuation multiples

19.2.3 Valuation Variables

Exhibit 19.1.2 depicts the following key variables to perform relative valuation:

- **Market Values**

19 For equity and EV valuation, market values are stock price and EV, respectively. They reflect the current market perceptions about company performance. For each

multiple, market values are numerators, indicating how much the market values a company's performance based on each of the value drivers (denominators)—the higher the multiple, the more the value relative to peers.

Value Drivers

Value drivers measure companies' performance on various aspects like earnings, cash flows, and tangible value. Exhibit 19.1.2 presents a few commonly applicable ones, but there can be several. For each multiple, the value driver is different so as to reflect a specific performance measure. Value driver application, therefore, differs depending on specific valuation needs and suitability. This aspect is further explained in ▶ Chaps. 20 and 21.

Multiples

A multiple is a ratio of the market value to value driver. It is, therefore, used as a valuation benchmark for peers—a benchmark can be an average or median of all companies in the peer group.

19.2.4 Value

Value is estimated as a product of a value driver and a respective peer benchmark. Therefore, the general equation to determine relative equity value (V_E) and enterprise value (V_{EV}) can be presented as follows:

$$V_E = \Psi_E \Theta$$

$$V_{EV} = \Psi_{EV} \Theta$$

where Ψ_E and Ψ_{EV} denote equity and EV value driver, respectively. Θ denotes a peer benchmark relating to a particular multiple.

In case it is impossible to estimate equity value using equity multiples (due to limitations like negative value drivers), it can be indirectly determined using operating multiples by subtracting the net debt (V_D) from the enterprise value as follows:

$$V_E = V_{EV} - V_D$$

▶ Exhibit 19.2 presents simple examples to calculate relative value.

Exhibit 19.2 Calculating Relative Value

Illustrative Example

Imelda Co Ltd. has just released its financials. Exhibit 19.2.1 summarizes the key information relating to its operating performance: earnings per share (EPS), sales per share (SPS), and EBIT. Imelda has 3.8 million common shares outstanding and currently trading at $10.8 per share, whereas its net debt is $18.8 million. Exhibit 19.2.2 shows valuation multiples for both Imelda and peer average during the

Exhibit 19.2.1 Imelda Co Ltd: value drivers

Metrics	Amount ($)
EPS	1.8
SPS	4.3
EBIT (millions)	5.0
[a]Sales (millions)	16.3

[a] Sales = SPS × number of shares outstanding (millions) = $4.3 (3.8) = $16.3 million

Exhibit 19.2.2 Valuation multiples

Multiple	Imelda	Peer average
P/E	6.0	5.4
P/S	2.5	2.1
EV/EBIT	12.0	12.2
EV/sales	3.7	4.0

same period for price–earnings (P/E), price to sales (P/S), enterprise value to EBIT (EV/EBIT), and enterprise value to sales (EV/sales).

Required:

(a) Compare Imelda's to peer average multiples and comment on the market perception of Imelda.

(b) Calculate Imelda's relative equity value based on EPS and SPS value drivers.

(c) Calculate Imelda's enterprise value using EBIT and sales value drivers.

(d) Calculate Imelda's equity value based on enterprise value.

(e) Interpret the valuation results.

Solution:

(a) Imelda's stocks are potentially overvalued because its multiples outperform the peer benchmark, but EV is undervalued because its multiple are below the peer benchmark.

(b) Relative equity value per share based on EPS and SPS:

$$V_E = \Psi_E \Theta$$

$$V_E = \text{EPS}(\Theta_{PE}) = \$1.8(5.4) = \$9.7$$

$$V_E = \text{SPS}(\Theta_{PS}) = \$4.3(2.1) = \$9.0$$

(c) Relative EV based on EBIT ($ millions) and sales ($ millions):

$$V_{EV} = \Psi_{EV} \Theta$$

$$V_{EV} = \text{EBIT}(\Theta_{EV/EBIT}) = \$5.0(12.2) = \$61 \text{ million}$$

$$V_{EV} = \text{Sales}(\Theta_{EV/Sales}) = \$16.3(4.0) = \$65.4 \text{ million}$$

19

(d) Relative equity value based on enterprise value: EBIT and sales value drivers:

If EBIT is a value driver:

$$V_E = V_{EV} - V_D = \$61 - \$18.8 = \$42.2 \text{ million}$$

$$\text{Value per share} = \frac{\$42.2 \text{ million}}{3.8 \text{ million shares}} = \$11.1$$

If sales is a value driver:

$$V_E = V_{EV} - V_D = \$65.4 - \$18.8 = \$46.6 \text{ million}$$

$$\text{Value per share} = \frac{\$46.6 \text{ million}}{3.8 \text{ million shares}} = \$12.3$$

(e) Interpretation:

- Based on equity value multiples (P/E and P/E), trading at a stock price of \$10.8, Imelda is overvalued. Its stocks should trade between \$9.0 and \$9.7 per share.
- Based on EV multiples, at an EV of \$59.8 million, Imelda is undervalued. Its EV should be between \$61 million and \$65.4 million.
- Based on EV multiples, at a market cap of \$41 million, Imelda is undervalued. Its market cap should be between \$42.2 million and \$46.6 million, trading between \$11.1 per share and \$12.3 per share.

Think 19.2

Is it appropriate to use an operating value driver to estimate equity value?

19.2.5 Usefulness

A survey conducted by the Chartered Financial Analyst (CFA) Institute (see Fabozzi et al. 2017) shows that, in comparison with other valuation methods, relative valuation is the most widely used for equity valuation mainly due to its estimation simplicity: it involves too many analysts' subjective decisions; it does not require complex formulas and computations; and it is easy to understand, apply, and interpret. Compared to intrinsic valuation (which is based on cash flows), the results from relative valuation tend to be closer to market values because multiples consider the most current reaction of the market on a firm relative to its financial performance indicators (ratios).

19.3 Basic Principles

Despite its simplicity, relative valuation involves some basic principles, which can be categorized as: assumptions, peer selection, valuation metrics, consistency, uniformity, and technical analysis.

▪ Assumption

The main assumption in relative valuation is that if firms are similar in comparable terms, they will have similar valuation multiples (e.g., P/E, P/S, EV/EBITDA, EV/sales, etc.). Therefore, valuation multiples represent realistic valuation benchmarks.

▪ Peer Selection

Relative valuation can only be applied in the presence of comparable firms, referred to as "peers"—meaning that peers are not only simply similar but also identical. A peer group does not necessarily relate to any industry or sector. For example, firms may belong to the same industry, the same sector, and the same geographical coverage but may not be identical—they may differ in several aspects like risk, returns, prospects, financial structure, and growth. Moreover, some companies tend to be classified by more than one sector or industry. For instance, mobile phone companies offer communication services as the primary product, but they also deal with other segments like baking, online retail, etc.—that is, a mobile phone company can belong to sectors like telecommunication, financial services, and retail. Although the industry or sector tends to determine a firm's characteristics, peer selection should consider identicality in the determinants of value such as risk, cash flows, and growth. A peer group is not absolute—a company can belong to more than one peer group.

▪ Valuation Metrics

There are three types of valuation metrics in terms of period: current, average, or forward. Relative valuation requires valuation metrics to be applied consistently to the peer group.

1. Current metrics apply the most current value drivers to determine multiples, such as trailing 12 months (TTM), trailing 4 quarters (TFQ), and current reporting period. The main limitations are misleading estimates if drivers are highly volatile or current performance is abnormal and will not be applicable for negative performance. ▶ Exhibit 19.3 presents an example of how current metrics can be misleading and the possible adjustments required.
2. Average metrics apply average (normalized) value drivers for a selected sample period (e.g., 4-quarter, 8-quarter, 5-year, 10-year, etc.). These metrics can address some limitations of the current metrics (volatile, abnormal, or negative performance).
3. Forward metrics are forward-looking measures, which apply forecasted metrics—also referred to as "leading" or "prospective" metrics. Analysts tend to use projections for the subsequent four quarters or the next fiscal year. Forward metrics are more consistent with valuation principles because they are based on expectations rather than history. However, inaccurate forecasts can cause misleading valuation. Forecasts tend to suffer from analysts' biasness due to over-optimism, which is not stable over time or across stocks—optimism tends to rise when investor sentiment is buoyant, particularly for growth stocks with hard-to-estimate future earnings. A company can have its own future estimates, but more reliable forecasts are based on analyst consensus.

What metric to use? There are two main decision criteria: availability of data and suitability of metrics. Generally, backward metrics can be irrelevant if a company changes its business nature—they simply do not reflect the company's future. Financial performance (value drivers) can be transitory due to a company's specific factors like business reconstruction, cycles in the company or industry, etc. A common solution is to use "normalized earnings," which are adjusted to the effects of cycles or seasonality. For companies experiencing business cycles, earnings from the most recent four quarters may be a relevant reflector of the average or long-term earnings performance of a company. While current and historical data tend to be easily available, it is not always the case for forward data—these tend to be available only for companies closely followed by analysts. Depending on data availability, combining several metrics provides a wider picture and allows profound valuation analysis. However, forward metrics should be given priority.

Exhibit 19.3 Current Metrics

Illustrative Example: Abnormal Earnings

On 30 June 2017, shares of ABC company, a car manufacturer, were trading at $122.76 per share. The income statement for the financial period ending on July 2016 reported EPS of $2.68. During the last quarter of 2016, the company recalled most of its cars worth $400 million due to technical defections, leading to an extraordinary loss of $1.34 per share. Moreover, during the second quarter of 2017, a nonrecurring expense of $1.85 per share was reported. The trailing EPS as on 30 June 2017 was $5.56, which includes the last quarter of 2016 and three quarters of 2017. This EPS is not adjusted for nonrecurring items.

Required:

(a) Show how abnormal items affected P/E on 30 June 2017.

(b) Calculate the trailing P/E as on 30 June 2017, considering adjustments for nonrecurring items.

(c) What is the effect of abnormal items on P/E?

Solution:

(a) Without adjustments for nonrecurring items:

$$P/E = \$122.76 / \$5.56 = 22.08$$

(b) EPS is adjusted (TTM) by adding back nonrecurring expenses to the reported EPS for the quarter that ended on 30 June 2017:

$$\text{EPS}(\text{adjusted}) = \text{EPS}(\text{current}) + \text{Abnormal expenses.}$$

$$\text{EPS}(\text{adjusted}) = \$5.56 + \$1.34 + \$1.85 = \$8.75.$$

$$P/E = \$122.76 / \$8.75 = 14.03$$

(c) The effect of nonrecurring expenses is to overestimate the P/E by 57%.

- **Consistency**

For more reliable valuation, value drivers should be (not obligatory) consistent with the type of valuation (equity valuation or enterprise valuation). That is, equity valuation should be based on equity-based drivers (e.g., EPS, FCFE, and book value of equity), whereas enterprise valuation should be based on operating drivers (e.g., EBIT, EBITDA, and FCFF). Nevertheless, operating drivers can be used for equity valuation if equity value drivers are inapplicable due to limiting factors like negativity and abnormality.

- **Comparability**

Value drivers are derived from financial statements, which tend to differ in several ways like reporting standards, financial reporting periods, reporting currency, and reporting frequency. Moreover, differences in accounting policies among firms can influence the reported results. Relative valuation requires these aspects to be comparable: financial information should reflect the same reporting standards, periods, currency, frequency, etc.

- **Analysis and Reasoning**

Relative valuation involves both objective and subjective aspects. Objective aspects mainly relate to obtaining financial data (value drivers). Subjective aspects relate to decisions such as peer group selection, financial metrics to apply (current, average, or forward), and so on. Valuation results, therefore, should be analyzed to determine sense-making considering subjective reasoning and objective aspects.

Banner 19.2 Peer Selection

Peer selection is the core of relative valuation. A wrong peer group will lead to inaccurate valuation.

Exhibit 19.4 Relative Valuation Process

The relative valuation process is not as complex as intrinsic valuation. It simply requires an existence of comparable companies (peers), availability of valuation data, some analyst judgments, and simple calculations.

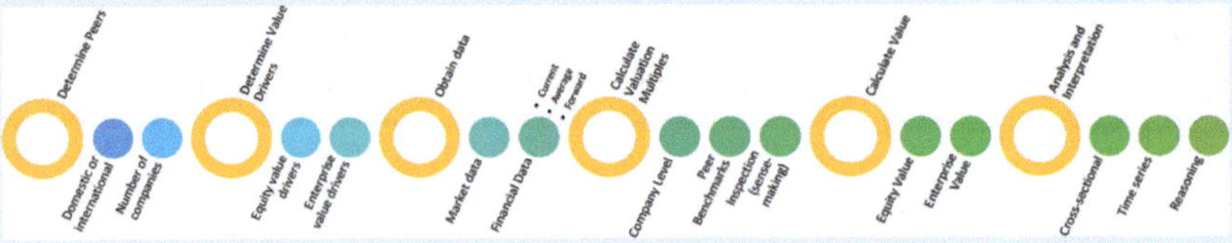

19.4 Relative Valuation Process

Relative valuation is a process involving several steps as depicted in ▶ Exhibit 19.4.

19.4.1 Determining Peers

This is the most challenging, yet the most important decision to be made. A wrong peer group will affect the accuracy of valuation. Peers are determined based on similarity regarding the key value determinants (cash flows, growth, and risk), among other factors. Practically, a perfect peer does not exist, but several identical peers do. ▶ Exhibit 19.5 outlines the key considerations for peer determination. While industry tends to define companies with similar characteristics, it should not be regarded as the main peer selection criteria—it should be supported by fundamentals and other factors. Overall, there is no standard peer group for a particular company. A single company can belong to more than one peer group depending on the selection criteria. ▶ Exhibit 19.6 shows how different sources define Netflix's peers, implying that peer selection involves both objectivity (similarity criteria) and subjectivity (what similar companies to include). Consider the following quotes based on empirical evidence.

About industry:

» We find strong evidence that product market space is amongst the most important factors in peer selection, but Standard Industrial Classification (SIC) codes, particularly three- and four-digit codes, do a poor job of categorizing related firms in this setting (Eaton et al. 2022).

» Peer selection based on the relative earnings stability takes account of some idiosyncrasies of companies, which remain uncaptured by traditional industrial classification-based peer selection methods (Janda 2019).

About subjectivity:

» This is the first large-scale study to examine the peer companies used by sell-side equity analysts in their research reports. … We find that analysts on average select peer companies with high valuations and that this effect varies systematically with analysts' incentives and ability. Our evidence provides partial support for the idea that analysts choose peers strategically (De Franco et al. 2015).

Banner 19.3 Peer vs. Industry

Sector or industry helps determine peers but not the main criteria for peer selection. The main consideration is on value determinants.

The process to determine peers from scratch is generally challenging. Thanks to specialized databases (e.g., Bloomberg, Reuters Thomson, Capital IQ) and analysts' sources (e.g., investing.com, globadata.com, comparably.com, Seeking Alpha, Yahoo Finance, Guru Focus, etc.), peers can be easily identified—but selection depends on an analyst's judgment.

One of the commonly asked questions is about the number of comparable companies in a peer group. Indeed, the is no standard number—the most important criterion is to select the most closely matching peers (see Bhojraj and Lee 2002). However, the number of peers can have valuation implications. The more the endeavors to improve peer closeness, the smaller the number of matches. In contrast, increasing the number of peers is likely to reduce their closeness. Practically, a reasonable number of peers tends to range between 4 and 8, but this is not restrictive.

Exhibit 19.5 Considerations for Peer Determination

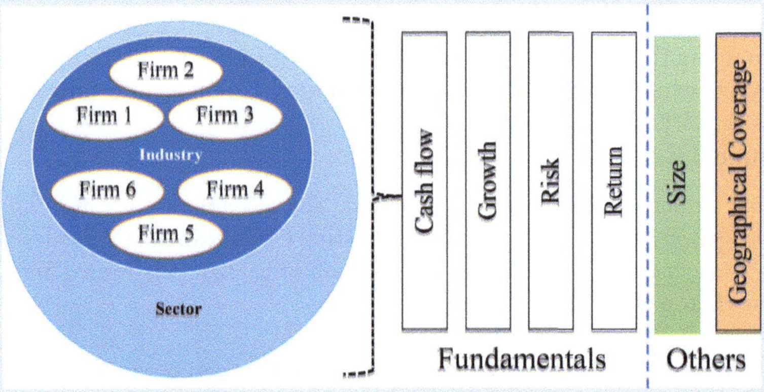

Sector or Industry

Many tend to think that peers belong to the same sector or industry—this conception is incorrect. A sector or industry is simply a starting point because firms in the same sector or industry tend to be identical in several benchmarks. A sector is a broad classification, which can have subsectors too. An industry is a narrow classification, but companies within it can have different characteristics. For instance, the energy sector can have industry classifications like oil and gas production, oil refining and marketing, coal mining, energy industrial machinery, natural gas distribution, electric utilities, oilfield services, etc. Companies in an industry (e.g., consumer discretionary) are not necessarily identical in terms of operational and financial characteristics (e.g., Amazon vs. Home Depot). Moreover, a company can be classified into different industries—for example, Amazon is classified as Internet retail (Yahoo Finance, CNN Money), retail specialty (Reuters), retail and whole (Forbes), and Internet and direct marketing retail (investing.com).

In some markets, where only a few companies are listed in stock markets, it may be impossible to have at least two companies in the same industry or sector—a peer is more likely to have companies in different industries.

Cash Flow

Cash flow is a key input in analyzing the financial health of a firm, estimating its intrinsic value, predicting its bankruptcy, bond ratings, and loan risk classification. Likewise, multiples in companies with identical cash flows will be more similar than those with significant differences.

Growth Rate

Growth rates are the key determinants of value, mainly as predictors of various aspects of company prospects like earnings, cash flows, and size. In turn, growth has an impact on the present value—the higher the growth rate, the higher the value. Hence, growth can be measured for specific value drivers (e.g., like earnings, dividends, sales, and cash flows) or fundamental (long-term) growth. Closeness in growth rates improves similarity of valuation multiples: high-growth companies tend to have higher multiples than low-growth companies.

Risk

Risk is a vital value determinant—the higher the risk, the higher the expected rate of return and the lower the present value of future cash flows, and vice versa. Risk can be measured in several ways depending on specific contexts like standard deviation of returns (volatility), beta (market risk), financial leverage (default risk), operating leverage (earnings risk), and so on. Credit ratings can provide a quick indication of companies with risk similarity.

Returns

Returns represent an incentive or disincentive for investing in a company—rewards to investors. Like risk, there are several concepts and measurements of returns such as market-based or forward-looking returns (cost of equity, cost of debt, weighted average cost of capital (WACC)), book-based or backward-looking returns (return on equity (ROE), return on assets (ROA), return on invested capital (ROIC), etc.).

Size

Size can be market-based (market cap and enterprise value) or book-based (asset value, sales, earnings, etc.). Generally, multiple similarities will be improved the more the similarity in size among peers. Significant size differences can affect valuation accuracy.

Geographical Coverage

Geographical coverage implies the presence of a company in different geographical locations such as a country, a region (for example, Latin America, Eurozone), or globally. A peer group can, therefore, be drawn according to its geographical presence. For example, a domestic peer for Walmart (United States) can be Amazon (United States), Costco Wholesale (United States), The Kroger (United States), and Target (United States), whereas an international peer can be Costco Wholesale (United States), Target (United States), Pan Pacific (Japan), Dollarama (Canada), and Coles Group (Australia).

Exhibit 19.6 Peer Selection

Illustrative Case: Netflix Inc.

This exhibit shows how Netflix's peers were defined by selected sources on 9 November 2022. It is noteworthy that a company can have several industry categorizations.

Peer groups	Company name	Domicile	Industry classification
Peer 1 By Seeking Alpha	**Netflix, Inc.**	**United States**	Movies and entertainment
	Walt Disney Co	United States	Movies and entertainment
	Warner Bros Discovery, Inc.	United States	Movies and entertainment
	Live National Entertainment, Inc.	United States	Movies and entertainment
	Spotify Technology SA	United States	Movies and entertainment
	Warner Music Group Corp	United States	Movies and entertainment
Peer 2 By Infront Analytics	**Netflix, Inc.**	**United States**	Broadcasting and entertainment
	Warner Bros Discovery, Inc.	United States	Broadcasting and entertainment
	Telenet Group Holding	Belgium	Broadcasting and entertainment
	Shaw Communications Inc.	Canada	Broadcasting and entertainment
	Comcast Corporation	United States	Broadcasting and entertainment
	Liberty Global Plc	United Kingdom	Broadcasting and entertainment
Peer 3 By CNBC	**Netflix, Inc.**	**United States**	Entertainment
	Warner Bros Discovery, Inc.	United States	Entertainment
	Walt Disney Co	United States	Entertainment
	AMC Networks	United States	Entertainment
	AMC Entertainment Holdings	United States	Entertainment
	World Wrestling Entertainment	United States	Entertainment

19

Peer groups	Company name	Domicile	Industry classification
Peer 4 By CNN Money	**Netflix, Inc.**	**United States**	Internet software/services
	Warner Bros Discovery, Inc.	United States	Cable/satellite TV
	Comcast Corporation	United States	Cable/satellite TV
	Charter Communications Inc.	United States	Cable/satellite TV
	Shaw Communications Inc.	Canada	Major telecommunications
Peer 5 By Yahoo Finance	**Netflix, Inc.**	**United States**	Entertainment
	Warner Bros Discovery, Inc.	United States	Entertainment
	Walt Disney Co	United States	Entertainment
	AMC Entertainment Holdings	United States	Entertainment
	Paramount Global	United States	Entertainment
	Roku Inc.	United States	Entertainment
Peer 6 By Zacks	**Netflix, Inc.**	**United States**	Media
	Warner Bros Discovery, Inc.	United States	Media
	Liberty Global Plc	United Kingdom	Media
	FOX Corporation	United States	Media
	Sinclair Broadcasting	United States	Media
	Sirius XM Holdings	United States	Media
	Grupo Televisa SAB	Mexico	Media

Apply 19.1 Peer Selection

Objective: Determine peer groups for a company.

Consider any public company of your interest.

1. Use several sources of information to examine its comparable companies.
2. Suggest a list of its peers as follows:
   (a) Domestic peers
   (b) International peers (if applicable)

19.4.2 Determining Value Drivers

There are several levered and unlevered value drivers for equity and enterprise valuation, respectively. All value drivers reflect comparability, but they have different valuation implications (refer to ▶ Chaps. 20 and 21). It is, therefore, recommended to use more than a single driver to arrive at a wide range of estimates. A careful inspection of financial data is required to determine the suitability of value drivers. Several factors can affect the suitability of value drivers. For instance, a value driver for one or more peers can be negative or abnormal on current metrics—this can be addressed by average metrics. Moreover, a value driver can jeopardize peer comparability: for example, EBIT may not be suitable for peers with significant differences in depreciation and amortization charges.

19.4.3 Obtaining Data

Obtaining data is a straightforward step once the preceding steps are properly performed. Market value data (stock price, market cap, and enterprise) can be easily obtained for most public companies: consider public domains like Yahoo Finance, investing.com, Bloomberg, Reuters, and many others. Value drivers (e.g., earnings, book values) originate from financial statements—sources should be reliable. Consider data frequency according to availability (it can be annual, semiannual, or quarterly) and timing (it can be current, average, or forward). Collecting historical data for several periods can help calculate averages and growth rates (for estimating forward data). It should be noted that averages (simple mean or median) intend to normalize value drivers. In some cases, however, multiples can still be misaligned even after normalization with simple mean—but median values tend to have better outcomes.

Banner 19.4 Use Several Multiples
Relative valuation should not rely on a single value driver or multiple. Several multiples should be used to improve valuation.

Think 19.3
Should values from different value drivers of multiples be consistent?

19.4.4 Data Compilation

Data compilation involves organizing both market and financial data to simplify calculation of multiples and the rest of the valuation process. Excel is probably the best tool to use. There is no standard format, but three key aspects should be presented: peer identification (company name or ticker, domicile country), market data (share price, market capitalization, enterprise value), and financial data (e.g., sales, EBIT, EPS, etc.).

19.4.5 Computing Multiples

Using compiled data, multiples (ratios) are first calculated for each company in the peer group. Then, peer benchmarks (mean or median) are calculated for the peer group. Multiples must be carefully inspected to determine any misalignments (outliers). In case of an unsolvable multiplier, several measures can be taken such as disregarding the respective multiple (not to be used for peer valuation) or redefining the peer group (omitting the company with an outlier from the peer group).

19.4.6 Calculating Value

This is the easiest task of all. For a particular target company, relative value is just a product of a value driver and a respective peer benchmark (refer to ▶ Exhibit 19.2).

Banner 19.5 Sense-Making
Relative valuation can be misleading if peers and the respective multiples are not properly selected. Sense-making intends to inspect multiples or value for possible misalignments (outliers).

19.4.7 Further Analysis and Interpretation

To become more useful, valuation results ought to be analyzed and interpreted by considering both quantitative measures and qualitative aspects. While valuation estimates provide indications of potential overvaluation or undervaluation, further analysis intends to provide reasons (why?). Generally, analysis can be categorized into two types: cross-company analysis and time series analysis.

■ **Cross-Sectional Analysis**
This is a cross-company analysis in which valuation multiples of the target company are compared with peer benchmarks. For a set of multiples, the analysis intends to determine whether the target company is overvalued or undervalued relative to other companies. There are always two possibilities:

1. Multiples can give consistent verdicts: all suggesting either overvalued or undervalued. For example, OPA company's stocks are trading at $4 per share. Using a peer group of five companies and three different equity valuation multiples, the results about equity value are as follows: $3.5 based on the P/E ratio, $3.8 based on the BP ratio, and $3.1 based on the P/S ratio. All three multiples suggest that the stock is overvalued.
2. Multiples can give contradicting verdicts: some suggesting overvalued, whereas some undervalued. For example, ERT company's stocks are trading at $4 per share. Using a peer group of five companies and three different equity valuation

multiples, the results about equity value are as follows: $5.5 based on the P/E ratio, $3.8 based on the BP ratio, and $4.3 based on the P/S ratio. Two of the multiples (P/E and P/S) suggest that the stocks are undervalued, whereas BP suggests that they are overvalued. The decision on whether the stocks are overvalued or undervalued will depend on the analyst's judgment about the most appropriate multiple among the three.

Regardless of the two possibilities, interpretation cannot be specific but general—value is usually recommended at a range between the minimum and maximum or on average. For example, in the OPA example, we can say that stocks should trade between $3.1 and $3.8 or at $3.5 on average. For the ERT example, stocks should trade between $3.8 and $5.5 or at $4.5 on average.

Time Series Analysis

Time series analysis is based on "historical multiples" to compare current valuation multiples to historical multiples at a comparable point in a company's life cycle. Usually, this analysis utilizes comparative graphs to examine the target company's historical valuation relative to peers. Time series analysis is useful in two major ways:

1. It intends to track valuation trends for the company to identify key events driving valuation multiples.
2. It can be used to determine forecasting variables for estimating forward-looking multiples.

Reasoning

Relative valuation can provide useful value estimates if applied appropriately. Suggesting whether stocks or firms are overvalued or undervalued is the basic purpose of relative valuation, but analysts can go further to reasoning—why overvalued or undervalued? The "why" question requires examining qualitative aspects—not directly related to relative valuation. ▶ Exhibit 19.7 outlines the most common reasons.

Nevertheless, the most important factor for over- or undervaluation is investors' expectations. Consider the following views from an investment manager John Archer during an interview with Forbes's contributor, Kam (2018). The interview was reflecting on the following quote:

> Facebook's well-publicized data breaches have resulted in a stock price that has declined over 25% since late July. So, what should an investor do? John Archer, one of my managers, says Facebook is undervalued by over 20% (Kam 2018).

In his response, John Archer considers Facebook as an undervalued stock mainly due to negative market perceptions following "bad news" about security breach issues. In contrast, his judgments were based on positive expectations due to Facebook's strong fundamentals, including a solid cash flow. In Kam's words "If you can make a five-year investment, this is a good time to buy Facebook." Similar views were provided by Robert Reisen, a portfolio investor, when comparing Facebook to Microsoft as follows:

» Microsoft (MSFT) and Facebook (FB) are two of my favorite stocks. It's hard to find any weakness in either's performance, balance sheet, or untapped potential. With that being said, I see Facebook's stock as having more upside potential right now. Facebook has had to fight a steady flow of bad press this year, which has hammered the stock price and presented a buying opportunity. The bottom line is that Facebook's performance is still impressive, its free cash flow remains strong, balance sheet is impeccable, and valuation is now at rock-bottom levels (Robert Reisen, Sept 2018).

Exhibit 19.7 Analyzing Why Overvaluation or Undervaluation

The following qualitative factors can be used to analyze why a company is overvalued or undervalued.

Market Behavior

- *Market trends*: The entire market can be down or up due to macroeconomic conditions. Most stocks will be undervalued during downs and overvalued during ups.
- *Misinformation*: The market can miss key information about a company's strong or weak aspects like new market, brand value, credit rating, etc. Missing strong aspects can cause undervaluation, whereas missing weak aspects can cause overvaluation.
- *Herd behavior*: Investors' decisions tend to follow general market momentum, taking similar trading decisions—buy during high market momentum and sell when the momentum declines.
- *Popularity*: Investors tend to aim at popular companies (even if they have weak fundamentals) more than unpopular companies (with strong fundamentals). High demand of stocks relative to supply can cause overvaluation, and vice versa.
- *News*: Bad or good news can cause temporary negative or positive market perception, respectively. Bad news is associated with undervaluation, and vice versa.
- *Profit mania vs. cash flow*: Markets tend to react negatively or positively based on profitability performance, ignoring cash flows. A high-profit company with weak net cash flows is likely to be overvalued, whereas a low-profit company with strong net cash flows can be undervalued.

Company Features

- *Cyclical performance*: Companies with cyclical sales and profitability performance can be overvalued during highs (even if they have weak fundamentals) and undervalued during downs (even if they have strong fundamentals).
- *Dividend payout*: A high payout implies low reinvestment: stock prices can fall temporarily.
- *Leverage*: Generally, investors tend to have a negative perception of high leverage (debt to equity). However, a good or bad leverage level is relative depending on the company's or industry's specific needs. A highly levered company can be undervalued if high leverage drives more value than low leverage, and vice versa.

Banner 19.6 Meaningful Valuation

More meaningful relative valuation should consider factors beyond qualitative measures because different multiples can have contradicting results.

Review Questions

1. Describe the meaning of relative valuation and its importance.
2. What is the difference between relative value and absolute value?
3. Explain the distinctions between the following:
   (a) Market value
   (b) Relative value
   (c) Intrinsic value
4. Explain the leverage effect of equity multiples relative to operating multiples.
5. Define the following relative valuation terms:
   (a) Peer group
   (b) Value driver
   (c) Valuation multiple
6. Provide any four examples of valuation drivers and multiples applicable for each of the following:
   (a) Equity valuation
   (b) Enterprise valuation
7. A company has just released the following financial data: earnings per share of \$23.5, sales per share of \$34.6, and EBIT of \$120 billion. The following peer averages are available: price–earnings is 6.4×, price to sales is 4.5×, and EV/EBIT is 15.4×. Calculate the equity value using both earnings and sales. Calculate the enterprise value using EBIT.
8. Clarify the following aspects as applied in relative valuation:
   (a) Assumption
   (b) Valuation metrics
   (c) Peer selection
   (d) Consistency
   (e) Comparability
   (f) Analysis
9. What factors should we consider when selecting peer companies?
10. Explain the implications of applying each of the following valuation metrics: (a) current, (b) average, and (c) forward.
11. What factors would you consider when determining a group of peer companies?
12. Why is a sector or industry not the main criterion for selecting peer companies for relative valuation?
13. Explain why it is a common practice to use a sector or industry when selecting peer companies and state the limitations of such a practice.

14. Why does relative valuation utilize both market information and financial information? Explain the role of each of them in equity valuation and enterprise valuation.
15. Explain the importance of inspecting valuation multiples during the process of relative valuation.
16. Under what circumstances can relative valuation provide misleading estimates? How would you overcome that problem?
17. What factors would you consider when explaining why a company is overvalued or undervalued?

Bibliography

Bhojraj, S., & Charles M. C. Lee. (2002). Who Is My Peer? A Valuation-Based Approach to the Selection of Comparable Firms. *Journal of Accounting Research*, 40(2), 407–439. http://www.jstor.org/stable/3542390

De Franco, G., Hope, OK. & Larocque, S. (2015). Analysts' choice of peer companies. *Review of Accounting Studies,* 20, 82–109. https://doi.org/10.1007/s11142-014-9294-7

Eaton, G. W., Guo, F., Liu, T., & Officer, M. S. (2022), Peer selection and valuation in mergers and acquisitions, *Journal of Financial Economics*, 146 (1), 230-255. https://doi.org/10.1016/j.jfineco.2021.09.006

Fabozzi, F. J., Focardi, S. M., & Jones, C. (2017). *Equity Valuation of Shares: Science, Art or Craft?* CFA Institute Research Foundation Volume 2017 (4), https://www.cfainstitute.org/-/media/documents/book/rf-publication/2017/rf-v2017-n4-1-pdf.pdf

Janda, K. (2019). Earnings Stability and Peer Company Selection for Multiple Based Indirect Valuation. *Finance a Uver,* 69(1), 37-75. https://www.proquest.com/scholarly-journals/earnings-stability-peer-company-selection/docview/2188843885/se-2

Kam, Ken (2018), Facebook Is Undervalued By Over 20%, available at https://www.forbes.com/sites/kenkam/2018/10/06/facebook-is-undervalued-by-over-20/?sh=c841bbf8a619

Relative Equity Valuation

Contents

Supplementary Information The online version contains supplementary material available at https://doi.org/10.1007/978-3-031-28267-6_20.

B. Kulwizira Lukanima, *Corporate Valuation*, Classroom Companion: Business, https://doi.org/10.1007/978-3-031-28267-6_20

20.1 Introduction

Relative equity valuation utilizes valuation multiples associated with value drivers that are directly relevant to equity holders. Value drivers differ across companies and industries and thus should be selected and applied depending on the specific characteristics of peers. This chapter, therefore, focuses on acquainting readers with an understanding of the most relevant equity value multiples. Selected cases are used to illustrate their practical application and limitations.

Learning Outcomes

- Understand the meaning and valuation implications of the following equity value drivers: earnings, earnings growth, sales, book value, and cash flow
- Decide on the appropriate equity multiples for a specific peer group
- Apply equity valuation multiples in real-world valuation
- Analyze equity value across peers and over time
- Explain valuation challenges and the limitations of equity value multiples

20.2 An Overview of Relative Equity Valuation

The rationale for relative equity valuation is that value drivers ought to represent residual claims to shareholders such as residual income, cash flows, assets, and so on. In conjunction with value drivers, valuation multiples reflect the market perception of a firm's financial performance, considering key value determinants such as risk, cash flows, and growth. Therefore, firms with low risk, good cash flows, and high growth are expected to trade at high multiples (more valuable), and vice versa.

Nevertheless, the suitability and application of equity multiples can be challenging due to several factors such as the nature of business, industry characteristics, and abnormalities. This section outlines the most applicable equity value multiples, focusing on their meaning, application, and limitations.

Banner 20.1 Equity Value Multiples
Equity value multiples should have relevance to equity holders' value.

20.2.1 Price–Earnings (P/E)

P/E is the ratio of price per share to earnings per share (EPS) available to common shareholders and can be presented as follows:

$$\mathrm{P/E} = \frac{P_0}{\mathrm{EPS}}$$

where P_0 and EPS are the current stock price and earnings per share, respectively.

20.2.1.1 Valuation Implication

The P/E ratio is a general measure of how much investors are willing to pay for a company's earnings. For example, a P/E of 12 times implies that investors have paid $12.0 for every dollar of EPS. Fundamentally, investors' perceptions of earnings depend on several equity-related factors such as expected growth, required rate of return, and dividend payout ratio (see Beaver and Morse 1978; Peasnell 1982; Leibowitz and Kogelman 1992; Fairfield 1994; Kane et al. 1996). Therefore, stocks with higher growth, lower risk, and a higher payout ratio tend to trade at higher P/E multiples, and vice versa. A higher P/E implies that investors are overall willing to pay more for a company's earnings, and vice versa.

20.2.1.2 Application

Since its inception in the 1930s (Graham and Dodd 1934), the P/E multiple has been the most popular equity valuation metric because EPS is considered a supreme driver of investment value compared to other measures like sales, book value of equity, and free cash flows (FCFs) (see Graham et al. 2005). Obsession with EPS stems from its ability to provide a clear summary of shareholders' earnings, with companies trying to outperform EPS estimates to meet market expectations.

20.2.1.3 Limitations

Despite its popularity, P/E has several limitations associated with the following EPS drawbacks:

- *Accounting Manipulation*: EPS is determined by net income, which can be subjected to accounting manipulations, thereby affecting comparability among peers—consider accounting policies on depreciation, amortization, extraordinary items, etc. Through "manipulative" practices referred to as "EPS management," companies can possibly increase EPS while destroying shareholder value. The case of Enron is a popular example—before its collapse, the company systematically embarked on a vicious EPS management cycle, hiding much of the debt used to finance EPS growth. Empirical evidence of EPS manipulation has been documented (e.g., Bergstresser and Philippon 2006; Myers et al. 2007).
- *Leverage Effect*: Peers can have identical operating income but highly unrelated earnings due to the leverage effect, such as the interest tax shield. Unlike sales, companies can increase EPS by simply borrowing more, without necessarily creating more shareholders' value (see Penman 2005). To overcome this problem, some analysts tend to use tax-adjusted EPS before interest expenses.
- *Negative Earnings*: Since net income is a bottom-line item, EPS can easily be negative and therefore not applicable.

Think 20.1

Why should investors prefer EPS to other vital value drivers?

20.2.2 Price–Earnings Growth (PEG)

The PEG ratio relates P/E to expected earnings growth, and it can be presented as follows:

$$\text{PEG} = \frac{P_0 / \text{EPS}}{g}$$

where g is the expected growth rate of earnings.

20.2.2.1 Valuation Implication

PEG is a modified P/E value that accounts for a company's growth at different stages or cycles, in which expected growth rates can vary across peers. It is, therefore, referred to as "forward PEG." Higher growth implies higher value in the future, and vice versa. Therefore, stocks with lower PEG (higher growth) are more valuable but are undervalued relative to EPS growth—that is, investors are currently paying less for higher EPS growth (a higher value) in the future. In contrast, a higher PEG implies overvalued (expensive) stocks relative to EPS growth—investors are currently paying more for less EPS (a lower value) in the future. Generally, a stock is undervalued if PEG is less than 1 and overvalued if PEG greater than 1. A stock is fairly priced if PEG equals 1.

20.2.2.2 Application

PEG is more relevant for analysis and investors wishing to relate P/E to growth and therefore is mainly applicable to value growth companies. Based on fundamentals, growth opportunities arise from reinvesting earnings at a premium rate of return. Investors who pay close attention to PEG consider themselves paying for earnings growth. Rational investors would typically prefer the EPS growth rate to be greater than the P/E ratio.

20.2.2.3 Limitations

Growth Assumption: PEG assumes constant EPS growth—a long-term growth rate. This assumption is always unrealistic as growth trends tend to change over time, especially for growth companies. Therefore, the "forward PEG" ratio must be cautiously interpreted in conjunction with other factors, both company-specific and overall economic factors.

Negative Growth: PEG is meaningful only if EPS growth is positive—hence, a negative PEG is irrelevant.

Interpretation: Interpreting forward PEG can be challenging for slow- and negative-growth companies. A company may look expensive based on its perceived growth rate but the reality may in fact be the opposite. For instance, Alphabet can be seen as expensive relative to its peers, but it is the strongest company with a strong investor reputation. It can, therefore, be a good value for investors seeking both safety and stability.

Dividends: PEG accounts for earnings growth but ignores the effect of dividend payouts—some companies return cash to shareholders in the form of dividends.

Depending on the payout ratio, dividend payments lower growth, thereby making PEG higher—stocks appear significantly overvalued. Therefore, PEG can be misleading as investors get a reward not only from earnings growth but also from dividend yield. Consider the case of the following investor (Fox 2022):

» I don't regularly invest in growth stocks, instead I prefer dividend stocks that provide me with a regular source of income. After all, it's worth remembering that many growth stocks fail, so it's not always worth taking that risk. Instead, I carefully pick my top growth stocks, looking at their performance, valuation, and the trends on which their growth is dependent.

Why now? Growth stocks tanked at the end of 2021 and into 2022. January's growth/tech sell-off came on the back of a surge in US Treasury yields. This hurt more expensive growth stocks that are valued on expectations for future earnings. Growth stocks often trade with very high price-to-earnings (P/E) multiples, or if they're not profit-making, high price-to-sales (P/S) ratios.

Despite a few small surges, growth stocks are yet to properly recover. One reason is that interest rates have been rising and this increases the cost of growth. So, right now, it can be wise to look at growth stocks with few debt obligations and plenty of cash.

20.2.2.4 PEG Adjusted for Dividends

The case of Fox (2022) reflects the limitation of PEG regarding dividends. To address this, PEG can be adjusted to account for dividends, thereby harmonizing peers' valuation multiples regardless of their payout ratios. The dividend-adjusted PEG ratio is calculated as follows:

$$\mathrm{PEG}_{\mathrm{DY}} = \frac{\mathrm{P/E}}{g + \mathrm{DY}}$$

where DY denotes dividend yield.

The following quote from Michal (2000) provides a clear picture of the role of dividend-adjusted PEG:

» While serving as portfolio manager of the Vanguard Windsor Fund from 1964 until his retirement in 1995, Neff employed a value investing approach using a stringent contrarian viewpoint. Neff perennially found undervalued, out-of-favor stocks in the bargain basement. He liked stocks with a combination of low price-earnings ratios, solid growth forecasts in earnings and sales growth, and an increasing dividend yield. Neff searched for stocks that were unattractive, and in his words, matched the fund's 'cheapo' profile.

During his 30-plus years at the helm of the fund, Neff delivered an annual average return that exceeded the rate of return of the S&P 500 by more than 3%. The fund did have its down years, however, and today, value investing has become an out-of-favor approach. Neff said his own contrarian nature told him that there was no better time to write a book on value investing than when it seemed out of favor.

A key point in Neff's case is the combination of several valuation criteria to make investment decisions: "low price-earnings ratios, solid growth forecasts in earnings and sales growth, and an increasing dividend yield."

20.2.2.5 Basic vs. Diluted EPS

These two types of EPS differ in the way we look at the profits reported in the income statement. "Basic EPS" reflects profitability of an entire company: net income available to common shareholders divided by the average number of shares outstanding. In contrast, "diluted EPS" reflects profitability based on a company's ownership structure rather than only common shareholders. It shows how much profit per share is available for everyone in the company's ownership structure, considering "additional securities" like new share issuances for mergers and acquisitions, executive stock options, equity warrants, and convertible preferred stocks or bonds—to determine diluted EPS, the number of shares outstanding considers additional securities as if holders would obtain common stocks. ▶ Exhibit 20.1 illustrates the difference between basic and diluted EPS.

Exhibit 20.1 Basic vs. Diluted EPS

Example

ABC company reported a net income of $440 million available to common shareholders for its fiscal year that ended in December 2017. Shares outstanding were $25 million in the beginning of the year and $20 million on 31 December 2017. In addition, the company had eight million shares of stock on convertible bonds and executive share options that could be issued at any time by investors at a conversion price lower than the current market price of $120 per share. Calculate P/E based on basic EPS and diluted EPS.

Solution:

Basic EPS

$$\text{Basic EPS} = \frac{\text{Earnings available to common shares}}{\text{Average number of shares outstanding}}$$

$$= \frac{\$440}{\left(\frac{25+20}{2}\right)} = \$19.6$$

Thus, basic P/E = $120/$19.6 = 6.1

Diluted EPS

$$\text{Diluted EPS} = \frac{\text{Earnings available to common shares}}{\text{Average number of shares outstanding} + \text{convertible shares}} = \frac{\$440}{\left[\left(\frac{25+20}{2}\right)+8\right]} = \$14.4$$

Thus, diluted P/E = $120/$14.4 = 8.3

The difference between basic EPS ($19.6) and diluted EPS ($14.4) is $$5.1. Considering the 20 million shares outstanding at the end of the fiscal year, this implies that share dilution transfers about $102 million of earnings from common shareholders to convertible bondholders and executives.

"What to use: based or diluted?" Consider the implication of P/E as a valuation multiple and the effect of share dilution on EPS as a value driver. Generally, P/E can help determine the following: the price paid for each earnings amount; whether the market is misconstruing the company; the payback period of basic EPS. Share dilution has the following implications: it increases the number of shares outstanding, thereby diluting EPS; diluted EPS ignores out-of-the-money conversions—that is, convertible securities that could not be converted, despite having the eligibility, as they were deemed not beneficial; and EPS dilution is likely to vanish if stock values decline due to several factors like recession, broad stock market collapse, or a company's internal problems.

Overall, there is no standard rule regarding application of basic or diluted P/E. The decision mainly depends on analysts' informed judgment about the dilution effect. Practically, for profitable companies, diluted EPS tends to be less than basic EPS because that profit is divided among more shares. In contrast, if a company suffers a loss, diluted EPS tends to show a lower loss than basic EPS because the loss is spread out over more shares. Depending on the stock structure, the difference between basic and diluted EPS can vary significantly across peers. Generally, aggressive analysts tend to prefer basic EPS to diluted EPS, whereas conservative analysts tend to prefer diluted EPS to basic EPS.

Banner 20.2 EPS Value Driver
Different versions of EPS-based multiples (P/E and PEG) consider EPS as a driver of value through growth and expected dividends.

Think 20.2
Why should dividends be considered with PEG?

20.2.3 Price to Sales (P/S)

P/S relates stock price to sales revenues—a value driver that is a topline item in an income statement.

$$\text{P / S} = \frac{P_0}{\text{SPS}}$$

where P_0 is the current share price and SPS denotes sales per share.

20.2.3.1 Valuation Implication

P/S indicates the number of times investors pay from their stocks for every dollar of sales revenue. For example, a P/S of 5.44 times implies that the investors have paid $5.44 for every dollar of sales generated by the company.

20.2.3.2 Application

P/S tends to be generally used to addresses some of the P/E limitations—negative or highly volatile earnings. Unlike earnings, sales revenues have the following general characteristics: they are never negative; they cannot be easily manipulated or affected by accounting conversions; and they are not as volatile as earnings. Moreover, P/S can be more relevant than P/E for valuing startup companies because earnings can be misleading—not reflecting the future.

20.2.3.3 Limitations

Equity Holders' Value: P/S is not consistent with shareholder value maximization—it does not consider whether equity holders benefit from sales. The value driver is levered and does not provide residual income to equity holders. The worthiness of revenues, therefore, depends on a company's ability to turn them into equity holders' earnings. Some companies tend to have high revenues but low or negative earnings due to high operating expenses. For companies in the same peer group, sales worth more for a company with higher earnings, than companies with less earnings. Consider the following case of HP, whereby sales are valuable because they are reflected in positive EPS (Team 2018).

> » HP Inc. is scheduled to announce its fiscal third quarter earnings on Thursday, August 23. In recent quarters, the company has reported growth across segments, with solid growth in compute and storage revenues. This trend continued in the April ended quarter as well, with the company reporting a 13% increase in net revenues to $14 billion. Much of the growth was driven by steady growth in the Computing and Printing segments, with both notebook and desktop sales contributing to growth. However, the company's non-GAAP operating margin was down 20 basis points over the comparable prior year period to 7.6%. Despite the slightly lower operating profit margin, high revenue growth led net income and earnings per share to increase in double digits. This trend is expected to continue in the third quarter as well.

The extent to which sales can be translated into earnings depends on the industry. For instance, average net margins (and P/S) for selected industries in 2018 were as follows: retail 2.32% (0.58), tobacco 43.37% (5.84), and air transport 7.03% (0.94). For equity holders, sales in the retail industry is less valuable than that in the tobacco industry—to generate a dollar of EPS, more sales is required in retail than in tobacco. Overall, the lower the net margin, the lower the contribution of sales revenues to EPS. Hence, the P/S ratio is particularly valid for analyzing a single firm over time or peer companies with similar profitability profiles.

Accounting: The use of P/S ought to be taken cautiously due to several accounting issues. For example, the P/S ratio will be inflated if a company makes a significant amount of credit sales. Moreover, valuation from the P/S multiple will be misleading when peer companies differ significantly in terms of their revenue recognition practices.

Banner 20.3 Sales Value Driver

When sales revenues are used as a value driver, the assumption is that they will be translated into shareholders' earnings.

20.2.4 Price to Book Value (P/B)

P/B is an equity multiple relating stock price to book value of equity as follows:

$$P/B = \frac{P_0}{BPS}$$

where P_0 and BPS are the current stock price and equity book per share, respectively.

20.2.4.1 Valuation Implication

Unlike P/E and P/S multiples, which are based on a company's operating performance, P/B is based on investment performance—equity holders' net worth in the company. For example, if XYZ stocks closed at $125.50 and BPS was $35.59 on 28 June 2021, then P/B is calculated as $125.50/$35.59 = 3.52 times. This implies that XYZ stocks were trading at 3.52 times their book value—investors paid $3.52 for every dollar of their net worth.

P/B, therefore, helps investors determine how much their net worth is valued by the market. A P/B greater than 1 implies that a stock is trading at more than its book value—that is, investors are paying more than the net worth because they expect the company to create more value. A P/B less than 1 implies that a stock is trading for less than its book value, thereby suggesting either of the following: the market believes that the book asset value is overstated and, as such, the company may be destroying shareholder value and the company is generating an extremely poor (or even destroying) return on equity (ROE).

20.2.4.2 Application

Since P/B is based on investment value, it is more relevant for companies with a significant tangible value. Its application, therefore, favors companies in capital-intensive industries (like banking, energy, airlines, etc.). It is not suitable for companies with significant intangible assets. To clarify this point, ▶ Exhibit 20.2 shows how intangible asset profiles (as a percentage of total assets or as percentage of book value) can significantly differ across industries and between peer companies. For a peer group, the smaller the difference, the more the suitability of P/B for valuing that peer group. Hence, P/B works better with Banco Santander's peers (◘ Exhibit 20.2.4) than Netflix's and Ecopetrol's peers (◘ Exhibits 20.2.2 and 20.2.3, respectively).

Think 20.3

What impact should P/B have in valuing companies with a significant amount of intangible assets?

20

Exhibit 20.2 Variations in Intangible Assets

Illustrative Cases: Companies in Different Industries and Peers in the Same Industry (See Excel Workings—▶ Chap. 20, Sheets E.20.3, E.20.4, and E.20.5)

Companies in Different Industries

Exhibit 20.2.1 compares companies in different industries at the end of the financial periods in 2021. The two companies in the technology sector (Alphabet and Microsoft) are noncapital-intensive and are relatively identical in size (based on their total assets) and other aspects, except for the proportions of their intangible assets and total equity (as a percentage of total assets). Compared to Alphabet, Microsoft has a higher percentage of intangible assets but a lower percentage of total equity—that is, its assets are financed more by liabilities. Chevron and General Motors are capital-intensive companies in different industries but identical is size (total assets). They have an identical percentage of intangible assets, but General Motors' assets are mostly financed by liabilities. Regarding the P/B ratio, the difference between standard P/B and tangible P/B is quite significant in Microsoft (14.4 vs. 24.1)—it will be misleading if used to value the company. For Chevron and General Motors, both standard P/B and tangible P/B are almost equal—P/B is a suitable valuation multiple.

Peer Groups

Exhibits 20.2.2, 20.2.3, and 20.2.4 use intangible assets as a percentage of book value (intangible assets to book value) to compare different peer groups and companies within the same industry over a historical period. Percentages are calculated as follows:

$$\text{Intangible assets\%} = \frac{(\text{Book} - \text{Tangible book})}{\text{Book}} \times 100$$

Variations Across Peer Groups

As a percentage of book value, intangible assets vary across different industries. Netflix's peer group (the entertainment industry) is characterized by significantly high intangible assets: the median percentage is between 105% and 185%, implying a negative tangible book value in most companies in the peer group (see Exhibit 20.2.2). This is quite different from Ecopetrol's peer group (oil and gas) and Banco Santander's peer group (banking): the medians are between 3% and 10% for oil and gas peers and between 12% and 38% for baking peers (see Exhibits 20.2.3 and 20.2.4).

Variations Within Peer Groups

Netflix's peer group, apart from holding the highest percentage of intangible assets, also features the widest variations among peers. The banking peer group has the narrowest variations, followed by the oil and gas one. Hence, the suitability of P/B can be described as follows:

1. Netflix's peer group: P/B can be applied with caution due to the significant size of intangible assets and wide variations among peers—valuation can be misleading.
2. Ecopetrol's peer group: P/B is generally suitable due to the small size of intangible assets, but variations among peers can affect valuation accuracy.
3. Banco Santander's peer group: P/B is suitable due to the small size of intangible assets and narrow variations among peers.

Exhibit 20.2.1 Companies in different industries

Financials	All in $ billions, except ratios				Percentage of total assets			
	Alphabet	Microsoft	Chevron	General Motors	Alphabet	Microsoft	Chevron	General Motors
Cash and cash equivalents	139.6	130.3	5.7	28.7	38.9%	39.0%	2.4%	11.7%
Total current assets	188.1	184.4	33.7	82.1	52.4%	55.2%	14.1%	33.6%
Net PPE	110.6	70.8	150.6	79.0	30.8%	21.2%	62.9%	32.3%
Intangible assets	24.4	57.5	4.4	5.1	6.8%	17.2%	1.8%	2.1%
Total assets	359.3	333.8	239.5	244.7	100.0%	100.0%	100.0%	100.0%
Total liabilities	107.6	191.8	99.6	178.9	30.0%	57.5%	41.6%	73.1%
Total equity	251.6	142.0	139.9	65.8	70.0%	42.5%	58.4%	26.9%
Minority interest	0.0	0.0	0.9	6.1	0.0%	0.0%	0.4%	2.5%
Book value	251.6	142.0	139.1	59.7	70.0%	42.5%	58.1%	24.4%
Tangible book value	227.3	84.5	134.7	54.7	63.3%	25.3%	56.2%	22.3%
P/B	7.6	14.4	1.6	1.5				
Tangible P/B	8.4	24.1	1.7	1.6				
Industry P/B	17.1	14.1	1.0	4.1				

Source of Data: Bloomberg (2022)

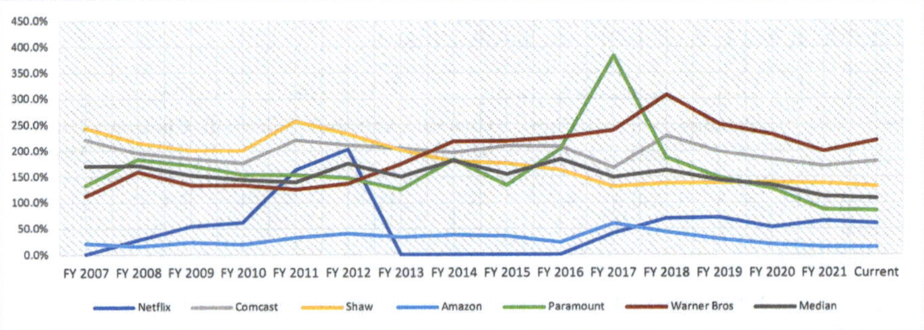

Exhibit 20.2.2 Intangible assets as a percentage of book value: Netflix's peer group

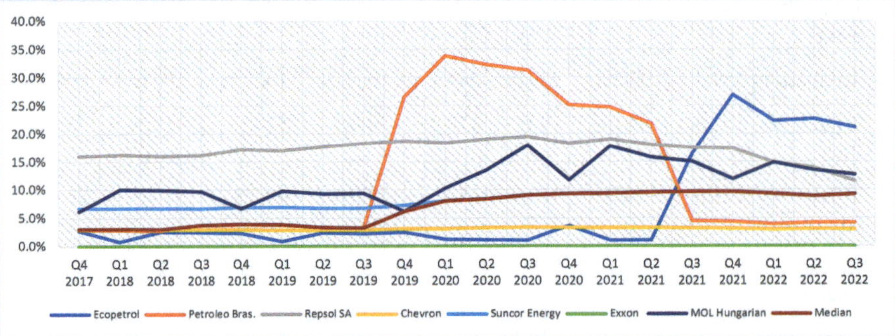

Exhibit 20.2.3 Intangible assets as a percentage of book value: Ecopetrol's peer group

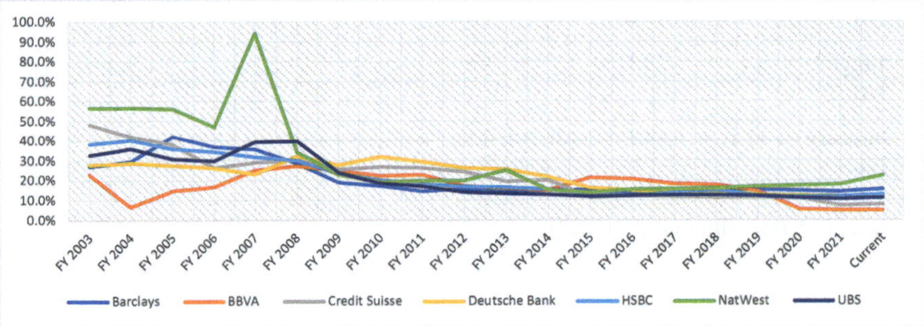

Exhibit 20.2.4 Intangible assets as a percentage of book value: Banco Santander's peer group. (*Source of Data*: Bloomberg 2022)

20.2.4.3 Limitations

P/B has several practical limitations. The most notable is related to comparability and interpretation, as outlined here.

- **Comparability**

Intangible Assets: As clarified in ▶ Exhibit 20.2, P/B can be meaningless for companies with a large proportion of intangible assets and significant variations among peers. Some analysts recommend the use of tangible P/B: obtained from tangible book value (by subtracting intangible assets from the book value). Nevertheless, the exclusion of intangible assets tends to be overly generalized and without a clear justification—what types of those intangible assets should be subtracted from the book value? For instance, some analysts do not consider goodwill as an asset because it is not separable when determining the price of a business acquisition. On the other hand, while other intangibles can be separated from the entity and be sold, justification can be difficult.

Unconventional Assets: Some valuable items (e.g., human capital) can be significant but not commonly recognized and disclosed according to conversional accounting requirements. To some industries (e.g., services), human capital tends to be more important than physical capital as an operating factor. Some companies tend to have significant spending in research and development (R&D), which is treated as expenses, thereby understating the book value. Adjustments may be required to account for such items.

Inventory Systems: Peer companies can have different inventory systems. If some companies use first in, first out (FIFO), whereas others use last in, first out (LIFO), then there will be significant differences in the reported inventory values—LIFO-based values will generally be understated. A possible remedy is to restate inventory values using LIFO as a common inventory system for all peer companies.

Historical Value vs. Fair Value: Accounting standards use historical cost, thereby ignoring the current value. For instance, lands reported at historical cost appreciate value over time, whereas equipment value may decline. A possible remedy is to determine the market fair value.

Debt Levels: P/B may be meaningless for companies with huge debts. This is because high liabilities may reach a point at which much of the tangible book value is depleted, leading to an artificially high P/B.

Overall, if it is necessary to adjust the book value, then the aim is to align P/B so that: (a) it correctly reflects the value of shareholders' investment and (b) it allows comparability among peers. However, adjustments can be complex and subject to analysts' discretions.

- **Interpretation**

Interpretation of P/B is not always straightforward, regardless of the nature of the industry. It is recommended to interpret P/B in conjunction with a company's ability to generate returns to common equity holders (ROE). However, these measures differ across sectors and industries, and, therefore, interpretation should consider peer benchmarks.

1. *A company's P/B is considered lower than ROE*: A company's P/B is less than the peer benchmark, whereas its ROE is greater than the peer benchmark. A low P/B with a high ROE suggests that the stock is possibly undervalued.
2. *A company's P/B is considered higher than ROE*: A company's P/B is higher than the peer benchmark, whereas its ROE is lower than the peer benchmark. A high P/B with a low ROE suggests that the stock is possibly overvalued.
3. *A company's P/B is considered consistent with ROE*: A company's P/B and ROE both are either less or higher than peer benchmarks.

Overall, interpreting P/B in conjunction with ROE constitutes using both sides of the same coin. Normally, a high ROE tends be associated with a high P/B, and vice versa, because investors will pay a high stock price when expecting a high return on equity. Similarly, companies with higher earnings growth rates tend to generally have a higher P/B because investors expect growth in the book value of equity per share. High growth may not have valuation meaning if associated with a high P/B ratio and a low ROE—it generally implies a potential collapse in the share price.

Banner 20.4 Book Value Driver
Book value is different from other value drivers (earnings and sales) because it focuses on investment value rather than earnings value: it reflects tangible shareholders' net worth.

20.2.5 Price to Cash Flow (P/CF)

PCF uses cash flow as a value driver and can be presented as follows:

$$\mathrm{P/CF} = \frac{P_0}{\mathrm{CF}}$$

where P_0 is the current stock price and CF denotes the different forms of cash flows per share (cash flow from operating activities (CFOs), FCF, or free cash flow to equity (FCFE)). For example, if a company's stock is trading at $50.5 per share and the FCFE per share is $24.5, then P/FCFE is 2.1.

20.2.5.1 Valuation Implication

Unlike other value drivers (e.g., sales, earnings, and book value), cash flows are true measures of value as they are consistent with shareholder value maximization. However, only FCFE reflects cash available to common shareholders—it can be used for shareholders' value creation in various ways such as paying dividends, repurchasing stocks, paying off debts, and making new investments. It is, therefore, the most important cash value driver to equity holders—the higher the FCFE, the higher the value expected. Cash flows from operating activities (CFOs) and free cash flows (FCFs) may not necessarily get into owners' hands but can have valuation implications just like sales revenues. Normally, comparing with peer benchmarks, a stock with a low P/CF is favorable because it is considered undervalued despite having an attractive value. A stock with a high P/CF is potentially overvalued.

20.2.5.2 Application

Since cash is "king," P/CF is more relevant for investment decisions. According to Block (1999), cash flow-based multiples compete hand-to-hand with the P/E multiples in terms of wide usage in investment practices. Overall, analysts give the following reasons for favoring P/CF multiples over P/E multiples.

- *Comparability*: Cash flows address the two major accounting drawbacks of earnings that can affect comparability: they are less subjected to accounting manipulation than earnings and they better handle the effects of accounting differences among peers related to the conservatism principle.
- *Positivity*: P/CF is especially useful for valuing stocks with positive cash flows even if they have negative earnings.

Overall, free cash flow profiles tend to vary across industries, and, therefore, P/CF is more relevant for peer companies within the same industry. Moreover, it is a useful multiple for analyzing a company's own performance over time (time series).

20.2.5.3 Limitations

Shareholders' Cash: The choice of a particular form of cash flow mainly depends on analysts' judgments and investors' expectations. Although FCFE is the most relevant to common shareholders, its application is limited by several factors like stability and leverage effects. In conjunction with FCFE, some investors tend to use cash flow from operating activities (CFOs) as a value driver, especially when FCFE is highly volatile or negative. According to the stock analyst Caveney (2018), some investors rely on P/CFO and P/FCF because "they trust in management's CAPEX spending decisions to be worthwhile and pay off."

Volatility and Negativity: Some companies tend to have highly volatile and even negative cash flows. This is a major limitation of P/CF and means that a company is destroying its value. For example, volatile or negative FCFE is related to firm's or industry characteristics—some companies tend to experience business and investment cycles while others tend to have stable capital expenditures. To address the limitation of volatile or negative FCFE, a typical remedy is generally to use normalized cash flows (if possible).

Cash Flow Profile: P/CF can be misleading if peers have significant differences in cash flow profiles: the main factors are operating strategy (affecting CFOs), fixed capital expenditure (affecting FCFs), and financing decisions (affecting FCFEs).

Banner 20.5 Cash Value Driver

Compared to other value drivers, cash flows are more consistent with shareholders' value maximization.

20.3 Practical Application

▶ Exhibits 20.3 and 20.4 present two practical cases to illustrate equity relative valuation based on the process described in ▶ Chap. 19. The first case focuses on a particular company (Netflix) to illustrate valuation with different peer groups. The second case focuses on several companies to illustrate valuation in a peer group.

Netflix Valuation: This case is about the valuation of Netflix (▶ Exhibit 20.4). The objective is to illustrate the valuation steps outlined in ▶ Chap. 19. Specific emphasis is on the following valuation issues:

- *Peer Selection*: Two peer sets are used to reflect international and domestic peers—US$ are used as the common currency for all companies. Companies in these two peer groups are not necessarily from the same industry classification, but they belong to the communications sector.
- *Value Drivers*: Several value drivers are used to consider different valuation implications and market perception. This illustrative case uses earnings per share (EPS), book value per share (book), sales per share (sales), cash flows from operating activities (CFOs) per share, and free cash flows (FCFs) per share . Free cash flow to equity (FCFE) is not used due to data limitations. All value drivers suggest that Netflix was potentially overvalued on 31 October 2022.
- *Organizing Data*: Using Excel, data are organized to enable easy calculations of multiples and values.
- *Negative Value Drivers*: Negative value drivers are one of the limitations of relative valuation. In this case, some peers have one or more negative value drivers. Usually, there are two possible remedies. The first is to completely ignore the value driver for the entire peer group—no valuation is performed with it. The second is to use a value driver without a company with a negative value—valuation is relative to a smaller number of peers on that specific value driver. In this case, the second remedy is applied.
- *Valuation Metrics*: Three different metrics (i.e., trailing 12 months (TTM), average, and forward) are used in this case.
- *Calculating Multiples and Values:* Calculation is straightforward but excludes a company with negative value drivers (when applicable).
- *Cross-Company Analysis*: The objective of cross-company analysis is to determine the potential valuation status: whether overvalued, undervalued, or fair. Netflix was potentially overvalued on the valuation date 31 October 2022.
- *Time Series Analysis*: The objective of a time series analysis is to track and reflect on a company's historical performance compared to its current period.

In this case, P/E is used as an example. Netflix has always been trading at a higher P/E than the peer median.

- *Reasoning*: Reasoning intends to make sense of the numbers. In this case, two key questions are probed: (1) why is Netflix overvalued? (2) why has its P/E been declining over time? To find out, consider the following quotes:

> Netflix (NASDAQ: NFLX) shares have outperformed the S&P 500 in 2021, generating a year-to-date total return of 25.9%. But after gaining 114.6% in the past three years, investors may be wondering if there's any value left in Netflix stock (Duggan 2021).
>
> The headlines in recent weeks have been filled with negative stories about the future of Netflix, Inc. (NASDAQ: NFLX) and whether increased competition from the myriad of new streaming platforms is finally eroding the company's subscription base…The company appears to be undervalued from a rearview mirror perspective, but forecasts utilizing cash flow in their models argue that it's overvalued. (Gigliotti 2022).
>
> I've been bearish on Netflix (NFLX) for years, not because it provides a poor service, but because the firm is a bait fish in a tank filled with sharks. I believe Bill Ackman's Pershing Square is wrong to purchase shares of Netflix and I fear that other investors will follow suit and purchase this dangerously overvalued stock simply because they trust and admire Bill Ackman…I expect Netflix will continue to lose market share as more competitors enter the market and deep-pocketed peers such as Disney (DIS), Amazon (AMZN), and Apple (AAPL) continue to invest heavily in streaming (Trainer 2022).
>
> Even after reversing its subscription declines and cutting down on costs, Netflix is still overvalued at around $260, Liberty Global Chairman John C. Malone said Tuesday. Speaking at the annual Paley International Council Summit in New York, Malone stuck to his long-term view of the stock, even as its price has gone down, saying that competition will limit Netflix's profitability in the future. 'The fact that Disney was able to launch and get to scale, pretty powerful and pretty quickly is a pretty good indication that that thesis is correct.' (Huston 2022).

Think 20.4

Based on the quotes above, suggest reasons for Netflix's overvaluation but at a declining trend.

20

Exhibit 20.3 Relative Equity Valuation

Illustrative Case: Netflix (See Excel Workings—▶ Chap. 20, Sheet E.20.3A and B)

In this illustration, Netflix is valued relative to two peer groups (international and domestic). Brief peer profiles according to Bloomberg are as follows:

Netflix Inc.: The company operates as a subscription streaming service and production company. It offers a wide variety of TV shows, movies, anime, and documentaries on Internet-connected devices. Netflix serves customers worldwide.

Telenet Group Holding: The company provides telephone and Internet services through a network of fiber-optic and coaxial cables. It offers customized packages to businesses and individual clients in Belgium.

Comcast Corporation: The company provides media and television broadcasting services. It offers video streaming, television programming, high-speed Internet, cable television, and communication services. Comcast serves customers worldwide.

Shaw Communications: The company provides broadband cable television, Internet, and satellite television services.

Liberty Global Plc: The company owns interests in broadband, distribution, and content companies operating outside the continental United States, principally in Europe.

Warner Bros. Discovery, Inc.: The company provides nonfiction entertainment. It operates a wide range of educational television channels as well as offers consumer and educational products and services and a diversified portfolio of digital media services. Warner Bros. Discovery serves customers worldwide.

DISH Network Corporation: The company is a satellite television company. It provides a direct broadcast satellite subscription television, audio programming, and interactive television services to commercial and residential subscribers. DISH Network operates in the United States.

Amazon.com, Inc.: The company is an online retailer that offers a wide range of products. Its products include books, music, computers, electronics, and numerous others. Amazon offers personalized shopping services, web-based credit card payment, and direct shipping to customers. Amazon also operates a cloud platform offering services globally.

Paramount Global: The company operates as a media company. It produces and distributes entertainment content through studios, networks, streaming services, live events, and merchandise. Paramount Global serves customers worldwide.

Peer Groups

Peer group 1 (P1) is based on international peers, comprising US and non-US companies as presented in valuation data sheets (▪ Exhibits 20.3.1, 20.3.2, and 20.3.3). Peer group 2 (P2) is based on US-based companies as presented in valuation data sheets (▪ Exhibit 20.3.4)—refer to Excel workings for more data.

Valuation

Exhibit 20.3.5 uses P1 to illustrate valuation multiples for all metrics (TTM, average, and forward): that is, market price divided by value driver. Negative drivers are excluded from valuation. Median is used as the peer benchmark. P2 multiples can be referred in Excel working sheets.

Exhibit 20.3.6 presents equity value (V_E) results calculated as $V_E = \Psi_E \Theta$, where Ψ_E denotes the equity value driver and Θ denotes a peer benchmark relating to a particular multiple. Both P1 and P2 are presented for wider comparative analysis.

Cross-Company Analysis

Regardless of valuation multiple and metrics, except for PEG, Netflix was potentially overvalued on 31 October 2022. However, the magnitude of overvaluation varies across multiples and metrics and between peer groups (refer to Exhibits 20.3.7 and 20.3.8). Netflix's valuation range is extremely wide—between 10.2 (lowest based on FCF) and 415.0 (highest based on PEG).

A verdict in this case is not straightforward due to significant variations: it depends on investors' perception about a particular value driver. For example, an investor in favor of EPS would suggest a trading range between US$120.1 and US$171.2 (overvalued), but a growth investor would suggest a trading range between US$298.3 and US$415.0 (undervalued); a conservative investor, who prefers book value would suggest a trading range between US$34.4 and US$85.9 (overvalued); and a cash-driven investor would suggest a trading range between US$10.2 and US$13.3. (overvalued).

NB: Other companies can be analyzed in the same way. Generally, Amazon resembles Netflix in terms of the direction and magnitude of valuation status—highly overvalued. For the rest, each company shows a consistent status (overvalued or undervalued) across most measures (multiples, metrics, and peer group). Overall, they differ in valuation direction but are similar in magnitude—not highly overvalued or undervalued (less than 100%). Some multiples suggest fair pricing on some stocks: this is because the respective stock multiples are equal or almost equal to the peer median.

Time Series Analysis

Exhibit 20.3.9 presents a comparative P/E time series (companies vs. benchmark). Netflix has been historically overvalued—its stocks have always been trading at a higher P/E than the peer median (and Standards and Poor's 500 (S&P 500) Communications Sector Index). However, a declining P/E trend has been noticed since 2012, implying that investors' expectations on Netflix value creation were previously higher than today. As predicted by stock analysts, the 1-year forward P/E (26.24) is less than the current P/E (30.03) and 5-year average (50.09), implying that investors are forcing Netflix price toward fairness. A similar situation applies to Amazon.

The Telenet Group was trading at higher multiples until 2018 when it started aligning with the peer median but slightly below. The rest have been trading at lower multiples than benchmark most of the time, except a few times: Shaw was above median in 2018, 2021, and current: forward estimates suggest more market optimism with a higher P/E (16.2) than current (14.8) but slightly lower than the 5-year average (17.6); Comcast was above the benchmark in 2020 but parallel in 2021 and currently. Analysts predict a lower P/E in 2023 (8.2) than the current P/E (9.8) and 5-year average (10.2).

Reasoning

To make more sense of valuation, let us consider investors' perception of EPS growth as reflected by PEG. Exhibit 20.3.10 depicts historical EPS growth for peers. Overall, Netflix and Amazon have experienced the highest growth. However, Netflix's EPS growth is the most stable at least since 2015. On the other hand, Netflix's PEG (see Exhibit 20.3.5) on TTM P/E (30.6), average P/E (54.1), and forward P/E (26.7) are slightly consistent with the peer median but below average (109.8, 69.1, and 105.5, respectively). This implies that high EPS growth makes Netflix more attractive (pushing the price high), whereas a low PEG makes it look cheap (also pushing the price high). Based on PEG, Netflix should be trading at a slightly higher price than US$292.84: valuation suggests a price range between US$298.3 and US$415.0 (see Exhibit 20.3.6). This could be one reason why investors are paying high for the stock than suggested by other valuation multiples. In contrast, this reason may not apply to Amazon because its PEG valuation is generally consistent with other multiples (i.e., overvalued).

Exhibit 20.3.1 Valuation data (TTM): the international peer group

International peer group	Country	Market perception (US$)		Value drivers (per share US$)				
Company	**Domicile**	**Price**	**EV (B)**	**EPS**	**Book**	**Sales**	**CFO**	**FCF**
Netflix	United States	292.84	140,638	9.75	46.13	70.84	2.65	1.61
Telenet Group Holding	Belgium	15.23	7557	9.40	−4.53	26.10	10.67	7.85
Comcast Corp.	United States	31.41	228,751	3.21	18.57	27.00	6.28	4.03
Shaw Communications	Canada	25.26	16,952	1.70	12.61	10.92	4.00	2.25
Liberty Global	United Kingdom	16.75	19,516	4.19	50.55	13.64	5.65	3.43
Warner Bros Discovery Inc.	United States	12.73	85,660	0.59	21.16	22.16	4.34	3.69

Exhibit 20.3.2 Valuation data (a 5-year average): the international peer group

International peer group	Country	Market perception (US$)		Value drivers (per share US$)				
Company	**Domicile**	**Price**	**EV (B)**	**EPS**	**Book**	**Sales**	**CFO**	**FCF**
Netflix	United States	292.84	140,638	5.52	27.22	46.62	−2.10	−2.84
Telenet Group Holding	Belgium	15.23	7557	3.17	−13.00	26.44	10.52	7.71
Comcast Corp.	United States	31.41	228,751	3.08	18.70	22.13	5.45	3.38
Shaw Communications	Canada	25.26	16,952	1.44	11.82	10.43	3.28	1.18
Liberty Global	United Kingdom	16.75	19,516	−0.03	30.21	16.55	6.85	4.89
Warner Bros Discovery Inc.	United States	12.73	85,660	2.53	18.26	21.11	5.36	4.82

Exhibit 20.3.3 Valuation data peer (1-year forward): the international peer group

International peer group	Country	Market perception (US$)		Value drivers (per share US$)			
Company	**Domicile**	**Price**	**EV (B)**	**EPS**	**Book**	**Sales**	**CFO**
Netflix	United States	292.84	140,638	11.16	55.27	76.32	5.81
Telenet Group Holding	Belgium	15.23	7557	2.95	−3.29	23.23	9.91
Comcast Corp.	United States	31.41	228,751	3.81	20.20	27.90	6.84
Shaw Communications	Canada	25.26	16,952	1.56	12.99	11.04	4.05
Liberty Global	United Kingdom	16.75	19,516	−0.59	54.77	14.24	5.93
Warner Bros Discovery Inc.	United States	12.73	85,660	0.83	20.13	19.11	3.72

20

Exhibit 20.3.4 Valuation data (TTM): US-based peer group

US-based peer group	Country	Market perception (US$)		Value drivers (per share US$)				
Company	**Domicile**	**Price**	**EV (B)**	**EPS**	**Book**	**Sales**	**CFO**	**FCF**
Netflix	United States	292.84	140,638	9.75	46.13	70.84	2.65	1.61
Dish Network Corp.	United States	15.11	29,039	3.93	31.21	32.96	6.14	2.18
Comcast Corp.	United States	31.41	228,751	3.21	18.57	27.00	6.28	4.03
Amazon.com	United States	102.01	1,126,589	1.38	13.48	49.35	3.90	−2.58
Paramount Global	United States	17.95	25,559	2.26	35.09	45.87	−0.38	−0.95
Warner Bros Discovery	United States	12.73	85,660	0.59	21.16	22.16	4.34	3.69

Exhibit 20.3.5 Valuation multiples: the international peer group

Company	Metrics	Valuation multiples					
		PE[1]	**PEG[5]**	**P/B[2]**	**P/S**	**P/CFO[3]**	**P/FCF[4]**
Netflix	TTM	30.03	30.60	6.35	4.13	110.51	181.89
	Average[3,4]	53.09	54.08	10.76	6.28	NA	NA
	Forward	26.24	26.73	5.30	3.84	50.40	
Telenet Group Holding	TTM[2]	1.62	3.98	NA	0.58	1.43	1.94
	Average[2]	4.80	11.80	NA	0.58	1.45	1.97
	Forward[2]	5.16	12.68	NA	0.66	1.54	
Comcast Corp.	TTM	9.79	31.13	1.69	1.16	5.00	7.79
	Average	10.20	32.46	1.68	1.42	5.77	9.30
	Forward	8.24	26.23	1.55	1.13	4.59	
Shaw Communications	TTM	14.86	115.43	2.00	2.31	6.32	11.23
	Average	17.59	136.66	2.14	2.42	7.71	21.37
	Forward	16.19	125.79	1.94	2.29	6.24	

Exhibit 20.3.5 (continued)

Company	Metrics	Valuation multiples					
		PE[1]	PEG[5]	P/B[2]	P/S	P/CFO[3]	P/FCF[4]
Liberty Global	TTM	4.00	4.68	0.33	1.23	2.96	4.88
	Average[1,5]	NA	NA	0.55	1.01	2.45	3.43
	Forward[1]	NA	NA	0.31	1.18	2.82	
Warner Bros Discovery Inc.	TTM	21.58	473.09	0.60	0.57	2.93	3.45
	Average	5.04	110.41	0.70	0.60	2.37	2.64
	Forward	15.34	336.29	0.63	0.67	3.42	
Median	*TTM*	*12.32*	*30.86*	*1.69*	*1.20*	*3.98*	*6.34*
	Average	*10.20*	*54.08*	*1.68*	*1.22*	*2.45*	*3.43*
	Forward	*15.34*	*26.73*	*1.55*	*1.15*	*4.01*	

Notes: NA means a value driver is not applicable due to negativity limitations. [1,2,3]Both the company and value driver are excluded from valuation relating to that specific value driver—EPS[1], book[2], CFO[3], and FCF[4]. PEG expected growth is based on a 5-year average of EPS historical growth.

Exhibit 20.3.6 Valuation on 31 October 2022

Company (price US$)	Peer	Metrics	Relative value (US$)					
			PE[1]	PEG[5]	P/B[2]	P/S	P/CFO[3]	P/FCF[4]
Netflix 292.8	P1	TTM	120.1+	300.9–	78.0+	84.7+	10.6+	10.2+
	P2	TTM	152.9+	332.8–	52.9+	61.6+	13.3+	11.9+
	P1	Average[3,4]	56.3+	298.3–	45.7+	56.7+	NA	NA
	P2	Average[3,4]	42.0+	298–3–	34.4+	47.1+	NA	NA
	P1	Forward	171.2+	415.0–	85.9+	87.8+	23.3+	
	P2	Forward	148.5+	298.3–	60.4+	68.4+	50.3+	
Telenet Group Holding 15.2	P1	TTM[2]	115.8–	290.1–	NA	31.2–	42.5–	49.8–
	P1	Average[2]	32.3–	171.4–	NA	32.1–	25.7–	26.4–
	P1	Forward[2]	45.2–	78.9–	NA	26.7–	39.7–	

(continued)

Exhibit 20.3.6 (continued)

Company (price US$)	Peer	Metrics	Relative value (US$)					
			PE[1]	PEG[5]	P/B[2]	P/S	P/CFO[3]	P/FCF[4]
Comcast Corp. 31.4	P1	TTM	39.6–	99.1–	31.4=	32.3–	25.0+	25.5+
	P2	TTM	31.4=	109.6–	50.3	21.3+	23.5+	31.4=
	P1	Average	31.4=	166.5–	31.4=	26.9+	13.3+	11.6+
	P2	Average	23.5+	166.5–	23.7+	22.4+	31.4=	24.5+
	P1	Forward	58.4–	101.8–	31.4=	32.1–	27.4+	
	P2	Forward	50.7–	141.7–	22.1+	25.0+	59.3–	
Shaw Communica-tions 25.3	P1	TTM	20.9+	52.5–	21.3+	13.1+	15.9+	14.3+
	P1	Average	14.7+	77.7–	19.9+	12.7+	8.0+	4.0+
	P1	Forward	23.9+	41.7–	20.2+	12.7+	16.2+	
Liberty Global 16.8	P1	TTM	51.6–	129.3–	85.5–	16.3+	22.5–	21.7–
	P1	Average[1]	NA	NA	50.8–	20.1–	16.8=	16.8=
	P1	Forward[1]	NA	NA	85.2–	16.4+	23.8–	
Warner Bros Discovery Inc. 12.7	P1	TTM	7.3+	18.2–	35.8–	26.5–	17.3–	23.4–
	P2	TTM	9.3+	20.1–	24.3	19.3–	21.7	27.2–
	P1	Average	25.8–	136.7–	30.7–	25.7–	13.1–	16.5–
	P2	Average	19.3–	136.7–	23.1–	21.3–	30.9–	35.0–
	P1	Forward	12.7=	30.9–	31.3–	22.0–	14.9–	
	P2	Forward	11.0+	22.2–	22.0–	17.1–	32.2–	
Dish Network Corp. 15.1	P2	TTM	61.6–	134.2–	35.8–	28.6–	30.7–	16.1–
	P2	Average	26.2–	185.8–	28.7–	30.3–	35.5–	36.0–
	P2	Forward	17.8–	49.8–	36.6–	28.0–	30.1–	

Exhibit 20.3.6 (continued)

Company (price US$)	Peer	Metrics	Relative value (US$)					
			PE[1]	PEG[5]	P/B[2]	P/S	P/CFO[3]	P/FCF[4]
Amazon.com Inc. 102.0	P2	TTM	21.6+	47.1+	15.5+	42.9+	19.5+	NA
	P2	Average	10.6+	75.0+	9.2+	31.5+	23.2+	8.4+
	P2	Forward	40.9+	114.2−	19.6+	50.8+	69.4+	
Paramount Global 18.0	P2	TTM	35.4−	77.1−	40.2−	39.9−	NA	NA
	P2	Average	34.8−	246.7−	26.7−	42.0−	17.3+	18.0=
	P2	Forward	23.3−	65.1−	41.1−	44.0−	11.7+	

Notes: NA means that a valuation was not performed with the multiples due to a negative value driver. [1,2,3]Both the company and valuation multiple are excluded from valuation relating to that specific value driver—EPS[1], book[2], CFO[3], and FCF[4]. +, −, and = denote that the stock is potentially overvalued, undervalued, and fairly priced, respectively

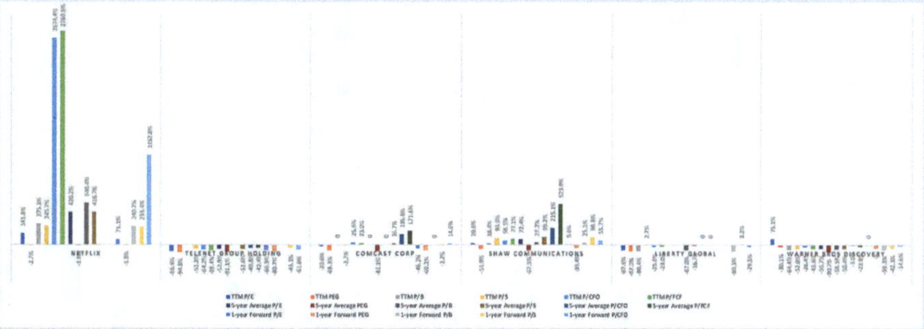

Exhibit 20.3.7 Valuation magnitude by percentage of overvaluation or undervaluation: peer group 1

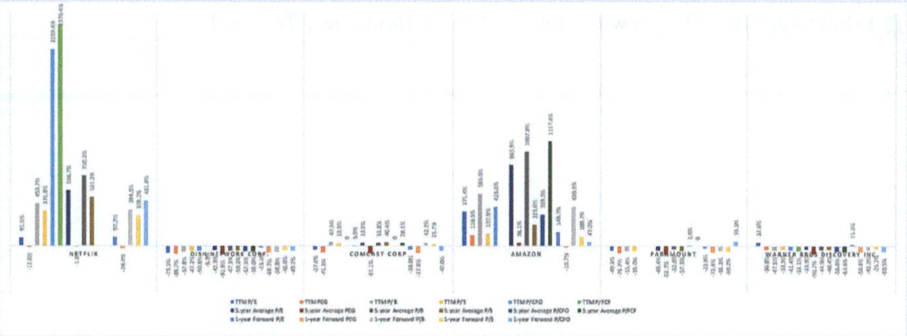

Exhibit 20.3.8 Valuation magnitude by percentage of overvaluation or undervaluation: peer group 2

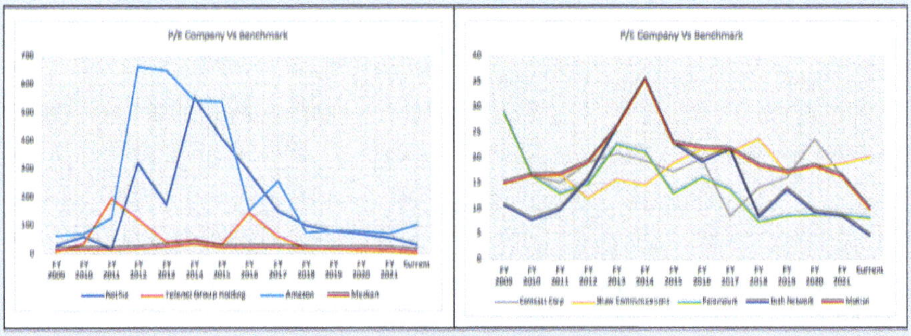

Exhibit 20.3.9 Time series P/E: company vs. benchmark

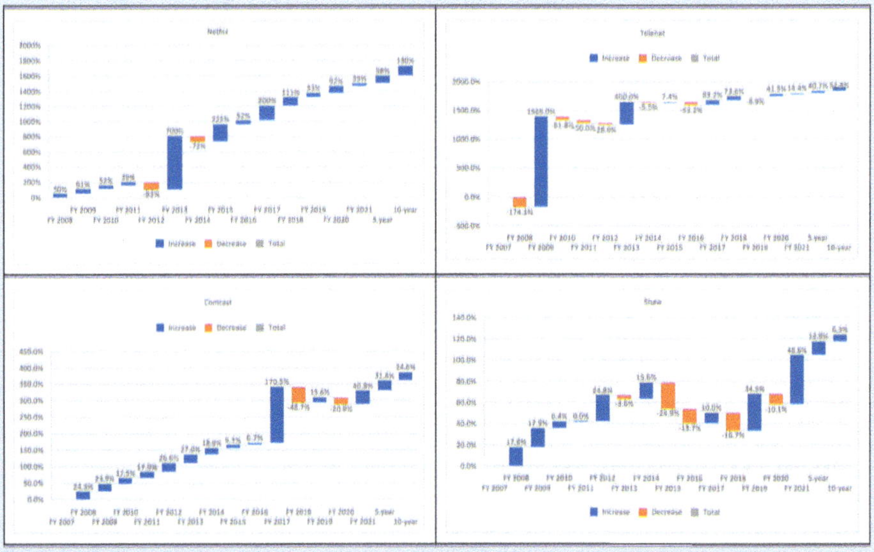

Exhibit 20.3.10 EPS growth. (*Source of Data*: Bloomberg Terminal)

Exhibit 20.3.10 (continued)

Banking Valuation: This case is for valuation of selected companies in banking (▶ Exhibit 20.4). Unlike the Netflix case, the objective is not to illustrate all valuation steps. Instead, it focuses on the following two major aspects:

- *General Interpretation*: Relative valuation utilizes different value drivers, which tend to arrive at different valuation results. This means that relative valuation does not aim at a specific value but recommends a valuation range.
- *P/B/ vs. ROE*: For capital-intensive industries like banking, P/B is generally the most important valuation multiple but should be interpreted with caution. This case shows how to analyze P/B in conjunction with ROE.

Exhibit 20.4 Relative Equity Valuation

Illustrative Case: Banking (See Excel Workings—▶ Chap. 20, Sheet E.20.4)

Peer Group

Peer selection focuses on large European banks with international operations. Brief peer profiles are as follows according to CNN Money, Yahoo Finance, and Bloomberg:

- *Banco Santander SA:* Banco Santander SA is a banking services company, which engages in the provision of banking services to individuals, companies, and institutions. It operates through the following segments: Europe, North America, South America, and digital consumer banking. The company was founded on March 21, 1857, and is headquartered in Madrid, Spain.
- *Barclays PLC*: Barclays Plc operates as a company that engages in providing retail banking, credit cards, corporate and investment banking, and wealth management services. The firm operates through two divisions: Barclays UK and Barclays International. Barclays was founded on July 20, 1896, and is headquartered in London, the United Kingdom.
- *BBVA SA*: Banco Bilbao Vizcaya Argentaria SA (BBVA) engages in the traditional banking businesses of retail banking, asset management, private banking, and wholesale banking. It operates through the following segments: Spain, the United States, Mexico, Turkey, South America, and the rest of Eurasia. The company was founded in 1857 and is headquartered in Madrid, Spain.
- *Credit Suisse Group AG*: Credit Suisse Group AG is a holding company, which engages in the provision of financial services. It operates through the following segments: Swiss Universal Bank; International Wealth Management; Asia Pacific; and Investment Banking and Capital Markets. The company was founded by Alfred Escher on July 5, 1856, and is headquartered in Zurich, Switzerland.
- *Deutsche Bank AG*: Deutsche Bank AG engages in the provision of corporate banking and investment services. It operates through the following segments: corporate bank, investment bank, private bank, asset management, capital release unit, and corporate and others. The company was founded by Adelbert Delbrück on March 10, 1870, and is headquartered in Frankfurt, Germany.
- *HSBC Holdings PLC*: HSBC Bank PLC provides banking and financial services. The bank offers personal and business banking, home loans, borrowing, investments, insurance, nonresident services, and online banking services. HSBC serves clients globally. The bank was established in 1865 in Hong Kong but is headquartered in London, the United Kingdom.
- *NatWest Group PLC*: NatWest Group Plc operates as a banking and financial services company. The bank provides personal and business banking, consumer loans, asset and invoice finances, commercial and residential mortgages, credit cards, and financial planning services as well as life, personal, and income protection insurance. NatWest Group serves clients

worldwide. It was founded in 1727 and is headquartered in Edinburgh, the United Kingdom.

- *UBS Group AG*: UBS AG operates as an investment management firm. The company offers wealth management, investment banking, and asset management services as well as renders a variety of financial services to individuals, institutions, corporations, governments, and financial intermediaries. UBS serves customers worldwide. UBS Group AG was founded in 1862 and is based in Zurich, Switzerland.

Valuation Summary
Valuation is for 17 November 2022 based on with several value drivers: EPS, tangible book per share, sales per share, CFO per share, and FCF per share. Each value driver is applied as current year and 5-year average. Negative value drivers are handed as follows: EPS (TTM), which applies to only one company is excluded only for the respective company (Credit Suisse); CFO (TTM) and FCF (TTM) apply to most of the companies and are therefore excluded for all companies. Average metrics (5-year) normalize the value drivers to eliminate negativity. Valuation currency is based on a company's reporting currency (not common currency). Peer benchmarks are based on the median. Calculations of multiples and values follow the same steps illustrated in ► Chap. 19 and ► Exhibit 20.3.

Valuation Results and Interpretation
Exhibit 20.4.1 presents all valuation results in graphical form—it shows stock market price against relative values for each valuation multiple (in the company's reporting currency). This form of presentation is useful for eyeball spotting and comparative analysis across peers and within a single company.

A starting point to interpret valuation results is to use cross-company analysis to determine market valuation status (over, under, or fair valuation). This analysis is depicted in Exhibit 20.4.2: percentages in which a stock market price deviates from the relative value for each valuation multiple—overvalued if positive, undervalued if negative, and fair if 0.

The next step is to consider valuation on two aspects: direction and magnitude.

- *Direction*

  This aspect gives a general indication whether a stock is overvalued, undervalued, or fairly priced. Interpretation is straightforward if all valuation multiples point in the same direction. For example, Banco Santander and Barclays are both in the negative direction (undervalued) and NatWest and UBS are both in the positive direction (overvalued).

  Complications arise if values point to different directions: this is the case for BBVA, Credit Suisse, Deutsche Bank, and HSBC. One way to deal with this challenge is to examine valuation multiples across peers to determine consistency or inconsistency in the direction status. For example, for all the four banks, the 5-year average cash-based multiples (P/CFO and P/FCF) oppose the rest of the multiples: for BBVA and HSBC, they show undervaluation, whereas for the rest, they suggest overvaluation; for Credit Suisse and Deutsche Bank, they suggest overvaluation, whereas for the rest, they suggest undervaluation.

Another multiple is the 5-year average P/E for BBVA and Deutsche Bank: in each stock, they contradict TTM P/E and the rest.

This analysis should be extended to determine which direction is correct. Several criteria can be used, but the most important is the suitability of value drivers for the peer. For example, P/B is a vital multiple in banking followed by P/E—directions based on them should be given priority. This implies that cash-based directions should be considered with caution as they contradict P/B and P/E. Next is about the contradictions between TTM and average, which applies to the case of BBVA and Deutsche Bank—the direction consistent with P/B should be favored.

It is always important to reason. For example, in this case—what is wrong with cash-based multiples? Referring to their limitations (volatility, negativity, and profile variations across companies), cash-based multiples could be unsuitable for the peers—historical data show high volatility and negativity (see ▫ Exhibit 20.4.3). Hence, the average metrics (normalized) can still be misleading.

Therefore, it is reasonable to suggest the following for the contradicting cases: BBVA (overvalued), Credit Suisse (undervalued), Deutsche Bank (undervalued), and HSBC (overvalued).

- *Magnitude*

When several valuation multiples are used, the magnitude of valuation in both percentage and monetary terms should be given as a range (between minimum and maximum) or an average of all multiples. The aim is not to give an absolute figure but estimates. To use Banco Santander as an example, we can say, Banco Santander, at a trading price of €2.5 on 17 November 20022, was undervalued between 11% and 54% based on three valuation multiples (P/E, tangible P/B, and P/S): it should be trading between €2.8 (minimum) and €5.5 (maximum) or €3.6 on average. It should be noted that cash-based multiples have been disregarded, but investors have discretion to use them.

P/B vs. ROE

▫ Exhibit 20.4.4 depicts historical trends comparing P/B and ROE to help make sense of market perception. Overall, P/B (for both individual stocks and the peer median) has been declining over time, implying a prolonged decline in investors' confidence on the companies' ability to create value—this is reflected in a persistent decline in ROE over time. The declining trend for both P/B and ROE is generally cyclical, within 3–4 years: the current cycle is upward, implying regaining market confidence after the 2020 drop.

On valuation date 17 November 2022, P/B multiples were less than 1 for four companies (Banco Santander, Barclays, Credit Suisse, and Deutsche Bank). This reflects the market's perception that book value is likely to be overstated or the investing return (ROE) is relatively low. P/B is greater than 1 for four companies (under all metrics in BBVA, NatWest and UBS, but only TTM in HSBC)—investors in these companies are willing to pay more in the market than the net worth of their investments because they expect more value.

Relative to the peer benchmark, a high P/B with a low ROE suggests that the stock is possibly overvalued—based

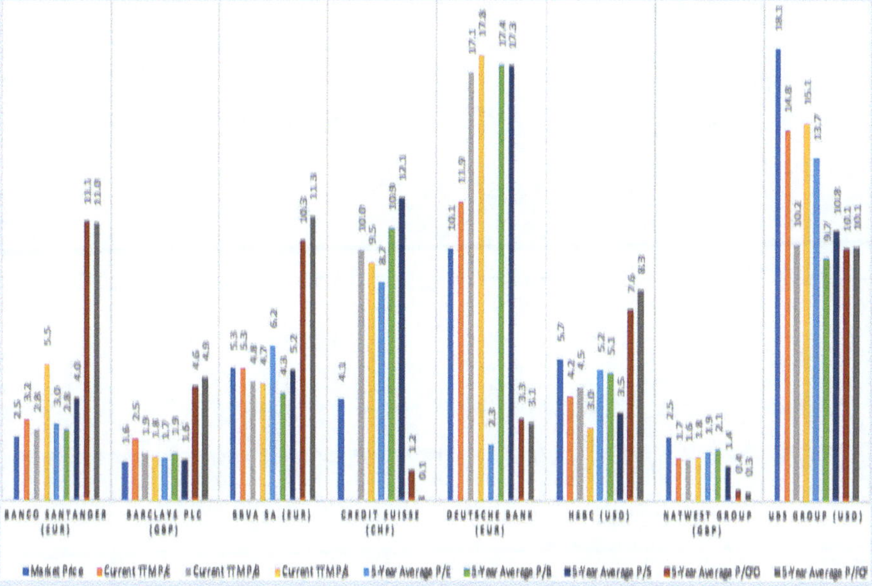

Exhibit 20.4.1 Market price vs. relative valuation: 17 November 2022

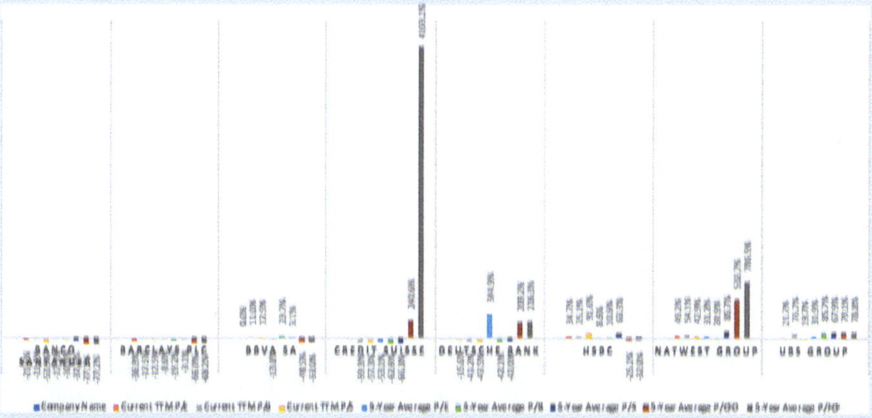

Exhibit 20.4.2 Percentage in which market price deviates from relative valuation: 17 November 2022

on the last 3 years, this situation applies to HSBC (overvalued on 17 November 2022). A low P/B with a high ROE suggests that the stock is possibly undervalued—based on the last 3 years, this situation applies to Barclays (undervalued on 17 November 2022). In the rest of the cases, both P/B and ROE are generally positively correlated—the two sides of the same coin.

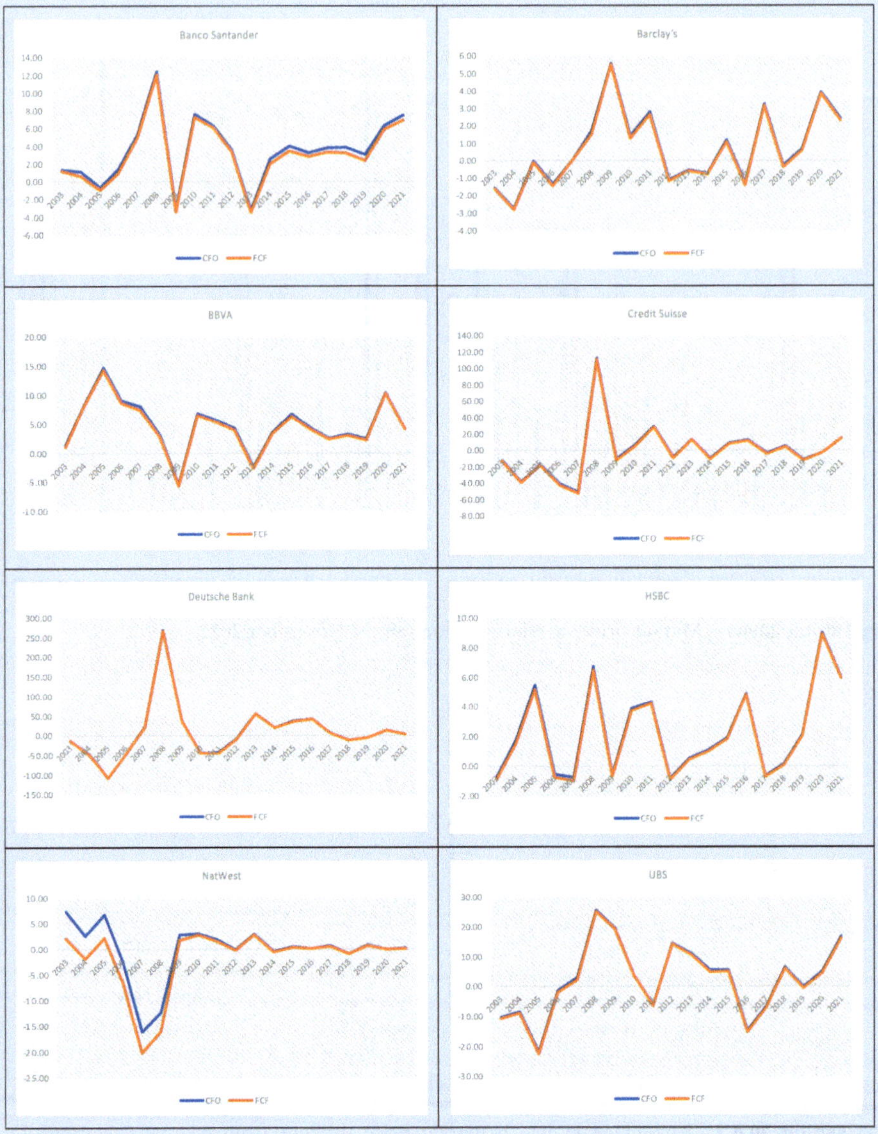

Exhibit 20.4.3 Cash flow patterns

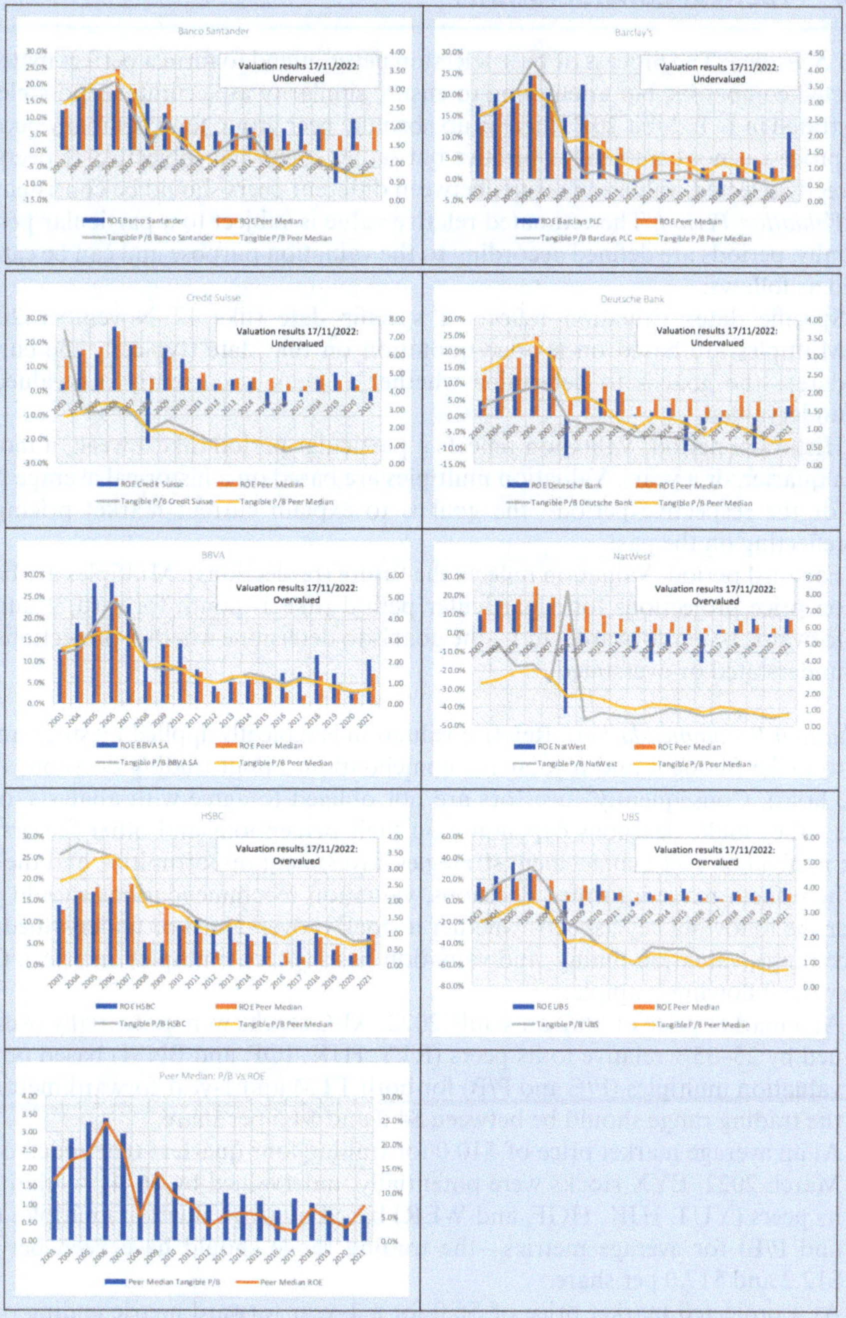

Exhibit 20.4.4 Historical trend: P/B vs. ROE. (*Source of Data*: Bloomberg Terminal)

20.4 Practical Considerations

Peer Selection: The process of peer selection never intend to form a perfect match of selected companies, but attempting to ensure similarity as accurate as possible. As illustrated in ▶ Exhibit 20.3, there is no absolute peer group for a company because the process is not completely objective but rather somewhat subjective. If peers are correctly selected, valuation results between different peers should be consistent.

Valuation Period: The estimated relative value is subject to a particular period. Usually, periods are defined according to the valuation purpose and can be categorized as follows:

1. Specific date: Valuation reflects a specific date (like 17 November 2022). Multiples are based on a price quotation on that date (typically the current date)—the goal is to determine whether a stock is currently overvalued or undervalued.
2. Historical period: Valuation reflects a particular period (like a week, a month, a quarter, or a year). Valuation multiples are based on a historical average price for the respective period—the goal is to explain current market pricing by reflecting on the past.
3. Forward period: Valuation reflects the future (projections). Multiples are based on price projections for a particular period (like 1-month forward, 2-quarter forward, 1-year forward, etc.)—the goal is to determine whether projections are understated or overstated.

Valuation Recommendations: Relative valuation is typically applied by stock analysis to make frequent and regular recommendations about trading decisions (buy, sell, hold). Consequently, investors are not obliged to agree with analysts' opinions—they make decisions depending on their perceptions and other factors like risk preference, risk management strategies, investment opportunities, and the like. To help them make informed decisions, valuation recommendations should consider the following key aspects: whether a stock is overvalued or undervalued, the price range, valuation timing, and valuation basis (peers, multiples, metrics). Consider the following examples:

1. At a market price of $6.2 on 4 July 2022, ABC stocks were potentially overvalued by 25–35% relative to its peers (RTY, HJK, IOP, and BNM) based on two valuation multiples (P/E and P/B) for both TTM and 1-year forward metrics—the trading range should be between $4.2 and $4.5 per share.
2. At an average market price of $10.0 for trailing four quarters that ended on 30 March 2022, EYX stocks were potentially undervalued by 16–41% relative to its peers (YUT, HJK, HGF, and WER) based on two valuation multiples (P/E and P/B) for average metrics—the trading range should have been between $12.2 and $17.0 per share.
3. At a projected market price of $6.0 for a 1-year forward metric ending on 31 December 2023, EYX stock price projections are potentially overstated by 24.8–34.6% relative to its peers (YUT, HJK, HGF, and WER) based on two valuation multiples (P/E and P/B)—the projected price range should be between $4.0 and $4.6 per share.

Apply 20.1

Objective: Perform equity relative valuation

Consider any company of your interest.

1. Determine its peer group.
2. Collect the necessary data to estimate the relative equity value using several value drivers.
3. Use Excel to perform valuation and present your results. Do they make sense?
4. Explain valuation challenges (if any) and how you have addressed them.

Review Questions

1. Outline the most relevant equity value multiples.
2. Briefly explain valuation implications and the limitations of the following equity value multiples:
   (a) Price–earnings (P/E)
   (b) Price–earnings growth (PEG)
   (c) Price to sales (P/S)
   (d) Price to book (P/B)
   (e) Price to cash flows (P/CF)
3. Why should EPS growth be considered when applying P/E?
4. Why should dividends be considered when applying PEG?
5. Why should the amount of intangible assets be considered when applying P/B?
6. Why are P/B and ROE regarded as two sides of the same coin?
7. When applying P/E multiples, what is the valuation implication of using either basic or diluted EPS?
8. Briefly explain the different ways to address the limitation of negative value drivers and their valuation implications.
9. What is the objective of the following equity valuation analysis?
   (a) Cross-company analysis
   (b) Time series analysis
10. How would you interpret relative value when several multiples and metrics are applied for the peer group?

Bibliography

Beaver, W., & Morse, D. (1978). What Determines Price-Earnings Ratios? *Financial Analysts Journal*, 34(4), 65–76. http://www.jstor.org/stable/4478160

Bergstresser, D., and Philippon, T. (2006), CEO incentives and earnings management, *Journal of Financial Economics*, 80 (3), 511–529. https://doi.org/10.1016/j.jfineco.2004.10.011

Block, S. B. (1999). A Study of Financial Analysts: Practice and Theory. *Financial Analysts Journal*, 55(4), 86–95. http://www.jstor.org/stable/4480185

Duggan, W. (2021). Is Netflix's Stock Overvalued or Undervalued? Available at Yahoo Finance, https://finance.yahoo.com/news/netflixs-stock-overvalued-undervalued-172159286.html, Accessed November 2, 2021.

Fairfield, P. M. (1994). PE, PB and the Present Value of Future Dividends. *Financial Analysts Journal*, 50(4), 23–31. http://www.jstor.org/stable/4479758

Fox, James (2022). I'd buy cheap growth stocks this autumn to try and get rich!, Available at Yahoo, https://uk.sports.yahoo.com/news/d-buy-cheap-growth-stocks-083314692.html?, Accessed November 13, 2022.

Gigliotti, G. (2022). Netflix And Its Real Value, Available at Seeking Alpha, https://seekingalpha.com/article/4506664-netflix-real-value, Accessed May 4, 2022.

Graham, J. R., Campbell, R H., and Rajgopal, S. (2005) The economic implications of corporate financial reporting, *Journal of Accounting and Economics*, 40(1–3) :3–73. https://doi.org/10.1016/j.jacceco.2005.01.002

Graham, B., & Dodd, D. (1934), *Security Analysis: The Classic 1934 Edition,* McGraw Hill Professional. New York.

Huston, C. (2022). Netflix Stock Is Still Overvalued, Billionaire Investor John Malone Says, Available at Hollywood Reporter, https://www.hollywoodreporter.com/business/business-news/netflix-stock-is-still-overvalued-billionaire-investor-john-malone-says-1235258086/ Accessed November 8, 2022.

Kam, K. (2018). Facebook Is Undervalued By Over 20%, Available at Forbes, https://www.forbes.com/sites/kenkam/2018/10/06/facebook-is-undervalued-by-over-20/#5d7c4b1e8a61, Accessed October 6, 2018.

Kane, A., Marcus, A. J., & Noh, J. (1996). The PE Multiple and Market Volatility. *Financial Analysts Journal*, 52(4), 16–24. http://www.jstor.org/stable/4479930

Leibowitz, M. L., & Kogelman, S. (1992). Franchise Value and the Growth Process. *Financial Analysts Journal*, 48(1), 53–62. http://www.jstor.org/stable/4479505

Michal, Kenneth J., (2000), Screening for stocks using the dividend-adjusted PEG ratio, American Association of Individual Investors AAII Journal, (August) 2-7, https://www.aaii.com/files/journal/pdf/6816_screening-for-stocks-using-the-dividend-adjusted-peg-ratio.pdf

Myers, J. N., Myers, L. A., & Skinner, D. J. (2007). Earnings Momentum and Earnings Management. *Journal of Accounting, Auditing & Finance*, 22(2), 249–284. https://doi.org/10.1177/0148558X0702200211

Peasnell, K. (1982), Some formal connections between economic values and yields and accounting numbers. *Journal of Business Finance and Accounting*, 9(3), 361–381. https://doi.org/10.1111/j.1468-5957.1982.tb01001.x

Penman, S. H. (2005), Discussion of "On Accounting-Based Valuation Formulae" and "Expected EPS and EPS Growth as Determinants of Value". *Review of Accounting Studies,* 10, 367–378. https://doi.org/10.1007/s11142-005-1536-2

Reisen, R. (2012). Microsoft Vs. Facebook: 2 Great Companies, 1 Stock To Buy, Available at Seeking Alpha, https://seekingalpha.com/article/4206580-microsoft-vs-facebook-2-great-companies-1-stock-buy, Accessed September 17, 2012.

Team, T. (2018), What To Expect From HP's Fiscal Q3 Earnings, Forbes, available at https://www.forbes.com/sites/greatspeculations/2018/08/21/what-to-expect-from-hps-fiscal-q3-earnings/?sh=ad99338f8ad3

Trainer, D. (2022). Netflix Is Still Overvalued By At Least $114 Billion, Available at Forbes, https://www.forbes.com/sites/greatspeculations/2022/01/27/netflix-is-still-overvalued-by-at-least-114-billion/?sh=1b7c46916fc3, Accessed January 27, 2022.

Relative Enterprise Valuation

Contents

Supplementary Information The online version contains supplementary material available at https://doi.org/10.1007/978-3-031-28267-6_21.

B. Kulwizira Lukanima, *Corporate Valuation*, Classroom Companion: Business, https://doi.org/10.1007/978-3-031-28267-6_21

21.1 Introduction

21

Relative enterprise valuation utilizes valuation multiples associated with value drivers relevant to all investors (equity holders and debtholders). Enterprise value (EV), therefore, is the relative value of a firm's operating assets. Like ▶ Chap. 20, this chapter clarifies different types of EV value drivers, their valuation implications, and their limitations. Selected cases are used for practical illustrations.

Learning Outcomes

- Explain the meaning and derivation of enterprise value (EV)
- Understand the meaning and valuation implications of the following EV value drivers: earnings before interest, taxes, depreciation, and amortization (EBITDA), earnings before interest and taxes (EBIT), sales, and cash flows
- Decide on the appropriate EV multiples for a specific peer group
- Apply EV valuation multiples in real-world valuation
- Analyze EV valuation across peers and recommend the direction and magnitude of valuation
- Explain the valuation limitations of EV value multiples

21.2 Enterprise Value

An "enterprise value" refers to the total value of a company, which includes all components of the capital structure such as common stock, debt, preferred stock, etc. Considering the accounting equation (total assets = total liabilities + total equity), an EV can be described as the market value of a firm's operating assets. Therefore, EV derivation can be presented as follows:

$$\begin{aligned}\text{EV} = {} & \text{Market capitalization} + \text{Debt} + \text{Preferred stock} \\ & + \text{Minority interest} - \text{Cash and cash equivalents}\end{aligned}$$

▶ Exhibit 21.1 outlines and describes each of the EV variables. The rationale for EV derivation is to focus on the financing components, by considering asset value should the company be an acquisition target—the amount to be paid to all investors. A business acquirer will have to pony up for the stock and pay off debts. Cash is received by the business acquirer—implying that the acquisition price is reduced by the cash amount received.

Think 21.1

Can an enterprise value be negative? If yes or no, what does it imply?

Example: ABC company has 2 million shares of fully diluted stocks outstanding, trading at \$30 per share. ABC's total debt is \$10 million. Cash and cash equivalents are \$2 million. If you acquire ABC, \$60 million (market capitalization) should be paid today while an obligation to pay \$10 (debt) stays—you should have paid \$70 million (equity + debt). If the acquired cash and cash equivalents

($2 million) are used to pay a portion of debt, then your total acquisition payment is $68 million.

It is noteworthy that EV can be negative if cash and cash equivalents exceed the value of capital structure components—that is, the company can be acquired by its own cash.

Banner 21.1 Enterprise Value
An enterprise value provides a quick indication of how much should be paid upon acquiring an entire company, including its debt and cash.

Exhibit 21.1 Components of an Enterprise Value

An enterprise value is determined by considering its implication in payment value upon business acquisition. One side of the accounting equation shows the value of the acquired assets, whereas the other side shows the net price paid for the assets.

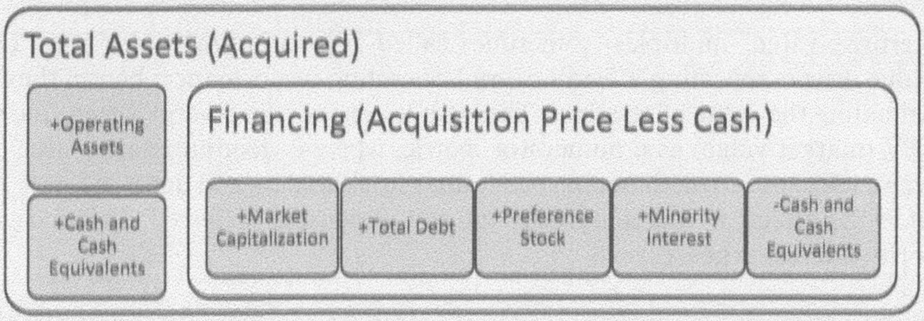

Implications of EV Components

All EV components reflect the current price (market value). Hence, like relative equity valuation, EV forms the numerator for determining EV multiples. Except for market capitalization, estimating market values of other components is generally difficult—hence, an acceptable practical solution is to use book values, assuming that they reflect realizable market values.

Market Capitalization: This is the total equity value, estimated by multiplying the share price by the number of diluted shares outstanding. To determine EV, market cap is added to reflect the minimum price to be paid to the target company's shareholders upon business acquisition.

Total Debt: This component typically includes interest-bearing debt (short- and long-term). However, depending on analysts' judgments, it is possible to consider other current liabilities as presented in company's balance except convertible debt (in-the-money) because they constitute equity. To determine EV, debt is added to reflect the obligation to pay.

Preference Stock: This is a financial security with features of both debt and equity. To determine EV, preference stock is added to reflect a fixed financial obligation just like debt. The focus, however, is on mandatorily redeemable and convertible preferred stocks, where conversion price is greater than the prevailing market price.

Minority Interest: Noncontrolling interest is a fraction of stocks that a parent company owns in a subsidiary or division, amounting to less than 50% of voting shares, and is fully consolidated in the parent company's financial results. This implies that value drivers (sales, EBITDA, EBIT, etc.) reflect financial results attributed to other owners (in subsidiaries). Hence, minority interest is added to determine EV to reflect minority stakes in a company, which are treated as a liability.

Cash and Cash Equivalents: These are the most liquid assets (regarded as non-operating assets), which could immediately be used to service a portion of the company's debt, consequently reducing the price paid on acquiring a business—for this reason, they are subtracted when calculating EV.

21.3 Enterprise Value Multiples

"Enterprise value" multiples (sometimes called "operating multiples") are based on value drivers reflecting a firm's overall operating performance: hence, they aim at estimating the value of the firm. These multiples exist in several forms, and they use EV (market value) as a numerator metric, whereas denominators (value drivers) have relevance to all financing claimants (stockholders and debtholders)—they exclude the effect of financing (i.e., interest expenses, preferred dividends, and minority interest expenses).

Banner 21.2 Enterprise Value Multiples and Debt Effect

EV multiples are used to value firms regardless of capital structure differences—they ignore the effect of debt.

Let us now examine the most common EV value drivers (EBITDA, EBIT, sales, and cash flows) and their valuation implications.

21.3.1 EBITDA vs. EBIT

Both EBITDA and EBIT value drivers are based on operating earnings but differ regarding the effect of depreciation and amortization (DA), such that:

- EBIT = EBITDA – DA
- EBITDA = EBIT + DA
- DA = EBITDA – EBIT

The respective multiples are EV/EBITDA and EV/EBIT. For example: A company has reported sales revenues as $60 million, cost of sales as $25 million, operating expenses as $15 million, and DA as $35 million. EBIT = $80 – $25 – $15 = $40 million. EBITDA = $40 + $35 = $75 million. ▶ Exhibit 21.2 presents case examples of EBITDA vs. EBIT for four companies: Chevron Corp. (United States), MOL Hungarian Oil & Gas (Hungary), Netflix (United States), and Liberty Global (United Kingdom). The wider the gap between EBITDA and EBIT, the higher the value of DA—implying a higher fixed capital and/or intangible assets (see Chevron, MOL, and Liberty). The narrower the gap between EBITDA and EBIT, the lower the value of DA—implying a lower fixed capital and/or intangible assets (see Netflix). It is noteworthy that companies in the same industry can have different DA profiles—for example, Netflix vs. Liberty.

Exhibit 21.2 EBITDA vs. EBIT

Illustrative Case: Chevron Corp. (United States), MOL Hungarian Oil & Gas (Hungary), Netflix (United States), and Liberty Global (United Kingdom) (See Excel Workings—▶ Chap. 21, Sheets E.21.3 and E21.4)

21.3.1.1 Valuation Implications

While EBITDA ignores noncash charges relating to depreciation and amortization (DA), EBIT recognizes them. Since DA is a measure of loss of asset value due to usage (depreciation) and market perception (amortization), EBIT considers them to reflect real expenses that will need to be replaced. As proxies for cash flows, EBITDA and EBIT can be described as follows:

1. EBITDA is a proxy for "cash from operations" (CFO) before the impact of capital structure and taxes. The main difference is that CFO considers the effect of fixed capital expenditure through DA, whereas EBITDA does not.
2. EBIT is a proxy for "free cash flows" (FCFs) before the impact of capital structure and taxes. The difference is that FCF considers capital expenditure fully, whereas EBIT considers only asset replacement costs (DA).

21.3.1.2 Application

"Which value driver is superior?" There is no straightforward answer. The decision depends on valuation purpose, the nature of the industry, and analysts' view on considering the effect of capital expenditure (depreciation) and intangible assets (amortization). The decision to use EBITDA implies completely ignoring the valuation impact of capital expenditure and intangible assets—in contrast, using EBIT implies factoring them.

"What are the general considerations?" The choice of a particular value driver tends to have an impact on multiples and relative enterprise value. The following aspects should be considered:

1. EBITDA is often preferred to EBIT by companies with heavy investment in tangible or intangible assets (high depreciation or amortization expenses). The main argument for ignoring the effect of capital expenditure and intangible assets is that noncash charges (captured by DA) can significantly differ across peers, thereby affecting comparability.
2. Because of DA, EBITDA is more suitable for valuing companies with identical investment profiles, usually in the same industry (consider Chevron and MOL in ▶ Exhibit 21.2.1). EBIT is more suitable when comparing companies from different industries or the same industry but with different investment profiles (consider Netflix and Liberty in ▶ Exhibit 21.2.2).
3. Capital-intensive companies tend to have lower EV multiples with EBITDA than with EBIT due to high capital requirements and high depreciation charge—they may look "artificially" overvalued. To avoid misleading valuation results, peers should be carefully selected by considering comparability in depreciation charges relative to capital expenditure. Significant differences can lead to misleading results.
4. When valuing firms with low investment in fixed capital (low depreciation) or with low intangible assets (low amortization), both EV/EBIT and EV/EBITDA tend to yield similar results, except if the value drivers are abnormal.
5. Overall, there is no definite argument for or against one another. Applying both EBITDA and EBIT helps depict a picture about investment characteristics of peers and assess the suitability of each value driver.

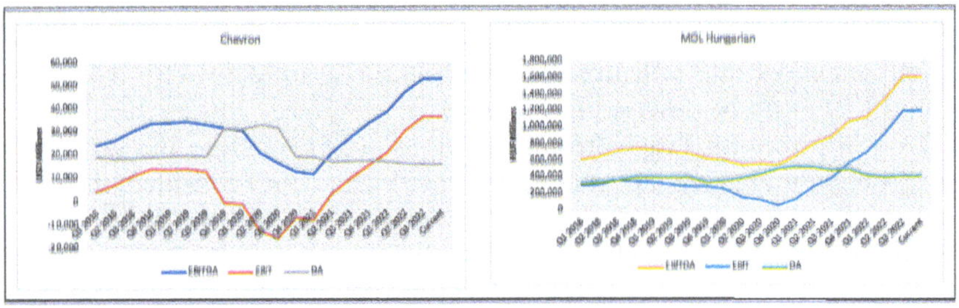

Exhibit 21.2.1 Chevron and MOL (Oil & Gas Integrated)

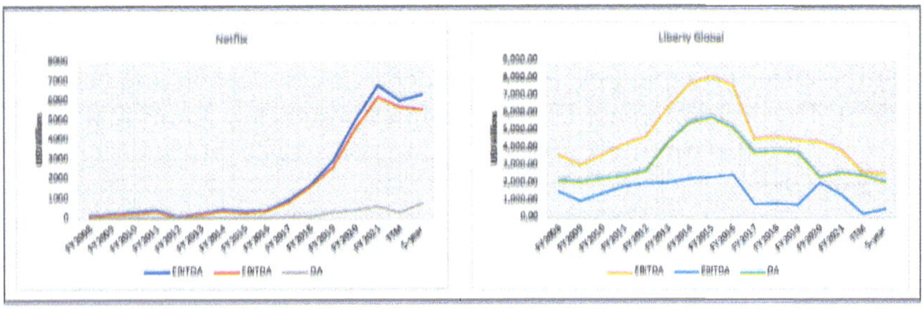

Exhibit 21.2.2 Netflix and Liberty (Entertainment)

Banner 21.3 EBITDA vs. EBIT Industry Effect
EBITDA is more sensitive than EBIT regarding industry characteristics. Hence, EBITDA is generally more suitable for valuing companies in the same industry.

21.3.1.3 Limitations

Comparability: Generally, the main limitation of EBITDA and EBIT stems from peer comparability regarding capital expenditure and intangible assets. Therefore, valuation can be misleading when peers' investment profiles are characteristically different even if they belong to the same industry. For example, consider two retailers, A and B, both utilizing buildings with an equal book cost but different forms—A's building was purchased, whereas B's was leased. B will have lower EBITDA because lease costs are expensed but there are no depreciation expenses relating to buildings. On the other hand, A will have higher EBITDA because depreciation expenses relating to buildings are not factored and hence there are no lease expenses. Regarding EBIT, it will be lower for A than for B due to depreciation charges on A.

Suitability: The main argument against EBITDA is that ignoring capital expenditure only intends to produce favorable multiples. However, for capital-intensive industries, investment in fixed capital is a vital valuation variable that should be considered.

Stability: Some companies can experience volatile or negative earnings (usually EBIT).

Banner 21.4 EBITDA vs. EBIT Proximity to Cash Flows
EBITDA is a proxy for cash flow from operating activities (CFO), whereas EBIT is a proxy for free cash flow (FCF). They both ignore the effect of leverage and taxes.

Think 21.2
How would you judge valuation if both EBITDA and EBIT produce conflicting results?

21.3.2 Sales

In relative enterprise valuation, the respective multiple is EV/sales. As already explained in ▶ Chap. 20, sales revenues do not represent earnings available to investors. However, unlike EBITDA and EBIT, sales revenues are more immune from accounting assumptions and manipulations because they are reported high up in the income statement.

21.3.2.1 Valuation Implications

When using EV/sales, the assumption is that they will be turned into earnings available to all investors (EBITDA or EBIT). Hence, even if peer companies have identical sales revenues, valuation can be misleading if costs of sales and operating expenses vary significantly across the companies. For example, three peer companies, namely R, T, and U, have reported sales revenues and expenses as follows: Companies R and T have equal sales ($50 million), whereas company U has sales of $80 million. The gross profit margins and operating margins, respectively, are 34% and 26% (R), 25% and −0.22% (T), and 20% and 10% (U). Clearly, the three companies have identical sales revenues, but returns to investors vary significantly—R and T have equal sales, but, whereas the former generates more earnings for investors, the latter generates loss. U, despite the highest sales, generates lower earnings than R. Hence, sales make valuation sense for companies with identical operating margins.

A lower EV/sales generally suggests that the company is potentially undervalued, and vice versa. However, this can be misleading. A low EV/sales, which implies an attractive company, may be due to investors' expectations about poor sales performance. Moreover, a high EV/sales may not necessarily imply overvaluation (an unattractive company) but positive expectations on sales performance.

21.3.2.2 Application

EV/sales is generally not a highly favorable valuation multiple. However, it is useful when EBITDA or EBIT are negative and redundant. This is always the case when a firm's operating costs exceed sales.

21.3.2.3 Limitation

Linking Sales to Earnings: Revenue is not a reliable metric for comparing firms because it is not uncommon to have firms with identical sales but completely different earning margins. Moreover, earnings tend to be more volatile than sales because they are susceptible to several economic variables.

Banner 21.5 Relevance of Sales

Sales ignores the effect of the cost of sales and operating expenses—they are only relevant if it can be turned into earnings.

21.3.3 Free Cash Flows

EV/CF multiples generally utilize free cash flows (FCFs) or free cash flows to the firm (FCFFs), which fully account for capital expenditure. The respective multiples can be expressed as EV/FCF and EV/FCFF. Refer to ▶ Chap. 20 for an explanation about cash-based value drivers.

21.3.3.1 Valuation Implications

A low cash-based multiple (EV/FCF or EV/FCFF) generally implies that the company is undervalued and its payback period for acquisition cost is relatively short. The opposite is true for high multiples. Hence, when comparing peers, lower multiples imply a higher value, and vice versa.

21.3.3.2 Application

EV/CF multiples are more appliable when valuing companies with stable and identical cash flow profiles. Overall, they reflect the valuation strength of a company's cash flows. As explained in ▶ Chap. 20, cash is a more realistic measure of value because it considers shareholders' or company's value maximization. The most relevant cash-based measures for EV multiples are FCF and FCFF because they fully consider the effect of capital expenditure.

21.3.3.3 Limitation

The main limitation of EV/FCF or EV/FCFF is that it becomes less useful when the cash flow items are subject to high volatility.

Think 21.3

Since EBITDA and EBIT can serve as proxies for CFO and FCF, should they produce consistent valuation results?

21.4 Practical Application

To illustrate the practical application of EV multiples, two cases are presented in ▶ Exhibits 21.3 and 21.4. Each case represents peers with different financial and operating characteristics to explain the following valuation aspects:

- *Value Drivers*: EV multiples are based on several value drivers to help compare and explain their valuation implications: EBITDA, EBIT, sales, FCF, and FCFF. When the results across multiples are inconsistent, analysis should be performed to determine which value driver(s) to disregard depending on suitability and reliability. Overall, the following points should be noted from the two cases:
  1. Valuation consistency of value drivers varies across companies—while results are consistent in most companies, inconsistencies are observed in few cases. Attempts are made to explain the reasons for such inconsistencies.
  2. Generally, average-based multiples depict more consistent results across value drivers than trailing 12 month (TTM)-based multiples. It should be noted that averaging tends to normalize values and serve as a proxy for forward-looking valuation.
  3. Negative value drivers are addressed in the same way as equity valuation in ▶ Chap. 20.
- *EBITDA vs. EBIT*: The two cases differ in investment profiles regarding fixed capital and intangible assets. This intends to explain the effect of depreciation and amortization and the suitability of each value driver. When the results from the two are conflicting, EBITDA should be favored for capital-intensive companies and EBIT for low capital-intensive companies.
- *Cross-Company Analysis*: Since results across multiples can be conflicting, analysis should aim at recommending an appropriate direction (overvalued or undervalued) and reasonable valuation range (the percentage at which a com-

21

pany is overvalued or undervalued). Consideration should be made on the following aspects:

1. What is the appropriate direction? If directions are conflicting across multiples, then decisions can be based on the most suitable value driver for the peer and company's specific issues.
2. What range of valuation magnitude is reasonable to recommend? Further analysis can be performed to determine the suitability of the value drivers, considering their data reliability and suitability. For example, a particular value driver can be suitable for the peer but not reliable for a particular company due to factors like stability and abnormality.

Exhibit 21.3 Relative Enterprise Valuation

Illustrative Case: Netflix and Peers (See Excel Workings—▶ Chap. 21, Sheet E.21.3)

In this illustration, Netflix is valued relative to nine peers (international and domestic). Refer to ▶ Chap. 20 (▶ Exhibit 20.3) for brief peer profiles. Valuation is as on 31 October 2022.

Valuation

▫ Exhibits 21.3.1 and 21.3.2 present several valuation multiples. To determine the relative value for each company, a particular value driver is multiplied by a respective peer average multiple (refer to ▶ Chap. 19). Value drivers are not presented here but can be calculated by dividing EV by a company's multiple: for example, since Netflix's EV is $140,638 million, whereas its EV/EBITDA is 13.35, then EBITDA = $140,638/23.35 = $6022 million. ▫ Exhibit 21.3.3 presents relative EV results (for each multiple) and market EV in graphical form for a quick comparison.

Cross-Company Analysis

▫ Exhibit 21.3.4 presents cross-company analysis of the percentage at which a company is overvalued or undervalued. Two aspects to consider are direction (it is overvalued or undervalued?) and magnitude (to what extent?).

Direction

The Same Direction: The verdict is straightforward when all multiples point to one direction: this applies to Netflix (overvalued), Telenet (undervalued), Comcast (undervalued), Shaw (overvalued), and Warner Bros (overvalued).

Different Directions: The following companies have conflicting directions, and, therefore, there is no direct verdict.

- Liberty: The company is overvalued based on EBIT (TTM) and sales (TTM) and undervalued based on the rest, except fair valuation based on 5-year averages (EBIT, FCF, and FCFF). Since the two conflicts relate to TTM, a verdict can be based on averages that tend to be normalized. Moreover, a high valuation on EBIT (TTM) implies an extremely low EBIT due to high depreciation or amortization charges (EBITDA and EBIT were $2668 million and $213 million, respectively), which misaligns the company's EBIT from peer comparability (misleading). Sales value drivers can be disre-

Exhibit 21.3.1 EV valuation multiples: TTM

Company	Domicile	EV ($millions)	EV/ EBITDA	EV/ EBIT	EV/ sales	EV/ FCF	EV/FCFF
Netflix	United States	140,638	23.35	24.61	4.47	77.60	104.16
Telenet Group Holding	Belgium	7558	5.25	11.60	2.66	4.03	4.82
Comcast Corp.	United States	229,615	8.12	16.02	1.89	7.56	11.33
Shaw Communi-cations	Canada	22,731	9.00	17.43	4.16	10.19	16.77
Liberty Global	United Kingdom	19,518	7.32	91.72	2.71	5.57	8.37
Warner Bros Discovery	United States	85,952	64.24	NA[a]	4.45	NA[b]	NA[b]
Amazon	United States	1,122,151	18.67	86.51	2.23	NA[b]	NA[b]
Paramount Global	United States	25,898	4.69	5.04	0.87	46.19	133.70
Dish Network Corp.	United States	29,023	8.15	10.85	1.66	8.91	24.95
Average			**16.53**	**32.97**	**2.79**	**22.86**	**43.44**
Median			**8.15**	**16.73**	**2.66**	**8.91**	**16.77**

[a] Not applicable due to a negative value driver
[b] Not applicable due to data unavailability. NA is excluded when determining peer benchmarks for the respective multiple: that is, relative valuation is based on the reduced number of peers regarding that multiple.

garded due to their inferiority. Fair valuation implies that the respective company's multiples equal its peers' median. From this analysis, it is reasonable to consider the company as generally undervalued.

- Amazon: The company is potentially overvalued by all multiples, except TTM sales (undervalued) and TTM free cash flows (fair). It should generally be considered as overvalued.
- Paramount: Most of the EV multiples suggest undervaluation. Two multiples based on TTM metrics (FCF and FCFF) suggest overvaluation,

21

Exhibit 21.3.2 EV valuation multiples: a 5-year average (including current)

Company	Domicile	EV ($millions)	EV/ EBITDA	EV/ EBIT	EV/ sales	EV/FCF	EV/ FCFF
Netflix	United States	140,638	36.12	39.17	6.31	509.82	NA[a]
Telenet Group Holding	Belgium	7558	5.09	11.31	2.58	5.18	6.59
Comcast Corp.	United States	229,615	7.31	12.43	2.19	7.80	11.60
Shaw Communications	Canada	22,731	10.40	21.17	4.29	11.95	25.89
Liberty Global	United Kingdom	19,518	4.72	19.71	1.83	NA[b]	NA[b]
Warner Bros Discovery	United States	85,952	28.86	66.68	7.29	25.08	27.51
Amazon	United States	1,122,151	25.60	73.33	3.29	27.20	89.25
Paramount Global	United States	25,898	4.99	5.59	1.03	11.70	13.66
Dish Network Corp.	United States	29,023	9.20	12.39	1.90	9.17	13.00
Average			**14.70**	**29.09**	**3.41**	**75.99**	**26.79**
Median			**9.20**	**19.71**	**2.58**	**11.82**	**13.66**

[a] Not applicable due to a negative value driver

[b] Not applicable due to data unavailability. NA is excluded when determining peer benchmarks for the respective multiple: that is, relative valuation is based on the reduced number of peers regarding that multiple.

valuation. Looking deep into free cash flows, TTM of FCF and FCFF was $562 and $194 million, respectively—they are extremely low compared to 5-year averages of $2213 and $1897 for FCF and FCFF, respectively. Hence, TTM free cash flows can be considered abnormal or nonrecurring (misleading). Based on this analysis, garded. Paramount is generally undervalued.

- Dish Network: Like Paramount, most multiples suggest undervaluation, except TTM FCFF (overvalued), TTM FCF (fair), and both TTM and average EBITDA (fair). Examining the suitability of value drivers, TTM FCFF and 5-year

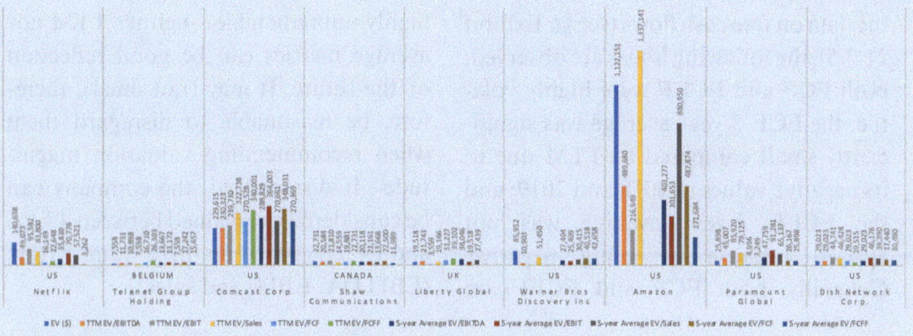

Exhibit 21.3.3 Relative EV vs. market EV

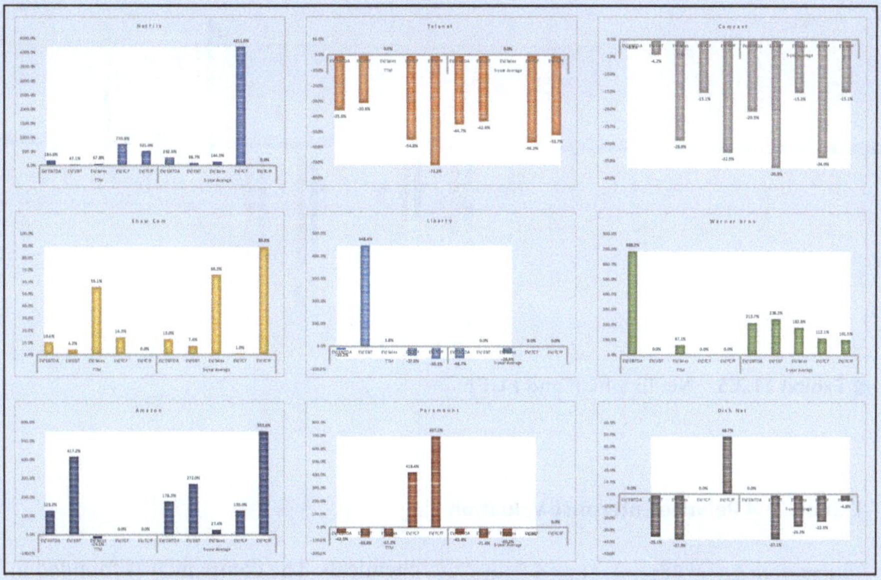

Exhibit 21.3.4 Cross-company analysis: percentages of overvaluation or undervaluation

average FCFF were $1163 and $2233, respectively—the TTM metric may not be a good reflection of the future and can be disregarded. Since the industry is less capital-intensive, EBITDA can be disregarded too. It is, therefore, reasonable to suggest undervaluation.

Magnitude

Based on direction suggestions (overvalued or undervalued), valuation magnitude should be stated in a range, as indicated in Exhibit 21.3.4. It should be noted that variations across multiples are due to different valuation implications of each value driver—there is nothing wrong about it unless a particular multiple is abnormal.

Let us look at Netflix as an example. The company is potentially overvalued but the average-based EV/FCF percentage of overvaluation deviates significantly from the rest. Why? Examining the data on free cash flows (see Exhibit 21.3.5), the following issues are observed: both FCF and FCFF were highly volatile; the FCF 5-year average was significantly small compared to TTM due to its negative values in 2018 and 2019; and the FCFF 5-year average was not applied because of being negative. Generally, both FCF and FCFF are highly unpredictable—neither TTM nor average metrics can be good reflection of the future. It may (not must), therefore, be reasonable to disregard them when recommending valuation magnitude—if disregarded, the company can be considered overvalued between 47.1% and 292.5% based on three value drivers (EBITDA, EBIT, and sales).

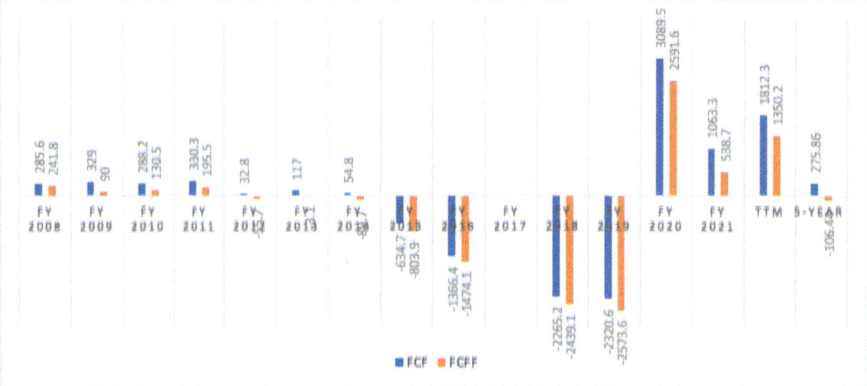

Exhibit 21.3.5 Netflix's FCF and FCFF

Exhibit 21.4 Relative Enterprise Valuation

Illustrative Case: Ecopetrol and Peers (See Excel Workings—▶ Chap. 21, Sheet E.21.4)

In this illustration, Ecopetrol is valued relative to seven international peers. Valuation is as on 17 November 2022.

Peers

Ecopetrol SA: This engages in the exploration, development, and production of crude oil and natural gas. It operates through the following segments: exploration and production; transportation and logistics; and refining and petrochemicals. The company was founded in 1948 and is headquartered in Bogota, Colombia.

Petróleo Brasileiro SA: This explores, produces, and sells oil and gas in Brazil and internationally. The company operates through exploration and production; refining, transportation, and marketing; gas and power; and corporate and other business segments. The company was incorporated in 1953 and is headquartered in Rio de Janeiro, Brazil.

Repsol SA: This is engaged in the exploration and production of crude oil, natural gas, and refined petroleum. It operates through the following business segments: upstream, downstream, and corporation and others. The company was founded on October 17, 1927, and is headquartered in Madrid, Spain.

Chevron Corporation: This engages in the provision of administrative, financial management, and technology support for energy and chemical operations. It operates through upstream and downstream segments. The company was founded in 1906 and is headquartered in San Ramon, California, United States.

Suncor Energy Inc: This operates as an integrated energy company, primarily focusing on developing petroleum resource basins in Canada's Athabasca oil sands and explores, acquires, develops, produces, transports, refines, and markets crude oil in Canada and internationally. The company, formerly known as Suncor Inc., was founded in 1917 and is headquartered in Calgary, Canada.

Exxon Mobil Corporation: This explores and produces crude oil and natural gas in the United States and internationally. It operates through upstream, downstream, and chemical segments. The company was founded in 1870 and is headquartered in Irving, Texas, United States.

MOL Hungarian Oil & Gas Plc: This engages in the exploration and production of crude oil, natural gas, and other gas products. It operates through the following segments: upstream, downstream, consumer services, gas midstream, and corporate, and others. The company was founded on October 1, 1991 and is headquartered in Budapest, Hungary

Valuation

Exhibits 21.4.1 and 21.4.2 present several valuation multiples. Exhibit 21.4.3 presents market EV against relative EV (for each multiple) and the extent to which a company is overvalued or undervalued (in percentages). To reach recommendations, analysis is performed on the direction and magnitude as follows:

Direction

The Same Direction: Consistency in valuation direction relates to the following companies: Petroleo (undervalued), Chevron (overvalued), and MOL (undervalued).

Mixed Directions: The following companies have conflicting directions, and, therefore, there is no direct verdict.

- Ecopetrol: The company is overvalued based on sales (both current and average) but undervalued based on EBITDA and EBIT (both current and average). Since sales is an inferior value driver, the EV/sales multiple can be disregarded. Hence, the company can be considered to be potentially undervalued based on EV/EBITDA and EV/EBIT.
- Repsol: The company is undervalued based on sales (both current and average) but slightly overvalued or fair based on EBITDA and EBIT (both current and average). Since sales is an inferior value driver, the EV/sales multiple can be disregarded. Hence, the company can be considered slightly overvalued or fair-valued based on EV/EBITDA and EV/EBIT.
- Suncor: The company is overvalued based on EBITDA, EBIT, and sales (both current and average) but fair-

21

Exhibit 21.4.1 EV valuation multiples: current

Company	Domicile	Currency	EV (M)	Current metrics EV/EBITDA	EV/EBIT	EV/sales	EV/FCF	EV/FCFF
Ecopetrol	Colombia	COP	219,887,234	3.13	3.74	1.45	NA	NA
Petroleo	Brazil	BRL	635,539	1.77	2.17	1.03	2.48	2.94
Repsol	Spain	EUR	27,152	3.22	4.39	0.36	NA	NA
Chevron	United States	USD	360,112	6.77	9.78	1.59	7.67	9.94
Suncor	Canada	CAD	79,148	3.66	6.24	1.42	5.26	7.80
Exxon	United States	USD	480,124	6.02	NA	1.24	6.24	7.98
MOL	Hungary	HUF	3,104,901	1.90	2.58	0.34	2.45	4.60
Average				**3.78**	**4.82**	**1.06**	**4.82**	**6.65**
Median				**3.22**	**4.07**	**1.24**	**5.26**	**7.80**

Notes: EV is in the company's reporting currency. NA means not applicable due to data limitations or unsuitability—it is excluded when determining peer benchmarks for the respective multiple: that is, relative valuation is based on the reduced number of peers regarding that multiple

valued based on FCF and FCFF (both current and average). Since fair valuation is the median, it can be disregarded—conservative analysts can consider the company overvalued.

- Exxon: The company is overvalued based on all value drivers, except for sales (fair-valued). Since sales is less favorable, and fair valuation is the median, it is reasonable to consider the company overvalued.

Magnitude

From Exhibit 21.4.3, the extent to which a company is overvalued (positive percentage) or undervalued (negative percentage) varies across multiples, reflecting different valuation implications of each value driver. To recommend a valuation range, do the following: (1) decide the direction as recommended above and (2) examine for abnormalities, and disregard if any. The following ranges are potential recommendations for each company as on the valuation date 17 November 2022:

- Ecopetrol: At an EV of COP 219.9 trillion, the company was potentially undervalued between 2.9% and 30.8% or 11.6% on average, based on EBITDA and EBIT EV multiples. Its value should range between COP 226.4 trillion and COP 317.6 trillion or COP 253.4 trillion on average.
- Petroleo: At an EV of BRZ 635.5 billion, the company was potentially undervalued between 17.0% and 71.3% or 50.0% on average, based on EBITDA, EBIT, sales, FCF, and FCFF EV multiples. Its value should range between BRZ 765.6 billion

Exhibit 21.4.2 EV valuation multiples: average

Company	Domicile	Currency	EV (M)	Average metrics				
				EV/ EBITDA	EV/ EBIT	EV/ sales	EV/ FCF	EV/ FCFF
Ecopetrol	Colombia	COP	219,887,234	5.73	7.79	2.44	NA	NA
Petroleo	Brazil	BRL	635,539	2.46	3.23	1.48	2.64	3.13
Repsol	Spain	EUR	27,152	6.01	11.25	0.55	NA	NA
Chevron	United States	USD	360,112	11.65	27.37	2.39	9.57	12.66
Suncor	Canada	CAD	79,148	6.45	14.84	2.07	6.42	10.18
Exxon	United States	USD	480,124	11.56	67.37	1.80	7.85	10.24
MOL	Hungary	HUF	3,104,901	3.03	5.75	0.53	2.81	5.47
Average				**6.70**	**19.66**	**1.61**	**5.86**	**8.34**
Median				**6.01**	**11.25**	**1.80**	**6.42**	**10.18**

Notes: EBITDA, EBIT, and sales are based on 8-quarter averages, whereas FCF and FCFF are based on 4-quarter averages. EV is in company's reporting currency. NA means not applicable due to data limitations or unsuitability—it is excluded when determining peer benchmarks for the respective multiple: that is, relative valuation is based on the reduced number of peers regarding that multiple.

and BRZ 2210 billion or BRZ 1429.3 billion on average.

- Repsol: At an EV of EUR 27.2 billion, the company was slightly overvalued by 7.9% of fair-valued based on EBITDA and EBIT EV multiples. Its value should range between EUR 25.26 billion and EUR 27.2 billion.
- Chevron: At an EV of USD 360.1 billion, the company was potentially overvalued between 24.4% and 143.3% or 70.0% on average, based on EBITDA, EBIT, sales, FCF, and FCFF EV multiples. Its value should range between USD 148.0 billion and USD 298.4 billion or USD 226.8 billion on average.
- Suncor: At an EV of CAD 79.1 billion, the company was potentially overvalued between 7.3% and 53.4% or 17.0% on average, based on EBITDA, EBIT, and sales: it is fair-valued based on FCF and FCFF EV multiples. Its value should range between CAD 51.6 billion and CAD 79.1 billion or CAD 70.9 billion on average.
- Exxon: At an EV of USD 480.1 billion, the company was potentially overvalued based on all multiples, except EV/sales. Nevertheless, an average EBIT provides a significantly low multiple (high overvaluation by 498.9%) compared to the rest. Inspection of data indicates that this is due to the extremely low average EBIT caused by a negative EBIT in four quarters consecutively prior to the

Exhibit 21.4.3 Valuation and the extent of overvaluation or undervaluation

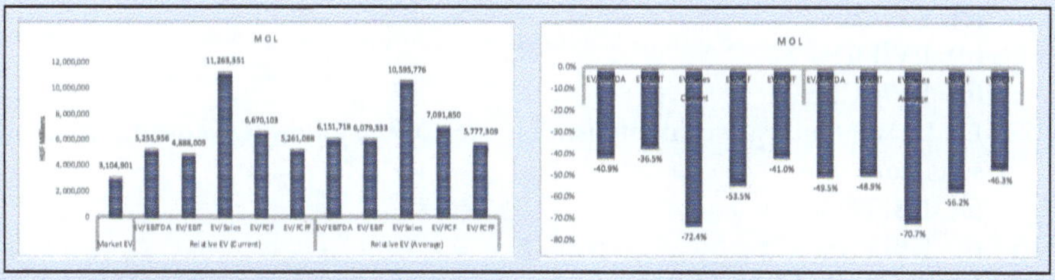

Exhibit 21.4.3 (continued)

four quarters of 2021, which do not reflect the subsequent and current trend. Hence, an average EBIT is generally misleading about the expected future—it should be disregarded. The company is then overvalued between 0.6% and 114.5% or 48.2% on average, based on EBITDA, EBIT, FCF, and FCFF EV multiples, or fair-valued based on sales. Its value should range between USD 223.8 billion and USD 480.1 billion or USD 353.4 billion on average.

- MOL: At an EV of HUF 3.1 trillion, the company was potentially undervalued between 36.5% and 72.4% or 51.6% on average, based on EBITDA, EBIT, sales, FCF, and FCFF EV multiples. Its value should range between HUF 4.9 trillion and HUF 11.3 trillion or HUF 6.9 trillion on average.

Apply 21.1

Objective: Perform enterprise relative valuation

Consider any company of your interest or use Excel data provided for banking companies (refer to Excel workings ▶ Chap. 21).

1. Determine the peer group.
2. Compile the necessary data to estimate the relative enterprise value using several value drivers.
3. Use Excel to perform valuation and present your results. Do they make sense?
4. Explain valuation challenges (if any) and how you have addressed them.

Review Questions

1. What is the meaning of enterprise value?
2. Outline and explain the variables for derivation of enterprise value.
3. Why should cash and cash equivalents be subtracted when deriving enterprise value?
4. Briefly explain valuation implications and the limitations of the following enterprise value multiples:
   (a) EV/sales

   (b) EV/EBITDA
   (c) EV/EBIT
   (d) EV/FCF
   (e) EV/FCFF
5. Under what industry characteristics is each of the following value drivers most suitable?
   (a) EBITDA
   (b) EBIT
6. Under what operating conditions can sales be considered suitable value drivers of enterprise valuation?
7. The suitability of EBITDA and EBIT is debatable. What are the common arguments for or against each of them?
8. Describe EBITDA and EBIT in the context of proximity to the following cash flows:
   (a) Free cash flow (FCF)
   (b) Free cash flow to the firm (FCFF)
   (c) Operating cash flow (CFO)
9. What valuation implications do EBITDA and EBIT have under the following industry characteristics?
   (a) High investments in fixed capital
   (b) High intangible assets
   (c) Low investment in fixed capital
   (d) Low intangible assets
10. Explain the limitations of free cash flow EV multiples under the following aspects:
    (a) Comparability
    (b) Stability
    (c) Industry characteristics
11. Why should different valuation multiples produce conflicting valuation results regarding direction (overvalued or undervalued)?

Application of Relative Valuation

Contents

Supplementary Information The online version contains supplementary material available at https://doi.org/10.1007/978-3-031-28267-6_22.

B. Kulwizira Lukanima, *Corporate Valuation*, Classroom Companion: Business, https://doi.org/10.1007/978-3-031-28267-6_22

22.1 Introduction

After grasping the technical and practical aspects of relative valuation from ▶ Chaps. 19–21, this chapter outlines its typical applications. Although applications can be broad, this chapter focuses on the most common ones such as investment decisions, initial public offering (IPO) pricing, merger and acquisition (M&A) decisions, performance analysis, and valuation of private firms.

Learning Outcomes

- Understand the role of relative valuation in various aspects of investment and performance analysis
- Apply relative valuation in performance analysis and forecasting
- Understand the use of relative valuation for stock price recommendations and investment decisions
- Apply relative valuation for determining terminal value in cash flow discount models
- Apply relative valuation in private firms
- Understand the role of relative valuation in IPOs
- Understand the use of relative valuation in M&A decisions
- Understand the key limitations of relative valuation

22.2 Performance Analysis and Forecasting

Since relative valuation multiples combine two key variables associated with companies' financial performance (value drivers) and market performance (market value), they play a vital role in performance analysis across companies and over time. For example, the following quote from Pruitt (2022) in his article titled "Time to Buy AMD or Intel Stock for 2023?" reflects on the performance of two semiconductor companies, AMD and Intel:

> Trading around $67 per share and roughly 56% from its 52-week high, AMD has a P/E of 20.5X. In comparison, INTC trades 49% off its highs at $28 a share and 14.7X earnings. From a valuation standpoint, both stocks are starting to look attractive relative to their past. However, Advanced Micro Devices stands out here too. AMD trades well below its absurd decade high of 5,985X and at a 49% discount from its median of 47.9X. When comparing this period, INTC trades nicely beneath its decade high of 16.7X but 15% above its decade median of 12.8X. Pivoting to growth, AMD's earnings are now expected to jump 25% to $3.49 a share in 2022. Fiscal 2023 EPS is projected to rise 1% to $3.52. However, earnings estimate revisions have declined for both FY22 and FY23 over the last 90 days (Pruitt 2022).

From this quote, performance analysis typically covers the past, current, and the future. ▶ Exhibit 22.1 presents two cases (Netflix and Comcast), both from the same industry. A typical performance analysis can consider the following aspects:

1. *Performance Measurement*: Relative valuation performance is generally based on multiples, which capture both market performance (numerator) and finan-

cial performance (denominator). For example, these illustrative cases use two multiples, price–earnings (P/E) and enterprise value/earnings before interest, taxes, depreciation, and amortization (EV/EBITDA) for each company.

2. *Cross-Company Benchmark*: Cross-company performance can be assessed using peer or industry/sector benchmarks. For example, Standards and Poor's 500 (S&P 500) index for the communications sector is used in these cases.
3. *Time Series*: This is about performance analysis over time in which three key questions can be asked: How did a company perform in the past? What is its current performance? What is its expected performance?

Banner 22.1 Performance Analysis
Relative valuation is useful for analyzing a company's market and financial performances historically, currently, and in the future.

Exhibit 22.1 Relative Valuation and Performance Analysis

Illustrative Cases: Netflix and Comcast Corp. (See Excel Workings—▸ Chap. 22, Sheet E.22.1)

The two companies' profiles can be referred to in ▸ Chap. 20 (▸ Exhibit 20.3). They are both based in the United States and belong to the same industry (entertainment) and sector (communications).

Performance Measurements

Both P/E and EV/EBITDA are used to measure performance. Comparison is based on S&P 500's communications sector benchmarks for the respective measures. Historical data cover 16 annual observations from 2006 to 2021 (current). To determine the expected performance (2022 and 2023), a 5-year average growth is used (see Exhibit 22.1.1). For example, Netflix's P/E for 2021 is 56.03, whereas its expected growth is −26.7%: hence, expected P/E for 2022 = 56.03 (1+ −26.7%) = 41.05 and expected P/E for 2023 = 41.05 (1+ −26.7%) = 30.03.

Performance Analysis

Exhibits 22.1.2 and 22.1.3 depict performance trends for Netflix and Comcast, respectively.

Netflix: Compared to the sector, the

Exhibit 22.1.1 P/E and EV/EBITDA: a 5-year average growth

Company vs. benchmark	5-Year growth	
	P/E	EV/EBITDA
Netflix	−26.7%	−19.6%
Comcast	7.6%	2.0%
S&P 500 Communications	8.0%	14.3%

22

company has been, still is, and is expected to trade at higher multiples on both stock value and enterprise value. Historically, market valuation can be viewed in two distinctive periods: increasing valuation until 2014/2015, followed by declining valuation from 2015 to current (which is also expected in 2022 and 2023). Generally, from 2016, Netflix's annual valuation changes (P/E and EV/EBITDA) have been lower than the sector's, implying deteriorating market confidence over the company (forcing its stock prices down).

Comcast: Compared to the sector, the company has been switching positions time after time in terms of valuation multiples. Over the past 4/5 years (2017/2018–2021) Comcast's equity and enterprise value multiples have been below the sector's but with an increasing trend. Forecasts suggest that the current position will persist in 2022 and 2023 (generally undervalued). Based on a 5-year average, P/E growth is consistent with the sector's (7.6% vs. 8.0%), implying improving market confidence over the company—expected to force stock prices up in 2022 and 2023. The company's EV/EBITDA growth is slower than the sector's (2.0% vs. 14.3%), but the market is still confident about the company.

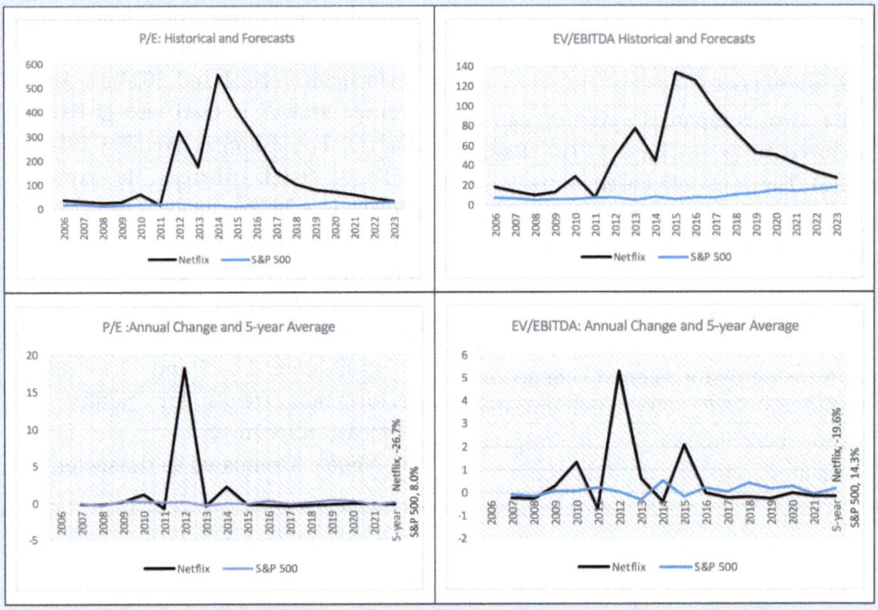

Exhibit 22.1.2 Netflix vs. the sector

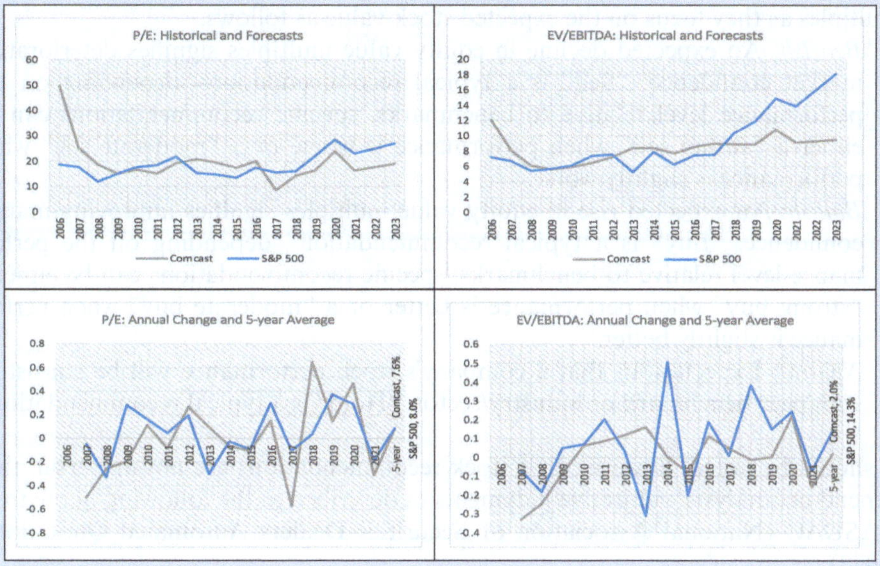

Exhibit 22.1.3 Comcast vs. the sector

Apply 22.1

Objective: Analyze Company Performance Using Relative Valuation

Consider any company of your interest or use data provided for oil and gas companies (refer to Excel data sheets for ▸ Chap. 22). Analyze the past, current, and projected performances using several multiples.

22.3 Price Recommendations and Investment Decisions

Investors in secondary stock markets make informed decisions about investment value. Among others, relative valuation is the most frequently used approach for guiding investors in their day-to-day decisions. Analysts provide recommendations or opinions about stock values (overvalued, undervalued, or fair) and whether it is reasonable to sell, buy, or hold. In conjunction with relative valuation, analysts perform regular research on financial performance, seeking customers' and managers' opinions.

Regular and frequent pricing enables dynamic investment decisions, which, in turn, reflect the dynamic pricing mechanism through demand and supply force. Undervalued (cheaper) stocks attract more buyers (high demand), thereby pushing prices up. Overvalued (expensive) stocks encourage selling (low demand), thereby forcing prices down. This dynamic process tries to maintain equilibrium (fair) price at least for a short time.

The typical valuation multiples for daily investment decisions are equity (price) multiples as they focus on the expected stock value as follows:

- *Bearish*: An expected decline in equity value multiples signifies deteriorating market confidence. "Sell" is a typical recommendation—depending on the performance level relative to benchmarks, specific recommendations can be either a "strong sell" when performance is worse or a "moderate sell" when performance is slightly worse.
- *Bullish*: An expected rise in equity value multiples signifies improving market confidence. "Buy" is a typical recommendation—depending on the performance level relative to benchmarks, specific recommendations can be either a "strong buy" when performance is better or a "moderate buy" when performance is slightly better.
- *Neutral*: Expectations that a company's stock performance will be consistent with peer benchmark or industry/sector. "Hold" is a typical recommendation.

It should be noted, however, that stock recommendations are not universal: they depend on analysts' subjective judgments as described in the following quote from NASDAQ (National Association of Securities Dealers Automated Quotations) (2022):

» Nasdaq Analyst Research provides analyst research for ratings consensus and a summary of stock price targets. Analysts evaluate the stock's expected performance in a given time period based on their research and their own opinions. Analyst ratings can be used in addition to other personal research work prior to making investment decisions.

For example, ▶ Exhibit 22.2 shows how different analysts recommended Netflix and Comcast in October to December 2022 (CNN Money). These recommendations reflect the information in ▶ Exhibit 22.1. For Netflix, the fact that the majority recommends "hold" followed by "buy" implies that the market is mainly neutral and somewhat confident about the company. For Comcast, the fact that the majority recommends "buy" followed by "hold" implies that the market is optimistic and highly confident about the company.

Think 22.1

Why do bullish stock recommendations tend to outshine bearish recommendations?

Exhibit 22.2 Price Recommendations

Illustrative Cases: Netflix and Comcast (See Excel Workings—▶ Chap. 22, Sheet E.22.1)

◘ Exhibit 22.2.1 presents Netflix's stock recommendations by 45 different analysts. ◘ Exhibit 22.2.2 presents Comcast's stock recommendations by 36 different analysts. Data were extracted from CNN Money for October to December 2022. The horizontal axis shows a typical recommendation scale from 1 (best performance)

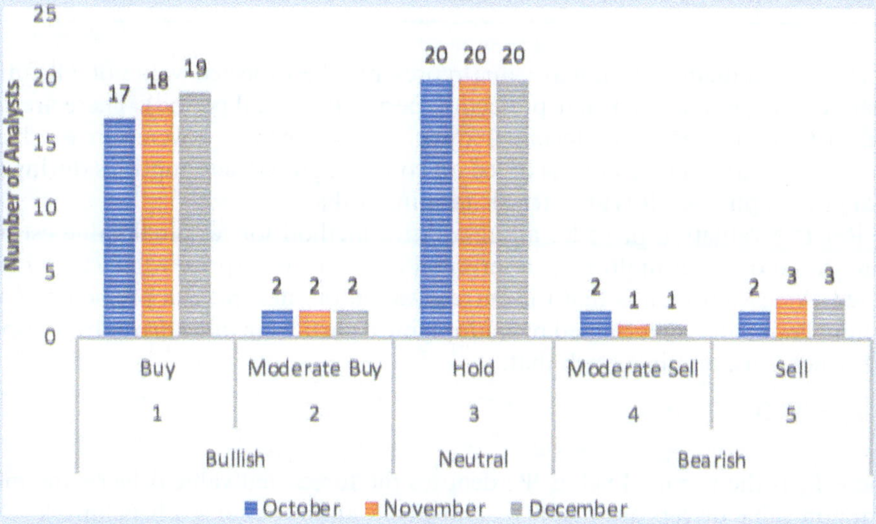

Exhibit 22.2.1 Netflix's stock recommendations

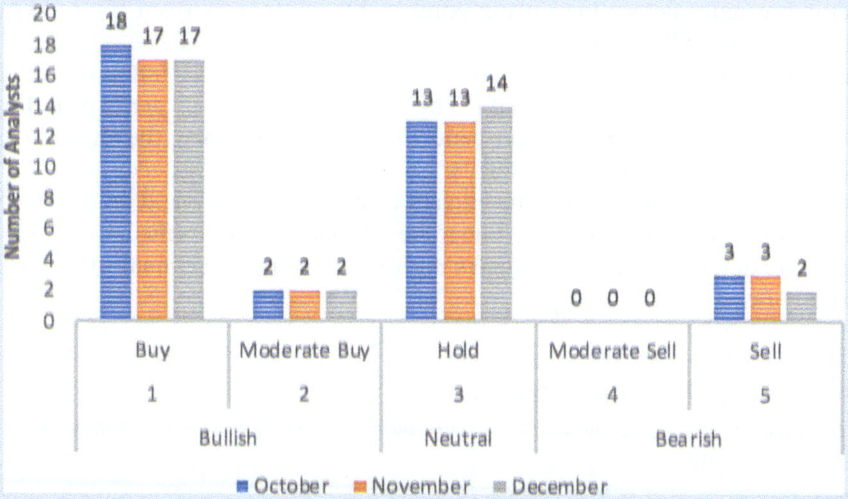

Exhibit 22.2.2 Comcast's stock recommendations

to 5 (worst performance) and descriptions about market expectations (bullish, neutral, and bearish) and specific recommendation along the scale. The vertical axis shows the number of analysts for each recommendation.

22.4 Terminal Valuation for Cash Flow Discount Models

In intrinsic valuation, terminal value represents the expected value of all future cash flows beyond a particular projection period (terminal period). There are several methods to determine terminal value. One of them is covered in ▶ Chaps. 15–17, where a terminal value is based on constant growth assumptions during the final growth phases—it is an intrinsic terminal value.

Relative valuation provides an alternative method for terminal value estimation. Based on "exit multiples," a terminal equity or enterprise value can be estimated. An assumption is that the current valuation multiple is a predictor of the terminal exit value, determined by multiplying a particular value driver by a respective benchmark multiple, such that:

$$V_{\mathrm{T}} = \Psi_{\mathrm{D}}\Theta$$

where V_{T} is the terminal value, Ψ_{D} denotes the forecasted value driver—the most common value drivers are EBITDA and EBIT, and Θ denotes a benchmark relating to a particular multiple, which can be determined using the following approaches (examples are presented in ▶ Exhibit 22.3):

1. Θ is normally determined using comparable companies from recent acquisitions (see ▶ Exhibit 22.3.1).
2. Θ estimation can be implied by the present value of free cash flows to the firm (FCFF) (see ▶ Exhibit 22.3.2). The same estimation is performed for all selected peers to determine peer benchmark multiples. Then, the terminal value is calculated normally as $V_{\mathrm{T}} = \Psi_{\mathrm{D}}\Theta$.
3. Θ estimation can be implied by current or average FCFF yield relative to market EV (see ▶ Exhibit 22.3.3). The same estimation is performed for all selected peers to determine peer benchmark multiples. Then, the terminal value is calculated normally as $V_{\mathrm{T}} = \Psi_{\mathrm{D}}\Theta$.

Banner 22.2 Terminal Exit Multiples

Terminal exit multiples should be forward-looking to reflect expectations about value drivers.

Overall, the following practical issues should be considered:

- The selection of peers should try as much as possible to ensure similarity in terms of business activities, growth stage, size, expectations regarding growth, risk, and returns.
- When Θ is implied by FCFF, the selected peers should be valued with the same FCFF growth assumptions.
- Terminal exit valuation should be forward-looking to reflect a company's expected dynamics beyond the terminal period and not the current period. This is captured by projected value drivers.
- The forward-looking exit multiple is generally implied by current market values.

Exhibit 22.3 Terminal Value Based on Exit Multiples

Illustrative Examples (See Excel Workings—▶ Chap. 22, Sheet E.22.3)

Exhibit 22.3.1 Based on Comparable Acquisitions

The following information relates to EV/EBITDA of recent acquisitions of four comparable companies E, F, G, and H: 6.9, 12.4, 8.7, and 10.4, respectively.

XYZ belongs to the same peer group and is being valued using discounted free cash flows to the firm (FCFFs). A valuation model assumes two-stage growth in which the first stage will last for 5 years, followed by stable growth indefinitely. Projected EBITDA in the beginning of the stable phase (year 6) is \$68 million. Estimate XYZ's terminal value using comparable multiples.

Solution:

To determine a comparable benchmark, an average or median can be used. Let us use an average in this example, which is 9.6 (median is 9.55).

$$V_T = \Psi_D \Theta = \$68(9.6) = \$652.8 \text{ million}$$

Exhibit 22.3.2 Implied by the Present Value of FCFF

The following information relates to ABC company: current enterprise value is \$450 million. The company is being valued using a two-stage FCFF growth model in which stage 1 will last for 4 years, followed by stable growth indefinitely. FCFF projections over the next 4 years (millions) are \$4.0, \$4.6, \$6.5, and \$8.2. Weighted average cost of capital (WACC) is 8.5%. A 1-year forward EBITDA is \$80 million, whereas EBITDA projection in year 5 is \$98 million.

Required:

1. Calculate the current priced EV/EBITDA based on 1-year forward EBITDA.
2. Calculate the terminal enterprise value in year 4 implied by 4 years' discounted FCFF.
3. Based on results in (3), calculate terminal EV/EBITDA in year 4.

Solution:

Current EV (\$ millions)	**450**
Less present value (\$ millions) of FCFF (years 1–4 at 8.5%)	18.6
Implied terminal value component of current EV (\$ millions)	431.4
Implied terminal EV (\$ millions) in year 4 = 431.4 $(1 + 8.5\%)^4$	597.9
Terminal EV/EBITDA in year 4 = \$597.9/\$98	6.10

Exhibit 22.3.3 Implied by the FCFF Yield

Use ABC's information in ▶ Exhibit 22.3.3 to estimate terminal EV/EBITDA using current and average FCFF yields.

Solution 1: Based on the Current FCFF Yield

Current FCFF yield = \$4.0/\$450	**0.9%**
Terminal EV (\$ millions) in year 4 = \$450$(1 + 8.5\%)^4$/ $(1 + 0.9\%)^4$	601.9
Terminal EV/EBITDA in year 4 = \$601.9/\$98	6.14

Solution 1: Based on the Average FCFF Yield

Average FCFF yield = [($4.0 + $4.6 + $6.5 + $8.2)/4]/$450	**1.3%**
Terminal EV ($ millions) in year 4 = $450(1 + 8.5%)^4/(1 + 1.3%)^4	592.4
Terminal EV/EBITDA in year 4 = $592.4/$98	6.04

Apply 22.2

Objective: Estimate the terminal value using relative valuation.

Consider any company of your interest. You can use any data from the previous chapters of this book.

1. Determine a group of peers.
2. For each company in the peer group, perform the following:
   (a) Determine a cash flow valuation model, projection of free cash flows, and cost of capital.
   (b) Determine the current and projected value drivers for estimating the exit terminal value.
   (c) Estimate terminal multiples implied by discounted FCFF and FCFF yield.
   (d) Determine both implied and relative terminal values for a target company.

22.5 Valuation of Private Firms

Unlike public firms, valuation of private firms tends to be complicated due to lack of observed market prices and data limitations. Relative valuation, however, can enable private firm valuation in the presence of comparable public companies.

To value a private firm, valuation multiples are based on market values and value drivers of comparable public companies. Then, to determine a private firm's relative value, its value driver is multiplied by a respective benchmark multiple of public peers, such that:

$$V_E = \Psi_E \Theta$$

$$V_{EV} = \Psi_{EV} \Theta$$

where V_E and V_{EV} denote equity and enterprise value, respectively; Ψ_E and Ψ_{EV} denote the private company's equity and enterprise value driver, respectively; and Θ denotes a benchmark relating to a particular multiple for public peers. A case example of Pemex in presented in ▸ Exhibit 22.4.

Exhibit 22.4 Valuation of Private Companies

Illustrative Case: Pemex (See Excel Workings—▶ Chap. 22, Sheet E.22.4)

Pemex (Petróleos Mexicanos S.A. de C.V.) is a private company owned by Mexico's government. It engages in oil and gas exploration, production, and refining and distribution and ranks among the world's largest vertically integrated petroleum enterprises.

The company can be valued using oil and gas peers. Exhibit 22.4.1 presents valuation data (all in USD millions). Public companies' data were obtained from Bloomberg, whereas Pemex EBITDA data were extracted from Fitch's rating commentary (24 Match 2022) and Form 20-F for the year that ended on 2021. Valuation is as on 31 December 2021 based on EV/EBITDA.

Pemex Valuation

Using EV/EBITDA peer median for public companies, Pemex's enterprise value is determined as follows:

$$V_{EV} = \Psi_{EV}\Theta = \text{US\$}23{,}300(4.86) = \text{US\$}113{,}238 \text{ million}$$

Its EV/EBITDA is approximately 4.86, calculated as US$113,238/US$23,300.

Reference items: The relative value can be compared with the following financial items (book value) as on 31 December 2021 (in US$ millions): total assets = US$99,700; total liabilities = US$205.121; total debt = US$112,180; and total equity = −US$105,421. Hence, Pemex's relative value is 14% higher than its total asset value. An approximation of relative equity value is US$1058 million (the difference between enterprise value and total debt).

Exhibit 22.4.1 Pemex and public comparable companies

Company name	Domicile	EV (US$ millions)	EBITDA	EV/ EBITDA
Pemex	Mexico	NA	23,300.00	NA
Ecopetrol SA	Colombia	51,699.20	9627.41	5.37
Petroleo Brasileiro SA	Brazil	114,671.20	47,581.41	2.41
Repsol SA	Spain	29,807.30	6565.48	4.54
Chevron Corp.	United States	256,532.70	34,022.90	7.54
Suncor Energy	Canada	48,829.60	10,047.24	4.86
Exxon	United States	312,586.40	43,841.01	7.13
MOL Hungarian Oil and Gas	Hungary	7842.90	3366.05	2.33
Average				**4.88**
Median				**4.86**

Note: NA means Pemex does not have a market value to determine EV and is excluded from calculating peer benchmarks (average and median)

Apply 22.3

Objective: Estimate a private firm's value using relative valuation.

Consider any private company of your interest and determine its public peer group. Collect data and use several multiples to estimate its equity and enterprise value.

22.6 IPO Pricing

Relative valuation is commonly used in conjunction with other valuation methods (intrinsic valuation) to determine a reasonable price to attract investors to buy an IPO stock. The valuation process is the same as secondary market equity valuation, except that IPO valuation takes place once (not driven by market perception). While investment banks use relative valuation to fix an IPO price, investors make decisions depending on other factors such as their own investment needs, strategies, and expectations.

IPO valuation is a complex process, in which IPO pricing can be right or wrong. Hence, the goal is to ensure a fair IPO pricing—neither underpriced nor overpriced. While underpricing prolongs time for listing gains (listing gains refer to the gains enjoyed by investors as soon as the stock is listed on exchange markets), overpricing limits IPO proceedings. Relative valuation is an ideal tool to determine a fair IPO price, which is consistent with peers' median or average multiples.

22.7 Mergers and Acquisitions

Determining an M&A value is a complex process. However, relative valuation provides a quick indication of a reasonable price range to bargain. Unlike IPO and secondary stock market valuation, M&A valuation utilizes enterprise value (EV) multiples, as stated in ▶ Chap. 21. It should be noted that EV valuation considers an acquirer's position—how much should be paid to another company without the effect of leverage (capital structure). Generally, the usefulness of EV valuation on M&A decisions is reflected in the value of the target company's components: equity value, debt value, and cash value.

A typical acquisition process involves a single target company but several interested bidders (potential acquirers). Hence, acquisition decisions involve both parties, i.e., the acquirer(s) and the acquired (target)—they must reach a consensus about value; this is like two sides of the same coin—pay for what is worth.

▶ Exhibit 22.5 presents examples to explain M&A's role in EV multiples. While an acquirer's attention is minimization of the "offer price," the target focuses on maximizing owners' value. This tension should bring both sides to a consensus price.

Exhibit 22.5 M&A's Role in Relative Valuation

Illustrative Example (See Excel Workings—▸ Chap. 22, Sheet E.22.5)

Acquisition Targets

Consider four peer companies in Exhibit 22.5.1. The companies differ in capital structure and cash balance. A valuation analyst has performed relative valuation based on two value drivers (EBITDA and EBIT). Exhibits 22.5.2 and 22.5.3 present valuation results and the extent of overvaluation or undervaluation, respectively.

Companies A and B are potential acquisition targets, and several bidders are contemplating acquisition bids. The two companies have equal enterprise value: Market cap + Debt − Cash = $510 million. However, company A is undervalued, whereas B is overvalued. What bid offer should potential buyers consider for each company? What ask offer should the targets consider?

Company A

- From relative valuation, the company is undervalued by 15% and 35% and should be valued at $597 million and $783 million based on EBITDA and EBIT, respectively. Since, the company is cheaper, its price should be competitive.
- The target (company A) will be evaluating several offers, which are likely to range between $597 million and $783 million—it can include a premium. Competition will determine the winner of the takeover bid, but the target will have bargaining power.

Company B

- From relative valuation, the company is overvalued by 18% and 23% and should be valued at $433 million and $414 million based on EBITDA and EBIT, respectively. Since, the company is expensive, its bid should be less competitive.
- The target (company B) will be evaluating several offers, which are likely to range between $414 million and $433 million—lower than the market value. Bidders will have the bargaining power (bid lower), but the target's goal is to maximize value (ask higher). Depending on the acquirers' motives, the acquisition bid offer can be around the market value ($510 million).

It should be noted that the acquisition price is determined not only by valuation but also other factors such as motive, risk, payment form (stock payment or cash payment), and so on. For example, potential buyers can consider financial risk (leverage), which is higher in company A than in company B.

22

Exhibit 22.5.1 Company performance and valuation multiples

	Market value ($ millions)				Value drivers		Valuation multiples	
Company	Market cap	Debt	Cash	EV	EBITDA	EBIT	EV/EBITDA	EV/EBIT
A	350	200	40	510	243	204	2.1	2.5
B	400	150	40	510	134	142	3.8	3.6
C	120	90	15	195	67	89	2.9	2.2
D	240	100	20	320	78	94	4.1	3.4
Average							**3.2**	**2.9**

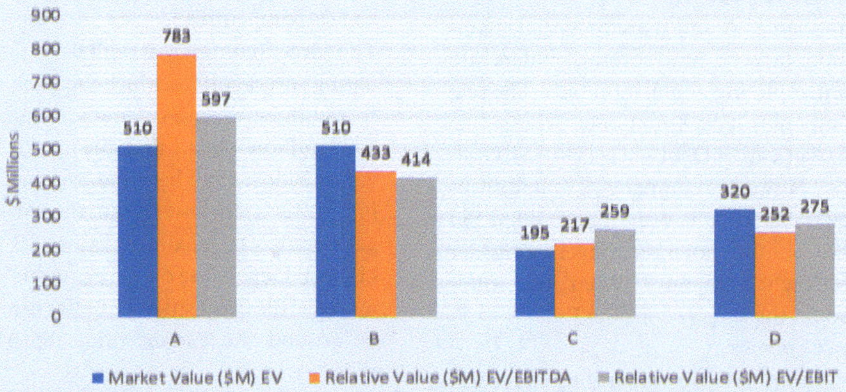

Exhibit 22.5.2 Enterprise value: market vs. relative value ($ millions)

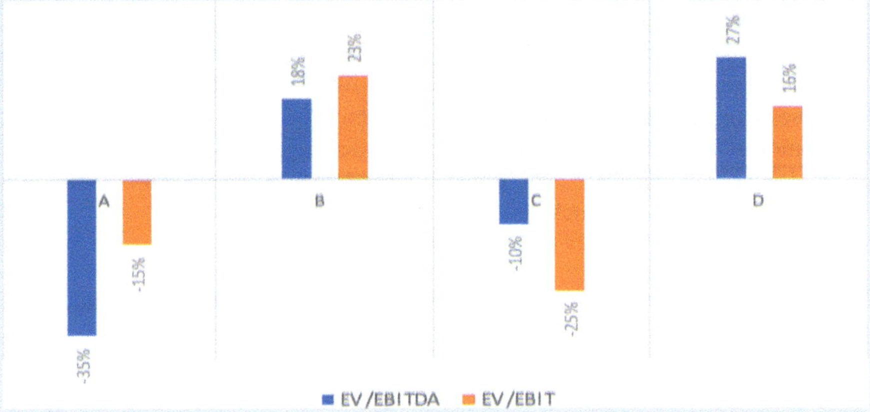

Exhibit 22.5.3 Percentage of overvaluation or undervaluation

22.8 Limitations of Relative Valuation

As we have seen, relative valuation is generally easy to apply compared to intrinsic valuation, but its simplicity comes with some limitations as outlined below:

- *Inconsistent Estimates*: Multiples are determined by value drivers and market values of comparable companies. Nevertheless, decisions about selecting peers and value drivers can differ among analysts due to subjective judgments.
- *Valuation Variables:* Relative valuation results can be inconsistent if peers are not properly selected to reflect key valuation variables such as risk, growth, or cash flow potentials.
- *Market Perception*: Relative valuation multiples are based on market perception and expectations. Valuation can be misleading if the market is incorrect—artificially too high or too low valuation.
- *Manipulation*: Analysts can easily use manipulative practices to arrive at desirable relative values. This is possible through judgments about peers, value drivers, and metrics (current, average, or forward).
- *Comparability*: Relative valuation assumes the existence of comparable companies. However, companies cannot be completely comparable in every aspect. Sometimes, finding the most suitable comparability can be difficult considering aspects like similar stages in a business cycle, risk profile, and return prospects.

Review Questions

1. What factors should be considered when using relative valuation as a tool for performance analysis?
2. How does relative valuation help in the following?
   (a) Stock price recommendations
   (b) Investment decisions
3. Describe the following approaches of estimating terminal value using relative valuation:
   (a) Based on comparable acquisitions
   (b) Implied by discounted FCFF
   (c) Implied by FCFF yield
4. Explain how to achieve a forward-looking terminal value when using relative valuation
5. Outline the key steps to estimate a private firm's value using relative valuation
6. What is the usefulness of relative valuation in M&A pricing decisions?
7. What are the limitations of relative valuation?

Bibliography

Nasdaq (2022). NFLX Analyst Research, Available at Nasdaq https://www.nasdaq.com/market-activity/stocks/nflx/analyst-research, Accessed December 16, 2022.

Pruitt, S. (2022), Time to Buy AMD or Intel Stock for 2023?, Yahoo Finance, available at https://finance.yahoo.com/news/time-buy-amd-intel-stock-013301432.html

MIX
Papier aus verantwortungsvollen Quellen
Paper from responsible sources
FSC® C105338
FSC
www.fsc.org

If you have any concerns about our products,
you can contact us on
ProductSafety@springernature.com

In case Publisher is established outside the EU,
the EU authorized representative is:
Springer Nature Customer Service Center GmbH
Europaplatz 3, 69115 Heidelberg, Germany

Printed by Libri Plureos GmbH
in Hamburg, Germany